ISBN 978-0-265-19045-6
PIBN 10187564

THE
HOMILETIC REVIEW

An International Magazine of Religion, Theology, and Philosophy
Treats Every Phase of the Minister's Work

Volume LXXXIV

From July to December
1922

PUBLISHERS:

FUNK and WAGNALLS COMPANY
NEW YORK AND LONDON
MCMXXII

GERTRUDE VANDERBILT WHITNEY
(Mrs. Harry Payne Whitney)

Born New York City; daughter Cornelius and Alice (Gwynne) Vanderbilt; Brearley School, New York; studied sculpture under Henry Anderson and James E. Fraser, New York, and took a course at the Art Students' League, New York; studied under Andrew O'Connor, Paris, France. Married Harry Payne Whitney, of New York City, August 25, 1896. Principal works: Aztec Fountain, in Pan-American Building, Washington, D. C.; Titanic Memorial, for same city; El Dorado Fountain, San Francisco; two panels for Triumphant Arch, New York; etc. Member American Federation of Arts, Association of Women Painters and Sculptors, National Institute of Social Sciences, International Historical Society, National Arts Club.

A new monument in bronze to the soldiers, sailors and marines of the Washington
Heights and Inwood districts (New York), who gave their lives in the World
War, by Gertrude Vanderbilt Whitney (Mrs. Harry Payne Whitney).

The HOMILETIC REVIEW

VOL. 84   JULY, 1922   No. 1

VAGABONDING IN BOOKLAND

The Rev. LESTER GEORGE SIMON, New York City

When I came to a pastorate in this metropolitan center, an observing friend who had lived here two score years remarked that the great majority of busy Gothamites did not have time for wide reading. The mass of folks rushing to, at, and from the business of this great city, seeking recreation in an occasional holiday excursion or an evening's amusement, can not find much time to read for enrichment and profit. Add to this circumstance the fact that reading is an art, requiring a properly adjusted mental attitude, and the difficulty doubles.

However, it is indisputable that we are the great losers, also that there are some things that ought never to succumb to the excessive rush of this era of super-business. By taking stock, clearing the ground of needless luggage, and readjusting our lives we can make a place, tho necessarily limited, for these greater values that are often sacrificed.

After a sermon calling for a larger cultivation of friendship with worthy books, I was gratified to receive in Monday morning's mail the following note:

My dear Mr. S., a word of appreciation never goes amiss and I, for one, enjoyed and needed your sermon of Sunday evening. It pricked my conscience with regard to the reading of good books—a habit that the busy years have caused me to drop. But now, thanks to your reminder, I am going to make a resolution for the new year to do some thoughtful reading and get acquainted with old friends. So, I say, Thank you!

"Have you read ———?" doesn't embarrass me in the least, unless reference is made to some seasoned worthy among the books which I have been guilty of neglecting. If the query has reference to the latest novel, which I have not read, it doesn't raise a blush. 'Tis not a serious reflection upon one's social standing or intellectual progressiveness to have passed by the latest fiction. Life is so full of a number of important things and of a great many good books that one is forced to select, resigned to the circumstance that in any case much must go unread. And busy folk simply can not afford the risk of a book that has not the verdict of time or a discriminating judge in its favor.

In my travels through bookland in the year of grace 1921 I find that I have maintained a double identity. In one person I have pursued studies and readings directly related to my work and its increased efficiency. In the other person I have just vagabonded. The diary records the course of my vagrancy, and as I attempt to account for the selection of books read I am convinced that I have been the most lawless vagrant in Vagabondia. However that may be, the trails have been delightful, and the books encountered have been, for the most part, the very best. They have yielded pleasure, diversion, information, inspiration, and tonic.

January entries in the diary record reading determined by holiday gift books. This reason lay back of my reading of *Mark Twain's Letters* in two volumes, Thayer's *Roosevelt, Roosevelt's Letters to His Children,* and the rereading of *Huckleberry Finn.*

I try to be as sure of my book before investing time in its reading as one should be in investing money. Books that have come through the test of time, or are recommended by friends and authors of discriminating judgment, immediately find a place on my waiting list. A reading of *Theodore Roosevelt and His Times, Shown in His Letters* suggested Trevelyan's *History of the American Revolution,* Cahun's *Turks and Moguls,* Balfour's *Decadence,* and Surtees' *Mr. Sponge's Sporting Tour.* I was deeply interested in Trevelyan's six volumes, and followed them with McMaster's *History of the United States,* the two giving a fair and complete portrayal of the course of national history to the Civil War. *Mr. Sponge's Sporting Tour* was unfailing in delight, its Pickwickian flavor clinching friendship from the start. Several unsuccessful attempts were made to secure a translation of Cahun, and I have not reached Balfour in the pursuit of my desires.

A friend with whom I happened to be dining on the eve of his departure for India mentioned F. T. Bullen's books on sea life. This was to me a real "find." One sample of the sincere writing and interesting substance from this man's pen has led me well into the list of his production. To his most fascinating *Our Heritage the Sea* I shall again make reference.

A series of nature and out-door books entered my list by reason of a hike taken in the Catskills during the spring. *John Burroughs; Boy and Man,* was immediately followed by his *Riverby, Under the Maples, Locusts and Wild Honey, Winter Sunshine,* *Wake Robin, Pepacton, Time and Change.* Then I turned to Longstreth's *Catskills,* and scattered readings dealing with birds, trees, flowers, and rocks. As part preparation for a hike in the Southern Appalachians I read *Carolina Mountains* by Morley, and *Our Southern Highlanders* by Kephart. In a period of quiet immediately following the hike I found exquisite pleasure in Stevenson's *Inland Voyage.* The geological structure of the mountains I had visited led me to a recent college text-book on geology, and while browsing among new books just received at the branch library, the interest aroused by the text-book induced me to take home *James Geikie; Man and Geologist.*

If, at the judgment, account is to be rendered for the use of our time, I shall be confronted with the necessity of confessing to hours and hours of browsing over bargain book-counters. This is not time wasted in tasting, mind you. For, to speak of only recent acquisitions, see what I picked up: Boswell's *Life of Johnson* in two volumes, *The Diary of Samuel Pepys, Life of Benvenuto Cellini, Essays of Elia,* and several uniformly bound volumes of Thackeray.

A few unoccupied hours in the midst of a vacation and a handy case of books gave me occasion and means for renewing acquaintance with the *DeCoverly Papers.* Later, during winter hours indoors, a fond inclination led me to seek the company of the genial Pickwickians. A cheap pocket-copy of *The Nigger of the Narcissus,* found while beguiling the hours in an Ottawa bookshop, gave me an introduction, tho not the best, to Conrad. Then came the sixth centennial of the death of the great Italian, and forthwith I took another plunge into *The Vision of Dante Alighieri.* Along about this time the paradoxical champion of the orthodox came to our shores, and, the only work of his ready to hand being *The Man Who Was Thursday,* I endured the weird suspense of this baptism of mystery. An unread book stared challengingly at me from my book-case in a moment calculated to get a favorable reaction; and I soon gorged Breal's *Rembrandt.* It is no great work, but surely a sweet morsel.

Some years ago a fellow passenger on an Atlantic liner called my attention to W. W. Jacob's collections of humorous stories dealing with British *Old Salts,* many of the stories containing a double-play, and now, during any slight indisposition, when just indisposed enough to enjoy a light diet, I am likely to reach for a copy of *Ships Company,* or *Sailors' Knots,* to laugh once more over the ludicrous escapades of Peter Russet, Sam Small, and Ginger Dick.

There are times when an irresistible spirit of adventure invades me. I must have new scenes and new thoughts. .The spirit rebels at the cramped and humdrum routine of life. I have been able to satisfy this recurring wanderlust in a limited degree by feasting my eyes and curiosity on foreign objects double-starred in Baedeker, and on some other things Baedeker has not gone out of the way to find. But this is expensive for the preacher. One other relief is always at hand, and not so expensive. I can take a good book of travel, together with a good map, and these, with the potency of a magic carpet, immediately sweep me into a new world of imagination. Then again, reading excursions into absolutely new fields give one a complete change of environment. I do not now refer specifically to travel literature. I have found myself among new, strange, and intensely interesting thoughts and pictures by turning to F. T. Bullen's *Our Heritage the Sea,* Osborn's *From the Greek to Darwin,* books on astronomy, economics, art, sociology, oceanog-

raphy, and glaciers. And recently a friend told me that I will be a thousand fold repaid by a perusal of Slosson's *Creative Chemistry.* These new fields are a relief to the mind that is daily driven into old pasturages. Once upon a time I came upon an effective cure for doldrums of the imagination. The end of the week was approaching, and a brother minister prescribed a highly exciting piece of fiction. I picked up the book, the first morsel of fiction I had touched in a long time, and was soon swung through a legion of entrancing improbabilities in the South Seas, and got back barely in time to finish Sunday's sermon. The tonic effect was appreciable.

For the sake of keeping old friendships in repair, and drinking at wells that never fail, I made occasional trips to Browning, Ruskin, Plato, Thoreau, Eliot, Thackeray, and the essays of our Yankee Plato. I have beaten paths to these springs, and never fail of inspiration here.

Strange diet this! Its food values may not be scientifically balanced. Nevertheless it has accomplished much. Some of it was informing, some gave pleasure, some inspired, some fed the soul, and much of it, now reduced to classification, will serve to enhance sermons.

Books, in the providence of God, have been assigned an honored and potent place. His own supreme revelation has been entrusted to a book. Individuals and nations have been molded by creative literature. The biography of a distinguished individual must list the literature that early influenced the life and later nourished it. Milton feeds on the Bible, Homer, Ovid, and Euripides; Dante on Virgil; Schiller on Shakespeare; Wellington on Bishop Butler, the Bible, and *The Wealth of Nations;* Lincoln on the Bible and Aesop.

Cicero and Paul are not often found

working together, but in the life of Augustine this thing happens. In the early part of his *Confessions* he writes,

> In the ordinary course of study, I fell upon a certain book of Cicero. This book of his contains an exhortation to philosophy, and is called "Hortensius. But this book altered my affections and turned my prayers to thyself, O Lord, and made me have other purposes and desires. Every vain hope at once became worthless to me; and I longed with an incredibly burning desire for an immortality of wisdom, and began now to arise, that I might return to thee. And since at that time apostolic Scripture was not known to me—I was thereby strongly roused, and kindled, and inflamed to love, and seek, and obtain, and hold, and embrace, not this or that sect, but wisdom itself, whatever it were.

Thus inflamed, he resolved to bend his mind to the Holy Scriptures, with the result that on that occasion when he heard the mysterious voice saying "Take up and read," he took up the volume of the apostle, "Seized, opened, and in silence read that section, on which my eyes first fell: 'Not in rioting and drunkenness, not in chambering and in wantonness, not in strife and envying: but put ye on the Lord Jesus Christ, and make no provision for the flesh.'" Instantly, at the end of this sentence, by a light as it were of serenity infused into his heart, all the darkness of doubt vanished away.

IS HUMAN NATURE GOOD OR BAD

Professor WESLEY R. WELLS, Ph.D., Lake Forest College, Lake Forest, Ill.

During the course of history two contrasting answers have been given to the question as to whether human nature is fundamentally good or bad. St. Augustine and John Calvin represent one view of their theory by innate depravity. The opposite view is well represented by Rousseau, who maintained that human nature is essentially good.

The theory of innate depravity has a theological setting, being connected with the account of the fall of man. St. Augustine and Calvin maintained that humanity has been corrupted because of Adam's fall, through which sin became hereditary in the race. The old *New England Primer* exprest this idea in the lines,

> In Adam's fall
> We sinned all.

The Calvinistic doctrine of infant damnation followed from this theory. Jonathan Edwards' sermon, "Sinners in the Hands of an Angry God," is a famous product of the Calvinistic view of human depravity. The doctrine of the original fall of man and of the natural sinfulness of the individual fits in well with schemes of salvation such as are taught by the Catholic Church and by those branches of Protestantism that place most emphasis upon the need of conversion or regeneration. In the more liberal forms of Protestantism, however, there has tended to be a rejection of this point of view.

No clearer or more influential expression has ever been given to the view of human nature than affirms its innate goodness, in contrast with such a view as that of the Calvinists than the one given by Rousseau. Rousseau is of great historical importance in many fields, and especially in political theory and in education. His *Social Contract* influenced modern democratic theories very materially, shaping some of the ideas exprest in the American Declaration of Independence, and becoming the handbook of the French Revolutionists. His *Emile* was the source of many educational reforms in the nineteenth century. This latter book is of interest in the present connection because of the view of human nature contained in it. The book begins with the statement, "Coming from the hand of the Author of all things, everything is good." The reference is especially to the nature of the child. Rousseau believed that the child is entirely good at birth, and that he degenerates only as a result of faulty education. As Rousseau exprest it, "In the hands of man, everything degenerates." From this it follows that a perfect educational scheme, were such possible, would maintain the original perfection of the individual throughout life. In pursuance of this thought Rousseau advocated a negative type of education, a keeping away from the child of educative influences of all kinds as much as possible, lest they should be bad influences. He advocated a "shielding of the heart from vice and the mind from error," believing that vice and error could come only from sources outside the child. And he was especially opposed to the use of external discipline in the nurture of children, in striking contrast with the Calvinistic type of education.

The more liberal branches of Protestantism have tended to go nearly as far as Rousseau in opposing the Calvinistic view of innate depravity; and the psychological basis, exprest or implied, of many present-day political theories of a radical type is precisely like that of Rousseau's theories. The fact of human dissatisfaction and suffering, as well as of vice and crime, is obvious; and many would place the blame entirely upon existing political institutions and industrial organizations, assuming that human nature, if only given a chance, would of itself be virtuous and happy. If human nature were inherently good, then a return to nature such as Rousseau advocated, and a throwing off

of institutional restraints, would obviously result in the increased happiness of mankind. An unprejudiced appraisal of human nature, however, in its original or hereditary aspect, must condemn Rousseau for his sentimentalism as much as it criticizes Calvin for his severely ascetic rigorism. Original human nature is not entirely bad, nor is it entirely good. It has enough good qualities to form a basis upon which moral education may build, but it has enough bad qualities to make impossible the speedy coming of a utopia of universal happiness such as many social theorists like to dream of.

Goodness and badness are ethical terms of approval and disapproval; and their existence is relative to human interests, which are furthered by those things that we call good and are thwarted by those things that we call bad. In saying that human nature is partly good, we mean that it possesses innate tendencies the unrestrained expression of which results in the furthering of personal and social interests, and a consequent increase in happiness. In saying that human nature is partly bad we mean that it possesses other inborn tendencies which, if fully exprest, lead to the thwarting of interests and a diminishing of happiness. The modern scientific view can not accept the Calvinistic theory of innate depravity, since it finds good traits in the natural man; nor can it accept the assumption of an original state of perfection at the beginning of history from which mankind has fallen, for the modern view is an evolutionary one, which traces the racial beginnings of man back to very lowly sources. And for the reason that the scientific view of human nature is based upon biological evolution, it must also reject Rousseau's theory that the individual is born in a condition of complete perfection. The fact is that the individual is born bearing in his physical organism the marks of the jungle existence of countless ages of ancestral life. Because of the persistence through heredity of ancestral traits and tendencies that come from a remote antiquity of pre-civilized and even pre-human life, present-day interests in civilized society are thwarted by the free expression of some of these tendencies. Those innate tendencies which must be checked for the sake of happiness under present conditions are bad, and the individual is innately bad to the extent that he possesses such tendencies. But, on the other hand, some of the remote ancestral tendencies of man are good since their expression enhances the welfare of present-day society, and the individual is innately good in so far as he possesses such tendencies.

Just what, specifically, it may be asked, are the innate tendencies of man, some of which are good, contrary to the theory of total depravity, and some of which are bad, contrary to the theory of the original goodness of man? The answer is in terms of instincts, of which man, according to modern studies, and in contrast with views prevailing as late as a generation ago, possesses through heredity a number even greater than do many of the animals below man. The late Professor James, and Professors Mc-Dougall and Thorndike, to mention no others, have made noteworthy contributions to the study of the human instincts, and in what immediately follows I shall be especially indebted to them.

In addition to numerous innate tendencies of a less specific sort, man possesses about a dozen well-marked instincts. Some of these instincts are present at birth, but most of them are delayed, not making their first appearance until after some months or years of the individual's life have passed. Their existence is inevitably determined by heredity, however, even tho educative influences may modify them in various ways. Professor McDougall, in his *Introduction to Social Psychology,* a book which has been called "as important in the development of this new science as was the work of William James in the development of general psychology," and "by far the most important contribution to this field that has yet been made in the present century" (Professor Wright, in the *Journal of Philosophy*, March 17, 1921), names eleven human instincts, as follows: flight (fear), repulsion (disgust), curiosity, pugnacity, self-abasement, self-assertion, the parental instinct, the sex instinct, the gregarious instinct, and the instincts of acquisition and of construction. Professors James and Thorndike have included other instincts such as hunting, for example. Then, of course, the food instinct is the most fundamental one of all. Man possesses these instincts partly because they were once useful and necessary to the existence of his pre-historic ancestors, whose lives depended upon success in hunting, fighting, and other activities involved in an animal or savage state of existence.

Under modern conditions of civilized life some of these instincts in their original form are good, and their exercise leads to good results. For example, the parental instinct is the source of sympathetic feeling and unselfish conduct in a much larger sphere than that of the family. Thus unselfishness is, at least to some extent, a part of original nature, which is for this reason not wholly bad. But, on the other hand, many of the instincts are bad if allowed free expression in modern society. The child has many bad tendencies in spite of the best of training, just because of his inherited instincts. The hunting instinct will serve as an example. Because his remote ancestors had to hunt for a living, the modern child manifests in his behavior some of the cruel aspects of the hunting instinct. As Professor Thorndike says:

There being no wild animals to pursue, catch, and torment into submission or death, household pets, young and timid children, or even aunts, governesses, or nurse-maids, if sufficiently yielding, provoke the response from the young. . . . Teasing, bullying, cruelty, are thus in part the results of one of nature's ways of providing self and family with food: and what grew up as a pillar of human self-support has become so extravagant a luxury as to be almost a vice. . . . Teasing, tormenting, and bullying are the most notable exceptions to childish kindliness (*Educational Psychology*, Briefer Course, pp. 19, 38).

Fighting, also, like hunting, constantly expresses itself, in young and old alike, in cruel and immoral ways.

Obviously, apart from bad training, and in spite of good training, but merely as a result of its racial heritage, child nature is not entirely good. This conclusion, however, leaves open another question of great importance, namely that of the possibility that the adult may finally outgrow undesirable instincts. Unfortunately none of the fundamental instincts ever entirely wane from disuse, nor can they be entirely repress or inhibited. Take, for example, the matter of adult expressions, direct or indirect, of the hunting instinct, the fighting instinct, and the sex instinct. As Professor Thorndike says of the hunting instinct,

Older [persons] indulge the propensity at great cost of time and money in hunting beasts, or at still greater cost of manhood in hounding Quakers, abolitionists, Jews, Chinamen, scabs, prophets (*op.cit.*, p. 19).

The fighting instinct is so strong that permanent world-peace seems an almost impossible ideal regardless of whatever improved educational methods and attempted substitutions of

"moral equivalents of war" may come. Rivalry and jealousy are variations of the fighting instinct, and these tendencies constantly express themselves in cruel ways. The instinct, however, that is most obviously difficult of social control is the sex instinct. This is so necessary to the continuance of the race that it has become very highly developed and strongly intrenched in human nature. Without it the race could not survive, but with it social disharmonies are inevitable. Even were mankind placed in a perfect environment, under a perfect system of government (so far as a human system of government could be perfect), with all industrial wrongs and other social ills eliminated, human nature would soon reassert itself in its vicious aspects of fighting, jealousy, cruelty, and sexual wantonness.

Those political radicals are recommending what is clearly absurd when they advocate a back-to-nature movement, a casting off of social and governmental restraints in the interest of the greater happiness that would result, as they think, from the free expression of the natural impulses. Discipline and restraint of many innate impulses are, and have been since the beginning of human society, the essential conditions of any sort of existence. Primitive man was not free to express himself without restraint. Customs, "folkways," taboos, and the force of tribal tradition, enforced numerous inhibitions in primitive society. In fact, with the growth of the institutions and laws of civilization there has come an enormous increase of individual freedom. Under no conditions, however, is the free expression of all the instincts possible. In the first place, man's instinctive desire for the approval of others conflicts with the free expression of many native propensities. In the second place, the necessities of group or social life render necessary the control of instincts that would otherwise bring individuals into conflict with one another, to the disadvantage of all.

Instead of being the cause of the degeneration of mankind, as Rousseau thought, an education that contains many elements of restraint and discipline is society's only hope. Undesirable instincts can not be destroyed, however. They are as irresistible as a river, the flow of which can not be checked by a dam. But, just as the course of a river may be changed, and elevated, by the construction of a dam, so the expression of an instinct may be changed through the process of sublimation. Sublimation is the elevation of the expression of an instinct to a higher channel, the substitution of new and better objects for the objects with which the instinct was originally connected. Thus fighting may be sublimated in the form of righteous indignation and of opposition to social wrongs. Curiosity, which often expresses itself in undesirable ways, may be elevated into intellectual curiosity, which is the motive of the best scientific research, and into religious wonder. According to Freudian psychology many of the highest types of religious aspiration and of artistic creation are sublimated forms of the sex instinct. Other instincts also may be sublimated and turned to good uses in cases where their original forms of expression are inimical to the best interests of society.

Thus, while the child's nature in its original condition is to some extent good, and in other respects bad, through proper education of a religious and moral as well as intellectual sort the good elements may be encouraged in their development, and the undesirable tendencies may be redirected, with resulting benefit to each individual and to society. A partial remolding of human nature is necessitated by the demands of personal morality and of social stability.

SCRIPTURAL MEANING OF "DESTROY," "PERISH"

The Rev. ERIC LEWIS, Cayuga, Ont., Canada

A correct interpretation of these words in the New Testament carries with it far-reaching consequences, doctrinal and practical. The word faces us in the great familiar passage, God so loved the world that he gave his only begotten Son, that whosoever believeth in him should not perish, but have eternal life (John 3:16, R.V.).

What in this message of God's love to a lost world did our Savior mean by this word "perish"? Did he mean his hearers to understand by it endless conscious suffering or the ultimate extinction of life in the fiery Gehenna of which he spoke elsewhere, of which the vale of Hinnom in his day was a fitting emblem? For the English reader of the New Testament it is necessary to explain that the words "destroy," "perish" are both represented by the word *apollumi* in the Greek original, the active voice of which is rendered "I destroy," the middle or reflexive voice, "I perish." And the argument that applies to the verb *apollumi* will be equally applicable to its derivative noun *apoleia*, commonly translated "destruction" or "perdition." Other Greek words are translated "destroy," "destruction," used occasionally of the doom of the impenitent; but space forbids their inclusion in one brief article.

A Greek word in the original will often be represented by several different words in our English translation; and *apollumi* has four English equivalents (alike in A. V. and R. V.), viz., to "destroy," to "perish," once to "die,"and secondary meaning to"lose."

As well as having primary and secondary meanings, the same word may be used either literally or figuratively, and besides its use in the natural or physical realm it may also have a special spiritual significance; *e.g.*, when we speak of a sheep as "lost," we mean it is missing, it has strayed from its owner; but when we speak of a sinner as "lost," we are giving to the word a spiritual significance; he is away from God, alienated from him, astray spiritually.

And here we ask attention to an important principle of correct exegesis, viz., that the primary meaning is the basic one from which all others are derived. To attempt to deduce from a secondary use of a word its primary meaning is a philological blunder from which erroneous interpretations inevitably follow.

Apollumi is fifty-nine times in the New Testament translated "destroy," "perish" (including John 18:14, where it is translated "die"); of these, forty-nine refer to animate beings, and the remaining ten to beings inanimate. To take the former first, here are a few instances culled without break from the concordance:

Seek the young child to destroy him (Matt. 2:13).

Able to destroy both body and soul in hell (Matt. 10:28).

Took counsel how they might destroy him (Matt. 12:14).

He will miserably destroy those wicked men (Matt. 21:21).

He sent his armies and destroyed those murderers (Matt. 22:7).

It will be at once apparent that in all these passages (omitting the second for the moment, as it raises the question in dispute) the meaning of "destroy" applied to animate beings is "to take life"; and this will be found to hold true of every other case in the New Testament where it is spoken of the destruction of animate beings in the physical realm. The taking of life is its primary basic meaning.

This meaning, of course, is inadmissible as applied to inanimate beings, such as wine-skins, meat, grass, gold or larger objects such as the world, the heavens. In these cases we are shut up to a secondary meaning of "destroy," easily deducible, however, from the first. If a wine-skin has no life to be taken, when we speak of it being destroyed or perishing we mean that its use and purpose as a wine-skin is ended; not that its substance is annihilated but that as a wine-skin it has ceased to be. Were we to argue from this secondary meaning of "destroy" exemplified in the destruction of a wine-skin and to assert that such should and must be its correct interpretation when used of living beings, we should only be demonstrating our inability to grasp or our unwillingness to submit to one of the reasonable principles of interpretation of language.

Yet this is precisely what we find our brethren doing, in their endeavor to establish the scripturalness of the doctrine of endless conscious suffering as the doom of the lost. I take the following from one of the most earnest and capable religious weeklies of this continent:

The word "destruction" as used in the Bible over and over again never means annihilation or blotting out of existence. The term destruction denotes ruin, but does not define the form of the ruin; it signifies to pull down, to separate a whole into its parts, or to reduce to disorder, to change the mode of existence so as to disqualify that which is destroyed from its original purpose.

These definitions might be accepted as fairly accurate when given for the meaning of the destruction of an inanimate thing; but when applied to its use in reference to living beings, they will be found to give a ludicrous result. The same magazine elsewhere gives us a right method for testing the correctness of a definition offered, viz., substitute the definition for the word itself wherever found. Let us try it here. Replacing the word "destroy" by the definitions given, we obtain the following result in the above citations:

Seek the young child to pull him down.

Took counsel how they might separate his whole into its parts.

He will miserably reduce those wicked men to disorder.

He sent his armies and changed the mode of existence of those murderers so as to disqualify them from their original purpose.

Here indeed is a *reductio ad absurdum*, showing that our interpreter has missed the track in his interpretation. And we now see the reason why—he has attempted to derive a primary meaning from a secondary, instead of *vice versa*.

Granted then that the true interpretation of the word "destroy" when spoken of animate beings in the physical realm is the taking of life, which will be found to be equally true in the middle voice translated to "perish," we ask what will be its meaning when applied to animate beings in the spiritual realm, i.e., when used of the destruction of man's spiritual entity in the doom of the lost? We shall naturally expect to find that its primary meaning in the physical realm, to "take life," will give us the key to its meaning in this spiritual realm. And further it will be obvious that if we find it anywhere applied at one and the same time to both the physical and the spiritual

realm, we are thereby shut up to its ascertained physical meaning as applicable likewise to the spiritual.

Let us now return to the second of the citations given above, which we passed over because it involves the question in dispute, viz.,

Able to destroy both body and soul in hell.

Here our word "destroy" is used at one and the same time both of the physical realm, the destruction of the body, and of the spiritual realm, the destruction of the soul. What other inference is possible than that its physical meaning gives here its spiritual meaning also? If the destruction of the body in hell means the taking of its life, so also must the destruction of the soul in hell involve the termination of its life there. And that this, the only possible conclusion under rational principles of interpretation, is the true and correct one is manifest also when we come to examine the context: Fear not them which kill the body, but are not able to kill the soul: but rather fear him which is able to destroy both body and soul in hell (Matt. 10:28).

What can any fair-minded reader conclude from this but that our Lord meant that to destroy the soul was to kill the soul, to take its life?

To establish further the correctness of the above conclusion, we have additional evidence supplied by the language both of our Lord himself and of his Apostle Paul. Speaking of the cruel death which certain Galilean worshipers met at the hands of Pilate, our Lord says to his hearers, Except ye repent, ye shall all likewise perish (Luke. 13:3).

And again, speaking of the tragic accident for those eighteen on whom the tower of Siloam fell, he utters the warning, Except ye repent, ye shall likewise perish (Luke 13:5). No one would suppose him to mean, "If you are impenitent, a similar cruel fate or a like tragic disaster will end your days on earth." He of course is thinking of their final doom, and his hearers would so understand him. What then would they take his meaning to be, alike from his use of the word "perish" and of the term "like-wise"? What could they conclude him to mean but that their spiritual doom, if they were impenitent, would be swift, fatal, cataclysmic, a termination of life in the spiritual realm, fitly portrayed by the illustrations which he chose of fatal and cruel termination of life in the physical? Whereas if the spiritual doom of the finally impenitent really were to suffer consciously and never endingly, where would be the congruity of our Savior's illustration?

The same deduction is to be drawn from Paul's use of the world "perish" in his great chapter on the resurrection. Allowing for a moment the hypothesis, If Christ be not raised, he shows the inevitable conclusion that would follow, Then they also that are fallen asleep in Christ are perished (1 Cor. 15, 18). Is it conceivable that Paul meant that if there be no resurrection, they that have fallen asleep in Christ are doomed to the eternal pangs of hell fire? Surely not: he meant, If there be no resurrection, then they are dead and gone like the beasts that perish: we have no assurance of a life beyond except in the resurrection of Christ.

We must not close our study of *apollumi* without a brief glance at its use in its secondary meaning of to "lose," to find its bearing, if any, on our present subject. We are familiar with its use in the parables of Luke 15, where the lost sheep, the lost coin, and the lost prodigal each in turn represent the sinner astray from his God. The Son of man is come to seek and to save that which was "lost," his sheep which had gone astray, but was still recoverable. When the term

is made applicable to the final doom of the sinner, it is noteworthy that it is used in conjunction with the Greek word *psyche*, which our Revisers have translated "life," giving the alternative and more familiar rendering "soul" in the margin.

For whosoever would save his life shall lose it; and whosoever shall lose his life for my sake and the gospel's shall save it. For what doth it profit a man, to gain the whole world, and forfeit his life? For what should a man give in exchange for his life? (Mark 8:35-36).

That Christ is speaking of the ultimate issue of life beyond the present is certain from his words immediately following, where he speaks of life's issues as manifested "when the Son of man cometh in the glory of his Father with the holy angels." Is it not patent then that the goal which the Savior had in view for man was the salvation of life as against the loss or forfeiture of life? And this is confirmed by the remarkable fact that in a parallel passage in St. Luke it reads, If he gain the whole world and lose or forfeit his own self (Luke 9:23). Now whether the Savior speaks of loss of life or forfeiture of personality as the sinner's ultimate doom, would this be appropriate language to describe a fate in which the sinner is forever living, conscious, with memory alive and active, and suffering agonies untold, whether physical, mental, spiritual, or all three combined? The fact thus emerges that the gospel of our Lord Jesus Christ in its pristine simplicity and purity was a gospel not of reward as against punishment, not of a life of bliss as against a life of loss, but of life itself against loss of life.

But it will be asked, what of the immortality of the soul? Where does that come in? We reply with Gladstone that this doctrine of the natural immortality of the human soul "crept into the Church by the back-door. . . . It is a doctrine wholly unknown to the Holy Scriptures, and standing on no higher plane than that of an ingeniously sustained but gravely and formidably contested philosophical opinion." The gospel as preached by Christ and his apostles was unencumbered by this guess of a pagan philosopher which to-day commonly passes muster as almost a Christian axiom, scarce needing proof, or established by probabilities. Let the faithful return to the fact that it was our Savior Jesus Christ who brought life and immortality to light through the gospel, and let us rejoice to give to him who is himself the resurrection and the life that most gracious title, "the Prince of life."

This conclusion obtained from the words "destroy," "perish," will, if our interpretation be correct, be harmonious with other Scriptures relative to the subject. And it is confidently believed that a careful inductive study of Scripture will show that every line converges to the same goal, yielding a separate and growingly cumulative proof.

IS THE CHURCH MEMBERSHIP SYSTEM CHURCHLY

HENRY H. BARSTOW, D.D., Auburn, N. Y.

The "Church Membership System" refers to our common custom of distinguishing between those who are members of a church and those who are not, on the practical assumption that it also marks the distinction between Christian and non-Christian— a thing which we all know it not always does. It includes of course the various ways in which people are tested for their Christian experience by church boards and pastors; "accepted" or rejected (since when was any one ever rejected?), inducted into membership, after some more or less adequate "catechumen" instruction, by standing before the congregation on Communion Sunday and being publicly "received on confession"; and then placed on the church roll by the clerk or pastor as members of the church after receiving the right hand of fellowship.

It is a time honored custom around which have gathered traditions and assumptions whose value in the past can not be lightly belittled, but that are themselves fair subjects for ex-amination" as to their future Christian standing and character. We may grant at the outset that many of the valid objections to the system as such are based upon its abuses rather than its intrinsic demerits. It has been made to mean more than it ever was intended to mean. It has been made a hiding place for unworthy men and women who have worn it as a cloak for godless lives. It has placed in a position of ecclesiastical recognition and Christian standing people who constantly disgrace the Christian profession and discredit the Christian Church. It has been mistaken for a guarantee of divine approval and of future felicity in heaven. Like infant baptism it has in the minds of ignorant people been accorded a superstitious quality, a spiritual effectiveness quite comparable with the Roman Catholic mass, holy water and extreme unction. This is less common than in former times, but every pastor has met it. On the other hand it is rejected by thoughtful men and women who see its fallacies and refuse to put themselves thereby in a false position before the world. They will not, however sincere their Christian faith, pretend to a virtue they believe they do not possess. However much we may insist it does not mean assumption of virtue they know that in the eyes of the world with which they do business it is regarded as marking moral professions which they hesitate to make.

Just what does church membership mean as the Church understands it? It does not mean to profess religion. It means to confess irreligion. It does not mean to proclaim our own goodness. It means to admit our own sinfulness. It does not mean that we claim exceptional knowledge of spiritual truth. It does mean that we acknowledge how little we know and our purpose to know more. It is like matriculation in college. We do it not because we know, but because we want to know. It does not mean that we think we are better than other people. It does mean that we know ourselves not to be as good as Christ, and accept him—not other folks—as our model. It does not mean that we think ourselves strong enough to live the Christian life. It does mean that we know we are not strong enough, and have put our trust in Christ to make us strong enough. It does not mean merely an amiable purpose to be good. It means a solemn purpose to let Christ master us for his own purposes. It does not mean that we merely like church society and want to get into its class. It means that we believe the Church is made up of people like ourselves who need the help of Christian fellowship, and are willing to unite with them for the sake of Christian growth and for service to the kingdom of God. The true assumption is that a person is willing to make a start in the direction of these things and join the Church as the institution that will help in their growing achievement. If a person refuses to do this, nobody is likely to know what he does think. He is hiding his light under a bushel. It is on this general assumption that the Church has felt justified in claiming that a Christian who refuses to unite with its membership has "denied Christ," and that one who has united with it has "confessed him."

Have we overworked that assumption? I think we have. Every minister with any pastoral experience knows that to make the line between church membership and non-church membership identical with or even parallel to the line between being in or out of the Christian life is an undeserved reflection on many without the Church and an unwarranted recommendation to many within it. "Inarticulate religion" is a phrase that had much vogue during the war. It unquestionably represents a number of people who are willing to touch the hem of the Master's garment in the press of the crowd but tremble at the thought of being caught at it. Such a person is not at all identical with the so-called "friendly citizen" of disastrous "Inter-church World Movement" memory. He is doubtless missing much in the Christian life. He ought, according to all the traditions, to join the Church and do it according to our program. But he just does not—or will not. We put him on our "prospect lists" in evangelistic campaigns; we assign him to "personal workers' committees"; we go after him, and get him out to suppers and church occasions, and in the mind of the regular church folk he bears a sort of subtle shadow upon his name and reputation. Doubtless all these things we ought and have a right to do—except the last. But he quietly stands by his guns, knowing that without pride his Christian life is just as true, often vastly better, than that of some who within the sacred precincts of church membership are so concerned about him. Christ's bitter word to the Pharisees, "Ye compass sea and land to make one proselyte; and when he is become so, ye make him twofold more a child of hell than yourselves," may be and probably is an unfair distortion of the situation to-day, but it is worth thinking about as a direful abyss to avoid. We would do well also to remember his rebuke to the apostles when they wanted to call down fire from heaven on the man who cast out devils in the name of Christ but who would not line up with them: "He that is not against us is for us." I am not commending the unattached brother's unattachedness. I am just trying to understand him and give him a square deal. He probably contributes to the church; or at least to the Ladies' Aid annual supper and bazaar as a concession to a harassed conscience, or as a sort of tip to the waiter.

Within the church membership we have four recognizable and concentric zones of "affiliation." They may be called for the sake of vividness the inside-inners, the outside-inners, the inside-outers, and the outside-outers. Every seasoned church pastor and officer and member will recognize the classification at a glance and will not need much further characterization of the groups named. The inside-inners are the heart of the church, the real spiritual remnant whom the world acknowledges, the church is proud of, and the Master honors. They are not necessarily identical with the official group tho often including part of it. Some of that group, God help them, were past due in heaven years ago; having neither learned nor forgotten anything, lo, these many days. The good Lord himself knows just who belongs in each group. The pastor knows them pretty well; but when the church by the artificial device of a membership roll attempts to draw the line between the outside-outers of its own membership and the nearest of the non-members it certainly assumes an impossible task, and assigns an unjustifiable distinction. At that point the whole problem becomes penumbral. It is the twilight zone of the Church and the world. At that point the "church membership system" hopelessly fails and becomes grotesquely unchurchly.

One only needs to recall to the mind of church clerks and pastors the hopeless muddle of "reserved lists," "suspended lists," "restored lists," &c., that eternally confuse their records and confound their faith in humanity both sanctified and unregenerate. The periodical necessity for "transferring" names from one list to another in order to keep down the church's tax and the interminable task of getting people who move away to "take their letters" only emphasize and make vivid the unreality of that phase of the "system." Furthermore, the "Minutes of the General Assembly" in Presbyterian churches and similar records in other bodies add weight to the contention that some better system should be discovered of recording the religious affiliations of the common peole. How inadequate a test of any church's quality is the record of its membership in these books, or of its additions or losses, &c. How subtly they minister to our pride or our depression! How little do they tell of the real heart-life of any church, or of its problems or conditions, or needs! How deceptive they are to the preacher who, becoming restless in his unfruitful field, looks for a fairer pasture and a fatter flock! How little they tell, to the solemnly burdened committee of some church seeking for a shepherd, of the abilities and qualities of the pastor whose apparent success or failure they assume to measure thereby! Granted the necessity for some such statistical setting forth of the quality of our churches and ministers, could anything be less revealing of the spiritual values involved! The church roll is not a measure of character any more than the census is a test of patriotism.

We are to-day continually being told that the Church is going through a period of radical change—or ought to be. Such words as "reconstruction," "new era," "social consciousness," &c., are becoming bromidic. I submit that one of the possible places where the Church might well begin to think readjustment would be in regard to its system of church membership. The present system undoubtedly has served a great and useful purpose. It has been the means of evoking Christian committal and witness from countless hosts of God's noblest children. It has served as a basis for devotion, clean living and sacrificial service. Most cheerfully one may concede much that may be claimed for it. But it is a fair question if the time has not come when church leaders should honestly ask themselves if there be not some simpler system by which the good in the present system can be preserved and its manifest evils avoided. Is the method of a definite, limited, specifically enrolled membership the best possible way of formulating the organized expression of the Church of God on earth? Is there no way by which the fellowship of the saints can be given a local habitation and a name that will not include so many who have no part or lot in the kingdom, nor exclude so many who not being against our Master are, by his own statement, for him? Most certainly it is worth the careful consid-

eration of forward looking Christian leaders.

Some of the most freely organized religious bodies have abandoned the present system and adopted a system whose basis of affiliation is a loose pledge of discipleship—literally, discipleship: that is, the mere expression of a purpose to seek open-mindedly the truths of Christian faith and life; but without any binding acceptance of a creed; or any confession that presupposes divine regeneration or assured salvation; or entrance into a membership compact with inclusive and exclusive features. I am not at all sure that this is a certain improvement on the present system. It involves pretty grave possibilities of serious abuse, perhaps more serious than those of the present system. But it is an effort to meet the situation.

The purpose of this article is frankly not so much to suggest a new form of church organization as to raise the question for farther consideration. The writer has no assured plan to propose. He would like to smoke out some one who has one. In his own church he is now trying the experiment on a smaller scale of a non-membership organization of his young people. Instead of one with fixt membership, pledges, dues, and all the rest he has a Young People's Association of which every young person in any way affiliated with the church is automatically a member by that very fact. It has enlisted a much larger number of young people than the old system; links them up to the work of the church; maintains a live Sunday evening service of prayer and religious education; and, while adequately officered and led, puts all the young people on a common plane of interest in the church and in Christian service. It works—that is the best word that can be said for it on the second year's trial.

CHRISTIAN CO-OPERATION THE CALL OF THE AGE[1]

The Rev. CHARLES S. MACFARLAND, Ph.D., New York City

Federal unity is simply denominationalism in co-operation. It is the effort to adjust autonomy and corporate action, individuality and social solidarity, liberty and social adaptation. According to the classic definition of Herbert Spencer, evolution is the process of passing from an indefinite, incoherent homogeneity to a definite, coherent heterogeneity during which the retained motion undergoes a parallel transformation. Thus the rise and existence of denominations, following the Protestant Reformation, was an indication of progress and not of deterioration.

A study of history, however, reveals another element in evolution—namely, that it is cyclical. Progress is not directly in one direction, it comes through both forward and backward movements. We go a long distance in one direction, we then pause, and to a certain point make a return. We then gather up our renewed forces and move on again.

In theology, we know of thesis and antithesis. First we move in the line of one proposition; then comes a proposition the antithesis of this, and out of the ultimate blending of the two we find harmony and progress.

These various theories of evolution seem applicable to our denominationalism. We have gone pretty far in carrying out the proposition which has resulted in the diversity of denominationalism. Those who hold to Rome have gone equally far, in their antithesis, in the direction of unity. Perhaps we are getting, among our Protestant denominations, to recognize in equal proportion the two principles of evolution and progress which we find everywhere in the natural order—diversity and unity.

Our various denominations and sects arose largely from the demand for freedom, and through much suffering we found our freedom. We are now recognizing as denominations, however, that the highest freedom we possess may be the freedom to give up some of our freedom for the sake of the common good. This was the kind of freedom to which

Paul referred in his discussion of those denominational differences which had already begun in the Apostolic Church. We are ready to acknowledge, without forgetting perhaps that in our intellectual expression of truth we have been of Apollos or Cephas, that we are all of Christ, and that in allegiance to him we must maintain or regain unity even in the midst of our diversity. We are following still farther our denominational search for freedom, and are seeking this highest freedom in our modern movements towards Christian unity.

For the past century or two we have been largely building up denominationalism, and now we have discovered the severe truth of the word of Jesus: "He that saveth his life shall lose it, and he that loseth his life for my sake and the gospel's, shall find it."

Meanwhile one of the most startling of modern discoveries is that we have been so sadly and thoughtlessly wasteful. We have wasted our mineral wealth, squandered our forests, and allowed the mighty forces of our streams to run out into an unneeding sea.

Worse still, in the development of industry and by social neglect, we have wretchedly wasted our human power and, as our new legislation witnesses, we have been criminally prodigal with human life itself. We have poisoned, neglected, maimed, and mangled by our inefficient speeding up, by our twelve-hour days and seven-day weeks. While we have wasted the forests that make the mines, we have also wasted by thousands our human brothers in the mines, have slaughtered and despoiled our women, and have consumed our babies beyond the count of Herod in our suffocated cities, while we had half a continent of fresh air. In our commercial development we have sacrificed innocent human life upon its altar and have given over our little children to an industrial Moloch saying, with outstretched iron arms, "Let little children come unto me, and forbid them not, for of such is the kingdom of mammon." And if we followers of Christ are content to disavow the

[1] From *The Progress of Church Federation to 1922*, Fleming H. Revell Company.

blame, let us remember that in the same breath in which the Master said that to neglect these little ones was to forget himself, he also condemned men, in his most severe and solemn utterance, for the things they didn't do.

But these are not an intimation of the worst of our dissipations, and indeed these wastes have been largely because of a deeper and more serious prodigality. We have let the very light within us become darkness, and the saddest of all has been the waste of our moral powers, our finer emotions, and our religious enthusiasms, through sectarian divisions, denominational rivalries, and unrestrained caprice often deluding itself as a religious loyalty.

If our effort for redemption had been given more fully to prevention, we should not now stand trembling, shamefaced, and bewildered before the results of our own social havoc. Our most serious profligacy has been the neglect to cultivate our ultimate power, the power of our religious enthusiasm and spiritual impulse, because they were neither socially concentrated nor socially interpreted and applied.

Let us consider a few examples. One of our most important Christian endeavors is that of our home missions, which is nothing less than the undertaking of the conquest and the moral development of a new nation. . . . A few years ago the Committee on Home Missions of the Federal Council of the Churches of Christ in America investigated the state of Colorado. One hundred and thirty-three communities were found ranging in population from one hundred and fifty to one hundred thousand souls, without Protestant churches of any kind, one hundred of them being also without a Roman Catholic church. And they were places of deep need in rural and mining sections. In addition to these there were four hundred and twenty-eight towns large enough to have postoffices, but without any churches, and whole counties were discovered without any adequate religious service.

The seriousness of the other problem of overlapping is indicated by a town of four hundred people in the same state with four churches, all supported by home-mission aid, and this but one of many like it. . . .

This investigation was followed by the Home Missions Council in fifteen western States, in what was called the Neglected Fields Survey. In one state seventy-five thousand people resided five miles or more from a church. A rich valley with a population of five thousand, capable of supporting fifty thousand people, had but one church. In another State fourteen counties had but three permanent places in each for worship. One county in another State had a rural population of nine thousand with no religious ministry except that supplied by the Mormon hierarchy. Another county with a rural population of eighteen thousand had regular services in only three of its school districts.

And these are but hasty suggestions from this report. The social problems raised by home missions have been a determining factor in the development of Christian unity.

Meanwhile the development of a new and complex social order about us was getting ready for the call of a persuasive and effective gospel. New foes were arising on every hand. They were all united, and we found ourselves facing federated vice, the federated saloon, federated corruption in political life, federated human exploitation. On the one hand were the federations of labor and on the other hand federations of capital, girding themselves for their conflict, waiting the voice which should speak with power and influence, that should quell their human hatreds.

Problems of social justice were looking to us with beseeching voice, and we found ourselves obliged to face them, or, worse still, to shun them, with shame upon our faces and with a bewildered consciousness, because we had no common articulation of a code of spiritual principles or moral laws. Our spiritual authority was not equal to our human sympathy, because it was divided.

On all these things we had a multitude of voices trying to express the same consciousness, but the great world of men did not know it. Why should they know it when we had not found it out ourselves? We spoke with voices, but not with a voice.

Very nearly up to our own day the Church has faced united iniquity while there has been scarcely a city in which it could be said, in any real or serious sense, that its churches moved as one great force. And in many a town and rural village we yet have churches wearying themselves to death in a vain struggle for competitive existence, or suffering from that worst of diseases, to be "sick with their brothers' health."

What wonder that we have lost our civic virtue! Why should we not lose, not only our Sabbath as a day of worship, but also our Sunday as a day of rest? Why are we surprised that we have lost not only temperance laws but also our temperate ways. Why should we be astonished that with the loss of these we have also lost our sons and filled our houses of refuge with our daughters? Why should we wonder that the rich have left us for their unrestrained, unholy pleasure and the poor because we had no united sense of power of social justice to restrain an industry that devoured widows' houses and that bound heavy burdens grievous to be borne, especially when this was sometimes done by those who for a pretense made long prayers? What wonder that, adequate sense of religion, the home should lose its sacredness and the family become the easy prey of easy divorce and unholy marriage? Still we went on singing: "Like a mighty army moves the Church of God." and when we came to resolve it to its final analysis the only trouble was that we did not sing together.

Leave for the moment the larger review and consider the work of our individual churches and the loss of their constituency. I say the loss of their constituency, because the Church cannot be said to gain or even hold its own if it simply fills its vacancies. Many churches have marked time, year upon year, and thought that they were moving because they kept their feet in motion. The age became a migratory one. Here was a root difficulty in our social disorder. The family left one city for another. It drifted, by the necessities of industry, from place to place. And because we had no provision for shepherding the sheep that left one fold for another, they wandered about just outside some other fold. If the family, say, from one Baptist church moved near another Baptist church, there was some hope. But in at least half the cases they did not.

For a study in efficiency visit the average city on a Sunday night and measure the power of, say one thousand people, scattered among twenty-five or thirty churches, when they might, with the contagion of human impact, be gathered into one, with a manifold and constantly increasing power which, with wise direction, would send them back to fill the empty churches whence they came and to become and to exert a social conscience.

As in the home-mission fields so in our cities. We have whole sections religiously dying and socially decaying because they are without any churches, while other sections right beside them die because they have too many churches to be supported. Effective distribution is as yet, in every city, either an undiscovered art or at best a feeble effort. Our rural communities are in a like situation because there has been no concert of action. The so-called rural problem as a social perplexity has arisen almost entirely from the disunity of our religious forces, and we might as well admit it.

Then, for many, many years we had fervently prayed that God would open the doors of the heathen world and let us in to take care of the heathen as our inheritance. God always gives us more than we ask; and so he not only did that, but he opened our doors and poured the heathen in upon us. When the immigrant came he became, as often as not, an American patriot before there was time for him to become an American citizen. He assimilated everything except our religious impulse. He learned the language of our daily speech because we have only one language to be mastered. But our religion presented to him too many tongues. And why should we wonder that he could not distinguish between them?

He met centrifugal forces which repelled and not a centripetal force which might have been an irresistible attraction. He found a united democracy and he became a part of it the day he landed. He saw the unity of ideal in our public schools, and he made it his own. And if we had met him with a united brotherhood of the Church, he would have felt the mass impact of religion as he felt everything else and he would have yielded to it.

Every once in a while, generally not oftener than once in four or five years, the wave of evangelistic power would strike the community. The evangelist came, rallied the united forces of the churches for a week, then went away, and we strangely supposed that what it was perfectly clear could be begun only by united action could be kept up and developed without it, and the churches fell apart sometimes a little farther than they were before.

Meanwhile every force, every movement, every single group gathered to oppose the Church was making its common compact with its common stock and its evenly divided dividends.

It was not because we were not thinking right. It was because we were not thinking alike. It was not because we were worshipping differently or because our politics were different. It was simply that we did not work and act together upon the tasks in which we were in absolute agreement. We were confused in our self-consciousness. We conceived our churches and our sects as ends in themselves rather than as the means to the one end that we have always had in common. We remembered that we were of Paul, or of Apollos, while we forgot that we were all of Christ, and that all things were ours. We were losing our lives because we were trying to save them.

So much for the facts of history. Let us now seek the vision of prophecy. This prodigality of moral power and spiritual impulse was not because the Church was becoming an apostate church. It was not because she was leaving an old theology or because she was rejecting a new one. Taken as a whole, her views were becoming larger and her vision finer. In certain ways she was creating greater forces. But her forces were spent because her attack on sin was not concerted, and because she was not conscious of her own inherent unity. The Church and ministry went on doing their unrelated work, gaining a keener moral sense and a stronger ethical gospel. The Church and her gospel were creating the very unrest that was crying out for social justice. And even while the Church was losing the toilers, she was preparing for their social emancipation. She was continually creating larger opportunities which, however, she was failing to meet because of her divided moral forces.

We now feel that something very different is to be done.

It is interesting that the first serious movement towards federation was in the foreign field. The missionaries began to send word that they could not make their way by using such confusing tongues. They sent imperative messages to us that they must get together, not only in order to impress the gospel upon the heathen, but for their own self-preservation. Both Christian unity and social service are largely reflex actions from the field of foreign missions.

This application of the gospel to the needs of the world is what is giving us our unity. When we get together upon our common task, we cannot help forgetting, for the time being at least, the things which have divided us because we find ourselves in unity upon these two laws upon which Jesus said the whole law and the prophets hung, on love to God and love to man. We are facing our common foe of commercialized vice, of human exploitation together, and we are receiving abuse. As we stand side by side it becomes impossible for us to do anything but love our fellow Christians, and we are willing that they should make their intellectual expression of religion according to their own type of mind, and that they should worship after their own forms and customs.

Is it any less holy to crush out a den of vice than it is to regenerate a vicious man? Here again our differences are only in our use of terms, and not in reality and fact. Go to commercialized vice and to industrial injustice and say to them, "We will make the laws tighter," and they will answer, "Very well, we will find ways to break them." Go and say to them, "We will make our courts stronger," and they will answer to themselves, if they do not to us, "The political power of our money is stronger than any court of justice."

But suppose you could go to them and say, "The churches of this city, all of them, have gotten together. They are thinking, planning, and moving as one man to crush you." They might doubt it; but if they did not doubt it, they would fear it as they have not feared even the Almighty himself.

Now for these common tasks we are discovering, faster than we admit it, and we are conscious of it faster than we express it to ourselves, that for these common missions we require no changes of our symbols or of the intellectual expression of our religious faith. We have passed the periods both of division and of toleration and we are entering that of serious co-operation. While Christian unity as a sentiment is everywhere in the air, it is taking perhaps three concrete forms.

The first is that which is expressed by the hierarchy at Rome. It is not our purpose here to discuss this form.

The second is that which finds expression in such movements as the Christian Unity Foundation and the proposed Conference on Faith and Order. For that we pause to offer a sympathetic prayer and to express our hope. Co-operation in service must precede it, or at least go hand in hand with it. Fellowship and unity of action must not wait too long upon it. We must come together for it with enough mutual faith and trust to believe that our aim and work are common.

There is therefore another form of Christian unity which is possible without waiting for the decisions of the Conference on Faith and Order, and is perhaps necessary or advisable before we can reach the common ground for any such conference. It might be called Christian unity at work. It is a unity not to be created so much as discovered and interpreted. We already have it. All we need to do is to exercise it.

God has put into our human order the mingling together of unity and diversity. While it is a unity on the one hand which is not uniformity, it must also be diversity on the other which is not divisiveness. I believe that the movement of which the Federal Council of the Churches of Christ in America is the most concrete expression is an illustration of this principle of progress.

Federal unity is stronger and more vital than the first form of unity, represented by the Vatican, because it is unity with freedom, and because unity is stronger without uniformity than with it. The social difference between the unity of the Federal Council and the unity of Rome is also thus: With federal unity the Church may give herself for the sake of the world regardless of what becomes of herself, she may give herself for the sake of humanity and not for the sake of herself; while under the unity of Rome she is obliged first of all to take care of her own life. We must be willing to save our life by losing it.

Federal unity, however, recognizes the two principles of progress, differentiation and coherence. It recognizes that the kingdom of God does not mean solitariness on the one hand or uniform consolidation on the other.

It is simply genuine co-operation without regard to the ultimate result to ourselves. It is not trying to get men to think alike or to think together. It is first willing that the army should be composed of various regiments with differing uniforms, with differing banners, and even, if necessary, with different bands of music at appropriate intervals, provided they move together, face the same way, uphold each other, and fight the common foe of the sin of the world with a common love for the Master of their souls, for each other, and for mankind. It is unity without uniformity; diversity without divisiveness; comprehensiveness, not competition or compulsion.

This unity we already have. It simply awaits discovery and use.

When the task is completed and the Church becomes the conscience, the interpreter, and the guide of the social order, and when the spiritual authority which she possesses is translated into one common tongue and her voices become one mighty voice, the gates of hell shall no longer prevail against her, and she will be no longer weak and helpless before the haggard, sullen, and defiant face of injustice, inhumanity, and heartless neglect, and she will be able to take care of all her children—and her children are humanity.

Finally then, the creative work of home missions can be conceived, to-day and to-morrow, only by a Church with the social vision and impulse, and can be performed only by unity and comity.

And only by these selfsame tokens can the heathen lands be redeemed, the heathen of those lands who came to us to be shaped into a Christian democracy; the Christian Sabbath be saved; the Christian home preserved in sacred purity; our boys delivered from the hosts of sin; our girls delivered from the lust of men; the people redeemed from injustice and oppression; our evangelism be redemptive, and the Christian Church itself be saved from becoming atrophied and from contempt of the world; by an immediate sweeping social vision and an instant sense of genuine and earnest unity, through which and by which alone her spiritual authority can make the kingdoms of this world the kingdom of our Lord.

It is true that the pages of federal unity are not free from interrogation points.

There is one comprehensive answer to them. As the writer is called to go from one to the other of the Federal Council's constituent bodies his one message to each is this: You can trust the other twenty-nine. The day for servile suspicion is gone. These other brethren will act with you in united freedom, in united faith, competing with you for the finest of Christian consideration that no principle held sacred by their brethren be derided, violated, or impaired.

Thus Christian unity will come, not so much by abstract process as by concrete experience; not by asking whether or not we shall come together, but, at least so far as our Protestant evangelical churches are concerned, by coming together first in order to find out whether or not they should come. It is the call of trust and faith and we are safe to heed it.

THE ONLY CURE FOR DISSATISFACTION [1]

Principal H. Maldwyn Hughes, D.D., Wesley House, Cambridge, England

The writer of Ecclesiastes is a born pessimist. The burden of his cry is, Vanity of vanities, all is vanity. There is no profit in the works either of nature or of man. The sun rises and sets, rises and sets, and so on, with endless regularity. The wind blows from the North, then from the South, then from the East, then from the West. Apparently its movements are endless. The rivers flow into the sea. The waters are caught up into the clouds, then they descend again in the rains to replenish the rivers, and so on, in never-ending cycles. All things are full of unutterable weariness. Vanity of vanities, all is vanity. As for man, what profit hath he in all his labors? The earth abides, but man who lives on the earth is but a fleeting shadow. One generation appears, pursues its way, consumed with desire, urged on by ambition, and then it is gone; another generation takes its place, and it, too, vanishes away. Life is a meaningless drama. Sense brings no satisfaction. The eye is not satisfied with seeing, nor is the ear filled with hearing.

Yet the eye is a very wonderful organ. Perhaps it is only those who have been stricken with blindness who fully realize how wonderful it is. Surely, you say, the things seen by the eye are very satisfying? By means of the eye we behold the wonders and glories of nature, the beautiful earth by day, the starry firmament by night. Through the eye we behold mountains and valleys, majestic forests, shining lakes, silver streams. Through the eye we behold the many-colored beauty of sky and sea and every living thing. By means of the eye we behold the masterpieces of sculpture and art, and we are transported by the world's ineffable beauty. By means of the eye we see man made in the image of God. We look into one another's faces and see the changing looks that are more eloquent than words. By means of the eye we read the masterpieces of literature, and are enabled to hold fellowship with seers and saints and sages of all generations. By means of the eye we look out on the wonderful and interesting world of man's manifold activities, and we ourselves are able to tread the intricate path of business and toil.

Yes, the eye is a very wonderful organ. None the less, this preacher is right. The eye is not satisfied with seeing. When we have seen all the beauty that the world has for us the heart is still unsatisfied, and in our eyes there is the far-away look that tells of unsatisfied desires.

The ear is a very marvelous instrument too; some people think, a more wonderful instrument than the eye. I have heard men say they would rather be blind than deaf. The ear is the organ of living fellowship. Have you ever thought what it would be to live in a soundless world? The music of the spheres, the murmur of the sea, the moaning of the wind, the hum of the summer day, the song of the nightingale and the lark, the melodies and harmonies of music, the rapture of oratory—all are yours if you can hear. But once again the preacher is right. The ear is not filled with hearing. You may drink your fill of the music of sound and your heart may still be unsatisfied. In your faces there is the wistful

[1] Specially reported for the Homiletic Review.

strained look of those who are listening for distant, far-away voices.

This preacher is right in his premises. He is wrong in his conclusions. The deduction that he ought to have drawn was not, Vanity of vanities, all is vanity; but, my soul thirsteth for God, for the living God. These phenomena of which he speaks demonstrate man's deep need of God. The eye is not satisfied with seeing until it has seen the vision of God. The ear is not filled with hearing until it hears the Word of God.

Now first of all, man needs a vision of God. That is man's deepest need. He lives for it. You can not understand life until you see God in it. To live without God is to live without hope. The key to the interpretation of life is God. We are accustomed to say of some crucial scene or situation that it is like Hamlet without the prince of Denmark. Just suppose that the great play was put on the boards without Hamlet; suppose that all his speeches and actions were left out. How dreary, meaningless, and chaotic the drama would be! Now re-enact the drama, letting Hamlet have his proper place, and immediately you see unity and order and meaning produced out of chaos. That illustrates what I mean when I say it is hopeless to try and understand the world and life without God. You are trying to understand the drama when you are leaving out the central, dominant, sovereign figure. Naturally everything is meaningless and chaotic. Let the scales fall from your eyes. See God in the world; immediately order and meaning and purpose are introduced into this drama we call life.

Let me give one or two illustrations of my meaning. You will remember that when Elisha was in the city of Dothan the Syrians came and encompassed the city in order to make him captive. His servant, a young man, came to him and told him his foes were besieging the city, and Elisha answered, Fear not, for they that be with us are more than they that be with them. The young man was perplext. There were the hosts of the Syrians outside the city, and there was Elisha, with his few faithful followers. Surely the prophet was mad! The young man was judging the circumstances, as he thought; but he did not see everything. You remember that Elisha prayed, Lord, open his eyes, that he may see. That must have seemed a very foolish prayer to the young man. He was wide-awake enough. Surely it was Elisha who was asleep, not realizing the seriousness of the situation. But read on. The Lord opened the eyes of the young man and he saw. And then! Behold, the mountain was full of horses and chariots of fire round about Elisha. That made all the difference. Now the young man saw the whole drama, whereas formerly he looked upon only a part of it, and that the least significant part. It meant that the vision of God and of the unseen world flashed in upon him, and he knew the great and invincible hosts of God were contending for righteousness. Are there not times when you are tempted to despair of the victory of truth and righteousness? You look around, and those who are given over to the service of unrighteousness are so many, while those who are devoted to truth seem comparatively so few. You are tempted to say there is absolutely no hope of victory. You are wrong in your arithmetic. Wrong in my arithmetic? you say; I have counted everybody I can conceivably imagine to have any sympathy with truth, goodness, and purity, and I find they are in a hopeless minority! Yes, but you have only counted those whom you can see. Pray, Lord, open mine eyes, that I may see. When that prayer is answered you will take into account the invisible hosts of God, and you will know that righteousness is always in the majority.

Or let me take another illustration, from the book of Job. It is a bold attempt to deal with the problem of suffering—that dark problem that has baffled men all through the ages, and still bewilders us today. Our agonized cry still is, Why do the innocent suffer, and why does tragedy hold the world in its cruel grip? You remember that Job was an innocent man. Innumerable, almost incredible, calamities overtook him. According to the theology of those days, a man's prosperity was a sign of his righteousness; if he was a sinner, sooner or later adversity overtook him. Job's friends came to him and presented the orthodox standpoint, hinting very directly that he must be guilty of some great sin, otherwise these disasters would not have overtaken him. Job refutes the orthodoxy of his day. He gives no cut and dried solution of the problem of suffering. When you reach the end of the book you are no nearer a philosophical solution. That is the greatness of the book: it gives us no cut and dried solution; but it does give us the only solution that can satisfy the human heart. Here it is: "I have heard of thee by the hearing of the ear, but now mine eyes seeth thee." That is his final word, but it is enough. What he says in effect is this: I have been arguing from insufficient data, speaking of things I did not understand, talking of things too wonderful for me. Now my vision is enlarged. It takes in the great unseen world. The whole problem is changed. It is not solved, but it is transcended. Job finds himself lifted up into a new region. He has not pierced the clouds, but somehow he has been lifted right above them. He is able to see the sun shining clearly in the heavens. Life is full of mysteries we can not unravel and problems we can not solve, but we may see the vision of infinite wisdom, infinite love, behind all thing. If we do not know and understand, we can trust if we have seen with the eye of faith him who makes the hurricane and the thunder and the storm the messages of his will, and makes even the wrath of man to praise him. When you get there you may not have solved the mystery but you have reached the secret of the peace of God that passeth understanding.

Let me take one more illustration of the same truth. Isaiah says: In the year that King Uzziah died I saw the Lord. Well, what then? It was then, he says, that I began to understand life and the ways of my own heart. It was then I realized the uncleanness of my own heart and the sinfulness of the world, and I said, Wo is me! for I am undone, because I am a man of unclean lips, and I dwell in the midst of a people of unclean lips, for mine eyes have seen the King, the Lord of hosts. It was then I heard the voice of duty, the voice that said, Whom shall I send? Who will go for us? There is a closer connection between sin and the dark problems and tragedies of life than we commonly imagine, and no man has realized the depth of the tragedy of the world's sin until he has seen the vision of God. Then he does not talk so much of the problems and mysteries. He does not spend too much time on profitless speculations. He cries, Lord, here am I; send me. He realizes the infinite possibilities open to him of cooperating with God in

lifting and purifying and redeeming the world. The eye is not satisfied with seeing until it has seen God.

The other thing I would say is that the world needs the word of God. Listen to all the world's wisest teachers and philosophers, and your heart is still unsatisfied. Man is always standing in the strained attitude of the listener, seeking to catch the sound of distant, far-away voices. What is the word of God? Again and again in the Old Testament you read that some prophet says that the word of the Lord came unto him. What he means is that he has grasped some truth which he could not have apprehended merely by the exercise of his own intellect. The spirit of God broodeth over the face of the waters, we read. The spirit of God broods over our hearts and minds and wills and consciences, bringing to birth thoughts, ideals, dreams, visions, and purposes which we could never have engendered of ourselves. We read and we think, and think and we read, until we are wearied. Often there comes no new light to us as the result of our intellectual travail. Suddenly the word of the Lord flashes in upon us. We are on the mount of vision and understanding. We have heard the words we long to hear. God speaks to us, spirit to spirit. We lose the strained, listening look from our faces as the voices of the other world break in upon us. Has not that experience been yours? Have you not wrestled and travailed again and again and found no relief? Have you not felt yourself weighed down by some heavy burden from which you could not get deliverance? Have you not felt yourself surrounded by thick darkness, lightened by no single ray of light, no solitary star? Then one day, as you are musing, as you are praying, the load is lifted from your spirit, the clouds are irradiated with light. The word of the Lord has come to you and your ear has been filled with hearing.

Well, you say, how am I to distinguish between the voice of God, the voices of the world, and the voices of my own heart? I can not give you any hard and fixt rule. The word of God attests itself. When it comes, you can not mistake its accents. Whoso hath felt the spirit of the Highest can not doubt him nor deny him. The word of God satisfies the deepest longings of our souls. It fills the ear with hearing. It gives us peace and courage and wisdom and confidence and understanding. It lifts our burdens. It does not solve our mysteries, but it lifts us far above them into that region where we see and know that eternal wisdom and eternal love are working for the best.

Yes, and the word of the Lord comes to us through him who was the very incarnation of the thought of God.

> Tho truths in manhood darkly join,
> Deep-seated in our mystic frame,
> We yield all blessing to the name
> Of him who made them current coin.

> For wisdom dealt with mortal powers
> Where truth in closest words shall fail,
> When truth embodied in a tale
> Shall enter in at lowly doors.

> And so the Word had breath, and wrought
> With human hands the creed of creeds
> In loveliness of perfect deeds
> More strong than all poetic thought;

> Which he may read that binds the sheaf,
> Or builds the house, or digs the grave,
> And those wild eyes that watch the wave
> In roarings round the coral reef.

When we listen to the voice of Jesus as it speaks to us through his word and his life and his works and the cross and the empty tomb, we know that the Word of the Lord has come to us. We have an inward confidence that can not be shaken. Our ears are filled with hearing, and we understand the mysteries of the kingdom of God. I say to you, if you doubt the revelations that come to you, if you wonder if they are the voice of God, test them by the revelation given to you in Jesus Christ. Learn of him. You will soon learn whether these inner revelations are born of God.

And let me say this: The word of the Lord still comes to you. Do not imagine that the word of the Lord came to the Old Testament prophets and the early apostles and since then has ceased to come to men. It comes in every generation. It comes to all sorts and conditions of men. There is a striking passage in Luke's gospel the significance of which I think we often miss. "Now in the fifteenth year of the reign of Tiberius Cæsar, Pontius Pilate being governor of Judea, and Herod being tetrarch of Galilee, and his brother Philip tetrarch of Iturea and of the region of Trachonites, and Lysanias the tetrarch of Abilene, Annas and Caiaphas being the high priests, the word of God came unto John the son of Zacharias in the wilderness." The word of God passed by the emperor on his throne, passed by petty kings and princelings, passed by high priests and priests, and came to the obscure John, the man of the people. And it came to him in the wilderness. So it has been in all ages. The word of God has come to all sorts and conditions of men, and it has come to them in the wilderness. If our ears are open, the word of the Lord will come to us to-day in the wilderness of our present perplexities and distresses. If we hear and obey, we shall know and understand. Our ears will be filled with hearing. Our souls will be satisfied. Here is the cure for pessimism and doubt. Here is the only cure for discouragement and disillusionment and disappointment. By faith—that is only another way of saying, by the vision of God—by faith, says the writer of the epistle to the Hebrews, we understand. The secret of understanding is to see God and to hear his voice as he speaks to us in Jesus Christ and in the solitary places of our own hearts.

The riddle of the world is understood only by him who knows that God is good. The solution of the riddle of the universe is God. The solution of the riddle of God is Jesus Christ.

What the Good Is Like

> Thou ask'st me what the good is like? Then
>   hear!
> The good is ordered, holy, pious, just,
> Self-ruling, useful, beautiful, and right,
> Severe, without pretense, expedient ever,
> Fearless and griefless, helpful, soothing
>   pain,
> Well - pleasing, advantageous, steadfast,
>   loved,
> Esteemed, consistent. . . .
> Renowned, not puffed up, careful, gentle,
>   strong,
> Enduring, blameless, lives from age to age.
>   —CLEANTHES.

Editorial Comment

We once heard an excellent man pass judgment upon a philosophical work with some of the conclusions of which he did not agree. "The author seemed to me," said he, "not at all to understand what he was talking about." At least one of his hearers went away wondering if it were not possible that the critic had failed to understand what he had been reading. Ministers are sometimes accused—and too often justly—of a tendency to "go off at half-cock"; that is, to speak loudly and positively, without adequate preparation and before a definite aim has been taken.

The Ethics of Controversy

Just now, when interest in the validity of evolution has been re-awakened, there is a new temptation to discuss it with more passion than knowledge and to emit more heat than light. This is a method of treatment which we rightfully resent when applied to ourselves. We do not like to have either act or motive judged by one who is ignorant of the real state of the case.

It were well to carry over the lesson suggested by that feeling into our discussions of all the great questions agitating the public mind. Burke, with his extraordinary gift for so viewing particular instances as to make them yield general rules, once remarked, "Men little think how immorally they act in rash meddling with what they do not understand." The minister, more than most men, ought, especially in his public utterances, to make sure of his premises, and then in drawing his conclusions to shun exaggeration. He should remember that his hearers, however widely they differ from him, can not reply, for the seemliness and dignity of a service of worship forbid. They can, however, fume inwardly, and if they have any reason to suspect that the preacher is hiding ignorance or prejudice under the veil of sanctity, not only will their indignation be righteous but the damage to the cause of religion as well as to the preacher's influence may be irreparable.

It is equally true that a too great cocksureness based on partial knowledge may lead logically to conclusions in the hearer's mind quite at variance with the preacher's purpose. To speak of the method of development known as evolution as necessarily "materialistic" and foreign to the idea of a divine plan in creation is to beg some very big questions. It is to set limits to God's power and ingenuity after a fashion calculated to belittle rather than to exalt him. He who rears the exquisite purity and fragrance of the lily from the mud of the pond may not disdain very humble paths for the progress of man himself. Just what these paths have been he has not always seen fit to declare in detail. But he invites inquiry, and where this is reverent and patient he rewards it. So Galileo and Kepler found, tho some of their conclusions seemed revolutionary to the theologians of their day. They were revolutionary, but, when rightly understood, they added to rather than subtracted from man's evidence of God's being and good-will. The swift-denouncer of the results of scientific investigation needs to be very sure of his ground lest he act "immorally in meddling with what he does not understand." Such immorality, such spiritual madness, is likely to result in belief in a God who is too small for his world, the immensities of which are being newly revealed with each increase of telescopic power and every new astronomic instrument.

The life of a nation corresponds to the life of the individual—the best is transmitted. There are nations that may be said to have arrived, and there are nations that are still coming. Shall those who have arrived stoop to senile petulance towards the future and ingratitude towards the past? When a fruit is ripe it begins to decay. Those who are dying, physically by a minus birth rate, morally by loss of virtue, who have had their turn at ruling land and sea and neglected to redeem its pledge to posterity: shall they get into the habit of abusing their rivals in oblivion? America will not have to wait ten thousands years for its New Zealander, to judge by its rapid growth; when he comes we hope he shall be able to say that we died game, without doing what poor sportsmen invariably do—maligning their antagonists.

Our Debt to The Nations

Babylon and Greece and Rome, Egypt and Palestine and Turkey, Portugal and Spain and Italy—they all lived their lives joyously and usefully, often against great odds and groping in the dark, as was the will of fate. The Turk once taught Christianity chivalry; the Moor brought beauty and truth to Europe; Italy, once, was the mistress of a thousand graces; Spain taught men the ways of bold venture; the Jew has been our master in a hundred points. The twentieth century would be a dark era but for the torch handed on through all the preceding centuries. The greater a man the more he owes to his mother; the cleverest nation is the greatest debtor to the past— its very prominence is a tribute to the greatness of those from whom it borrowed or stole or inherited. Land and sea, knowledge and art are not the property of any nation, they are but a temporary trust, like the possessions of a short-lived man, to be passed on, with an increment, to its wiser and better successors.

With the present-day habit of national self-glorification, rampant on this long-suffering globe, we are in danger sometimes of forgetting this simple and obvious fact.

✠

The crime wave which for months past has spread over many of our American cities appears to be the genuine article. Not only the record of the police blotter but the reports of the daily press and common observation confirm the impression that an exceptionally large amount of criminal behavior is taking place.

The Crime Wave

Many answers have been given to the question as to the causes. Most of these lay stress on some phase of the post-war psychology. Some say that crime is a natural reaction from the stress and excitement of warfare. Others hold that the sanctioned killing involved in war destroyed the natural inhibitions against inflicting death and suffering which usually deter people from acts of violence, and that an analogous effect was produced in the case of respect for property rights. Still others find the causes largely economic, and call attention to the fact that any period of industrial depression and unemployment is likely to be accompanied by an increase in crime.

A different set of explanations accounts for the situation by some rather ill-defined influence of prohibition. Usually the relationship is not as direct as in the report from Chicago that prohibition had increased the efficiency of the criminal class by making it difficult for them to befuddle themselves with alcohol. The customary explanation is that any prominent law which conflicts with a considerable body of public opinion and so is constantly violated tends to lower the respect for all law.

There is an element of truth in all these explanations. Two general influences seem to be at work. First, the industrial depression and unemployment; second, the fact that the war produced an abnormal acceleration of social change which resulted in breaking down old standards, disorganizing established institutions, and encouraging individuals to set themselves up as judges of their own conduct. The psychology which results in "flapperism" and "jazz" in the so-called higher circles produces lawlessness in groups where the temptations are of a different character.

Equally important with a knowledge of causes is an understanding of remedies. As always in such a period, the unthinking and uninformed desire to rush to the expedient of increased severity of punishment, in disregard of the fact that thousands of years of penal experience have proved the ineffectiveness of severe punishments as a deterrent against crime. More hopeful is the movement which has made some headway in Chicago and New York to secure speed and certainty of punishment. If the potential criminal were certain that he would be detected and punished, the gravity of the punishment itself would be of minor importance. At present, unfortunately, there is altogether too good a gambler's chance on the side of the criminal.

One interesting commentary on our social situation is the tendency to organize unofficial agencies to back up the legal representatives of the government—a sort of sublimated and law-abiding vigilance committees.

INTERNATIONAL IDEALS OF THE CHURCHES OF CHRIST [1]

1. WE BELIEVE that nations no less than individuals are subject to God's immutable moral laws.

2. WE BELIEVE that nations achieve true welfare, greatness and honor only through just dealing and unselfish service.

3. WE BELIEVE that nations that regard themselves as Christian have special international obligations.

4. WE BELIEVE that the spirit of Christian brotherliness can remove every unjust barrier of trade, color, creed and race.

5. WE BELIEVE that CHRISTIAN patriotism demands the practice of good-will between nations.

6. WE BELIEVE that international policies should secure equal justice for all races.

7. WE BELIEVE that all nations should associate themselves permanently for world peace and good-will.

8. WE BELIEVE in international law, and in the universal use of international courts of justice and boards of arbitration.

9. WE BELIEVE in a sweeping reduction of armaments by all nations.

10. WE BELIEVE in a warless world, and dedicate ourselves to its achievement.

[1] From the Commission on International Justice and Good-will of the Federal Council.

The Preacher

JACQUES BÉNIGNE BOSSUET
THE BRILLIANT FRENCH PREACHER[1]

Bossuet (1627-1704) is called by Sainte-Beuve, "the glory of France." He had a genius for form. The French language was never better used. He is the best known of that brilliant group of preachers associated with the reign of Louis Fourteenth—Bossuet, Bourdaloue, Massillon. He is recognized by all good Catholics as the chief theologian and controversialist of the Gallican Church.

But Bossuet has never been a popular study in the English-speaking and Protestant world. In thought he has been connected with the court of the Grand Monarch, with its artificial social life, its confusion of thought, its inconsistent religious life, devotion to all the forms of religion and complete worship of mammon. Then Bossuet is so wrapt up in the religious controversies of the age, and in the conception of authority that finally drove the Huguenots from France, that he has lost interest for a freedom-loving world. Only a few have gone back to the great French preacher—critics like Matthew Arnold in the matter of style, and high-churchmen like Canon Liddon who was attracted both by form and doctrine.

The fact that there has been no adequate biography or study in English, accounts in part for the lack of interest in Bossuet. There have been many such works in French, but in English only such brief studies as are found in the histories of preaching, as Wilkinson's *French Classics in English*, Broadus' *History of Preaching*, and the more recent history by Dargan. So Bossuet has been a splendid figure, like a snow-peak glistening from afar, rarely explored. He has been almost an unreal figure, wrapt up in legend. In this book by E. K. Saunders he is brought forth into true human interest. We see the age and

its influence upon him, the growth of those forces that gave him place and power and fame, and the revelation of that inner life of faith and single devotion and sincere love of individual souls. The man of two worlds is carefully traced, and the honest effort to reconcile them is made, at least, to show us how such contradictory elements make up a man. I think the reader will feel that the effort to justify or harmonize is sometimes overdone, but that it is honest, critical work there can be no doubt. It is a book of great interest, full of genuine life.

First of all Bossuet was a preacher. He felt the fascination of an audience, the power of speech, and the praise of men. As a student at Paris he was thought a prodigy and at sixteen preached before the court circle. The king encouraged preachers, however little he regarded their doctrine, and so hearing sermons was a fashion. Bossuet had the sincerity and courage to turn away from Paris and devote the service of his early priesthood to the provinces. It seemed a definite renunciation to the religious life. A veteran priest, and a noble scholar and preacher, warned him that "learning and reflection rather than constant practise were the best preparation for a preacher." And Vincent de Paul had taught him the sacredness of holy orders. His tastes were trained by classic learning, his message was formed by the constant study of the New Testament and Catholic doctrine with Augustine as guide, his character was formed by the severest priestly discipline and sincere devotion to the interests of his people. Under such education his genius became the facile servant of the Church. After the early experiences of the priesthood, he was for a short time court preacher, ten years as tutor to the Dauphin, and

[1] *A Study*, by E. K. Saunders, S.P.C.K., London. The Macmillan Company, New York, 1921.

most of his life bishop of Meaux. His fame as preacher first came from his funeral orations, for the queen of Charles First of England, the daughter of the duchess of Orleans, and for Prince Condé. He was the preacher for special occasions. But his life was devoted to teaching his own churches. He was above all a doctrinal preacher. He did not analyze character and lay bare the ugliness of individual sins as did Bourdaloue, nor persuade through beauty of form and sentiment as did Massillon. He was always an exponent of the Catholic faith. "His own faith was as a fire that burned within him and he sought to impose the same conviction of the truth on the minds of others." He studied, he served, he believed, he was full of his subject, and he spoke as he believed. His famous saying was true and made him the preacher: "Style is the man."

Bossuet was a bishop—devoted to his flock in teaching, in trying to win converts, in ministering to the religious. This was the best, purest part of his life. Here his fame is the least clouded. He did not gain the higher honors of the Church and so satisfy his natural ambition and fulfil the promise of his early fame. But he was known to his own priests and churches as making religion supreme, and his own life a sincere service to the Church.

His devotion to the Catholic Church led him to use his great learning, his keen logical powers, and his matchless style for her defense and for the propagation of the faith. Bossuet is best known as a controversialist. He gave the strength of his life to it. He anticipated H. G. Wells by more than three centuries in his *Universal History*. He had one thing in mind and did not suffer any contradictory evidence. He thought the faith might be proved by secular history either of persons or nation. It was his philosophy of history. That "God gave free-will to man, but he retained the power to mold the effect of its misuse and so fulfil his purpose for the universe" was his constant theme.

His faith in the Catholic Church was so single and his idea so fixed that he could not think of any salvation outside of his Catholic Church. So he constantly labored to win back the Huguenots, and to this end prepared his great work on *The Variations of Protestantism*. Bossuet was not naturally cruel, but he lived in an intolerant age and his zeal made him hard and inhuman, and led him to approve the revocation of the Edict of Nantes, though he tempered his persecution by individual kindness.

His conception of the unity and supremacy of the Church also interprets his controversy with Fénelon. He could not understand the latter. He felt that the idealism and mysticism of Fénelon depreciated the offices of the Church, and led to fellowship with men of good will whatever their creed. To him, this was a fatal blow at religion. And so he fought with bitterness one of the purest and most spiritual men of the age.

Through the fixedness of his intellectual faith there grew unconsciously the love of authority. He wanted victory for his church, and his love of victory brought a shadow on his great fame. All reform seemed hateful to him as a weakening of the Church. In his mind the authority of the throne was bound with the unity of the Church. He held that absolute monarchy was God's rule of men; and so he tolerated or ignored the unreality and inconsistency of Louis XIV and felt with the pomp of power, while in his heart he tried to be a servant of the lowly Christ. The "will of God" was as supreme with him as with Faber, and he accepted everything as a charge from God, from teaching the Dauphin and fighting the Protestants and Quietists to the charge of a soul like Madame d'Albert. As to faith he was autocratic, but humble towards souls. By nature gentle, he became the stern guardian of orthodoxy, relentless in his search for heresy. His zeal betrayed his charity. He tried to be the censor of all theological opinion, and he became the terror of critics and younger men.

The story of Bossuet is full of surprises and contradictions. Two natures are revealed by this careful biography, the idealist and the worldling. He is a genius, but not always great in character, with weaknesses that so often mar great lives.

KINDLING AND INSPIRING THOUGHTS

The ideal is only truth at a distance.—LAMARTINE.

The fashion of this world passes away, and it is with what is abiding that I would fain concern myself.—GOETHE.

When two countries begin to laugh at the same jokes there is real hope that they will become united on other matters also.—JOHN J. BANNINGA.

Religion is caught rather than taught; it is the religious teacher, not the religious lesson, that helps the pupil to believe.—DEAN INGE.

A universal and absolute toleration of everything and everybody would lead to a general chaos as certainly as a universal and absolute intolerance.—D. G. RITCHIE.

Nothing counts in the world of pure science except facts and the interconnection of facts.—ROBERT J. WARDELL.

The breadth of my life is not measured by the multitude of my pursuits, nor the space I take amongst other men; but by the fulness of the whole life which I know as mine.—F. H. BRADLEY.

It is a man's sincerity and depth of vision that makes him a poet. See deep enough, and you see musically; the heart of nature being everywhere music, if you can only reach it.—CARLYLE.

So far as human agency can operate to bring on a better era to the church, he who despairs of it, hinders it, to the extent of his influence; while he who expects it, hastens it, so far as it may be accelerated.—ISAAC TAYLOR.

The equilibrium we want is not the equilibrium of a boulder that has been sitting in the same place for ten centuries without a quiver. The equilibrium we want is the equilibrium of a moving wheel that can keep its equilibrium only as long as it keeps rotating.—GLENN FRANK.

The present degradation of human life is due to man's refusal to accept Christ's estimate of its values and duties. It will endure so long as the work and person of Christ are refused their right place in human thought and aspiration.—CANON E. W. BARNES.

It is a singular proceeding to discredit the historical method while professing to hold fast to the psychological, since history is neither more nor less than the objectifying of psychology and psychology the inner side of history.—C. A. BECKWITH.

True religion takes up that place in the mind which superstition would usurp, and so leaves little room for it; and likewise lays us under the strongest obligations to oppose it.—BISHOP BUTLER.

There is a great deal of good about us, you know; a great deal of good—more or less. We are like the fruits of a certain island in the Pacific, which are very plentiful, but all imperfect in one way or another—very good, only there is something the matter with each one of us.—W. L. WATKINSON.

How can we hope to get a true system of education from politics. Is there any atmosphere more degrading? Plato has warned us that no man is fit to govern until he has ceased to desire power. But these men think of nothing else. To be in power; that is the game of politics. What can you expect from such people?—Dr. L. P. JACKS.

Among the microbes which are very dangerous and to be guarded against with all diligence is the taking oneself too seriously. To be a fool may not be set down as a sin, and yet it leads to chief sins. "Thou shalt not be a fool," would be a good commandment and one for which there is real need and one which would be kept right busy all days of the year.—W. A. QUALE.

Where the State has bestowed education the man who accepts it must be content to accept it merely as a charity unless he returns it to the State in full, in the shape of good citizenship. . . . Only a limited number of us can ever become scholars . . . but we can all be good citizens. We can all lead a life of action, a life of endeavor, a life that is to be judged primarily by the effort, somewhat by the result, along the lines of helping the growth of what is right and decent and generous and lofty in our several communities, in the State, in the nation.—THEODORE ROOSEVELT.

The Pastor

THE MINISTER'S SIDE LINE

BY A MINISTER WHO HAS ONE

Much of the talk about the minister's side line is altogether too narrow. Many of its advocates take the position that it is a necessary evil rather than a virtue in itself. It helps the minister to right an injustice rather than standing on its own strength. This article is written because the writer, after some years of experience with a fairly profitable side line, feels that more can be said for it than has been said.

I remember back in the days when the idea was in my mind. The question of the morality of the side line was a real issue. I wondered if one could be fair to the high calling and still use part of his time for financial renumeration. It was the advice of a prominent bishop of the Methodist church which finally brought the decision. He advised all ministers to give their entire time to the ministry. In reading and pondering over his book the thought came to my mind that he didn't really believe that, for he himself had a side line. With his fairly remunerative salary he still took time from his religious duties to write books. His statement, then, was a sort of camouflage.

My side line, like his, led to writing. I had had experience in that line and knew that I could turn odd moments into profit. From that day to this I have utilized the gift more or less. And now, occupying the pulpit of a church of some influence with a visitor provided to help with the parish activities, I still keep my hand in at the writing business. Not all who would seek a side line will find it in the writing field, for it is a crowded field and one enters slowly; but there are many others of virtue which the minister can turn to and each will offer some advantages.

First among them we find the virtue of increased compensation. It will help the minister to get a living wage. He is entitled to it. The average minister can face his church fairly and tell them that he and his family are going to have enough to eat and wear and even a share of the luxuries of life. He can tell them that they can have all of his time if they will pay a living wage. Otherwise he will divide himself with some other job. A church will take offense, perhaps. But in the end the members must see that the shame is upon themselves. I remember that my father, a Methodist minister, was asked to leave one field because he insisted on putting on his overalls and jumpers and working at his trade. He insisted that his family was going to live and that a false dignity as to the calling was not going to keep him from work. A great many congregations would do well to study the passage in the seventh chapter of Mark where Jesus discusses the meaning of *Corban* and the obligation to his family of one engaged in religious work.

Another effect of the side line, if it is remunerative, is psychological: it puts the minister, in his own mind,

[33]

more on a level with his fellow men. When a preacher knows that, if he should be turned from his church to-morrow, there are other paying fields of activity for him, he is not going to bow before any of the petty or the strong bosses of churchdom. I believe that I am a better preacher because I know that I am not dependent upon my salary. If it should stop to-morrow I should still have a good income. And there is a psychological law which works here. The church gains respect for the man who is independent; and if the minister doesn't seem too anxious for his job, the church is usually the more anxious to keep him on the job.

There is a physical and intellectual effect upon the minister. Every parish at times offers problems which nearly break the heart of the conscientious minister. Intense application may solve it. But on the other hand if he can turn directly away from it and turn his mind in another direction to give it a rest, it will come back strong in the end. It is well to have a hobby. It may be golf or fishing. Or it may be some remunerative side line which saves the minister from a nervous breakdown and brings him back to his job with a new vision.

There is a social effect upon the minister. The side line will give him a contact with the business and professional problems with which the layman of his church come in contact. For instance, last winter I wrote a series of interviews with men in the city on religious problems. I knew more about their attitude when I was through than when I begun. In the same way the minister who has had trade experience can appreciate the problems of the worker, and the farmer-minister knows the problems of the soil and the social life of the farmer. These qualities certainly make the man a better preacher, for he has a better and truer attitude on life.

Now, how about the effect on the parish. A study of the parishes ministered to by ministers with side lines will not reveal a series of failures. There are many instances of unusual success. Isn't it a fact that many small parishes receive more pastoring than is good for them? A minister is placed in a small parish and with plenty of time on his hands is apt to become petty himself and to yield to petty desires of his congregation. The church soon interprets all of its activities in the terms of the pastor. He is expected to make a dozen rounds of calls each year and to enjoy all of the petty gossip of the neighborhood. Many adults are like children. The more attention you give them the more they will expect and the less they will grow in character.

A minister who is known very well to the writer retired about ten years ago. The present ministerial dearth has drafted him into part time service. He has charge of a church thirty miles from his home which is on a farm which he supervises. He can give but a limited time to the church. But despite of that fact the church is enjoying the greatest prosperity of its history. One of the trustees volunteers the information that its finances are in the best of shape. It is building a new structure which will be completed and dedicated inside of two months. How can that be explained? Knowing both the man and the field, I offer an explanation. The man is of such temperament that when giving entire time to a field he becomes irritable and is apt to monopolize the work of the parish. Limited in time he developed the ability to put others to work. The parish had workers but had had too much pastoral oversight.

The present arrangement is the best for both parties.

We have many men in the ministry who haven't big enough fields to keep them busy. A well known Presbyterian minister who followed the advice of his seminary to choose a small village to begin with recently expressed the conviction that the advice was all wrong. "It gives a man too much chance to be alone with himself and become petty. He should go to a field expansive enough to challenge all of his youth." Double the fields up. Give a man an automobile and a secretary, if necessary. Get away from the pin hole parish idea and get a field. Many a minister will testify that, while he had good intentions in starting in his work, the small parish with petty detail work became so monotonous that he was led into strange ways of thinking and into temptations which might have led to strange ways of living. The saving grace for many men is a job big enough to tax their vision and their strength.

This article is not a plea for every minister to try to handle two jobs. If a man has a field which is taxing all of his strength with adequate financial remuneration, the wisest plan is probably to devote all of his time to it. But the man who needs more money to live on need not hesitate to use a side line to secure it. He will profit financially and the chances are that the church will profit because of his wider experience with life. If they feel that he should devote all of his time to the church, then the challenge comes to them to pay a living wage. If their objections are serious they will meet the challenge.

Indirectly it is the intention of this article to break down the superstition that the minister who seeks a remunerative hobby, rather than one which merely takes time but gives little in return, is not true to his task. He may be doing the biggest work in the kingdom of God. In the end the minister must be his own judge of his temperament, strength, and ability. But if he feels that he must have a side line, he can choose one with clear conscience and definite conviction.

Suggestions for Children's Sermons

A card issued by the Kenwood Church, Chicago (Dr. A. J. McCartney), has on one side the quotation "Thy Way Is in the Sea" as the heading of an announcement of the resumption of talks for children. At the top of the reverse side of the card are the words "Seven Sea-Side Sermonettes for the Junior Congregation." The titles are listed as follows:

And I stood upon the sand of the sea.—REV. 13:1.

Let your light so shine.—MATT. 5:16.

As an anchor of the soul.—HEB. 6:19.

"There is a tide in the affairs of men."—SHAKESPEARE.

As fish that are taken in an evil net.—ECCLES. 9:12.

In wisdom hast thou made them all.—PS. 124.

"There's a wideness in God's mercy like the wideness of the sea."—F. W. FABER.

1,488,948 in U. S. Can't Speak English

Eleven per cent of the foreign-born white population in the United States ten years of age and older, according to the 1920 census, was unable to speak English, the Census Bureau announced recently. The number was 1,488,948, out of a total foreign-born population more than ten years of age of 13,497,886. These figures compared with 2,953,011 non-English-speaking foreign-born residents, or 22.8 per cent of the total enumerated in the 1910 census.

The bureau attributed the decrease to several causes, citing that many immigrants who could not speak English in 1910 had since learned the language, died, or returned to their native countries; that the number who could not speak English arriving during the last decade was smaller than in the previous ten years, and that a majority of these had come to this country prior to August 1, 1914, and therefore had had time to learn the language before the census was taken.

In Texas, New Mexico, and Arizona, where more than two-thirds of the foreign white inhabitants were born in Mexico, the percentages unable to speak English were, respectively, 51.7 per cent, 49.4 per cent, and 51.9 per cent. The next highest percentages unable to speak English were in West Virginia, 18.8 per cent, and Florida, 18.8 per cent, while the smallest proportions were shown in South Carolina, 1.8; Georgia, 1.8; Kentucky, 2.2; North Carolina, 2.7; District of Columbia, 2.8; Washington, 3.2; Oregon, 3.3; Tennessee, 3.3; Montana, 3.4; Virginia, 3.7; Utah, 4.1; Alabama, 4.2, and Iowa, 4.3.

MID-WEEK PRAYER MEETING

July 2-8—The Law of Liberty

(Rom. 8:1, 2)

Christ is the liberator of the human race. He has come to bring "liberty to the captives." Wherever his gentle reign extends, slavery of every kind is doomed and melts away. He strikes off not only outward fetters but also spiritual fetters. He brings true freedom to the spirit of man.

The great problem of government in all ages has been how to unite law and liberty. Without law there can be no order, without freedom there can be no development. To attain the true end of his being man has not only to be under law, he must be free to work out his own destiny. These conditions Christ supplies in "the perfect law of liberty."

The teaching of Jesus marks the advancement from outward to inward authority, from outward restraint to inward constraint, from object lessons of the kindergarten to the deeper truths of the spirit. Many seem to regard only external law and to ignore "the law written in the heart." But the things written in a statute book are merely signs of spiritual realities; the things written on the heart are the spiritual realities themselves; just as the letters of a friend do not contain love, love is in the writer's heart. External laws, written laws, are only symbols of authority, they are real things only when they have been transcribed into the heart and are freely obeyed.

"The law of the spirit of life in Christ Jesus," by which Christians are governed, marks also advancement from rules to principles. Rules are necessary for the regulation of conduct in childhood, but are outgrown in later life. Christ did not attempt to control human actions by specific rules but by guiding principles. Many duties he leaves undefined. In our present complex social life we find many things for which there is no definite rule. When a certain college president, holding up a copy of the New Testament, said, "This book teaches me how to run a college," he did not mean that it contains a system of rules on college management, but that it contains guiding principles which can be applied to every department of college life. Children when left at home alone may have given to them by their parents a piece of paper containing specific directions for each hour, or they may be left on their honor. In the latter way Christians obey the Christ who is out of sight. When we go to the bottom of the matter, we find the perfect law of liberty in the first and great commandment which inculcates love to God and man. Love is the fulfilling of the law; it leads to free and joyous obedience, so that the saying of one of the ancient fathers, "Love God and do what you please," is justified, inasmuch as those who love God will be pleased to do only what pleases him.

It must not be forgotten, however, that liberty is not an end in itself. It merely affords opportunity for higher development. Hence the apostolic admonition, "Brethren, ye have been called unto liberty; only use not liberty for an occasion to the flesh" (Gal. 5:13). Liberty in itself changes nothing, and is a blessing only when used wisely for higher and nobler ends.

The highest form of human government is democracy; but democracy has its dangers, chief among which is the tendency to emphasize personal freedom at the expense of obedience to constituted authority. Witness this, in the present outbreak of lawlessness among citizens otherwise law-abiding, in reference to the eighteenth constitutional amendment prohibiting the manufacture and sale of intoxicating liquors in the United States. Unless this lawlessness, which substitutes license for liberty, be speedily checked, it will undoubtless spread into wider areas and we shall find ourselves on the road that leads to national dishonor and ruin.

J. M. C.

July 9-15—The Imperishable House
(Matt. 9:24-27)

There is no more conspicuous instance of the sublime audacity of Jesus than is to be found in the closing words in his Sermon on the Mount. There he sets himself forth as the world's supreme spiritual teacher, to whom it has been given to utter the last word on morals. He contrasts his teaching with that of the past, saying that things set forth by "men of old" had been outgrown, and that to his "verily, verily, I say unto you" finality belongs. His word may be better understood, but it can never be superseded.

The expression, "These sayings of mine," looks back over the three preceding chapters in which Jesus lays down the principles which are to govern his kingdom and are to control human life and all its personal and social relations. He declares that the man who builds upon them builds an imperishable house, whereas the man who builds upon aught else builds a house which will one day become a heap of ruins. It is not, however, his words taken by themselves but his words as practically applied that form the secure foundation for a man's house of life. He says, "He that heareth these sayings of mine and doeth them is like a wise man who built his house upon a rock." It is not enough to hear the word, to assent to its truthfulness and to rhapsodize over its beauty; it must also be obeyed. "If ye know these things," says Jesus, "happy are ye if you do them"; not "happy are ye if ye talk about them, or pray about them, or magnify their importance," but happy are ye if ye carry them into practical effect. Faith and obedience are to be conjoined. One can hear the words of Jesus with interest and may have a correct understanding of their meaning, and yet come short of being a true follower. The scribe who gave strong endorsement to the teaching of Jesus regarding the first and greatest commandment was said by him to be not far from the kingdom. He had only to put into practise what he believed in order to step over the threshold.

Applied Christianity is thus the only secure foundation upon which to build. The words of Paul, "Not the hearers of the law are just before God, but the doers of the law shall be justified," are only an echo of the words of Jesus. See also James 1:22-26. When a rich young ruler asked Jesus, "Master, what shall I do that I may have eternal life?" Jesus answered him, "If thou wilt enter into life, keep the commandments." There is no other way into life but by obedience to the divine commandments." And to produce that obedience is the end of all God's effort on man's behalf within the sphere of spiritual influence.

The two builders described are very different; the one is wise, the other foolish; the wisdom of the former is seen in the kind of foundation which he selects. He builds his house upon rock, and when the rains descend and the winds beat upon it with wildest fury, it remains intact because its foundation is immovable. The folly of the latter is seen, not in selecting a foundation of sand, for in certain conditions sand may be a very excellent foundation, but on selecting a foundation on the edge of a dry river bed, so that when the rain descends it is undermined and the wind beating upon it causes it to fall with a crash. When the storm has rolled past, the two houses are seen merging into view, the one stands erect and unharmed, the other is a heap of ruins—mute witnesses to the declaration of Jesus that in the day of testing the only life that will abide will be the one which is founded and built upon his teachings. And with this graphic picture, the most sublime discourse that ever fell from mortal lips ends.

In the heart-gripping little book by Dr. Henry Kingman, entitled *Building on Rock* (Association Press) we find this apposite illustration:

Many have seen a certain unforgettable cartoon by the Dutch artist Louis Rae-maekers. It shows the German kaiser riding down the highway on his war-horse, stern and masterful, the incarnation of relentless power. Around him are his mounted staff, with cloaks and swords and helmets, silent and terrible in the pride of war. But at his side upon the road, trespassing on the high company, is a humble man mounted on an ass, as Jesus once rode in Palestine, his bowed face eloquent of love and sadness—the Man of Sorrows. And the kaiser pointing indignantly to the intruder, exclaims to his staff, "Who is this man?"

Had he but known it, that silent man was his divine Master, who intercepts every one who is thrusting aside his teachings, and seeks to prevent him from riding to a fall.

J. M. C.

July 16-22—The God of Things as They Are (Ps. 99:1)

Our topic is taken from the familiar poem of Kipling, entitled "When Earth's Last Picture Is Painted," in which the poet, forecasting the perfect life in the great hereafter, says:

Only the Master shall praise us, and only
    the Master shall blame,
And no one shall work for money, and no
    one shall work for fame,
But each for the joy of working, and each
    in his separate star,
Shall draw the thing as he sees it, for the
    God of things as they are.

But the God of things as they are is also the God with whom we have now to do. To his omniscient eye all things are naked and open. He is the God of reality, the God who judges things not by their outward appearance but by their inward essence. From such a God honesty and sincerity are demanded; he requires truth in the inward parts. In his presence the last vestige of pretence is stripped off and things are judged by what they actually are and not by what they seem to be.

The God of things as they are is constantly looking over our shoulder to see how we perform our allotted task. He is the "Master of all good workmen" and will approve only of what is genuine. With all shoddy and show and sham he will have nothing whatever to do, Longfellow reminds us that

In the elder days of art,
Builders wrought with greatest care
Each minute and unseen part;
For the gods see everywhere.

It is said that since the great World War things have been so disrupted that altho wages have gone up the quality of work has gone down, so that good, honest work is scarcely to be found. And this deterioration has entered into every part of our social and religious life.

Life and religion are one. The distinction between the secular and the sacred has been obliterated. Instead of making a business of religion, we are seeking to make the business of life religious and to connect religion equally with the shop and with the sanctuary, yet there are certain parts of life which have more distinctly to do with our inner religious experience, and when God comes to make inquisition it is about these that he is primarily concerned. He wants to know about our relation to himself as well as about our relation to our fellowmen; he wants to know about our character as well as about our conduct, about our motives as well as about our deeds; and in dealing with us he seeks to bring into view the hidden man of the heart so that we may see ourselves as he sees us, which means that we may see ourselves as we actually are.

Self-judgment is frequently wrong. It flatters, it exaggerates virtues, it conceals unpleasant facts, and makes the worse appear the better reason. When self-judgment is honest, it is as humbling as it is wholesome. Daniel C. French, the sculptor who made the bust of Emerson which is now in Memorial Hall, Harvard University, tells that at one of his sittings Emerson rose up suddenly and walked over to where the sculptor was working. He looked long and earnestly at the bust, and then, with an inimitably droll expression, said: "The trouble is the more it resembles me the worse it looks." That is generally the verdict when a man's true self is brought to view. A self-made man was boasting of what he had made of himself when a friend remarked that it was a good thing for him that there was no inspector around to pass on the job.

From the scrutinizing eye of the divine inspector there is no possible escape.

In the psalm which forms the background of the present study we have a vivid picture of a holy God whose eyes of flame search the hidden recesses of the heart, before whom we are to tremble. He accepts and forgives the penitent whose confession is genuine; but even while pressing him to his bosom he allows him to suffer the consequences of his misdeeds. Forgiveness does not wipe out as with a sponge the natural effect of one's wrongdoing; but it does restore the penitent soul to the favor and fellowship of God. Let any one truly repent of his sin, confessing not some abstraction called his sinfulness but his actual sins; saying with the psalmist, "against thee, thee only have I sinned, and done this evil in thy sight," and the God who wounds that he may heal, who kills that he may make alive, "will be faithful and just to forgive his sin, and to cleanse him from all unrighteousness." J. M. C.

July 23-29—International Christianity
(Micah 4:3; Acts 17:26)

One Sunday morning not so very long ago the writer heard one of our leading preachers tell his well-to-do congregation a little incident that will serve as an introduction to the subject before us. The church was located in one of our best avenues and there was at least one pew in that church shared by two families. These two families came to the same pew, they heard the same message, the same prayers and joined in the same songs. But just here the sameness ended, for they never exchanged words. Strange things, however, happen, as was the case with these two families. On a beautiful summer day Mr. and Mrs. ———— made the ascent of a mountain in Switzerland and just as they had reached the summit whom should they see but the couple who shared the same pew in the big church on the avenue at home. Of course they were surprized, the old time silence, conventionality, and unneighborliness of the city and the church had to give way to the unconventionality and neighborliness of the open spaces.

In view of such an incident is it any wonder that we have to ask such a commonplace question as, Who is my neighbor? The answer is beautifully set forth in the parable of the Good Samaritan (Luke 15:25-37). There we see that it is not a question of whether one belongs to our persuasion or whether one is of our nationality. It is not a question as to whether the person is near or remote; the one thing to settle is, does that person here, there, or anywhere need our help. The man who was beaten on the Jericho road was befriended by a Samaritan and the Samaritans were despised by the Jews. So today there are some nations who look with envy, with jealousy and malice, towards other nations. "National hatreds and rivalries and ambitions are hotter than ever" (Bryce). While this spirit is alive it is futile to look for swords being "beaten into plowshares and spears into pruning hooks." The most desirable and urgent thing today is for each individual and each nation to seek the good of his neighbor. This is God's way of solving problems. Such an attitude of mind in all conferences would be a tremendous step in the right direction.

The Washington Conference on the Limitation of Armaments was a most encouraging sign of the conference idea. Now that we have had a conference of a few nations the time is ripe for a conference of all the nations. One of the most promising results of the Washington Conference was the awakening of our own people to a larger interest in international affairs. It is said financially and commercially we are inextricably bound up with the world. That is true, but we must not stop there, for humanly and spiritually we are inseparable.

The oneness of the world is a fact. That was brought home unmistakably during the Great War. While some countries suffered more than others, no country escaped injury.

In James Bryce's recent book on *International Relations*, the concluding chapter is on Possible Methods for Averting War. There is one paragraph there that fits into this question of International Christianity.

You may ask, What is it that any one of us, you here or we in England, can do as individual citizens to improve the character of international relations, and especially to provide security against the outbreak of future wars. . . . What can private citizens do? Well, the State is made up of private citizens and such as they are such will the State be. Each of us as individuals can do little, but many animated by the same feeling and belief can do much. What is Democracy for except to represent and express the convictions and wishes of the people? The citizens of a democracy can do everything if they express their united will. The raindrops that fall from the clouds unite to form a tiny rill, and, meeting other rills, it becomes a rivulet, and the rivulet grows to a brook, and the brooks as they join one another swell into a river that sweeps in its resistless course downward to the sea. Each of us is only a drop, but together we make up the volume of public opinion which determines the character and action of a State. What all the nations now need is a public opinion which shall in every nation give more constant thought and keener attention to international policy, and lift it to a higher plane. The peoples can do this in every country if the best citizens give them the lead.

The needs of the world, whether it is in Armenia or Russia, have found the hearts of Americans responsive and is not this responsiveness an evidence that we are all the children of one Father, who "made of one every nation of men to dwell on all the face of the earth."   R. S.

July 30–Aug. 5—God in the Heart of Man

(Rom. 2:14, 15; Jer. 31:33)

With regard to the heathen Paul affirms that "they having not the law, are a law unto themselves; who show the work of the law written in their hearts." By the term law he means the *torah*, the divinely authoritative instruction given not to the Jew as a Jew but to the Jew as a man. His words might be freely rendered, "These having not the Bible are a Bible unto themselves, who show the very substance of the Bible teaching written in their hearts." God has not left himself without witness to his presence in the heart of any man. To every man is given inward illumination. Whatever outward light be denied him, he has an inner light sufficient to guide him in the way which he ought to take.

The two revelations, that written in a book and that written in the heart, must be in perfect agreement, seeing that they have the same author. The inward revelation is personal and comes first. It is peculiarly a man's own. The written revelation is simply a commentary upon consciousness and finds a responsive echo in man's heart. A Chinese scholar who assisted a missionary in translating the New Testament paused in his work and said, "Whoever made this book made me. It tells of my struggles, speaks to my soul, and shows me the true way."

The heart was made by God and for him, and it ever responds to his voice. "When a message comes to a man from heaven, he need not ask if it is true," for "he that believeth hath the witness in himself."

The moral nature of man testifies to God's presence and continuous activity. Conscience is an inward monitor. It is God's witness within the soul; more strictly speaking it is the mouth of man's moral nature through which God speaks. The word conscience itself when broken up means *con-scio*, "to know with." The one along with whom man knows, whose voice of approval or censure is heard in his heart, is God.

Man is not left alone to grope his way in the dark. "His primal duties shine aloft as stars." The great principles of morality such as those set forth in the decalogue are inscribed in the soul. They are written not on tables of stone but on the fleshly tablets of the heart. Men may refuse to read the written word, they may tear it to pieces and cast it to the winds, but from the mandatory voice within they cannot escape. And it is by this standard of action that those who have not the written word shall be judged at last.

In Prov. 20:27 it is said that "the spirit of man is the lamp of the Lord." Through man's moral nature God speaks, giving him light sufficient to guide his faltering feet into the way of life. Man is ever open to God, he is the recipient of communications from him. God comes into inner contact with him that he may give him the light which he needs for the journey which he is to take.

In the present age we are called upon to enjoy the direct tuition of the Holy Spirit. He is the source of inward illumination, bearing concurrent testimony with the written word, and hence is the source of equal authority. It is said that before his departure Jesus gave to his disciples "commandment through the Holy Spirit" (Acts 1:2). To his inward voice they were ever to give heed. By him they were to be led "into all the truth" which was necessary for them to know in order to receive direction in all the practical affairs of Christian life. As exprest in terms of the present, God in the heart of man means the brooding presence of the Holy Spirit as enlightener, comforter, and guide. To resist or grieve the Holy Spirit is the climax of iniquity. This age of privilege has its added responsibilities. "Unto whomsoever much is given, of him also shall much be required."   J. M. C.

The Book

THE EXILE AND THE RESTORATION

Professor JOHN E. McFADYEN, D.D., United Free Church College,
Glasgow, Scotland

July 2—Ezekiel, the Watchman of Israel

(Ezek. 2:1—3:27)

Last quarter's lesson carried us to the destruction of Jerusalem in 586 B.C., in this lesson we go back six years, to 592. There were two sieges of Jerusalem by the Babylonians; the one which ended in 586 with the destruction of the city and the deportation of its people was preceded by another, in 597, which also involved the deportation of King Jehoiachin (2 Kings 24:15) and many of the leading men. With this group "Ezekiel the priest" was carried into exile, and the vision which opens his book came to him, he tells us, "in the fifth year of Jehoiachin's captivity," i. e., in 592. Ezekiel differs from the earlier prophets, such as Amos or Isaiah, in this, that while they addrest themselves to the nation, he, as chap. 3 admirably illustrates, is supremely concerned with the moral welfare of the individuals whom he addresses, and he is the first example of what we should to-day call a pastor.

Chap. 2 shows how hard his task was. He was very conscious of addressing a "rebellious house," impudent and stiff-hearted, who were vastly more likely to reject than to accept his message. But he was not asked to face them until he had had the glorious vision of the power, omnipresence, and omniscience of God

which occupies chap. 1. Ezekiel, prostrated by the vision, was then addrest as "son of man" (a phrase designed to express his frailty in contrast with the majesty of God), and bidden to rise and accept his commission for service. That service was to declare the message of God, which, tho in the last half of his book (chaps. 25-48) becomes a message of hope and promise, in the first half (1-24) and expressly here (2:10) a message of doom—he is thinking of the destruction of Jerusalem and the consequent exile—a doom justified by the past and present infidelity and idolatry of the people (cf. chap. 8). There was every temptation on his part to refuse to embark upon so perilous a course, to "rebel" in one way as the people had rebelled in another; nevertheless he must speak his message without flinching or fear.

His inspiration is suggestively described by the symbolical swallowing of a bookroll: the discovery of the book of the Law (Deuteronomy) which we discust six weeks ago, had doubtless suggested the idea of a book as a source of divine revelation. Ezekiel was to swallow the roll, that is, to digest the book and make its ideas his very own. When he ate the roll, bitter as were its contents, it was as sweet as honey in his mouth, for it is sweet to do the will of God and to be trusted with tasks for him. The task, he was again reminded, would

---

¹These studies follow the lesson topics and passages of the International Sunday-school Series.

be unspeakably hard, for his stubborn hearers would be less responsive to the divine message than even heathen foreigners would have been; but he was to go resolutely forward, trusting in the God who had called and could equip and sustain him. He then found his way to Tel-abib, a colony of his fellow-exiles, where he remained for a week in a state of utter stupefaction, dumb and motionless.

Then he received another message. His task was then defined as that of a watchman. As it is the watchman's business to detect and give warning of danger, so it was the prophet's business to warn individual men of the coming catastrophe which he himself so clearly saw. And it was not enough to warn the crowd; he had to deal personally with individuals, good and bad, and warn them solemnly, each and all, the good no less than the bad—the bad to turn from his evil way, and the good to persist to the end without swerving from the good way; for the destiny of men will be determined by the character and conduct they exhibit when the hour of judgment strikes.

The passage suggests that it is almost impossible to overestimate the importance of the teacher, and in general of education, in the process of reconstructing a world shattered, as Ezekiel's world was and as ours is, by war and its tragic consequences; and in connection with it, it would be well to read H. G. Wells's fierce insistence on the inconceivable importance of education in his recent book on The Salvaging of Civilization. We learn (1) that the teacher must have a vision of what he would be at. In our time he must clearly understand that the ultimate aim of education is to create an intelligent world-citizenship. If the nations can not all learn that they are members one of another and that each needs every other, then

civilization as we know it is doomed to perish. How a clear conception of this would put purpose and fire into the detail of history and geography, much of which now seems so dreary! To speak powerfully and truly we must first see clearly. (2) The teacher must make the message his own. This is what is meant by the strong language of 3:3. He must not repeat it in parrot-like fashion, he must work it into the very fiber of his being until it is his very self that he is uttering; and he must speak it out with courage, whether people like to hear it or not. Small-hearted patriots may resent the invitation to think internationally; but it is either that or chaos. The teacher should teach himself and his pupil to remember that God "loved the world" (cf. John 3:16). (3) The teacher must give time and thought, like Jesus, to the individual as well as to the class or crowd. His business is not only to give information, but to create an outlook and to mold character. If he does not do that, what is he there for? He is there, in Ezekiel's words, to "warn" of the doom which will overtake us all if we do not think large and generous thoughts. He is responsible for the individual souls of his class, and the prophet sternly maintains that, if one of them dies unwarned, the teacher is his murderer. Good and bad alike need warning, for the individual life and the world of today are alive with dangers.

July 9—Daniel Interpreting Nebuchadrezzar's Dream

(Dan. chap. 2)

The world-outlook for which we pled in the last lesson is brilliantly set forth in this long and fascinating chapter. Very briefly the story is this. In chap. 1, Daniel and his three friends, Jewish captives at the court of Babylon, proved their fidelity to their religion by refusing to defile themselves with the king's food. At the end of the three years they showed themselves superior to the "wise" men of the empire. Then follows in' chap. 2 a dream of Nebuchadrezzar in which a great image was shivered to pieces by a little stone, which grew till it filled the whole world. Daniel alone could retell and interpret the dream: it denoted a succession of kingdoms, which would all be ultimately overthrown and succeeded by the kingdom of God.

To the view of history underlying this dream there is a parallel in the vision of Daniel in chap. 7, which should be read alongside of chap. 2. In chap. 7, four great beasts are seen coming up out of the sea—the last of them especially cruel and terrible. Before the Judge who is seated upon his throne is brought one like a son of man, who comes with the clouds of heaven—this human and heavenly figure being in striking contrast to the beasts that rise out of the sea. Daniel is informed that the beasts represent four kingdoms, whose dominion is to be superseded by the dominion of the saints of the Most High, *i.e.*, by the kingdom of God, which will be everlasting. Evidently the vision and the dream are parallel.

What were those kingdoms or empires? With 11:1, 2, in view, the answer is very simple. Without enigma or symbolism of any kind, the Persian empire is mentioned in 11:2, as preceding the Greek, and in 11:1 as being preceded by the Median, which in its turn has been preceded by the Babylonian. Here, then, in the plainest terms, is a succession of four empires—Babylonian, Median, Persian, Greek—the last

to be succeeded by the kingdom of God; and the book was written in a time of persecution to console and strengthen the faithful and to confirm their hope in the coming kingdom of God, when the empire of brute force would once and for all be over.

The aim of chap. 2 has been well described by Professor Driver. It is to show (1) how the heathen king is brought (verse 47) to acknowledge the supremacy of Daniel's God; (2) how the sequence of empires is in the hands of God (verse 21); and (3) how a divine kingdom is destined ultimately to be established upon earth. The representation of the magnificent but hollow splendor of earthly empire in the form of a "huge, gleaming, terrible colossus, of many colors and different metals," brilliant at its summit, but gradually deteriorating, both in material and appearance, toward its base, and, when struck by the falling rock, instantly collapsing into fragments, is fine and striking.

In reading these words we are irresistibly reminded of the career and fate of the German empire, but we dare not forget that all the nations of the world have been involved in a common ruin, and that not one of them is a worthy representative of the kingdom of God. That is yet to come.

These chapters (2 and 7) embody a fine vision of history as not a mere tangle of events but the march of a purpose. In particular they teach us (1) that there can be no permanence for nations that worship and build upon force. In time the brass and the iron shall be shattered no less surely than the clay. The ferocious nature of the policies of earthly empires is even more graphically portrayed in chap. 7 where they are compared to four wild beasts. It is the author's way of suggesting that those policies are brutal, the sort of thing you might expect from wild beasts rather than from sane men. How truly the writer has anticipated the modern world, with its nations which draw their symbols from fierce, cruel animals—

the Russian bear, the British lion, the American eagle. Now you can not build a world on mere force; a world poised on bayonets is very insecurely poised indeed. The spirit of militarism must die out or be destroyed in every nation, before the kingdom of God can come. As Havelock Ellis has recently said,

Surely at no period of the world's history has it been so necessary as it is to-day to strike hard at militarism. Never before has it been so clearly visible that all civilization, even all the most elementary traditions of humanity and brotherhood, depend on the absolute destruction of militarism.

(2) But we must cherish the faith that the era of force will pass and that the kingdom of God and the era of peace will surely come. The mighty image will be shattered by the little stone: or more plainly in chap. 7, the brute beasts will be followed by the man, i.e., the rule of force will one day give place to the rule of humanity. It is in this faith that, amid the disillusions of peace, men must continue to work and pray.

July 16—The Handwriting on the Wall (Temperance Lesson)

(Dan. 5:1-31)

This chapter ushers us into the magnificent banqueting-hall of the palace at Babylon. In a drunken humor Belshazzar ordered to be brought upon the table the gold and silver vessels that had been taken away from the temple at the sack of Jerusalem, and out of those sacred vessels he and his heathen company drank, praising the while their heathen gods. The pious Jew who heard this tale would shudder at the profanity and impiety into which the king had been led by indulgence in wine. But the gaiety was speedily transformed by a weird message written on the brilliantly illuminated wall by a mysterious hand. Terrified and sobered, the king summoned his wise men to interpret the enigmatic words, but they could not even read them, far less interpret them. On the suggestion of the queen-mother, Daniel was summoned, whose wondrous power had many a time been tested (cf. chaps. 2 and 4). Here, as in chap. 2, the writer means us to feel that the only wise God is the God of the Hebrews, and the only wise men are the men whom he inspires.

Conscious of his power, Daniel calmly offered to read and interpret the mysterious writing, but he would accept no reward. Before, however, the fateful words were uttered, he paused to remind his royal listener how much he might have learned, and how little in reality he had profited, from the humiliation of his haughty predecessor, Nebuchadrezzar. He too had been lifted to power and sovereignty, but power had bred pride and pride had been chastised by unspeakable humiliation (cf. chap. 4). Belshazzar, however, had repeated Nebuchadrezzar's mistake: he had been guilty not only of pride, but of wanton profanity and impiety as well, in touching with sacrilegious hands and wanton lips the sacred vessels of Jehovah. Then, after this unanswerable charge, came the solemn moment when the mysterious words, which had so baffled the wise men, were uttered and explained. The words and their explanation raise for us difficult problems into which it is not needful here to go, but probably they were meant to carry a double sense: on the one hand they seem to have indicated weights, and on the other to have denoted the ideas, "numbered, weighed, divided." In any case the awful words sounded the death knell of Belshazzar and the Babylonian empire, the last word announcing plainly enough that it was to fall before the Persians. That night which had been begun in gaiety and continued in mystery and terror ended in death. The proud and impious king was slain.

From the weird and brilliant story we see that drink begets insolence and irreverence. It was after he had tasted the wine that Belshazzar committed the impiety of desecrating the sacred vessels of the temple. Strong drink destroys a man's balance, his sense of the fitness of things, his self-control, his sense of reverence. It leads to insolence, profanity, and a blasphemous disregard of the most sacred things. Last September it was my unhappy fate to travel by rail a good many miles in a car with three young men who, after a football match, had allowed alcohol to pick what brains they had. They made the journey not only uncomfortable but hideous by their silly shouting and maudlin screaming of songs: and—what was much worse—one of them playfully addrest a child sitting opposite in language of vulgar profanity. When drink comes, self-control goes—and with it goes also a decent regard for the rights of other people, to say nothing of reverence for the sanctities of childhood. On Tuesday afternoons and evenings, when licensed premises in Glasgow are closed in terms of the half holiday closing order made by the local authority under the Shops Act, men and women have been streaming out in the tramcar in search of drink to neighboring villages where the public houses (or saloons) were open, with the result that the work of the car conductors on the return journey is carried out under the gravest difficulty, and, as the local press states, "some of those who traveled displayed a disposition to quarrel with anybody and everybody, and made fluent use, in the presence of women travelers, of language of the most offensive charac-

ter." Drink drives out reverence for God and respect for woman and child; the fate of Belshazzar suggests that the end of indulgence is destruction.

July 23—Daniel and the Lions
(Dan. 6:1-28)

A fortnight ago it was pointed out that the book of Daniel was written to strengthen the faith of men who were suffering bitter persecution for the religion of the fathers, and this general purpose is happily illustrated by the vivid and familiar story before us today. The Hebrews were fond of telling how their countrymen came to posts of highest dignity and power in foreign lands; and, like Joseph in Egypt, Daniel had reached a position of supreme eminence in the government of the Babylonian empire. This drew upon him the jealousy of the other high officials, a jealousy enhanced by the fact that he was an alien, and they plotted his destruction. His public record, however was so unimpeachable that he could be successfully attacked only on the ground of his religion. They accordingly induced the unsuspecting king to establish a stringent interdict forbidding any of his subjects to offer a petition or prayer to any power in heaven or earth except to himself for the space of a month, and any who violated this interdict were to be cast into a den of lions. As Oriental monarchs were accustomed to adulation, honors, and titles which amounted almost to worship, this decree would by no means have seemed so monstrous to the ancient world as it seems to us.

Daniel was well aware that this decree was practically his death warrant, but this did not in the least appal him or affect the habits of his religious life. On the flat roof of his house there was a chamber with latticed windows, such as may still be seen in the East to-day, and these windows faced Jerusalem. To a devout Jew Jerusalem, and especially the temple, was the most important spot in all the world, for Jehovah, tho the God of all the earth, was believed to have made it in a unique sense his home. Consequently nothing was more natural than that worshipers should turn to it in prayer (1 Kings 8:44). So in his roof chamber whose windows faced Jerusalem Daniel, nothing daunted by the decree, regularly went on his knees three times a day (cf. Ps. 55:17) and prayed; and it is worth noting that special mention is made of his thanksgiving. The awful fate which now seemed so certain did not dull his capacity for praise and gratitude.

This was the hour for which Daniel's jealous rivals had been waiting. They denounced him to the king as a deliberate law-breaker, and demanded the extreme penalty. The king, who saw the trap too late, did what he could—but all in vain—to save Daniel; but after a night of sleepless anguish he went to the pit and discovered with joy beyond measure that Daniel was still alive— saved by his God from the cruel lions and the still more cruel men. Then the tables were turned. The king delivered the enemies of Daniel over to the fate which they had contrived for him, and he made a decree that the God of Daniel who had proved his power in so marvelous a way should be honored and feared throughout his dominions as the living God whose kingdom knows no end.

(1) Incidentally we learn the folly and the doom of envy. Jealous of Daniel's gifts and position, the Persian officials plotted his ruin, only in the end to find themselves and not him torn to pieces in the lion's den.

With great frequency and power the Old Testament portrays this nemesis which runs through human affairs, involving the guilty often in the very ruin in which they had hoped to involve others. (2) But the chief aim of the story is to emphasize the duty of maintaining religious habits when tempted to neglect or abandon them, and the certainty with which such fidelity will in the end be rewarded. If any one should raise the question, "But did these things really happen?" the answer should be sought along the following lines. (a) It has to be remembered that the book of Daniel was written about the year 165 B.C., *i.e.*, about four centuries after the events with which it deals, and is therefore not contemporary history. (b) The difficulties occasioned by the miraculous element in this book—the deliverance of Daniel from the lions and of his friends from the fiery furnace (chap. 3)—recall the similar difficulties that gather round the stories of Elijah and Elisha with which we dealt in January and February. We then saw that to the Hebrew historians the idea was more important than the fact, and that their aim was not so much to convey historical information as to create religious impressions and convictions. The book of Daniel, we repeat, was written to sustain the tried and tempted faith of the loyal Jews under the fierce assaults made upon their religion and their sacred books by Antiochus Epiphanes; the writer desired to assure them that fidelity was to be fully rewarded by deliverance from cruelty as personified by the lions and from the flames of persecution. And brilliantly did he succeed in his aim; for he kindled his comrades to a passionate endurance and enthusiasm which won them victory after victory. That was the writer's intention, and it is with that

that we should be concerned. He looked at Daniel praying with his windows open to Jerusalem, and asked his countrymen to be like that, and to trust God for the consequences. There are times when to perform a religious duty silently or stealthily is to play the coward. It is a cheap and flabby religion which is afraid to take the consequences; and if the men who do face them are not invariably delivered from danger and death, they will assuredly find their place in the end in the everlasting kingdom of God.

July 30—The First Return from Exile

(Jer. 29:10-14; Ezra 1:1-11)

A month ago our studies brought us to the destruction of Jerusalem and the exile. The false prophets had proclaimed that the Jews would soon be back in their own land (Jer. 28:3); Jeremiah knew better, he knew that a discipline, long and severe, would be necessary before the people were worthy to return; not till seventy years had passed would the exile be over and the return begin (Jer. 29:10). Seventy we are to understand as a round number—in point of fact the exile lasted scarcely fifty years (586-538 B.C.). The return of the Jews was made possible by their emancipation from the yoke of Babylon, and that was effected by Cyrus, here called "king of Persia," who overthrew the Babylonian empire. Notice how completely the opening verse assigns the control of history to God and the interpretation of it to the men whom he inspires; it is he who stirs up Cyrus to make his famous proclamation and it is he who had inspired Jeremiah to announce in advance the return which this proclamation made possible. It is worthy of note, too, that the instru-

ment chosen by Jehovah to effect the emancipation and restoration of his people was a foreigner—the king of Persia.

Cyrus, tho a great conqueror, was also a man of singularly humane and gracious temper and a statesman of extraordinary political insight. His official permission to the Jews to return to their own land was in accordance with his noble and tolerant policy, generally allowing the deported inhabitants of conquered countries to return to their original homes and to restore there the worship of their ancestral gods. His own words are: "The gods I restored to their seats and made for them a dwelling-place forever. All of their people I gathered and restored to their homes." This latter concession is not a mere piece of clever statesmanship designed to make a contented people: himself a man of deep religious feeling, he respected the religion of others. What is reasonably certain, says Dr. McCurdy, is that

he abhorred the idea of using force to spread his religious views; that he saw sufficient good in all the greater religions to justify him in both tolerating and encouraging them; and that he promoted the happiness and welfare of his subjects by giving them the opportunity of serving God according to the dictates of conscience.''

The decree not only permitted the Jews to return and rebuild the temple, but it made provision that the returning exiles were to be helped by the gifts of money, goods, cattle, etc. Many devout souls must have taken advantage of the decree to go back to Palestine, but all did not go, only those who felt the divine constraint; for the prospects opened up by the homeland, whose fortunes must have been very low since the fall of Jerusalem, were far from inviting. We hear nothing of the journey, our attention is concentrated upon the temple vessels, because with the compiler of Ezra, who was no doubt also the writer of the book of Chronicles, the dominant interest is public worship.

This baldly written passage conceals some important thoughts: (1) The sure fulfilment of the divine purpose. The word of the Lord had to be accomplished (1:1). Israel's work for the world could be completely wrought out only in her own land; and so, in his mysterious providence God, through Cyrus, brought her back. Each nation has its own contribution to make to the welfare of the world; the contribution of the Jews was religion, and God made use even of foreign soldiers and statesmen to bring to pass his purpose through the Jews. Behind history is a purpose of God, often thwarted, but never defeated. (2) The importance of religion. "They rose to go up to build the house of Jehovah." It would seem as if the returning exiles had no other thought in their hearts but the reestablishing of the temple worship. If immigrants were bent on creating opportunities for worship, and on strengthening and extending the influence of the Church in the countries to which they go, how well it would be both for them and for the land of their adoption! (3) The duty of generosity in religion. The exiles gave each according to his ability. People should be willing to pay for what they pretend to value, and if they believe in the Church, they should support it.

THE LORD'S SUPPER[1]

In the first part of the story (verses 17-25) note two points: (1) The disciples assume that Jesus will observe the religious custom of the day. "Where wilt thou that we prepare for thee to eat the passover?" They were right, but he had already arranged with an unknown disciple to have a room ready. Probably the words, "My time is at hand," were the pass-word which had been fixed upon. In any case, the disciples find that Jesus has been already thinking of the future and planning for them; they are soon to discover that he plans a very different kind of feast from what they had been accustomed to expect. So God outdoes our expectations. (2) The honesty of the disciples. Hitherto the predictions of betrayal had been general; now, to their dismay, Jesus declares, "One of you shall betray me." We know (from verses 14-16) it was Judas, but the eleven did not know. And, instead of wondering who it was, instead of Peter wondering if it would be John, or of John wondering if it would be Thomas, each asked, "Lord, is it I?" That is, they were conscious of their own unsteadiness of heart. The first impulse was not to criticize some one else but to examine their own hearts. None of them regarded himself as too good for this temptation, dreadful as it must have sounded to them. There is no better preparation for the Lord's Supper, or for any fellowship with Christ, than this humble, searching sense of personal weakness. For, after all, Christ is betrayed by people inside his circle. It is among those who bear his name that his interests are abandoned and injured. And no outward tie of membership can avail to safeguard us against such a temptation.

In the story of the supper (verses 26-30) note (1) the gladness of the Lord. He "blessed," he "gave thanks," over the bread and wine; they meant, as he said, his own body and blood, the sacrifice of his life. But it was a gift of God to men, the

[1] A Study of Matt. 26:14-30.

inauguration of a "new testament" or covenant of forgiveness and fellowship. This note of joy is preserved in the term "Eucharist," and ought to be struck at every communion service. (2) The assurance of future life and fellowship "in my Father's kingdom." The supper was not to be an end of his relations with them. Hope as well as memory was to pervade their communion.

The latter thought recurs in Paul's word: "As often as ye eat this bread and drink this cup, ye do show forth the Lord's death till he come." But the apostle's counsel carries with it a further reminder. "As often," he says. Now what we do often tends to become formal, unless we are careful. The repetition of the supper may abate our freshness of wonder and reverence. The word, the actions, are so familiar to us that they may become almost a thing of rote. The Lord's death must never be a commonplace to us; it must stir faith and love and hope, whenever we remember it at his table.

Should the Revision Be Revised

In the *Contemporary Review* for January Dr. John E. McFadyen, so well known to readers of the HOMILETIC, discusses the question—Do we need a revision of the Old Testament, especially in view of our possession of the Revised Version? The real advance of the R. V. over the A. V. is acknowledged (and in many respects the American Standard Version is still better). But even the R. V. leaves much to be desired. It retains many archaisms, the elimination of which would appeal to the modern mind. It embodies the "curious result" that the better readings are often in the margin rather than in the text. It retains LORD instead of the "proper name" of the God of Israel (Jehovah, Yahweh). It often perilously approaches nonsense in its renderings (Isa. 10:22, 23, &c.), sometimes through sheer timidity or through slavish adherence to the Hebrew when the Septuagint gives a better reading. The Revisers, too, were singularly averse to quite obvious and simple conjectural readings which would have carried out the sense of the passage. Dr. McFadyen approves the suggestion of Duhm in Ps. 34:10, substituting "liars" (*i.e.*, apostates, "those who deny [God]") for "young lions." [This is a meaning that appears in the Talmudic Aramaic.] Moreover, at times the Revisers adhered slavishly to Hebrew idiom, as in Isa. 40:24, for which Dr. McFadyen supplies a better rendering as follows: "Scarcely have they been planted, sown, &c., when he bloweth upon them." The American version of Jer. 4:19 in substituting "anguish" for "bowels," raises the translation from bathos to pathos. In like fashion the Revisers employ "inelastic and conventional ways" of translating "great recurring words" like "judgment," instead of using such a word as "justice" (cf. Amos 5:24; Mal. 2:17). Literal translation of a Hebrew idiom may be misleading. "Son of a prophet" means a professional prophet; son of God means a supernatural being; son of man (Dan. 7:13) means "a figure in human form." Indeed, Dr. McFadyen points out that sometimes paraphrase gives a sense in the rendering closer to the original than literal translation. "Lamb of God" to an Eskimo would mean little or nothing. But care is needed here.

A paragraph or two, which might well have been extended, refer to the often condemned ignoring of poetic form, especially in the prophetic books. The author quotes Cheyne's beautiful rendering of the "Song of the Vineyard," Isa. 5:1ff., and notes the possibilities in such passages as Isa. 1:3; Song 2:11, 12; Isa. 5:21ff.

Another advance is suggested in the separation of history and legislation. Remove from its context Ex. 35, Num. 10:28, and there is left in the narratives before and following "a connected and intensely human story of the fortunes of Israel in the wilderness." Indeed, "would a modern version of the Old Testament be under any obligation to incorporate legislative actions at all?" However this may be, "it would still be worth while to have a thorough revision of the Old Testament, in its completeness, 'perfect and entire, wanting nothing.'"

ON THE SIGNIFICANCE OF RECENT ASTRONOMICAL DISCOVERY

HARLOW SHAPLEY, Director of the Harvard Observatory, Cambridge, Mass.

SCRIPTURE LESSON: Read Ps. 19:1-6; Job 38:31-33.

INTRODUCTION: The newest of scientific developments have profoundly affected the oldest of all sciences, the study of the heavenly bodies. Laboratory experiments in physics and chemistry now aid in the interpretation of the tenuous atmospheres of stars. The new knowledge of the structure of the atom has given us a better insight into the methods by which a star shines. The conspicuous advance during the last decade in all branches of astronomy, particularly in those divisions that may be grouped under the term "astrophysics," is, however, only partly due to the concurrent developments in other physical sciences. The main cause appears to be the rise of the great American observatories. The private endowment of nearly a dozen large institutions for astronomical research has placed this country, noted for its materialistic interests, ahead of all other nations.

In the following discussion of recent progress I shall touch briefly on five phases of the science of the sidereal universe that seem to be of particular significance to students of spiritual things. I hope that this untechnical survey of present knowledge of man's relation to his surroundings can be of direct service in relating the tangible material scheme to the non-material. Deductions from these plain statements are of course left wholly to the individual reader.

It happens that I finish writing this article at Easter time, on a ship off the coast of Palestine. We have just returned from Jerusalem and Bethlehem, which are full of pilgrims—full of impulsive proponents of a variety of religions. The variety and the impulsiveness impress one greatly. I feel all the more strongly that in formulating or promulgating our individual religious systems it can not be amiss to know what science can tell of the extent, the composition, the workings, of that universe where we play a hurried part.

July 2—New Dimensions for the Stellar Universe

The physical universe was anthropocentric to primitive man. At a subsequent stage of intellectual progress it was centered in a restricted area on the surface of the earth. Still later, to Ptolemy and his school, the universe was geocentric; but since the time of Copernicus the sun, as the dominating body of the solar system, has been considered to be at or near the center of the stellar realm. With the origin of each of these successive conceptions, the system of stars has appeared ever larger than was thought before. Thus the significance of man and the earth in the sidereal scheme has dwindled with advancing knowledge of the physical world, and our conception of the dimensions of the discernible stellar universe has progressively changed. Is not further evolution of our ideas probable? In the face of great accumulations of new and relevant information can we firmly maintain our old cosmic conceptions?

As a consequence of the exceptional growth and activity of the great observatories, with their powerful methods of analyzing stars and of sounding space, we have already reached an epoch, I believe, when another advance is necessary; our conception of the galactic system must be enlarged to keep in proper relationship the objects our telescopes are finding; the solar system can no longer maintain a central position. Recent studies of clusters and related subjects seem to me to leave no alternative to the belief that the galactic

51

system is at least ten times greater in diameter—at least a thousand times greater in volume—than recently supposed.

Let us first recall that the stellar universe,[1] as we know it, appears to be a very oblate spheroid or ellipsoid—a disk-shaped system composed mainly of stars and nebulae. The solar system is not far from the middle plane of this flattened organization which we call the galactic system. Looking away from the plane we see relatively few stars; looking along the plane, through a great depth of star-populated space, we see vast numbers of sidereal objects constituting the band of light we call the Milky Way.

The loosely organized star clusters, such as the Pleiades, the diffuse nebulae, such as the great nebula of Orion, the planetary nebulae, of which the ring nebula in Lyra is a good example, the dark nebulosities—all these sidereal types appear to be a part of the great galactic system, and they lie almost exclusively near the plane of the Milky Way. The globular clusters, tho not in the Milky Way, are also affiliated with the galactic system; the spiral nebulae appear to be distant objects mainly if not entirely outside the most populous parts of the galactic region. This conception of the galactic system, as a flattened, watch-shaped organization of stars and nebulae, with globular clusters and spirals as external objects, is now pretty generally agreed upon by students of the subject. Possibly the most convenient way of illustrating the scale of the sidereal universe is in terms of our measuring rods, going from terrestrial units to those of stellar systems. On the earth's surface we express distances in units such as inches, feet, or miles. On the moon the mile is still a usable measuring unit.

Our measuring scale must be greatly increased, however, when we consider the dimensions of a star—distances on the surface of our sun, for example. The large sun-spots can not be measured conveniently in units appropriate to earthly distance—in fact, the whole earth itself is none too large. The unit for measuring the distances from the sun to its attendant planets, is, however, 12,000 times the diameter of the earth; it is the so-called astronomical unit, the average distance from earth to sun. This unit,

93,000,000 miles in length, is ample for the distances of planets and comets. It would probably suffice to measure the distances of whatever planets and comets there may be in the vicinity of other stars; but it, in turn, becomes cumbersome in expressing the distances from one star to another, for some of them are hundreds of millions, even a thousand million, astronomical units away.

This leads us to abandon the astronomical unit and to introduce the light-year as a measure for sounding the depths of stellar space. The distance light travels in a year is something less than six million million miles. The distance from the earth to the moon, in these units, is 1.2 light-seconds. The distance to the sun is eight light-minutes. But the nearest star is more than four light-years away.

In some phases of our astronomical problems (studying photographs of stellar spectra) we make direct microscopic measures of a ten-thousandth of an inch; and indirectly we measure changes in the wave-length of light a million times smaller than this; in discussing the arrangement of globular clusters in space, we must measure a hundred thousand light-years. Expressing these large and small measures with reference to the velocity of light, we have an illustration of the scale of the astronomer's universe—his measures range from the trillionth of a billionth part of one light-second, to more than a thousand light-centuries.

It is to be noticed that light plays an all-important role in the study of the universe; we know the physics and chemistry of stars only through their light, and their distance from us we express by means of the velocity of light. The light-year, moreover, has a double value in sidereal exploration; it is geometrical, as we have seen, and it is historical. It tells us not only how far away an object is, but also how long ago the light we examine was started on its way. You do not see the sun where it is, but where it was eight minutes ago. You do not see faint stars of the Milky Way as they are now, but more probably as they were when the pyramids of Egypt were being built; and the ancient Egyptians saw them as they were at a time still more remote.

We are, therefore, chronologically far behind events when we study conditions or dynamical behavior in remote stellar systems; the motions, light-emissions, and variations now investigated in the Hercules cluster are not contemporary, but, if my value of the distance is correct, they are the phenomena of 36,000 years ago. The great age of these incoming pulses of radiant energy is, however, no disadvantage; in fact, their antiquity has been turned to good purpose in testing the speed of stellar evolution, in indicating the enormous ages of stars, in suggesting the vast extent of the universe in time as well as in space.

Taking the light-year as a satisfactory unit for expressing the dimensions of sidereal systems, let us consider the distances of neighboring stars and clusters, and briefly mention the methods of deducing their space positions. For nearby stellar objects we can make direct trigonometric measures of distance (parallax), using the earth's orbit or the sun's path through space as a base line. For many of the more distant stars spectroscopic methods are available, using the appearance of the stellar spectra and the readily measurable apparent brightness of the stars. For certain types of stars, too distant for spectroscopic data, there is still a chance of obtaining the distance by means of the photometric method. This method is particularly suited to studies of globular clusters; it consists first in determining, by some means, the real luminosity of a star, that is, its so-called absolute magnitude, and second, in measuring its apparent magnitude. Obviously, if a star of known real brightness is moved away to greater and greater distances, its apparent brightness decreases; hence, for such stars of known absolute magnitude, it is possible, using a simple formula, to determine the distance by measuring the apparent magnitude.

It appears, therefore, that altho space can be explored for a distance of only a few hundred light-years by direct trigonometric methods, we are not forced, by our inability to measure still smaller angles, to extrapolate uncertainly or to make vague guesses relative to farther regions of space, for the trigonometrically determined distances can be used to calibrate the tools of newer and less restricted methods.

For example, the trigonometric methods of measuring the distance to moon, sun, and nearer stars are decidedly indirect, compared with the linear measurement of distance on the surface of the earth, but they are not for that reason inexact or questionable in principle. The spectroscopic and photometric methods of measuring great stellar distance are also indirect, compared with the trigonometric measurement of small stellar distance, but they, too, are not for that reason unreliable or of doubtful value. By one method or the other, the distances of nearly 3,000 individual stars in the solar neighborhood have now been determined; only a few are within ten light-years of the sun. At a distance of about 130 light-years we find the Hyades, the well-known cluster of naked eye stars; at a distance of 600-light-years, according to Kapteyn's extensive investigations, we come to the group of blue stars in Orion—another physically-organized cluster composed of giants in luminosity. At distances comparable to the above values we also find the Scorpio-Centaurus group, the Pleiades, and the stars of the Big Dipper.

Much greater distances have now been measured for globular clusters and faint variable stars. The Hercules cluster, at a distance of 36,000 light-years, is one of the nearest of that remarkable class of objects. One-third of the globular systems now known are more distant than 100,000 light-years; the most distant is more than 200,000 light-years away, and the diameter of the whole system of globular clusters is about 300,000 light-years.

Since the affiliation of the globular clusters with the galaxy is shown by their concentration to the plane of the Milky Way and their symmetrical arrangement with respect to it, it also follows that the galactic system of stars is as large as this subordinate part. During recent years, we have found Cepheid variables [1] and other stars of high luminosity among the fifteenth magnitude stars of the galactic clouds; this can mean only that some parts of the clouds are more distant than the Hercules cluster. There seems to be good reason, therefore, to believe that the star-populated regions of the galactic system extend at least as far as the globular clusters.

One consequence of accepting the theory that clusters outline the form and extent of the galactic system is that the sun is found to be very distant from the middle

---

[1] For "Cepheid stars" see near end of lesson for July 16, p. 57.

of the galaxy. It appears that we are not far from the center of a large local cluster or cloud, but that cloud is at least 50,000 light-years from the galactic center. Twenty years ago Newcomb remarked that the sun appears to be in the galactic plane because the Milky Way is a great circle—an encircling band of light—and that the sun also appears near the center of the universe because the star density falls off with the distance in all directions. But he concludes as follows:

"Ptolemy showed by evidence, which, from his standpoint, looked as sound as that which we have cited, that the earth was fixt in the center of the universe. May we not be the victim of some fallacy, as he was?

Our present answer to Newcomb's question is that we have been victimized by restricted methods of measuring distance and by the chance position of the sun near the center of a subordinate system; we have been misled, by the consequent phenomena, into thinking that we are in the midst of things. In much the same way ancient man was misled by the rotation of the earth, with the consequent apparent daily motion of all heavenly bodies around the earth, into believing that even his little planet was the center of the universe.

If man had reached his present intellectual position in a later geological era, he might not have been led to these vain conceits concerning his position in the physical universe, for the solar system is rapidly receding from the galactic plane, and is moving away from the center of the local cluster. If that motion remains unaltered in direction and amount, in a hundred million years or so the Milky Way will be quite different from an encircling band of star clouds, the local cluster will be a distant object, and the star density will no longer decrease with distance from the sun in all directions.

July 9—The Evolution and Dimensions of Stars

Altho direct observation has never been made of the evolving of a luminous star out of primordial nebula, astronomers nevertheless believe that the circumstantial evidence for such a development can be accepted as proof.

The stars are highly organized spheroidal masses of exceedingly hot and luminous gases. The diffuse nebulae from which stars are supposed to have evolved are, in general, disorganized or unorganized masses of gas, sometimes luminous, sometimes not. The luminosity of a star such as the sun is due to the high temperature of its constituent gases. The luminosity of the diffuse nebulae is probably due in some cases to the reflection of starlight (in the same way as zodiacal light represents the reflection of the sunlight from small particles in the solar system) and in other cases to a phosphorescent kind of radiation, excited by neighboring stars in the atoms and molecules of the gases that are known to exist in these nebulae.

The stars differ little in form, but greatly in size, and still more remarkably in the character of the light they emit. Diversity in size and light appears to depend largely on the length of the time that has elapsed since the organization out of nebulosity.

The prevailing theory at the present time pictures the newborn star of enormous dimensions, with a low temperature at its surface, and a feeble luminosity. It differs little from a nebula—it is merely at an early stage of condensation. As the new star grows in age it shrinks in size. In operating under the laws of gravitation, maturity means high density rather than great stature; and youth is the stage of rarity, therefore of monstrous dimensions. As the "growing" star contracts, the falling together of its various parts generates heat. The heat from this and other sources is radiated away from the surface, and the star tends to cool. This act of cooling, by losing the heat of radiation, brings about further contraction, with the further generation of heat. The final result sounds paradoxical. The more heat the young gaseous star radiates away, the more heat it acquires, and the temperature at the surface steadily increases.

At the low temperature possest by a star when it makes its first steps in luminosity, the surface has a reddish appearance, according to Russell's widely accepted theory. If the astronomer then analyzes the light with a spectroscope he finds radiation characteristic of certain chemical elements. With increasing contraction and temperature, the average color changes to orange, then yellow, green, blue; and other characteristics of the spectrum change as well. When the star shines as a reddish young giant the surface temperature is about 4,000 degrees Centigrade. When later it becomes yellowish the temperature lies between 6,000 and 8,000 degrees; and the bluish-white stars radiate with temperatures from 12,000 to 20,000 degrees or higher.

The density, or specific gravity, of the contracting star of course steadily increases. Beginning with a rarity much less on the average than that of the best vacuum obtainable in a terrestrial laboratory, the average density increases to about one-tenth that of water for the highly luminous white stars. At that point, because of this relatively high density, the star ceases to behave as a perfect gas. It no longer follows the rules, one of which prescribes that the more heat it wastes in radiation the hotter it becomes. From that stage in its contractional life-history the star loses heat by radiation faster than it generates it by contraction. As a result, the surface temperature begins to fall off, the total brightness begins to decrease; the star passes the prime of life and starts down a decline.

We call the stars giants while they are in that part of their career where surface temperature increases. We call them dwarfs throughout the decline toward senility and extinction. The declining dwarf star runs through the series of colors and spectral characteristics in the inverse order, from blue to green, to yellow, orange, red.

Our sun is a yellowish star in the dwarf age apparently far past the turning-point in its life history.

The diameter of the sun is less than a million miles. We have not as yet measured directly or indirectly the diameters of red dwarf stars. A few of the yellowish dwarf stars are known to have dimensions comparable with those of our sun. The diameter of the components of large numbers of bluish-white double stars have been estimated from mathematical analyses of their orbits, to be from two to twenty times the solar diameter. It is, however, only among the young and yellow giant stars that striking dimensions are encountered. Theory, as well as the experiments with the interferometer as applied by Michelson and Pease at Mount Wilson, shows the great size of the giant stars. The interferometer, for instance, has measured the angular diameter of Betelgeuse, a bright reddish star in Orion. The distance of the star has been measured trigonometrically; combining these two data, distance and angular diameter, it is simple to compute that the linear diameter of Betelgeuse is more than 200 million miles—considerably greater than the diameter of the orbit of the earth. The space occupied by that star is therefore much more than ten million times the space occupied by the sun.

The red star Antares, in Scorpio, has been found to be of still greater size; and on theoretical grounds a considerable number of distant stars that appear exceedingly faint in our biggest telescopes are believed to be as large or larger.

July 16—The Source of Stellar Power

The origin of the heat that the sun radiates wantonly upon the earth has long been a subject of speculation and investigation. Clearly the simple combustion of the matter the sun is composed of would be quite insufficient. The earth intercepts less than one billionth part of the solar radiation, and, of the fraction of that billionth part that gets through our atmosphere, only a very minute fraction is utilized by terrestrial organisms. The total daily output of energy from the sun is obviously enormous, and the interval of time during which the sun has radiated is beyond expression in days. Our theories of the origin of radiant energy must therefore account for a vast store in the sun and other stars.

The names of Helmholtz, Lane, and Ritter have been associated with the theory of the gravitational source of solar heat. The Helmholtzian hypothesis that the gravitational contraction of the sun supplies ample energy for radiation has been generally maintained until recently. That source now appears to be secondary, but the gravitational mechanism is probably an important regulatory device for the control of the radiating energy, which comes, not from the gravitational infall of the atoms of the gases that make the star, but chiefly from the energy within the atoms.

The forsaking of the Helmholtzian theory is made necessary by the newer conception of the extent of the sidereal universe. His temporal gravitational hypothesis would be sufficient if we were content to limit the age of the sun (radiating at its present rate) to a few million years. Kelvin and others long ago computed that the energy derivable from contraction could support the observed output for an interval of ten to fifty million years. But now at least three lines of evidence from three different sciences indicate that the present solar rate has been maintained for a much longer interval.

First we shall consider the geological side of the operation. It is generally admitted that the sun has advanced very little in age during the whole interval of historic geology. For instance, certain animal forms common in the Paleozoic times are in essentials unchanged to-day. The terrestrial temperature has of course oscillated slightly throughout geological ages, but the average temperature must have remained nearly constant during the evolution of metazoan organisms.

If we measure present rates of denudation and erosion, present rates of sedimentation, present rates of deposition of salts in the seas, we can estimate the whole duration of geological times. Barrell, Chamberlin, Holmes, and others have recently pointed out, however, that present rates are deceptive. We are living in an age of great land elevation. The average rate of geological processes is undoubtedly much slower than the present rate. Moreover, there have been long intervals of time when the processes have nearly or completely come to a standstill. Taking this into account in his Theory of Rhythms, Barrell is led to conclude that the age of the Paleozoic fossils is to be measured in hundreds of millions of years. This result is clearly in opposition to the Helmholtz-Kelvin deductions.

The physics of the last two decades has also contributed an instrument important for the measurement of geological ages, and hence of value in the measurement of solar evolution and in the search for the true source of solar power. This physical device is based on our knowledge of the behavior of radioactive elements in the rocks. The speed with which the elements uranium and thorium automatically decay and resolve themselves ultimately into the inert gas helium and the common element lead is known with considerable accuracy. By measuring, for instance, the relative amounts of uranium remaining and lead found in radioactive minerals of various geological epochs, it has proved feasible to date those epochs—to set up a time scale for the whole of geological history.

The radioactive minerals appear in many formations all over the earth's surface, and have been extensively studied in recent years. According to this method, the earliest known pre-Cambrian rocks date from 1,100 million years ago, and the beginnings of the fossil-bearing Cambrian formations are over half a billion years old. This result from physics, therefore, also clearly disagrees with the contraction theory of the source of solar (and of stellar) energy.

The astronomer's contribution to the problem is equally definite. The mathematical theory of the evolution of a gigantic mass of luminous gas has led, in the hands of Eddington and Jeans, to a remarkable knowledge of the interior of a star. For the present discussion the most significant deduction from that work is that such a gaseous body will run through the giant stage of its evolution in a few thousand years, if the energy for radiation comes solely from the gravitational infall of its parts. Observation shows no such brevity in the giant stage. I shall cite two relevant contributions.

a. My own work on the globular star clusters with the big reflecting telescopes at Mount Wilson has brought out the interesting fact that these remote systems are composed of just such giant stars as Eddington's theory analyzes. Because the velocity of light is finite, the more distant of these clusters are, as far as our earth-made records go, much younger than the nearest globular cluster. Their recent history is still en route as light-waves. The system N.G.G. 7006, the remotest object on record at the present time, is, for us, nearly 200,-000 light-years younger than the cluster in Hercules. My analysis of the giant stars in both systems shows, however, no evidence of different ages. The same result is found from the study of many other clusters.

We have no reason to believe, of course, that the more distant clusters came into existence later than the nearer ones; it would be preposterous to think that distance from our earth has anything to do with the order of origination. Hence, this similarity in near and distant clusters must mean that an interval of one or two hundred thousand years is not sufficiently long for a measurable evolution of giant stars. And we must conclude, therefore, because of the clear implication of the mathematical theory, that the radiant energy of a giant star comes not from gravitation.

b. One type of variable star, called the Cepheid because the star Delta in Cepheus was the first known example, owes its oscillations in brightness to pulsations, according to the theory advanced some years ago by the present writer. These pulsations, with their consequent variations in light, are periodic, the period or interval of time between successive geyser-like outbursts depending on the density of the star. Recently it has been shown that the pulsations for Delta Cephei could not have been maintained, as observed for a century, unless its radiant heat is generated by something more than gravitation.

Science is not yet ready to describe how the stars use the energy of the elemental atoms. In a few years we shall no doubt be able to speak more advisedly on the subject. At present we surmise that the building up, of the heavier chemical elements such as iron, lead, gold, out of the lighter elements such as hydrogen and helium, releases energy for stellar radiation. There appears to be a transformation of a part of the mass of hydrogen atoms into energy when that fundamental material is compounded into more complex elements. The energy that stars shine by and which as a passing incident operates the earthly planets and animals, appears, therefore, to be a by-product of the material evolution of cosmic gases.

July 23—On the Origin of Planetary Systems

Serious attempts to set up a natural explanation of the origin of the earth and the other planets of the solar system, in the place of the supernatural accounts, followed as a matter of course the acceptance of the Copernican theory. The deservedly famous hypothesis of Laplace, more or less coinciding with similar explanations by Thomas Wright, Immanuel Kant, and others, held its place in scientific thought for a century. It is now generally abandoned by astronomers. Its attempt to account for the origin of planets from cast-off rings of a condensing, rotating nebula fails in certain dynamical details. The present speed of rotation of the sun on the one hand, and the distances and velocities of the planets on the other, are mutually irreconcilable in the Laplacian scheme.

The planetesimal theory proposed by Chamberlin and Moulton, and the subsequent variations upon it, have led to a conception of the origin of the planetary system that is compatible both with the demands of celestial mechanics and with those of sidereal probability. Difficulties are found with all proposals. But the so-called tidal-evolution theory, which deviates in detail and method rather than in principle from the planetesimal hypothesis, is at present considered to be quite satisfactory. It differs from the nebular hypothesis in many ways, but most in deriving the planets from the sun through an accident, rather than through a natural process of contraction.

According to the tidal evolution theory, the planets originate from the sun. They are the product of eruption, of solar catastrophe, incited by the passing of another sidereal body. They represent the debris of a disaster that occurred some thousands of millions of years ago. When two gaseous stars wandering in space come near together, the mutual gravitational attraction raises tides upon them both. The case is analogous to terrestrial tides, generated by moon and sun; but the greater masses involved in stars raise relatively higher tides, which, for a sufficiently close encounter, must become unstable and break down, causing stellar matter to fly out in streams. In the case of the solar system, the ejecta were apparently concentrated in a few large masses which now appear as the planets. Assuming such an origin, Jeffreys has computed that the present shape of the orbits of the planets indicates that the genesis of the sun's planetary system occurred not less than 3,000 million years ago.

Presumably the disturbing star, which we must thank for our present existence, was reciprocally disturbed at the time of the encounter. What happened to it depends on its mass, its stage of evolution, and its velocity of rotation at that time. We have no clue to the identity of this hypothetical object. It has had sufficient time since the affair with our sun to be lost in space.

The planets, born of the sun, are made

of the same chemical constituents. The earth, originally gaseous, being of relatively small mass, has cooled and formed a solid crust. Meanwhile, no doubt, it has picked up a certain amount of the surrounding fragments, but the biggest of these, the moon, has remained as a companion planet. Even now, in the form of meteors and meteorites, the earth and the other planets are picking up small gleanings that may date from the ancient creation.

Some of the other planets—Mercury, Venus, Mars—have also formed superficial crusts; but the planets of greater mass—Jupiter, Saturn, Uranus, Neptune—apparently still retain their gaseous nature. The average density of Saturn is even less than the average density of its solar parent, but probably it is much denser than the outer layers of the sun.

Altho we find the Laplacian theory not suited to the interpretation of the planetary system, it has been found by Jeans capable of explaining satisfactorily the origin of still greater systems, the spiral nebulae. The shape of the nuclei of these great nebulous masses conforms more or less with the suggestions of Laplace. For stars, however, the amount of material is too small for such an operation. If about equal to the sun in mass, a star contracts as a single body, and only an accident can bring it a planetary system. If the contracting star is several times as massive as the sun and rotates rapidly enough, a double star is a natural outcome of evolution.

July 30—Life and the Physical Universe

We have suggested above that other stars may have planetary systems. We often wonder whether some of those planetary systems are analogous to our own—whether other planets are similar to the earth—whether terrestrial life exists elsewhere in the universe. It is far beyond our telescopic power to detect visually other planetary systems. As reflectors of light stellar planets are of no consequence at stellar distances. As gravitational disturbers of the motion of their primary suns, they are essentially weaklings. We can not prove the existence of a single non-solar planet. Yet we infer with cause that they exist.

For the sake of furnishing material for contemplation, one can reasonably assume that there are among the thousands of millions of known stars a great many with attendant planets. Indeed the chances favor the existence of planets especially suited to some kind of unstable, chemical evolution which we might call life, and for all we know that development may sometimes be very high compared with ours. But the chance that terrestrial forms of life are duplicated, or closely paralleled, is much more remote. And to hold that there now exists an organism of the exact physical and chemical character as the predominating terrestrial primate, man, is asking too much of the law of chance, even in a sidereal system as large as we know ours to be. For the existence of man depends on a delicate balance of physical conditions and laws. The astronomer can emphasize a few of the factors absolutely essential to life of the terrestrial type.

In the first place, the abode of life must be near a source of energy—a star. The star must not be double; otherwise a sufficiently stable planetary orbit could not exist. The single star must have had its planet-breeding disturbance to just the right degree. Once disturbed, it must be left in peace for an enormous interval of time; it can not have passed through a nebula, or in any other way flashed up as a nova (a new star), if the delicate animate evolution on its planets is to avoid fatal interruption.

The planet that is to give birth to organisms must be neither too large nor too small. If too massive its meteorological phenomena (rainfall, windstorms) would be of too violent a nature for earth-like life. If its mass is too small it can not retain an atmosphere. Earthly creatures, for instance, could exist neither on Jupiter nor on the moon.

The favorable planet must have an atmosphere of the proper density and constituents. Its crust must have a salutary chemical constitution. Probably most important of all it must possess water in a liquid state, because that is an essential of the protoplasm that is the basis of life. Therefore the planet must be at an appropriate distance from its sun. At the small distance of Mercury the temperature is too high. At the too great distance of Mars the water would be mostly in a solid form. Other restrictions involve the rotation period of the planet, the inclination of its axis, and the eccentricity of its orbit.

THE AUTHORITATIVE VOICE OF JESUS[1]

J. H. JOWETT, D.D., London, England

He taught them as one having authority and not as the scribes.—Mark 1:22.

Who does not know the difference between the voice of a fountain and the voice of a cistern? Who does not know the difference between a speaker whose words carry no cargo and a speaker whose words are deeply laden with a precious freight? "He taught them as one having authority." That authority was not couched in oratory, nor did it borrow anything from the charms of eloquence. The authority was not in the form and color of his words, but in their weight. His thought did not suggest flowers of rhetoric, but rather a deep and vital rootage. What Jesus said always seemed to come out of mysterious depths, those tremendous depths where the ultimate secrets of life are born. It was not cleverness that was speaking; it was character. It was not the voice of learning; it was the voice of wisdom. He taught as one having authority.

I think we have the contrast in purely human relationships. Who does not know the difference when a man of authority intervenes in a debate? It is not necessary that he should be a man of the front bench. A man may be on the front bench, clad in a little brief authority, yet there may be no authority about the man, or about the word he speaks. The authority which is derived from office is something like the awe which sits upon the judge. It is divested with his ermine robe, and ceases to exist when he steps into the street. Real authority is quite independent of office and station. It is independent of place. A man may rise in the back benches of the house, he may be an unfamiliar presence, he may never have spoken before, yet he may not have spoken for two minutes before the house knows that authority speaks. Was there ever a poorer speaker than the late duke of Devonshire?[2] His style was un-

impressive, his manner was drowsy, he stammered, everything about him was heavy and laborious. Yet somehow or other, when he brought out his cumbrous lantern, there was light on the road. Whether in or out of office, he always spoke with authority. It was born in a deeper realm than that of the intellect, deep down among intuitions of character. With whatever clumsiness he spoke, he was always trafficking with the primitive secrets of life, and always there was something in his word which to his fellow-countrymen seemed to run parallel with the controlling law and order of the universe. It is always so with men of that order. Whenever a man of this order speaks to us, he always unveils a little of the strata of the fundamental constitution of the world.

I think all this may lead us just a little way in the understanding of this contrast between the scribes and our Lord. Who were the scribes, and what were they like? The scribes were men whose business it was to be learned in the law. They were experts in their familiarity with not merely the original law, but with all the accretions and encrustments which had fastened upon the original law, like some huge fungus upon the trunk of an old tree. They were experts in the traditions of the elders. Their memories were bulging with legalities, stored with the most burdensome care. You can see the same process of acquisition going on today in any of the great Moslem mosques of the Orient, at Damascus or Constantinople. If you went you would find there young Moslems, training for the priesthood, memorizing the Koran, drawling it with dreary monotony, paragraph after paragraph, page after page, until they have piled up vast deposits of their sacred book with all the unenlightened detachment of a parrot. So it was with the scribes. I

---

[1] Reported for THE HOMILETIC REVIEW.
[2] Marquis of Hartington, one time member of Mr. Gladstone's cabinet, at other times in the opposition.

said their memories were bulging with legalities. They exercised their memories more than their reason. They packed their mental lockers with statutes, and rules, and precepts; with thousands of jots and tittles. They were just incarnate codes of law. When they gave counsel to anybody it was always a bit of legality, always a fragment of tradition, something taken down from the dusty shelves of the past. If you want a symbol that stands for the life and business of a scribe, take a roll of parchment, heavily and thickly inscribed with legal trivialities of a past age.

Among these men, filled with legal technicalities, Jesus came. If the symbol of the scribe is to be a roll of parchment, what should be the symbol of Jesus? It shall be his own symbol, a well of water springing up into everlasting life. When you pass from a scribe to Jesus, you pass from the dusty shelves of ancient trivialities to a natural fountain, up-gushing from inexpressible and fathomless depths. When you pass from a scribe to Jesus you pass from a reciter to a creator. You pass from laws to the spirit of the law, from knowledge to wisdom, from the echo to the voice. You take your thirst to a scribe and he leads you to a cistern and to the stale deposits of a cistern. When you take your thirst to Jesus he leads you to a spring whose waters have all the freshness of a new creation.

The contrast was just this. The inspiration of Jesus was not meditated through a long, long line of rabbinical tradition. It was new, original, immediate. He spoke with authority. Well then, I want to listen to him. I want to see, if I can, what his authority is like. The first thing I would like to say about the authority of Jesus is this: he spoke with authority by reason of the amazing intimacy with which he talked about the deep things of God. There was no guess work. There was certainty. The scribes had spoken of divine things in such a way as to make men feel that no end of distance stretched like a chilly waste between the soul of man and God.

Well, Jesus came, and he began to speak about God, and he spoke in this way: "I speak that which I have seen of my Father. I come forth from God. I speak that which I have seen, I justify that which I know." That was a new sort of word! I do not

wonder that the people were held in amazement. There is such imperativeness, such a strange impressiveness, in it. No scribe talked like that! The scribe talked in this way. He told you what Rabbi A. had to say, who borrowed it from Rabbi B, who had it from Rabbi C, and so on, until God was lost in words, dissolved in unreality by long ranges of rabbinical triviality. Jesus quietly and confidently said, I have seen. "We speak that which we know." I have been there, I have just come from there. I come from God, whom I have seen. A tremendous note of authority, altogether unlike the scribes. It was an awe-inspiring intimacy with God that held the people in such surprise. It was a first-hand view of God. What did he tell them? What did he say he had seen? My brethren, I would like you to feel the tremendous impact of it. I want you to realize that these people had been dealing with God through multitudinous statutes, countless rules and precepts, which instead of giving them wings only seemed to add to their burden. Then Jesus came, and what did he say about God? A word like this: I have just come from God, and I will tell you what he is like. He is like a shepherd. He is like a shepherd who had lost a sheep, and spent a day and night scouring every ravine, every gully in the mountains, until he found it. He is like that! He is like a woman who has lost a precious piece from a necklace, so that there is a great ugly gap in the chaste design, and she searches every corner of the house until she finds it. He is like that! He is like a father who has lost his boy, who goes down every road looking for him; who one day, when he is well on the road, sees the boy a long way off, runs, and falls on his neck, kisses him, and brings him home in joy and peace. He is like that—just like that! And when Jesus thus speaks, the people are filled with wonder, because after all their statutes, their rules, their legalities, their trivialities, their formalities, it is like some sweet summer morning after a night of pain.

And Jesus went on to talk to them, and he told them about the Father's house, where no one has trouble any more, and about the open way which anybody can find, for it is just where everybody needs it. Then he told them the Father would wash away their stains and their shames and clothe them with eternal garments befitting the children of royal blood. Then he told them that God looked after them like the birds of the air, like the lilies of the field. He told them that God did not want to see the care-lines on their faces, the wrinkles in their hearts. Your Father does not want that, he said. I know. I have seen. Be not anxious, your heavenly Father knoweth that ye have need of these things. So Jesus put his strong, calm, enquieting hand on the care-lines and smoothed them out. As he spoke to the people the wrinkles went out of their hearts, and they were filled with a strange peace. That is how he talked to them. It was just as if they had gathered at a dry cistern, with not a drop to quench their thirst, and suddenly close by the cistern there came a stream from the mountains. He spoke as one having authority.

I would like to look again at the contrast between the two: between the voice of the scribes and the voice of the Lord. Try again to feel the impact of the contrast upon the hearts of the people of his time. Do you know the difference between the law courts and the House of Parliament? What is the difference? Pay a visit to the law courts. What are they doing there? They are administering the law. Pay a visit to the high court of Parliament. What are they doing there? They are making the law. The one is administrative, the other is legislative. The one interprets the law, the other creates it. The one studies the law as it is, the other shapes the law as it shall be. The one expounds, the other explores. The one gathers precedents and makes inferences, the other brushes precedents aside, disregards them, leaves them as abandoned roads, and begins to make new roads. The law courts exercise memory and recollection. A law court never uses the organ of vision—I mean the organ of hope, and of foresight. The law courts exercise the faculties of memory and recollection—Parliament exercises the faculty of vision. The law courts look backward, never forward. Parliament looks forward. The law courts say, It hath been said by them of olden time. Parliament says, I say unto you, The law courts repeat, and repeat, and repeat. Parliament renews. I think this contrast between the law courts and the House of Parliament will tell us something of the supreme difference between the

scribes and the Lord. If I may reverently say it: The scribes spoke with the voice of the law courts; Christ spoke with the voice of Parliament. The scribes interpreted the law, or interpreted interpretations of the law, being expert in all the marginal notes and comments on the original law. The scribes fenced the law, regarding it as a most precious deposit. Jesus put the law on one side, or rather, he re-shaped it, he handled it as if it were plasticine. "It was said by them of olden time, love thy neighbor and hate thine enemy, but I say—" That is the voice of Parliament, the high court of the universe. It is the imperative note. It is the creative word. He spoke with authority.

And the supreme wonder about his word is this: It never becomes an anachronism. It never passes into the museum. We never leave it behind. It is always up to date. It is the light of tomorrow. It is always in front of us. It is always the expanding ideal for the ever-progressive crusade. It is always the dawn that is beckoning us on the horizon. Jesus, in front of every reform, in front of every crusade. We are not leaderless. He is leading. The word he spoke is life. It never, never dies. He spoke with authority. Jesus was and is the moral legislature of the human race.

I would mention a third point. I have said Christ was incomparable in his intimacy with the deep things of God, and incomparable in the way in which he declared the creative law of God. I would add this. If he was incomparably intimate with the heart of God, he was also incomparably intimate with the hearts of men. I did not say with the heart of humanity. Jesus Christ never used a word which could be translated "humanity." It was not in his vocabulary. You will not find it in your Testament. Our Lord never dealt with abstractions. His intimacy was not with man, but with men; and his understanding sympathy was not with woman, but with women. He never dealt with a type as tho a single type represented everybody else. He always dealt with us, not as standardized members of the race, but as individuals, as tho we were separate creations. "I know my mass." Did he ever say that? "I know humanity." Did he ever say that? "I know my flock." Did he ever say it? He said, "I know my sheep." What is finer and dearer still, he said, "I call my sheep by name. No one is lost in the crowd." That is how he knew folk. He spoke to every single person as tho there were no others in the world. Did you catch that! I will repeat it. He spoke to every individual as tho there were no others. He knew all their highways and all their byways. It seemed to everybody as tho he had trodden their ways, every inch of them. He spoke to a woman at the well, and when she told her story she said, He told me all things that ever I did. He had a word with Nathaniel, who was almost speechless with wonder. Whence knowest thou me. He spoke to a publican, and the publican melted at the word, just as old Scrooge melted under the genial influence of Christmas, and rose and followed him. He knew everybody. Nothing was standardized. He knew a certain rich young ruler, and spoke one word which disclosed his chain. He knew a certain woman who was a sinner. He spoke one word, and her dungeon flamed with light. He knew everybody. He knows everybody. "I know my sheep." And knowing everybody and everything about everybody, he loves everybody, and he proclaims himself absolutely sufficient to save and heal them. "Come unto me all ye that labor, and I will give you rest." My God, there is authority there!

What do you think about my Jesus? Incomparable in his knowledge of God, incomparable in his moral imperative, incomparable in his moral insight into the hearts of men; with his wise, rare smile, with his sweet certainties, I reverently present him to this congregation as the Son of God. I reverently present him as the Son of man. With all the homage of my heart I present him as Savior of the world. He and he alone can meet all our necessities. He, and no other, can lead the world out of its present chaos into paths of pleasantness and ways of peace.

> Thou O Christ art all I want,
> More than all in Thee I find.

He speaks with authority. Let us listen!

TRIFLES AND TRIVIALITIES

The Rev. MARK WAYNE WILLIAMS, Brooklyn, N. Y.

But Martha was cumbered about much serving.—Luke 10:40.

I. Martha was fortunate in having Jesus for her guest; she was extremely unfortunate in her way of expressing hospitality. She was an efficient housewife, a good provider, generous, industrious, and painstaking. She had the mothering instinct to a pernicious degree. She fussed and bustled about, busy with the chores, crockery, and cooking. So I have seen a fluttering plymouth rock, clucking to her brood, scratching for choice worms, ever alarmed about hawks, never giving her offspring any initiative nor allowing them to grow up. How feckless and futile becomes divine motherhood when it wastes its glory on the accidental and the transient. I have seen such quivering and befuddled service when the old preacher came to dinner down on the farm. Scarcely has he been made effusively welcome, and settled comfortably in the ancient rocking chair, wishful of a restful chat, when the devastating bombardment of good will begins. First, Mary must run intermittent errands to the neighbors for superfluous dishes or forgotten table linen; and Martha must rush about to prepare delicious knickknacks and succulent relishes. Lazarus must run up to the delicatessen for additional supplies. Whatever preparation had been made beforehand, nothing is too good, nothing is quite sufficient, to give this good man of religion. In the pauses, Martha commends certain magazines, or points out interesting books, or rearranges the furniture, or invites him to try half a dozen different easy chairs or tells Mary to turn on certain tunes on the phonograph, or makes Lazarus show him over the farm. Then at dinner, the discourse on immortality is interrupted by something burning in the kitchen; discussion on political tendencies yields to inconsequent gravy; and the parable of the prodigal loses its artistic point by the passing of inadvertent potatoes and inappropriate pie. Even Jesus could scarcely work miracles here, because of such cluttered and cumbering kindliness. Martha invented the word "service" for us to exaggerate. How mournfully and quizzically Jesus says, "Martha, you are careful of many things. One thing is needful, and Mary hath chosen the better part." [1]

II. Trifles make perfection, and perfection is no trifle. But it is obvious that we are bogged, dragged down, and smothered by the multitude of piffling and insignificant objects of our attention. One mosquito in the wakeful night sings as loud as any nightingale; a myriad such, nestling up to humanity, breed malarias, fevers, and death. A grain of dust is indistinguishably small, but cuddled in the corner of the eye it commands more attention than this round world; and multiplied by thousands and swept by the bosom of the simoon, it buries ancient civilizations in innocuous desuetude. A grasshopper is an insignificant fiddler, yet his armies stop transcontinental expresses, strip the cornfields of whole States, devour the granaries of opulent Egypt herself. We harness ourselves to the treadmill of unnecessary drudgery. We can not see the forest for the trees. We postpone Shakespeare until we have mastered our unabridged dictionary. We regulate our activities by the clock, and become efficiency experts. We rush from duty to duty, from committee to committee, from call to call, from club to club, until we crack, and go to recuperate in Florida or Greenwood. Then folks shrug their shoulders and say, "She wore herself out trying to do too much." Not too much, but too many little, unrelated, impertinent things. Instead of driving our business our business drives us. A drop of water is a tiny thing; a humming bird can sip it from the calix of a flower; a morning ray can dry it off a dewy thorn. Yet you may stand by the ocean's marge and sweep and sweep and sweep, but you can not keep back the tides of tiny, incalculable molecules. Your boat may swim the upper reaches of Niagara, you may thrill or startle with the sense of the nearing cataract; but however you despise the warning shout from the shore; however you may boast your ability to stop when you please; suddenly the river gets its claws upon you, and you are dragged to an exhilarating but terrible doom. In vain you row and call and pray; those innocent waterdrops become a stream, that stream a river, that river a

flood, and that flood a Niagara. Such is the cumulative power of littleness.

It is a foolish ambition, to get all the experience there is in the earth. At the old home-town fair they had a pie-eating contest. I recall that they lined up ten ardent youths at a table groaning with assorted pies, baked by estimable and convincing housewives. At a signal, with fork and knife and fingers and elbows, by pick and shovel and hook and crook, and might and main, those eager striplings, amid laughter and applause, urged pie after pie, pumpkin, apple, raspberry, blueberry, quite regardless of taste or appetite, into their assorted faces. I remember how one by one the contestants dropped out, too full for utterance. How at last amid universal approval, the victor, who was also the victim, smeared with the trophies and gorgeous with accomplishment, advanced to the tune of "Here the conquering hero comes" and received from the mayor the prize, which was, as I recollect, a noble mince pie. The world has praise for its gormandizers and cheers its worthiest pie eaters.

III. Because we allow ourselves to be tyrannized over by trifles we come inevitably into the tragedy of trifling. For our greatest tragedy is this, not that we do not give great powers to great ends, but that we dedicate our finest effort to little and mean purposes. The marvelous inventions of the mind are devoted to the perpetuation and dissemination of standardized stupidities. An ardent neighbor woke me Sunday morning up-State as he clambered over my roof. He was making an aerial for a wireless telephone. "Can you hear sermons?" I ask. "Oh, yes," very eagerly, "from Springfield, and Syracuse, and Chicago." I wanted to ask him what was in the sermons, but that apparently made no difference so long as they came over the wireless. Perhaps tomorrow every light socket will be tuned to the gossip of the universe.

They carry wireless parasols in Paris, so that as you promenade down the Rue de Rivoli you may hear if baby is crying at home, or Galli Curci is singing in New York. What fascinating mixed music we shall have. I long to listen in to the duet by Caruso and the old clothes man. The Iliad of the *Congressional Record* will drone like a bourdon pipe through all our telephonic souls, interlarded by flageolets from the fogbanks

---

[1] See a Russian painter's conception of this scene in the frontispiece for the April number of this REVIEW.

of Newfoundland and the chirps of "Katy did; Katy didn't" from the meadows adjoining the United States Senate.

Sunday morning I saw a father leading his wife and three children to the house of God. I was pleased and entranced. Here was an old Puritan father, a patriarch, a real saint, who outdid the plesiosaurus in being alive and present. I said, "I will now draw near, and see this thing which is come to pass. Surely he is expounding foreordination to his offspring or descanting on the ways of divine Providence to his assenting spouse." I was disillusioned by his actual converse. "Yes, the engine is only one cylinder, but it can run eighty miles on one gallon of gasoline." Our Pilgrim forebears did carry their muskets on their shoulders to church, but they kept their minds free to think great thoughts and their hearts open to believe great ideals.

Then, too, we take our geniuses and, because we can not understand them, or dislike them since they are not exactly like us, we starve them into acquiescence and set them to Cinderella tasks. Napoleon's sword he must now use to whittle toothpicks; Angelo uses his chisel to quarry stone; Moses we make a village alderman; Isaiah sips tea and chats with the old ladies; Solomon stays home to take care of the children, while his 900 wives attend the Republican caucus and nominate the new mayor for Jerusalem. Paul guides tourists around the Mediterranean, pointing out his various shipwrecks and stonings; while John has quit writing the Apocalypse and has become chief scenarist for a moving picture company. To such uses does this housewife world, cumbered with much serving, put its prophets and dreamers and interpreters.

There was a man who carved the Lord's Prayer on a dime. It was a difficult task; nobody but he ever did it. It took him a long, long time and it was very hard on his eyes. It was not a work of art, it gave him no skill for a larger work. It was, as the heathen say, a stunt. Yet he set himself to the work, neglected his wife, his meals, his business, and finally completed the job. He had put the biggest prayer in the world on one of the smallest coins in the world, a coin so small that it represents only twice the average offering of the American church audience. There was the tragedy—he had spent his whole enthusiasm in putting the kingdom of God on a dime. Why didn't he think of putting it on at least a quarter, or even more audaciously on an almighty dollar? Why couldn't the Lord's Prayer be inscribed on all eagles and double eagles and offspring of eagles, notes and bonds and stocks, and farms and factories and governments? Alas, the Lord's Prayer is assiduously carved on dimes, while the devil writes his signature on all the big currency.

IV. Faith is the transcending of triviality. What has become of all the bird's eggs and marbles and bright pebbles and stamps that we used to collect when we were boys? Some oblivious garret hides them; their charm vanished and their lure departed. By what meticulous and incredible labors did you build up their ephemeral value, as worthless now as the dust of the apples of Sodom. Some day you will look back on your present accumulations and wonder at the childish enthusiasm that could hugely and sacrificially marshal machines, and houses and lands, a supposititious wealth that, like Russian roubles, becomes less valuable as more innumerable. Rousseau perceived the superficial nature of civilization and urged us back to nature. Gandhi, the Hindu mystic, avers that Occidental methods are fatal to the genius of the Indian race. The greatest of ancient cities have been overthrown; time has crumbled their bastions and temples, but beside the ruined marbles the peasant still follows the plow, and the harvests ripen amid the stones of Baalbek. The mediæval monk, opprest by the futilities rather than the enormities of his age, solaced his heart in the mighty thoughts, the saintly companionships, the noble sacrifices, the unceasing labors and prayers of Cistercian abbeys. He could forget, if he could not dispel, the pall of littleness that overhung the worldly life.

Mary indeed chose the better part when, neither through indolence nor unconcern but through a true perception of the values of life, she sat uncumbered by many things at the feet of Jesus. "But few things are necessary," says the older text. These indispensable things are doubtless: First, the soul of man is bigger than the stars. You are the true center and focus of the universe. The further ethereal horizons, the fire mist of unbelievably distant ages, the roar of primeval gigantism; the long eons of cosmic explication must not, shall not, blind us to this greater truth nor deafen us to this higher voice. You are the epitome of all evolution; you are the teleologic heir of all elemental processes; you are the right interpreter of this transmogrifying spectacle. You are the answer to all earth's obstinate questionings, fallings from us and vanishings. Beyond seas and suns, leviathans and megalosauri, you persist beyond the bounds of time; you are worth a hundred million constellate flaming orbs.

Secondly, we perceive the associate truth, that you are greater than all your works, however cumbered and busy you may be. Incomparable soul of man, creator of piled ranges of cities, of vivid and angelic art, of intricate and multiplex pathways of commerce, of sublime and profound cogitation on this universal flux, why dost thou fall down and worship the mere product of thy genius, the shadow of thy substance, the echo of thy voice? Man is greater than any and all his work. Nor books, nor symphonies, nor constitutions, nor societies, magnificent as they may be, are in any sense comparable to him that flung them off. Civilization is but the garb of man, as nature is but the garment of Deity. And truly the life is more than meat and the body more than raiment. Lilies and sparrows remember this, which man, alas, forgets.

And thirdly, you are of infinite meaning and worth, not as the housekeeper of this third class planet, this economist of a doubt-ful hospitality, but as you listen to the voice of the infinite Teacher himself and realize the image of him who made you to be like him.

They tell us that Armenia is going blind, that trachoma, that terrible and contagious disease, is spreading rapidly, that the sorrows of these awful years have so weakened the people's bodies and shattered their souls that they are fast becoming a prey to this new sadness. The tears of Armenia are turning her eyes to stone. Would that they might turn their hearts, too, to stone, that they might not remember the orgies of agony through which they have passed. Ah, to be blind and have written indelibly on sightless eyeballs the unforgettable terrors of her wo. But there is another blindness, fast growing here, in which the prince of the powers of the air hath blinded the minds of them that believe not. The mists of pettifogging trifles is in our eyes; the dust of trivialities has shrouded our vision; we grope darkly in the way, we stare and behold not the vision; we stumble and fail of the task. Better the blindness of Armenia, who through the fogs of bereavement beholds the apocalytic purposes of God, than this moral blindness which can not see because it will not look. "If to feel, in the ink of the slough and the sink of the mire, veins of glory and fire run through and transpierce and transpire—that the smooth shall bloom through the rough. Lord if that were enough."

SAVOR AND ILLUMINATION

The Rev. T. Robertson McBride, Mowbray, South Africa

Ye are the salt of the earth.
Ye are the light of the world.
—Matt. 5:13, 14.

Under the able editorship of Professor Cairns of Aberdeen, Scotland, some time ago a book was published, entitled *The Army and Religion.* The army, in this case, was the citizen army of the empire, and the opinions obtained from the soldier may be taken to reflect the attitude of many who today are engaged in the ordinary pursuits of civilian life. In the army were men drawn from all classes of society: men of different training, upbringing, and outlook. The army reflected many diverse opinions; it was a little world in itself. In touch with it, in-deed forming part of it and in intimacy more or less close to it, were chaplains and Y. M. C. A. workers. And among the men, sharing their life and their hardships, their joys and their sorrows, were some who had been closely identified with the work of the Christian Church; some indeed in the days of peace had been ministers and office-bearers. Thus it was that the army presented an almost unique field for religious enquiry, an opportunity for understanding men's minds in relation to religion, the Christian gospel, and the Christian Church. Two things emerging from that enquiry I wish to note just now: and they are not unrelated. The first is that it was evident that men had the most extraordinary ideas about the Church and its place and function in the world. Many of them seemed to imagine that the Church had no other purpose than to get people together into a building on Sunday, and that ministers would be perfectly satisfied if the Sunday congregations were more considerable. The essential meaning of worship and the idea of a Christian life, fostered and built up through the preaching of the Word and the means of grace, had no essential place in the minds of large numbers of our fellow citizens. And let us remember that these men had been born and bred in what are called Christian countries, and many of them must have had some sort of religious education. I do not stop to offer an explanation of a fact so strange, so disconcerting. But when every allowance is made for the perversity of human nature and the determined obtuseness of the human mind (when it so wishes), it seems to me that we must conclude that the churches themselves must carry some of the blame and must confess that they have failed to make a true and adequate impression on men's minds. The further related fact is this: Professor Cairns—a great Christian apologist and a man of marked power, especially among university students both in Britain and America—makes the confession that if Christianity, if the Christian gospel, were indeed what many of these men assumed it to be, he would not very readily avow himself a Christian. Plainly there is a clear case for a more definite mode of Christian living and a plainer statement of the simplicities of the Christian faith.

For the age in which we are set has one question that it is never tired of asking, namely, "What's the use?" Sometimes it is a very irritating question in that it disturbs old habits and old modes of thought. Sometimes it is the reflection of a shallow mind and shows simply an inability to appreciate any values other than those of the market. It is often the question of those whose minds are on the same level as that of the men who were indignant at the woman who poured the precious ointment over the head of Jesus, and cried out, "To what purpose is this waste?"—which was just the same as saying, "What's the use! Look at the waste!" But however the question is put, even if it be put in a hostile spirit,

the Christian Church can't resent it. For the Church must have patience with the slowness of men's hearts, even as Christ had. Nor is the question, "What's the use," to be brushed aside because it sometimes indicates a shallow mind or a cynical spirit. In essence it is a right and proper question. If rightly answered, it may help to open blinded eyes and direct attention to undreamed-of horizons. When a man asks this question in a spirit that betrays no sense of value other than the material, a true answer will at least direct his attention to the fact that there are other values—values of mind and character and soul, values that are spiritual and eternal. It was so that Jesus answered the grumbling remonstrances of those who grudged the poor woman her costly tribute of devotion to himself. "She hath wrought a good work upon me. Verily I say unto you, wheresoever this gospel shall be preached, in the whole world, there shall also this that this woman hath done be told for a memorial of her."

Men are asking today: What's the use of the Church? It is at bottom a reasonable question. It is a question we must answer for our own sakes, as well as for the sake of others. We must make it our business to let men know that the Church has a great purpose and function to perform. And it is more necessary to exercise patience and sympathy than to indulge in rhetorical denunciation.

For the Church is not a little private concern, going its own way and caring nothing for the great world in which it is set. That is one of the misconceptions that must be removed. It is designed to touch men's minds at a hundred points, to disturb men's lives, to make them discontented with themselves that they may seek and find the peace of Christ.

When the Church of Christ is really alive and active, it is bound to rouse a certain amount of resentment. It is the height of foolishness to imagine that it will do anything else. It will not leave the world to go its own way. It will not leave a man to go to the devil in his own fashion. If it has the mind of Christ, it will not look calmly on at deeds and practices that are unjust and evil; it is bound to put forth its strength to protect the weak and helpless. When the Church does not act as an irritant on society, when it does not come into collision time and again with the natural man, you may be certain that it is somnolent. Christ did not come to send peace, but a sword.

We all like to be popular with our fellows, and people who are at cross purposes with all whom they meet and are so cross grained that nobody has a kindly word for them are not likely to accomplish much in influencing their fellows. But popularity of a certain kind is something that a Christian man has no right to covet. There are men who ought to feel uncomfortable in the presence of Christian people, and there are men in whose presence a Christian ought not to feel happy. "Woe unto you, when all men shall speak well of you; for so did their fathers to the false prophets." One remembers that the earliest recorded criticism of the Church made by the onlooker was in these words: "These are they which have turned the world upside down." Evidently in those days Christianity did not suggest to men's minds acceptance of present conditions, or a set of quiet, decent people, well enough content to lead a quiet existence and leave their neighbors in peace. Far from it. In those days the Christians were turning the world upside down. And that is part of the essential work of a live Church. When you have a perfect world, it will be time enough to cease trying to disturb it. But till then the Church must be the Church militant, active and aggressive. And whether it be said in bitter opposition by those who do not wish to be disturbed in their iniquities or in glad appreciation by those who have heard the summons of the King to warfare and to battle, it matters not. It is a sign not of strength but of weakness, not of life but of death, if it cannot still be said of the Christian Church: "These are they which are turning the world upside down."

When questions are asked about the place and function of Christian fellowship, there should be no great difficulty in answering them. The real difficulties do not arise so long as we keep in contact with the realities of New Testament religion. We often befog our minds by too much cleverness and too great subtlety, and so we depart from the simplicity which is in Christ.

"Ye are the salt of the earth; ye are the light of the world." What words can be more suggestive than these of the place and function of the Christian Church? They stretch out beyond private satisfactions and aspirations and happiness to the duties of Christian men; they denote a function of the Christian society; they contemplate the reaction of the life of the Christian Church on human society and development. Quite obviously, Jesus contemplates for his Church a great work in the world.

Salt and light, are, of course, metaphors, and metaphors of a plain and simple character. Salt is essentially a preservative; it saves from wastage, decay, and corruption. And this is a part of the function of Christian society, to save the world from running to corruption and waste. Try and picture the world today without the hope and promise of the gospel, without the labors and enthusiasms, the sympathies and enterprise, of Christian men and women. Think of what society might become if there were no Christian homes, and no Church of Christ! What would the world be? It does not require great stretch of the imagination to think of such a world as unfit for human habitation and ready to be blotted out, like the cities of the plain.

And light is life giving. Darkness is displaced only by the stronger force of light. The Christian society is designed to carry the light of the gospel to the souls that are in darkness. All evil things are dark things. It is before the light of the gospel of Jesus Christ that darkness disappears; it is through the activities of light, shining in the souls of the disciples of Christ, that good is revealed and the ghouls of the darkness are driven into their lurking places. And despite all the imperfections of the Church, despite all that can be alleged against it in the way of priestcraft and superstition and persecution, the simple historical fact is that the lives of Christian men and women have exercised an incalculable influence for good upon the world.

"It is simply a fact of history," says Dean Church, "that Christianity and the Christian Church have exerted on human society a moral influence which justifies the figure by which it has been described—an influence more profound, more extensive, more enduring, and more eventful than any the world has seen."

To the question, "What's the use of the Christian Church?" the answer, in the words of its Founder, is to be read in such a text as this: "Ye are the salt of the earth, ye are the light of the world." Such is or ought to be, the relation of Christian men and women to the world in which they are. Certainly they have a relation to the world—and Jesus never sanctioned for a moment the idea that the proper place to lead a Christian life is in a safe seclusion or behind the walls of a monastery.

But let us notice that salt and light display their active principles in a very quiet fashion. They do their work without a great blare of trumpets. When the dawn arrives, you do not need to advertise the fact. It carries its own witness and its own message. And the Church did not accomplish its greatest tasks or achieve its greatest success when it was much concerned about dinning into the ears of the world its own greatness and importance. That sort of activity generally leads to much dissipation of energy and too little attention to the king's business.

Preach the gospel, proclaim the gospel, placard before the world's eyes the greatness of Christ and the beauty of his sacrificial love—but let the lives of Christian men and women work in the world quietly and steadily, like salt and light.

As I have indicated, history offers more than one convincing illustration of the essential truth of our text—that the presence of Christian men and women in the world has saved the world from corruption and waste, and, through them, the darkness that covered the earth has at least grown less dense. When the old Roman empire was crumbling to pieces, when the civilization of centuries was like to be swept away before the advance of the northern barbarians, it was the Christian gospel that saved European civilization from destruction; the darkness of the heathen mind was conquered by the light of Christ.

Today we look abroad upon a world which seems almost on the verge of self-destruction. The wisest of our statesmen and thinkers are appalled at the thought of what the years may hold if some great preservative principle be not found to stay the corruption. "If," said Lord Crewe, speaking in the House of Lords after the signing of the Peace Treaty: "if knowledge comes and wisdom lingers, the future not only of this country but of the world is dark." One has only to glance at the daily papers to realize that there has been a big loosening of moral restraints, and that the wastage and corruption of debased ethical principles are spreading in many quarters.

Faced as we are today with a world which is changing before our eyes, the old words come to us with a new force and meaning, "Ye are the salt of the earth; ye are the light of the world." There is no doubt about it, there is a use and purpose for the Christian Church, if it can only fulfill it. Today the Church as well as the world is on trial, and the judgments of God are abroad upon the face of the earth. Jesus did not contemplate a useless church, a powerless church, a church too feeble to do anything to stay the destructive energies of evil. He had no place for a religion that had no power of service, no place in his kingdom for men of flabby purpose and little zeal. "But if the salt have lost its savour, wherewith shall it be salted? It is thenceforth good for nothing, but to be cast out, and to be trodden under foot of men."

Of whom does Jesus speak, when he says, "Ye are the salt of the earth; ye are the light of the world?" Of the men and women, who are his disciples: of those who call him Lord and give to him the service of heart and life, of those who carry into the world in life and character the principles of his teaching.

My Christian friends, what a responsibility Jesus lays upon his disciples. Yes—but what a trust he places in them! Let that trust be our challenge. Let it ever direct us to the grace that is sufficient for every need.

This is a time in which we hear on every hand criticism of the Church in varying shades and degrees It is being continually pointed out that the Church should do this, that, and the other thing. Much of such criticism may be helpful. But it must ever be borne in mind that the essential function of the Christian is that he fulfill the description, "Ye are the salt of the earth, ye are the light of the world."

The light we have must come from the Source of light; our souls must receive their sacred fire from him who is The Light of the world. Ye are the salt of the earth—then the corruption of our own nature must first be stayed: and the death that is in us transformed into life. "Ye must be born again."

THE EVOLUTION OF NATIONAL IDEALS[1]

(INDEPENDENCE DAY SERMON)

In his days shall the righteous flourish; and abundance of peace so long as the moon endureth.—Ps. 72:7.

The story of the beginning of governments is interesting. In the earlier history of the world men lived in separate families with the father of the family as the sole law-giver. The code of laws was, of course, oral and dependent upon the will of the patriarch. As the family developed into the clan, and the clan into the tribe, and the tribe into the kingdom or the State, little by little the foundations of written law were laid. At first, these laws were crude, because the people for whom they were made were no less crude, and law is always intended for the people, never the people for the law. Law is, in fact, nothing more than crystallized public sentiment, and never can be anything more. The conflict over laws arises because public sentiment is always in a state of ferment, and in every case the old teaching holds over by virtue of its position until the new can clearly establish its place. A people's laws are not, and can not be, any better than the general sentiment of the nation. I remember hearing Woodrow Wilson say in his jurisprudence class at Princeton that the Czar was the best governor for Russia until Russia itself put him away. Of course, he said, there were doubtless at that time millions of people in Russia who had gotten even then beyond the Czar, but there were many more millions who had not reached that stage in development. Since the time this remark was made Russia has overthrown the Czar, public sentiment having reached a stage where the monarchist rule no longer represented the voice of the people.

1. Law is the servant of the people at large just as every individual considered by himself is the servant of the law. For this reason, national ideals must be evolved and become recognized before they can be crystallized into laws. In the early history of the world progress was slow. In the three fundamental spheres of personal rights, family rights, and property rights only the simplest rules prevailed. In the sphere of personal rights, safety of life and limb was the goal of the earlier, as it has been of the later, laws of nations. The methods, however, by which it was guaranteed have changed almost infinitely for the better. In the family sphere, while things are still far from perfection, much progress has been made. In the palmiest days of the Roman code a man might put his wife to death, without any hindrance from the law, for the most trivial offenses; for example, if she purloined the key to his wine cellar, or if she tasted wine without his consent, or for other derelictions of similar character. In the terms of Roman law woman was denominated not a person but a thing. To-day, she has at last achieved equal rights and privileges under the law.

With regard to property rights, laws have multiplied and higher ideals prevail. For one thing, human slavery, which in early history was universal, has disappeared almost entirely from the face of the globe. Another improvement has been in the enactment of laws prohibiting cruelty to domestic animals; still another enacts the destruction of property rights, when they become a nuisance to the community at large. In Shakespeare's day, only four centuries ago, every citizen, if he cared to do it, could keep a garbage heap before his front door and no man could say him nay. This, too, even tho the neighbor's family took the fever and died as a result of unsanitary conditions. In these earlier days the common sense of the community took no note of the most ordinary axioms of general welfare.

II. The progress of national and social ideals is admirably shown by going through some of the castles and prisons of the older time. In London you will find rusted models of the rack which a few centuries ago was ordinarily and nearly universally used to pull people's bodies apart until they told anything to get rid of the pain. In European prisons you will find worse things in existence than even the rack. Nowadays, they torture a witness by cross-examination but, with occasional exceptions upon the part of ignorant and brutal public officials, in

[1] From *Sermons For Special Days*, by Rev. Frederick D. Kershner. George H. Doran Company, New York, 1922.

no other way. Two or three centuries ago, the rack and other instruments of torture were in common use all over Europe.

Another thing which has gone along with the torture is the custom of arbitrary imprisonment. Before the days of habeas corpus a man might be arrested at any time, kept in jail any length of time, and given no chance to establish his innocence. In the days of the French kings, Louis XIV and XV, only a little over a century ago, the king signed blank forms of arrest, and a favorite of the king filled them in. The unhappy wretch whose name went on the blank was arrested some dark night, hustled off without a chance to say good-by to his family, and buried alive in the Bastile or some other dungeon of the king. The French Revolution made that sort of thing impossible forever.

Still another evil which is disappearing rapidly, but has not yet quite disappeared, is the union of Church and State, or the enforcing of religious views by the secular arm. No provision of the United States Constitution has met with the general approval of our people more than its doctrine of the. separation of Church and State. It is everywhere recognized that religion is, and of right must be, purely a matter of conscience, and that the arm of the civil law has as little to do with a question of conscience as a gadfly has to do with the higher mathematics.

III. It is not so much the history of the past, however, which should concern us today, as it is the problems of the future. It is true that we should be grateful for what has been accomplished, but our duty does not end in effervescent gratitude. Upon our shoulders lies the burden of today and the responsibilities of to-morrow. Much remains to be done, and in the few minutes which are allotted for this sermon I can hope to do no more than to mention briefly a few of the more important ideals which are in the most immediate need of realization.

One of the first which should be mentioned is the ideal of humaneness, if I may put it in that way. This refers to a number of excrescences which still burden the body politic and help to encourage pessimism among decent people. One side is the child-labor question which has been so largely .discust in recent social reform literature, to

which one of America's foremost poets has largely devoted his life. We have done a great deal to elevate the living conditions of the ordinary laboring man and woman. Much remains still to be done before every human being is given a fair chance to make the most of his life.

Another consideration which demands attention is the problem of prison reform and the treatment of criminality in general. One phase of this question relates to the medieval character of our legal executions in many presumably civilized commonwealths. The matter of capital punishment itself may be left out of discussion, but the barbarity of method is beyond apology. The time will come, and before long, when the gallows will be exhibited along with the rack and the guillotine and the garrote as specimens of days of forgotten barbarism. A little over a hundred years ago capital punishment was inflicted in England for over a hundred offenses. That is, the law said it should be so inflicted. If a man stole sheep, he was to be hanged; if he broke into a house to pilfer, he was to be hanged; if he stole over five pounds (twenty-five dollars in our money), he was to be hanged; if he resisted arrest, he was to be hanged; if he defaced Westminster bridge, he was to be hanged. Of course, the consequence of all this was that eventually no jury could be found to return a man guilty of these crimes. If a man stole ten pounds, or twenty pounds, or fifty pounds, the jury would find that the amount did not exceed four pounds and nineteen shillings in order to save his neck. And so, by and by the Draconian laws slid off the statute books. To-day in certain sections of America popular sentiment has gotten so strong against capital punishment that it is a common thing at a murder trial for scores of presumptive jurors to be disqualified because they do not believe in the infliction of the death penalty for any cause. In my own home county, in one of the Eastern States, it is extremely difficult to secure a conviction of murder in the first degree. In the case of the only capital sentence which was imposed in that county for years the condemned man was not hanged because of the pressure brought to bear upon the governor for a commutation of the sentence from the very section where the crime had taken place. Perhaps as a people we have not yet evolved to the point where we are willing to rid the land of the barbarity of legal executions, but it seems to me that we ought to be rapidly approaching it. Beyond any question the recent war has turned the clock backward in this particular respect, as well as in countless others. Nevertheless, we ought to recognize the fact that the disappearance of cruelty in any form is, and always has been, the distinguishing mark of the upward progress of civilization.

In this connection, attention should be called to the increase of lawlessness throughout our country as a whole. The mob spirit has shown itself with renewed emphasis since the recrudescence of animal passions in the world war. The barbarity of many of these exhibitions of mob violence can not be duplicated outside of the records of the Inquisition or of criminal procedure in the middle ages on the continent. It is time for Christian people throughout our land to awaken to the necessity of maintaining law by peaceful procedure in order that we may wipe out the terrible stain which the mob spirit is placing upon our history.

IV. Perhaps the most important ideal of all, the one which is receiving most consideration nowadays, is the ideal of worldwide peace. It is possible that we are not yet quite civilized enough for universal peace, but it is to be hoped that we are heading rapidly in that direction. Just what the practical result of the recent disarmament conference will be we can not say, but the mere fact that such conferences are being called is an item of no little importance. The infinite folly of war, the stupidity of settling disputes by brute force instead of by common reason of mankind, will some day become apparent to everybody; then the torpedo boats, the armored cruisers, and the battleships will go to the museums, and the war budget, which now swallows over ninety per cent of our funds, will be spent building libraries and colleges and parks and public roads and art galleries and in providing comforts for people instead of providing approved methods of killing them. The day when the swords will be beaten into plowshares and the spears into pruning hooks is sure to come, and it may be nearer than most of us think.

V. One of the hopeful signs of the future, in which we are all especially interested at this time, is the withdrawal of government protection from immoral agencies. That the nation should become a silent partner in the perpetuation of vice and vicious habits, thereby lending aid to agencies which have for their aim its own destruction, is a form of suicide as peculiar as it is indefensible. Of course, the drawback hitherto has been the toleration or indifference of public sentiment. It is gratifying to say, however, that things are progressing toward a higher level. Lottery schemes have been put under the ban of the law, and gambling, which has been a function of government many times during the past, no longer has the support or approval of the State. It is an exceedingly disgraceful thing that vice is still harbored in certain sections under the protection of the law, and that on the ground of expediency it has found defenders among the ranks of professedly decent people. It is only a question of time when this attitude must and will change. Of the three chief foes of social progress—gambling, social vice, and the saloon—the first and the last, after making the most strenuous fight for legal tolerance, have at last been put under the ban. The saloon was fought energetically in city precinct after city precinct, in crossroads town after crossroads town, in county after county, State after State, until the national sentiment became crystallized to the point where it was outlawed by the voice of government itself.

VI. The advocates of this or the other reform sometimes forget the necessity for the slow and the gradual, but none the less sure and powerful, development of public sentiment, in order that permanent progress may be made. The prophet has such clear perception of future needs that he is apt to become impatient because things move so slowly. But things must move slowly at first, and after all they move more rapidly than many of us imagine. The function of the true reformer is to blaze the way; to keep hammering at the problem; to beat down prejudice; to endure calumnies; to suffer persecution, detraction, and misunderstanding, but at last to win the goal. The public at large is a great unwieldy sort of animal which has to be coaxed at times and goaded at times into what is necessary for its health, perchance even for its salvation. But when the unwieldy animal is once fairly set in motion the reform soon comes. This, too, is preeminently the mission of the pulpit. It is the chief business of the preacher to develop national ideals as well as to emphasize the individual welfare of his auditors. To keep men's eyes fixt on the true goal of individual and social life; on something higher still to be realized; to fight the agencies which are pulling in the downward direction; assuredly the pulpit can have no greater mission than this. Moreover, this is the special reason for the existence of memorial occasions, like Independence Day, when in the light of past sacrifices we rededicate ourselves and our nation to the task which lies ahead.

The life of a man and the life of a nation can rise no higher than the goal which is placed before them. Against this goal there is always the constant pressure downward, the desire to stand still, which always means to go backward, so that progress is achieved only by constant effort and struggle. "Look thou not down but up," is the watchword of success in the moral, social, and national realms. He only is a true citizen who strives, day by day, to develop higher national ideals, and by adding his own mite of effort to the cause of righteousness brings the gates of the Golden City a little closer to our view.

"Be what thou seemest, live thy creed,
  Hold up to earth the torch divine,
Be what thou prayest to be made,
  Let the great Master's steps be thine.

"Fill up each hour with what will last,
  Buy up the moments as they go,
The life above, when this is past,
  Is the ripe fruit of life below."

THE CHALLENGE TO ENDURANCE[1]

If thou hast run with footmen, and they have wearied thee, then how canst thou contend with horses? and though in a land of peace thou art secure, yet how wilt thou do in the pride of the Jordan.—Jer. 12:5.

Behold, we live through all things—famine, thirst,
Bereavement, pain; all grief and misery,
All wo and sorrow, life inflicts its worst
On soul and body,—but we can not die.
Tho we be sick, and tired, and faint and worn,—
  Lo, all things can be borne!
                    E. A. ALLEN.

Sweet are the uses of adversity,
Which, like the toad, ugly and venomous,
Wears yet a precious jewel in his head.
                    SHAKESPEARE.

Jeremiah's position in Jerusalem, to all appearances, was not an enviable one. His fidelity as a preacher of righteousness had won him a host of enemies. His fearless pronouncement of the impending doom entailed by their apostasy had made him the most hated man in the city. And when with longing eyes he turned toward Anathoth, his old home, he found that even there the bitterness had spread. The men of his native place were plotting against his life and saying, "Let us destroy the tree with its sap, and let us cut him off from the land of the living, that his name may be no more remembered." This was the hardest blow he had yet been dealt, and it was tremendously discouraging. He pictured himself as a tame lamb that is led to the slaughter. We do not wonder that his patience began to waver.

And to make it all worse, the very men whose wickedness brought the anguish to his soul were happy and prosperous. There was no question in the mind of Jeremiah, of course, concerning the ultimate fate of those who opposed him. He was confident that the corruption of his people would meet its judgment. He thoroughly believed that sin resulted in suffering—every time. So close did the connection between the two seem to him that he could argue with equal ease from sin to suffering or from suffering to sin. If any one sinned, he would suffer; if any one suffered, he must have sinned. But now his own persecution brings this old faith to a very severe test. For surely, he was not the outstanding apostate of his time, that all the punishment should be inflicted on him. He was God's spokesman, the one man in his generation, apparently, who was interested in righteousness and truth. Why should he alone suffer? It would not have been so hard, if all the rest had been afflicted, too. But the prosperity of the wicked only served to throw the

[1] From *The Rock That Is Higher, and other Addresses*, by TEUNIS E. GOUWENS. Fleming H. Revell Company, New York, 1922.

greater emphasis on the painfulness of his own lot.

And so Jeremiah takes his case to God. This is perhaps the first time that the problem of the suffering of the righteous is definitely raised. "Righteous art thou, O Jehovah, when I complain unto thee," he says, "yet will I reason the case with thee: wherefore doth the way of the wicked prosper? Wherefore are all they at ease that deal faithlessly?" And for answer he was told, "If thou has run with footmen, and they have wearied thee, then how canst thou contend with horses? And tho in a land of peace thou art secure, yet how wilt thou do in the pride of Jordan?" In other words, "If your lot is hard now, summon your energies and out upon it! For it will be harder still." That was a strange answer, was it not? There was apparently small comfort in that. And yet, it was the very answer Jeremiah needed. It was a call to patience, endurance, perseverance.

What God was interested in here was the development of Jeremiah. Thus far Jeremiah had been courageously contending against adversity. But now his patience was almost exhausted. He felt that his oppression was being unjustly prolonged. Suppose, however, that the resistance to his righteous endeavor had suddenly collapsed. Or suppose he had abandoned his struggle against existing conditions. Suppose circumstances had now suddenly changed so as to give him luxury and ease. It would, in all probability, have meant the ruin of his life.

Many a young man who is strong and full of promise so long as his difficulties are great and many goes into decay as soon as the demand for the struggle is over. Many a man, upon retirement from business, finds that he really has nothing into which to retire. His life is in his work, and his work is a preparation for higher service. To abandon it for idleness means decay and death. The contention against footmen can never come to a successful issue by giving place to ease and self-indulgence. It must go on to the contest with horses.

To confront a man with such a truth as that with which Jeremiah was here challenged is to make him or mar him. The mettle of a man shows itself in a situation like this. If he has any gold in him, this test will bring it out and refine it. Had

Jeremiah quailed before his test, his name would have dropt from the memory of man. But so far from crushing him, his trial put new stamina into his soul. What business had he to be weary with a race against footmen, when a contest with horse was in store for him! What business had he to desire escape from a land of comparative security when he might have to dwell some time in the pride of Jordan! The pride of Jordan was that jungle along the banks of the river where confusion and trouble reigned, where fever spread and where lions roared. What business had he to complain faint-heartedly about the burdens of today when tomorrow would make so much greater a demand on his strength! This was the spirit the answer of the Lord aroused in his soul, and the result was that Jeremiah was one of the finest, strongest characters the world has known.

No small part of Jeremiah's victory must be attributed to the fact that he felt himself to be God's man. He was Jehovah's spokesman to that generation. It was a tremendous commission. And it could be fulfilled only by one who was himself Godlike. Thoughts of God's unwearied patience with the children of Israel in all their wilderness wanderings and throughout their later history when, time after time, they showed themselves to be an ungrateful, stiff-necked, and rebellious people, must have been a mighty inspiration to the prophet in his moment of weakness. Fidelity and endurance had characterized Jehovah throughout his disappointing experience with the faithlessness of the people of his choice. If this was the kind of God with whom he was working, how could he, with even the slightest self-respect, permit himself to be crusht by this little trial! As God's man, he must be able to endure with utmost loyalty anything that his work may involve. And how, if in running with footmen he was wearied, could he hope to contend against horses? How, if in a land of peace he was tempted to flee, could he stand in the pride of Jordan?

The Christian life is a life that calls for endurance unto the end. Dr. Lyman Beecher, when asked whether he believed in the perseverance of the saints, replied, "I do, except when the wind is from the east." But perseverance means nothing, if it disappears when the wind is from the east.

For misfortune and trial are the very things that test it and bring it out. If there was one thing Jesus was careful to impress upon those who came after him, it was that persecution was certain. If the Master did not escape without it, the faithful disciple could not expect to do so. "If any man would come after me, let him deny himself, take up his cross daily, and follow me."

Look over the biographies of the whole world, and where will you find a life that can match the Master's in endurance? Driven about from place to place, considered insane even by his own family, harassed by priest and ruler, forsaken even by his most devoted friends, spit upon and scourged, he finally, of his own free will yielded himself to the shameful death of the cross with the prayer, "Father, forgive them, for they know not what they do." Has the Master asked of his disciples anything that he himself has not fulfilled? He who can stand calmly tied to the stake and let the fire leap up and consume him is a hero indeed. And they of whom such a story is oftenest told are they precisely who draw their inspiration and strength from Jesus. The martyrs of the world are Christians. And it is from their Master they learn how. But to submit to death when tied in place by a cord, what is that compared with the heroism of standing there unbound! No man took Jesus' life from him; he laid it down. And if the Master asks nothing of his followers that he himself has not fulfilled, neither is he content with a spirit which will withhold anything of that full measure of devotion. There never was a leader who made a bigger demand than Jesus. Loyalty has its full meaning only when thought of in relation to him. The greatest task any man can assume is that of following Christ.

It is hard to live a Christian man. And the only reason we have not found it so, if such indeed be the case, is that we have been content with a name instead of a life. We have been too ready to sacrifice principle for convenience, duty for pleasure. We have chosen ease in preference to loyalty. The Christian life seems easy only when we are not living it. It is because the little demands it does make upon us often elicit only murmurings and excuses that the real struggle of the Christian life is beyond us and that, consequently, its real joy eludes us. The unconquered does not lure us because we permit ourselves to be disheartened by the obstacles we meet in the small territory we have invaded. We have been too ready to mingle with the Canaanite in the land and thus to compromise our highest convictions. We fool ourselves tremendously in our Christian lives when we think that the small trials we have to bear are almost beyond our strength and when we consider our little endurance worthy of supreme recognition, commendation, and reward. We forget that we are running only with footmen and dwelling in a land of security.

It seems that our daily experience in other things would teach us that the duty which looms large today, when it is accomplished, only opens our eyes to the far more exacting duty of tomorrow. The thing that baffles us today becomes trivial tomorrow. And in its place comes something else, something far more important, something the existence of which we probably never suspected till the matter in hand had previously been successfully disposed of. The boy in school struggling with the multiplication tables considers them an end in themselves. He little dreams of the intricate accounts they will enable him to keep in his later business career. Yet it is there his real test in that sphere comes, and his success in it will depend on his faithfulness and endurance in the earlier years when the contest is only with footmen. There can be no ability for a successful grapple with the greater in any undertaking, there can be no vision even to see the greater in the lesser, until there is first fidelity in the lesser.

It is in the daily round of life where things soon grow monotonous and commonplace that the test of loyalty is made. It is when little unpleasant circumstances and trials accumulate that we become weary and long for the wings of a dove that we may fly away. The suffering and sorrow that mingle with the ease and joy of our experience and cast clouds over the sun of our peace—these are the things that draw out our complaints. The little temptations, which annoy us by their very comparative insignificance and make us wonder why we must always be good while those around us have their fling, these are the things that make us murmur against so much of Christ's ideal as we have appropriated. The small tasks that devolve upon us as Christians, the little burdens our profession of Christ casts upon us, the trifling inconvenience of tending the small portion of the Lord's business allotted us, these are the things that make us look back with Peter and ask, "Lord, what shall this man do?" How jealous we are of another's ease! How weary we get running with footmen! And when we have jogged along for a while in fretful obedience, we cry, "How long, O Lord, how long?"

But, my friend, there is nothing in the Christian life to indicate that the reward of victory over minor hardships and of half-hearted fulfilment of little tasks is intended to be ease and comfort. The true reward is more strenuous conflict. The severer trial results in stronger, more Christlike character, and that is the end in view. The ideal can be reached only through endurance. And the endurance must begin here and now with the burdens we are called upon to bear and the evils we are called upon to resist and the service we are asked to render.

For if we run with footmen, and they weary us, how can we vie with horses? And if in a land of peace we are uneasy, how can we endure the pride of Jordan?

We need, like Jeremiah, to get a conception of ourselves as God's men. The question is not, "Am I enduring more than my neighbor?" The question is, "Am I enduring for Christ's sake and in Christ's spirit that which in his judgment the welfare of my life demands?" Get a true conception of what the spirit of Christ means and involves and brings, and all that is best in you will arise and say, "Jesus is right. Than his there is no higher, no nobler life conceivable. And if the attainment of such a life depends upon endurance such as his, then God grant me strength not to murmur but to continue steadfast, with a spirit triumphant, in my race with footmen, that I may not fail in my contest with horses and grant me courage to stand for the highest in this land of slight danger, that I may pass unscathed through the pride of Jordan."

THE CHILDREN'S SERVICE

THE FLOWER CLOCK [1]

The Rev. Hugh T. Kerr, Pittsburgh, Pa.

I make all things new—Rev. 21:5.

The other day I heard about a new sort of clock. I had heard about grandfather clocks, and banjo clocks, and eight-day clocks, and electric and radium clocks, and clocks that would not go. I had even heard of John B. Gough's clock. When it pointed to three o'clock, it struck six, and then he knew it was half-past nine. But I had never heard about a flower clock. That was a new sort of clock.

It was made by a great lover of flowers and shrubs and trees. He was called Linnaeus and he lived in Sweden. His real name was Karl Von Linne. When he was four years old he began to ask queer and interesting questions about plants and flowers, and when he became an old man he was as reverent in a garden as he was in a church. His motto in life was, "Live quietly. God is here."

His garden was full of rare and strange plants, and it was in the garden that he kept his flower clock. The hours of the clock were marked by flowers that opened and closed at exactly the time of day where they appeared on the dial of the clock. The first flower to open was the goat's beard which marked the hour of three o'clock in the morning and from that hour on to midnight, every hour was marked by the opening of a new flower. At midnight the large flowering cactus closed its petals and then until three o'clock the great flower clock rested. What a strange clock it was and what a wise man he was who made it. He knew every flower and the hour when it opened and closed its petals. Each hour was thus marked by a beauty and fragrance of its own.

Every true life ought to be like a great flower clock. Every hour and every day and every year should be bright and beautiful. The Christian life is full of pleasant surprises and is like a continuous springtime. The hours are full of joy and beauty,

[1] *Children's Gospel Story-Sermons.* Fleming H. Revell Co.

and youth and old age have always their own delights. Did you ever notice how often in the Bible life is compared to flowers and plants and trees?

"As a flower of the field so he flourisheth."

"Consider the lilies of the field how they grow."

"He shall grow like a cedar in Lebanon."

"Every good tree bringeth forth good fruit."

If you will call to mind the words of the first psalm, which is one of the psalms boys and girls should know by heart, you will discover that it almost exactly describes a good life in terms of the flower clock:

"He shall be like a tree
Planted by the rivers of water,
That bringeth forth his fruit
In his season;
His leaf also shall not wither;
And whatsoever he doeth
Shall prosper."

In the very last chapter of the Bible, we read of the tree of life, which bears twelve manner of fruits and yields its fruit every month. The Christian life is like an unfading flower and like unfailing fruit.

OUTLINES

Need of Patience

For ye have need of patience, that, having done the will of God, ye may receive the promise.—Heb. 10:36.

None but would readily assent. Consider the text under two aspects—

I. As endurance. 1. Under opposition and persecution. Christ warned his disciples of such. They encountered such frequently. Ours are of different kind. Must meet them in spirit of Christ. "He endured—for the joy," &c. 2. Under pain and suffering. Pain is real, not "error of mortal mind." Patiently endured, a blessing. Beauty of a patient sufferer. Test of Christian character. 3. Under limited and trying conditions. Poor in this world's goods. Limited education. Disagreeable surroundings. Without home or friends.

II. As persistence. 1. In secular things. a. Farming. Seed, blade, full corn. Drought, blight, frosts, &c. Weeds, bugs, worms. b. Education. Primary, secondary, college, university. Result is worth the effort. c. Manufacturing. Competition, dishonesty, depressions, reverses, &c. d. Social and political reforms. Slavery, intemperance, disarmaments. Selfishness, graft, short-sightedness. 2. In spiritual things. a. Personal religious attainments. Encounter sinful tendencies. Weakness of moral fiber. Evil temptations without. Requires persistent struggle. b. Personal work for others. Sometimes seem to offend. Many times seem ineffective. Persistent effort will tell. Christ, apostles, missionaries. c. Church work. Sometimes divisions in the Church. Coldness among the members. Loss of some supporter. Lack of efficient leaders. Outside opposition. d. Missionary endeavor. Difficult to finance. Dense ignorance among heathen. Disappointing converts at times. Does it pay for all sacrifices?

Learn patience from God's patience with men. How trying this attitude toward him. How long he has borne with them. Learn patience from Christ's example. What opposition and persecution. How imperfect his followers. How slow the progress. "Let patience have her perfect work, that ye may be perfect and entire, wanting nothing."

The Trinity of Prayer

Prayer was made without ceasing of the Church unto God for him.—Acts 12:5.

Prayer is as necessary to the Christian as "the air we breathe, the food we eat, and the sunlight of the house." Prayer to be effective must be definite, with a three-fold aspect—(1) the petitioner, (2) the petitioned, (3) the thing petitioned.

I. The petitioner. 1. The Church—"Prayer was made of the Church." Just a few devout souls in need of God, in the home of John Mark in Jerusalem. The small struggling church or mission and the large flourishing city church must be sterile and futile but for prayer. 2. Each individual. Private prayer is as essential to the life of the Church as is public prayer. Prayer is the individual's and the Church's (a) equipment, (b) ammunition, (c) shield, (d) fortress of protection.

II. The petitioned. "Prayer was made unto God." 1. We must know God—(1) by revelation, (2) by personal experience. 2. We must believe in God—(1) in his power, (2) inclination, (3) readiness to hear and answer us. 3. We must understand God. We are not praying to (1) a blind force, (2) one who has predestinated all the minor acts of life (fatalism), (3) unchanging law; but to a flexible and ready will. III. Thing petitioned. "Prayer was made for him." 1. We must have (1) a definite desire, (2) a fixt object, (3) a certain specific aim in prayer. 2. We must take stock (1) of self, (2) of Church, (3) of community, (4) of the world as to a worthy end and a fit object of prayer. Of the many things for which this band of early Christians might have prayed, they chose one definite object on which they all agreed, St. Peter's freedom from prison. We must cultivate the habit of prayer—they prayed "without ceasing."

The New and the Old

Old things are passed away; behold all things are become new.—2 Cor. 5:17.

This is an age of novelty, of newness, of progress. The new and the novel are more alluring than the old and the familiar—but not always so substantial or dependable. "Be not the first by whom the new are tried, nor yet the last to lay the old aside." Many old things have passed away.

I. In point of time. "We take no thought of time, but by its loss." 1. The old year is gone in respect to time, thought, action, life. 2. In respect to customs, fashions, habits. "Yesterday is a record, tomorrow a dream—today only is real."

II. In point of science. "All things are become new." 1. In medicine—old things are passed away; all things are new—(1) anesthetics, (2) opiates, (3) radium. Even diseases are new—(1) appendicitis, (2) hook-worm, (3) pellagra, etc. 2. In invention—(1) telegraph, (2) telephone, (3) "wireless," (4) automobiles, (5) airships, (6) victrolas, etc. 3. In point of chemistry, astronomy, electricity, etc.

III. In point of fashions, social relations, education, politics, and international outlook—all things are become new.

IV. In point of religion. 1. New thought, Christian Science, new theology, "twentieth century religion," etc. These all indicate that people are tired of shallow formalism, antiquated theology and "unpractical religion." We are spiritually on the brink of danger by reason of ultra-conservatism and ultra-radicalism. What is needed is a readaptation of religion to the new day and a readjustment of life. But we need today a reorganization of life, of habit, of all our relations more than a restatement of faith. We need less of the mystical and more of the practical, the ethical, the spiritual in religion.

Steering or Drifting

Abram dwelt in the land of Canaan, etc. —Gen. 13:12.

Character study interesting and profitable. Abraham and Lot present great contrast. Start together, but end far apart. Actuated by different motives. Case of steering and drifting.

I. Abraham steered by God's chart. 1. He heeded God's call from Ur. "He obeyed, not knowing whither," implicitly, promptly. 2. He followed the divine leading. Followed what light he had. Kept in close fellowship with God. 3. He believed the divine promises. Should be father of a great nation. Should be a great blessing. 4. He persevered to the end. Journey was long and hard. Blazed the way by numerous altars. 5. He obtained the great reward. Called the "father of the faithful." All nations blest in him. Entered the "city which hath foundations."

II. Lot simply drifted. 1. Accompanied his uncle Abraham. Perhaps from personal attachment. Perhaps from love of adventure. But without apparent aim. 2. Had regard only for self. See his selfish choice with Abraham. No evidence of seeking God's will. 3. Heedless of tendencies. "Lifted up his eyes" toward Sodom. "Pitched his tent toward Sodom." "Lot sat in the gate of Sodom." 4. Made an awful failure of life. Disgraced his family. Nearly destroyed in the city. Left no heritage of value.

Heed the failures of an aimless life. It is easy to drift with the current. The longer one drifts the farther from God. Mark the blessings of a well steered life. Commence early in life. Never leave the wheel, nor disregard the chart—the Holy Scriptures.

Sin at the Door

Sin lieth at the door.—Gen. 4:7.

Sin is at the threshold of the life of every individual, every group, and every nation of people. Sin is a thing not to be "defined" but to be "refined."

I. What sin is. (1) In the life—angry passion, secret unbelief, folly of youth, curse of age, poison in the cup, flaw in the title, enemy in the camp, fool that rocks the boat, discord in the song, blood stain on the soul. (2) In the Bible—Unclean spirit, father of lies, enemy sowing tares, thorn in the flesh, mote in the eye, beam in the eye, Satan desiring to get possession of the soul, expulsion from Eden, thorn-cursed soil, brand on brow of Cain, overwhelming flood, shattered Babel, fiery tempest over Sodom, wars, plagues, disasters, captivities, death. "Sin is the lighted candle carried into the powder-magazine of the human citadel."

II. What sin does. (1) Causes shame, pain, fear. (2) Makes a hole in the soul, letting in a never-ending stream of evil.

(3) Casts a shadow in the night, forecasting death. (4) Creates darkness where God intended light. (5) Turns life's diamonds into black coals. (6) Cuts us off from God, goodness, peace.

III. Remedy for sin. Since sin is the "unrefined inner life," the remedy is a refining process. This process proceeds through (1) confession, (2) penitence, (3) prayer, (4) praise.

There is only one remedy for sin, namely Jesus Christ, "one mightier than I." "If any man sin, we have an advocate with the Father, even Jesus Christ." We must (1) love him, (2) serve him, (3) obey him. The remedy for "evil" is "goodness." The cure for Satan is Christ, who is (1) our strength in weakness, (2) light in darkness, (3) hope in despair. "I can do all things through Christ who strengtheneth me."

ILLUSTRATIONS AND ANECDOTES

The Rev. F. C. Hoggarth, Bradford, England

The Moment of Splendor

"Ruskin says that the full splendor of the sunset lasts but a second and that Turner went out early each evening and watched with rapt attention for that one second of supreme splendor and delight. He lived for sunsets and while others were balancing their accounts or taking tea he went out to see the daily miracle. . . . For one second in the day he caught the glamor of earth and heaven and went back to his untidy studio blind to all but the splendor that he had seen." So writes a padre friend of mine, and that explains why so many think Turner's sunset exaggerated. "I never see a sunset like Turner's," said one young critic to Ruskin. "Don't you wish you could?" was Ruskin's penetrating reply. The masters see splendors that the crowd misses. For there are visions, that are caught only by prepared hearts—moments of glory that swiftly pass and leave us all unblest unless we know the time of their visitation and go out to greet them. Nature has many such moments. There are great and wonderful happenings in the heavens and on the earth, that are easily missed except by enlightened souls. There are in some parts of the world rare flowers that bloom and

fail in a night. The flower of wheat lasts only fifteen minutes and common as wheat-fields are, how few have ever caught that moment of glory. There are spectacles in the heavens that those who know most carefully prepare for, that when the moment of vision comes, nothing of its revelation may be missed.

Nor is it otherwise in the spiritual visitations of life. There are moments of splendor there also, hours of transfiguration and communion on the mount that swiftly pass. Only those chosen and choice souls who have climbed the mount, those who are disciplined and prepared, behold the glory. No vision is granted to the dull and unprepared souls at the foot of the mount. And as we never know which may be the moment of splendor we must be out early, expectant, prepared, for in "the hour that ye know not, your Lord cometh"—cometh in some revelation of beauty, in some vision splendid.

Chirps or Songs

A writer in *My Magazine* has recently reminded us of Darwin's idea that sparrows might sing like other birds if they would. "The unattractive chirp of the sparrow is the result not of physical inability but rather of inherited laziness." Young sparrows if reared by canaries sing canaries' songs, not perfectly, yet quite recognizably. So there is one more indictment against this much maligned bird—the bird that makes its way everywhere though no one particularly wants it. It not only works havoc among the crops, and ousts other more desirable and useful birds, it is too lazy to live up to its possibilities. It is content to chirp when it might sing. Its inherited tendency to sing lies undeveloped. It might do so much better in the way of song if it only would.

Not a few people resemble this bird in living below their possibilities. If they would, they could do far greater things. A friend said to me recently, of a minister we both know well, that tho he had preached a good sermon, one got the impression that it was not the best he could do. In his student days that man gave the same impression. He had great gifts, the garnering of knowledge was no difficulty, mentally he could leap where others had to bridge, yet he never did anything outstanding, nor ever will, because he will not pay the price in laborious application. The gifts are there, but not raised to their highest powers. He chirps, whereas he might sing. So do not a few in the pew as well as in the pulpit, outside as well as inside the Church. Sometimes it is because their lives have lacked the proper environment, the challenging and inspiring example of friendship, more often, perhaps, it is because men are careless and lazy in the higher disciplines of life. They just refuse to take the trouble to develop their spiritual capacities. They are content with some chirping average of attainment.

Real Estate

In one of Professor Jack's books, there is a conversation between two train passengers as follows: They are looking out of the train window at the snowy ranges of the Rockies. "What mountains!" exclaims one. The other, puzzled for a moment, replies, "I guess I haven't got any use for those, but if you're thinking of buying real estate. . . ." That was his line, land with a chance of rising in value, land that one day might be wanted for cities or by railways, land with a chance of oil or minerals underneath it. In a word, land with money in it was his interest, his reality.

It is a curious tho not uncommon attitude. Our civilization produces quite a lot of people who have no use for snow-capped mountains or for the starry silences of the night, or for sunsets. Their hearts do not leap up where they behold a rainbow in the sky. Amid the vastness and quietness of nature they are ill at ease. They prefer Broadway or Piccadilly. So that to take a man out into the great presence of nature, to watch what he says and how he acts is a pretty reliable test of character. The man who does not consider that sunsets and snowy heights are also real estate, rather more real than your accurately measured and fenced city plot, is at any rate blind. He needs an operation for cataract of the soul.

On Going with the World

Sir Charles Doughty in his book on Arabia tells how at one place in the midst of desert sands he saw the caravans of pilgrims—the Haj—pass through on its way from Bagdad to Mecca. One of the pilgrims drest as an oriental stopt and spoke to him in French. "I am an Italian," he said, "but have become a Moslem and have given up the Bible for the Koran." Doughty exprest amazement that the man should give up his privileges as a Christian to become brother of Asiatic barbarians. "A man," he answered, "can not always choose, but must go sometimes with the world. When I return to my native land I shall wipe off the rust of this Mohammedan life." How familiar the excuse sounds! It is heard in other places than desert sands. Man's easy surrender to environment, his acceptance of the world's way for the sake of ease or profit, with the accompanying delusion that when the time comes he will be able to obliterate all marks of his surrender. It is never so easy as men imagine. The rust gets in deeper than we intend. In any case there is loss of self respect, and the very real loss of all the strength and nobility that come through loyalty to great convictions.

The Awakening of Honor

Professor David Smith has recently told how the sense of honor was first awakened in him. "I was," he says, "a little lad some twelve or thirteen years of age, hopelessly crippled by an accident. My dead father's books were my chief resource. Among them was Stanley's *Life of Dr. Arnold of Rugby*, which, for some occult reason, strongly attracted me. Towards the close there is a contribution from one of the 'old boys' where he explains the secret of the famous master's influence over his scholars. 'In the higher forms,' he says, 'any attempt at further proof of an assertion was immediately checked: "If you say so, that is quite enough—of course, I believe your word"; there grew up in consequence a general belief that "it was a shame to tell Arnold a lie—he always believes me." "Child as I was," observes Dr. Smith, "that sentence gripped me, and it has ever since been engraven on my soul. It awoke my instinct of chivalry; and looking back I recognize there the crisis of my life. It was a challenge to my honor and it enkindled within me an ambition to play the man. Without it I am persuaded I would never have made a fight; I should have acquiesced in my disabilities and remained a dependent weakling all my days."

It is a significant confession, valuable in its testimony to the incalculable good that comes through books, specially through biography. To put the right book into a youth's hand at the right hour is one of the most beneficent of human services.

On Learning to be Blind

Sir Arthur Pearson in his book, *The Conquest of Blindness*, makes frequent use of the rather curious phrase—"learning to be blind." Just as men have to learn to see, as the eyes have to be trained in discrimination, so have men deprived of sight to learn to be blind. Especially do they need to learn the right attitude to their disability. On that he lays the utmost stress. The training lasts six or eight months, by the end of that time the men have "conquered a foe that threatened to destroy the spirit as well as the sight." "They have pulled themselves out of the dark morass in which they were plunged and set their feet on the roads of endeavor and happiness again." It is a wonderful education. From St. Dunstan's, the famous institution for blinded soldiers, have gone out scores of blinded men, to lives rich in the prospect of worth-while human service and the happiness born of endeavors. Visitors to the hospital can hardly believe that the men are blind, there is such an air

of happy usefulness abroad. Sir Arthur tells of one man who is not only blind but without hands and who in spite of that double handicap is doing excellent organizing work in the offices of the National Institute for the Blind. Special devices enable him to use a typewriter. He feeds himself and does many things which his great handicap would seem to make impossible.

Such are the victories men have won in the place of their limitation. The phrase about "learning to be blind" is spaciously suggestive for all upon whom calamity has come. May we not speak of learning to be poor, or bereaved, or deaf? The spirit in which the blinded soldiers win their victory, is equally potent with all other handicaps. It is at least good to know that whatever may have befallen us, life may still have its service and its victories and its joys.

Personal Responsibility

Of the famous defense of Lucknow, when a small British garrison was besieged by a rebel army and yet held out week after week until relief came, Brigadier Inglis has written the following words: "Owing to the extreme paucity of our numbers, each man was taught to feel that on his own individual efforts alone depended, in no small measure, the safety of the entire position. This consciousness incited every officer, soldier and man, to defend the post assigned to him with such desperate tenacity and to defend the lives which Providence had entrusted to his care with such dauntless determination, that the enemy, despite their constant attacks, their heavy mines, their overwhelming numbers and their incessant fire, could never succeed in gaining one single inch of ground within the bounds of this straggling position which was so feebly fortified, that had they once obtained a footing in any of the outposts, the whole place would inevitably have fallen."

It is a vivid picture in which we see that personal responsibility is far more important than numbers. Almost all things are possible to even a small army, once the rank and file vividly realize how much depends on them. The Church's weakness is largely due to the absence of any such sense in numbers of people who are supposed to be members. A general reawakening of responsibility is one of the needs of the hour.

Of Luther it has been said, "he felt himself part of every situation he was placed in. The aloofness of the mere observer was not his." Our day needs that spirit.

Life's Seed Time

Writing to a young minister who after some year's service found himself still in an obscure place and who was becoming impatient for the prizes and recognitions of life, Professor David Smith recently wrote, "I bless God daily for the long years which I spent in a remote corner of Scotland, ministering to a little congregation. It was oftentimes a disheartening experience but it did much for me. It was the seed time of my life. . . . True and abiding influence is slowly won and there is no more precious experience for youth than a protracted season of obscurity." They are true and timely words. Early popularity often means early barrenness. The quiet, obscure years, with their steady and unremitting discipline of mind and heart may be made the most enriching of all the years. Not a few of those who have won great influence have had long foregrounds to their life. Over an old rectory garden door at Linton in Devonshire is the motto: "Live Unknown." It is a useful motto for young manhood. Youth has to learn to labor and to wait. "Be content to go on working in obscurity a little longer," said Ruskin once to a young artist, impatient for recognition. It is the only way. There must be a seed time, before there can be a harvest of wisdom and of influence.

"If It Was My Boy"

At the opening of a reformatory some years ago, the statement was made that if only one boy were saved by it, it would not have cost a dollar too much. Some critic challenged the statement. He considered it an exaggeration. One boy! Why boys are more plentiful than blackberries and not half so sweet. "No," said the speaker, "I should not think it had cost a dollar too much if only one boy were saved, if it was my boy who was saved." Personal relationship makes all the difference in our estimates and values. One of our social reformers has said that for years she read and quoted with a certain cold detachment, the figures of infant mortality. But when her own boy died, those figures suddenly became living and tragic. From the day of her own sorrow they spoke to her with new meaning. So was it with the casualty lists during the war. The moment some dear name was found in those lists, we each of us realized what those lists had meant to millions of other people. Only when the personal relationship enters in do our judgments become deeply sympathetic and true. The Christian ought to try to think of people in that way. For being children of the one Father in heaven, we are personally related to all the rest. In a real sense they are brothers and sisters however ignorant or degraded or unprivileged. Once we get that spirit into society what different outlooks and estimates there will be!

PREACHERS EXCHANGING VIEWS

The Long Sermon

EDITOR OF THE HOMILETIC REVIEW:

I want to urge the continuation of printing long sermons and articles. Those are the ones that appeal to me. I want articles and sermons which discuss a subject or text thoroughly from all viewpoints so that I can get help to treat subjects in such a way that those to whom I preach can get the mastery of any subject upon which I preach. There is no short cut to a good sermon or address. No man is or has a right to be too busy to prepare first-class sermons. That is the main business of the preacher. Continue the present plan.

E. F. WIEST.

Lebanon, Pa.

Christ Coming on the Clouds

EDITOR OF THE HOMILETIC REVIEW:

In the March number of the REVIEW, page 237, you print an article by Albert D. Belden, on "Christ Coming on the Clouds" in which he makes the following statement: "The phrase, the second coming of Christ is both misleading and unscriptural, the New Testament does not speak of Christ's second coming, but only of his coming again."

I am wondering just what one should think

of that statement, and especially when published in THE HOMILETIC REVIEW. Does the writer of that article really think he is telling the truth, being unaware of what is in the Bible to the contrary? Or does he know better, and is wilfully trying to deceive those who read his writing because he hates the truth of this matter?

Does our friend recognize the book of Hebrews as belonging to the New Testament? and if so what is to be done with Heb. 9:28? which reads:

"So Christ was once offered to bear the sins of many; and unto them that look for him shall he appear the second time without sin unto salvation."

Is it not trifling with the word of God to try to dodge the force of what he has written on this great and important truth? Would it not be the smallest kind of work to try, on a technicality, to twist the meaning of that statement? I believe this should be corrected for the readers of the REVIEW in the interest of the word of God.

P. A. KLEIN.

Seattle, Wash.

Women and the Ministry

EDITOR OF THE HOMILETIC REVIEW:

I have read with considerable interest in your magazine for May, the arguments put forward by Miss Royden as to women being permitted to a recognized place in the ministry. But I note, and not with surprise, that she has carefully omitted any mention whatever of the administration of the Lord's Supper by women.

It appears to me that for a woman to dare to attend at the altar for that purpose is a presumption more glaring than that recorded in Numbers 16, and it would be thoroughly out of order, and for this alone if for no other cause, women should not be admitted to the priesthood.

And as to taking part in the other phases of the Church service, beyond that of a deaconess, it is questionable anyhow if the novelty is worth trying. Certainly the Bible teaching is thoroughly against any such schemes as those women agitators propose. They are ready to "expound" Bible teachings to others, yet are not inclined to follow its laws themselves. Both the Old and New Testaments are against women assuming too much.

It is some comfort to know that the female unrest of the present day has not affected the majority of women, for most of them are free of the microbe of shiftiness. They have their duties to attend to and do them, and are in no way anxious to be either Amazons or He-She's. They have sense enough to bear in mind that whatever outward changes a woman may make, she must remain a woman and can never be a man.

There is no doubt but that a pretty young priestess would draw a number of young men to the church over which she presided. But there certainly would be also a marked absence of the young ladies who would rather see and hear a young curate speak. I am not assuming that such attendance at church is valuable, but am endeavoring to show that a lady preacher would have no advantage in mere numbers, and in no other way when the novelty wore off. And as there is no demand for lady preachers, it is foolish to start experiments in so serious a cause.

ORLANDO JAMES ROBERTS.

Gibbons Station, Alberta, Canada.

Themes and Texts

"SAY IT IN A WORD"

Miracles. "This beginning of his signs did Jesus in Cana of Galilee, and manifested his glory; and his disciples believed on him."—John 2:11.

Climbers. "Till we all attain unto the unity of the faith, and of the knowledge of the Son of God, unto a fullgrown man, unto the measure of the stature of the fulness of Christ . . . but speaking truth in love, may grow up in all things into him, who is the head, even Christ."—Eph. 4:13, 15.

Fun. "I said of laughter, It is mad; and of mirth, What doeth it?"—Eccles. 2:2.

Trails. "And thine ears shall hear a word behind thee, saying, This is the way, walk ye in it; when ye turn to the right hand, and when ye turn to the left."—Isa. 30:21.

Others. "Not looking each of you to his own things, but each of you also to the things of others."—Phil. 2:4.

Quitters. "Upon this many of his disciples went back, and walked no more with him. Jesus said therefore unto the twelve, Would ye also go away?"—John 6:66-67.

Men. "Watch ye, stand fast in the faith, quit you like men, be strong."—1 Cor. 16:13.

Neighbors. "But he, desiring to justify himself, said unto Jesus, And who is my neighbor?"—Luke 10:29.

Dollars. "But they that are minded to be rich fall into a temptation and a snare and many foolish and hurtful lusts, such as drown men in destruction and perdition."—1 Tim. 6:9.

Recent Books

WHAT IS THE MATTER WITH OUR CIVILIZATION[1]

Here are three books dealing with the same general theme—the apparent intention of civilized men to dig their own graves by the very means which they have created to raise them from the stage of savagery. It may be an aftermath of the war, or it may be our over-sensitiveness to suffering, but the number of books with a pessimistic outlook has increased since 1915 and there is presumably no way of stopping the flood. One of the authors believes that we are killing ourselves by lack of reproduction, another by having too much machinery, the third by ruthlessness in war. Each has called attention to a problem which it would behoove us to take to heart and ponder over.

The author of *The Trend of the Race* is professor of zoology at the University of California, and is thoroughly familiar with the biological factors of the human race. His thesis is that of the eugenists—mankind has advanced by virtue of its more capable specimens. All through history the innovators and initiators have opened new paths for men to walk in and advance to a higher stage of development. Yet this very class has ceased to hold its own in numbers, and the outlook is, to say the least, not encouraging. In sixteen chapters he takes up the different problems of heredity and eugenics. The tendency of civilized men is undoubtedly in the direction of a lower birth rate, but the reasons seem social rather than biological. The author holds out just one hope, that education must be directed to this important problem by having the attention of the young called to the need for eugenic marriages and a larger number of children among the mentally and physically favored. He refuses to discuss financial aid to these families as lowering their morale.

Social Decay and Regeneration attacks

civilization from another point, its too extensive use of machinery, which has reduced the worker to a slave, or rather to an appendix of a machine. The inventors have always promised that a particular machine would reduce human labor, but we are busier than ever; that it would save time, but we have less leisure than our forbears. A feverish activity which robs us of our sleep and makes us swallow our meals in haste, is undoubtedly the most striking characteristic of the age, and the lunch counter is its sign. A return to craftsmanship and a rejuvenation through eugenics are advocated as remedies.

It seems a peculiar blindness of some writers to look for remedies in the past and not in the future. Yet return to the past is impossible; craftsmen may have produced some very excellent utensils, but how small was the number of men who were able to procure them! And many men who had learned a trade laboriously, simply repeated over and over the tricks they had learned. To the writer's personal knowledge shoes are still made in eastern Europe fitting, or rather not fitting, either foot; they are hand-made, too, by a man who spends from three to five years as an apprentice and several more as a journeyman. The Europeans who prefer American machine-made shoes to those made by their own craftsmen, presumably know what they are doing. Many articles can now be bought in a ten-cent store which have three or four uses and are beautifully made and nickel-plated. A craftsman of a century ago simply could not make them if he spent a year on the job. Our future lies before us, not behind us. The mechanization of the worker is not as serious as more sensitive and creative minds imagine. The average worker has always moved in grooves; his redemp-

[1] *The Trend of the Race*, by SAMUEL J. HOLMES. Harcourt Brace & Co., New York, 1921. 396 pp. *Social Decay and Regeneration*, by R. AUSTIN FREEM. Houghton, Mifflin Co., New York, 1921. 345 pp. *The Folly of Nations*, by FREDERICK PALMER. Dodd Mead & Co., New York, 1921. 408 pp.

tion lies in better education and shorter hours—an education which will fit him to use his leisure properly instead of frittering it away in soul and body-destroying activities. Our education must become social by paying heed to this problem, instead of teaching the extraction of the cube-root and other futilities.

The Folly of Nations is written by a man who has had excellent opportunities for observing wars and their evil effects. In the Balkans, in the Russo-Japanese war, and in the World War he has seen the soldiers and learned their mind; in the councils of the statesmen he has observed the crafty, incorrigible reactionary attitude. The young men are willing to fight, and always will be —just because they are young. Is it fair for the schemers for profits and enlargement of territory to take advantage of the soldier? Will society much longer permit that secret diplomacy which regards peoples merely as pawns on a chessboard? The thought is too horrible when we consider that some 7,000,000 men were killed and some 13,000,000 wounded during the late war. What is to be done? The League of Nations has taken hold of the imagination of many peoples; it has already done some excellent work, and its influence is increasing. For an enlargement of its power and prestige it needs America. Are we going to join? We must, or the folly of nations will be repeated on a larger scale. We cannot withdraw from world affairs now, even if we would, because isolation for any one nation is impossible in this age of rapid transportation and world-wide commerce.

Public Opinion and the Steel Strike of 1919. By the Commission of Inquiry, Interchurch World Movement. Harcourt Brace & Co., New York, 1921, 346 pp.

"The Report on the Steel Strike of 1919" which was made by a committee of ministers and laymen interested in the betterment of the working classes, met with greatly divergent views. The companies which were proved to be doing many things provocative of strikes naturally complained and had the support of all their confrères among the employers of the old individualistic type of mind.

The book under review contains the documentation for the report, or rather, further documentation. The Commission of Inquiry could not very well keep quiet when lack of evidence, bias, and even bolshevism were charged against the report. The result is interesting, to say the least. The new book contains a vast amount of material which can not be summarized, but all of which is valuable. The following chapter heads give a mere glimpse of the richness and variety of topics discust: Under-cover men; the Pittsburgh newspapers and the strike; civil rights in Western Pennsylvania; the mind of immigrant communities; welfare work of the United States Steel Corporation; the Pittsburgh pulpit and the strike; the steel report and public opinion; addenda, containing letters to and from Judge Gary.

This book suggests a number of reflections. The press was almost unanimously against the strikers, the employers were liberal with the epithets of "red," "bolshevist," "anarchist," against anyone who even mildly defended the strikers; the private detective agencies are fast becoming not only a nuisance, but a public danger; the cheap labor of southern and eastern Europe was lured over by the employers as an antidote to English-speaking organized labor, and was praised for its docility and obedience, but condemned when it attempted to get better living conditions.

Perhaps most interesting is the attitude of the pulpit. Nearly all the ministers whose congregations consisted of workers favored the strikers, while those whose pews were filled, or at any rate paid for, by the employers, decried the strike. Were both parties hypocrites? Did they care more for the bread basket than for the truth? The employers certainly lauded the men who stood by them! It may be simply a case of the source of one's information, and not malice at all.

The World as Power Reality. By Sir John Woodroffe. Ganesh and Company, Madras, 1921. 7¾ x 5¼ in., 118, xix pp. Rupees 2.

The author of this little book is the one non-Hindu authority on Shaivite Tantrism, one of the most important of modern native religious cults in India. Under the pen name of Arthur Avalon he has to his credit a long list of texts and expositions, some of which have been noticed in this Review. The present little book sets forth the metaphysics of the system, especially in its Vedantic phase. He undertakes to show that the latest science in the Occident is coming into ever closer accord with Indian basal philosophy in its conception of what is real. Here he has in mind the physico-chemical results which have already, in our book-review column, been laid before our readers. The investigation of the atom, the discovery of the positively charged nucleus and the surrounding negatively charged electrons bring Western notions concerning the ultimate constitution of the universe wonderfully close to the Hindu idea, which is "fundamentally realism." The volume constitutes a defense of modern Indian thought as sound. It is not easy reading—Sir John's exposition and style are difficult. He is a master of the technical Sanskrit terms and uses them constantly, often to the confusion of the reader who is not a Sanskritist. But it is the most appreciative exposition of the subject in brief form that we have in English, and well worth studying out.

An Introduction to Mahayana Buddhism. With especial Reference to Chinese and Japanese Phases. By WILLIAM MONT-GOMERY McGOVERN. Kegan Paul, Trench, Trubner & Co., Ltd., London; E. P. Dutton & Co., New York, 1922. 8¾x5¾ in. 233 pp. $3.00.

Asian Cristology and the Mahayana. By E. A. GORDON. Maruzen & Company, Ltd., Tokyo, 1921. 9¼x6¼ in., 334 pp. $5.00

The complexion any religion takes in a given environment depends largely upon the mentality of the people. Hence, for example, Mohammedanism in pantheistic India and semi-pantheistic Persia is a different thing from Arabian Islamism. Similarly Buddhism in India, Ceylon, and Burmah differs greatly from the same religion in Thibet, China, and Japan. This all students know, and they recognize two branches —the Southern, called Hinayana ("lesser vehicle," because it has a relatively small "bible"), and the Northern, called Mahayana ("greater vehicle," because it has a very extensive "bible"). The latter branch has been little studied until the last few years, and light is sadly needed. Dr. Mc-Govern has presented an able exposition of the philosophy and principal ideas of Northern Buddhism as found in China and Japan, particularly in its sects. The fundamental differences between the two branches he finds are in the conception of the means of salvation. Southern Buddhism attains sal-

vation by works; Northern, by knowledge; and a large sect of the latter proceeds by faith. Of course, many other diversities exist, such as the doctrine of the Buddhist Trinity. The growth of doctrine, after the death of the Buddha, is well set forth, with its epistemology and metaphysics. And this might afford a ground for comparison with the growth of dogma in Christianity which would prove splendidly illuminating.

Miss Gordon's book is in quite a different category. She has based her work on a reprint of Thomas Yeates unreliable Indian Church History, published in 1818. This was in turn based upon Asseman's Bibliotheca Orientalis (1719-28), which is an uncritical collection of heterogeneous documents. Our author's thesis is that the "roots of the symbols everywhere prominent in Korean and Japanese temples" are found in the frescoes of subterranean Rome—the catacombs. A prodigious amount of work has been done in gathering materials from art, ritual, legend, and literature, all of which, Miss Gordon thinks, is due to stimuli and suggestion from the West. The huge fallacy which underlies this entire presentation is two-fold: Yates' book lacks authority; and the supposed derivation and similitude of forms are due not to borrowing but to the normal working of the essentially similar human mind.

Studies of Contemporary Metaphysics. By R. F. A. HOERNLE. Harcourt, Brace and Howe, New York. 5½ x 8 in. ix, 314 pp.

The writer of this notice had several times come upon the name of this author signed to reviews of various works in philosophy, religion, and metaphysics and had been profoundly imprest with the insight, sobriety, fairness, and value of his contributions. The hope that he might soon come upon some production by this poised thinker was gratified when this book was put into his hand; his expectations have been more than met as he has read it all once and much of it several times. Having defined the "Philosopher's Quest," the author proceeds to discuss present-day tendencies in philosophy and the immediate difficulties which beset one who will understand the world he lives in. This is followed by a constructive presentation of the reality of the world of sense, Mechanism and Vitalism, Theories of Mind, and the Self in Self-Consciousness, with an epilogue on Religion and Philosophy of Religion. From beginning to end he moves with the step of one who is carefully feeling his way, courteous and just to those from whom he differs, appreciative of those to whom he is under obligation, frank in the acknowledgement of difficulties which no philosophy has solved and perhaps can not solve, always courageous with the confidence of brave and heartening leadership. His fundamental conviction is that "experience, taken as a whole, gives us clues which, rightly interpreted, lead to the perception of order in the universe, a graded order of varied appearance." Material for deep and further reflection is provided in his chapter on Mechanism and Vitalism, or perhaps better Mechanism and Order or Teleology and Value in the world. The nature of self as interpreted by self-consciousness and his final discussion of religion. Religion is defined as "a response to, or acknowledgement of, that character of, or in, the world for which we have the words 'God' or 'divine'."

This work will appeal first of all to students of philosophy, but also to multitudes of inquiring business and professional men, and not least of all to thoughtful ministers whose task is to solve as far as possible the problems of life and mind, the world and God. Ministers more than most other men ought to have a well-worked-out body of philosophy in which the values which they are striving to realize shall be those for which the world itself cares. This book will aid one to gain a deeper assurance that "the total scheme of the universe is not indifferent to the values to which it gives rise and which it sustains."

The author intimates that this treatise is to be followed by another bearing on the controversy between realism and idealism. This will be awaited with an interest which has been justly aroused by the present work. Incidentally it may be remarked that Professor Hoernle adds another laurel to fair Harvard's philosophic wreath.

The Find Yourself Idea. By C. C. ROBINSON. Association Press, New York, 1922. 7½ x 5¼ in., 134 pp. $1.40.

There is no greater service which one man may render to a younger man than to help him to "find himself," to open his eyes to see the great needs of the world for service, and to help him to answer for himself the question, "How can I, such as I am in ability, health, character, and opportunity,

find my best place for service and use that place for my own betterment and that of humanity?"

This quotation is well worth passing on. It is taken from the Introduction by Jesse B. Davis, Supervisor of Secondary Education for the State of Connecticut.

In this little book the author aims to give—

a brief statement for the purposes and practicability of vocational guidance with suggestions for making such work effective among older boys. In includes instructions for the use of self-analysis blanks, the selection and coaching of interviewers, and a particular emphasis upon the character-building values of such service with boys.

The article on "Vocational Guidance" which we published on page 50 of the January number of the REVIEW is well worth the serious attention of our readers in connection with this book.

Radioactivity and Radioactive Substances. By J. CHADWICK. Sir Isaac Pitman and Sons, Ltd., London and New York, 1921. 6½ x 4¼ in., 111 pp. $.85.

Until 1896 the smallest body conceived by science was the atom, out of which molecules are composed. In that year it was discovered that the atom is itself composite, being built up of a nucleus carrying a positive charge of electricity and "electrons" or particles carrying a negative charge. The discovery of radioactive elements (that is, elements which are in process of breaking down by discharging particles from their substance) and subsequent study of these elements has thrown even new light on the construction of matter.

Mr. Chadwick's little book in pocket size reduces almost to a formula briefness the results of twenty-five years' investigation of the radioactive elements. It diagrams the apparatus employed, expresses in scientifically accurate but brief statements the meaning of the experiments, and for the advanced student gives the mathematical formulas for investigation of the principal radioactive substances. The layman can follow with comparative ease the descriptions furnished. He can discover that there are many forms of this kind of matter—for instance, several forms of uranium and radium, eleven of thorium, besides ionium, and actinium, &c. It is a revealing book, to be read with Mills' *Within the Atom* (See March HOMILETIC, p. 256.).

We can conceive a Sunday's two services presenting the contrasts between the infinitely great and the infinitely small of our universe. The morning sermon could show the glory of God as even the psalmist could not conceive it—building upon the latest researches in astronomy through the telescope, the spectroscope, and the grating. The evening sermon, using this book, could present the same glory in the almost inconceivably small—the structure of the atom, built up from particles one two-thousandth as big as the atom itself! Sermons in stones?—there's a sermon in every speck of dust that reveals itself in a ray of sunlight, if you only know how to make it!

An Encyclopaedia of Religions. By MAURICE A. CANNEY. George Routledge and Sons, Ltd., London; E. P. Dutton and Co., New York, 1921. 10 x 8½ in., 397 pp. $10.00.

It is a coincidence that this work and the *Dictionary of Religion and Ethics* (see our January number, p. 86) appeared almost in the same month. The outstanding difference between the two—which set out to cover practically the same ground—is that this is the product of a single scholar, that of over 100 specialists and two editors. The author of this one is conscious that his was "a bold undertaking" in so enormous a field as the history of religions. He justifies (in part) his accomplishment by the large number of new vocabulary entries. So that the student of comparative religion will find many terms defined or discust which are not in any other encyclopedia. That is so much to the good, provided the information is clear and reliable. And tribute is due to the prodigious industry evinced, which has included much that is odd and unordinary as well as most of the topics normally expected.

On the other hand it was perhaps inevitable that single authorship should omit many subjects that would be looked for. For instance, "Brahmanism" is often referred to but not treated. Incubation is another important but missing theme. Neither sin nor salvation find place as vocabulary terms, significant elements tho they are of religious belief. And no geographical articles are to be found, tho they are so useful in nucleating facts and indicating origins and progression. Apart from these and numerous other omissions, some of the discussions are disappointing. Atonement is treated almost solely from the Anselmic position. The novice reading "Canon, Buddhist," would wrongly suppose that the Sikhs' sacred *Adi-Granth* and the Jains' *Gaina Sutras* belong to the Buddhist bible.

Letters of Principal James Denney to W. Robertson Nicoll, 1893-1917. Hodder and Stoughton, Ltd., London, New York, Toronto. xliii—270 pp.

These letters were not written with a view to publication. Whether Dr. Denney would have approved of their appearance in such a volume is not essential. When a man has achieved as much influence as he did, the benefit of the doubt in such a question may be given to the public. And the public will unquestionably welcome the volume as a service not only of the deepest interest, but also of the fullest enlightenment respecting a transitional period in the history of religious and political thought in Great Britain. Being written as expressions of personal views to a friend they are frank, simple and sincere. They reveal the workings of a great mind; and, tho the reader may not always share the writer's philosophy, theology or politics, he can not but be filled with admiration for the sterling qualities of the man and ennobled by his lofty idealism.

A Gentleman in Prison. Translated by CAROLINE MACDONALD. George H. Doran Company, New York, 1922. 7¾ x 5½ in., 164 pp. $1.75.

This is the story of Tokichi Ishii, written in Tokyo Prison. It is surely a story of intense human interest by an uneducated man, who—

steeped in crime, condemned to death for murder, waiting daily for the unescapable end to which his crimes have brought him, is touched by one of another nation, and a woman at that, with traditions and history and education as different from his as night is from day; but the universal message of the love of God flashes across the gulf of human differences and the man's soul responds.

Dr. John Kelman has written out of a full heart a most appreciative foreword. He says he is responsible for the title of the book. It seems to us an unfortunate choice and we may add also that his estimate of this story and the man may seriously be questioned. For example, he says: "It is indeed one of the world's great stories" and that "Ishii was one of God's aristocrats."

Is it not time that experienced and cultured Christian people placed a higher estimate on the well-disciplined life, the life of steady growth in knowledge and love from childhood to manhood, the life that is free from the catalog of crime as set forth in this book. Magnifying the cataclysmic type of conversion has been very much overdone. The grace of God is present, it seems to us, in a much larger degree in the nurture and growth of the young child than in the sudden conversion of a criminal.

The Art of Thinking. By T. SHARPER KNOWLSON. Thomas Y. Crowell Company, New York, 1921. 7½ x 5¼ in., 165 pp. $1.35.

The author of this little book—which by the way is a revision of the work which was first published in 1899—quotes from Madame Swetchine a remark which is pertinent to the subject discust:

To have ideas is to gather flowers; to think is to weave them into garlands.

More garlands, then, are needed and this manual is designed to help in that direction.

Henry Scott Holland. Memoir and Letters. Edited by STEPHEN PAGET. E. P. Dutton and Company, New York, 1921. x, 336 pp.

Henry Scott Holland occupied a prominent and influential position in the English Church. As teacher at Oxford and as Dean of St. Paul's, he was a leader; as editor of *Commonwealth*, he was the distinct hope of progressive young men; he was one of the half dozen men who were the heart of the Christian Social Union. The editor of the memoir knows all this, but he does not make it evident to the reader. With the exception of Bishop Gore's chapter on "Holland and the Christian Social Union" there is little in the volume to account for Holland's well-deserved place in the English Church.

A Short History of the Papacy. By MARY I. M. BELL. With two maps. Dodd, Mead & Co., 1921. xiii, 390 pp.

An excellent book. Systematic, clear, unpartisan, readable. It should be in the hands of students. Laymen who wish to know the outline of papal history will like it. Here and there one can discover a point one would rather have treated in a slightly different way. For example, not enough time is given to the Forged Decretals; the immediate ef-

fect of the founding of the College of Cardinals in securing the independence of the papacy is over-stated; insufficient attention is paid to the significance of the reforming councils. But these limitations are rare. As a whole the book shows scholarship and insight.

Children's Gospel Story-Sermons. By HUGH T. KERR. Fleming H. Revell Company, New York, 1921. 7½ x 5¼ in., 190 pp. $1.25.

The fifty-two "story-sermons" in this collection are well above the average. They stick closer to the gospel stories or texts on which they are founded than do most such talks, and yet retain the present-day interest that is necessary in speaking to children. We give one of the stories on p. 75 of this issue.

Sermons for Special Days. By FREDERICK D. KERSHNER. George H. Doran Company, New York, 1922. 7¾ x 5½ in., 223 pp. $1.50.

Volumes covering special days have been quite numerous of late. Our readers have sampled them as they came along. We are going to give them an opportunity to read one from this volume (see page 69). The book contains fifteen discourses for church year occasions and three under the general title of Passion Week Studies.

The author mentions in the preface that he kept a record of the number of times several of them had been delivered "and in one case at least the figures run to over three hundred." The keynote to this thoughtful collection may be found in this thought, "the life worth while can not be achieved without the firmest confidence in an all-wise, an all-powerful, and an all-good captain of our souls."

The Rock That Is Higher, and Other Addresses. By TEUNIS E. GOUWENS. Fleming H. Revell Company, New York, 1922. 7½ x 5 in., 160 pp. $1.25.

Concerning this volume Dr. Macfarland of the Federal Council has this to say in his Introduction:

These utterances do not strive to lift us, in mere dreams, out of the realm of our common life, nor do they labor to obscure its drudgery by any priestly pretense. They face life honestly, unevadingly, as it is and as we all know it.

We take pleasure in giving one of the sermons in another part of this number.

JOHN FREDERICK KENSETT

American landscape painter; born at Cheshire, Conn.; March 22, 1818; died in New York, December 14, 1872; studied note engraving under his uncle; in 1840 began a five years' study of painting in England, continuing his work as engraver; for two years painted landscapes in Italy; exhibited at the Royal Academy in London and (returning to the United States in 1847) in the National Academy in New York, becoming a member of the latter in 1849, and being ranked with the "Hudson River School" of painting. Many of his works are in the Metropolitan Museum of New York, quite a number not exhibited, and others in the Corcoran Gallery, Washington, D. C. His "White Mountains," hung in the Metropolitan Museum, is regarded as a masterpiece in its class.

LAKE GEORGE IN LATE SUMMER

By John Frederick Kensett

The HOMILETIC REVIEW

VOL. 84   AUGUST, 1922   No. 2

IS THE COMMUNITY CHURCH A FAD

The Rev. DAVID R. PIPER, La Grange, Mo.

The Church of the living God can not well be a dead thing. And if it lives, it must, like all other social institutions, be in a state of evolution. Sectarianism has existed for only about four hundred years, in spite of its seeming stability. Before that for a thousand years we had a stagnating uniformity in which liberty of religious thought was supprest. Just as this gave way through the Protestant Reformation to sectarianism, so sectarianism in a living Church must eventually give way to something else. Keen observers believe that the evolution out of the sectarian organization of religion into that something else which is to follow is now rapidly taking place. While some conservatives warn us against the community church movement as a dangerous fad, others see in it the beginnings of a transformation destined to be the most far-reaching and profound in its effects upon organized religion since the days of Martin Luther.

The community church movement is as yet small as compared with the great Protestant denominations. The most complete list thus far compiled contains the names of 710 churches, and 143 of these are denominational churches which have not really broadened their basis of membership, but are the only churches in their communities and are trying to serve the whole community. As it stands, the number of true community churches thus far listed exceeds the number of Unitarian churches in the United States and almost equals the number of Universalist congregations. And the movement exerts an influence out of all proportion to its recorded strength. New community churches are being organized at the rate of about one per week, and news of community churches hitherto unlisted in the statistics of the movement, but which have existed for some years, are constantly coming to hand. Large groups of people in hundreds of villages are becoming convinced that the community organization of religion is the only solution of their church problems. Thus while denominational leaders are conferring and drawing up timid resolutions full of reservations, which their respective legislative assemblies reject, amend, table, and kill in committee, the people themselves are actually getting together. The get-together movement in religion is proceeding by local option. It is coming not because a few officials see the beauty of dwelling together in unity but because "things" have "got so bad" that the people see that something has to be done.

And this is not my theory of the matter. It is a statement based upon thorough investigation. Questionnaires were mailed to the pastors of more than 500 community churches, asking them to tell what considerations induced their people to repudiate sectarianism in favor of a single community-serving religious organization, and who were the leaders in the movement. Answers received show that in 56.2 per cent of the communities laymen were solely responsible for the movement and for the actual organization of the community church. Laymen led also in 17.7 per cent of the communities, but with the active cooperation of one or more local pastors; 13.5 per cent of the churches investigated were organized under the definite advocacy of local pastors, and 12.6 per cent through the leadership of non-resident ministers, evangelists, or denominational officials, with the cooperation of the people. In about half of the last-named instances the non-resident leaders were called in by laymen to assist in organizing a community church for which there was already a strong demand. Thus, 80 out of 100 community churches are formed because of the spontaneous desire of the people themselves, and almost three-fourths of these are actually organized without the assistance of ministers. Many authentic cases are on record of communities whose Christian people have come together in spite of the active opposition of denominational officials. One of the most striking examples is that of a village where recently two congregations ruled by the monarchical form of government voted almost unanimously to join with other Christian people of the town to form a strong unsectarian church. The district superintendents declared that they would maintain sectarian preachers in that town if they had to preach to empty benches. Accordingly, $2,500 home mission money has been appropriated by the two denominations to make good these assertions. It is re-

ported that the largest audience one of the home mission preachers has had thus far is 24, and that the other has preached to a maximum crowd of 5—this in a town of 1,500 people. The incident is mentioned here merely to make vivid the fact that the community church movement arises from the people themselves. Moreover, it has the sympathy and support of the unchurched "masses" as no other religious movement has had in modern times.

To the question, what factors led the Christian people of these 500 communities to get together into one church, the answers are various, and often recite superficial, secondary causes. Economic considerations of one sort and another are most frequently mentioned. The competing churches had become too weak to support separate pastors; increased expenses, combined with the removal of some of the chief "pillars," is another way of stating the financial difficulties; the church edifice of one of the competing congregations burned at a time when it seemed impossible to raise funds to rebuild; two or three churches were influenced by the shortage of preachers, and one community decided magnanimously to share its surfeit of this commodity with another community which was preacherless; fuel shortage during the war led congregations to worship together, with the result that union was discovered to be more blessed than separation—a fact which Jesus mentioned some 1900 years ago; people saw that the law of self-preservation demanded that they quit fighting each other and begin fighting the devil; and more of the same kind. Reasons other than economic were also given, in smaller number and variety; the desire to render a more efficient community service; to secure more capable pulpit ability and social leadership; and one pastor said that the reason his folks got together into a single unsectarian church was that most of them were really Christians!

There is no doubt of the power of the economic factor in the religious reintegration of community life. But economic considerations have operated not so much as a fundamental cause, but rather as a practical incitement. The influence of the economic factor must itself be regarded as a symptom of a most significant transformation which has taken place in the religious consciousness of America. Yesterday the problem arising out of the inability of two or more competing churches to support pastors would not have been solved by the merger of the churches. As a matter of fact the problem was solved yesterday by the division of the minister. Either the preacher divided himself between several churches in different communities or he divided himself between his sacred calling and a secular avocation. Divided communities produced preachers with divided interests. The financial weaknesses of competing congregations yesterday did not draw them together, but embittered them toward each other and led them to the unholy business of trying to steal each other's best-paying members by proselyting methods. But to-day the same problems are answered by the community church. Why?

Because of the development of a community consciousness stronger than the group consciousness. Slowly but surely the telephone, automobile, farmers' cooperatives, chautauquas have broken up the little groups by the power of larger interests. For years agricultural journals have preached cooperation. During the war farmers faced the necessity of practising this preachment. Better roads have not only increased neighborliness, but have increased the size of communities. Consolidated schools

have been introduced and in many places have helped directly to foster the community church. This has been notably true at Revere, Mo., and in the Sargent community, near Monte Vista, Colo. The influence of co-operation in secular pursuits upon the religious life and thought of rural communities has been nothing less than profound, altho it is not often consciously felt.

In a certain community in Lewis County, Mo., in the 'sixties there was a thriving Methodist church. Two miles to the south of the church building ran a creek which in spring became an inundating torrent. An influential family of the church moved over on the south side of this creek. For weeks each year these good folks could not ford the stream to reach their church services. So, seeing himself thus deprived of religious privileges, the head of the family built a church of his own on his side of the creek! That little incident is characteristic of the period in which it occurred. It would have been quite as cheap to build a bridge over the stream. And that would have served the whole community. But yesterday was a day of church-building, dividing communities. To-day is a day of bridge-building. We are building all sorts of bridges to-day to span all sorts of social barriers. The community church is a bridge to span the sectarian barriers erected in the past. It merely applies the present-day trend to religion.

The changed emphasis in religious thought manifesting itself in the multiplication of interdenominational agencies and in the social application of religion through such agencies as the Y. M. C. A. is sifting down into the most isolated corners of America and bearing fruit after its kind. The demand for a more efficient program of service and for a more capable religious leadership, which has been a factor in the community church movement, finds root in this changed emphasis in modern religious thought. The social implications of the gospel are being recognized in the remotest villages. People in small communities are conceiving of the Church no longer as a divinely commissioned agency to pluck elected individuals from the general damnation, but as a leavening influence to penetrate into every phase of community life with the transforming power of the religious spirit.

That is why sectarian churches are being found wanting. The whole theory of sectarianism depends upon the individualistic view of the gospel. Sectarian competition is justifiable only on the ground that "my" church has a better interpretation of the truth than "yours," or that it has the most Biblical doctrine and offers the surest way of salvation. This, in fact, is an argument actually used to-day in many communities where the community church movement is meeting opposition. But when once the social gospel becomes recognized, sectarianism loses its reason for existence. The instant one conceives of the big task of the Church as that of fostering the kingdom of love in the community and in the world, that instant sectarianism is perceived to exert a divisive and inimical influence within that kingdom. It becomes clear that the limitation which sectarianism places upon Christian people must be overcome. And the community church is the only practicable means yet offered for overcoming the limitation.

RELIGIOUS AND ETHICAL CONDITIONS AND OUTLOOK IN GERMANY

Professor EDUARD KÖNIG, Ph.D., Th.D., Bonn, Germany

It goes without saying that two such events as the defeat of Germany in the World War and the complete revolution in conditions of State could not be without profound results for both theory and practise in the life of the nation. Can there be more important factors of national life than religion and morals? It is therefore a matter of the highest interest to set forth the results of the World War as shown in present religious and ethical conditions in Germany. To do this is the purpose of this article.

I. A natural starting point is found in the question: How has the relation between Church and State resolved itself since Nov. 9, 1918? With the end of the Kaiser's rule as king-emperor there came also the end of his status as supreme bishop of the national church. The rights which he used to exercise fell at first to three ministers, but now are taken over definitely by the Church itself and are exercised through three authorities constituting the supreme Church Council in Berlin. The Church, consequently, has become more nearly autonomous than it ever was. Nevertheless, the fact that is to be feared, namely, the complete separation of Church and State, has come to pass neither in the nation as a whole nor in the separate States. The Social Democrats did include in their "Erfurt Program" the statement that "Religion is a private affair." But in the establishment of the German republic's administration they could not get this principle applied—or, perhaps, they did not really desire to carry it through. The majority in their ranks at the decisive moment discerned that even a democratic State, as protector of rights, can not dispense with morals as its deepest root, and as the nurse of culture dares not destroy religion which is its most vital blood. Consequently, as yet the relation of Church and State in Germany is comparatively friendly—practically like the conditions existing in the United States of America. For there, altho since 1783 the principle of the separation of Church and State has been practised the quiet of Sunday is legally protected by the State, which also appoints chaplains for the land and naval forces.

Those who adhere to Marx's socialistic theory, who are committed to the cause of communism, have been obliged to content themselves with an urgent agitation for dramatic withdrawal from the Church. They have indeed raised loudly the old slogan, "The Church is reactionary, is a stupefying institution," or have shouted out in the popular services, "The Church is protected only by the priests." These agitators senselessly disregard the fact that many leaders in science—a Copernicus, a Newton, a Robert Mayer (enunciator of the principle of the conservation of energy), and many others—have treasured their Biblical faith as their choicest possession. It is easy to understand, however, that their success is very great especially in the larger cities, since many men stream toward them who together with their appreciation of home have lost their sense of ancestral religion. An example of this can be cited from Hamburg. In the early days after the war at the offices where declaration of withdrawal from the Church was made the rush was so great that announcement had to be made in the newspapers that "today at this place only 200 could be registered, at that place only 300," and so on. Indeed a sufficient staff for purposes of record could not be maintained. But the rush was short-lived. So that, for instance, from Halle, where Tholuck taught, the report came that "in 1921 only 211 withdrew, but 378 came into church connections." The cases increase in which people who had left the Church have returned to it.

II. The financial situation of the Church. While, as set forth above, the radical adherents of Marxism and all declared foes of Biblical religion are not agreed upon an absolute separation of Church and State, it has not reached the point where the income of the clergy of the great ecclesiastical corporations or "State churches" depend upon the free-will offerings of the membership. Especially in Prussia the majority of the deputies to the Landtag have not risked losing sight of what happened in 1803 ff. They recall the loss to the State, after the dissolution of the Holy Roman Empire, caused by the secularization of numerous church properties—which have not even yet been restored. In order to pay at least the interest on the millions of church property seized at that time and in general to do its full duty to the Church as one of the weightiest factors working for civilization, the government has decided further to remunerate the ministry and the ecclesiastical administration (Consistories and the like). Also in those divisions of German Christendom in which the preachers are endowed with their claim upon the free-will gifts of the membership, the spirit of self-sacrifice is much in evidence. To cite a concrete example, the very active body of pious souls in Bonn who call themselves *Gemeinschaftschristen* ("Community Christians") support their own special preacher, altho they are under obligation also to pay the general church tax. We observe the very same readiness to make great sacrifices for ecclesiastical purposes among the Baptists and other small circles of non-Catholic Christianity.

It is nothing less than astounding how much, Sunday after Sunday, is deposited in the collection plates, in part for the deaconesses of the particular local churches and in part for other church work—this all in spite of the colossal increase in the cost of living. Illustrative figures can again be drawn from the evangelical membership in Bonn: On March 5 for the work of the deaconesses the sum of 503 marks was bestowed, and 697 marks went into the collection for the *Lutherstiftung* ("Luther Foundation"). The following Sunday 481 marks went to the deaconesses, and a collection for "The Protestant Germans in South America" amounted to 632 marks. In November of last year there was an extra "Gift-week" for home-mission institutions, inasmuch as they were unmistakably in great financial straits because of the rapid rise in living costs. In Bonn alone 140,000 marks were gotten together, altho in this city the population is only one-third "evangelical" (*i.e.*, Protestant) in affiliation. In a similar period the membership at Bonn taxed themselves in great sums (reaching into the millions) for the cause of foreign missions. This was necessary in order to extinguish the debt which had been incurred, and during the war had accumulated, for instance, under the well-known Barmer Missionary Society.

There were, moreover, collections for the activities of the Gustav-Adolf-Verein, for the Evangelical Union, and for the Evangelicals in Palestine. On June 14, 1921, to the well-known Syrian Orphan Asylum in Palestine its distinguished founder, Ludwig Schneller, was given back, and further assistance was undertaken in connection with the work for 50,000 orphans cared for by the American "Near East Relief." Meanwhile neither the support of Evangelical Christians in Russia nor the need of the Christian Armenians was forgotten. Special organizations were built up in Germany to look after these distressed classes. Thus the practise of Christian love—the leading trait in the first of the three triads of fruits of the spirit of Christ (Gal. 5:22)— is carried out in far-reaching and manifold ways even in the present narrowed circumstances existent in Germany.

III. How stands the case concerning the strength of the inner religious life of evangelical Christianity in Germany? We note first a matter that lies on the borderland between the externals and the internals of living of a division of Christianity. The need of the time has brought about what has been in vain sought for centuries, a union of all evangelical churches in all the constituent parts of the German realm. This most noteworthy result was accomplished at the evangelical Church Diet at Stuttgart on Sept. 12, 1921. Germany's evangelical Christianity consequently composes a compact unity comparable with that of Roman Catholic Christianity in this land. It is therefore in a position to insist upon its rights as against the State and other forces with an emphasis stronger than ever before. When we pass from this fact to look within at the heart of evangelical Christianity, God be thanked that we need miss none of the varied indications of a living power. One significant pointer of earnest religious life is diligent attendance upon divine service. This is in evidence stronger than before the war, not merely on fast and festival days (like Good Friday and Easter Sunday) but also on the Sundays throughout the year.

Other signs of real inner life in the German Evangelical Church are the following: First the earlier "alliances" of the different church circles continue to exist and extend, like that of the positive union of confessional Lutherans. There is also the creation of an active "Union" of all the smaller circles of friends of the Biblical faith and the purpose strongly to maintain their position against the strivings of the so-called "Liberals." Next we may remark on the formula of confession which was shaped for the Prussian Church by the Commission referred to above:

Faithful to the heritage from the fathers stands the Church of Prussia upon the gospel given in Holy Scripture by Jesus Christ, the Crucified and the Risen One, our Lord and Savior, as the creeds (the Apostles', etc.) attest and confess.

It is beyond question that, to the great astonishment of Germany, the "Positives" make up four-fifths of the deputies that will carry through this formulation of the Confession of the New Testament gospel.

Another symptom of wide-awake consciousness in the evangelical circles of Germany is the earnest protest which was lodged in October, 1921, in the republic of Thuringia when the radical *Kultusminister* (Minister of Public Worship—a "cabinet" officer) forbade celebration on a week-day of the anniversary of Luther's publication of the *Ninety-five Theses*, since October 31 fell on such a day. To this may be added the important fact that commemoration of the day when Luther returned from the Wartburg to Wittenberg (bringing the first volume of his translation of the Bible) 400 years ago was celebrated with great unanimity in this city, March 4-6. In this celebration three high church dignitaries from Sweden (Archbishop Söderblom), Norway, and Finland took part and commemorated the association of their countries therewith. What a tribute it is to the force of the piety of the evangelical circles in Germany that the celebrated materialist Ernst Haeckel

(in Jena), who through his book on *The Riddle of the Universe* had destroyed in thousands of men their faith in God, before his death became one of these same evangelicals. So that the founder of the League of Monists was compelled at last to pay his tribute to the Biblical faith that was in evidence all about him.

IV. An important chapter in the history of the religious life of New Germany has reference to the influence which the revolution has caused to be experienced in the relations of the State to religious instruction in the official schools. At first it appeared as tho a dreadful storm had appeared in the sky of spiritual life in that it looked as tho the theological faculties were to be eliminated from their places in the universities. But the time of activity of the first communistic minister of public worship soon passed, and his successor Haenisch returned to the earlier order of scientific procedure in Germany. Consequently the theological faculties hold their place among the former departments of general science. Sharper was the conflict concerning the position which religious instruction should take in the other schools supported by the State. The principal turns which this contest took are the following:

Great numbers favored a so-called undenominational school (*Simultanschule*) which would be attended equally by the children of atheists and of Christians, religious instruction being eliminated from the plans. According to their desires these schools alone were to be supported by the State and to be developed with reference to the rights of their entering students. But these plans were met by a storm of indignation from those who stood by their ancestral faith, and protests against these "worldly schools" were signed by millions. In the development of this conflict many thousands of unions sprang up in the cities and villages which enforced the demand for confessional schools as those which alone guarantee a unified instruction of youth. In the autumn of last year these unions were organized into a National League of Parents which by the end of last Febuary counted a million members. There may be differences of opinion as to the result of all this strife. But according to the facts as they lie before us it seems certain that the issue will be like that in Holland. There existed during the period from 1806 to 1888 a time of persecution for the confessional schools. But finally the hour of freedom struck, and those schools were recognized as having equal validity with the State schools and, like them, as equally entitled to the protection of the State.

The achievement of this victory for the confessional schools is the earlier to be expected as greater numbers of leagues, made up of faithful teachers of both sexes, fight in the front lines. Examples of these leagues are the "Union of Positive Evangelical Teachers of Religion" (from the High Schools), and the "Alliance of German Evangelical Teachers," which latter exists through all Germany. Finally, as tending to assure the victory, there is a host which we may call the Junior Guard—the "Alliance of the League of Youth for a Resolute Christianity." This alliance includes 967 leagues with 33,712 members, strengthened by 462 Sundayschools with 40,093 members. In general, Biblical religion in Germany now seems to be secured for the future, inasmuch as, like the Romans, it regards the youth of the land as the ultimate hope of the Fatherland. This thought will be expanded in the following paragraphs.

V. This article would be but a fragmentary torso did it not take up the matter of the influence on the morale of Germany caused by the World War. This is, to be sure, a comprehensive theme; nevertheless, I may hope, in the following, to be able to present an essentially correct statement respecting the results referred to.

In many circles of the population there is evident an almost frantic mania for amusement and in other circles a senseless eagerness for gain. These do not, however, form the majority of the people, least of all are they its heart. The soul of the nation . is bent on the aim of not trembling before the application to themselves of Christ's words, By their fruits shall ye know them.

First, the State as well as unofficial leagues are striving with all earnestness against the further spread of such epidemics as the craze for the "movies," and against planting in the soul the germs of deadly disease by means of shameless representations on the screen. Second, there exist leagues of earnest men and women who are combating prostitution with all boldness. Significant is the fact that in Hamburg after a ten years' struggle with the city senate the "Midnight Mission" won the victory at the end of last year. The brothels in the city were closed, and the streets that were notorious because of vice were cleansed of their filth. Third, into these regions youth comes as an important factor. At the time when the so-called "enlightenment films" (Aufklärungsfilme) overflowed Germany and our large cities presented such a picture of moral filth as can hardly be imagined, the youth of our high schools and universities rose of their own initiative to take up the battle against the "smutfilm," against the lewd picture-card, against plays that dealt with dishonor of marriage, against indecent advertisements and theater presentations. To take one scene out of this series of battles—the "sexual" picture card was distributed in Dresden from some twenty shops. The police were helpless, since for a city of half a million only a single officer was available for this purpose. But the youth succeeded in making the cards disappear from all shops within fourteen days. And how did they go at it? Scarcely was a particular shop opened in the morning before a high-school student entered with "Good morning, Madame X. I would gladly make some purchase from you, but since you display such and such postcards in your window, I can not do it." Ten minutes later another student would come and say, "Good morning, Madame. Do you know that when anyone passes your display-window and sees such and such cards there, he feels really ashamed?" So it went day after day, and in two weeks Dresden was swept clean of that disgrace.

Where such fruits spring up on the soil of belief in the Biblical gospel, we may anticipate that, after the words of the parable in Matt. 13:23, the seed falling on good ground drives its roots deep and produces an abundant harvest.

The conclusion which we may reach from this review must be the following. While we look back with deep sorrow at the devastating influence wrought by the World War upon the religious life and the ethics of large circles in vanquished Germany, we yet may feel confidence that not merely a Biblical faith in God but also the illimitable gospel of the New Testament will retain its assured and roomy place among the German people.

HOW FAR AWAY IS NEXT DOOR

VINCENT M. BEEDE, Washington, D. C.

Terence wrote, "I am the nearest relative to myself." Remarked Ovid, "Our own house is hard to save when the neighbor's is on fire." Said an unknown author, "A friend is more needful than fire or water."

Some of us live out West, on the prairie, where there is no front yard, and no back yard, but just one big, big lawn, with very few fences to bother about. To get to our friend (or enemy) next door we may have to hop on the horse or the motor-car, unless we are extra fond of hiking; and altho we can give the approximate number of miles that lie between us, we should need a surveyor to make an accurate report.

Or perhaps we dwell in an up-and-down sort of place, and can't even see our neighbor's windmill with a pair of binoculars, for the reason that he lives around a tremendous corner consisting of a Rocky Mountain.

If we inhabit a village, a town, or a small city, we would have little trouble in measuring the feet, yards, or rods that separate us from our "nigh-dwellers," but unless we are engaged in a lawsuit, it would hardly occur to us to go through so tedious a performance with the tape and the stakes.

Oddly enough, some of our nearest neighbors are the furthest away—so far as we care about them.

How far away is next door?

This morning I was talking about neighbors to my cousin, Wanda, whom I hadn't seen for a long time. Wanda lives in New York City—at least, she is to be found there most of the time.

Neighbors? smiled Wanda, in that same old-time, teasing way. What is a neighbor, pray tell? I have seen the word, and when I spend the summer in the country, I meet what are called "the neighbors," but here in New York—impossible! I don't believe we have such a thing! Most of us live in apartments or hotels, and if anyone is so fortunate as to have a whole house to himself, it is just a slice of a long block of houses that look as tho they got melted in July, and are trying to be one big house: but the people inside will have no such thing. Sometimes I think that the only homey people in a skyscraper are the janitor's household on the top floor. I knew of one literary janitor who had a Swiss chalet built on the roof of an apartment house, yes, and he kept real chickens, too. But as for the office occupants, how they do not love each other! Oh, I am so sick of these stone beehives and whole acres of gigantic cracker-boxes! Actually, I have seen a biscuit factory that takes up a whole square! Think of the windows! And the human ants that crawl in to work, and then out again, in and out, in and out!

But by neighbors, I explained, I mean, my dear Wanda, primarily the people who live next door to you. Surely you have a next door.

Oh, yes, but of course we don't know much of anybody close at hand except the grocer and the druggist. So many people move into our apartment house that half the time I am not even familiar with the names of the people who live across the hall on the same floor.

How many feet across is your hallway?

How absurd you are! laughed Wanda. Why, about six or eight feet, I should judge.

Hm! a grave is usually dug six feet down, isn't it?

Don't be so dolorous, you crazy boy! burst out my cousin. I don't forget them as completely as all that! I had an odd experience the other day. A woman rang our bell, and asked through the speaking-tube whether Mrs. Charles Cranberry were at home. I told her that I had never heard of such a person. The voice then wanted to know whether there were not a Mrs. Cranberry in the building? I replied that I had no idea, but that I would gladly come down to the front door, and look over the names that were printed on the mail-boxes in the hall. Really, I was rather annoyed by the interruption, for I was in the middle of writing invitations to my Thursday tea.

No such name as Cranberry was visible. I called the janitor, and after he had consulted his book, he decided that there must be a mistake. As the woman had a little child with her, and looked clean, and very tired, I asked her upstairs for a cup of tea. Our new cook, Annie, came into the room, squealed with pleasure, threw her arms about the neck of the newcomer, nearly ate up the little girl, and exclaimed, "Cousin Lottie!" Well, it turned out that the last name of our latest domestic was Cranberry. When we hired her, it didn't come into my head to ask her last name.

Very illuminating, I commented. I imagine that you have had other curious adventures, or at least experiences in dealing with—with persons who happen to live within a few feet of your flat?

Not many that I recall, but I shall never forget the time that we thought burglars were in the apartment. Jim was away on one of his trips, and Flitta, Honora, and I were waked about 2:00 A.M. by a strange crash on the roof,—we could hear the noise through the court-window of our bedroom—as tho a chimney had blown down. Pretty soon we heard the dumb-waiter machinery groaning, and then the sound of a man getting out of that dumb-waiter into our kitchen, mind you! No one but a schoolboy had ever before thought of squeezing into our package-lift, and only the repairman would dare to ride in the top, so that we three whispered, "Burglars!"

Now we heard footsteps—heavy footsteps! Then came a loud, official, authoritative knock on the closed door of the dining-room,—the door was open that led from there into our bedroom. Turning the key of the kitchen door, I said through the keyhole, in a rich, firm, dramatic chest-tone, "Who is there? The pistol is ready!" This was not a fib, because my husband's automotic lay loaded and ready, so to speak, in the top drawer of the chiffonier.

"Pardon us, please, and don't have any apprehensions," came a nice voice with a laugh in it. "We are merely a pair of army aviators from Mineola, and after a bit of an accident, we happened to plump down on your roof. We're awfully sorry that we made such a racket. . . . Thank you, no, we are not at all nicked up. The roof stairway door was locked, quite naturally, and after we had boarded the upper deck of the dumb-waiter, it got stuck at your floor, instead of taking us down to the basement. Of course, we are more than pleased to have the honor of calling on you. Otherwise, we should have paid our respects to the janitor, at General Headquarters."

Delighted to hear your voice, Major, I answered in my usual tone. Kindly stir up the fire, and put on some water. My daughters and I will shortly join you, and we shall have an enjoyable breakfast together.

Most extraordinary! I breathed. Please go on!

Well, pursued Wanda, they proved to be very fine young men of the best families, and last week Honora was engaged to one of those officers, Lieutenant John Townley.

Congratulations! By this time I suppose you are quite reconciled at having birdmen tap at the window, or glissade to the fire-escape. But now that we are on the subject of neighbors, do you mind if I satisfy my curiosity as to whether you have had any commonplace, or actually disagreeable encounters with fellow apartmentarians?

Continuing, my apartment-house cousin Wanda said, It is disagreeable to live under the same roof with a lot of jumbled-up human beings whom we have little or no desire to get acquainted with. The only reason that we live in this way is because we haven't the money to stay in New York and do otherwise.

One time, in a particularly crowded street-car (we are too poor for taxis, except now and then)—a car that smelled horribly of garlic—my daughter Flitta gasped, "Mother, darling, in all this car there is not one person that I would want to meet socially!"

Wanda and I laughed together, but I fear that my own contribution to the mirth was of the acid variety. Poor Flitta! What a weazened apple this world of ours must already have become to her!

However, I said, your apartment house can't be so intolerable as a trolley car, for you can always creep inside your four walls, can't you, and shut the door?

Not at all, my dear coz, came back Wanda. We haven't four genuine walls, or even one wall. Our ceiling is somebody else's floor, and our floor is somebody else's ceiling, and we have to keep up some of the windows, even in the dead of winter. There are noises from the court, and street, and back yard, and up and down the dumb-waiter shaft; noises in and on the steam-pipes, and noises from the telephone, not to mention noises from above and below, paticularly from above.

I can not describe the lineaments

of the new family that has moved in over us within the last two weeks, but I should estimate that there are fifteen or twenty children, ranging from one year to manhood. I can detect the patter of small, but heavy feet on my kitchen ceiling, which isn't padded, you know: "bump" would be a more exact term than "patter." Sometimes I am inclined to guess that beside the children, there is a Shetland pony. Every boy in the group must own a toy locomotive and a baseball bat, and every daughter a flat-iron and a pair of roller-skates, and all of these possessions are constantly being dropt, or thrown. Oh, those endless games of tag! And that tinny piano! And those dancing feet! It is providential that our chandelier hasn't come out by the roots. If it did, we should all be asphyxiated before I could insert a cork!

Youngsters, I agreed (I have seven of my own), are often given to self-expression. It takes the quiet business man to snore all night in the sleeping-car as tho he were the locomotive and not the passenger.

Apartment houses and hotels, groaned Wanda, with deep emotion, are no places for growing children. Thank my stars, Flitta and Honora have passed the pigtail stage, and when they were in it, I took no nonsense from them. I don't wonder that the most exclusive hostelries refuse children. I heard of a family man who became so exhausted from being turned down by landlords that he got his words mixed and begged for an apartment of six baths and a room. If my two girls had been boys, I would unfailingly have packed them off to boarding-school in the winter, and to a Maine camp in the summer. Not that I don't like children. You remember the wonderful games that we used to play at your father's during the holidays?

Perhaps, I wickedly suggested,

there ought to be no cities at all, just towns and country, and every one the baron of his own little castle, or private park.

Not at all! disagreed Wanda, with that decided set of the mouth that has distinguished woman for the past few thousand years. I just love a big city, and all its excitements!

I can see that you do, I dryly commented. But let's return to those proximate people across the hallway, and below your apartment.

Don't ask me! objected Wanda, but on the other side of the court, in the next building, there is a young woman who does vocal exercises until I am nearly frantic. There ought to be a municipal "Howling Alley" where such people could be penned.

How are Flitta and Honora getting on with their music? I remember with what distinction they used to play a piano duet called, "The Twins at Breakfast."

Our Flitta is doing well with the tenor saxophone, and Honora is developing a charming contralto. But it's amusing when she catches a cold, and tries to practise, and her contralto becomes a positive bass. I'm thankful that my dear girls show real musical talent. I don't let them take all of their exercises in the house; they spend a good deal of time in the studio with Dr. Mel and Professor Zizzini.

Wanda here left the room to return with some wonderful chocolate cake.

Do you find apartment house life fairly healthful? I questioned, after we had talked on other subjects, such as the hoped-for motor-car that my cousin was dreaming about. We country people do not necessarily keep well during the winter.

To tell you the truth, we hardly ever hear of sickness being prevalent on our block. I have occasionally visited friends in the hospital, and at their homes. We are careful to keep away from those germ-laden slums and side streets. No social settlement nonsense for my girls! I fancy that it is the policy for apartment house proprietors to hush up sickness and death as much as possible. One time I saw a piece of crape on the opposite door, and I tell you it didn't take me long to pack off Flitta, Honora, and myself for a visit with Aunt Nettie in Roselle Park. Funerals and mourners are terribly depressing.

How old a person had died? I inquired.

I'm unable to say. There were no white ribbons. I can't remember whether they were lavender, violet, or plain black. But one very sad thing did happen three years ago. It was thrust upon us, so to speak, I heard the police smashing into the apartment below us, and when I questioned them, they told me that they had been sent around with a man from the telephone company. An old man and his sister had been living all by themselves. The woman must have fallen ill, and her brother must have tried to phone. It seems as tho, after he had taken down the receiver, he must have stumbled and struck his head: perhaps he also was ill at the time. In any case, when the police arrived, both of these people were lying dead in the winter's cold. (You remember that fuel famine, when we all had to take to kerosene- and gas-heaters.) I was sorry that I had not gone in to see them, now and then. What was their name? I have such a poor memory for names!

When I had reached home again, my wife said, It's all very well for you to make fun of your cousin Wanda for being so unneighborly, but you and I are mighty feeble neighbors in comparison with two South African lepers that Dr. Holbeck watched at work. One leper had no hands; the other had no feet. The man without hands was carrying the man without feet, and he, in turn, carried the seed bag, and dropt a seed now and then, which the handless man pressed into the ground with his feet; and so, between the two of them, they did the work of one man, and showed how much they cared for each other.

True enough, my dear, I responded. And speaking of responsibility to our neighbors, did you ever hear what is done by the officials of a certain Chinese province when a son murders his father?

No, but I suppose that you are trying to go my South African story one better!

The governor of this midland province, I went on, had the houses of all the neighbors pulled down as a punishment for their not having had a better influence over the criminal!

We will do well to cherish these words from the records of Merlin: Therefore men seyn an olde sawe, who hath a goode neighbour hath goode morowe.

If everyone, wrote Barnett, who professes to care about the poor would make himself the friend of one poor person, there would soon be no insoluble problem of the masses, and London would be within measurable distance of becoming the city of happy homes.

Neighborliness, then, goes far deeper than saying a jocund "Good morning! How is everybody?" or than purring out dozens of "My dears," and "So sorrys." It goes way down deeper than loaning the lawn mower, or sitting beside the sick-bed. It goes far, far below being "nice" to people who belong to the same lodge, or political club, or regimental company, or religious body. Neighborliness must begin in the mind, the heart, and the tongue.

THE ENCHANTED GROUND OF IMAGINATION

The Rev. Ralph Baxter Larkin, Berkeley, Cal.

"There is an enchanted middle ground between virtue and vice, where many a soul lives and feeds in secret, and takes its payment for the restraint and mortification of its outward life."

These words were written many years ago by Dr. J. G. Holland and they have a sharp point. They probe to the heart of nearly every moral disaster that ever overtakes a human soul. The "enchanted middle ground" is a region that lies in the realm of the imagination. It is in this realm that human destiny is almost wholly determined. Dr. Holland was speaking of that very great number of people who lead outwardly correct lives, who nevertheless perform acts in imagination which they would not dare to perform in actual fact. They have enough sense of right, enough conscience, to keep them outwardly upright; but they are not so controlled by right principle but that they will willingly allow their secret imagination to revel in forbidden fields.

This is pitifully in accord with the facts of human nature. People permit themselves in thought to commit acts which they would not dare to commit in practise. They exult, even if not always recognizing the fact, in the "enchanted middle ground." It is a kind of compromise with their souls, in which they try to even up matters — seeking reprisals, so to speak, to compensate them for being so correct in outward life. Missing so much in practise, they try to make it up to themselves in secret thought! There may often be no intention of doing wrong in this. It is "only an attempt to filch from sin all the pleasure that can be procured without its penalty."

This may be the purpose in it, but let him who does it understand very well that he does not escape the penalty. The detested practise is sin whether it leads to outward act or not. No man has any right to dally in thought with sins which he dare not commit. He that does needs a purifying moral bath and disinfectant.

There is virtually no such thing as a sudden moral downfall. Moral disasters are a result, not an accident. They have been prepared for. Thought has preceded act. Sudden temptation is usually harmless unless the soul to which it comes is in a state of impaired moral resistance. Impure imaginings or unworthy empty thinking inevitably bring about in a soul a condition of low moral resistance. Dr. Holland puts this strongly:

A pure soul sternly standing on the ground of virtue, or a pure soul standing immediately in the presence of vice, not once in ten thousand instances bends from its rectitude. It is only when it willingly becomes a wanderer among the wiles of temptation, and an entertainer of the images it finds there, that it becomes subject to the power that procures ruin.

Dr. Holland has a very graphic illustration which I am loath to omit. He likens the realm of forbidden imagination to a voluptuous fairy island in the sea of life, known only by individual personal discovery. The voyagers to it are all unseen to each other and the voyages themselves are secret.

Out toward this charmed island, by day and by night, a million shallops push unseen of each other, and of the realm of real life left behind, for revelry and reward! The single sailors never meet each other; they tread the same paths unknown of each other; they come back, and no one knows, and no one asks where they have been. Again and again is the visit repeated, with no absolutely vicious intention, yet not without gathering the taint of vice. If God's light could shine upon this crowded sea, and discover the secrets of the island which it invests, what shameful retreats and encounters should we witness—fathers, mothers, maidens, men—children even, whom we had deemed as pure as snow—flying with guilty eyes and white lips to hide themselves from a great disgrace.

"The pitcher that goes often to the well gets broken at last."

How much leeway shall a man give his imagination in this middle ground between virtue and outward vice? To ask the question is to answer it. It has only one answer—in principle. But in actual practise—ah, that is another matter! My brother, here you need the grace of God if ever you need it anywhere.

EVOLUTION, THE BIBLE, AND RELIGION [1]

By Frederic J. Gurney

[In the June number we printed two articles on God and Evolution. One of our subscribers, after reading them, propounded to us the following question: "Would it not be well to ask some one who has some first-hand knowledge of the subject to contribute an article on evolution?" We deem the following a fair and constructive treatment of the question as stated in the title, and it is here reproduced, in part, by permission of the University of Chicago Press. We purpose later a fuller discussion of the facts of evolution. —Eds.]

THE ISSUE: Evolution as a principle in nature has come to be accepted in practically all departments of knowledge and all lines of investigation. It is only because of a supposed hostility to religion that there are still some people combating it. So much is being said and written against it in certain quarters as an enemy of the Christian faith that a plain statement of the case is not untimely. . . .

THE EVIDENCE: Evolution is the process through which God made the world and all that dwell therein. This is what the theory means. It includes the entire universe—all the heavenly bodies, even the most remote, our own solar system, the earth in its formation, and all forms of life, vegetable and animal, which inhabit it. So it embraces astronomy, the study of the heavens; geology, the study of the earth; botany, the study of plant life; and zoology, the study of animal life; and it includes man with all his capacities and all his achievements. The principle underlying it is—development, from the simplest forms to all the infinite variety and the infinitely complex and highly organized forms that now exist. So it is commonly called the development theory. From time to time during many centuries thoughtful observers of nature had felt their way toward this theory, but the working of it out into a thorough-

going system has taken place within the past seventy-five years. It was in 1859 that Charles Darwin published his *Origin of Species* and in 1871 followed his *Descent of Man*. These were epoch-making books, which, together with the works of Alfred R. Wallace, another great English scientist, put the subject of the evolution of living things prominently before the world. So the term "Darwinism" is not infrequently used, tho scientific men restrict this term to certain phases of the subject.

Within a few decades the development theory, by the sheer force of its reasonableness and its helpfulness in understanding the material universe, established itself in all the natural sciences. More than thirty years ago, Professor Joseph Le Conte, an eminent geologist and a devout Christian man, said:

Evolution is no longer a school of thought. The words *evolutionism* and *evolutionist* ought not any longer to be used, any more than *gravitationism* and *gravitationist*, for the law of evolution is as certain as the law of gravitation.

When once the pathway was made clear, there was a great stimulus to the first-hand study of nature, and men gave themselves to the task with keen ardor and in increasing numbers. The result was that in every department of natural science facts in most amazing array have been discovered

---

[1] The University of Chicago Press, Chicago, Ill., 10 cents.

by observation and experiment and have been most carefully studied, both minutely in themselves and comprehensively in relation one to another. The knowledge of nature as a whole has been extended and systematized to a degree that may well excite the admiration and enthusiasm of every intelligent person. More important still is the establishing of evolution as a principle. Not only is it seen to be true as a theory of how things came to be as they are, but it also furnishes the method of study for advance along all lines. . . . In existing animal and vegetable life, from the highest forms to the lowest, the vital process is traced back to the simplest beginnings. In the structure of the earth a like continuity is found in the formation of mountains and plains, rocks and soil, and all other features that go to make up the planet on which we live. In the remains of extinct life, found in such abundance beneath the surface, the same is true. Again and again have various "missing links" been found by further explorations. New forms, intermediate between those already known, are frequently unearthed. So far as evidence is concerned, the chain is practically complete. In all departments of human knowledge and investigation men work on the basis of evolution as a matter of course and find it a valid and trustworthy principle.

THE OBJECTION: When this point in the story is reached, we meet objections from two classes of people. Some see the force of these facts and the irresistible inferences from them, but are perplexed and bewildered because they do not see how to square all this with their belief in the Bible. . . . It will help them greatly if they will go with open mind along the line of argument . . . here following. The outcome will give them a sense of relief and freedom, as it has already given to thousands of others. They will get a new vision of truth, an enlarged conception of God and of man's relation to him that will be of priceless value. Others seem hopelessly sure that everything scientific is wrong or at least is open to suspicion of being antireligious. One can but wish that they would open their minds and look, without fearing that newly discovered truth will undermine the Christian faith.

Just here the question is raised, But what about the Bible, particularly the first chapter of Genesis? The answer is, essentially: Nothing about it; so far as the study of external nature is concerned, it forms no part of the evidence.

The earth is the Lord's and the fulness thereof;
The world and they that dwell therein.

It is as truly our privilege and our duty to study the world before us, of which we are a part, and to accept its testimony in the material field as it is to study the Bible and accept its testimony in the spiritual field. We had to use our minds to decide whether we would believe the Bible. Why not enlarge our vision and consider also what God has to tell us through other channels? The testimony of the material world is this: Careful and thorough and unprejudiced study points unmistakably and unavoidably to a process of evolution as the method by which the world came to be as it is. Why not accept that testimony? But is not the Bible the inspired and infallible Word of God, and must we not accept what it says at face value as against any human theory however plausible, and does it not tell us very plainly how the world was made? Now this is the crux of the whole matter. If we must regard the Bible as a first and last word on all subjects, dictated by the Creator to human amanuenses and binding our understanding without reference to what may be learned from any and all other works of God, we are in a serious dilemma. The visible works of God tell us one thing and the dictated words of God seem to tell us another and very different thing.

This difficulty took shape in the minds of religious leaders as soon as the theory was clearly set forth. Forced to admit the reality of much that had been discovered in the realm of natural science and yet fearful for religion, they began to devise various lines of argument in order to save the faith without denying the plain facts of nature. The commonest and most plausible theory has been to regard the six days of creation as six ages, and try to make them correspond to the successive periods of which the geologists have found evidence in the history of the earth. The figurative statement in the Bible that one day is with the Lord as a thousand years gave color to this theory, and certain broad parallels between the geologic ages and the creative acts on successive days as narrated in Genesis seemed further to support it.

Concerning such efforts Professor Henry Drummond, another eminent scientist, . . . wrote:

Science is tired of reconciliations between two things that ought never to have been contrasted, and the critics have rightly discovered that in most cases where science is either pitted against religion or fused with it, there is some fatal misconception to begin with as to the scope and province of either.

Indeed, the more thoroughly we read the rocks and the more candidly we read the Scriptures the plainer does it become that such harmonizing devices are ingenious and interesting rather than convincing and satisfying.

THE RECOGNITION OF SCRIPTURE: But we are not under any obligation to interpret the Bible in such a mechanical fashion. There is a far easier way to avoid the difficulty, a way that is also better because it is true, and that is, simply to recognize the fact, that the dilemma is imaginary and not real. The Bible is a library of books whose one concern is religion, not natural science. They were written ages before natural science was born. They reflect the conceptions of nature that were current when they were written, but it is religion, spiritual truth, which they aim to impart, not a knowledge of nature or the history of the earth. To force the Bible or any part of it into service as a scientific treatise confuses people's ideas about nature and also does violence to the spirit and purpose of the Scripture itself. The Bible displays an intimate acquaintance with nature and a love and appreciation of its beauties, for it is the literature of a people who lived largely in the open and were familiar with God's out-of-doors. . . . In the first chapter of Genesis itself the evident aim is to set forth God as the Creator and man as made in his image, the crown of the creative process, whom God set over the works of his hands. Simple, dignified, lofty in conception, poetic in form, it contains lessons of priceless spiritual value for the men of the writer's time and of all time, but it has nothing to teach the twentieth century as to the actual process of creation. God left mankind to discover that for themselves, just as he has left them to discover

many other things in life, by observation and experience. The primitive ideas concerning nature have merely been outgrown. It was vitally important, however, that man's spiritual training should begin in the childhood of the race. This is precisely our way now in family life, that is if we are wise. We begin to teach our children the difference between right and wrong at the very outset. We train them in morals, we strive to lead them into a conscious spiritual life just as early as they are capable of it, and they are capable of it earlier than many people suppose. Children can appreciate the essential spiritual things long before they can understand the things which eventually make up their intellectual equipment. That is the way God has dealt with the race, as we find recorded in the Bible. . . .

THE WORDS OF NATURE: When it comes to understanding nature, the natural and reasonable thing to do is to open and read the book of material things which the hand of the Creator has laid before us. The way to find out how God made the earth is to look and see how he is making it now. Formative processes are going on all the time.

The waters wear the stones,
The overflowings thereof carry away the dust of the earth.

Rivers are carrying down their silt and building flood plains in their curves and deposits on the bed of the ocean, the wind is drifting the sand, volcanoes and earthquakes are making changes in the earth's surface, and other forces are at work each in its own way. Most of these processes are slow and are unnoticed by the casual observer, but they are quite apparent to one who will take the time to look. The formations they produce are precisely like those found below the surface, even in the vast strata very far below, which are manifestly very, very old. There is no reason at all to doubt that these earlier formations were made by the same processes as those now at work. And as they are far more vast in extent than the visible surface formations, it is manifest that the time occupied in forming them must have been incalculably longer. The way to find out how God made living creatures is to see how he is making them now. Of all the myriad forms, animal and vegetable, which people the earth, not one individual of any kind springs into being full grown, unless it be the very simplest organisms consisting of only a single cell. They all come by growth—from germ to lily of the field, from germ to sturdy oak, from germ in the egg to full-fledged eagle, from germ in the womb to full-grown man. This is God's way of making living creatures at the present time. There is no reason at all to doubt that the vital processes now at work have been working throughout the ages, or that God made the race in the same way that he now makes the individual, by gradual processes. And as the race is incalculably greater than the individual, so the time occupied must have been immeasurably greater. A vital force, divinely implanted, continually urging upward, and a marvelous power of adaptation to external conditions, have in the course of ages brought into being the wonderful world that now is.

THE REACTIONARIES: What we are considering is process. We need not raise the question as to the origin of all things. That is a philosophical question, and may be left to the philosophers. The important thing is to recognize frankly what nature teaches us about God's way of doing these things. But the reactionaries, the people who are suspicious of everything scientific and are afraid for the faith, are not willing to be convinced, no matter how cogent the evidence may be. "No," they say, "we must hold the old ground and not concede anything to the unbelievers. If we yield at all the faith is gone." But the difficulty is that the old ground will no longer hold us. It long ago became utterly unstable, and it is folly, worse than folly, to try to maintain an argument for religion on ground which for years and years past has been crumbling under our feet more and more completely every day. . . . The development theory has come to stay. . . . It is the carefully wrought product of the most painstaking, thoroughgoing research by men who have given their lives to the study of nature. It is not speculation but investigation that they have carried on. Their work has been done at first hand and with unshrinking intellectual honesty. Their findings all lead to the same general conclusion. No man who denies this conclusion has a right to demand, on religious grounds or on any other, that we accept his contrary judg-

ment until he, too, has gone through the same thorough investigation and can show valid reasons for denying it. The theory is being modified in details and will continue to be modified as time goes on and further facts come to light, but this does not affect the principle; that is established beyond debate. . . . The traditional conception . . . is simply the inheritance from past ages, when men judged only by casual appearance and thought about nature as children do now. It is as completely outgrown as the belief that our earth is the center of the universe.

"But the development theory," it is said, "rules out God entirely and leaves us in a universe of mere matter and blind force." It does nothing of the sort; it opens our eyes to see how God works. It enables us to discover behind the wonders and beauties of his world the still greater marvels of the method by which he has produced it. It does not solve all problems, does not pretend to, but it does answer the question How? in the realm of visible and tangible things. "But," it is objected once more, "this theory makes us nothing more than animals. We are not made in the image of God after all." It does nothing of the sort. Humanity is what it is, however it came to be. A man is no less a man because he was once a baby in arms. It is just as true as it ever was that man is a spiritual being. It is just as true as it ever was that he has intellectual capacities which can not be filled by material things, that he has spiritual aspirations which can not be satisfied with the things of time and sense. On the other hand, it is no more true than it was before, but only just as much so, that man has a physical being, that in his body there is an undeniable kinship to the lower animals, and that in dealing with human nature, whether theoretically or practically, this fact must be taken into account. . . .

Another objection that is often put forward as an argument is, that scientific men themselves do not agree in regard to evolution. Of course they do not. Why should they? How can they be expected to? Is not the same thing true in every realm? What two theologians agree in their statements of Christian truth? There are theological tenets without number by which teachers of religion attempt to state Christianity in terms that may satisfy their intellectual conceptions. Many of these tenets differ widely and some contradict each other, yet all these men base their teachings on the Bible. Nevertheless a man would be a fool who would argue from this disagreement that Christianity is false and the spiritual teaching of the Bible is not worthy of belief. In the great basic facts of Christian life and the saving power of the gospel they all agree. It is in the explanation of the facts that they do not see alike. Precisely the same thing is true in the realm of natural science. As to the fact of evolution there is no disagreement at all among scientific men, but the field is vast beyond conception, the forces of nature act in ways innumerable, and their operations are exceedingly complex. It is therefore not only natural but inevitable that in studying these things, in order if possible to ascertain the causes and method of evolution, men should differ in their views. Some put more stress on one set of forces and others more on another. No one claims to have explained everything but they keep on investigating, confident that further study will reap further results.

THE REVOLUTION: The development theory can not be put as a patch on the old conception of nature; it takes the place of it entirely. . . . It is a great advance in our knowledge of the world and of human nature. It is of inestimable value in the solution of the problems of life, personal, social, and religious. The theory is revolutionary, as the Copernican theory was. . . . Men proved from the Bible that Columbus was wrong when he said the earth was round. Nevertheless his ships, when they ventured on unknown seas, did not sail off the edge of a flat world into the void, and it was only a few years later that Magellan's fleet sailed all the way around. Men proved from the Bible that Copernicus was wrong and made Galileo recant on his knees the belief that the earth moves around the sun. Yet it really does move around the sun and it had always been doing so.

"But," say the reactionaries, "this theory raises many serious difficulties. If we take our stand on the new ground, we encounter more difficulties than on the old." So be it, but they are difficulties of another sort. They do not involve us in absurdity. They do not require us to shut our eyes to well-ascertained facts or try to explain them

away. . . . They are difficulties of unsolved problems and unexplored fields. Such difficulties offer a splendid challenge to Christian scholarship. They call to men who know that humanity is not all included in terms of biology to give their lives to the solution of these problems and not leave the field to men whose interest is in the material side of the subject alone. They offer a noble appeal to faith; that faith is . . . a calm confidence that the Creator who gave us eyes to see and minds to think will not disappoint us when we study without hesitation all the things he has made, that all truth is from him and is for us, and that things material are intended as helps to the spiritual life and can be made to serve it.

THE FALSE ALTERNATIVE: Indeed, precisely this result is coming to pass. In the earlier period of the controversy many scientific men were repelled and took an attitude that was non-religious, tho not necessarily antireligious, because of the violent attacks made by many well-meaning but shortsighted defenders of the faith. These attacks did a vast amount of harm to the cause of religion, not a little of which continues to this day. They confused the issue by raising a false alternative, and forced men into opposing camps while both parties were really seeking for truth. In recent years, however, a truer view has been arising, and many men of truly Christian spirit are working in these fields with the Christian faith as their spiritual ground. It is childish and absurd to stigmatize men as unbelievers because they are scientific scholars.

THE UNSETTLING OF FAITH: In the renewed controversy at the present time it is the zealous but unperceiving religious leaders who are doing the most harm. They have raised again the false alternative. They are saying, in effect: "You must believe everything in the Bible as being literal fact just as it stands, or you can not be a Christian. You must believe that the world was made in six days of twenty-four hours or you can not follow Jesus Christ." The position is false. Jesus himself said nothing like that, and there is nothing of the sort in the Great Commission. His appeal is to the heart and the life. His religion is a spiritual matter, not a matter of belief concerning the material world. Faith in him, obedience to him, living his life, does not depend on the rejection of evolution or on the rejection or acceptance of any view of the external world.

The charge is frequently made that the faith of young people is wrecked in the schools, particularly in the state universities, by the scientific teaching which they get. It is quite true, more's the pity, that there are still scientific men who seem indifferent to religion and some whose attitude dislodges a young person's faith from the ground it occupied in childhood, quite unconcerned as to whether he finds a surer ground. But the remedy lies not in denouncing science or even the scientist, but in helping the youth to find the surer ground. . . . Far more harm has been done, far more young people have suffered the wreck of their religious faith, by the attitude of short-sighted religious advisers who have insisted on erroneous views of nature as essential to religion. .

On the other hand, these critics ignore the fact that thousands of young people have had their religious thinking clarified and their faith confirmed and deepened by contact with teachers who have shown them the surer ground. They have come to see that the object of their trust is not the form in which they held it but the eternal reality behind the form. It is one of the most hopeful aspects of the present situation that there are already many able teachers who recognize this need and are earnestly endeavoring to meet it. Their students are going out into the world with clear mind and high purpose, ready to help others solve their problems as they themselves have been helped. Again, there are not a few young folks who come from homes and churches where the religious stress has been laid on the spiritual side of life, on purpose and conduct and personal relation to God, who find no difficulty on religious grounds with any scientific teaching which they get. Having grown up with an appreciation of realities rather than a mere devout literalism, they find that knowledge of the material world is a help not a hindrance to their faith.

THE RECONSTRUCTION OF THEOLOGY: At this point the question is asked, Must we, then, reconstruct our theology? Some religious leaders surely must do so or they will be left stranded beside the unresting sea of human inquiry and human spiritual need. This is not the first time in Christian history that men have had to reconstruct their theology and it will not be the last. Theology is not a closed science any more than other departments of human thought. But what basis is there left if the old-time reliance on the Bible is taken away? The answer to this question is immediate and final: "Other foundation can no man lay than that which is laid, which is Jesus Christ." As Jesus is the corner-stone of the Christian's faith, so is he also the foundation of the Christian's theology. Just here the reactionaries make a stand with an objection which they think is fatal to the whole case. "The development theory," they say, "does not account for Jesus Christ, and it should do so if it is really comprehensive." True, emphatically true, it does not. But let us ask in all seriousness, does the theory that God made the world in six days by a series of creative fiats by which he spoke all things suddenly out of nothing, account for Jesus Christ? Men have been trying for nineteen hundred years to account for Jesus Christ, and neither his foes nor his friends have succeeded in doing so. He is one of the unsolved problems, perhaps the greatest problem of all. When a person sets out to account for an ultimate he is undertaking a very difficult task. And Jesus Christ is the ultimate man; no human being at all comparable to him has come within human knowledge. But he is no less real because we can not explain him. He is both real and accessible. We can recognize him as God's message to the world, the "Word" who "was made flesh and dwelt among us." Tho we can not comprehend him, we can apprehend him. Tho we can not account for him by our philosophy, we can come into personal relation with him in spiritual life; we can lay hold on him and be laid hold on by him. And precisely this is the personal experience of millions of people to-day, as it has been the experience of millions throughout the Christian centuries. Herein lies the power of Christianity. "Progressive experience," says William N. Clarke, "makes an ever-growing Church, and out of the ever-growing life of the Church comes an ever-growing theology, with the indwelling Spirit of God as the guide of its progress."

Now when we say that Jesus Christ is

the foundation of Christian theology we are on strictly scientific ground and are using the scientific method. The scientific method is: first get your facts, then build your theory. Jesus Christ is the supreme outstanding fact of all history. The influence of his brief earthly career on human events surpasses immeasurably the influence of all other moral and spiritual forces put together. The power of his living personality over men's thoughts and conduct and character at the present time is incomparably the greatest uplifting force in human life, both individual and social. The fact of Christ and the facts of Christian experience are as real as the facts of the material world. They are as valid data for constructing a science of theology as the other facts are for constructing a theory of evolution. Build theology directly on Christ. . . .

In reconstructing theology, then, so far as it may need reconstruction, we may safely begin with Christ. On the vital themes of human life and conduct and character he speaks with the assurance of one who knows what is in man, and as one living in conscious harmony with God. His teaching has behind it the self-evidencing power of truth, his gospel meets the deepest human needs. So when we come to the great underlying questions of the being and nature of God, the nature of man and his relation to God and his fellow man, the destiny of man, the authority and value of Scripture, the nature and constitution of the Church, if we learn first of all what Christ has to teach us concerning these things, we shall have theological material of lasting value to lay on our foundation. And as we go on in our work and our study, interpreting history and life in terms of Christ and meeting present problems in his spirit, we shall not build

amiss. We do not need to wait for a completed theological system in order to do the work of Jesus Christ in the world. And if we are wise, we shall receive truth from any and every source and recognize it as material to be used in that work, in absolute confidence it is all from the one Eternal Source.

THE OBLIGATION: Practically, therefore. we find ourselves free to study God's word in Scripture, God's leading in human history, God's providence in our own experience and that of our fellow men, untrammeled by any fear that we are doing wrong by honest investigation. As reasonable beings we are logically bound to accept that which is shown by the evidence to be true and to adjust our thinking thereto. As spiritual beings we are morally bound to accept that which manifestly makes for righteousness and to conform our lives thereto. This is an eternal obligation. It is upon us to open our hearts, to dedicate our wills, to devote our strength to that which is highest and truest and best. Recognizing the truth of evolution does not in any way lessen our moral obligation or our spiritual privilege. It does not in any way hinder us from following Jesus Christ, from believing his gospel and acknowledging him as Lord and Master. On the contrary, it enables us to see that in so doing we are entering into the divine plan and putting our wills into harmony with the divine nature.

The following books are helpful to the ordinary reader: Lyman Abbott's *Theology of an Evolutionist*, Scribner's; Drummond's *Ascent of Man*, James Pott & Co.; Lo Conte's *Evolution and Its Relation to Religious Thought*, E. P. Dutton & Co.; Drummond's *Natural Law in the Spiritual World*, A. L. Burt & Co.

COMMENT AND OUTLOOK

BY OUR LONDON CORRESPONDENT

The Tomb of Lazarus

Pilgrims to the Holy Land hardly ever fail to visit a ruined house near Jerusalem of which only an archway and the foundation remain—the house in which, so tradition has it, our Lord spent the last few nights before his crucifixion. A door into the wall leads into what is supposed to have been the garden of Simon the leper, and further on at the roadside there is a square opening in the rock alleged to be the entrance to the grave of Lazarus. Twenty-six steps, slippery with damp, lead into a cave, and from that cave further steps, evidently once covered by a stone, lead to the actual grave.

The Rev. T. Francis Forth, writing in *Theology*, recently visited this spot, and on examining the Greek text of St. John's account of the raising of Lazarus, concludes that it is morally certain that tradition is right in honoring that spot as the actual scene of Lazarus' resurrection. He finds that the word used by St. John, *epekeito*, could not have been used to indicate a stone that stood against the opening of the grave, as was usual among the Jews, but only to describe the unusual method of laying a stone upon the opening, as is the case in the traditional grave. Also, the Greek word used for removing the stone, *airo*, distinctly means "lifting up," it being the same word as that used in the sentence, "Jesus lifted up his eyes." Moreover, Mr. Forth visited many other tombs in the Holy Land and was struck by the fact that this was the only instance of a grave from which the stone had to be lifted, not rolled away. He holds, therefore, that tradition is right, and when we remember the gospel narrative of the number of people who came to Bethany to see Lazarus after he was raised from the dead, we feel there must have been a very strong tradition as to the site of the tomb.

The Retreat Movement

Twenty years ago, or even ten years ago, the very word "retreat" roused general supicion as being something specifically "popish"; to-day it has become a matter of course within the Church of England, and many Free-churchmen are longing for the time when it will be accepted as a common means of spiritual advancement within the Free-churches. In Anglicanism the retreat-houses are multiplying. Whereas until comparatively recently retreats were regarded as the amiable fad of wealthy and leisured folk—mainly of the gentler sex—there are to-day an increasing number of retreats for working people, especially for working men and for factory girls. It is a matter of surprize to those responsible for these retreats how readily working men take to meditation, how fully they appreciate the period of complete silence, and how enthusiastically they testify to the practical good derived from quiet self-examination and the forming of genuine resolutions. The list of retreats in England for 1922 would occupy many pages of this REVIEW, and what strikes one very vividly is the high skill and training of the conductors as compared with, say, ten years ago, and the increasing influence of the retreats upon the lives of the retreatants. More and more the Ignatian ideal is accepted, *i.e.*, the ideal of a retreat the object of which is not to provide exalted thoughts and emotions, but to strengthen the will for self-sacrifice and heroic service. The psychology of the retreat as a means of producing virile souls, ready to venture their all, is increasingly recognized, and a leading Free-church leader, who has made a study of these retreats, remarked to me lately that non-conformity would never regain its ancient force until both ministers and peo-ple ceased "this endless noisy 'yapping'" and took stock of themselves in silence and self-discipline. Retreats for clergy and ministers are rapidly increasing and many a ministry, once stale and unprofitable and now at once prophetic and sacramental, owes its rebirth to a well-made retreat.

The Ministry of Healing

Nothing is more notable as characteristic of religious life in England to-day than the growing interest in the question of the ministry of healing. Since M. Coué's visit especially the attention of church people has been drawn to the question of healing as never before. One good result of the publicity given to healing movements is that Christian people are learning to distinguish between healing by mere auto-suggestion and healing by an opening of the whole personality to divine influences. There can be no doubt that healing by a process of auto-suggestion such as M. Coué advocates is fraught with danger just in proportion to its success. It often results either in the suppression of painful symptoms where these symptoms are a danger signal, and their suppression means that help is not sought and death often supervenes when least expected. Or the cure may be genuine and radical, but the effect upon the personality, the soul, is the fostering of egoism and sometimes of megalomania. Over against this, Christian healing goes to the root of the matter and recognizes as the primary condition of a cure not the assertion of self but an attitude of penitence, trust, and whole-hearted concurrence in the will of God. It is significant that so well authenticated a healer as Dr. Pakenham-Walsh, bishop of Assam, whose healing ministry is one of the most remarkable spiritual phenomena of the day, insists upon resignation as a condition of being cured. In his experience a feverish grasp upon life and an unchecked assertion of the will to live so far from promoting a cure either prevent it entirely or make it a cure of the body only, with detrimental effects upon the personality. In every case in which he has cured people—and his cures extend to the most serious organic diseases—it has been when they have ceased to count life a thing to be grasped at and quietly acquiesced, not in slavish submission but in free and virile concurrence in the unknown will of God for them.

Mr. Hickson's Healing Mission

Among Christian healers Mr. J. M. Hickson, who has recently returned from a prolonged visit to the Far East and has again started on a world tour, occupies a unique place. A loyal and devoted Anglican, he regards healing as a corollary of Christ's redemption. He repudiates the cult of mere physical well-being. Mental healing, he contends, shows the power of mind over matter; Christian healing, on the other hand, reveals the power of the spirit—and specifically the power of the spirit of Christ—over both mind and matter. He does not want his audiences to think of him as one endowed with a gift of healing, for he has no power at all to heal the body. All he is prepared to do is to lay hands on the sick in the name of Christ and pray to him to have mercy and help them, first in soul and then in body. That sounds elementary, but the results of Mr. Hickson's healing missions, results which are claimed to have included the restoring of sight to the blind and the healing of lepers, have given occasion for serious thought to some of the best minds in the Church. Mr. Hickson demands faith from his clients—but it is not faith in his power to heal, or belief in the certainty of a cure, but personal faith in Christ, faith which involves penitence—a genuine desire for the amendment of life and for freedom from all that is known to be sin. His recent mission in Aberdeen bore testimony to a deep and wide-spread desire for such comprehensive Christian healing. Thousands came to the altar rails for the laying on of hands, and among the first to kneel there was the bishop of Aberdeen and many of the leading clergy, both Anglican and Presbyterian.

The Martyr Church of Russia

The Russian Church continues to travail in anguish and we must not be misled by the reports of the so-called All-Russian Church Convention which is comprised of representatives carefully selected by Bolshevist officials. The arrest of the Patriarch Tikhon and the noble appeal of Archbishop John of Latvia speak for themselves. The patriarch was arrested for refusing to surrender church property for alleged famine relief, offering instead to undertake genuine famine relief on the Church's own account. Archbishop John, in appealing to the Protestant churches of England and America to come to the defense of the Russian Church, does not deplore the confiscation of its property, for this has served to strengthen it spiritually.

Among prominent Russians who, keeping aloof from the Church in the time of her prosperity, have identified their fortunes with her in the hour of persecution is M. Serge Bulgakof, a well-known professor of economics. Beginning as a Marxian, he was converted to the mystical faith of Soloviev and Dostoyefsky but kept aloof from the Church on account of her subservience and deadness. But when the martyrdom of the Church began and she spoke once more from out the fire with a voice of her own, he not only returned to her but gave up his academic career and became a priest. "Russia is living," he declares, "and Christ is still the Savior. Christ is walking on Russian soil in the ragged garments of a slave. The Russian soul will soon re-echo with the cry, 'Christ is still the Savior,' and will fall at the feet of its Master. There is nothing left but this hope and faith." To-day in Russia the scenes of the nativity are repeating themselves. Once more "simple shepherds" come to see the Holy Child, and once more wise men pour their treasure at his feet. And it is perhaps only in Russia that the Christian soul discovers Christmas joy in the agony of the cross, smiles while it is tortured, and weaves wondrous tales while its heart is breaking.

Portraits of St. Peter and St. Paul

The recent discovery in Rome of portraits which, according to so great an authority as Professor Lanciani, are authentic likenesses of St. Peter and St. Paul by a contemporary has set Dr. Rendel Harris off once more on his pet theory, viz., that St. Peter and St. Paul were always depicted together because they replaced the Heavenly Twins in Roman worship and they frequently appear either as twins or in charge of twin saints. He instances a picture in which the two apostles are depicted as presenting to Christ St. Cosmas and St. Damien, who were twins. Dr. Harris, while evincing the highest respect for the scholarship of Professor Lanciani, believes he dates his discovery a century too soon. The portraits in question, by the way, show St. Peter as possessing a round head covered with curly hair, a beard, strong jaw-bones, and a slanting forehead, while St. Paul is depicted as a bald man with a heavy beard and an aquiline nose. It is characteristic that while Dr. Harris casts doubt upon the portraits, he is quite ready to believe that the carved figures on a silver chalice discovered at Antioch during the war and pronounced by some archeologists to be first century work were contemporary representations of the two apostles.[1]

---

[1] See the HOMILETIC REVIEW for April, 1917, opposite p. 312.

Editorial Comment

The story is told of an old Quaker woman who, while quietly piloting her way to the entrance of a large auditorium, was subjected to discourteous treat-

Civility as an Asset

ment at the hands of an inconsiderate and impatient group of young men. Her niece standing near her was a witness to the unseemly behavior and exclaimed, "Auntie, I should think you would be boiling." "I am boiling, my dear," she answered, "but without steam." She felt the indignity but will power and common sense won a moral victory. In this connection it is pertinent to note that any one who commits a wrong has done himself more harm than the one wronged.

Self-restraint and forbearance under slight or strong provocation are not only educational; they are sure to evoke admiration and make for promotion.

In the hurry of our modern life no one can afford to disregard the little niceties, the charming amenities, the rewarding civilities so essential for the best work in the home, in the school, on our crowded highways, and in the business life of the world. The fact is there is no more hopeful field for the practise and cultivation of civility and its twin sister courtesy than the particular spot where one happens to be. For example, if for a moment one is wedged in some throng and gets very much perturbed, or perchance should enter one of our large stores on bargain day to find every salesman engaged, or should fail in the attempt to stop a bus on signal, the wise and agreeable thing to do then and there is to withhold the steam and let patience do its perfect work.

That choice bit of philosophy, ancient tho it may be, is just as relevant to modern conditions and the strengthening of character as when first uttered:

"He that is slow to anger is better than the mighty;
And he that ruleth his spirit, than he that taketh a city."

This statement reenforces what all experience teaches, that the strong man is the man who governs and controls his temper.

Every life has within itself untold potentialities, and every life has unlimited resources to meet every emergency, every crisis.

Life yields only what one puts into it—this is his capital.

A man's real capital is made up of sterling qualities like chivalry, courage, civility, reverence, and self-control. These are necessary for a well-ordered society.

Incivility should be tabued for it never has aided in the settlement of any dispute. The poet, the philosopher, and scientist all agree in this—that pleasant emotions and

"Pleasant words are as a honeycomb,
Sweet to the soul, and health to the bones."

Recognize the fact that all belong to a moral order in which mutual self-respect is fundamental. Civility, therefore, is something each one owes to the other, regardless of class, color or creed. In the performance of that obligation what is there that compares with it in results?

[113]

"He died at forty-six." These words recently headed a "display ad" in front of a Central Y. M. C. A. building. The idea it was intended to convey
For the Fun of It was that the supposititious individual referred to took no exercise, indulged in no recreation, and as a result did not live out his full measure of days. Many of us have known men who did not know how to exercise or to play and died "old" at a comparatively early age.

The value of varied and systematic exercise has long been recognized, especially for those in sedentary occupations; but giving full scope to the recreative principle in all our activities is only just now coming to full appreciation. Even when the value of play has been perceived it has been thought of as applicable merely to children. School play-grounds, even in the city, reservation of streets for after-school play, public recreation piers, testify to the knowledge that all healthy young animals, including children, must play. But the adult's need of recreation has been less in the mind's eye. We have inherited somewhat of the Pilgrim grimness, and we have sometimes thought of playfulness in a man or woman as "frivolousness" or waste of time.

Implicit testimony has been borne by the world's wise men and women to the value of laughter—which is the spontaneous response to the stimuli of enjoyable experiences. "A good laugh is sunshine in the house," said Thackeray. "The laughter of man is the contentment of God," is the way John Weiss put it. Cheery Ella Wheeler Wilcox coined the much-quoted and variously paraphrased "Laugh and the world laughs with you." And Mr. "Anon." declares that a laugh is worth a hundred groans in any market. We ourselves are inclined to agree, provisionally at least, with him who said, "Beware of the man who never laughs."

This is recreation time. Let us not be afraid of sore muscles and relaxed risibles. God has provided in his varied world many fine touches of the humorous side of life—in the woods, in the fields, and in the waters—lakes, streams, and seas. God's great open spaces have a message and a blessing in store for all vacationists.

✠

The relations between conservatives and progressives in the Protestant churches have reached a point of strain greater than at any time in the past twenty-five years. Can we continue to fellowship one with
Can We Fellowship One With Another another? The answer, it is to be feared, must be No, unless we can find a basis of fellowship other than doctrinal. There is another bond, if we may trust the New Testament, one that is strong enough to hold us all together in spite of our doctrinal differences—and that is Christ himself. Not something about Christ, but Christ. It is the bond of a common experience and not of a common set of beliefs. It goes beneath intellectual formulations to spiritual verities.

If this bond of union in Christ is accepted it is simply impossible for one body of believers to say to another: "You must believe as we do or you can not be Christians." To take that attitude is to set aside the fundamental teaching and spirit of Christ. True fundamentalism founds faith upon Christ and not upon any doctrines or theories about him.

But is it possible for those who differ so widely in all their mental ideas and attitudes to have any real fellowship with each other? To many true

Christians on both sides it seems impossible, and they are frankly saying so. With all due respect to their judgment, it should be pointed out that this position is true neither to original Christianity nor to a genuine comprehensiveness of mind and spirit. Peter, when he became a leader of the Church, was strongly tempted to adopt the Judaistic attitude, but overcame it and became a true catholic. Paul was sorely tried by those who sought to limit Christianity to those who accepted certain beliefs and practises and vigorously opposed those who tried to impose these limitations on others. His own fundamental conviction and principle was: Neither Greek nor Jew, for all are one in Christ. That did not mean that the Jew was called upon to abandon his peculiar ideas and practises, nor the Greek his, but that the uniting possession of both was Christ and in him they could be and are one.

Unless we can adhere to this essential unity in Christ—united in him and agreeing to differ in our doctrinal interpretations and ideas—we shall be untrue to our common faith; and the result will be reproach to ourselves and disaster to our cause.

✠

A hospitable attitude, a warm-hearted greeting, and the cooperative spirit will always do much to calm, encourage, and inspire. An example of this kind of mind is given by Dr. Joseph Fort Newton in his recent book **The Tie That Binds** on "Preaching in London." The occasion is his first preaching service in the City Temple. We cite a few words from his diary indicating his own frame of mind at this time.

Something like panic seized me. . . . It was terrifying. Pacing the vestry floor in my distress . . . my sermon and almost my wits began to leave me.

That, however, is only one side of the picture, and a dismal and discouraging side at that. There is something which his diary did not contain, something infinitely greater in that vestry than an uncomposed and perhaps over-conscious individual. There was an object—a vase of flowers—that represented, yes, was the manifestation of an imminent and an unseen presence.

In the midst of my agony, as I bent over to enjoy the fragrance, I saw a dainty envelop tucked down in it. Lifting it out, I saw that it was addressed to me, and, opening it, this is what I read:

"Welcome! God bless you. We have not come to criticize, but to pray for you and pray with you. THE CITY TEMPLE CHURCH."

Just as soon as this was brought into the foreground nervousness was forgotten, and a gracious ministry of good will was happily inaugurated.

SERMONS I'VE NEVER PREACHED

The Rev. Wm. J. May, Wellingborough, England

I am probably in the midst of the years as far as my active ministry is concerned, and it has been good, if in some ways humiliating, to look before and after and take stock of my work. I have tried to estimate what I have done with my opportunities and to see the influence my ministry has had upon my people. I have made many discoveries, and one of the most interesting has been the discovery of the sermons I ought to have preached but never have. My preaching has been as wide in its range as the ministry of most men, I believe, but I have been too fond of favorite themes and familiar texts, and large areas of Christian truth have been neglected. Here are some of the themes of the sermons I have never preached.

I have never preached on the greatness of humility. I am going to do so, but I ought to have done it before. I know the peril of choosing the chief place and lusting after platform seats, and I know it is one of the deadly lusts which war against the soul. Yet I have allowed my people to live in a world which is forever insisting that the only test of success is to get to the top, even tho it means pushing others aside and stepping on their fingers as you climb the ladder. And I have never warned them of the real failure that is hidden in that apparent success.

Nor have I preached upon courtesy as a Christian virtue. I have often been pained by the sheer rudeness of professing Christian people to each other. They never seem to realize that it is as un-Christian to wound another person's feelings as it would be publicly to strike him on the face. Politely we call it a "well deserved snub," and in our secret hearts we feel a little proud of our smartness. Really it was wounding a soul, and some wounds are a long time healing. That "cutting retort," that "well deserved snub," ought to have meant penitence instead of pride. I want to go back to my people and tell them so.

There I am up against a problem. How can I say these things to them without hurting them? If my people have been blind to these truths, I have been blind also, and it will be fatally easy for me to whip them for their frailty, scourge them for their foolish blindness, and commit all the sins for which I am condemning them. Even preachers have been known to go home after a service and rub their hands and say, "Ah, I made them sit smartly to-day." That is not the test. Did I do them good? Daily I pray to God for mercy. It should be to me a daily reminder how much other men need my mercy. And my people do not need to be chastised so much as to be educated that they may repent and be forgiven. That suggests another theme for an unpreached sermon: "Our Need for Each Other's Mercy."

I shall have to go beyond that. "He that showeth mercy, with cheerfulness," wrote St. Paul. So evidently St. Paul, too, had to do with the people who shew mercy with head shakings, and dismal prophecies, and dark foreboding fears. When I have preached on shewing mercy I shall have to go on to preach on the duty of friendliness, of being friendly to the people it is not easy to be friends with; the people who are not likeable, who rub me the wrong way, who make large and constant demands upon my mercy. For it has occurred to me of late that it can not be very easy for God to be friends with me. There is so much in me that he can not like. I like the schoolboy's definition of a friend: "Some one who knows all about you and still sticks to you." That is the kind of friend I have to be.

These discoveries of new aspects of God's character are delightful and wonderful, and they are always coming. Yet I have never preached on "God's Ministry of Surprise," and asked my people to recall the unexpected blessings, the unhoped for deliverances, the surprizing opportunities which have come to them and invited them on that ground always to be looking forward, always expecting the best, always believing that God has still more surprizing riches of his grace and love to make known to them as the days come and go.

Think of it, you can never come to worship without a feeling that all sorts of wonderful things may happen, all manner of new truths may be revealed to you. Few people remember it, and I have forgotten how many there are in my pews to whom divine worship has become an old habit which has lost most of its meaning. Because I dislike preaching to the people who are not there, I have scarcely ever preached on the duty and value of public worship. I shall have to do so more often in the future.

I remember how during the war I preached in the days when ideals were bright and clear, on "Are We Worth Fighting For?" I shall have to preach again on that topic: "Are We Worth Fighting for Now?" I read descriptions and see pictures of those awful cemeteries in France. I see the war memorials in every little village, but I wish some Sunday I could gather all the people of my town together round the war memorial and ask them: "Are you worth the sacrifice the memorial represents? The ideals you are pursuing, the things you are living for—how do they look in the light of the ideals for which that memorial stands?" I have got to ask myself that question, too.

We are all saying to-day, some cynically and some despairingly, that ideals are as unreal and illusory as dreams, and that it is not worth while living for them. As I face my people week by week and preach ideals to them I see it in their eyes. I am preaching to so many men who have failed, men who have seen the vision and have not had faith enough and power enough to be obedient to it; men who are saying to-day that it is not worth while trying. I have got to create in their souls a spirit that will make them say: "Even tho my dreams prove impossibilities I will not be content with realities. I will go on dreaming my dreams. I will fight the fight, even tho I am beaten. I will finish the course, even if I fall exhausted; I will keep the faith, and I know that my faith will not be in vain."

So I face the future. Even tho I have done it so poorly, I am in love with my job. I would not change it for any position on earth. I am eager for the possibilities opening before me in the days ahead. I am fascinated by the vast new range of material opening out before preachers to-day. There are whole continents of thought and feeling in the religious consciousness which I must explore, open up their wealthy possibilities to my people, be their Joshua as they face the promised land. If I fail to lead, my people will go forward without me. They will not refuse to avail themselves of its possibilities because I decline to press on. I have to serve the present age, to talk the language of the men of my day, and to keep abreast of modern thought that I may know what men are thinking and guide them.

I have to help to guide that new movement which is sweeping the world like a great tidal wave. In theology it is the revolt against "tradition" and a cry for "reality." In music, art, and literature it is a despising of the old standards and a search for new forms of expression.

In international politics it is the passionate demand for liberation, self-determination, and nationality. In domestic politics it is the spirit which, impatient of the limitations of "'democracy," restlessly turns to "Bolshevism." In home life it becomes a surging demand for individual liberty and unrestricted opportunity of self-expression. I am not condoning it. I am not judging it. I am only trying to understand it, endeavoring to conserve all its vast possibilities of good and seeking how best to save it from the awful perils with which it is faced. I know that in the immediate future, at any rate, that is the atmosphere of thought and feeling in which my work must be done. It is a wonderful opportunity. "Good is it in these days to be alive, and to be a preacher."

SUNDAY MEDITATIONS

The Rev. THOS. F. OPIE, Red Springs, N. C.

Liberty Still Calls

"What will you give us?" was the query of the Italian peasants when Garibaldi was trying to raise an army to fight for liberty. "I will give you long marches, heavy loads, hard fighting, and wounds and death," came back the reply—"But with it, 'Freedom'!"

This is indeed the challenge of life. The worth-while achievements—especially that greatest possession of all, "liberty"—come only after toil, warfare, hardship, and even death itself! There is no royal road to freedom—to liberty. The life of the race, the history of nations and the experience of individuals have demonstrated it. *Ad astra per aspera.*

The call to fight the battles of liberty did not end with Garibaldi, nor with Joan of Arc—nor with Washington, nor yet with Foch and Pershing! Not until the entire human race has been liberated and men everywhere are brothers in God will the call of liberty and the hard battles of freedom cease!

The call is heard now in the Church as it never has been before, perhaps. Men are needed to sound the call to service and to duty and to freedom. Men are needed for leadership in the great fight for God and humanity—against the enslaving forces of selfishness and oppression and evil. Never has the Church needed men more than now.

In the past five years the number of men answering the call of the Church, which is the call of liberty in its idealist form, has decreased alarmingly. Every Protestant body has lost in respect to candidates for the ministry.

The call comes to every young man choosing a profession and to men in middle and later life, to come to the help of the Lord and to leadership in his army. And the pay? What can the Church offer? What will be the reward? A hard road and a heavy load, yes! Many a hard battle, yes—and big tasks, yes—and sacrifice and hardship, yes! But it is the battle of liberty. It is the fight for freedom.

And this call in one form or another comes to every aspiring soul. Either you are fighting the battles of disintegration and of evil or the battles of liberty and construction and progress. The call comes as of old, "Where art thou?" May the answer come as of old, "Here am I. Send me"—and, with David Livingstone, "Send me anywhere, if it be forward!"

The Message of the Flowers

Many are the lessons conveyed to us by the flowers, silent messengers of God—beautiful children of the summer. Christ observed them and taught the great lesson of the Father's care by reference to the lilies of the field (see Matt. 6:28). These God has clothed in his own radiant beauty—so that even the regal Solomon was not arrayed like them!

God's loving care and creative temperament, the infinite variety of his mind; his singular attention to detail in its extreme minutiæ; his love of the beautiful—these are all evidenced by the life and beauty of the sweet flowers with which he has embroidered the earth. They speak to us of hope and joy. They signal to us with a subtle sort of botanical wireless telegraphy to appreciate the joys of the present—because these joys, like the fragrant blossoms about us, will soon be passed.

They speak to us of forgetfulness of the disappointments of the past, and of anticipation of the glories of the future. The sweet radiant flower that bloomed and faded and died yesterday leaves its seed—and others more fragrant, richer, and more beautiful will spring up from the soil enriched by its decadence! Yes, the flowers assure us of the continuity of life and of the perpetuity of God's love and care.

As a great artist God has painted marvelous colors and tones into plants and flowers and all the verdant things of the woods and the fields. He uses the rays of the sun as his brush, the clouds of heaven as his palet, the universe as his canvas; and his colors?—the very soul of love and beauty!

But the noblest work of the Great Artist is not in the realm of nature, but in the realm of human nature! It is God's part to paint out the lines of care and worry, the ugly things of selfishness and sin and the repellent things of hate and vileness in the human family and to paint in the graces of patience, resignation, sympathy, tolerance, peace, amity, and love.

This is what God would do with the world to-day. He would paint out the dull grays and the dark reds, and the blacks and yellows which have lowered over the earth and put in cheerfulness and bright colors of peace and international harmony. But men must be the willing subjects of God in this transforming process! Nations and peoples must co-operate with the Almighty if the world's pathway is to lie amid flower beds of beauty and if human life is to be sweet like rare and radiant roses.

The Mountains

Who has never stood on a pinnacle of the mountains and looked out over the ranges stretching like great billows of the sea off in the distance in seemingly endless tiers of mighty hills?

To stand so in the springtime when nature is putting on her new green robes, or on an evening in the summer when she is veiled in rich royal purple, "as tired day sinks into the lap of restful night"—or else in the autumn when golds and yellows and reds run into a riot of russets and browns—this is enrichment and grandeur indeed.

But to view the mammoth ranges on a bright winter morning after a sleet storm, when hills and trees and shrubs are decked in silver sheen, bespangled in pearls, and diamonds, and radiating star-light, and sparkling gleams of glistening grandeur, from a million reflecting points—this is the luxury of divine art! It is matchless and superb.

The hills are the source of our water-power, of our wealth of coal and iron and timber. The mountains afford us our best atmosphere and within the circle of our exalted hills thousands have found health and vigor and the joy of living, which they had lost in the heat and congestion, sharp practise, and enervating climate of the lowlands.

In the mountains the air is fresh and invigorating and one seems closer to God and exalted above sordid selfishness and the clamor of relentless commerce and competition, and the sorrow and suffering of cities.

Go to the woods and the hills—no tears
Dim the sweet look which nature wears.

KINDLING AND INSPIRING THOUGHTS

What we love, that we see; and what we see, that we are.—DEAN INGE.

The most living thought becomes frigid in the formula that expresses it.—HENRI BERGSON.

Man has in religion at least always been more autocratic than God.—EDWARD B. POLLARD.

It is the common human heart that makes us philosophers and theologians.—JOHN A. HUTTON.

A man who keeps his word and makes good his promises will attract friends of equal worth.—WILLIAM FEATHER.

Definition of poetry: "I am truth singing in disguise and unconscious of an audience." —GEORGE MATHESON.

Life is a great glad game, Elisha, to those who play it gladly; a high adventure, to those who enter upon it with a high heart.—DAMON DALRYMPLE.

The crying need for to-day is for some great reconciling power that would still the war of creeds which set men fiercely fighting when they should be cooperating.—E. WAKE COOK.

A nation is a body of people united by a corporate sentiment of peculiar intensity, intimacy, and dignity, related to a definite home-country.—ALFRED ZIMMERN.

He who wrestles with us strengthens our nerves and sharpens our skill. Our antagonist is our helper.—BURKE.

The God we worship is the God still suffering over the sorrows of humanity, the God with tears in his heart for the sorrows of this world—the God who is like Jesus Christ.— STUDDERT KENNEDY.

There are telescopes, microscopes, spectroscopes, and other instruments for assisting the eye in the vision of objects and phenomena. There is also a "theoscope" with which God and his glory may be seen. It is purity of heart.—SAMUEL JUDSON PORTER.

Unless it be in religion, there is no field of human thought where sentiment and preju_ dice take the place of sound knowledge and logical thinking so completely as in dietetics.— STEFANSSON.

It is a commonplace in religion that the pondering gaze of reverence sees farthest into the mysteries of God. So the sympathetic soul, attuned to what it studies, sees farthest into the nature and meaning of animate creation.—W. L. DAVIDSON.

I remember that the Lord never said, "Blessed are the dignified,"—but I know that Paul said that "the Lord loveth a hilarious giver." To be sure, we camouflage that under the more dignified term "cheerful," but the hilarity is there, in the original Greek.—HELEN BARRETT.

Only that picture is noble which is painted in love of the reality. . . . If you desire to draw that you may represent something that you care for, you will advance swiftly and safely. If you desire to draw that you may make a beautiful drawing, you will never make one.—RUSKIN.

Happiness must be earned, like other good things, else it can not be held. It can be deserved only where its price has been somehow paid. Nothing worth having is given away in this world,—nor in any other that we know of. No one rides dead-head on the road to happiness. He who tries to do so, never reaches his destination. He is left in the dumps.— DAVID STARR JORDAN.

Lastly, tho much more might be said, Japan needs an artistic presentation of Christianity and she has not yet been offered it. "Art," says Dr. Anesaki, "is an international language," and he makes a strong plea for introducing his people to the great things of Christian art. They go in millions to art collections. Why not send a loan collection of Christian masterpieces to Tokyo? It would help mightily toward mutual esteem and understanding. —KENNETH SAUNDERS, in *The Journal of Religion.*

FUNERAL SERMONS

The Rev. EDWARD H. EPPENS, Ann Arbor, Mich.

Conducting funerals is one of the most important and one of the least satisfactory functions of the pastoral office. Its importance is due to the acute needs of a race that craves comfort; its shortcomings are measured by the artificial demands which custom has been allowed to make upon suffering and superstitious mortals.

We are all going to die. And somebody is going to grieve over the death of the most worthless person. There is always a mother or a son or a neighbor with a heart. And grief wants to be assuaged. It is the business of religion to offer comfort to the bereaved. Death and the minister of religion meet at the bedside and at the grave of most mortals. The Egyptian priest, the medicine man, the father confessor, the modernist in practical brotherhood, the chaplain of the order—all are expected to do something that will dissipate the gloom of death. How many are equal to the demand?

It is this incessant demand that makes the funeral sermon so generally a bore to the mourner and the despair of the preacher. The appreciation rarely gets beyond the hackneyed "It was such a beautiful sermon!"—a praise which is not altogether unequivocal. After a thousand failures the identical demand comes yet again. The small group of mourners changes—in a small parish even that consolation is lacking!—but the preacher remembers the leaden monotony, the Scripture selections, the usual texts, the illustrations of the grass, the cloud, the butterfly, the broken bowl, the shock of corn, and often squirms, if he is sensitive, under the compulsion to find the delivering word.

For it should be noted emphatically that there is a delivering word. Death is not finality. Death, like a blow, like a war, settles very little. It answers few questions. It raises a thousand. For every question, however puzzling, there is, we trust, somewhere in this vast universe a definite answer. It is the business of the spokesman of religion not to find the answer but to help tide over the painful period during which the bereaved grope for the clue that will lead to the answer.

What can he do? The following suggestions are in no sense an attempt to give formal advice. The manuals and text-books supply an abundance of that. But experience, the mother of invention, may stumble upon some facts that work havoc with all these well-articulated theories. At any rate, the preacher will do well not to write his sermons by the book, and he will always be suspicious of the ready-made, second-hand material.

Every funeral is really *sui generis.* There are Scripture passages which would be grotesque at some graves; there are graves where the finest tribute is silence. Some deaths are an inditement; some are a deliverance; some are a judgment. Experience alone can teach a man what to say and what not to say. The best part of some sermons consists in what the speaker leaves unsaid.

One of the lessons a young preacher soon learns is that of discretion. The things that count are not the absolute pronouncements. The truth comes by indirection, on tender wings of hint and hope rather than by the imperious push of dogmatic claim. Let the speaker be positive, by all means, but in the name of truth let him avoid, like poison, the cheap and discredited tone of absolute certainty. Job is still asking questions of the universe which no humble preacher can expect to settle. Even the *ex cathedra* pronouncements of the Holy See make but a poor showing in the presence of real seekers after the truth.

The first and last rule, the safe and sensible rule in practically all cases, is to be brief. The speaker may have to wait with the beginning of his remarks until the chief mourner or the choir arrives; he is under no compulsion to wait with the conclusion until the undertaker nods. Where so little can be done to relieve the pain that attends a final parting words are hollow, and the professional comforter needs to be on his guard lest he be put into the same class with the hired mourner and the claqueur who earn their fee at the price of sincerity. The more we sympathize the harder it is to say anything worth saying, and many words are a weariness to the flesh.

The days of fulsome panegyric are over, except in a few medieval localities where the funeral sermon still contributes to that horrible spectacle of the advertizing undertaker called "viewing the remains," thus adding to the vulgar and senseless display which the deceased one's former station in life makes an insult and a fraud. The rhetoric of a Bossuet, for all its rolling periods, offers poor consolation to real mourners, and the hangers-on who "wouldn't miss a

funeral for anything"—as a sort of mild and free entertainment and social function—generally have neither the desire nor the capacity to sift the mass of words for the grain of comfort hidden within. Those who have pierced the veil and caught a glimpse of heaven no longer try to describe the ineffable; the experience strikes a Paul dumb, and a Lazarus is discreetly silent too; and those who have never looked into heaven are mere word-mongers anyway.

There still cluster about even the most Christian funerals so many pagan rites, so many practises which are crude survivals of pure fetishism, that the wise comforter will always aim at simplicity and naturalness. All display, all argument, all learned and subtle reasoning is an offense against good taste. "Proofs" of immortality (N. B.—A proof of personal survival after the crisis of death is very interesting, but it is not a proof of immortality!) are of no value whatever, especially when they resolve themselves, as they so often do, into mere quotations from Scripture, many of which require careful manipulation before they yield the desired result. At funerals one can encounter some queer interpretations of the Bible!

Science offers little that is helpful. This must be said in spite of the fact that much can be predicated of death in the evolutionary process of growth. Here is a fertile field for the psychologist and the psycho-analyist. But science has nothing to do with comfort; it deals with spiritually inert matters which may comfort and which may disconcert, and never asks how its conclusions react upon the hopes of man.

What, then, is left? The personal touch. This means an interest in the thousand and one little details of life, an instinctive, sympathetic appraisal of the whole business of life. Not

God only, not heaven and eternity merely, but the inquiring glance of an eye, the smile of the babe, the needle-pricked finger of mother, the quaint turns of speech, the hobbies, the tricks of gesture, the ambitions, all these mortals "desired to be—and were not": this is the tissue out of which life's fabric is woven.

In our normal moments we are not interested in death. The saddest mourner must get back to life's business. Death, in the Christian view, is but an episode in the endless life. Therefore it must not crowd too hard upon life's issues. Here is where so many set funeral sermons fail. They are weighted with tears and sighs, leaden as death itself, not tense with the vigor of life. To be convincing a person must speak of the things he knows. We know something of life; we know nothing of what comes after life.

It was with an acute sense of this fact that one pastor of twenty years' experience once said to the writer: "I have never yet preached a funeral sermon." To him a so-called "funeral sermon" suggested a manufactured piece of intellectual carpentry, planned, built up, polished, according to certain traditional specifications, not to forget a liberal application of whitewash at times, and delivered at a certain place and date. He knew what he was saying. No poet-laureate can deliver a masterpiece at the nod and caprice of a sovereign, and no speech rings true when it is manufactured over a given last. His expedient was as follows: "I have," said he, "about one hundred and fifty ideas to draw upon (lucky is the man who has so large an armory of sermonic material for *all* occasions!). These I use, making my selection with an eye to the need of the particular group addrest, in connection with something of local importance, suggested by the life, the

habits, the beliefs, the personality of the deceased."

In other words, the personal touch, which is everything.

This determines to a large extent the choice of material. As said, the jejune arguments and the florid rhetorical outbursts are equally in poor taste. Where many words are a mockery the few words spoken must come from the heart and must be addrest to the heart.

It is the poets who are the most helpful and satisfying; the prophet, the psalmist, the parabolist of the Bible are ever fresh. Sir Thomas Browne's *Urn Burial* touches heights which no mere logician ever dreamed of. *La Saisiaz, Abt Vogler, A Death in the Desert, In Memoriam, Ulysses,* a score of poems by Wordsworth, Whittier, Hugo, Whitman, Arnold, a dozen books by Russian mystics and Catholic saints, here are inexhaustible springs.

What does the voice of the ages tell us? Out of death comes life. The world is ever rejuvenating itself. The classic inspirers of a robust faith tell of God, youth, the wisdom of age, seasonal changes, companionships, the depths of love, the kinship of Jesus, the touch of the friendly hand, the miracle of spring-time, the strength of hope, the joy of service. Death, to most great thinkers, is a friend. What seems an end is only a beginning.

Dostoyefsky's Job-like flights in *The Brothers Karamazoff* can teach us what strength and beauty may come out of corruption. The motto of this abysmal work, John 12:24, strikes the key-note: "Except a grain of wheat fall into the earth and die, it abideth by itself alone; but if it die, it beareth much fruit."

The Ingersoll lectures on immortality and Myers's monumental production with its wealth of suggestion are good for the ground-work; they present what the intellect can grasp of the great mystery. And Maeterlinck knows how to make the great cathedral bells ring in the heart, starting memories and aspirations that lie too deep for words—to such as can adjust themselves to the somewhat somber tones.

Of course, the mystery remains. Perhaps most men with the practical duty of conducting funerals facing them can appreciate what J. F. Genung says in *The Life Indeed*:

It is forever too late, with their (Ostwald's, Osler's, James's, Royce's, Fiske's, etc.) weighty contributions in mind, to reecho that cheap sneer of Omar Khayyam,
"Myself when young did eagerly frequent Doctor and saint and heard great argument About it and about: but evermore Came out by the same door where in I went."
And yet—can we say that any of them have really touched the spot?

We may be permitted to reserve judgment about the alleged cheapness of the astronomer-poet's so-called sneer. But as for "touching the spot" most preachers of the word have surely felt the same difficulty. Hence the drag, the nervous exhaustion, the disappointments associated with funerals.

In justifying the ways of God with man it is well to remember that the commandment not to take the name of the Lord in vain applies to the clergy as well as the layman. When a babe loses its life in a tub of hot water left standing by a careless mother or when a reckless driver races with an express train to the "fool-killer curve," with the natural result, it is inviting the scorn of the community to tell how the Lord gave, the Lord hath taken away, blessed be the name of the Lord!

It is evident that this caution is not always to be taken for granted. The line between a suicidal action and an "act of God" is frequently so delicate a one that the utmost care is necessary to avoid giving offense. Often the physician and nine-tenths of the community know more about the cause of the death than is good for the speaker's reputation for perspicacity and love of the truth. The pious sentiment may tempt the knowing ones to put him down either a fool or a liar.

Once a preacher dwelt upon the Lord's taking away a notorious drunkard. "Och," said a plain-spoken rustic, "the Lord had nawthin' to do with it. Mike died on his own hook!" The teleology of the retort was not above criticism, but the rebuke implied was justified in the circumstances, and the criticism stuck.

When all is said, what can a preacher do? Men will not give up and bury their dead in a brutish way. They have aspirations which make a burial into a solemn rite, imposing sacred duties. Only the cult of brutal force, with its apotheosis in war, makes men forget that life is sacred and that the affections reach out for pity in the hour of death. By many the consolations of religion are regarded as the one sovereign anodyne to be applied. It is still the pastor, the priest, who is expected to help.

The most he can do is to bow before the mystery, to speak a few simple words of sympathy, to show poor humanity how to cling to hope, to share the pain and the sorrow, to point to those whom grim death could not conquer, beginning with the first-born of the new creation, to help those who are left behind to take up the load of the future with courage and faith.

This is little enough; but it is much when measured by the hopelessness in which most expedients leave the stricken ones.

All this is not to be learned out of books, but in the daily and hourly struggle of life and death.

The Salvage of a Nation

The Armenians form the oldest nation which has been continuously Christian as a people since its conversion. They are perilously close to extinction. Abdul Hamid literally decimated them in 1895. The Young Turk massacres of 1909-10 were less widespread but more destructive. The end of the war found the numbers in Turkish territory reduced by half or more through the ruthless massacres by their rulers. The Angora Turks recently promised to rebuild the destroyed mosques of Asia Minor "with the skulls of the — Armenians."

Of this people now only a remnant is left, and this remnant consists largely of orphans. The purpose of the Near East Relief is not merely temporary relief, it aims at the reconstruction of the Armenian nation through the 100,000 children whom it is feeding and training. It must rebuild the bodies weakened by famine and exposure; it must educate them and build character; it must fit them to earn a useful livelihood by giving them trades. By doing this for the children whom it can accommodate it is working toward the re-creation of a self-respecting and respected nation.

It must be remembered that outside the orphanages there is at least an equal number of starving orphans for whom nothing can be done because there are no funds for the purpose.

As an adjunct to all that is done for the children Near East Relief is furnishing opportunity for work for adults by which they earn food and shelter; it is building industries in the devastated areas and establishing scientific agriculture; it is training for agriculture, industries, and business the surviving youth of both sexes. So far as possible, seeds and tools are being provided, and tracts of land for farming and settlement are secured on which crops may be raised.

Permanency of results is the watchword throughout. Not just saving from present starvation, but the basing of the security of the future in healthy and competent bodies and character.

Believing that only action by the United States government can save the remnant of Armenians from further persecution and probable extermination on account of their faith, the Federal Council of Churches is making a nation-wide appeal to 150,000 congregations in America to urge Congress to take proper steps to ensure the permanent protection of Christians under Turkish rule.

The appeal to the churches summarizes the present plight of Armenia as follows:

First, the Armenians were one of the Allies in the late war, and fought for its ideals.

Second, in consequence of their loyalty, they suffered untold persecutions, almost to the verge of annihilation.

Third, the Allies as well as our own country pledged them a safe area for themselves and their children, and they have a right to expect nothing less.

Fourth, the American public has given millions of dollars to save the remnant of this shattered race, in confidence that they will be given a protected home.

Fifth, this remarkable response to a nation's need will be lost if these promises are not fulfilled.

Sixth, the Allied Powers are preparing a treaty with the Turkish Nationalists which threatens to return the Armenians to unrestricted Turkish control.

Seventh, responsibility for protecting the Armenians has been referred to the League of Nations.

Eighth, America can not escape her responsibility upon the ground of non-membership in the League. Our vast relief contributions, the cause of humanity, and our own moral welfare demand not expressions of sympathy but action.

The appeal then suggests that pastors and church members express their opinion to their congressmen and senators so that they may have the viewpoint of people back home.

Child Labor—Is It to Return

Chief Justice Taft of the Supreme Court of the United States on May 15 rendered a decision that has set socially minded people thinking. The court has decided that it is unconstitutional for the Federal Government to levy a tax (10%), avowedly for purposes not of revenue but of prohibition, on the products of industries employing child labor when sold outside the State in which they were produced. This law has been in operation since 1919.

Justice Taft's decision has been accepted as based on a purely legal analysis of the law, unprejudiced, uninfluenced by any "interests." There seems to be little disposition to dissent from this decision on the part of those who most ardently desire the present abolition and the future prohibition of child labor; but rather a new determination to accomplish their end, and, since all other expedients have failed, to advocate an amendment to the Federal Constitution.

Since in almost every one of the forty-two State legislatures in session in 1921 some measure relating to child labor or child welfare was on the program, it would seem that public conscience is aroused and that ratification would easily follow the proposal of a federal amendment that would for all time put an end to the labor of little children by placing every State on an equality in the production and distribution of goods where child labor might be employed.

The National Child Labor Committee reports that because of the limited scope of the present federal law and the variations in the State laws one child out of every eight from the age of ten to fifteen years has been gainfully employed outside the protection of federal or State laws:

"Each year 1,000,000 boys and girls of these ages leave school to go to work, perpetually swelling the ranks of the great army of men and women handicapped in respect to health, education, vocational fitness. The greatest vocation of all is life and the ultimate employer is society" (*Child Labor Facts*, 1922).

The general secretary of the committee now declares: "In the States with lower standards than those provided by the federal law we may anticipate an immediate return to the employment of children for the maximum hours and at the minimum age the State law permits." This would mean that in some States children of fourteen years may work ten hours a day (54 a week) instead of eight; in North Carolina eleven hours a day (60 a week). In Georgia, Massachusetts, Maine, Rhode Island, Florida, and Missouri the mines and quarries may employ child labor.

MID-WEEK PRAYER MEETING

Aug. 6-12—The River of Life

(Rev. 22:1-5)

St. John borrows from the prophet Ezekiel the figure which he here employs, and improves upon it. His vision is wider, his canvas is larger. Seer and prophet agree in ascribing to this mystical river a divine origin. It is not formed from tributary streams flowing adown the hills of time, but comes directly from God. Ezekiel represents it as flowing from under the sanctuary, John pictures it as "proceeding from the throne of God and of the Lamb," signifying that from God through Christ all our blessings flow.

This river is at its source "clear as crystal." Its waters have not yet become contaminated by the muddy impurities of earth. We instinctively seek for a pure religion at the beginning of things, just as a city seeks for a pure water supply at a river's fountain head. For a pure gospel we have to go well up-stream.

The figure of a river is suggestive of perpetuity. Men may come and go, successive civilizations may wax and wane upon its banks, but a river flows on forever. The outgoings of God's eternal love are not like a mountain stream that dries up in summer, but like a river fed from an unfailing source, which never ceases to flow.

Every river is literally a river of life. It has life-giving power. Upon its banks vegetation of every kind springs up. "Everything shall live whithersoever the river cometh," exclaimed Ezekiel as he contemplated the ever-widening, ever-deepening flood of God's grace sweeping over a nation that had become a desert land. The tree of life, with its delectable fruits and its healing leaves, which John saw on the banks of his river, has been rightly taken to symbolize the richness and variety of blessings which ever mark the course of the river of God's redeeming love. In the vision of St. John the river of life is connected with a city, and is indeed the center of its life. The world's great cities have, with few exceptions, been built on rivers, and sometimes the drying up of a river has meant the extinction of a city. A river has therefore been regarded as indispensable to a city's life. "There is a river" says an ancient psalmist, "the streams whereof shall make glad the city of God." That river is the emblem of the bringing down of the heavenly life into the earthly, the descent of the divine into the human.

All the blessings typified by the river of life are in the first instance realized on earth. They belong to the holy city, new Jerusalem, which John saw "coming down out of heaven from God." They are therefore things to be enjoyed in the present dispensation. But the scene keeps shifting from earth to heaven, and these blessings in their fulness can be realized only in the heavenly life. This Christian saints in all ages have felt, and have voiced their longings in such words as,

My feet are weary with the march
Over the steep hill-side,
City of God! I fain would see
Thy peaceful waters glide.

In all ages souls who have received the divine anointing have caught comforting glimpses of this mystical river, from whose waters they have often been refreshed, and have anticipated the time when the vision of the seer of Patmos shall come true. In the abiding city of God, through which ceaselessly flows the river of the water of life, all they longed for, hoped, prayed, and labored for will be abundantly fulfilled.   —J. M. C.

Aug. 13-19—The Fruitless Tree

(Luke 13:6-9)

This spoken parable must not be confounded with the acted parable in Mark 11:12, 13. Both are parables of judgment; both have to do with fruitless fig trees; but there is a touch of mercy in the one which is absent from the other.

The first thing that strikes one in connection with the fig tree now under consideration is its advantageous position. It was not growing by the road side, nor in some barren and waterless spot, but in a vineyard where it had protection, good soil, and the owner's personal care. This description points directly to Israel, to whom God had given peculiar advantages; but it is equally applicable to all who enjoy special privileges or means of grace. They possess the conditions favorable to spiritual productivity and are under responsibility to bring forth fruit accordingly.

The owner had every reason to expect good returns from this particular fig tree. It had been well cared for, had made excellent growth, and bore a fine show of leaves. But its appearance was deceptive; for when closely examined it was found to be fruitless. It had nothing but leaves. It did not answer the end of a fig tree—which is to produce figs. For that end it had been planted. Like a fig tree a Christian should be fruit-bearing. He should be known by his fruits. Among the green leaves of his profession there should be found "the fruits of the Spirit," the fruits of holy living. A fruitless Christian and a fruitless fig tree show the same failure to function.

The owner was deeply disappointed. This was the third year he had come personally seeking fruit from this highly favored tree, and had found none. The expression "three years" has had read into it many mystical meanings. It has been taken as referring to Moses, the prophet, and Christ, to the three years of our Lord's public ministry; and to the three periods of life—childhood, manhood, and old age. But these are fanciful interpretations. The obvious meaning of the phrase is that the owner had given a fair trial, having come for three successive years after the time that the tree ought to have borne fruit. To many individuals Christ has come for fifty years, and more, and has turned away empty handed. A Christian of marked spiritual maturity was asked, "What is the quality in God that impresses you most?" He at once replied, "His patience."

The sentence of the owner has nothing harsh about it. The fruitless tree was taking up room which might have been more profitably occupied. It was cumbering the ground, being utterly worthless as a fig tree. After the manner of many Christians it took in more than it gave out; it absorbed without being productive.

As touching the intercession of the vine-dresser care must be taken not to read into it an idea which it was never intended to carry. It has been taken as representing Christ as pleading with a stern judge so as to induce him to relent and delay in carrying his sentence out. The suggestion is abhorrent; there can be no such schism in the Godhead. All that the vine-dresser asked was that the fruitless tree might have another chance to make good, so that the labor that had been expended upon it might not be lost. Another chance! and in this case a final one. Nations and institutions have their complete judgment here. Not so with individuals. With them life is a succession of chances; their completed judgment is in the hereafter. With every soul God is ceaselessly working to make his life spiritually productive, and what else can he do with the profitless fruit tree but hew it down and cast it into the fire? It has made itself fit only for fuel.   —J. M. C.

Aug. 20-26—The Storm on the Lake
(Luke 8:22-28)

It was at the express invitation of Jesus that the disciples launched their boat to convey him across the lake that he might have a brief respite from the throngs that prest upon him to hear his message and to receive his healing touch. Did he know into what danger he was taking them? Did he purposely seek to test their faith and to strengthen it by testing it? Could their faith have been strengthened, or could the faith of any one be strengthened, in any other way? And did he put the preservation and confirmation of their faith above every other consideration? (See 1 Peter 1:6, 7.)

One thing is certain, sailing in the same ship with Jesus did not secure immunity from danger, but it did imply immunity from destruction. To his followers Jesus says, "In this world ye shall have tribulation; but in me, peace." He does not promise exemption from the troubles common to humanity, but he does promise grace to triumph over them.

It was a peaceful evening when that little fishing wherry, which carried the one in whom was centered the hopes of humanity and the seed of his Church which was yet to be, set out on its eventful voyage to the other side of the lake. The sky was calm, the waters of the lake unruffled, and everything presaged a pleasant and prosperous voyage. For a time all went well, but all at once a squall arose. The wind which rushed down one of the gorges which surround the Galilean lakes struck the boat and sent it dancing over the waves like a cockle-shell. In the midst of the storm the Master, wearied with the labors of the day, was asleep in the hinder part of the boat. At first the disciples hesitated to awaken him. But the situation grew desperate. The hardy fishermen had exhausted all their strength and skill to keep their little craft afloat. Then they came to Jesus and awoke him, saying, "Master! Master! carest thou not that we perish?" Their words must have cut him to the quick, for never had he given them the slightest ground to doubt his tender care. Their reproach was born of fear, and their fear was born of a temporary breakdown in their faith. That their faith had not failed utterly is evident from the fact that they appealed unto him to save them. In words of loving rebuke he asked, "Where is your faith?" It was about their faith that he was mainly concerned; and to him its wreck was a more serious matter than the wreck of the ship. Surely their previous experiences of him ought to have conserved their faith in the crisis of the moment. Faith banishes fear, as on the other hand fear banishes faith. Those who have had experience of Christ feel well assured that

No water can swallow the ship where lies
The Master of ocean and earth and skies.

The ship in which he sails is unsinkable. The soul that receives him can never perish, no matter what may befall the body in which it is encased. Because he is in his Church it has weathered, and will weather, every storm.

Having rebuked the disciples for the breakdown of their faith, he arose and rebuked the winds and the waves; then, as he uttered the omnific words, "Peace, be still!" the tempest ceased.

Does someone exclaim, "Oh, where is he who rebuked the sea? Has he gone away leaving us to battle alone with the storms which sweep over the waters of our troubled life, leaving us only a beautiful legend of his wonder-working power?" Wisest are those who cling to the simple faith that he is ever with us, who behold with Francis Thompson,

Christ walking on the waters,
Not of Gennesaret but Thames.

This simple faith was the solace of William T. Stead in his long and active public career. The hymn which he learned at his mother's knee, to which he often referred as his favorite, was the familiar one by John Newton,

Be gone, unbelief!
My Savior is near,
And for my relief
Will surely appear;
By prayer let me wrestle,
And he will perform;
With Christ in the vessel
I smile at the storm.

And we doubt not it came to him with all its comforting power when he stood serene on the deck of the ill-fated *Titanic* as she sank into the waters of the Atlantic. —J. M. C.

Aug. 27-Sept. 2—The Christian's Appreciation of Hinduism
(Missions)

Carrying on the series of subjects begun in February and continued in May, we consider this month the faith held by over 200 millions in the great Asian peninsula.

It is interesting to note that the sectarianism of Christendom with its scores of denominations and its host of churches has a close parallel in India. But the lines of cleavage follow quite variant principles of division in the two religions. The differences of Hindu sects are based upon the particular phases of deity which are attributed respectively to the momentary object of worship. Thus the great Hindu trinity represents God as Creator, Savior or Preserver, and Destroyer—destruction (for re-creation) being considered one of the many divine operations. Besides these great deities, there are hundreds of local "godlings" who are thought of as local protectors and benefactors. Each of these has his own greater or lesser circles of devout worshipers.

While this "sectarianism" is the obvious fact in Hindu religious life, it is fundamentally modified by what is basally the theological belief of India. This is the deep consciousness that God is one. The great deities— Brahma, Vishnu, and Shiva—and equally the "good little gods" (as Kipling makes a Hindu call them) of the villages are but phases or manifestations of the One.

This One, Hindus hold, is eternally active in his world, everywhere and always present and working. So far is this thought pushed in the relentless logic of India's thinkers that they regard the world as a manifestation of God's self. They are open to the imputation of pantheism. The doctrine is the extreme of what Christians speak of as "God's immanence." While we distinguish between the being of God and his operations, we may realize that Hindus in identifying Deity with his creation intend to honor him, and manifest that by profound respect for the visible things about them. In no other land is life in all its forms so extensively regarded as a sacred gift and its preservation so carefully guarded.

Flowing from this comes the Hindu sense of the high worth of man. It nearly approaches the conception of Sir H. Davy in his poem "written after recovery from a dangerous illness":

A sacred spark created by his breath,
  The immortal mind of man his image
    bears;
A spirit living 'midst the forms of death,
  Opprest, but not subdued, by mortal cares.

Or Pope's

  Vital spark of heavenly flame.

The object of man's striving is his salvation, conceived, however, in a manner different from the Christian's. Salvation of man is the return of the spark to the central flame from which it issued.

Another result of the central Hindu doctrine of God is the thought of all relationships, tasks, and operations as inherently sacred, as having definite relations to religion and to God. No other system—even rabbinic Judaism—has developed this thought in so great detail. For every activity an appropriate ritual of dedication has been charted. The idea of consecrating all acts, of creating and conserving consciousness of their essential religiousness, dominates life. This worshipful attitude underlies the vast compends of ritual and law. By these the learned seek to make the impression that every material, earthly, temporal deed has its spiritual, supernal, eternal aspect. Hence the forms of invocation and prayer are huge in number and instinct with reverence. "Millions upon millions of pilgrims are traveling in a never-ceasing quest for the Eternal. . . . Nowhere on earth, not excepting even Christian lands, is there such universal spiritual earnestness."

Items that are strest in Hindu thought are those of perfect intelligence as an aim, the fact of incarnation, the value of asceticism (here carried to most extravagant extremes), and regard for parents.

With much that is unworthy and distorted the Hindu reveals a devotion, a simplicity or childlikeness, and a sense of the presence of God that must evoke admiration.—G. W. G.

The Book

THE EXILE AND THE RESTORATION [1]

Professor JOHN E. McFADYEN, D.D., Glasgow, Scotland

Aug. 6—The Temple Rebuilt and Dedicated

(Ezra 3:1—6:22)

In the last lesson we saw that a goodly band of exiles returned from Babylon to Jerusalem and Judah (Ezra 2:70); the chapters for study to-day tell us how they spent the next twenty years or so (538-516 B.C.). After chap. 1 we are not surprized to learn that they spent them largely in the effort to reestablish their religious life. A brief summary of these chapters will enable us to see their drift.

A great gathering was held at Jerusalem, at which, under the leadership of Joshua the priest and Zerubbabel, the altar was built, that the sacrifices might regularly be offered. But the foundation of the temple was not yet laid (3:1-7). Measures, however, were at once taken with this end in view. The returned exiles address themselves to the work, and the foundation was laid to the accompaniment of music and song. The joy of the young was mingled with the tears of those who had seen the glorious temple of Solomon (3:8-13). The Samaritans requested permission to assist in the building of the temple on the ground of their common worship of Jehovah. On the Jewish leaders' refusing, they hampered the activities of the Jews and kept plotting against them till 520 B.C. (4:1-5, 24). The omitted verses refer to a later period. Then under the stimulus of the

preaching of the prophets Haggai and Zechariah, the real work of building was begun (5:1, 2). But their efforts were challenged by the suspicious Tattenai, Persian governor of the western provinces. He, however, before prohibiting them, formally communicated with Darius, intimating the rapid progress of the building, the names of the leaders, and the reply of the Jews to his challenge, in which they had appealed to a decree of Cyrus granting them permission to return and rebuild the temple, and had pleaded the uninterrupted progress of the building since the laying of the foundation stone (5:3-17). On Tattenai's recommendation Darius instituted a search for the alleged decree, which was at length discovered at Ecbatana, whereupon he not only warned Tattenai not to interfere with the work, but passed an irrevocable decree that part of the royal tribute be placed at their disposal, that they should be regularly supplied with all that was necessary for sacrifice, and that prayer be offered for his dynasty (6:1-12). Thus under the stimulus of the preaching of Haggai and Zechariah, the returned exiles kept the dedication of the temple with joy, offered liberal sacrifices, and arranged for the worship (6:13-18). A great passover feast was held in which all, with glad gratitude, participated—both the returned exiles and all who had separated themselves from the filthiness of the heathen of the land.

[1] These studies follow the lesson-topics and passages of the International Sunday-school series.

Perhaps by the latter are meant those who had not been carried into exile (6:19-22).

In brief, the first thing the returned exiles did was to build an altar for sacrifice; then apparently they laid the foundation stone of the temple; but, as many difficulties soon emerged —drought, poverty, opposition of neighbors, etc.—the building was not actually completed till 516 B.C.

The passage, which is so interesting historically, well illustrates the condition of successful religious work. (1) The importance of enterprise in religion and reconstruction. Pious aspirations and good resolutions must be translated into act. The exiles came home with the ardent desire to build their God a worthy house in Jerusalem. Much that they saw when they returned to their poverty-stricken land must have filled their hearts with disappointment and dismay (cf. Hag. 1:11); but they went on with the work—first the altar, then the foundation stone, and finally, in the teeth of malicious opposition, the building. And so, in our sorrowfully shattered world, must each of us work steadily on at his task, whatever it be, with energy and hope. (2) The possibility of obstruction from well-meaning people. The Samaritans were Jehovah worshippers, willing and eager to help in the building of his temple. But, in point of fact, their worship was of an inferior and tainted order and compromised, at any rate in earlier times, by the worship of other gods (cf. 2 Kings 17:28ff., 41); so their overtures, well-intentioned as they were, were not unnaturally rejected by the Jews, with the result that their friendship was turned into persistent and malicious opposition. The most deadly enemy of religious enterprise is often the spirit of professedly religious men themselves. (3) The need of preserving the purity of religious enterprise. When help is sorely needed in such enterprise, we are sometimes inclined to welcome it with open arms, without too closely scrutinizing the quarter from which it comes. But the Jews rejected the offer of the Samaritans' help, tho they needed it and tho it was politely and sincerely made. The value of help in religious matters depends upon its quality, and men like the Samaritans were little likely to advance the true interests of Jerusalem. To accept in church work the help of men of doubtful character under the stress of great need is to compromise the whole character of the enterprise, to lay up for its future possible ruin, and for the workers inevitable trouble and sorrow. The Jews by their refusal may have seemed ungracious, but they knew what they were doing and they did it deliberately.

Aug. 13—Esther Saves Her People
(The Book of Esther)

The stories of Joseph, Ruth, and Esther have been described as miniature novels. Within the compass of a very few words the writers created scenes as dramatic and characters as fascinating as any in modern fiction. If to these we add the stories of Daniel and Jonah we shall see how interested the Hebrews were in tracing the fortunes of their countrymen in foreign lands. We shall see, too, how conflicting was their attitude to the alien problem; some of them were friendly to the foreigner, others were not—they longed for his extermination or at any rate his subordination (cf. Isa. 61:5, 6).

Here is the story of the book in brief. The queen of Xerxes, king of Persia, was deposed for contumacy, and her crown was set upon the head of Esther, a lovely Jewish maiden. Not long afterward Mordecai, the foster-father of Esther, saved the king's life by communicating to him through Esther a plot against his life, and Mordecai's deed was put on record. Presently, however, a certain Haman, promoted by the king above all the other nobles, conceived a deadly hatred of Mordecai for persistently refusing him obeisance, and he sought to gratify his revenge by destroying the Jewish people throughout the empire. By representing them to be seditiously inclined, he obtained from the king a decree for their annihilation, to take effect in eleven months. The decree prostrated the Jews with grief. Mordecai contrived to inform Esther of it and charged her to implore the king on behalf of her people. Esther well knew the peril of such a course; yet, nerved by Mordecai's appeal, she eventually made up her mind to intercede with the king, cost what it might. The king received her graciously and offered to grant her request even to the half of his kingdom. She only asked, however, that he and Haman should come next day to a banquet prepared by herself. There the king renewed his promise, but again she invited them to a second banquet. Haman's joy, however, was still clouded by Mordecai's refusal of obeisance. On his wife's suggestion he prepared a gallows, hoping to secure next day a decree for Mordecai's execution. With Mordecai's unrewarded service in mind, the king next day asked Haman what should be done to the man whom he delighted to honor. The extravagant honors which Haman suggested he was himself compelled to bestow on the hated Mordecai, and afterwards he was hanged on the gallows that he had prepared for Mordecai, who was then installed in Haman's post of honor. Thus were the tables turned; and also later, on a more public scale, when the Jews, whom the initial decree had doomed to extermination, actually slew 75,000

of their enemies throughout the empire, including the ten sons of Haman.

(1) The first thing to note about this brilliantly told tale is its evil and vindictive temper. It is inspired by an aggressive fanaticism and thirst for vengeance; it is with a shudder that we read in 9:13 of Esther's request for a second butchery. The vehemence of the book is doubtless thoroughly intelligible when we remember that it was written in a generation that had already smarted under persecution and shed its blood in defense of its liberty and ancestral traditions, which had been cruelly assailed by foreigners; but it is a comfort to know that it is never quoted or referred to by Jesus or his apostles. Many of the troubles from which the world has been suffering since the war have been created by political arrangements inspired by the vindictive spirit; and to any Christian who would venture to quote the book of Esther in defense Jesus would have said, as he said to other apostles of vindictiveness, "Ye know not what spirit ye are of" (Luke 9:54f.). Hatred can only beget hatred and plunge nations deeper into the mire. The book of Jonah is a fine foil to the book of Esther, pleading as it does for magnanimity towards the enemy, and exhibiting the love and pity of God as being extended even to the nation from which the writer's people had suffered much in war. It is not by cherishing vindictive thoughts and by passing vindictive measures that the friendly world for which we long will ever come into being.

But over against this intolerant temper there are striking and helpful thoughts in the passage selected for special study, (4:10—5:3) and they are gathered up in the immortal words of 4:14, 16 and 5:2.

(2) Ability and opportunity involve responsibility. "Who knoweth," says Mordecai to Esther, "whether

thou art not come to the kingdom for such a time as this?" (4:14). These words instantly lit the whole career of Esther with a new and solemn meaning. It was not for nothing that she was queen, and it was not an accident that had set her upon the throne. This was the crisis to which, throughout the brilliant, happy years, she had all unconsciously been moving; and now she was to prove to the world whether she was a queen in name only or also in deed and truth. She had the training, she had now the opportunity; how will she act? So should Mordecai's appeal come home to every one of ourselves. We, too, have come into some kingdom; there is something that we have trained ourselves to do, some particular service that our education, experience, or money enables us to render; and "at such a time as this," when the world is more disillusioned, needy, and shattered than it has ever been before, shall we not recognize that God is presenting us all with a supreme opportunity to render, like Esther, saving service to our generation?

(3) Responsibility must be assumed heroically. "If I perish, I perish" (4:16). Important duties are very often associated with great dangers—sometimes to life and limb, often to reputation and comfort. Let us thank God that millions of men all over the world went forward with unflinching heroism to all the terrible risks of war; why should we be less concerned to be heroes in time of peace? If one hundredth part of the skill and money and devotion which were gladly given in war were offered in the cause of peace, the transformation of our world would speedily come. At the call of duty, whether in home or church or public life, it is for us to play the hero, cost what it may.

(4) Responsibility must be assumed hopefully. The anticipated danger often vanishes when we approach it. "When the king saw Esther, she obtained favor in his sight, and he held out to her the golden scepter that was in his hand" (5:2). It is often our imagination of the peril that unmans us; the resolution to face it brings the requisite strength and often, too, the victory. We quail at the thought of the king upon his throne; but lo! when, with brave tho beating hearts, we appear before him, he holds out to us the golden scepter. "Behind a frowning providence he hides a smiling face."

Aug. 20—The Second Return from Exile

(Ezra 7:1—8:36)

A fortnight ago we saw that twenty years or so after the return of the exiles from Babylon, the building of the temple was completed in 516 B.C. Then follows a gap in the record of sixty or seventy years, a period of which we know nothing except that it must have been one of tragic disillusion. The happy reconstruction of the national life to which the people looked forward had not been achieved, the people had grown dull and apathetic, even the services of religion—as we learn from Malachi (1:8, 14; about 460-450 B.C.)—had degenerated into empty and disgraceful formalism. The chronology of the period is also very obscure. The two certain dates are 444 and 432 B.C., the years respectively of Nehemiah's first and second visits to Jerusalem. But it is not even certain whether Ezra preceded or followed Nehemiah. If he followed him, as many modern scholars incline to suppose, the date of the journey we are about to consider will be 398 B.C.; if he preceded him, it will be 458 B.C. The decision of this question, however, does not affect the interest or importance of the story, which runs as follows:

Headed by Ezra, a company of Babylonian Jews, including both laity and the various grades of the clergy, arrived at Jerusalem after a four months' march from Babylon. This expedition had the express sanction and support of the Persian government, and its object was to investigate the religious condition of Judah and Jerusalem and to teach the law. Ezra brought with him a letter from Artaxerxes, embodying a decree that empowered any Jew who pleased to accompany him, and offering liberal contributions towards the sacrifices and for other needful purposes. The decree further instructed the treasurers of the western provinces to give Ezra, within certain limits, anything he might require, exempted the clergy from taxation, and commissioned Ezra to appoint judges to teach the law with varying penalties for disobedience. This considered and deliberate emphasis upon "the law" marks a stage of the most far-reaching importance in the development of Judaism.

After gratefully acknowledging Jehovah's grace to the people and to himself at this juncture, Ezra gathered at a short distance from Babylon all who were to accompany him, priests, princes and laymen. The prospect of return had little attraction for the Levites, to whom Ezekiel (44:10-13) had assigned a distinctly subordinate place in the reconstituted church, so we need not be surprised that there were no Levites in Ezra's company. Like a practical man, however, he immediately took steps to have their places filled by Nethinim, who were servants of the Levites. Then he proclaimed a fast, with public humiliation and prayer for protection by the way (for, after having assured the king that their God protected all who sought him, he could not well ask for a bodyguard), and their faith was justified; for either they were not assailed at all, or, if they were, at any rate they suffered nothing. But the pilgrim band were not to go to the holy city empty-handed. They had costly presents, collected from many sources, to take to the temple. The Persian king and his counsellors had made a handsome contribution (cf. 7:15), but of course the greatest proportion had been contributed by the Jews themselves—in the form of money and vessels, representing (if the text has been correctly transmitted) sums almost fabulously high. Ezra then committed these offerings to the charge of certain select priests, taking needful and scrupulous precautions to have them safely delivered at Jerusalem. Then they took their departure, and eventually reached Jerusalem in safety, being preserved by their God from the dangers of the way. The offerings also were found on inspection to be intact.

The passage finely illustrates the condition of successful organization in religious enterprise. (1) There must be genuine and practical recognition of God. When Ezra secured the men whom he needed for Levitical service, he attributed his success not to his own business capacity, but to "the good hand of our God upon us" (8:18). His company fasted and prayed before embarking on the expedition, and offered sacrifice at its close. Most significant of all, however, was Ezra's refusal to ask for a military escort for a journey likely to be so full of danger. We need not maintain that Ezra's course was the only one possible for a man of real religion; for on a similar occasion, Nehemiah, one of the most devout men in the Old Testament, accepted an escort (Neh. 2:9). But God and his power must have been very real and vivid to pilgrims who were willing, on so dangerous a journey, to dispense with the help of armed men. (2) The leaders must be capable of real initiative and authority. Priest and scribe as he was, Ezra showed fine practical sagacity throughout. He held a muster of men before the start, took steps to have the gaps filled up, and was not afraid to charge his officers very plainly to look scrupulously after the gifts entrusted to them. (3) Leaders and led alike must be devoted to their cause. The absence of Levites from the first muster shows that nobody went who did not want to go. It is only a willing and enthusiastic band that can achieve anything worthy. (4) Business methods are necessary. The men in charge of the money and the vessels were consecrated men, but that did not deter Ezra from weighing and tabulating very carefully the property of which they were in charge, nor the Jerusalem authorities from checking it on its arrival. The moneys and property of the Church should be handled in strictly business-like ways. This is not a wordly demand; it is made no less in the interests of religion than of common sense. It was no worlding but the devout Ezra who insisted that this should be done; and five hundred years after we find Paul taking similar precautions in connection with a collection of money for the poor at Jerusalem, and defending his arrangement in the business-like words, "For we are careful for good appearances not only in the Lord's sight, but also in men's" (2 Cor. 8:21).

Aug. 27—Nehemiah's Prayer

(Neh. 1:1-11)

In the Old Testament we have not only history and biography but even some autobiography, and it is a singular piece of good fortune that a large part of the story of Nehemiah's important career has been preserved for us in his own words. If Ezekiel gave Judaism its ecclesiastical framework,

it was largely due to the political and civic enterprise of Nehemiah that the community had any real social coherence.

The date of the opening chapter is December, 445—the twentieth year of chap. 1:1 being the twentieth year of Artaxerxes, head of the Persian empire (2:1); the place is Shushan, the winter-palace of the Persian kings, where Nehemiah was officiating as cup-bearer. In that month a deputation from Judah, headed by Nehemiah's own brother (cf. 7:2), arrived at Shushan. Nehemiah, like the true patriot that he was, immediately proceeded to question them about the home-land—in particular, how were the people (the descendants of the returned exiles) and how was the dear city of Jerusalem? Sorrowful indeed was the answer to both these questions; the people were suffering, the city walls had been broken down, and the gates had been burned. (The dilapidated state of the city and the walls is vividly described in Nehemiah's fascinating account of his midnight ride in chap. 2:12-15 when, on reaching Palestine, he made a personal investigation of conditions.) Unfortunately we do not know for certain to what catastrophe these allusions point; but it must have been an experience very much more recent than the sack of Jerusalem over 140 years before. The sorrows of Jerusalem have not all been recorded in history. The deputation probably came to Persia in the hope that their countryman Nehemiah, who belonged to the court, could do something directly or indirectly to remedy their distress.

Nehemiah's first emotion was one of uncontrollable grief; then, like Ezra (8:21) on the eve of his expedition to Palestine, he fasted and prayed. The form and contents of the prayer are alike suggestive; it is made up of an ascription of glory, an appeal, and a confession, and only at the end does the petition emerge which is the real object of the prayer. From this order have we not all something to learn of the proper approach to God? The opening words, which, in a sense, are the keynote of the prayer, emphasize on the one hand, God's majesty, and on the other, his grace. Then comes a general appeal that God would be attentive to his prayer, and this is followed by the very significant confession of sin, for no progress can be looked for till sin is confessed and forgiven; and note that Nehemiah confesses not only the national sin but his individual sin. He then pleads the ancient promise made through Moses, that national repentance would be followed by restoration. The allusion appears to be Deut. 30:1-5, the words of which, however, are not exactly reproduced. The petition which closes the prayer is simply that God would grant prosperity to Nehemiah, and mercy in the sight of King Artaxerxes, whose cup-bearer he was. The real bearing of this somewhat general request is only understood when we read on to chap. 2 and find that he desired the royal permission to be sent to Judah to help to restore the fallen fortunes of the province and in particular of the city and people.

The chapter may be described as a study in patriotism. Nehemiah describes himself in 2:10 as a man who "sought the welfare of the children of Israel." This did not prevent him from being a loyal subject and a faithful official in the land of his adoption. The welfare of one land is not only quite consistent with, but is even necessary to, the welfare of every other land. But as patriotism is so often vulgarly, and even mischievously, conceived, it will do us good to look this ancient Hebrew in the face, and learn what a true patriot is. He is (1) a public-spirited man, deeply concerned in all that concerns his land. Nehemiah was grieved unto tears at his country's misfortune. It is not enough to do our duty, we must be profoundly and intelligently interested in the affairs and the welfare of our country. (2) The true patriot acknowledges his own share in the national responsibility. "The children of Israel have sinned against thee; I and my father's house have sinned." It was one of the best men of his time who made this confession. It is the men of sensitive conscience who recognize that they have not been as true and as brave as they might have been. For the decline or depravity of our nation every man of us must bear his share of blame. (3) The true patriot prays for his country. Nehemiah is an almost romantically energetic figure, every inch a man of action, yet no less a man of prayer. There are many allusions to prayer in his memoirs (cf. 4:9; 5:19; 6:9; 13:31), perhaps the most winsome of all being the silent prayer he offered up (2:4) before he answered the Persian king. (4) The true patriot will not only pray, he will do and dare all for his country. The whole book of Nehemiah is an eloquent testimony to the skill, the resourcefulness, and the courage which he brought to the task of restoring the fallen fortunes of his countrymen.

HOW CLIMATE INFLUENCES HUMANITY

WILLIAM A. MURRILL, Ph.D., of the New York Botanical Garden

Aug. 6—The Effects of Climate

SCRIPTURE LESSON: Job 38:19-38; Matt. 16:2-3.

On a clear, sparkling day we feel cheerful and our work seems light. The weather is said to be stimulating. Now, it is a law of nature that any stimulus from without invigorates an animal, and through the influence of many small stimuli acting through the ages man has risen to his present high estate. The effect of little things like rivulets of water on hard stone is well known to the student of geology. In a similar way man's mind, as well as his body, has been influenced by climate. The Nordic race, with fair complexion and great intellectual power, originated in a temperate climate; while races inhabiting tropical countries are usually slow in thought and movement and are protected from the sun by more pigment in the skin.

According to Professor Ellsworth Huntington, our great authority on this subject, human progress depends upon three great factors: Inherent mental capacity, material resources, and energy. All progress, whether material or moral, arises from ideas in the minds of individuals. Some races produce great men, others are lacking in this respect. The Greeks in the age of Pericles, their golden age, were far superior to the average man of today in their ability to think. Environment allows some types to endure, and climate is a most important environmental factor. Climate has kept the American Indian from developing mentally, leaving him patient, enduring, and observing, but lacking in many things which the Japanese, for example, have. Their long sojourn in the frozen north when migrating from Asia to America by Bering Strait doubtless caused this difference. The long icy night is torture to a man of nerves, and only the phlegmatic can survive it. The Japanese pushed out from central Asia in the opposite direction from the Nordic race and has never felt the retarding influence of a very cold or very hot climate. The African negroes were represt by the heat. In the tropics energetic people kill themselves with over-work, because the

---

WHAT THE WEATHER DOES

The farmer complains of his rheumatism and predicts rain; the fat man complains of the heat and mops his brow; the anemic woman shivers with cold on a frosty day; while the nervous woman fusses about to little purpose when the air is unusually dry. The professional man comes into his office in the morning and finds the thermometer around forty. Work is impossible. He walks about, shivers a little to stimulate circulation — and accomplishes nothing. In the afternoon, he returns to find the thermometer registering eighty-five. Work is again impossible. He becomes uneasy, restless, his brain burns and whirls, his blood boils, the manufacture of thoughts is impossible.

These and many other effects of climate on human beings are commonly looked upon as merely incidental or of little moment, but is this really the case?

heat and the activity both generate toxic substances in the blood, and there is no rest period for their elimination. The Australian bushmen are still worse off, because they contend with heat and also desert conditions.

No man, however inventive or energetic, can accomplish much in the frozen North where there are no material resources, nor in the desert. Put a New Yorker in the land of the Eskimo and he would soon retrograde almost beyond recognition. The Pueblo Indians were well advanced in civilization, while the Utes were of a very low type. This difference seems to have arisen entirely from the districts in which these tribes lived. Nine-tenths of the world's resources are dependent on climate. All kinds of food and clothing and most of the materials used for shelter depend absolutely upon it. Where coal and iron occur, their use is largely dependent upon climatic conditions.

Energy moves the world, and energy is very closely related to climate. Think of the good ideas that go to waste because we lack the energy to develop them, and think of the efforts of reformers that are wasted on a generation too inert to appreciate and accept them! Energy is partly the result of proper food, clothing, shelter, etc., and partly the result of inherited ability and freedom from disease. All of these depend largely upon climate; but the right kind of climate is needed to furnish the additional stimulus to do our best work. Even if one is free from malaria and other enervating diseases in the tropics, he can not accomplish the same amount of work because he lacks the energy.

Blonds are adapted to cool climates, if their circulation is normal, and brunettes are the result of warmer climates. It is exceedingly important to change our climate at times when we find that the particular location in which we live is not adapted to us, but, in general, blonds have nothing to fear from the New York winters. Why are New Yorkers so energetic? Altho they complain bitterly about the ups and downs of their climate, it is doubtless the cause of their energetic life and accomplishment. We work best and we think best in a changeable climate, where the barometer goes up and down and the wind changes every few days, bringing clear weather and rain, cool spells and hot ones in quick succession. The region of cyclonic storms suits us best because we have been made by these continually recurring climatic stimuli and we have become adapted to this particular sort of weather. The direct effect is probably through stimulating the circulation of the blood, as in taking hot and cold baths alternately. The changes in temperature should not be too great, as sometimes happens in New York City, when colds become prevalent after a violent drop in the thermometer. The delicate mucous membranes of the nose and throat may become irritated and congested by sudden, severe cold spells. Humidity also has a decided effect on one's health and energy by checking the evaporation from the skin and in other ways. Some people are peculiarly sensitive to changes in temperature, humidity, wind, sunshine, air pressure, and the amounts of ozone and electricity in the air; while others are little affected. All of us, however, appear to work best at the end of a storm, after the various weather changes have fully imprest their stimulating effects.

Different seasons show different effects on our physical and mental efforts. In the region from New York to the Rocky Mountain October is generally the best month for accomplishment. After that the cold weather becomes more and more depressing and by the end of January there is a drop of probably 25 per cent in health and efficiency. Conditions improve with the coming of milder weather until May or June, but July and August are often as bad as midwinter, when stomach troubles take the place of colds as an irritant and the severe heat may cause a feeling of general debility.

Aug. 13—The Ideal Climate

The purpose of human life is to accomplish some useful work, and we next inquire what climate is best suited for such work. The first important element to be considered in this inquiry is temperature. After observing and experimenting over a wide range of territory under varying conditions, experts have decided that the optimum temperature for the physical well-being of the human race is an average of about 64° F. for day and night, or 68° to 72° F. in the day and 56° to 60° at night. For the best mental work, a much lower temperature is required, averaging about 40° F. for day and night, or 45° to 60° F. in the day and 32° F. at night. In New York City, the best temperature for mental work is usually early in December and during March, the brain requiring a considerably lower temperature for full stimulation than the body. The effect of extremely hot or extremely cold weather on the human system is much the same, causing irritation of the sensitive mucous membranes and increasing the tendency to nervousness. The injury is augmented during severe cold spells in winter because we overheat our houses, dry up the air, become more susceptible to colds, and more sensitive to petty annoyances.

Variability in temperature within moderate limits is much better than uniformity; a cool spell is stimulating. We get accustomed to changes and the effect is like exercise. It is much better to go to California than to stay there, for example; it is the change that does us good. Storms are exceedingly stimulating, altho not without bad effects in cold weather at times. This is balanced by their good effect in warm weather. All races of men have the same optimum, around 64° F. Altho the negro has lived in Africa for thousands of years and the Finn has lived in a cold climate for many generations, they are not yet essentially changed as to this optimum. The Nordic, the Chinese, and other races are the same. Black skins have been developed to protect men from the heat and fair skins are adapted to a cloudy, northern home, but this is all. It looks as tho man's adjustment to climate were like the temperature of the blood, a matter settled before the various races were formed. Mental activity is quite different from physical activity. Tests have shown that the negro has undoubtedly been retarded in his mental development by the hot climate, the mental development having taken place to a great extent after the white and negro races were separated. Extremely hot weather is more injurious, both to body and mind, than extreme cold.

The optimum humidity for the human race is about 80 per cent saturation for day and night taken together, or about four-fifths as much moisture as the air will hold. If the amount drops to one-half, it becomes too dry and the nose, throat, and skin suffer, causing nervousness and other troubles. The fact is that the relative humidity of the air in our living rooms during wintry weather is usually about 30 per cent instead of 80 per cent—a condition which should be remedied by hanging out wet cloths, placing pans of water on the radiators, etc. Moist air feels warmer than dry air, and one should keep the humidity up to 60 per cent if possible, when a temperature of 64° to 68°

would be ample. As shown by an analysis of the death rate at different seasons in various countries, moist conditions are much better for us than dry in cool weather, altho it is hard to bring ourselves to believe this. The effect of varying degrees of humidity is easily observed in animals as well as in human beings. During rainy weather, the hunting dog lies sluggishly before the fire; before a storm sheep and cattle eat the grass greedily, while the raincrow gloomily predicts bad weather from some sheltering tree. Every hunter knows that animals are good weather prophets. Primitive man also lived in close contact with nature, but civilized man has lost the sensitive touch—unless he is afflicted with rheumatism.

Another essential characteristic of stimulating weather is variability. All men, as well as the lower forms of life, must have variety in food, climate, and other conditions of this earthly existence. Monotony is deadening to both body and brain. The north temperate zone of cyclonic storms is the best region in the world because of the great variety of weather it has to offer. Even a cold wave in winter, if not too severe, brings a healthy glow to our bodies and quickens every faculty within us.

An ideal climate, then, should have moderately cool winters as a mental stimulus; moderately warm summers as a physical stimulus; a rather high relative humidity, except in warm weather when the air is capable of holding more moisture; and frequent changes in temperature, humidity, sunshine, electricity, and barometric pressure. At Lake Placid, New York, which is ideal in many ways, including elevation, the winters are too cold; and this is true in general of the northern United States and Canada east of the Rockies. From Maine northward, the winters only are bad; but farther south the summers are too hot. In central Florida the summers are too long; while the California climate is too monotonous. Parts of New Zealand and Australia are rather good; northern Japan is better; but the eastern central United States and western central Europe are the best regions in the world.

"If we can conquer climate," wrote Huntington at the end of his book on civilization and climate, "the whole world will become stronger and better." From time immemorial, human beings have attempted in various ways to control the weather, because excessive heat or cold or dampness or dryness are alike disagreeable to them. But most of the attempts made thus far—whether with charms, or cannon, or bombs, or dust, or electricity— appear to have been failures when viewed scientifically. However, when the causes of the weather are more fully known, it may be possible to control it, at least so far as precipitation is concerned. According to Professor Hering, it is already possible to avert damage by hailstones to maturing grapes in certain districts of France by bombarding the threatening clouds with large, funnel-shaped cannon charged with powder. The quantity of heated gas and smoke rings issuing from the cannon seems to dissipate the cloud, either by disruption or by reason of the extra amount of heat introduced into it.

What a wonderful thing it would be to be able to control the time and amount of rainfall! It might be difficult to use such power to everyone's satisfaction, but we can all recall periods of widespread drought when a few inches of rain would have checked forest fires, made crops, and entirely changed the face of nature. Climatic changes, like pandemics, may be due to variations in solar activity and students of electricity and magnetism may some day conquer them. In the mean time, we shall continue to imitate the migratory birds and hibernating animals, seeking the sunny South or hiding in warm caves during the winter; while in summer we shall live in the cellar or cool our rooms with ice or fans, or go often to the mountains and seashore. A certain amount of stormy weather even the rich should endure for the sake of their health; and it may become the fashion, for economic reasons, to send laborers from one part of the country to another at different seasons to increase their efficiency and give them greater opportunities for work. One great advantage of moving to a warmer climate during the winter would seem to be the chance to work and sleep in the open air; still, experiments in ventilation are not yet conclusive. Man always did live in a cave and cover his body more or less with skins and rags. Even our sleep seems to depend much more upon the coolness of our bedrooms than upon the relative amounts of oxygen and carbon dioxide in the night air.

The question is often asked, "Does civilization depend upon race or place?" Looked at in a broad sense, one might answer that "place" has had much to do with the formation of "race." But even if we limit the discussion to the present time, there are many important ways in which the climate of a given region affects the people of that region. Man is hampered in his efforts to advance civilization by storms, floods, cold, desert conditions; by the scarcity of food, clothing, shelter, and materials with which to work; and by the lack of health and energy in regions where body and mind are affected by extremes of climate or disease.

Changes in the weather from day to day, which set the blood in motion and tone up the system, seem to have largely controlled human progress. The great centers of civilization, where great ideas have been born and developed, seem to have always been where the climate was best for human activity. Apparent exceptions to this rule may perhaps be explained by the shifting of the regions of cyclonic storms. The climate of Persia and Egypt, for example, was doubtless more variable and stimulating centuries ago than it is at the present time. Three of the earliest and greatest steps in civilization were the invention of tools, the invention of speech, and the discovery of the use of fire. Man's primeval home had a climate similar to that of modern Greece, but was much more variable from day to day. Fire was first employed as a source of heat; the climate must have been cold and there must also have been plenty of wood. Only after heat was used for cooking food did the use of fire extend to the tropics. In the case of iron, there must have been ore lying about where large fires were kindled in order to melt out the iron, and a man of genius must have been present with a generation of alert men to put his discovery into operation. The use of iron probably originated in northern Africa about six thousand years ago, when the climate of Egypt was cooler than to-day.

Few things have had more influence on civilization than agriculture, which depends on climate, and all of the great staple foods except rice and corn seem to have arisen in temperate regions, where agriculture has made far greater strides than in the tropics. Moreover, where irrigation was necessary man developed more rapidly, because it required care and a social organization. Farming develops independence. It is a great stimulus to effort to be forced to depend upon one's self for supplies.

The invention of writing marks the great boundary line between barbarism and civilization. It was developed by the Mayas in Guatemala and Yucatan and by the Babylonians,

Chinese, and Egyptians, separately or together, in the Old World. With writing, anything that was useful could be handed down for thousands of years and thoughts could be spread far and wide. Where would we be today but for the recorded ideas of the Greeks and Egyptians? No great man except Mahomet has arisen within 25° of the equator, and even Mahomet's ideas were developed in a cooler region than the one in which he lived. In Egypt the great men lived from Thebes northward, outside the 25° limit. Civilization today is the highest where climatic energy is the greatest; and civilization, looked at broadly, has followed the lines of organic evolution as influenced by climate. Civilization that originated in the tropics, as in Mexico, Yucatan, Peru, etc., depended upon pulsations of climate, or eras of cold, succeeded by warmer periods. We no longer believe that only one glacial epoch has visited the world, but many periods of cold have come and gone in the various geological ages. We can even find pulsations of climate by examining the rings of the big trees of California. Why did the civilization of the tropics not make a great impression on the world? Because the climate did not change sufficiently to afford a stimulus necessary for continual progress. Men went a certain distance and then stopped. In Central America, however, the Mayas evolved a remarkable architecture, a calendar based on observation of the stars, and a system of writing better than that even now used by the Chinese; but Yucatan was visited by what are called "northers," periods of stormy, cool weather, which furnished the stimulus needed.

The fall of the Roman empire has been explained as fundamentally due to climate. In the golden age of Rome storms and rainfall were abundant, but in the third century much less rain fell and the storms diminished in frequency and violence. Agriculture declined while malaria increased. No longer had the Romans energy to resist malaria and to overcome agricultural difficulties, and Rome fell.

Aug. 20—Climate and Character

The wise man no longer expects either superlative greatness or superlative goodness from the far North or from the tropics. The leaders of mankind, both in thought and morals, have come and will doubtless continue to come from regions having a temperate climate. Not even in the delightful elevated plateaus and mountainous districts of the tropics can one expect any very great achievements under present conditions, because the climate there is usually too monotonous. The writer has many times visited and carefully observed the inhabitants of various parts of Europe, North America, and tropical America; and he believes that the influence of climate is fundamental. Race, religion, government, and educational opportunities are important; but climate seems more important and far-reaching in its effects. Take two white men of practically the same advantages and character, and send one to the tropics, while the other remains in Delaware, for example. What is the result? The first begins to degenerate within a short time after he sets foot on tropical soil, while the second should be improving with every passing day. Character depends mainly on will-power, and the will is almost invariably weakened by tropical conditions. A temperate climate makes for honesty, sobriety, industry, initiative, truthfulness, self-reliance, self-control, and high standards of living and attainment; while in the tropics one may expect laziness, carelessness, drunkenness, untruthfulness, immorality, and generally low standards of living.

Comparative studies have been made by experts of countries differing widely in climate when settled by men of the same race and character. One of the best comparisons of this kind is between Ontario and the Bahama Islands, both settled by Englishmen, but one having a stimulating climate and the other sapping the energy that man needs to initiate and carry out inventions and reforms and to live on a high plane of thought and action. The man who is truly successful under such adverse conditions deserves large credit.

Aug. 27—A Glance Backward and Forward

Life originated on the earth when the climate was ready for it and when suitable food was present to support it. The physical conditions were probably nearly what they are now. The temperature range of active life is from 32° to 104° F. or from freezing to fever heat. Spores of fungi can resist much greater extremes. The lowest fungi are bacteria, which were probably the first forms of life and appear to be the simplest of all and most resistant. For a long, long time the world knew only a very low order of life. Plants must have come before animals. The law of development was gradual change from simple to complex. The great variety was due to the tendency in the protoplasm to vary, and to differences of environment, in which latter climate figured very largely. The amount of water vapor and carbon dioxide in the atmosphere greatly influenced climate by preventing radiation and increasing absorption of the sun's heat. Warm climates have been the rule throughout geologic history, when the north and south poles were inhabited by plants and animals, but a number of short cold eras have separated the longer warm periods during which the land was elevated, mountains

formed, and wide destruction ensued.

There came a time when great forests covered the earth and our coal was formed. Only in recent times did flowering plants, and broad-leaved trees, and swarms of insects appear, with great development of the mammals, followed by brute man and then men like those of the present day, who have probably existed from thirty to fifty thousand years.

The pulse of life through the ages has been largely dependent upon climate, and the extinction of one race to be followed by another was largely due to changes in climate that were too rapid to allow for adaptation. The complex, over-refined types then died off and the lower types came to the front. These periodic changes of climate have been due mainly to the elevation of the land into cool regions, and to rhythms of solar energy by which the earth received more or less heat and light. The giant trees of California exist there and there only because the climate is similar to what it was when they had a wide distribution over the earth.

Improvement has always come through facing difficulties, struggling against severe conditions, and these conditions have usually been the result of climate. We say that a man rises to meet responsibilities. They bring forth his best effort. This is true also in the world of plants and animals. The vertebrates, or animals having a backbone, arose through this struggle and became active, dynamic forces. From water, they passed to the land and to the air. Terrestrial limbs were formed, as in the older reptiles, and feathers and skins appeared to protect birds and mammals from the cold.

The dinosaurs, or giant reptiles, developed into birds in the cold regions, while in the warmer climates they simply grew larger and more terrible. A cataclysm appeared in the Laramide revolution which destroyed these terrible monsters and allowed the mammals to develop.

Man originated in Central Asia on the great plateau just north of the Himalaya mountains, where the climate became gradually colder and drier. A portion of the original tribe migrated to Java when it was still connected with the mainland and this was the origin of the Pithecanthropus. The main tribe remained as hunters, and appeared in Europe as cave men, the Nordic race being the one most highly developed because it remained in the temperate climate of central Europe and Asia.

Struggle to obtain food was a large element in man's development and this was dependent upon climate. Man naturally was a wanderer, a nomad, a hunter, and in Egypt this wandering life finally became impossible because he was confined to one tract, and, not being able to migrate, he had to devise means by working his brain in order to increase his supply of food, hence agriculture arose and the taming of animals. Social life developed from the necessity of getting together to get food and protect it and the colony. This caused the development of language. Agriculture was a female invention and occupation. Wives were selected for their strength until prisoners were used as slaves and woman was set up for adoration.

We have glanced at the past. What of the future? The climate of the earth is becoming drier and men more nervous. Central Asia is no longer a fit place for the making of a race. As in the past, the adaptable types will survive and the others perish. Our strong men were made by fighting physical obstacles; our thinkers have behind them a long ancestry of knitted brows and compressed lips. Civilization is full of dangers; with its easy life, its temptations, its luxuries, its petty cares, its selfishness, and its lack of incentive. The smooth ice is apt to trip us if we are not very careful. If we want our children to amount to anything, we should give them the same chance to struggle that we had. Even the trees must feel the chill of winter in order to flourish in summer. Vigilance and activity have been the basis of improvement in the past and work is still necessary to progress and happiness.

"God toward thee hath done his part, do thine," said Milton, stuggling against the affliction of total blindness. Our Longfellow exprest it another way:

Know how sublime a thing it is
To suffer and be strong.

Let us work, let us endure the icy blasts of winter and the no less icy mental and moral sufferings incident to human life with a calm fortitude, knowing that all these things are necessary to perfection, which is the ultimate justification of being. It takes a rough sea to make a perfect sailor. If we face the future sensibly and bravely, and escape the bad effects of civilization, then we may confidently look forward to a rapidly approaching golden age for the human race,—the highest type of life on the earth, for whom this planet seems eminently fitted, with its plants and animals, minerals and precious stones, mountains and rivers, grandeur, and beauty, and variety. Man will use his intellect as he has already done to assist in the struggle against the all-conquering cold. He will live in glass houses, harness the sun and wind and tide, and draw upon the energy of the atom to furnish heat and other forms of power. He will conquer most diseases, prolong human life, become stronger physically, mentally, and morally, and settle business troubles by brotherly kindness rather than by force and cunning.

PROVIDENCE VIEWED AND REVIEWED

The Rev. CHARLES RUMFITT, LL.D., London

All these things are against me.—Gen. 42:36.

The God which fed me all my life long unto this day.—Gen. 48:15.

What a great contrast there is between the words and the spirit of these texts. Yet they were said of the same events, tho at different periods of Jacob's life. The first was when he was passing through them; the second many years after when he was realizing the good they had brought to him and his family. Thus he viewed and reviewed the providence of God. In his review he altered his opinions, was sorry for his murmuring against the dealing of God with him, and acknowledged that all was for the best, especially those things which he had thought were for the worst. His experience and conduct were typical of those of God's people in every age. The way by which God leads them is mysterious, and causes suffering and apparent disaster, so we cry out that we are being brought down in sorrow to the grave; but when the things are finished and we enjoy the good they have brought and the peaceable fruits of righteousness, we change our opinions of God and of his ways and thank him for the very events for which we were tempted to curse him. A careful study of the conditions and circumstances of Jacob at these two periods of his life will give us the principal reasons for this contrast.

I. Jacob lived in the first period by sight instead of by faith. The law of life for all God's people is faith in God's promises even against appearances. This was especially so with the patriarchs who, as the fathers, were to be examples for all their generations. Jacob had succeeded to the birthright, had been instructed in the traditions by both his father and grandfather, had longed for the birthright, and was determined to have it in all events. And he obtained it. But like his fathers he must

be tried. "All these things" were therefore sent and arranged by God to try his faith; and they were severe because of his deep disposition and cunning plots which he had used to secure the birthright.

He was tried especially with respect to the life of Joseph. His trials were made to arise, as are most of the temptations of God's people, out of the ordinary conditions of life. The hatred of his brothers and the business of their occupation were used by God to fulfil his plan for sending Joseph away. Joseph was missing, and his coat, which Jacob had made as the symbol of his love and of Joseph's heirship, was placed before Jacob saturated with blood. Jacob immediately came to the conclusion that Joseph was "without doubt" rent in pieces and dead. He had not sufficient ground for this. The sons did not say their brother was dead, but that they had found the coat. Jacob was misled by appearances and reason and feeling. He ought to have had faith in God; he should have remembered the promises. God had sworn to his fathers and had promised him many times that his seed should become a great nation and a blessing to the world; and that was to be through the life of Joseph. Jacob should have believed God even against appearances, should have been confident that God's promise could not fail, that therefore Joseph would be found and that he himself would see his son again. This was the first reason why Jacob was so overwhelmed with sorrow, because he looked at appearances and was led by reason rather than faith in God. If he had trusted in God as his grandfather had done in a greater temptation, he would have been supported and blest and would have endured the temptation. It is through living by sight instead of by faith that Christians are so overwhelmed with trouble and induced to declare, "All these things are against me."

II. Jacob, at the time of the first text, did not know the real facts of his own life. "All these things" which he so sadly thought were against him were not true; he only supposed them to be true. He had been shamefully and wickedly misled. His sons had deliberately conspired to deceive him so as to cover their own sin and to get rid of their hated and envied brother. He said "Joseph is not," but Joseph was the governor of all Egypt; "Simeon is not," but Simeon was safe in the hands of Joseph and safer in the care of God; "Ye will take Benjamin also," he thought into danger, but really he was going into the protection of the brother who so longed to see him. Jacob therefore, building upon untrue information and supposing "things" that had no foundation, came to wrong conclusions of God's dealings with him and was troubled and full of foreboding. His experience and conduct were the same as many of the people of God in such circumstances. We do not know the facts of our lives; what we do know we know only "in part," and what is told us is also in part and much of it untrue. Hence, to form an opinion of God's providence on all we know or suppose is to do an injustice to God, to make ourselves miserable, and to lay up future trouble. "Judge nothing before the time," nor by feeble sense, but wait until we are told. Soon all shall be known.

III. Jacob, when he spoke the words of the first text and was passing through the dark providences, thought all these things were pure misfortunes, disconnected and accidental, or caused by the spite or errors of men. Afterwards he saw that they were part of a great plan of God, carrying out a fore-ordained purpose and a fore-promised blessing. He was perplexed; he could not see why these things should be. He would blame himself for showing so much love and preference for Joseph when he knew that his brothers hated and envied him, for sending Joseph to Shechem when he knew that it was a dangerous place after the affair of the massacre. But he was anxious for the safety of his sons; he would blame his sons for their envy of Joseph and for their want of care for him and their lack of prudence before Pharaoh. He would look upon the action of strangers as accidental. That these things were of God he could not think, and might have refused to believe that God would do such things to him. Therefore he refused to be comforted, and believed that all these things worked against him. Afterwards, however, when in his last days he looked back upon the whole perspective of his life, he could trace everywhere the hand of God. He would remember that his grandfather Abraham had told him that his seed should go into a land that was not theirs, and that this was the beginning of the prophecy. He would be able to see the connection of all these events; that Joseph's brothers had left Shechem for Dothan which was on the highway to Egypt; that the Midianites had come just at the time to carry Joseph to Egypt; that Joseph had been in prison and falsely charged, but used by God to interpret dreams and then placed in high position to preserve life— lives of his own family and also of the Egyptians. And seeing all these things in close connection and the good they had done, he acknowledged that God was the first cause of all. He thanked God for all the way he had led him and fed him and redeemed him. Such is the experience of the people of God.

IV. Jacob thought that "all these things" were against him, because they caused him suffering and loss; afterwards he knew that they constituted the discipline sent by God to change his name and character and thus to fit him for his high calling as the type of spiritual life to all his descendants. Each of the three patriarchs was a type of a principal element of the Christian life: Abraham was the "friend of God," Isaac was the son of God, Jacob became the prince of God through struggling in prayer. Jacob, the "Heel-catcher" became "Israel," the wrestler with God; and he prevailed over men because he first prevailed with God. But he so attained only by "all these things."

He was the elect of God for the birthright, and by his natural qualities he was the more fitted for it; but at the first he thought to secure it by cunning rather than by the providence of God. This method of life he practised for many years, until he was taught that it would not succeed. "All these things" were sent by God to discipline him. He was driven from home; he had to contend with Laban; he was met on his return by Esau with we know not what intention; he was bereaved of his beloved wife and of his children. All these were judgments, retribution, and chastening to make him know that as the successor to the promised blessing he must live not by deceit but by faith in God. God appeared to him at various times to teach him this; at Bethel, in the house of Laban, and at the Jabbok. Eventually he learned the lesson God intended. He was born again; his name was changed, and he became a true Israel of God, humble, penitent, prayerful, and spiritual, the father and pattern of all his generations. But it was the discipline of "all

these things" that by the grace of God worked this change. So it is with all the people of God.

"Now all these things happened unto them for examples and they were written for our admonition." God's way is often dark, rough, mysterious, chastening, and grievous. But let us walk in it by faith believing that we shall know what we know not now and shall thank God for those very things which we thought were for our ruin but have found were for our good.

THE CONTEMPORARY CHRIST

Edward Yates Hill, D.D., Philadelphia, Pa.

Have I been so long with you and yet hast thou not known me, Philip?—John 14:9.

Philip called him "Lord," indicating that he already had enough knowledge of Jesus to yield to him the sovereignty of his life. Nevertheless, he was disturbed with dissatisfaction because he felt that Jesus could make a disclosure not yet given to the disciples, and that he, as a disciple, was competent to see something divine in Jesus which had not yet been vouchsafed to him. He was quite like all students who know their subjects, yet realize that one of the joys of their student-life is to make fresh discoveries of what they already know, and from the basis of the known to press on into the unknown. The greatest mind of the Church was the Apostle Paul; and yet, after uttering truths about Christ, the full beauty and overwhelming sublimity of which still enrapture the human mind, Paul confessed that his highest ambition remains, that he might know Christ and the power of his resurrection. Every generation must discover anew and make contemporary the great souls of the past. These great souls must come into our time, become near to us, and we must commune with them, if we are to feel the power of their spirits. It is reimpression that deepens impression and makes it permanent. The first reading of a book flashes its outstanding ideas before the mind, but the second reading integrates the whole book into our being. We are always asking for the new books to tell us over and over again the old thought, revised, illumined, and enriched by the new experience of our time. We shall always require

poets and prophets, philosophers and teachers, to take the same everlasting realties in God, in man, in nature, and pass them through their living minds on to us with the freshness of rediscovery. The miracle of the incarnation came once in human history; but, Christ is reborn in many lives, and must be if he is to be our contemporary.

There was once a book written called, *The Larger Christ.* It is a misnomer. There is no larger Christ, for he is the same yesterday, to-day and forever. Out from the bosom of God he came with all spiritual and moral perfection to be the ideal and Savior of all generations and the goal of all history. Progress is following him and him alone. But, if the idea of a larger Christ is false, it is true that we may have a larger thought and experience of Christ. The limitation is on us and not on him.

We glory in the labors and contributions of those lofty minds of the ancient Church who left us the Nicene creed. They saw that nothing would ultimately bind earth and heaven except the very God incarnate in Jesus of Nazareth. We glory in the rediscovery by Martin Luther that the spiritual and moral triumph of man is determined solely by his vital union with this dying and risen Christ. We glory in all those blessed mystics who, in all ages, have seen the Christ walking up and down through all the avenues of creation as the immanent God, clothed in forms in whic only the rarest souls could see him.

Now it would be a strange thing if this universal Christ, who is God's expression of an eternal humanity, should not be discovered in our time in some new light. Our generation is unique in that it is the last thus far.

> Heir of all the ages
> In the foremost files of time.

We have had a new experience. The changes that have come over the world are staggering in their immensity and significance. We look out upon life from an angle never reached before. The intense and detailed study of every human interest has caused generalizations to be made, and principles and laws to come into view which are very revolutionary in much thinking. The whole world is so changed, except in elemental human nature, by the new ideas and their application that our forefathers would think they were dreaming if they should return to us.

Now you naturally ask the question: What deeper discovery of Christ are we making to meet the special exigencies, needs, and problems of our time? What is it that your modern Philip sees or wants to see that will suffice to give him firmer faith and deeper encouragement? Let us see if we are making Christ our contemporary, and wherein we are knowing him or trying to know him in some new and deeply needed way.

First, our modern psychology is showing the deeper significance of human want, and that Christ alone can give satisfaction to the soul. The materialistic explanations of the nature of the soul are breaking down of their own weight. This generation is aware that it has more nearly demonstrated the exhaustion of all temporal things to satisfy life than any generation in history. It has defined life in every possible term. It has sought to express life by every adjective and verb. It is about to be seen that the more thorough students of the human soul are right when they say that the finite implies and demands the infinite. Moreover, this generation is in the process of discovering afresh the truth of St. Augustine's dictum, that the only rest for the finite is on the bosom of the infinite; and that what we require is nothing that man can do, but only what God, through Christ, can do. Many to-day are restless, worried, and have the sense of being robbed of something fine and elemental—something harboring peace and quiet joy, which they know belongs to them, but which they know not how to grasp. There is for them a life which eludes, tantalizes, but does not come

to them. They hunger for God, but they have not learned to name their hunger. They have an instinct for Christ; look wistfully, yearningly, toward him; but do not dream that in their very longing he is near. Ah! it is the vacancy in man; the failing search for satisfaction; the confused and erratic struggles in the domain of thought; the hungering for new emotions; the cheapening of the material riches of the world; the disgust with worldly ambition as futile to compose the spirit; the sickening sense of satiety with the world's pabulum in all its forms; the distrust of man's devices to heal the hurts of society or to improve the relations of the nations—it is the feeling that our ideals, artificially created and blown up into iridescence by propaganda, are as evanescent as bubbles; that there is no power in man alone to bring either peace or satisfaction—it is this, the very cynicism and despair in so many hearts that will bring a rebound to the spiritual realities. The result of it all is that religion is becoming a watchword in the most surprising quarters, even down in the marts of trade, and that multitudes are hovering about in the neighborhood of Christ with a vague but growing consciousness that they must make discovery of him.

Moreover, our nation is haunted by this Christ, whom it repels but would embrace. No nation can rise to a great height of idealism, where it sees and exultantly accepts its share in the weight of the cross, and then fall back into sordid selfishness, demobilizing both its spiritual and moral powers, without a biting sense of betrayal. And the betrayal itself only brings out from the shadows the sad and accusing face of him against whom the wrong has been done. Never did disciples feel more poignantly than disciples feel now those burning eyes turned upon them. Never were Christians more aware of disappointment which they have thrown into the soul of their Lord. Truly, America is pursued by the inescapable presence. There is one upon us like the "Hound of Heaven," of which Thompson wrote in such immortal lines. The best spirits of America are terribly aware of one before whom they are in judgment. There is a deep sense of failure in the consciousness of our thoughtful people, a sense of sin, and it is all because of him who is with us always and whom we, like Peter, through our very moral lapse, know more deeply every day. But while he is our rebuke he is also our encouragement and our hope, for he never despairs of us, knowing that ideals which we have once enthroned we can never ultimately abandon, but will enthrone again.

This leads me to say that much of the prevalent criticism of Church and State, of industry and economics, of education and social life, is the articulate conscience of a better known Christ. I say much of the criticism, but not all. For there is a thoughtless and malicious criticism which deserves contempt. The Church, just because she heralds the Christ and claims to follow him, is most naturally the object of fault-finding and abusive scorn. Much of the criticism of the Church by the outside world is stupid and deplorable, issuing from ignorance and sin and propagated by imitation and contagiousness. Jesus said, "I will pray the Father and he shall give you . . . the Spirit of truth; whom the world can not receive; for it beholdeth him not, neither knoweth him; ye know him, for he abideth with you, and shall be in you." We may, therefore, expect much but certainly not the most helpful criticism from the world. It has not the spirit of truth. But it is just because of this spirit of truth at the heart of the Church, this glorious Christ himself who is always the animating and informing center of the life of the Church, that out of the deeps of the Church come the most searching criticisms of the Church. Every year the Church enters more profoundly into her Masters mind. Every year she looks more closely into his reflection of the eternal realities. More books are written to-day by Christian students upon the life and thought, the purpose and methods, of Jesus Christ than ever in these nineteen centuries. And students do not feel to-day that they have exhausted his significance when they view that matchless life, death, and resurrection as central facts and powers in an eternal economy, but they demand the scientific study of his principles in the conviction that they should be applied to the whole of this temporal life. So intimate is the heart of the Church with her creative Lord, so closely has she viewed his standards, so deep is her communion with his mind, and so fresh and vital are her discoveries in him, that the Church wrestles in an agony of disappointment that she is not a better

Church. All along the line, in all communions, there is trouble and pain because the Church is aware of inadequate procedures, because of reliance upon unspiritual resources and methods, because of too narrow definitions of the Church's task, because of excess of machinery and the waste of vital powers. The living conscience of the Church is astounded when calmly told that she is more interested in the safety of property and the comfort of the privileged than she is in the personal opportunity for growth in character of man, woman, and child. She is made ashamed when it is hinted that by compromise of her devotion to the interests of the unprotected multitudes she may save her institutional prestige and have the resources for institutional success. Such sensitiveness, such recoil, reveals a heart of loyalty. There may be waverings and vibrations, but there is a center, strong and true, sure at last to rule. Hidden in the soul of the Church is the Master's throne of moral judgment.

So Christ is the conscience of the Church and, through the Church, the conscience of the nations. Some are very pessimistic now. They think that the end of the age has come and that God has lost all patience with humanity, having given us over to greed and hate, to passion and mutual destruction. They seem to think that we have reached the nemesis of wickedness and that we now totter at the edge of an abyss, and that this civilization is to be hurled into the darkest deeps of chaos. I do not believe a word of it. The dispensation of the Holy Spirit of Christ will not prove such a fiasco. On the contrary it would seem that such dismal views are possible only because a present Christ has sharpened to an extraordinary degree the moral perceptions of our time. Men detect iniquity as never before. We see the shadows just because the light is so bright. Many things—customs in business, practises in social life, political methods—that passed unchallenged in the years gone by are frowned upon and regarded as intolerable at the present time. The reason is that Christ walks up and down the land, the most colossal and controlling figure among us. He has created a standard, inspired a sentiment, produced an atmosphere, which even the most crass, sordid, and obstinate worldling can not wholly ignore. In every council and convention of whatever class of people, dealing with whatever subject, there is the tilt of heads and the bending of ears to hear what this imperious conscience is dictating, what the best informed public opinion will tolerate, what his Spirit is saying unto the churches. He makes more and more uncomfortable those who would oppose his Spirit and ethic, and he continually gives the comfort and joy of deeper views into his beauty and divinity to those obedient to his ideals.

Students of the development of human life make much of heredity and environment. But the induction of facts is not complete that omits the most dominant elements. The Church has an inheritance of power, unconquerable and all-persuasive. Nor is there anything in our environment closer to us than Christ.

Speak to him thou for he hears, and Spirit with Spirit can meet—
Closer is he than breathing, and nearer than hands and feet.

Adaptation to environment is the law of nature. If there were no Christ in our environment then our adaptions would be solely to the sordid battle of the world, to the battle in which animals fight for survival, and humans, by more cunning than skill, seek selfish ascendency. But we know that there is something higher touching us all the time to which we, by the very law of the Spirit within us, must adapt ourselves. A soul is near who awakens in us and draws out from us powers of love, who elevates, refines our vision, who inspires in us hope, and who builds our faith in the goodness of God, in the reasonableness of his methods, and the superlative worth to him of man, his child.

In our deeper knowledge of Christ we should miss something of transcendent importance if we did not recognize in him our sovereign creative ideal. Comprehensively he and he alone creates the spiritual life in man. Men are new-born by his power. Born in him they are forever associated with him in his creative work. By him they seek to find the way and the truth, to do a better thing, and to excel in the fine art of the highest living. By the divine which he brings into humanity he awakens all beautiful visions and noble dreams, bringing an infinite urge into the soul to express the infinite and the eternal in many ways. To him we owe all those resources so necessary for the recreational and reconstructive work now demanded of us. Our inspired moments, our visions of a better life, our yearning for an improved social order, our dreams of a divine kingdom, our struggles for brotherhood and liberty and the realization of personal possibility, our faith in the highest values and their attainability by man, our sense of high calling, our consciousness of responsibility and of reserves of power to meet it, our determination to press on with courage and with hope until the divine pattern is reproduced on earth and the kingdoms of this world shall become the kingdom of love—all we have making for spiritual and moral victory are from him, from him!

It is everywhere acknowledged that we are in an era of necessary reconstruction. The Spirit of him who said "Behold I make all things new" is upon us. But something more than external reconstruction is the first demand of our creative Christ. There must be a reconstructed soul before there can be a reconstructed society. And a soul can not be reconstructed except by processes of life from within. And that life never comes within save as it first comes down from above. A great accession of new life is the primal need of the hour. Our first duty is evangelism. The most philosophic, statesmanlike, and effective voice pleading for reform and reconstruction to-day is the voice that cries, often with emotional pleading in a revival hymn, "Come to Jesus." The recalcitrant and disobedient elements in society will never come under mastery until the Master is given his rightful throne in human hearts. And the inalienable duty of the Church is to bring the people to a living and deepening knowledge of the Savior. If we are ever to lift this world to the heights of God, we must resort to those heights for the power.

I speak intensely of evangelism. It is a right beginning for reconstruction, for if the Church moves upward, all society will move upward with her. Waves of crime come with spiritual depression; waves of moral interest and living come with thoughtful, spiritual quickening. But, let us remember, evangelism is much more comprehensive than emotional elevation. The fires that kindle in the heart must awaken the mind to clear and accurate thinking. The "evangel" is the whole love and thought and work of Christ for life in all its relations. It is the vision and enthronement of the human values as of the highest worth. It is the proclamation of eternal ideals hovering over us in all our daily life. It is the pledge to the soul of heavenly power not only to love supremely, but to love with all the mind and strength the things of Christ, that they may continually unfold their principles for our unfolding life as, by our obedience, we come into deeper fellowship with him.

In the work of reconstruction, one of the deepest concerns of the present moment is to see the employers and the workers at one in fraternal cooperation, recognizing one another as partners in the enterprise of true living, holding all they have and are as stewards for the good of all. Such a consummation will be far on the way when the Church sincerely, thoroughly, courageously, adopts what she already knows are the two sovereign principles of Christ's work; the renewal of souls, and the application of his principles to the whole industrial, economic, and social life of the world—when, like a martyr, she is ready to fill up the measure of crucifixion for the entire program of Christ.

We long for pure politics, to know that our liberties are not secretly bartered and desecrated. We seek a democracy so thorough, real, and all-inclusive that the thoughtful purposes of the people can not be diverted, nor those purposes formed in darkness or bewilderment. We want a country where the quality of living shall be more important than the quantity of things. We want a government where our laws shall be just and right; where no man or set of men, of their own license, shall set them aside, or foil their operation, or seek to change them save by orderly persuasion and process. That day will come when the Church visualizes and understands what the kingdom of God means, when the prayer-life of a dynamic Church so enters and spiritually dominates political life as to make low political ideals impossible.

Millions are the prayers to-day for peace among the nations. And that day will come whenever there is a disarmament conference that will invite the spirit of the Prince of peace to come and counsel effectively in the discussions. So long as diplomacy remains pagan, and great States put their ambitions above the law of God, so long as the Church

fails to call the nations, as such, before the divine judgment, that long will there be wars and rumors of war.

Searching is the thought at present into the methods and ends of education. Those who can see deep and far know that we can not close the windows looking toward spiritual culture and values above all markets, without impoverishing and enfeebling this republic and making existence a sordid boon. The contemporary Christ would have us read: "Man does not live by bread alone."

Some day we look for a united Church. We humbly bemoan our divisions. We are not adequately comforted in our attempts to explain them as providential. We know that only an overruling Providence can endure them. Our divisions cause much mutual crippling. They create artificial limitations of power. They impose burdens upon towns. They make for failure of opportunity. They induce reasonable complaints from the world, bring a burden upon the enlightened conscience, and are adverse to the Master's prayer. Our vigorous effort in this new age should be first to unite the family groups. Then, if the people are good enough to be trusted with anything so great and glorious, possibly the whole Church may come into organic unity. But it can not come, and we do not want it to come, unless it comes out of the hearts of the people burning for the unity of the Spirit in the bond of peace. Unity imposed by human contrivance would be a failure, but, springing from loving devotion to a better-known Christ, it would be a glorious success.

There is only one master-builder for our shattered times, only one to whom we can trust the work of reconstruction. He alone is wise and strong. No other contemporary is sufficient for our needs. He lives and works in the sphere of eternal reality. What is new to us is the everlasting in him. His concern is to lift us higher into God, to disclose the new demands of righteousness, to correct and perfect our morality, to open up other areas of love, to make beautiful and sacred all experience, to interblend the realms of heaven and earth, and interlock forever the human with the divine.

Philip wanted the Christ to make a larger revelation. Behold, the Philip of to-day sees the great Lord as never before. Philip also knows what must be done. God grant he be not disobedient unto the heavenly vision.

TURNERS OF THE OTHER CHEEK

The Rev. SYDNEY STRONG, Seattle, Wash.

Ye have heard that it was said, An eye for an eye and a tooth for a tooth; but I say unto you, Resist not him that is evil; but whosoever smiteth thee on thy right cheek, turn to him the other also.—Matt. 5:38.

Jesus said, there is a law of society with which you are familiar. It is that when men do evil, they shall be punished according to the rule of an eye for an eye and a tooth for a tooth. This may be called the law of retaliation, or exact justice. The rule appears just; and is indeed higher than that which actually obtains among us to-day. Among all those punished in America to-day thousands get less than exact justice, while other thousands get vastly greater punishment than exact justice; while other thousands get off entirely. No rich woman ever goes to prison; few rich men ever stay long.

Jesus said, in this world of evil, there is a better and higher way and he proceeded to give it by saying: "I say unto you, resist not him that is evil, but whoever smiteth thee on thy right cheek, turn to him the other also." There has never been, I think, any doubt as to what that meant. Doubts have arisen entirely around the application of these words. Is that the way to treat evil men? Or, is it impossible? Can one actually be a turner of the other cheek; and if so, would it be for the good of the world?

The practically uniform practise of people for centuries is against it. Mankind, however, has a way of throwing off some agelong habit or idea. Mankind for ages believed that, the earth was the center of the universe, with the sun circling the earth; believed that some were destined to be slaves; believed that cannibalism was proper; believed that woman was an inferior being; believed that dueling was the practise of gentlemen; that drunkenness was an everlasting habit; that God made man out of dust, woman out of man's rib.

While the uniform practise of mankind, in any specific way, is an approval almost conclusive, yet there are so many exceptions as to make one pause before declaring against the practicability of a teaching, especially if it comes from one who has won the confidence of the world as much as Jesus has. One must be ever open-minded lest some long-neglected or misunderstood truth may become one of the Messiah-truths of the world, and he be found with those who crucify this truth.

I was, therefore, greatly interested in the story of Bertha W. Clark, who visited the Huterite people, living in the James River Valley of South Dakota, whom she describes in the *Survey* as "Turners of the Other Cheek." They constitute one of the oldest communistic societies in existence, being 400 years old, organized by Joseph Huter, in the Tyrol. The colony in South Dakota has been in America for fifty years. They are trying, in matters social and religious, to pattern their lives after the earliest Christian disciples. They are progressive in the use of modern machinery and have "diligently developed some of the finest farms in America." No one was aware of their presence until, during the war, they were brought before the courts, fined, imprisoned, and at last by these things, forced to begin another exile —into Canada. After 400 years of seeking they have not yet found a country where they may freely insist that it is a sin to fight.

The story of the wanderings of the Huterites is as interesting as that of the "Children of Israel" and possibly may become as important; for they, too, have their "Chronicles."

During the war they were taken into court and accused of following a "black book," and when this book was ordered to be translated, so that all might see the blackness of the contents, there were found such sentences as these:

"Thou shalt not kill." "Resist not evil." "If thine enemy hunger feed him." "If he smite thee on one cheek turn to him the other also." They had declined to buy liberty bonds, but they had offered money to the government generously for anything except war. Some of the young men had gone to prison. Some had lost their lives in prison.

It seems that a delegation interviewed Canadian government officials, who showed them the statute book, which indicated that everyone's religious belief was respected and excused from service if there was a conflict between it and his church creed. The Mennonite people were spoken of by name. As a result, the people began to move to Canada. Just as those remaining in the United States were planning to follow, a wave of ill feeling swept over Canada, against those who had not gone to fight; and an edict went forth from the Canadian government that no more could come. Meanwhile, the two sections are apart.

.The movement had its beginning in 1520. When Luther led a movement for reform, there were those who thought he did not go far enough; and wished to go still further toward the primitive simplicity of the Apostolic Church. These people were called Anabaptists—meaning that people were baptized again. Among some of them it was felt that the shedding of blood in battle was directly against the teachings of Jesus. Because of this they met the most violent opposition, equally from Catholics, Lutherans and Calvinists, and especially from government officials.

In five years a thousand of these were put to death in a small section of Europe, which marks the birthplace of the Huterite church in Bavaria and the Tyrol. The men, after slow torture, were burned at the stake. The women were drowned in sacks in the rivers and lakes. They fled in all directions—just as the early Christians did when persecution broke out in Jerusalem. A large band of them fled to Moravia, and because of the extreme dangers surrounding them, adopted a communistic form of life, just as the early disciples had done. Jacob Huter, founder of the church, was burned at the stake in the year 1536. In Moravia the Huterite people lived for a hundred years and prospered greatly; then came the war between Bohemia and Moravia, and they suffered from the invading armies of both sides—every sort of plunder, ravaging, and indignity. These armies—

Were like wild swine
Falling on God's vineyard
With gluttony and violence;
Bringing an awful tyranny,
Great injustice, every kind of wantonness
On young and old.

They gave themselves to the wild forest.
In the raw, sharp winter's cold.
They suffered direst need.
Nothing beautiful was left to them.
Some were condemned to die.
Men traversed all the land:
Village and market-place were burned.
And what they had endured before
They must keep on enduring.

They fled to Hungary to begin life anew. Again they went through the hardships of pioneer days. They began to see the fruits of their labor in prosperous homes and easier life. Again persecution arose, again they fled, this time to Transylvania. Again the old story repeated itself. Here there were Turks and Tartars to invade and plunder. Then they moved on to Wallachia, but soon the armies of Russia and Turkey overran them.

And then they heard of the great offer made by the Empress Catherine to the Mennonites. She had great tracts of devastated lands in Southern Russia and needed colonists. She offered them free lands, exemption from taxes for a period of years, religious freedom and entire exemption from military service. So they "went to Russia, built up villages and prosperous homes." For a hundred years, all went well; in fact they were too prosperous. Those Russians living around them became jealous of their prosperity and privileges. When the 100 years were up, the government refused to renew the old contract, but under a new one proposed that they should do military service and give up their Swiss-German dialect. These two demands were impossible to them. So they started another exile. Thousands upon thousands set out, until the government was alarmed over the loss of thrifty farmers. All who went into exile, came to Canada and the United States. Those who came to South Dakota came in 1874.

Miss Clark was deeply imprest by what she saw during repeated visits among the Huterites in South Dakota. Their social life centers around the home and the church. The most modern conveniences are to be found in the homes. There is no cooking and no kitchen work done in the house. In each colony there is one building for all the laundry work, one for all the baking, one for the milk, one where the little children eat, and one for the men and women. Work is arranged by groups in turn, making it less arduous than work usually falling to the lot of farmers' wives. For hours women and girls sit out under the trees spinning and talking, or spinning quietly while one reads aloud. They say that their communism is different from that advocated by many socialist thinkers of to-day. One said to Miss Clark:

The Socialist plan of communism can never succeed because they are not based on religion. I can not do justice to the richness of the spirit of Christian love and forgiveness which characterizes all their speech. They do not believe in resenting evil in any way. This has been their one refuge through now the four centuries of their existence. Attacked and plundered, and seeing many of their band put to death, the rest of them have never retaliated, but have simply moved on. Their faces show the heritage of four centuries in their rare kindliness of expression—a sweetness mingled with tremendous strength.

The wandering of the Huterites is full of pathos and power. It is unfortunate for us that they are being exiled from the United States; for they carry certain treasures that are sorely needed to enrich our life. Too much is the policy obtaining that we should "inflict everything we have chosen to do on all who come to our land." Far better would it be to encourage all groups of honest people who are striving to arrive at a solution of social life.

The question I now ask about these people is: Are they but wandering Arabs in mankind's life, who will become absorbed; or are they wandering Israelites who bear with them the ark of God, to whom belongs the land of promise, who are seeking for the city of God? I am not disposed to assert that they carry the candle of the Lord, tho I confess they are strangely like those whom Christ described as his followers—strongly like Christ. The progression of human life is full of surprises. Jesus is described as a plant grown out of dry ground; so, many of the great personages and events have proceeded from humble origins. The kingdom of heaven is likened unto a mustard seed—the smallest of all seeds—which was to become the largest tree in the garden. Is this non-retaliation, non-resistance method of the treatment of evil and evil men, which was proclaimed by Jesus and applied by the disciples, which has appeared and re-appeared in small groups of people in every age and in divers manners—persistingly and conqueringly—is it at last to become the acknowledged law for treating evil, the head of the corner of the "social system"? I would not be dogmatic. However, there are signs that the non-resistance idea and movement are adding territory, breaking down opposition, attracting more attention than ever before in the history of the world, and being discust seriously by the rank and file of mankind.

Several things are noticeable. First, the people who are leading in the reconstruction of humanity, the Quakers, in feeding the hungry, binding of wounds of homes and nations, keeping alive the spirit of reconciliation and trusted by all partisans alike, are known far and wide for the practise of non-resistance. The experience of the Quakers in Britain and America stands as an argument for the power of persistence of the principle of non-retaliation and non-resistance.

Second, the most influential personality of the last 100 years is probably Tolstoy. He was endowed with genius and tireless energy that would have compelled attention wherever he went; but the conspicuous feature of his life and its hold on mankind is the fact that he preached and practised non-retaliation, non-resistance, love of enemies. Tolstoy's personality seems to persist, and the only way he explains it is by the fact that he tried to personalize the Sermon on the Mount.

Third, undoubtedly the greatest political and religious movement in progress to-day is in India. There is on in India a people's movement to drive out a foreign power—the most powerful military power that man ever saw—which has at command most efficient economic and military forces for the accomplishment of human purposes. In India are Moslems and Buddhists and Brahmins—heretofore hostile in their partisanship to one another. India has become united under the leadership of one man, whose name is Gandhi. He goes about the country, as unarmed as did Jesus. He tells it far and near, that the only way for India successfully to treat the foreign invader is to treat him with non-resistance. "If there is any blood shed, let it be our blood." So the principle of non-cooperation, non-resistance, gives more promise of winning India's independence (and the same method has spread to Egypt and Persia) than would the arming of her millions. Where did Gandhi get hold of this method with its power. Why, he says he was greatly influenced by Tolstoy and Thoreau; these got it from the teachings of Jesus.

I do not mean to claim too much. I am saying that there are signs in the experiences of mankind's life which indicate that men in great masses (no longer small groups) are beginning to understand and apply the power of non-resistance—which has marked the Huterite church now for 400 years. Men far and wide recognize the utter insanity of appealing to the sword to heal the world of its evil. Those who try to cast out the devil of militarism (called Prussianism a short time ago) are themselves soon inflicted with the same disease. Men are recognizing they must find some other principle of life than that of revenge and retaliation. "The thoughts of God are long, long thoughts"—but by them the worlds were made. Is not this teaching of Jesus one of the thoughts of God?

If the gospel could work in the first century it can work in the twentieth.

Can the principle be worked in this city —as it is worked by the Huterites in the James River Valley? It is far more difficult, yet the early Christians began to work it in the city of Jerusalem. There are many signs of hope. I listened last week to a group of men talking about prisons, and there was a general agreement that modern prison methods are failing to stop evil, are, instead, increasing it. The modern prison method is based on the principle of "an eye

for an eye, a tooth for a tooth." I met a woman last week who has spent a year in prison—because she was opposed to the war —and she referred to the loneliness, the woman being cut off from all that was human and natural and elevating, and yet even expected to improve. Prisons are a logical effect of "an eye for an eye"— enforced by coercion.

Gandhi's soul was burdened—as was the heart of Moses—with the cries of his people, who were opprest, he thought, by a foreign invader. If he thought of guns, swords, aeroplanes, bombs, as possible weapons—he did not take second thought. So, he turned to another kind of power, a higher form of resistance. And it is going on to-day in India—non-cooperation and non-violence. I am not declaring he will secure the independence of his country in this way. I am saying—what is evident to all newspaper correspondents—that he has unloosed a power that, so far, has proved to be more formidable than arms. It is soul power. The spiritual power of men who love their enemies, who turn the other cheek instead of striking back, will some day, I think, be seen to be invincible. Anyway, this is a power worth trying, worth encouraging. If here is a power, armed with which a man or a group may be superior in endurance, in character—then it's worth examining. Jesus says it is the true way to power: that it is the way to cure the evil man; it is the way to conquer enemies.

REALIZING THE MASTER'S IDEA

The Rev. W. H. HOPKINS, Manitou, Colo.

That they may all be one; even as thou, Father, art in me, and I in thee, that they also may be in us: that the world may believe that thou didst send me.—John 17:21.

In the Master's great prayer no thought was more emphasized than that of the unity of his people. Three times it is repeated in this one chapter. It was the great burden of his heart on that last night of his earthly life. The two great reasons for his prayer stand out and appeal to every Christian heart. First, a longing for heart fellowship, the longing that comes to every Christian, that all who love him may be united;

may work, plan, and pray together. The second reason is that the world may believe and be won to him. The surest test of our Christianity is seen in the way in which we follow him in seeking to win those about us. If complacently we can go on and do nothing toward winning the world to him, it is certain that we have but little of his spirit.

I. In these transition days since the war his prayer has received a new emphasis. First, because we have been compelled anew to study the weakness and failure of the Christian Church. There are some facts which are alarming. We are told that there are twenty-seven million boys and girls in America receiving no instruction in either church or Sunday-school. The universal testimony of the chaplains and the "Y" workers in the war was that most of the boys had no Christian foundation. It is a well-known fact that there are thousands of communities in which the church has been and is a waning quantity.

That man who last summer made an automobile trip from Chicago to Colorado Springs and wrote up his observations in one of the papers recited a fact which every student of conditions knows. He said that as he went through the country in all the small towns he would note the fine high-school building with its well-kept grounds and its evidence of being the center of interest. After seeing the high school he would look for the church and would find two, three, four, or more dilapidated, poorly-kept buildings. He asks the question—"Is is true that America is thinking of education and forgetting Christianity?" As every one knows, the answer is the over-churched community—too many churches frequently standing for divisiveness and strife, rather than for unity and fellowship.

Another alarming fact is that for some time there has been a dearth of candidates for the ministry. Business and professional life openings are overcrowded, but in the ministry there is a lack. In many of the colleges there are scholarships awaiting the student for the ministry, and as a rule they are not taken. Is it because our young men have lost their ideals and their idealism? No one who saw the enthusiasm with which they went into the World War can believe it. There may be other reasons but it is certain that the multiplicity of little churches in the average community is one of the reasons. The young man does not see a man's job in the ministry. A re-study of conditions since the war has tremendously emphasized the need of an answer to Christ's prayer.

II. During the war there was a new discovery of the community. We were surprised to find what could be done when all worked together. The changes which came in many communities through the united war work were simply marvelous. There was the discovery of latent talent, and what could be done when men and women worked

together. It will be a long while before those people who worked together in war days will be content with the divisiveness which is frequently created by the large number of churches in the small community.

III. There is a new get-together spirit in the world. Since the Washington Conference the new way to settle difficulties is around the table, working out the new program. The council table method is now in vogue. In this new day a good many see that the church can no longer be the only divisive organization in the community.

The story is told of one village in Texas in which four boys grew up together. They were chums, visited one another's homes, and did everything together. The time came for them each to go to his church school. Each of the four boys became a minister; one a Roman Catholic priest, claiming that his denomination was the only church; another became an Episcopal rector, claiming his church to be the church; another boy became a Baptist minister, refusing to his other three friends the Lord's supper; and the fourth became a Disciple minister, professing that he did not belong to a denomination, and inviting all his friends to the Lord's supper, and none of them accepting the invitation. As the story is told, the fellowship of their boyhood days was entirely ended. It is but a picture of what is happening all the time. Our unfortunate divisions are making impossible the answer to his prayer.

IV. The fourth reason for the new emphasis grows out of the fact that the reason for denominations is largely of the past. It is a matter of tradition, rather than of present-day reality. Once the name Presbyterian, Methodist, Baptist, stood for something. Now these names mean but little. The differences in doctrine in any given church are greater than the differences between that church and sister churches. There is a universal feeling that some change is necessary; that in some way the great prayer must be answered.

What shall it be? Coming from our ecclesiastical leaders there are two answers. Ever since the collapse of the Interchurch World Movement there has been a new emphasis upon denominationalism. We are told that the only way to save the world is through denominations, that any one who touches upon or belittles the denominational spirit is ruthlessly putting his hand on the ark and in great danger. We are given many fanciful and pitiful interpretations of his word, "that they all may be one." Many of these explanations show wonderful ingenuity, but they fail to convince. The average layman in our churches knows better. In a pitiful way there is a trotting out of the old shibboleths. There is the effort to show that it was not unity for which the Master prayed, but a continuance of the present program.

Then there is constantly emphasized that the one thing needed to be done is for Christians everywhere to wait for the outcome of the various conferences. The word is ever going out that local bands of Christians must wait for the ecclesiastical leaders to settle the question. Until New York acts, Smith Corners must keep up the old strife and the old jealousies, the petty stifling programs. It sounds good and deceives some, but the problem with all its difficulties remains. Is there then no outcome? The students of history know that never has any great reform come in that way. Waiting for ecclesiastical leaders has always meant defeat. Christ tried it and the old Jerusalem church leaders sent him to the cross. Paul tried it and in every city he was compelled to shake out his garments and go forth to the Gentiles before the real program began. Girolamo Savonarola tried it in old Florence, and it ended in his being burned at the stake. Luther tried it, but turned to the common people for his only hope. Wesley tried to stay with the ecclesiastical leaders, but his followers did not. It has always been true that the forward movements or reforms in history came not from the ecclesiastical leaders down, but from the common people up.

What is the way out? Where will we find hope? These are not the days for dogmatic statements, but they are days in which we have need to walk humbly, following the best light we have. There are many trying to solve the problem. We have federated churches and independent churches. In many communities there has been an honest desire to get together and to end the stigma which rests upon our Christianity. To an ever-increasing number the one bright ray of light is seen in the community church. It has in it more of promise than anything

else. Since the war the growth of the community church idea has been surprising. Entirely without human leadership, there has grown up a large community church movement. This movement now has its own magazine, and is growing every day. For months now the Brooklyn *Daily Eagle* in its Monday edition has every week featured the community church movement. It is the most hopeful thing on the religious horizon.

The community church, however, in these transition days needs to be defined. There are so-called community churches which satisfy no Christian heart. They are a travesty upon the Christian name and one of the greatest hindrances to the real cause of unity. What is a community church?

First: In the thought of the great majority of community church leaders a community church is a church, and not a club; a church made up of men and women who accept Jesus Christ as Lord and Savior. However broad and varied its work, however much it may seek to touch its community, the basis of its work must be the consecration of hearts to the great Head of the Church. In all our thinking we must keep the Church foremost.

Second: It is a church welcoming on an equal basis all evangelical Christians belonging to church bodies affiliated with the Federal Council of the Churches of Christ in America. It is necessary that there be a working basis. At present the best unity program the country knows is that of the Federal Council of the Churches of Christ. The community church receives all Christians, leaving each one to keep his own denominational affiliations. It asks only that each member recognize the rights of the other one to his peculiar views. In hundreds of communities this type of church is being blest. It is realizing the real spirit of unity.

Third: It is a church aiming to meet all the unmet moral and religious needs of the community. Through its community program it aims to reach every person in the community. The denominational church picks out the members of its denomination and more or less neglects the rest. The community church feels a responsibility for every person in the community. At present the community church has no desire to break away from denominational affiliations. In one community it will be Methodist, in another Presbyterian, and in another Congregational.

"That they all may be one" is now the great longing desire of millions of Christians. It will some day be realized. The old emphasis placing the denominational good above that of the community good will not long hold people. We are hearing the call to the ends of the earth, and we are seeing anew that it must be "beginning at Jerusalem." The goal of the unity is not far off. It is coming even tho there are some ecclesiastics who have not seen the light. How can we hasten the day?

First: By a continual emphasis upon the teaching—one church for each community.

It is far more important that we have community churches, making good friends and neighbors, ever creating the spirit of co-operation and good-will, than it is that we have denominational churches, far too frequently creating strife and jealousy. It takes time for any new teaching to grip the lives of men and women. In every possible way the community church idea must be kept before Christian people of America.

Second: We can hasten the day by multiplying the illustrations of successful community churches. There are hundreds of such churches now doing fine work. Each one is hastening the day when his prayer, "that they all may be one," will be answered.

FROM BOYHOOD TO THE MINISTRY[1]

WILLIAM LAWRENCE, D.D., Bishop of Massachusetts, Boston, Mass.

We then, as workers together with him, beseech you also that ye receive not the grace of God in vain.—2 Cor. 6:1.

A young man stands before you in the pulpit about to preach; as you look at him, you probably assume that he has been an ecclesiastically-minded young man for some years, and then you wait for his sermon. Where did that young man come from? What about his boyhood and early manhood?

Twenty years ago, he with his brothers and sisters was tumbling around his father's house, just a schoolboy. Ten years ago he was carrying a football across the line, amidst the cheers of his fellow students. Five years ago, in darkness and midst shrapnel and shell, he was leading his company up to the trenches in France, was inspiring and steadying them. Only five years ago a captain, and here he is in the pulpit preaching. What sent him here? What has gone on in those few years since? What has driven him towards the ministry? It is in answer to those questions that I want to speak this morning.

The minister comes from the home. He is, to a large degree, what his home, his education, his stock, and his surroundings have made him. Men and women are saying, "Why aren't there stronger young men entering the ministry? Why aren't there more of them? Have we the best; or is medicine or banking getting the best?"

If the stronger men are not coming into the ministry, whose fault is it? Is not the trouble largely with the homes? Is there an atmosphere in the home which is sympathetic with the boy's going into the ministry? Let each parent think this out, "Is my home and its spirit and temper such as makes it natural for my boy to think of the ministry as a possible profession?" I know, for I speak from experience and from some knowledge of young men, that one of the greatest obstacles the young men have in entering the ministry is that their parents do not want them to enter it. A college student came to me last year, saying that his great desire was to be a minister. "What do your parents say?" I asked. "They don't like it," he answered, "and one of the family has been in the university for the last week talking to some of the professors, trying to persuade them to keep me out of the ministry. My father wants me to go into his business."

I know another young man whose mother has led him toward the ministry, and whose father, a man of great culture, says that he hates to see his boy waste his life in the ministry. Only last week I was asked about another, whose father is bringing all the pressure that he can on his son, a university graduate of high promise, to keep him from going into the ministry because he wants him in his business.

[1] This is part of a sermon preached in behalf of the Cambridge Episcopal Theological School.

Is it not a fact that, as we think it over, we say to ourselves, "I can imagine my boy in a broker's office, or as a doctor in a hospital, or as a lawyer, but I can not quite imagine my boy and his wife and children, —my grandchildren,—in a mill city, or living on a 'Main Street' in the Middle West"? That attitude of mind, of course, sifts into the boy, and he assumes that the ministry is not for him.

What sends a young man into the ministry today over these and other obstacles? In old days it used to be assumed that before entering the ministry he should have some vivid or emotional call, and many men are waiting for that kind of a call, which they will never get. The young man of today thinks the subject out somewhat in this way: "I want to put my life where it will do the most good." His mind then runs over the different opportunities—business, law, medicine, engineering, and somehow the idea of the ministry comes to him. He talks these over with his college mates. He thinks them all out; perhaps decides to try one of them, and starts in for business; but there gradually comes over him the thought, "I want to strike at the deepest, strongest part of human life, at the motives of men. The calling of a physician is a noble one; it is a great thing to heal men's bodies; but I want to go deeper than that, and try to do something for their lives, their souls; the Church stands as the great institution for that sort of thing, and the work of the ministry is right at that point. I know nothing of theology and mighty little of the Bible, but God has been good to me, Christ is my leader, and in his name I will start for the ministry. I may not get in; they may put up a five-barred gate of doctrinal obstacles which I can not leap over, but I am going to try it." He enters the theological seminary, and begins his preparation. Free to change his mind, his interest develops into enthusiasm and consecration; and he gladly passes through the gate of ordination.

Now, when he is in, what is his work? Perhaps the best thing I can do is to suggest three instances of men whom I have known and known well among many.

Twenty-five years ago a young man of physical and moral force, the orator of his college class, was under me as a theological student. He had determined that he would

put his life where it would do the most good; and so, during the last year, he went into a hospital and learned how to nurse, for his first work was to be in a Western mining camp where were accidents and illness among the men. After two years he came back into a Massachusetts mill city, and for several years lived in the tenements of the mill hands. After several years of strenuous work he went to a large parish in Chicago, and became a force in the parish and city. Today he is the missionary bishop of a great State in the Northwest, and has an influence far beyond its borders. How interesting that career is! And it is a real one.

Here is another man. Twelve years ago he graduated from an American university; then spent a year in an English university, another year in teaching in a school in the Orient. Entering the ministry three years later, and starting in a mill city, he went to France as chaplain with the first troops to cross, and stayed to the end. Back again in his parish, he is, tho only thirty-three years of age, the guide and spiritual leader, friend and comforter, to some two thousand people. Are there many young men in any other calling in life that have that great opportunity for development and leadership?

Here is a third instance. The war found this man five years ago in the theological seminary. He dropped his books, went to Plattsburgh, crossed with his company to France, rose to the rank of major, went back to the theological school, finished his course, and is now the rector of a large parish in a city of one hundred thousand inhabitants, and is on the way to be one of the spiritual forces of that city.

Can you think of anything more interesting, more varied in life, more calculated to develop all that is finest and strongest in a man than the work of the ministry as illustrated by these three men? Each one of them is following a vision, and he is following it with devotion and enthusiasm. He is moving, too, in a cross-section of society, —far more interesting than moving in a horizontal section. The broker moves largely in a horizontal section. He meets his fellow business men and his clerks. The lawyer has a broader constituency, and the doctor still broader; but the minister is moving every day from the highest to the lowest, and touching every phase of social life.

I came of merchant stock. Until I went into the ministry I never knew any poor people; I had never been in a tenement. To that side of life my eye was blind; but during the first eight years of my ministry I lived with working people, and was in their tenements all the time. I got a different point of view.

Now that is what comes to every man entering the ministry,—a broadening influence, together with an appeal to judgment, leadership, humor, sympathy. Moreover, he is forced to make his own way. You can not compel a lot of people to sit and listen to a stupid preacher, or to follow a lazy pastor. They may do it for two or three months, but the parish will dissolve and no influence of bishop or warden can keep him to the front unless he keeps to the front himself.

The enjoyment of the work, too, is great! He does not sit like the young lawyer or even the young doctor, waiting for clients or patients. They tumble in on him; and seven days in the week, morning, noon and night, he is on the job. It is a joyful work, stimulated with gratitude from those who want his help, sympathy from others, response from the boys. Think of one example of response. I know a young minister, not ten years in the ministry, who wanted to go to the war as a chaplain, but he had a big parish, and his first duty was there. He had two hundred and ninety men and boys in the service, and he sent each of them a message, either by letter or by picture postal card once every month while they were in the service. Think of the satisfaction of keeping in touch with two hundred and ninety such men and boys, and imagine the gratitude of those who returned!

Now, how is the minister prepared? I go back from the work of the minister to his preparation, for it is of this that I want particularly to speak.

There is much talk about the lack of numbers in the ministry. There is lack of numbers, but to my mind, what the Church wants more than numbers is quality.

Have you ever thought? You know about law schools, you know about the College of Physicians and Surgeons, but how much do you know about the theological seminary?

There has, I believe, been almost as much change in the methods of teaching theological students within the last forty years as there has been in the methods of teaching

law or medical students. People do not appreciate it. In old days the students used to be "crammed." The theological teacher gave him the correct theological material; he took it and went off and distributed it. Today no theological professor can hold his own a month if he attempts that process. The theological school must be and is on a level, if it be doing its work, with any graduate school of a university.

Such a school must have certain conditions. For instance, the locality of the school is of great importance. In old days it was thought best to put the theological seminary up on a hill in the country, to be a kind of Protestant monastery, where nobody could touch the young men, and where they could not get into contact with the wicked world. Today the right sort of a theological seminary is right next to the university, in the midst of those who are seeking for the truth, in touch with a great population,—for in these days every young man must prepare himself to live in a large population, and train himself to use his time and strength with method and self-restraint.

A theological seminary which hopes to develop spiritual leaders should, in my judgment, have no official relation with any diocese or convention or council of the church. England has been right in making Oxford and Cambridge the chief centers for theological training. The Church as an institution is naturally and rightly conservative; it moves slowly, slowly along with the average; but the young men who are going to be the next generation and hope to lead the life and the thought of the next generation, can not afford to keep with the average. They must be in the front, and their teachers must be in the front. Hence their teachers, steeped in the literature and history of the past, must have full sympathy with the thought and life of today, for although they may be misunderstood or distrusted for their advanced thought and radicalism, they must keep in the van of thought and spiritual life, if they are leaders of young men who are going to be leaders. Hence these teachers are loyal to the Church and to the faith, their thoughts are open to the truth, and in the air of the theological seminary is a sense of freedom.

Thus young men who are going to meet heavy problems and hard questions later will not have to meet them first in the loneliness of a rectory, but under the guidance of wise teachers. Under such leadership the students will usually pass through doubts and questions which seem at the time to strike at the very vitals of their faith, but deeper thought, fresh interpretations and patient experience will mature and strengthen their faith; and as they leave the school they are kindled with a deeper and truer enthusiasm for Christ and his Church; they will teach and preach the gospel and the faith in the towns today. To men who having a living faith, speak in living language of Christ, the people listen gladly.

REFLECTIONS ON THE SEA

"The sea is his, and he made it." All day long the great words of the Bible about the sea have been coming to mind, with meanings I had never guessed before. "There is sorrow upon the sea: it can not be still"— what words they are as one looks out upon these restless, reinless waters! And there are those other words, so freighted with meaning just now: "And the sea gave up the dead that were in it"; but best of all the line of the psalmist, "Thy way, O Lord, is in the sea."

Truly, if I were a rich pagan instead of a poor Christian, I would build a temple to the sea. It is so patient and strong to ship or soul that bravely casts loose upon its mighty promises; so variable and stern to the unpiloted and unseaworthy. It is a great burden bearer. It can not be overloaded. It never breaks down. It never needs repairs. It is not only a helper, but a teacher and friend. It rests the eye with its vastness and its infinite variety. It calms the heart with its never-ending music. It speaks to the mind of that divine depth over which the mystics brood, but never fathom. It is responsive to every mood—now sad, now troubled, now quietly meditative, now bright with what the Greeks called its "inextinguishable laughter." It preaches more sermons than all preachers; and as we listen, the sighs of human care are lost in the murmur of its many waters.

Why did St. John leave the sea out of his vision of heaven? No doubt the exile of Patmos, longing for the sight of familiar faces, grew a-weary of the imprisoning sea. Sundered by leagues of tumbling waters from the sorely tried little church he loved, he dreamed of a land where there would be "no more sea." But it is not so now. Once a symbol of separation, the sea has become a bond between lands and peoples. The sea in the Bible, like the sea of which Homer sang, is the unknown, untamed sea. To-day we sail a sea whose ways and winds are known, and whose forces have yielded to the power of intelligence.

Still, Matthew Arnold speaks of an "unplumbed, salt, estranging sea," by which he means the awful isolation of each soul in an unfathomable universe. More often in English poetry—and, indeed, in all poetry, since Homer, that has in it the sound of the sea—its tidal rhythms, its measured waves and measureless horizons, have been symbols of the deep, mysterious thoughts of God; as the stars round off the three divisions of the *Divine Comedy.* . . .

How can a man be irreligious on the sea! Are we not, all of us, out on the bosom of the deep, with the Infinite above and beneath us! We feel secure enough, thanks largely to the cheerful company, the dear faces, and the duties and pieties of the day. Still, when we look over the edge of the ship, up starts that primitive terror which only faith can allay. Religion is a thing of the depths and for the depths. "Have mercy upon me, O Lord; my boat is small, and thine ocean is great"—was the prayer of the old Breton fisherman; and it has in it the profound instinct which lies at the heart of faith. There will be companies of believing souls so long as there are deep, unplumbed places in this life of ours.

Last night I sat up on the deck of the ship near the prow, at midnight, long after others had gone below. It was "a clear, cool night of stars," and the great sea lay spread out beneath. Never did the old words, "What is man, that thou art mindful of him," come home to me with such awful majesty of simple truth to subdue the heart and still it. Then the ship bell rang out the hour, and the watchman from above cried, "All's well," and I went to my couch knowing that if I sank it would not be into the sea, but beyond it!—JOSEPH FORT NEWTON, in *Preaching in London.*

THE CHILDREN'S SERVICE
NATURE THE ORIGINATOR [1]

ROBERT SPARKS WALKER, Chattanooga, Tenn.

In nature we find originality. In her raw original material she challenges man to interpret. Through man's interpretation he becomes a discoverer, but never an originator. In all art nature first made the suggestion, man grasped the idea, then as a result we have music, painting, drawing, poetry, and other arts. In challenging man to become a painter, she gave him the tints of the rosebud, the apple blossom, the lily, the sunrise, the sunset; she placed the raw material by his side, gave him an intellect and then an ambition, and now we have artists and art schools. The harmony of the universe is poetry, and man becomes a poet when he can translate this into language. Through the little potter-wasps that build out of sand and clay wonderful designs of pottery nature has taught mankind the art of making pottery. The little caddis-worm that lives in cool springs and constructs its cocoons of stone and cements them together taught humanity the art of building houses out of stone. The mud-dauber was the first builder of the apartment house. The camouflage used in the world war was copied from animals which have been using it for centuries for purposes similar to those for which the armies employed it. The pelican, through his expert knowledge of catching fish in the bag that he carries on his throat, has taught man the art of catching fish with the seine. A certain cricket is an expert ventriloquist and might have suggested to man the idea of ventriloquism.

In many countries nature with the tools of wind and weather has done some splendid sculpturing and has left statues to many of her great men.

The dog knew the value of cold storage of perishable products long before man constructed buildings for the purpose, and the dog's remedy of green vegetation for a sick stomach is worthy of practise by the human family. Electricity has been used by certain fishes for years as a means of defense and for killing food. The spider may furnish the mechanical engineer some splendid practical ideas in the construction of bridges and tramways. The wonderfully symmetrical snowflakes furnish an endless variety of patterns for artists and for textile manufacturers.

The invention of the aeroplane is the interpretation of the secret of the creatures that fly—especially illustrative are the successful modern airplanes modeled after the common dragon fly. Certain species of spiders have been constructing balloons and taking pleasure-flights for centuries past. The ants have long been keeping plant aphis to produce honeydew and for these insects the ants care as tenderly as we care for our milch cows.

It is man's duty to interpret nature, not only in words, but in deeds. In the spiritual realm it is man's business not to try to discover or originate a new religion but to interpret and put into practise God's own religious laws. In this interpretation, as in the material world, there should be a steady and healthy growth; then, as man advances, a better understanding and broader conception of the meaning of religion and religious ideals should harmonize in the great plan of the Creator of the universe, who through nature is originator of everything that is good in both the material and the spiritual world.

[1] These nature studies are given as the raw material for the children's sermon, which each pastor can adapt in his own way to the needs of his own situation.

SUGGESTIONS FOR FUNERAL ADDRESSES

S. B. DUNN, D.D., New York City

When Two are Better than One [1]

Two are better than one, etc.—Eccles. 4:9, 10.

Saddest lot in human life is loneliness. Man is gregarious. Two lobes of brain. Two ventricles of heart. Marriage. Society. I. Common causes of loneliness. 1. Commonest is death. 2. Close second is selfishness. 3. Most serious is unreligion. A soul apart from God, a Robinson Crusoe. II. Common occasions of the multiple life. 1. In the family. 2. In church membership. 3. In the several brotherhoods. The solidarity of man. The fraternal spirit.

"Laddies," said a canny Scotch daddy, "one stick 'll never burn. Put more wood on the fire."

A commonwealth of any sort is a common wealth of soul and society.

A Mother in Israel

I, Deborah, . . . a mother in Israel, etc. —Judges 5:7.

Noblest title woman ever bore. What world needs most is mothering. I. Deborah—Mother. Biography: Widowed, leader in Israel. Palm-tree home. Deborah —A bee: honey-bee. Won a victory to sing over and wrote the song. 1. Deborah's industry. 2. Deborah's valor. 3. Deborah's piety. II. Serious loss, the loss of a mother. 1. Queen of the home. 2. Motherless home a sahara. 3. Memory of pious mother a child's richest heritage. 4. If active in church work, death a calamity. No lifemission a failure whose activity has been service; nor silent if it has enriched the song of life.

The Dead to Live Again

Thy brother shall rise again.—John 11:23.

Natural to turn to John's gospel for comfort. Story of the Bethany Lazarus richest comfort-mine. I. Mark how Jesus comforts Martha. 1. By assurance of future life. 2. By the tender of his own tearful sympathy. 3. By

his claim to power over death and grave. II. Mark how Martha reacts to Jesus. 1. In asseveration of her personal faith, verse 27. 2. In her errand to Mary, verse 28. 3. In her battle against her senses, verse 39. 4. In her gratitude, chap. 12:2. Scientist gave servant beautiful solid silver cup. Servant accidently dropt it into vessel containing nitric acid. Cup dissolved. Servant heart-broken. Master infused a chemical which precipitated silver from solution, and then had the silver fashioned again into another cup more beautiful than the first. "The dead shall so live again."

The House in the Heavens

For we know, etc.—2 Cor. 5:1.

What impresses one is Paul's confidence and hopefulness. Some things are settled. "We know." One thing we know is: What is now a tabernacle shall be a building—of God—not made with mortal hands, but eternal in heaven. I. Paul concedes the temporary. Paul has in mind the tents he made. Had in mind, too, perhaps, tabernacle in wilderness. 1. Body subject to dissolution. 2. But is shrine of immortal soul. 3. And even mortal life is sacred. II. Paul anticipates the eternal. An eternal abode: 1. To be thought of. 2. To be hoped for, verse 2. 3. To be awaited with patience and fortitude. 4. Whose chief attraction is, presence with God. How empty at best is mortal life! What a fulness of life is before us!

Hidden Springs

All my springs are in thee.—Ps. 87:7.

Sorrow is a time when soul seeks for springs. Needs a lot of them. A life that has no fountain is a desert. Soul cannot live on tears. May I unseal some springs? I. Of course, main spring is God. "Are you the woman with the great faith?" asked one. "No, I am the woman of a little faith in a great God." II. A gushing spring is the heart of Jesus. In his love, sympathy, and promises.

[1] An address for funeral of member of a brotherhood.

III. A veritable geyser is the sanctuary. A warm spring to heal and soothe the soul. A cool spring to refresh the fevered heart.

IV. A perennial spring is the memory of our dead. Don't you recall love-lit eyes? Don't you hear echoes of sweet voices? Don't you feel on your brow their very breath? With so many bubbling, welling springs, why be so tearful?

The Arithmetic and Craft of Life

So teach us to number . . . and apply, etc. —Ps. 90:12.

The passing of a man is always an event. It gives one pause. "An arrest of thought." Like blowing out of light. Like bugle-blast. At such a time test most opportune. Voice from long past. I. The arithmetic of life. 1. Digits are our days. 2. The number of the digits. 3. Sum, dewy with youth, vigorous with maturity, or, frosty with age. 4. In any case our years are our assets. II. The craft of life. To "apply our hearts unto wisdom." 1. Wisdom is knowledge and sound sense put to use. 2. The craftsman is the heart. 3. The craft must take into its perview the end. 4. The appeal must be to God. 5. Such a craft must be acquired—taught. The pay is appealing.

A Message from Heaven

And I heard a voice from heaven, etc.— Rev. 14:13.

While such a message falls we do well to pause. Comes from yonder sky; from God.

Rub eyes; prick ears; prepare the heart. What, then, is our message? I. Announces blessedness of pious dead. 1. What a crowning consummation of Christian life! 2. What a consummate comfort to the bereaved! II. Specifies wherein blessedness consists. 1. Rest from labors, as original means, as well as wearying, wearing activities. 2. "Their works do follow them"; that is, their business is continued: 1. Of obedience. 2. Of devotion. Cultivate what you would perfect. Begin what you would consummate. Engage in a business you would continue in. Reflections: 1. Our pious dead ask no condolence. It is we who need commiseration. 2. Our message is a call to come.

Turning One's Face to the Wall

Then Hezekiah turned his face toward the wall, etc.—Isa. 38:2.

Hezekiah is warned of death. 1. Turns face to wall. 2. Turns soul to God. Wordsworth, "The Excursion":

He wept, he prayed
For his dismissal day and night compelled
By pain to turn his thoughts towards the grace,
And face the regions of eternity.

I. Facing the wall. 1. Recognizing the inevitable. Victor Hugo: "The tomb forgets me not." 2. Cultivating a calm anticipation. 3. Yet realizing its import. II. Praying unto the Lord. 1. Shut up to and closeted with God. 2. Making one's peace with him. 3. Spending remnant of life in his service. Soul's concern demands absorbed attention. The set of the face determines direction of feet.

THEMES AND TEXTS

By WILLIAM S. JEROME, White Pigeon, Mich.

Three Disciplines. "Why do John's disciples and the disciples of the Pharisees fast, but thy disciples fast not?"—Mark 2:18.
A Double Parentage. "Now the sons of Eli were sons of Belial."—1 Sam. 2:12.
The Men Who Got There. "And they went forth to go into the land of Canaan; and into the land of Canaan they came."—Gen. 12:5.
Strength in the Soul. "Thou didst encourage me with strength in my soul."—Ps. 138:3.
Names and Nature. "Wo to them that call evil good, and good evil."—Isa. 5:20.
The Teaching of the Trees. "Behold the fig tree, and all the trees."—Luke. 21:29.
Father and Son. "God dealeth with you as with sons."—Heb. 12:7.

Accepting the Universe. "Let us run with patience the race that is set before us."—Heb. 12:1.
Use and Abuse. "I gave her the grain . . . which they used for Baal."—Hos. 2:8.
The Profit of Piety. "Doth Job fear God for nought?"—Job. 1:9.
Right and Might. "Their might is not right."—Jer. 23:10.
Reception and Reward. "He that receiveth a prophet . . . shall receive a prophet's reward."—Matt. 10:41.
The Vision and the Voice. "I saw a vision . . . I heard also a voice."—Acts 11:5, 7.
The Fearful Followers. "And they that followed were afraid."—Mark 10:32.

ILLUSTRATIONS AND ANECDOTES

The Rev. F. C. HOGGARTH, Bradford, England

Lost Treasures

Speaking at the Society of Engineers in England, Lord Headley, who is an authority on foreshore protection, suggested that the Goodwin Sands might be explored for buried treasure. The Goodwins are a treacherous spot off the coast of Kent wherein is the accumulation of centuries of disasters. Within a few square miles many millions of pounds worth of treasure are hidden. Various schemes to recover these treasures had been turned down, but he thought it possible to sink a good floating concrete tower in Trinity Bay and to run tunnels from this base of operations in any direction. And tho the adventure may not immediately be undertaken, it certainly looks as tho the day will come when the Goodwins will yield up their treasure. Storm and sea at least have not spoken the last word. Man will yet have something to say and to do concerning these disasters so old and apparently so final. The end is not yet and who knows what may be as the skill of man increases and his spirit dares to challenge the finality of nature's destroying powers?

It is a thought with far horizons in it. In other ways also disasters may be less final than they seem. For when we have to do with the power of God, working in love in the place of our tragedies, who will limit the possibilities?

The Instinct of Direction

Canon Barnett, the founder of Toynbee Hall, had, we are told, an unerring instinct of direction. He could not explain it, but there it was, "an animal sense of the points of the compass." He said that he always knew by day or night which was north, south, east, or west, and that he guided his ways by that conviction. "His power," adds a writer in the *Times Literary Supplement*, "he also possest in his mind and spirit. His greatness lay in his sense of direction, he himself was like a compass, except that he was not stationary; and those who knew him well knew that they could steer by him, as if he were not a man of human caprices, but a spiritual instrument pointing towards

the kingdom of heaven." No wonder Clemenceau, after a visit to England in 1884, said, "I have met but three really great men in England and one was a little pale clergyman in Whitechapel!"

This sense of spiritual direction has ever been the hallmark of the prophet. The prophet is a man who has come to such a point of spiritual insight that he knows the way. In perplexing circumstances he senses the right way and the right word. He is a master in the scout lore of the soul. Christ himself suggested that there was a spiritual instinct parallel to that of ear and eye by which men guided the situation of the day. His indictment of the men of his day was that whilst skilled in sky signs, able to forecast the weather, they were unskilled in the soul's scout lore.

It Is Humanity that Counts

In the life of Canon Barnett there is an amusing picture of Herbert Spencer, that erstwhile idol of the philosophic and scientific. The Barnetts traveled with him in Egypt and knowing the man ceased to be imprest by his theories. When they went to see the tomb of Tii, Spencer stayed outside impatiently, for, as Barnett says, "when any one has seen the class of thing, it is quite as efficacious, less fatiguing, and more convenient to study the facts from books and pictures." Gradually they discovered the truth about Spencer, "that he was one who found all reality fatiguing and prepared a formula for it." Privately the Barnetts called him a mummy. Reality in the shape of Arab boys drove him almost to distraction and he would pursue them, with coat-tails flying and umbrella lifted, shouting "Confound you, I say." It is not an attractive picture, this of the man who was something of an oracle to our fathers, at whose seemingly spacious genius men marveled. The fate of the author of the Synthetic Philosophy is something of a warning to all men who live much among theories and formulae and who are thereby in danger of getting out of touch with the realities of life. Living human contacts are needful to keep our lives fresh and our theories true. Barnett, with his kindly human service in Whitechapel, his close contact with the realities of life in the slums of London, is an infinitely more impressive figure than Spencer. After all it is humanity that counts. In the noble phrase of Bacon's, "the more objects of compassion a man has, the nobler he is."

"Waters in the Desert Rise"

A coal strike, with its consequent danger of flooding in the mines, calls attention to the fact that underground there are immense supplies of water. Underground work of all kinds is made possible only by constant battle with these waters. Pumps have to be kept going unceasingly. "The amount of water underground must be far vaster than all the rivers of the world put together, for they are, in reality, only a small outlet for the enormous bulk of water that has soaked into the earth, and been constantly added to by the rains and dew." Not the least interesting fact is that it is found everywhere if we dig deep enough. Scientists say that all round the earth, just below its crust, is a layer of water-bearing strata containing immense reservoirs of water. It varies in depth. In a desert a well might have to be a mile deep to touch it, while elsewhere it may be only a few yards beneath the surface. The water is there even underneath the world's deserts—moisture enough in the depths, which science may yet bring to the surface, to turn deserts into watered gardens. For with such enormous underground supplies, all things become possible. The difference between the real Christian and the worldling is that one has this secret of the depths and the other has it not. There is an old promise about life being "as a watered garden" for Israel, and another about the righteous man not fearing when the heat cometh. Not a few Christians, content with surface supplies, do fear when the heat cometh. Yet the promise and the privilege for them is the boundless supply of the depths. For them waters in the desert rise. It is a great thought to remember that underneath every experience of life, however parched and forbidding the aspect, there are boundless and adequate supplies, available for all who believe.

Swimmers and Drifters

Professor J. A. Thomson divides the animals of the open sea into active swimmers, such as the whale and the herring, and into drifters, or easy-going swimmers, such as many kinds of sea worms and jelly fishes. Jelly fishes are often borne into shallow water and are left stranded by hundreds on the beach. As he says, they represent two different attitudes of life, and both attitudes may sometimes be found in one family, crustaceans, for instance, belong partly to the swimmers and partly to the drifters. It would be possible to divide people into the same two classes. There are the active swimmers, who steer their way through the waters and win some mastery over circumstances, and there are the drifters, who are merely at the mercy of wind and wave— passive, rudderless barques on a wide sea. Browning and Meredith are the poets of the active swimmers. They sing of the joy of struggle and of the glory of the life that strives. Their heaven is reserved for those who having their loins girt "dare and never grudge the throe." The Bible, too, is the vade mecum of strivers. All its promises are to "active swimmers." It has no hopes, no heaven for drifters. Glover points out that whilst painters have often pictured Jesus as "something of a dreamer, a long-haired, sleepy, abstract kind of person," the real Jesus is a man of energy, of straight speech, vigorous in thought and venturesome in deed. Not a few of the parables turn on energy. The real trouble with men, he seems to say, is again and again sheer slackness—the parable of the talents turns on energetic thinking and decisive action and so do many of the others. Paul's metaphors are drawn from camp and field. He presses on like a racer. He strives like a warrior. In the book of Revelation the promises of its early chapters are all to "him that overcometh."

On Starts in Life

The pigeon, we are told, tho a strong flier, after being made to rise from the ground and fly a short distance five or six times in succession, refuses to rise again. It remains on the ground, panting with open beak. Marey, who observed his own pigeons, calculated that the energy expended per second in a pigeon when taking flight is five times as great as when it has acquired a certain velocity. When starting a flight a bird has to make more rapid strokes with its wings which move through a larger angle. When speed has been required the flaps are slower and the angle is smaller. Once under way it gets more support from the air.

Thus I read—I forget where—in some book on birds. The fact seems rather suggestive for human life, especially suggestive for those who in youth are always making fresh starts, who never continue in one stay. To-day they will be this; to-morrow they desire to be that. They are forever falling in love and as quickly falling out of love with successive vocations. They never achieve anything. In life it is necessary as early as may be to get under way. New starts are more than doubly exhausting. And what a glorious feeling to know that you are under way, making progress with a certain ease, conscious of gaining mastery over your task, conscious, too, of manifold helps and supports, able to use even high and contrary winds for your purposes.

Statistics that Fail

Dr. Francis E. Clarke wrote some months ago about the cold in Paris. Everybody felt it. The Parisians were muffled up to the eyes, with necks enswathed in numerous folds of cloth, and even with heads and mouths tied up, lest the fog should invade them. For a thick fog enveloped the city and you seemed, he said, to breathe in little ice crystals. The air had a peculiar bone-chilling, blood-freezing property. Yet he asked why he, who had stood forty degrees below in a New Hampshire winter, should mind a mere fourteen above in France? The American Consul told him that ten degrees above zero in Paris is colder than ten degrees below in Boston. Evidently the mere figures on a thermometer are no adequate guide to climate. There are other factors of which the mercury takes no cognizance, so that we need to know about situation, humidity, fog, and many other things in the environment before we can accurately know a climate. Figures often have such a weakness. They leave out so much that we need to know before we gauge a situation, often the most important factors are just those that are not and never can be put into statistics.

The Church often seems to have a rather pathetic trust in statistics. It measures so much by numbers. Every year it keeps thousands of people busy, for many hours or days filling in schedules. It collects assiduously the numbers of scholars and teachers, of members and preachers, and as the figures rise or fall, the Church is presumed to have found success or failure. It is a presumption. It may be even one of our presumptuous sins. For there is so much that is of vital importance not indicated in schedules.

Clean Athletics

I have a friend who is an alumnus of Wesleyan University at Middletown, Conn. Recently he has told me of a baseball game played twenty-eight years ago in Middletown. It was between Amherst and Wesleyan. In the last inning the score stood a tie. Amherst batted first and scored a run, which put them ahead. Wesleyan came to bat and her runners reached second and third. Two men were out. A ball was hit by a Wesleyan batter into center field. The fielder stopt the ball, threw to second. The second baseman made a pass at the runner coming down from first to second. The runners on second and third meanwhile had scored on the hit, but the umpire called the runner going to second "out." So the runs did not count.

The second baseman, who was captain of the Amherst team, walked into the diamond and told the umpire that he did not touch the runner, thereby allowing the runs to be scored and Wesleyan to win.

The incident made a profound impression upon my friend. It put a mark of superiority upon the captain among college players and regard for the college he represented rose tremendously.

One act like that helps very greatly to clean college athletics. Manhood counts more than victory.

The illustration would not be complete without the name of the captain, who was "Al" Stearns, or Principal Stearns, of Andover, beloved by all Amherst men.

J. H. OLMSTEAD,

Homer, N. Y.

Recent Books

A Student's Philosophy of Religion. By WILLIAM KELLY WRIGHT, Ph.D. The Macmillan Company, New York, 1922. 9x6 in., 472 pp. $3.75.

The basis of Dr. Wright's volume is a series of lectures delivered to Cornell students representing Protestantism, Roman Catholicism, and Judaism. One has not to read far before he finds that a sense of the concrete is dominant. So, if this book presents a "philosophy of religion," it is a philosophy that never becomes footloose from the facts of history or experience.

The author defines religion as "a certain kind of systematic effort to secure the conservation and enhancement of values." Necessarily the things valued differ according to the grade of civilization and religion. Hence (to illustrate) "magic" is not to be condemned offhand as either the precursor of religion (Frazer) nor as a degenerate form of religion. If "magic" is used to conserve some "socially recognized value" (as, for instance, the ethical virtues among the Egyptians), it is religious. This is distinctly an advance.

The discussion is in three parts: I. Religion and the Conservation of Values; II. Religion and the Self; III. Religion and Reality. The first part is a survey (a) of three types of primitive religion as typical —those of Australians, the Todas of Southern India, and of the Bagandas in Africa; (b) of the great historic faiths of India, Greece and Rome, Palestine, and Christendom.

Great good sense abounds throughout. To illustrate once more, our author does not find the "origin of the idea of God" in any one source—as specialists are inclined to do. He specifies at least half a dozen lines of development of this idea as suggested by the proved facts of early culture. He finds the outstanding achievements of Christianity to be "the purification of home life and of the relations between the sexes, . . . it has been zealous in all forms of humanitarianism, . . . (and) it has usually stood for social justice."

But "is Christianity ultimately true?" Here is the answer:

In a strictly metaphysical sense, the author supposes that it must be said that no religion can claim ultimate truth. All try to express by means of symbols what is infinite and unknowable, as well as what is knowable, but has not yet become scientific knowledge. But the symbols of Christianity have proved their adaptability to twenty centuries of more varying conditions than ever confronted any other religion (except the Jewish), and they have grown and become enriched in the process.

Part II is especially instructive in its exhibition of the recent findings of psychological science in relation to religion. Among the headings of either chapters or sections we find The Subconscious, Instincts, Habits and Sentiments, The Development of the Self. Under the latter subheads are: Religion in Childhood, Adolescence, Adolescence and the Religious Sentiment, Role of the Subconscious in Adolescent Awakenings, and so on.

In Part III one chapter deals with Mechanism and Teleology, three with various phases of the idea and relations of God, and one with Immortality.

In spite of the number of good books on the subject, the reviewer is decidedly inclined to award this one the palm of excellence because of its adherence to concrete facts, its conspicuous clarity in exposition, and especially for its practical value to pastors and teachers of religion.

The Resurrection of Christ: An Examination of the Apostolic Belief and Its Significance for the Christian Faith. By JOHN MACINTOSH SHAW. T. & T. Clark, Edinburgh, 1920. 215 pp.

Scholars will differ very widely in their findings on the resurrection of Jesus in the light of the modern discussions of the subject. Perhaps they differ more widely than ever. Nevertheless these discussions have yielded at least one net result of great value for the future investigator, namely the conviction that the center of the field of investigation must be not so much the sepulchre of Joseph of Arimathea as the mind of the earliest believers in the Messiahship of Jesus. It is the belief that Jesus rose from the dead and not the fact of the rising that must serve as the starting point and ground of research. Without question this inquiry will lead back to the more fundamental question of the fact or facts that produced the belief and then forward into the full significance of the belief for all the ages that have followed; but the inquiry is more likely to yield satisfactory results if it begins on the sure ground of the belief than on that of the facts behind. Dr. Shaw, without saying so, approaches the subject from this point of view. He passes under review all the allusions to the resurrection in the New Testament and finds that they can only mean the physical re-entrance of Jesus into the life from which he had been withdrawn for a time by his death. This conclusion is then brought to the Christian faith; it is shown that it explains the vitality and strength of it as a force in the spiritual life of the world. These results contain nothing new but the discussion is conducted by Dr. Shaw in a fresh and forceful manner.

The Origin of Paul's Religion. The James Sprunt Lectures. By J. GRESHAM MACHEN. The Macmillan Company, New York, 1921. 329 pp.

The problem of Paul's relation to Jesus on one side and to historic Christianity on the other has, generally speaking, in recent years evoked a tripartite controversy. At one angle of the triangle stand those who contend for the essential identity of the Pauline system and the teaching of Jesus. These deny the claim that Paul and not Jesus is the true founder of Christianity. It is scarcely necessary to say that Professor Machen belongs to their number. Professor Bacon of Yale is also a member of the same group. The second party to the controversy (if it may be called such) holds with Wrede and Brückner that Paul must be affiliated with the pre-Christian development of Messianism and owes very little to Jesus. The third group of scholars interested in the subject believe that Paul is indebted for his "gospel" to the Gentile world. Here they find an inchoate religious system, redemptive in its central thought, which gave Paul his conception of a "Savior" and "Lord." Professor Machen finds that both

camps of his opponents are fighting in the interests of "naturalism" and that it is necessary to enter the lists against them and vanquish them if supernaturalism shall survive. Even Bacon's position is to him a dangerous one and must be repudiated. He thus enters into a minute examination of all the historical data, sifting and testing their value, and endeavoring to show that they support his position and militate against that of his opponents. So far as the conclusion is concerned that Paul's system is a legitimate outgrowth of the teaching of Jesus the historical evidence is undoubtedly on his side. But that it is necessary to establish this position in order to save the authority of Paul does not necessarily follow. On the contrary, even if it were possible to demonstrate with mathematical precision that Paul had derived every idea he ever entertained from the historical Jesus, the supernaturalness of these ideas would need to be proved in some other than a historical way. As orthodox and evangelical a scholar as the late Principal James Denney admitted many years ago that even the authority of Jesus must be accepted not upon historical grounds, but because somehow we have learned to believe in him as a divine teacher. On the whole, however, Professor Machen makes a notable contribution to a debate of the deepest interest in the field of New Testament study.

Painted Windows. Studies in Religious Personality. By A GENTLEMAN WITH A DUSTER. G. P. Putnam's Sons, New York and London, 1922. 9¼x6½ in., 299 pp. $2.50.

These brief studies in religious personality—twelve in all, and all of them Englishmen—are fascinatingly penned. The author seeks to discover a reason "for the present rather ignoble situation of the church in the affections of man." After examining the kind of Christianity he lights upon a cause "for the confest failure of the church to impress humanity with what its documents call the will of God."

When he comes to the final chapter in the volume he states his remedy for the powerlessness of the church. It is to be sought in the world's great Teacher of Reality.

There were two things to which he set no limits: one, the love of God, and the other, the power of faith.

Let all schools in the church revise their definition of the word faith, and unity will come of itself. Faith, as Jesus employed that term, meant making use of belief— belief that the spiritual alone is the real. Faith is the action of the soul. It is the working of a power. It is mastery of life. Let the church realize that Jesus taught this power of the soul. Let her begin to exercise her own spiritual powers. And then let her understand that she is in the world to teach men, to lead the advance of evolution, to educate humanity in the use of its highest powers.

While there are sentiments in the volume that ring true there is an undue obtrusion of the author's own personality, and an over-belaboring of the church that does not digest very well. "Something is wrong with the church," the author says. Of course there is, and the reason is not far to seek, for as we all know there is something wrong with humanity and humanity will not be headed in the right direction until the church takes up seriously the problem of the moral and religious education of the young. We must get back far enough in the life of the child to give him the kind of training and education that will fit him for his duties as husband and as citizen.

Epilegomena to the Study of Greek Religion. By JANE ELLEN HARRISON, D.Litt., LL.D. The University Press, Cambridge, 1921. 8½x5½ in., vi—40 pp. 3s 6d net.

This little but weighty pamphlet summarizes and supplements the results of the author's *Prolegomena* and *Themis* (published in 1908 and 1912 respectively) in the area of primitive religion. The thesis she presents is the social origin of religion. This is the result of facts coming recently to light in four related fields—totem, tabu, and exogamy; initiation ceremonies; the medicine man and king-god; the fertility-play or year-drama. The first has to do with the family or clan. It is concerned in part, in some regions, with production and enhancement of life, with the ideas of sanctity, sacrifice, sin and sacrifice, animal and plant worship, continuance of life and ancestor worship (but not god-worship) looming up. The second is concerned with the tribe and the passing of the youth to adulthood, and a great spirit comes into view. The third has to do with divinity of a sort, the preservation of the king (divine right). Incense and sanctity attaching to a person are two of the marks. The fertility or folk-play, which has survived so often in harvest

homes and that sort of thing, with ritual dances and mimes, is shown to be important. The two brief concluding chapters are on primitive theology and the religion of to-day.

Miss Harrison always affords stimulating and informing reading, even tho she follows perhaps a little too closely Frazer and Freud. For example, it is not probable that the one source of conception of deity is the leader of the choral dance.

Contemporary Science. Edited with an Introduction by BENJAMIN HARROW. Boni and Liveright, New York, 1921. 6¾x4½ in., 253 pp. $0.95.

The twelve chapters of this pocket volume are by as many authors, all high authorities in their respective fields. They tell the latest concerning physics, atoms, engineering, gas warfare, enzymes, death, aviators, bacteriology, asepsis, mental tests, psychoanalysis, Einstein and gravitation. Here are quotations from the two opening chapters:

We may then picture with considerable confidence this whole physical world as built up of one positive and one negative electron. The positive electron is the nucleus of the hydrogen atom. It is very minute in comparison with the negative, but much more massive. When two free positive electrons are tied together we have the helium atom. We don't know why these positives cling together.—R. A. MILLIKAN.

According to the well-established Rutherford-Bohr theory, all the positive electricity in an atom is concentrated in a nucleus at its center. The dimensions of this nucleus are negligibly small compared with those of the rest of the atom, its diameter being of the order of 0.00001 of that of the atom. The charge on the nucleus is an integral multiple of the charge of an electron but of course opposite in sign. The remainder of the atom consists of electrons arranged in space about the nucleus, the normal number of such electrons (called the atomic number) being equal to the number of unit positive charges on the nucleus, so that the atom as a whole is electrically neutral.—IRVING LANGMUIR.

Ministers ought to include science books (like this) in their reading lists.

The Isle of Vanishing Men. A Narrative of Adventure in Cannibal-Land. By W. F. ALDER. *The Century Company, New York,* 1922. 7½x5 in., 184 pp. $2.00.

The "Isle of Vanishing Men" is New Guinea—a large part of which is for white men virgin territory never trodden by them. The "Vanishing Men" are whites who come into touch with natives away from the coast, being transformed into "long pig," their skulls decorating the homes of the cannibals; or they are the natives themselves who fall in the fight or as victims of vengeance.

It seems that one "long pig" may be stretched to satisfy ten hungry men, but "it is better," says a native, "to have enough . . . so that one body need to be divided among only five or six." But more subjects than this come into the story—something of customs of adornment, marriage, and the like, as well as the travel experiences of the author. It ·is a diverting tale, easily read, not, however, very valuable to the anthropologist.

The Habit of Health. How to Gain and Keep It. By OLIVER HUCKEL. 7½ x 5 in., 128 pp. $1.00.

Spiritual Health and Healing. By HORATIO W. DRESSER. 7½ x 5 in., 314 pp. $2.00. Both published by Thomas Y. Crowell Company, New York, 1922.

These two books may be said to have much in common, for spiritual living lies at the heart of both of them. This may be seen from a quotation from each work:

Let a man think in the spirit of Jesus, let a man speak in the spirit of Jesus, let a man live in the spirit of Jesus and that man is a victor over the body. A man who has the ideal of Jesus dwelling in his thoughts continually, will have there the inspiration of the noblest living.

From the book by Mr. Dresser we read:

To be normal, to live in spiritual health is to be in accord with the universe: to think, will, live by the Divine order. Spiritual health is the standard set for man by God's purpose in bringing him into being. It is man's birthright as heir of the heavenly kingdom. . . . Christ bids man so live that health shall always radiate from him as virtue radiates from one whose religion is "to do good."

The World in Revolt. By GUSTAVE LE BON. The Macmillan Co., New York, 1921. 256 pp.

Professor Le Bon has added another worth-while psychological study to those already published by him. He works out in a new department a thesis applied along other lines. Peoples are not guided or controlled in their national aspirations by reason but by feeling. There are the age-long attitudes, customs, viewpoints, which act as real motives to action. Over against

these biological and emotional causes, reason is helpless.

This thesis he elucidates in seven parts: The mental evolution of the peoples; conflicting principles in modern warfare; the influence of psychological factors in battle; the propagation of beliefs and the orientation of opinions; the new revolutionary tempest; political illusions of to-day; the political disorganization of Europe. The World War furnishes the text for most of these discussions.

The author is an intense individualist and deprecates anything which may weaken the initiative and resourcefulness of the individual. This leads him to pay his compliments to bolshevism in Russia and socialism in Germany. The intelligentsia of Russia was killed or exiled, and debacle was inevitable. In Germany the scale of wages has changed completely. In Berlin an alderman gets 10,000 marks, an assistant clerk 18,000 marks; a city engineer receives 6,600 marks, his office boy 8,000 marks. These and many similar figures are for November, 1920. These facts are illuminating and explain the enormous deficits of the German republic. But—they will convince no one; for if a person prefers turnips to beef, nothing more can be said; it is his emotional privilege.

The Book of Job. By MOSES BUTTEN-WIESER. The Macmillan Company, New York, 1921. 370 pp.

Alike to the student of literature, religion, and textual criticism, the book of Job is a subject of perennial fascination. Eight years ago Dr. Buttenwieser proved his competence in all these lines by his acute study of "The Prophets of Israel," and his new book will not belie the reputation he then won. He believes that the text is in extreme disorder, due to the hostility with which the original book was received, and he attempts a revision and re-arrangement of the Hebrew text, which is printed at the end. It may be doubted whether the disorder is as drastic and pervasive as the author would have us believe: in all such criticism there is an inevitably subjective element. But the writer has weighed his arguments well, and they are plausible, even when not fully convincing. He regards the prolog as integral to the book, but not the epilog, and he presents a novel view of chaps. 32—37, assigning only chaps. 32 and 33 to Elihu, and dividing 34—37 between Bildad and Job. In the famous passage 19:25-27, the text of which he regards as perfect, he finds no hint of immortality or resurrection. The date he puts about 400 B.C. The meaning of the book is suggestively discust in a long chapter. He offers a fresh continuous translation in his own rearrangement, and follows it by copious and illuminating notes. The whole book is the work of a vigorous and independent mind, and is a really valuable contribution to the already voluminous literature on the immortal book of Job.

Four Pilgrims. By WILLIAM BOULTING. Kegan Paul, Trench, Trübner and Co. Ltd., London; E. P. Dutton & Co., New York, 1921. 8¼ x 5¾ in., 256 pp. $4.00.

The "four pilgrims" were Hiuen-Tsiang, a Chinese Buddhist who journeyed to India A.D. 627-643 to visit the sacred scenes of his faith's birth; Saewulf, an English pilgrim to Palestine in 1102, shortly after the first crusade; Mohammed Ibn Abd Allah, a Moslem traveller of 1304-77; and Ludovico Varthema, an Italian, an inveterate wanderer who travelled in Moslem lands and to Mecca at the beginning of the sixteenth century. All of these were intelligent and acute observers of the peoples they saw in their wanderings, and left accounts, now highly prized classics, of the countries they visited. Mr. Boulting has condensed into reasonable length and in his own words the narratives of these wanderers, retaining the spice, giving also the historical background, and accompanying the stories with seasoned elucidation. The travels covered nearly the entire Orient east of Egypt. Little that is more interesting than these is found in recent "journeys in foreign parts," especially if one hold to Terence's maxim—I am a man, and nothing human is uninteresting (or "foreign") to me.

As a minister's vacation book—interesting and profitable—this book makes a strong bid.

Bible and Spade. The Bross Lectures for 1921. JOHN P. PETERS. Charles Scribner's Sons, New York, 1921. 239 pp. $1.75.

He will indeed be a well-equipped student who has not much to learn from this book, the writer of which is not only an unusually competent Biblical scholar, but a highly distinguished archeologist. Many incidental touches remind us that he has seen in Babylonia and Palestine the things whereof he speaks. On this wide experience has reacted a mind of uncommon independence, and the result is a book stimulating and illuminating from the first page to the last. In successive chapters Dr. Peters deals with The Ancestry of the Hebrews, Cosmogony and Folk-Lore, History and Prophecy, Hebrew Psalmody, The Exploration of Palestine, and New Testament Times, and everywhere he has something interesting, and often something challenging to say, as, e.g., when he argues that "so far from our Psalms not being ancient, we must even carry them back in rudiment before the time of David." The volume helps us to feel that the Bible can never be completely intelligible without some knowledge of Semitic antiquity, while this knowledge inevitably enhances our conception of the Bible's inestimable worth.

Truly Rural. By RICHARDSON WRIGHT. Houghton Mifflin Company, Boston and New York, 1922. 7¾ x 5¼ in., 219 pp. $2.00.

Here is a "dee-lightful" book to read in the summer—just then and no other time. It's about the development of a country house and "seven acres 'more or less'" by a "city man." You had better not read it in the winter, because you'll be fidgeting about spring buying of bulbs, shrubs, etc.; nor in the spring because you will be still more imprest with the importance of immediate large outlay on all such things; nor in the autumn because that's the time to put in hardy roots and the like. In the summer it's too late for spring planting, too early for fall; too tardy for regrets and too soon for resolutions; so read it then—be sure and read it!

That the Ministry Be Not Blamed. By JOHN A. HUTTON. George H. Doran Company, New York. (Second edition.) 7½ x 5¼ in., 202 pp. $1.50.

In Scotland a foundation for lectures on preaching has been established similar to that of the celebrated "Yale Lectures" at New Haven. These are delivered in Aberdeen, Edinburgh, and Glasgow—three noted centers of theological education. The first series was given by Dr. Hutton, and are here collected. They are good reading—intimate and "informal" in the sense that they are "talks" drawn from the font of a ripe experience. Not only students but seasoned ministers would do well to read them—we are all likely to form habits, not all of them good, which such advice as is here given may help to correct. And it may prove also a preventive of what some one in our pages once called "pulpitantics."

Peace and Happiness. By H. L. PAGET. Longmans, Green & Company, New York and London, 1922. 7½ x 5 in., 127 pp. $1.25.

"Peace and Happiness," "Truth and Justice," "Religion and Piety" form the main chapters of this readable and helpful book. Religion, says the author—

must assert its claim to a place in any adjustment of human life, if life is to be worth living; and men are ready, more widely perhaps than ever before, to own their need of it. A plain, strong, coherent faith, a faith that can hold men in close and practical fellowship, a faith that reckons with the actual facts of human life, and covers the whole area of human work and effort, speaking to men in their own language that is the sort of faith men need to-day.

Third Report of the Joint Commission on The Book of Common Prayer. Appointed by The General Convention of 1913. The Macmillan Company, New York, 1922. 7½x5¼ in., 231 pp. $1.50.

The Book of Common Prayer is not the exclusive possession of the Anglican Church and its daughters. Being a repository of devotions from all the generations in the Church, it has approved itself widely as an expression of worship and is used by many outside the Episcopalian communion. This report, by the Joint Commission appointed in 1913, which will in all probability be adopted by the next General Convention, is consequently of interest to others than Episcopalians. The changes are conservative, but generally in conformity with the demands of the newer age.

A Correction

The American publishers of *The Remnant*, by Rufus M. Jones (noticed in the June number, p. 517), are George H. Doran Company, and the price is $2.00.

The Case of Korea

Editor of THE HOMILETIC REVIEW:

In your January number you review *The Case of Korea* by Henry Chung. In your review you say:

From that time, especially during the last three years, Korea has been under a rule of oppression, terror, massacre, and arson! Especially the object of attack, accompanied by assault, beatings, murder, and burnings, are the Christian villages. Japanese propaganda is often particularly directed against the missionaries and their work. . . . A friend of the reviewer, after reading it, said that he could almost forget now the atrocities of the Hun.

I am sorry that such an honorable and responsible journal as the REVIEW should lend itself to such a misrepresentation of Japan in Korea. No one can condone the police brutalities and atrocities in the suppression of the independence movement three years ago. But to describe the Japanese rule in Korea in general as a "rule of oppression, terror, massacre, and arson" is an ugly misrepresentation of the facts.

There has been no governmental oppression of the missionaries or their work or of

Christianity in general in the sense of anti-Christian propaganda. Under-officials have taken occasions to work out their hatred or prejudice against Christianity, but that is a very different thing from what you represent.

Korean propaganda in America is filled with exaggeration and thus it is most untrustworthy. We are grieved that Christian people and Christian papers in America should be so easily taken in by this exaggerated and often lying propaganda. The result is the distorted and unfair views of Japan now so common in America. We ought to be able to rely upon our Christian journals to give to the American public a fairer and juster and therefore a more righteous view of Japan.

ARTHUR D. BERRY.
Aoyama Gakuin, Tokyo.

[We are glad to give publicity to the above letter, but we are assured by the reviewer of Henry Chung's book that the evidence for the facts stated in that volume is so extensive and abundant that no denial can blunt the facts.—EDS.]

FINAL SCENE IN THE PAGEANT OF JOB. (See p. 175.)

JOB (ON THE RIGHT), THE THREE FRIENDS IN ORDER OF AGE, AND ELIHU (ON THE LEFT).   (See p. 175.)

The HOMILETIC REVIEW

VOL. 84   SEPTEMBER, 1922   No. 3

DRAMA OF JOB

The Rev. CLAUDE S. HANBY, Ph.D., Rolla, Mo.

[The editors take pleasure in presenting this record of an unusual study of one of the great books of the Bible by a Bible class such as may be found or formed in almost any of our churches, and of the reproduction of the drama by local talent in the church building. It may well be taken as an example of what can be done, as a stimulus to do as well or better, and of the spirit in which it may be undertaken. The following is the author's introduction to the record:

Interest in the Bible defies extinction. Study groups may be large or small, and gleaned results commensurate with preparation. The society engaged in the study experience herein related has been conducted through a ministry of seven years in the college town of Rolla, Missouri. We have made a serious attempt to be sensitive to the accent of the historical, the literary, and the spiritual. After a rich experience in the New Testament writings, we undertook a course in the Old Bible.

No book has proved more profitable than the drama of Job. A course of lessons was prepared and directed by the writer. At the conclusion of the course our class gave a dramatic presentation of this stirring masterpiece. The following is a description of the methods we pursued.]

I. The name of Job has been a household possession for centuries. Many proverbs have been woven from the thread of his life story. The patience of Job, his poverty, his comforters, have been familiar expressions from antiquity. The opinion grew upon the Rolla Bible Class that intensive study was essential in order to acquire a just interpretation.

The drama divisions were first in interest. We made use of convenient boundary lines; the prolog, comprising chapters one and two; the dialogs, reaching from chapter three to chapter thirty-one; the intervention of Elihu, concluding with chapter thirty-seven; the theophany, extending to verse six of chapter forty-two; the epilog, beginning at verse seven of the last chapter of Job. The prose of the prolog and epilog was observed with care; and the poetry of the other divisions disclosed rich tintings, and rewarded us with exalted emotions.

The literary emphasis was examined without exhaustive methods. We learned that Job has the nature of a drama, with entanglement, development, and solution. However, the action is chiefly internal and mental. Lofty dramatic qualities were recognized; but it was also agreed that Job is very largely a law unto itself.

We enjoyed the comparison of our text with sections of Isaiah. As in many a masterpiece, one literary offering supplies inspiration for another. It would appear that Job has profited by the imagery, eloquence, and rhythm of earlier works of art.

Using the American Standard Version of the Bible, we searched for the high peaks of poesy. It was nearly unanimous that no rhetoric was found richer than that in 3:11-19. Many quotations from eminent writers were introduced, classifying Job with Dante's *Divine Comedy*, Carlyle's *Sartor Resartus*, and Browning's *Rabbi Ben Ezra*.

Historical implications were garnered thoughtfully. The Bible was searched for mention of Job; Ezekiel in the Old Testament and James in the New offered the only valid texts. Vivid pictures of patriarchal life swung the pendulum of opinion toward a great age for the drama. However, this sentiment was overcome when we were confronted with mention of houses, troops, populous cities, kings, priests, and other evidences of culture and conditions far later than pre-Mosaic years.

Following reputable precedent, we considered the history of Job from the standpoint of its chief subject matter, the problem of suffering. We found Job dealing frankly with disaster and human misfortune. Our class leaned to the side of the scholars who find Job to be the first great work to deny that misfortune is always a punishment for the bad. We considered it altogether plausible that the drama of Job should come out of one of the exile periods. Hebrew commerce and politics would be destroyed and society in dire confusion. Overcome and driven out of their land, the author's countrymen would require heroic treatment to sustain their faith.

The identity of the author soon became an issue. Thus early in the study we were entertaining a constantly deepening respect for the stately music of Job. We were assured that the reaction of modern life to these profound chords and to their author is that of unmixed reverence. Like Shakespeare, this dramatic masterpiece nowhere bears the author's signature. Tho unsigned, the massive productions of these two immortals are everlasting monuments.

It was altogether essential that we should get the viewpoint of the author in order to sympathize with him, think with him, see with him, and feel with him. Therefore, we went questing for traces of the author. With sheets of notepaper at hand, we jotted down references identifying our author as a traveler, master of the Hebrew language, versed in foreign learning, a leader, and an influential public man. Many verses reminded us of Elijah, John the Baptist, and Saul of Tarsus, all desert trained.

The author's versatility impinged upon us from every angle. His range and depth inspired us with awe. We trembled in storms, bathed in sunshine, reveled in ancient legends, in fancy wore the robes of patriarchal customs, and paid homage to lofty statesmanship. Whirlwinds, swelling seas, caravans, and the wailing dirge of a troubled nation were always clamant, but never obscured the expectant questioning of an eager soul. We felt that the piety of the author never lagged behind his genius. Biblical references to Job, scarcely more than hints, are not so brief as to conceal our author's spirit of religious devotion.

Tho scholars are not unanimous, we considered our action trustworthy in classifying this excellent author as a Jewish exile. As such, he would see just men suffering. Doubtless, he would observe tyrants, thieves, and possibly murderers avoiding punishment. Such a thinker would reflect upon the troubled thoughts of innocent martyrs. He would know the stories of good men, suddenly reduced by galling misfortune. These incidents would thrust two questions upon his sympathetic mind: What do such men think about God? How does God justify such apparent injustice? To us, it seemed that our text was the attempt of a gentle, devout, and cultured scholar to answer these two questions.

II. The incomparable artists enacting the drama have exercised an irresistible spell for untold generations. Our class, while studying the drama, tried to see the characters in action through the eyes of the inspired author. Thus, we imagined the actors coming upon the stage so that we might study their features and gestures. At this point plans for our own dramatic presentation began to take definite form. That we might make the personality of each actor the more nearly indelible, we determined to reenact the world-famous drama. Impelled by this decision, we scrutinized with great care the achievements of the hero, Jehovah, the Satan, Job's wife, and Job's friends.

Job, the hero, was a radiant character study in the opening scene of chapter one. His personality dominated the stage. His moral worth, religious devotion, eminence of position, and love for his home and children were distinctive in every movement and posture.

To find that the dramatist had prepared a non-Jewish setting for his stage was a surprize to some class members. However, Job's name had a foreign origin; he sacrificed without the help of priests, very possibly without knowledge of them; he spoke no word about the laws of Moses, the Jewish temple, or Palestine's desolate cities; and his chief friends were not Hebrews. Thus class interest deepened in following a Jewish dramatist as he elevated a non-Jewish hero, who became a popular figure among Hebrew people far back in the dim centuries.

As our class became more and more absorbed in the study of the drama, it was inevitable that the question should arise whether Job was a fictitious character. No effort was made to evade any such query. Flewelling's *Christ and the Dramas of Doubt*, and Dr. Jastrow's *Book of Job* were examined by several class members. The former was constructive and helpful. The vivisection of the latter was somewhat bewildering. However, both contributed to the solution of Job's reality.

We discuss the evident inspiration of the far famous narrative. We dwelt upon the breadth of the drama in making use of a non-Jewish hero. We reviewed the traditions concerning the piety of the cultured author. We weighed the theory of the tolerant and patriotic exile reviving his comrades. We examined the searching questions which confronted the hero. Is pain evil? Why do the innocent suffer with the guilty? Does worldly comfort become a greater blight than poverty and suffering?

With Job we tried to plumb the depth of human wo and scan the peak of God's glory. In Job we found deep despondency, bitter anguish, and, finally, a prophetic cry that would not be supprest, breaking through storm and night. As we looked at the hero Job we voted with that great school which accepts this deathless work as a richly dramatic poem with a foundation of history. In the gospel of John we can not always distinguish between quotation and sentiment of the author. So, in Job, we acknowledged that the line between history and tradition, and the boundary between character of hero and personality of author, might not always be determined. The unprejudiced disposition of the class found a brilliant author drawn to a genuinely human hero. To this class of business men, matrons, and college professors the virile and blameless life of Job was the explanation of the selection of his mind, soul, and voice as one of the chief battle-fields of all time.

The character of Jehovah was second in order of consideration. We attempted to examine the various conceptions of Jehovah, such as the Mosaic view; that of the prophets; and the New Testament thought of God. In Job's conception of Jehovah was much of stateliness and strength. We studied the authority of the Jehovah of the drama, his knowledge of the world, his interest in humanity, his claims upon human service, and his appreciation of human loyalty. It was brought out that the old gods were arbitrary; men tried to keep them in good mood. We examined our artist's impression of Jehovah for possible intimations of arbitrary qualities. We studied the postures of Jehovah to find whether his own glory was his chief thought. We wanted to learn whether the Jehovah of the drama wished to ennoble the race through the testing of the hero.

Two important questions were raised early in the study. Were we following an artist who would exalt his drama with a Divinity capable of inspiring affection? If such was in any large way the conception of Jehovah in Job's day, would such magnetism remain when temporal blessings were dim or destroyed? One striking thing in this dramatic development was Jehovah's affection for Job. Another unforgetable feature was that Jehovah's rights in the affairs and affections of humanity were never absent from the plot.

The Satan demanded attention. We sought to compare him with the "Accuser" of Zechariah, and the "Tempter" of the New Testament. We seemed to find it a bit difficult to renounce prejudice and give the author a chance to experiment with his daring actor. We were obliged to admit that Job's Satan was not chief of evil spirits, nor was he hideous in form, nor was he a fallen angel. In this dramatic creation we witnessed a restless, inquiring spirit, venturing to dispute the judgments of Jehovah. He sneered at faith and virtue. To us, he seemed an unbelieving, misrepresenting spirit, a sort of eternal skeptic, a tireless searcher after flaws in human faith.

We discuss the value to the drama of Satan's opinion of Job; Jehovah's reason for seeking the Satanic expression; whether the Satan's slander against the faith of Job was a disguise for the judgment of sneering men; and whether the drama implied that the Satan had authority to strike humanity only with the permission of Jehovah. We did concede, perhaps grudgingly, that our author had invested this self-conscious actor with a limited honor, shrewdness of thinking, and at least a superficial reverence.

Job's wife provoked conflicting emotions. One thing appeared very clearly at this point, however, namely, that the cast of supporting actors, including Job's wife, the Satan, and the friends, were as so many mirrors; from this point to the conclusion of the drama, their chief accomplishment was to reflect various degrees of light upon the personalities of Job and Jehovah. And yet we found strength, of a sort, in this feminine character. She too had "integrity"; otherwise she had not recognized that quality in Job. It requires some sense of goodness to pay homage to virtue. We thought her counsel to Job as much a tribute as a thrust. We found in her admonition some proof of her honesty of character. Whatever creed she had held hitherto, she imputed to Job no infidelity to Jehovah. We concluded that the shrewd and sympathetic dramatist had created this personage as an intimate and perhaps unconscious witness of the sincerity of Job. Thus she corroborated the testimony of Job's children, the wise men of his day, people of all walks, and of Jehovah.

The appearance of Eliphaz revealed to us a gentleman of culture and position. Teman, a center of thought (Jer. 49:7), was the home of this friend. That Eliphaz was oldest, wisest, and best of Job's friends was the theory accepted by our class. Analyzing his strength, we traced lines of originality, courtesy, and genuine sympathy for Job. To us, his features indicated frankness. We felt that Eliphaz could steel himself to the performance of a disagreeable duty, even tho confronted with memories of a rich friendship.

Bildad suffered in comparison with Eliphaz. Indeed, in order to be just toward him, we had to remind ourselves that he had shown traits of real friendship. We would not allow ourselves to forget that he made a journey of at least a few hundred miles across the dangerous deserts of Arabia to sympathize with Job. Bildad displayed less dignity and more directness than his older companion. Lasting sympathy implies deep understanding. We could find little of either in Bildad, the fair-weather friend of Job.

Zophar's bearing indicated intelligence, without which he would scarcely have been a friend of the thoughtful Job. Could we have located the homes of Bildad and Zophar, we might have found thereby some reason otherwise unknown for their veneer of friendship for Job. Of the trio who made the unhurried call upon tormented Job, Zophar appeared to be the youngest. His first words were hot and heedless of wounds. He risked a promising friendship to clasp a threadbare creed, which proved little better than a fetish.

Elihu played the part of the youthful "bystander." In *Greater Men and Women of the Bible* Dr. Hastings speaks well of Elihu. The poetry of his eruption may have been somewhat inferior. Tho self-conscious, he disclaimed prophetic wisdom. His sincerity was his own best advocate. We

appraised Elihu as far more wisely zealous than Zophar; clearly broader than Bildad; at least the moral equal of Eliphaz; but visibly inferior to Job.

Authorities were generously consulted in our study. No exposition was saner and sweeter than that of Dr. Robert A. Watson, in *The Expositor's Bible*. We levied upon history, geography, archeology, the evidence of old manuscripts, and accredited Jewish scholars. Some members felt that our attention given to Job and to Jehovah was disproportionate. But our chief disclosures of the Infinite always have taken human form. In Job we tried to become intimate with a mystic whose pure soul became more and more sensitive to the secrets of the unseen.

III. Having decided to present the drama, a management committee was named. This body indicated smaller groups to select the characters, arrange costumes, build and equip the stage, and prepare the music.

The stage was arranged to represent a patriarchal encampment. At the extreme right appeared Job's tent. At the back, was a paper screen, painted as a jutting wall of desert rock. Half a dozen small pine trees were firmly placed at intervals about the tent and wall. Talented fingers converted a piece of canvas into a background of mountain summits. This transformation was wrought with colored crayons and suspended across the pipe organ alcove. "Drops" were made of tissue paper. At the left of stage burlap wings were hung, and we had a front curtain of the same material controlled from the wings.

For a moderate sum costumes were rented from a city dealer. A few other garments were borrowed from a local society. Turbans, mantles, tunics, flowing robes, and sandals were much in evidence. Thorough study, originality, and discreet adjustment characterized the work of this faithful committee.

The music was altogether appropriate. A quartet of our best voices sang a few choice selections. The pipe organ was reenforced by stringed and wind instruments. The selections were reverent, glad, or tender, as demanded by the progress of the drama. Handel's Largo, Haydn's Shepherd Song, and Nevin's Song of Sorrow, were indispensable. A great oratorio supplied the line, "I know that my Redeemer liveth," which was sung with fine interpretation.

The author of Job has been hailed as a very great dramatist. We had many a thrill as we detected the research and culture of centuries gleaming in a single touch. Nor did we have any doubts about the intensity of the action. And yet this drama was well adapted for our use, tho we were all amateurs. The dramatic webs entangled the hero in disaster with the least possible stage machinery. No real necessity existed for the changing of scenery, which our limitations made impossible.

With the parting of our sackcloth curtains, criers in somber costume appeared at right and left of stage, reciting the opening lines of the drama. Presently, Job entered in prosperous oriental attire. While he was engaged in devotion, the heavenly council convened. The Satan ascended a stairway, concealed behind the desert wall. He was garbed in Mephistophelian garments. He sneeringly discust the unsuspecting Job with the invisible Jehovah.

Immediately the messengers panted to the door of Job's tent. At the close of a happy day they burst upon him with crushing reports. The slaughter by the Sabians, a dreadful electrical storm, bands of piratic Chaldeans, and a fierce tornado had slain Job's herds, servants, and children. One messenger followed another with confusing rapidity. They delivered their information of multiplied calamities, and then sank exhausted before the tent. As in the long ago, Job was bewildered. His calm spirit was staggered by the breathless reports of the swarthy survivors of disaster. Recently rich, suddenly destitute! Solicitous for children, violently bereft! Believing serenely in Jehovah, suddenly scarred by frowning destiny.

Immediately the second council convened. Jehovah's original confidence was emphasized. Job still held fast his integrity. The Satan was forced to yield a point. Jehovah strengthened his position. Job was not in the council. He was unconscious alike of the Satan's sneer and of Jehovah's approval. Yet it was made clear that the immediate consideration of the celestial council (and of the heavenly drama) was the testing of the faith and life of Job.

The council adjourned, the Satan descended to earth. He subdued Job with a spell of evil magic. Thus smitten, Job writhed in agony. After a time, his wife emerged from the tent. Tortured with the grief which had come to her, as well as to Job, she flung wild words of depravity at him. There were moments of disappointment in Job, and this was one of them. And yet, she merited Job's reproof, which was softened with a temperate note of faith.

Dirge-like music tolled off a period of time. Travelers approached and seated themselves in silence. Scholars have talked of verse thirteen of the drama's second chapter as a commentary on oriental friendship. But, working out the drama as we did, we wondered with Job not at the length but at the character of the silence. Did their grief for Job keep the visitors dumb? Doubtless, all of them, including Job, had believed that suffering implied sin. Were they applying their grim doctrine to him? He may have felt their unspoken inquiries about the cause of his humiliation. He must have read their suspicion in their averted looks.

We tried to think with Job. Altogether we found excuse to think that Job finally chose between an unhinged mind and volcanic speech. As Job's heat subsided, his lament became a tragic chant. We found at this point one of those moments of convulsive pain wherein Job welcomed death. Within his breast raged a cyclonic revolt against old beliefs that dared not face the whole of life.

The part of Eliphaz was taken by one of our church men, who has had much experience as a Masonic lecturer. In musical periods he tried to show the perplexity of Job's scholarly visitor. He began with gentle dignity, paying tribute to the former benevolence of Job. But presently our twentieth-century audience was listening to the polished Eliphaz challenging Job to remember, if he could, any innocent or upright man suffering such adversity as Job's. Eliphaz believed Job's suffering was due to secret guilt.

Job's reply to Eliphaz was most vigorous. The dogmatic logic of his visitor stimulated the accused man. Job's interpreter tried to make clear the coherency and variety of the hero's thinking. Job's burning reply conveyed to us a new sense of the merciless pain and violent struggle of the drama's chief human character.

Bildad was impersonated by a robust young college professor. We heard him accuse Job of impiety merely because Job dared to think for himself. Bildad's belief in Jehovah included no personal investigation. When he advised Job to seek for the Infinite, he might as well have substituted antiquity for Deity. He acquiesced with his older friend's assumption of Job's impurity.

Forthwith, Job responded, and found Bildad's position insufficient. Eloquently he confirmed all reference to the greatness of Jehovah. With votive awe Job reflected upon the majesty of earth, and the mystery of the far planets. We witnessed Job as a Bunyan, imprisoned but pressing against bars that could not long confine him.

Zophar's impetuous personality was portrayed by the obliging pastor of a neighboring church. With utter disregard of Job's prostration he upbraided the sufferer for alleged offenses deserving extreme penalties.

Job resented the contempt and loose reasoning of the youngest of the three visitors. He contended for a religion appealing to the reason. The visitors were unanimous as to Job's guilt, but they identified no sinful acts. Job repudiated such a verdict, and rejected their admonitions to repentance.

The second and third cycles were followed in the same manner.

Elihu's part was played by a stalwart young lieutenant from our College Military Department. With many apologies, he tried to explain his position. He agreed with the visitors that Job had spoken foolishly. He concurred with Job concerning the greatness of Jehovah. Elihu and Eliphaz were in harmony about sacred visions. Not all of the young intruder's professions were fulfilled. His offensiveness was less and his egotism no greater than the same qualities in Bildad and Zophar. In support of his arguments, Elihu made shrewd use of the gathering tempest.

With Elihu's dramatic disappearance, our storm scene developed. Switches, rheostats, a large number of electric lamps, and quantities of insulated wire were borrowed from our College of Mines. Thus was made possible the spectacular play of lightning. The accompanying thunder was cleverly executed. We made a further contribution to realism by spraying water upon the windows nearest the stage.

The dialog between Jehovah and Job was impressive. The words of Jehovah were voiced by an expert reader, unseen, but clearly audible. When the invisible Jehovah spoke, all smaller lights were extinguished, leaving one large globe illuminated. This light was subdued by a screen of crepe paper, so that a soft glow suffused the blue background where sky and summits converged.

Everything led up to the point where Jehovah answered Job. In the written drama, three friends visited with Job. In our spoken drama, Job's circle of friends included the whole of the audience. We watched the ebb and flow of burning pain. We were lifted high on the rising tide of thought, more intense than the agony of boils and leprosy. A supremely masterful author, our actors, and a dramatic atmosphere inspired us to live the drama over again. We saw and felt that a great heart was breaking to regain association with Jehovah. "Then Jehovah answered Job." There could be no other climax for this drama of the soul.

IV. In a final survey of spiritual lessons, we reviewed, first, the dialogs. Rich devotional intimations were found in Job's discussions. In chapter nine, we reflected upon the suggestion of the daysman or umpire. We regarded this compelling note as no mere suggestion of chance. Half logic, half prophecy, Job's hunger for a daysman lingered with us as one of the drama's fadeless spiritualities.

The breadth of the Golden Rule nowhere was more incandescent than in verses four and five of chapter sixteen. The morning air of the New Testament was radiant with Job's assurance that he would console his friends if conditions were reversed.

Second, we collected the votive implications from the suffering of Job. Agony could not silence the triumphant exclamation of the drama's nineteenth chapter, "I know that my Redeemer liveth."

Third, we were animated by the religious radiation of Jehovah's response to Job.

Fourth, we reviewed the display of spiritual truth in the pageant. As in the prolog, our pantomime included white-robed maidens, paying deference to Job, and venerable men bestowing gifts. Job's unassuming dignity was in sharp contrast with his former degradation.

Some considered the drama weakened by the scene of renewed health and returned prosperity. But we reflected upon the more abundant health of many a man and many a race, due to recognition of God's laws. Prosperous America has been a land of churches and school houses, since Colonial days. Neither her history nor the record of many a tithing church would justify the abolishing of the dramatic pageant.

With our study as foundation and our stage effort as "background," we constructed in four paragraphs our views of the author's purpose, and the meaning of his book. First, Job is a drama of the testing of faith. We are assured that a good man may suffer violent pain, and still believe in the mercy and justice of God.

Second, Job encourages the individual soul to claim the attention of God. In the drama, Job was vindicated. Had he suffered again, he would not have been so violently disturbed, since Jehovah had spoken to him. Job justifies emphasis upon the Infinite's recognition of distrest human personality.

Third, Job persuades us of God's friendship, notwithstanding darkest surroundings.

Fourth, Job demonstrates that

character may be deeply strengthened in suffering. Job has become one of our mighty immortals. He has left us the questions which agitated him, the thoughts which absorbed him, the hope which strengthened him, and the faith which glorified him; all of which

the masterful author has set to ever lasting music.

By our willingness frankly to approach such questions and reasonably to consider them we disclose our degree of faith in God, and our depth of sympathy with our human fellows.

BIBLE TEACHING CONCERNING CREATION

Professor JOHN WRIGHT BUCKHAM, D.D., Pacific School of Religion, Berkeley, California

If the question were asked: What is the Biblical teaching concerning creation? virtually the only answer would be, the account found in the first chapter of Genesis. And if it were then asked if there is any other and later account, the answer would probably be: No, that is, aside from the "creation psalms," such as Ps. 104. Yet there is another and later account; and by all the tests of reasonableness, maturity, and centrality of position it rather than that in Genesis is the Biblical account. It is in all respects in full and complete accord with philosophy, history, and science. Moreover, it suggests, if it does not actually teach, evolution. It is, in fact, one of those "pools of Scripture" spoken of by Augustine, "in which lambs may drink and elephants must swim."

This account commences in precisely the same way as the first chapter of Genesis—"In the beginning"; and it assigns creation to the same source, God. But it proceeds to interpret creation in the light of truths which had come to the human mind after that early interpreter of creation spoke—above all in the light of the truth revealed in Jesus Christ.

The reason why this New Testament passage is so little understood to be an account of creation is that it is at once so profound, so comprehensive, and so comprest. In order to get more of its significance let us attempt to expand and paraphrase its wealth and meaning.

1. "In the beginning was the Word" —i.e., the Logos, reason, order, law, revelation. This right reason (the writer affirms) is not derived, created, produced. It is of the very nature of God himself. It is in his every thought and deed. It has entered into the very structure of the universe—into the whole and into every part. "Without him was not anything made." Moreover the Logos is not something mechanical, instrumental, impersonal, but inherent in the divine mind— therefore conscious, rational, personal.

2. In this eternal rational potency there was enwrapt from the beginning not only order, relationship, structure, symmetry, but life. Not only is it (or he) the key to the inorganic but to the organic realm. The scientific search for the intimate secret and origin of life has been long and fruitless. According to this interpreter of creation it lies here—in the eternal Christ of reason through whom God gave being to all that is, and in due course life.

3. Out of the inorganic, life; out of life, intelligence—the light of men. "And the life was the light of men." In men life flamed up into self-conscious rationality, in the light of which the whole cosmic order stands disclosed as such, interrelated, uniform, law-governed, progressive, purposeful.

4. "And the light shineth in darkness"—a reminder of the Genesis description of primeval darkness. Yet darkness seems to have for this author a deeper than a mere physical aspect. It appears to stand for that negativity which is the essential counterpart, or antithesis, of light, and as such is not in itself evil, but which by its very ineptitude provides a medium for the rise of evil. Thus we have a suggestion of something which—if not itself as yet opposed to the good—has within it the capacity for such opposition. There is no gnostic dualism here, but only the suggestion that within creation itself there lay the possibility not only of a positive self-development but of a negative self-development.

5. "And the darkness apprehended it not." Was this, then, the beginning of disharmony, of devolution, of sin? —in the refusal of a part of the creation to be illumined, the preference of darkness to light, the inertia and selfishness, perhaps, which led so many forms of life to choose ease and sloth and stagnation rather than to advance through the strait and narrow way that leads to life?

6. "There came a man, sent from God." Now enters the individual, divinely chosen, a witness to the light, the man who emerges from his fellows and stands out historically selected and endowed for a special service. The very name John—gift of God— is significant. The divine purpose can not be fulfilled without the intrepid individual, the hero, the leader, the witness. Yet the mere individual, the witness, is not, can not be, the full revealer. The way now opens for his appearance.

7. "There was the true light, even the light that lighteth every man coming into the world." Within each man and all men is the Logos light, the rational intelligence, the divine principle, the guide to true and immortal living—dim, broken, rejected by many souls, clouded and hindered by the lower, physical nature; yet in other souls burning clear, tho dim, ready to be augmented and to become regnant by means of a fuller revelation. Thus operative and decisive is the will—either receiving not the revelation, even on the part of his own, or receiving it and entering thereupon into divine sonship. Now comes the climax.

8. "And the Word became flesh and dwelt among us." There is the crowning creative act—incarnation— not mere diffused and general incarnation but historic, concrete, individual incarnation so complete and unique as to justify the assertion that the Word became flesh. Not that this perfect and complete incarnation denies universal incarnation. Complete incarnation would be incomprehensible and meaningless without partial incarnation. The Light lighteth every man. The Word is in everything that is made. But only when the Light shines full is the partial light made effectual. Only as the incarnation is complete and convincing, only as the Word is enfleshed and dwells among men, does the partial incarnation become fully conscious of itself, making its possessor a true son of God.

Here, then, in the prolog of the Fourth Gospel, is the clearest, profoundest, most satisfying account of creation that has yet been produced in any literature—whether of science, or of religion, or of philosophy. Not that it is in any respect a detailed description. The methods and forms of the creative process are matter for scientific rather than religious knowledge; but its ultimate principles are here in clear and convincing outline. This account, too, is virtually the teaching of Paul (see Col. 1:15-17) and also of the author of the epistle to the Hebrews.

Whether one accepts this version of

creation or not, it is no more than just to the Bible that, instead of reverting to the early narratives in Genesis—remarkable for the age in which they were written, but necessarily limited—this profound, succinct, comprehensive, progressive interpretation through the divine operative reason should be recognized as the Biblical account of creation.

THE MINISTER'S USE OF FICTION

Professor CHARLES ALLEN DINSMORE, D.D., Yale University, New Haven, Conn.

What one writes or preaches is of small value unless the thought and emotions issue from personal experience. Therefore, my words may be a little more persuasive if they reflect somewhat intimately my own adventures in the wonderland of fiction. When a boy, just awakening to the responsibility and glory of life, I read with avidity Dr. John Todd's *Student's Manual*, an austere, lofty, stirring book, immensely inspiring to an ambitious lad. But it nearly killed me, for it induced me to drag myself out of bed at four o'clock on cold Vermont winter mornings to study some three hours before breakfast. The sure road to fame, I foolishly believed, was through early rising. The book also deflected me from a proper appreciation of the literature of the imagination. Dr. Todd strongly advised against the reading of fiction—life was too serious, too much knowledge was still unappropriated to waste one's time on such trivial stuff. In order to speak from experience the good doctor had read the whole of Scott, and, with scarcely less thoroughness, Bulwer and Cooper. It was his deliberate opinion that these authors, who had squandered such brilliant talents merely to amuse men,

must meet the day of judgment under a responsibility which would be cheaply removed at the price of a world . . . When you have read and digested all that is really valuable, and which is comprised in what describes the history of man in all lights in which he has actually been placed, then betake yourself to works of the imagination.

And if you would train the imagination, so runs his counsel, read "Chalmers on Astronomy" rather than fiction. For a long time I conscientiously tried to follow this advice, and in the end I was a prig, half dead. The mind of the ordinary man can not endure being crammed continuously with such massive food any more than the stomach can digest a constant weight of solids. It is fatal both to character and to the tone of the mind to keep the faculties stretched to the utmost; one needs relaxation to escape from the wheel of things, to let the fancy run free. Life is not quite so serious as the old Puritan war-horses imagined. God causes the rivers to meander leisurely through the meadows, the birds to sing, and the lambs to gambol. Beauty is his law as well as righteousness. The artist is as dear to him as the reformer. Laughter as well as prayer has a place in his home. I am confident that, while Dr. Todd was reading Scott for the purpose of warning the rest of us to refrain, the people of Pittsfield said, one to another: "How well the doctor is preaching lately! His sermons have more lively imagination, more human sympathy."

There is a literature of knowledge, but more valuable and permanent is the literature of power in which moral truth and human passion are molded into forms of beauty. An editorial in the *World's Work* for May, 1922, calls attention of all workers to the part the imagination plays in every field of action. It instances a business man who declared that unless he occasionally read Shakespeare he was conscious of becoming a mere routine man. To keep his imagination alive he must ever and anon enter the poet's magic realm. Only thus could he deal with affairs in a large way. True in business, it is doubly true in the ministry, for the imagination is the faculty by which the mind sees the heart of truth, forms it into images of beauty, and sets it in its proper atmosphere. It sees, it shapes, it glorifies truth. Moreover it enables one to put himself in the place of another. Next to a clean heart, a sane and vigorous imagination is a minister's best endowment. And for the training of a creative and sympathetic imagination the literature of power is indispensable. Here fiction holds a high place.

Truth embodied in a tale not only enters into lowly doors, it enters clothed with power and amazing glory. When in the midst of Hugo's *Les Miserables* I was lifted up to the lofty places of emotional experience. I walked the streets feeling that I was a mile high, the mountains and the hills spoke with strange voices, and the trees of the field rejoiced. In Bishop Bienvenu I felt the redeeming power of Christian good-will as I have not realized it in any historical saint, not even in St. Francis. Jean Valjean's tragic struggle with an unescapable past has not only been a vivid picture in my mind for thirty years, it has helped me again and again to see life steadily. That scene in the court-house where the cleansed soul of Jean, to save another, takes up voluntarily a hated and unjust past with all its terrible entailment for the future, who can ever forget it! Every novel of George Eliot's has been a distinct epoch in my intellectual and spiritual life. She has given me a sense of the majesty and the inviolability of the moral law which I have received nowhere else save in Dante and the Greek dramatists. In fact, no writer of the first class lacks this instinct for the moral order of life. It is the little authors who minimize sin and retribution.

A great artist renders us this service. First, he enables us to see life whole. In the actual world a long time often elapses between a deed and its consequence. One generation witnesses an act, another sees the judgment. The artist within the compass of a drama, or of a story, brings the action and the results together. We read the nature of the cause in the effect. Thus we are made to comprehend vividly what we believed only vaguely.

Moreover, truths which we hold in our minds in a shadowy, ineffective, commonplace sort of way the artist shapes into living characters. The truth, the passion, walks before us tingling with life. We feel it, we know it, we can not forget it. Afterward everywhere we see similar people, we recognize the passion, the truth, and we are certain whither they are tending. Having learned from the seers how inevitably character is destiny, we do not need to read the stars to learn the future.

The great writer also by the magic of his art takes us down into the hearts of men of all sorts and conditions; and, living for a time in others, we have thereafter the understanding heart, the tempered judgment, the kindlier feeling.

This three-fold service the authors of clear vision and steady mind render to us: they help us to see life vividly, to apprehend it truly, and to feel it sympathetically. These insights can not fail to give us much sermon material fashioned into the imagery of power.

But there are times when the grand wizards tax too severely our mentality. We need rest and utter relaxation, we crave a refuge for our jaded spirits. The fiction of retreat and refreshment is much more abundant than the fiction of power. Mark Twain has helped me forget many a miserable sermon and sent me to bed with a laughing heart. Gilbert Parker's exquisite short stories—*An Adventure of the North, Pierre and His People, A Romany of the Snows*—have taken me up into a far, strange world, cast over me the spell of the North, of burning stars, of vast silent places, and then returned me with a rested and tranquil mind, invigorated through the simple story of human heroism to fight more courageously my own peculiar battle.

Joseph Lincoln's stories are sure to be good and diverting. One is rarely disappointed in the recreational value of O. Henry's yarns, yet upon my mind he leaves no impression. I read his tales with joy and then a few months afterwards, if I pick up a volume of his, I may read it half through ere an expression or an incident will remind me that I have read all this before. Why I have this experience with the prince of story tellers I know not, for writers in every way his inferiors leave a deeper mark on my memory.

There are some unfortunates among brain workers who are afflicted with the "terror by night." About three o'clock in the morning we suddenly awake and all the spectres of the mind come trooping hideously forth. Fears and troubles which in the day or when in a perpendicular position we would easily waive aside, now that we are horizontal rise before us monstrous and horrific and will not down. One of the best ways to banish the "Terror," which the Bible tells us we are not to fear, is to recall some pleasant story and follow languidly its un-folding until gentle sleep comes again. *T. Tembarom,* by Frances Burnett, has been more effective than any other.

But how difficult it is to find clean, sweet, interesting stories! Much of our fiction is written by beardless boys, or romantic, immature girls; the pages are drenched with sex, or are the vehicles of half-baked sociological theories; we are asked to associate by the hour with people with whom, were they living, we would have nothing to do except to marry them, convert them, or bury them. Why drag our imaginations through all their inanities of speech and experience? Here Archibald Marshall comes as an immense relief. He introduces us to people whom it is a pleasure to know, carries us along easily through quite ordinary events, and leaves us as refreshed as tho we had been spending an evening with clever and interesting folks.

Occasionally a rattling good romance, like Jeffry Farnol's *A Broad Highway,* will restore to us the zest of youth. Here the lady is inexpressibly fair, the invincible hero daily performs prodigies of valor, and a villain is killed in every chapter. A thoroughgoing romance does not pretend to be true. One therefore can park his critical judgment while the imagination performs double loops and nose spins in the high ether.

The number of eminent professional men who have a selected library of detective stories is perfectly amazing. The reason seems to be that men in middle life and over have grown utterly weary of sex problems, sentimental love stories, the high lights and stage machinery of the ordinary novel, and turn to a type of literature that can engage the tired mind without nauseating the delicate stomach. He who makes two good sleuth yarns grow where one grew before is a benefactor of humanity. Would that

Conan Doyle might get an authentic message from Sherlock Holmes! That would be more interesting than some of the communications which he is giving to the public.

There is another type of literature especially healing to tired nerves. What minister, prest by a thousand petty and distracting engagements, has not dreamed of a cozy home in the country where he could enjoy a garden, open his soul to the cleansing strength of the great out-of-doors, and read at his leisure the books he had longed all his life to know? Inexpressible was the pleasure which came to me when David Grayson gave shape to my dreams in *Adventures in Contentment* and *Adventures in Friendship*. I was tempted to resign immediately that such tranquil joy and ripened wisdom might be mine. But, alas, I have found that these stories and all similar ones are pipe-dreams. Did you ever know a minister, or any other nerve-racked professional man, who wrote an idyll of his serene contentment out of anything resembling his actual experience on a farm? Such books are not written. It is the busy men of the cities who write delightful stories of the joys of retirement. The men who have really made the experiment are not publishing books of any kind, or even reading them, but are sitting by their fireplaces with their chins in their hands, utterly disillusioned, wishing they were back again in the harness, with a steady job, a stated salary, and an opportunity to do something worth while.

There is another use of fiction which remains to be mentioned; it reflects quite accurately the trend of modern thought and emotion. To attempt to read comprehensively the flood of books being issued from the press is impossible. Most of it is certainly inferior, yet we can not quite follow Charles Lamb's impulse: "When a new book comes out, I read an old one." As leaders we must know what the people are having served up to them, therefore it is well to take two or three of the outstanding novels of the year to read in the leisure of vacation. If they are good, then our minds are at rest to receive their beauty and truth; if they are poor, well, time is not worth much in vacation anyway.

In order, I suppose, that I might form some judgment on the drift of popular reading, the editors of this magazine sent me a large package of recent fiction of all kinds.[1] On the whole the reading has been disheartening. The sex problem looms large, the married people are uniformly ill-mated and unhappy, true love seems to be an infatuation with another's mate; the conventions of life seem to these jungle animals a form of slavery from which they must escape. "Their honor rooted in dishonor stands." The romantic yarn-spinners are bad enough, but the realists are unspeakable. Apparently they think that real life is known only in debauchery, they not only ask us to follow their characters into orgies of lust, but they literally strip them naked that nothing by any possibility be hidden. Our modern realists know the animal in man so much better than they know his soul.

---

[1] *Success.* By Samuel Hopkins Adams. Houghton Mifflin Co., New York, 1921, $2.00.
The Young Enchanted. By Hugh Walpole. George H. Doran Company, New York, 1921, $2.00.
Trouble-the-House. By Kate Jordan. Little, Brown and Company, New York, 1921, $2.00.
Enter Jerry. By Edwin Meade Robinson. The Macmillan Company, New York, 1921, $1.75.
Beggars' Gold. By Ernest Poole. The Macmillan Company, New York, 1921, $2.00.
Mr. Waddington of Wyck. By May Sinclair. The Macmillan Company, New York, 1921, $2.00.
Maria Chapdelaine. By Louis Hemon. The Macmillan Company, New York, 1921, $2.00.
The Wasted Generation. By Owen Johnson. Little, Brown and Company, New York, 1921, $2.00.
If Winter Comes. By A. S. M. Hutchinson. Little, Brown and Company, New York, 1921, $2.00.
Simon Called Peter. By Robert Keable. E. P. Dutton and Company, New York, 1921, $2.00.
Princess Salome. By Burris Jenkins. J. B. Lippincott and Co., Philadelphia, 1921, $2.00.

Some of the stories would make capital films for the cheap movies, the characters are exaggerated, the lights are red and yellow, the staging bizarre. If the books sent to me were a cup taken at random from the stream of modern fiction, then I can say that the water is muddy and tastes of the sewer. I endorse Dean Cross's recent characterization of the new fiction: "Out of nothing into nowhere." It rises in the springs of shallow sentimentalism and perverse fancy which is not imagination, it flows through a squalid country, and is absorbed in a desert. I make a few exceptions. Hugh Walpole's *The Young Enchanted* leaves a pleasant light on the mind. Robinson's *Enter Jerry* delightfully unlocks the memory of one's boyhood; *Maria Chapdelaine* is a sweet prose-poem, and *Mr. Waddington of Wyck* starts some interesting questions. *If Winter Comes,* vivid, clever, intense, is so good that it ought to have been better. Would spring have come had it not been for divorce and death? And was it spring after all that came? No wonder that the book is popular, for it so accurately represents our age. Puzzled! Seeing a scene distinctly, but not the horizon or the trail! "Odd affair! Mysterious and baffling conundrum to be mixed up in! . . . Life!" Life is confused and mysterious enough, no doubt; but it is not quite so inexplicable as modern writers seem to think. The supreme seers have felt darkness, winter, tangled wilderness, but they discerned a way in the jungle; they found a pillar of light and of cloud to guide humanity; they heard a voice above the storm; they saw a light in the darkness; they recognized a divine meaning in suffering. Life indeed is a puzzle, but it can be put together with some sort of meaning, and a glorious meaning too. It is a great and terrible wilderness, but there is a Light and he that followeth after the Light shall not walk in darkness or lose the path.

Read the supreme works of fiction for culture, some lighter stories for refreshment, a few of the best sellers to catch the drift of the times, and then pray God for the coming of a genius who will "see life steadily, and see it whole."

HIGHER WAGES FOR LOW-PAID WORKERS

WORTH M. TIPPY, D.D., New York City

A breakfast conference was held on a mid-August morning last summer at the Lake Junaluska Assembly, at which business men and church leaders discust the possibility of permanently higher wages for lower-paid workers relative to cost of living. All agreed that better living conditions for the families of workers were desirable, and two of the manufacturers present decided to undertake to raise the wages of lower paid men in their own factories. One of them was overheard to say to his wife after breakfast, "You may have to walk or ride in the street car, for we shall probably not be able to buy the automobile this fall."

One of those who attended the breakfast was Mr. John J. Eagan of Atlanta, Georgia, then majority stockholder, now president, of the American Cast Iron Pipe Company of Birmingham, Alabama. On taking office, Mr. Eagan made a public statement to the effect that

The directors of this company are all church members. They have elected another professing Christian as president on a basis that the teachings of Jesus Christ are to be the ruling principles of the business. I am glad if the action of the directors of our company will cause other profest followers of Christ to give this question their thought.

The platform adopted by the directors declares for a reasonable living wage to the lowest paid workman, constant employment for every member of the organization, and actual application of the Golden Rule to relations between employee and employer.

Quite as interesting as these declarations is Mr. Eagan's comment on the publicity which his announcement received. He remarked that it was an unfortunate commentary on modern business life that when a Christian, among Christians, announced a simple Christian program the papers should treat it as "news."

Two others at the breakfast were the president, and the vice-president and general manager, of the Stockham Pipe and Fittings Company of Birmingham. This firm also, but by different methods, is working on the same policy, namely, living wages, rewards for skill and faithfulness, good will and fair dealing between management and men, certain forms of cooperative service such as medical, dental, and surgical care for the men and their families, and a gradual development of democratic relationships. One can not enter these factories without sensing an atmosphere which is human and quickening.

A dispatch to the *New York Herald* from Cincinnati under date of January 2, announces:

Six hundred employees of the Nash Clothing Company, of which Arthur Nash, known as "Golden Rule" Nash, is president, will go to work to-morrow richer and happier as the result of action taken this afternoon increasing the wages of all employees 10 per cent. and adopting a forty-hour week instead of a forty-four hour week as in the recent past.

This is the firm which increased certain low paid workers from $4 to $12 per week when the organization of another clothing factory was taken over two years ago, and, as stated above, has reduced the week to forty hours and five days, mainly for the sake of the large number of mothers who are employed. It is Mr. Nash's theory that these mothers should meet their children at home when school is out, and that they should have Saturdays for work and shopping in order to have Sunday as a day of rest and worship. Mr. Nash in March still further shortened the day of his women operatives to seven hours, or thirty-five hours a week.

These are factories which have come before public notice because of striking features of their experiments. Mr. Nash, for example, has been in great demand as a speaker, and has made above 500 addresses in the last two years. Mr. Eagan's experiment has attracted public interest because of the policy which was announced when the new management assumed control. As a matter of fact in thousands of factories the managements are pursuing the same general principles to the best of their light, but without announcement or publicity. This is the heartening side of American industry at a time when the land is agitated by menacing disturbances. One has but to visit widely scattered industrial centers of the United States to realize how powerfully the leaven of good will is at work. Thousands of factories have no labor troubles and have not had for years, and it will be found usually in these establishments that the Christian principle is being followed, either deliberately or instinctively. Employers often hesitate to talk about what they are doing, lest they be subjected to criticism and misinterpretation. They prefer to go ahead, taking responsibility and hoping to approximate the Christian ideal, satisfied if they can feel that in the sight of Christ, "that great Shepherd of the sheep," they themselves may be considered also as good shepherds.

I have yet to talk with an employer who does not desire a permanently higher level of wages for all workers over the pre-war period. There are doubtless selfish and hard-hearted men who do not, and unquestionably wages have been unnecessarily reduced in many industries; but most employers realize that the families of workingmen must live better and that they are determined to live better. They agree with a Western banker

Of all the evils which contribute to the undoing of the average workingman—particularly the so-called unskilled laborer—that of low wages, or more precisely the non-living wage, is far and away the principal one. It is bad in its immediate and direct results, and worse in its more or less remote effects, for it can be shown that overcrowding, bad housing, child labor, much of the sickness in workingmen's families, are largely, in many cases entirely, due to low wages.

It is my own experience, and I think I speak for social workers generally—certainly for workers in settlements—when I say that it is the rare family among unskilled

ANNUAL BANQUET
Colored Workmen, American Cast Iron Pipe Company, Birmingham, Alabama.

who said to me in October, 1921, that "labor is justly entitled to a larger share in the product of industry." This is especially true of unskilled and low-paid workingmen, who constitute the great majority of toilers. They must have more for their families, and to see that they get it should be the united object not only of organized labor and the churches, but of employers as well.

Rev. Wm. E. McLennan, head worker of Welcome Hall, Buffalo, a social settlement in the Italian quarter under the control of the First Presbyterian Church, made a striking study of the incomes and living conditions of some families in the neighborhood of the settlement during the war. His comments are significant.

laborers that has a large enough income to insure even a minimum standard of living. Even in normal times—I will go further and say that even when industry is prosperous—the average non-technical worker seldom or never earns enough to provide for the legitimate needs of his family.

It is not a simple or easy matter to increase the wage of large numbers of working men at a given time. In many factories, however, the profits are such that to pay all a living wage is possible, and therefore obligatory. An employer can not be right in the sight of God who receives a large salary and high profits, while considerable numbers of his workers struggle to keep their households from want. This ought to be said, and said again and again, by every pulpit in the land. Employers are sorely tempted by the lure of large profits. They desire money for all kinds of good purposes. But we shall have to come to a more Christian ideal of business, namely, current interest on capital, moderate dividends on stock, sinking funds for unemployment, as well as a reserve to assure dividends in lean years, living wages for all workers, and wages above minimum subsistence according to skill and faithfulness, and made as high as the industry will justify. Surplus above these items is being divided with labor by an increasing number of firms.

If wages of low paid workers, both men and women, are to be lifted to a level of independence, so as to provide American standards of living for such households, two things are necessary: first, research into the cost of living in the community where the factory is located, with concerted action by the employers when that is possible, and second, increased production.

As to the first, the matter is fairly simple. Numerous studies into cost of living have been made during the last four or five years. An admirable summary of these is given in a recent monograph on the Wage Question by the Research Department of the Commission on the Church and Social Service. The following family budgets for a workingman's family of five persons provides for a small margin above reasonable subsistence, and indicates the needs of such families in various industrial centers:

Seattle, October, 1917, by Wm. F. Ogburn	$1,505.60
San Francisco, October, 1917, by Jessica Piexotto	1,476.40
New York, July, 1918, by Wm. F. Ogburn	1,760.50
Philadelphia, October, 1918, by Philadelphia Bureau of Municipal Research	1,636.79
Washington, D. C., August, 1919, by U. S. Bureau of Labor Statistics	2,243.94
Bituminous Mining Towns, 1919, by W. F. Ogburn	2,243.94
Chicago, November, 1921, U. S. Bureau of Labor Statistics	2,445.65

It is but necessary to check these up locally to know what it costs a workingman's family to live in any community. A competent social worker, such as could be secured in most communities, might gather the information. If the employers were to act together, as was proposed in the Junaluska breakfast conference, the problem would be made easier and its competitive complications lessened.

But any considerable wage increase for large numbers of workingmen is dependent upon elimination of industrial waste and increased production. At present labor does not believe this but turns its attention to what it considers to be an unjust distribution of the products of industry. The recent and very important volume on *Income in the United States,* by the National Bureau of Economic Research, shows a total national income for 1918 of $61,000,000,000, an average of $55- per capita; or an average of $2,77(for a family of five persons. This i too little above the living wage se for a family of five to offer much relief if it were divided equally, which it could never be.

Writing on "Strikes, Wages an Values," in his new volume, *What W Want and Where We Are,* Mr. W. A Appleton, Secretary of the General Federation of Trades Unions of England, has this to say:

The standard of living depends upon the standard of production. If the latter is low the former can not be high. The world abounds with proofs of the fact that the nation which produces little enjoys little. If the miner refuses to produce coal, the poor have no fires. If the railwaymen refuse to carry goods, the poor have no food. What applies to the miner and the railway men, applies equally, tho perhaps not so obviously, to the whole gamut of human enterprises and affairs. . . . Questions of fairness or unfairness in distribution are of profound importance, but they are secondary in importance to the need for production. Those who imagine that they can successfully reverse the order in which these two functions must be performed are indeed chasing shadows.

These are sober and challenging

statements coming from the late president of the International Trade Union Congress. However, encouraging possibilities of improved standards of living lie ahead of American working men, if united action can be secured to reduce the waste of strikes, lockouts, unemployment, business cycles, seasonal and intermittent industries, limitation of output, inefficient training, incapable and inexperienced management and other sources of loss; and if the full power of machinery, invention, improved processes, and scientific management can be brought to bear upon the life sustaining processes. The Christian employer is bound by his principles to do his best, as a good shepherd, for his workers; and his workers are bound also by the same principles to respond with the best skill and productive power which it is within their power to give. The interest of the one is bound up with that of the other. What more inspiring work could any man set before himself than to help put stronger and deeper economic foundations underneath the lives of our people? Marriage, homes, food, clothing, education, recreation, religion: all of these are largely dependent on income. If the mass of toilers, hewers of wood and drawers of water, are to progress and have their chance at abundant life here and now, it will be mainly because the leaders of industry refuse to be profiteers and choose rather to be good shepherds like the Master. The problem is, "The transition from an organization of society attuned to the major motive of profit to one attuned to the dominant note of service."

ABOUT IT AND ABOUT [1]

Professor JAMES MOFFATT, D.D., Litt.D., United Free Church College, Glasgow, Scotland

These four books produce upon the mind of a reader the same impression that is voiced in the stanza of Fitzgerald's "Omar Khayyam":

"Myself when young did eagerly frequent
    Doctor and Saint, and heard great argument
    About it and about: but evermore
Came out by the same Door as in I went."

It is certainly something to read men who are in earnest. None of the writers is a dilettante; all of them have zeal; tho whether it is a zeal according to knowledge, is another question. Each writer has more than an amateur's interest in the subject. Each has his solution of the problem, and if the arguments are not always great, they are prest with great force and faith.

Professor Ellwood starts from the assumption that "the religious revolution of the last two generations, which undermined theological Christianity, has left the Church all but prostrate and powerless before the immense social task which now confronts it." But if this means that "theology" is bankrupt, it is a misreading of the situation. Forms of theology may need to be revised, but Christianity must be "theological" if it is to live and move at all. The danger, no doubt, is that theological orthodoxy is allowed to cover indifference to social duties and even to personal religion. As our author remarks, "It has been theological Christianity which has tolerated practical paganism in the Church, covering it with the cloak of respectability by making the acceptance of a theological creed count for so much." But this has been the abuse of theology. And, for all the vigor-

[1] The Reconstruction of Religion. A Sociological View. By C. A. Ellwood. The Macmillan Company, New York, 1922. $2.25.
New Churches for Old. A Plea for Community Religion. By John Haynes Holmes. Dodd, Mead and Company, New York, 1922.
The Fundamentals of Christianity. By Henry C. Vedder. The Macmillan Company, New York, 1922. $2.00.
The Crisis of the Churches. By Leighton Parks. Charles Scribner's Sons, New York. 1922. $2.50.

ous arguments about the need of producing a Christian world by means of transforming public opinion, the plain truth remains that Christianity is a personal religion first and foremost, that personal religion does not mean selfish religion, and that some theology is essential if Christianity is not to be more than a diffused form of good-will. Little that Professor Ellwood brings forward is new, but much of it is true enough, however. In many circles still it is needful to urge that the Church is responsible for creating a social environment in which the good life is possible, and for attacking conditions of economic oppression in which faith and character are handicapped unfairly. This book summons such reluctant Christians to their duty in this respect.

Mr. Holmes is equally against theology, indeed, more so. He believes that "Protestantism in all its forms, both orthodox and liberal, is as dead a religion to-day, and therefore as subversive a social influence, as was medieval Catholicism in the fifteenth and sixteenth centuries," that in the blessed beginning of "democracy" as fellowship all hope lies, and that the real Church of the future will be not a church at all, in the old sense of the term, but "itself the community, functioning spiritually." How far he is prepared to go may be seen from his answer to the question, "But what is your community church? Is it Christian?" Well, he replies, when the community is Christian. But "in its ultimate form the community church can not be a Christian Church," for religion is an instinct of human nature which is broader than Christianity. This is logical with a vengeance. "The minister," we are told, "may work out to a belief in God, or he may not." And so on. Mr. Holmes has parted with the idea that there is anything distinctive and final in Christianity, and we may cheerfully part with him, wondering only whether it is more pathetic or tragic to see a man trying to save mankind by calling it to worship its magnificent democratic self.

Professor Vedder takes the matter much more seriously. Before trying to apply Christianity to democracy or to anything else, he sensibly sets himself to discover what Christianity is. Unfortunately he finds himself compelled to throw over the Apostle Paul, who "never got the social point of view." "The ethics of Paul," we are told, "are individualistic." Poor Paul! How-

ever, we are better off than he was. For "we are able to profess as our faith, 'God is democracy' with quite as much confidence as when we say, 'God is love.'" To read a sentence like this is almost enough to disgust one with the term "democracy" altogether. There is vigorous analysis in the earlier part of Professor Vedder's book, but vigor is misapplied when it is devoted to proving that Christianity was deflected when it passed from the Galilean gospel of Jesus into the hands of Paul. Such a reading of history is antiquated. There is a continuity between Jesus and Paul, and redemption in some form or another is organic to Christianity. The failure to recognize this has made a large part of these conscientious pages unhistorical and exaggerated. Professor Vedder does recognize that "a Christian theology will be a necessity so long as there is a Christian life; for religion must not consist of mere vague emotions and aspirations, but must be founded in a definite philosophy of life, corresponding to our scientific knowledge as well as to our inner experience, or it can not successfully appeal to a world that more and more demands reality as a basis for its living." But he does not see that the teaching of Jesus implies a profound theology, and that it is playing with words to call the message of Jesus "ethical" and "prophetic," and to denounce the early Christians for deifying, and so defying, their Master.

The fourth volume, by Dr. Parks, is in another world. Here we meet a man who writes with knowledge, responsibility, and a sense of central issues. He addresses himself to the practical problem of unity among the Protestant churches of America. He is not a sectarian, but he speaks some frank words about the "sentimental idealization of the Roman Catholic Church" in certain quarters, where people forget that "its estheticism is pagan, not Christian," and that "its discipline, which it is the fashion to applaud among those who have lost faith in democracy, is autocratic, and would use democracy for the reestablishment of a discredited autocracy." He fully agrees with Dean Inge that "it is the *ignis fatuus* of reunion with Rome which blocks the way to reunion with our Protestant brethren." It is the latter that he has in mind, organic union. As a clergyman of the Episcopal Church he believes, in no arrogant spirit, that his church possesses items of central value for the ideal American church of the future, in doctrine, discipline, and worship. His book is a thoughtful, persuasive statement of these items. He has no sympathy with the Anglo-Catholic sectarians, and regards everything as relative except unity of spirit among true Christians. How far his practical proposals will meet with acceptance, is a matter for doubt. No one can pronounce upon that who is not inside one or other of the American churches concerned. But on the other hand, a book like this is certain to promote the atmosphere in which alone such intricate problems can be solved. "The churches should be ashamed to continue longer in the spirit of Jonah," Dr. Parks writes toward the close, "the spirit which fails to see good elsewhere than in the little company of which he forms part; the spirit which, on the eve of a great revelation of God's wide-spread mercy and redeeming love, is angry because the little system which helped us is about to be destroyed, but cares not if the whole world perish provided that can be perpetuated." The two main temptations of those who write and speak about Christian unity are facile optimism and a secret desire to merge others in their own particular system. Dr. Parks is too profound a Christian to fall into either error. Whatever we may think of his opinions about creeds or the ministry, he impresses us by his genuine candor and truly catholic spirit. He has the essential note of sympathy with the past and at the same time a keen sense of the fresh problems awaiting us to-day; and it is the combination of these two convictions which saves his book from anything like crudity or hectoring. It is a sincere pleasure to say with what profit one has read the book; there is nothing patronizing about it, as—perhaps Dr. Parks will forgive me for saying—is sometimes the case with upholders of his communion; also, there is nothing vague, no escape from difficulties under a cover of pious platitudes. This is the sort of book that brings people together by helping them to understand one another, and further by suggesting to them the pressing duties and claims of the great cause in which after all the motives of unity are to be found. It ought to be circulated widely. Few books on the subject have contributed to the ventilation of what is vital.

THE CHURCH AND THE PUBLIC CONSCIENCE

[The following extract from Professor Ellwood's new book (reviewed above) we regard as worthy of the widest publicity.— Eds.]

If the business of the Church can not be summed up as looking after the physical and spiritual welfare of its members, or even as educating them into Christian ideas and ideals, what then is its work? Plainly its final work, as we have so frequently said, is the social redemption of mankind—the creation of a Christian world. But this means something more than a ministry to individuals as individuals. It means the transformation of customs and institutions. It means the shaping of the policies and conduct of groups as well as of individuals. Beyond the Church's mission of individual evangelism is the Church's mission of social evangelism. The subject of redemption is not the individual, but the world of individuals. How can the Church undertake this larger work of social control to secure the social redemption of mankind? Manifestly the Church must undertake to deal not only with individuals, but with mass movements and the forces that lie back of mass movements, which we vaguely call public sentiment, public opinion, and popular will. The Church must undertake the work of creating conscience, a public conscience, upon the behavior of groups as well as of individuals. Not until the Church is willing to grapple with this problem, which we might call that of "Christian statesmanship," can it create a Christian world.

It must be evident to all who desire a Christian world, that if such a world is ever to become a reality, the Church, animated by the true spirit of Christianity, must assume the moral leadership of the opinion of mankind. A Christian society, we have seen, can not be realised by merely developing Christian character in individuals. That has been a mistaken idea of the Protestant Church. "No individual," says one of the profounder social thinkers of the present, "can change the disorder and iniquity of this world. No chaotic mass of men and women can do it." Such change can come only through public opinion, organized popular will, and social control. The transition from non-Christian society, then, to Christian society can only be effected by the formation and guidance of an effective public opinion which shall express itself in an appropriate mode of social control, because that is the only mechanism through which conscious social changes are effected in human society. Individual education, individual conversion, individual repentance, and the whole development of individual Christian character are, of course, necessary foundations; but if the Church desires a Christian world, it must have a vision of its work beyond these fundamentals. It must see that its higher work is the creation of public conscience—that is, an effective public opinion—regarding the conditions under which men and groups of men live together. It is only thus

that a Christian world can come into being.

There can be no doubt about the power of public opinion to make a Christian society, and ultimately a Christian world; the only doubt is, as to whether the Christian Church will use its opportunities to make, guide, and control public opinion. Probably no one would claim that there has been much organized effort on the part of Protestant churches in the United States in the past to guide and control public opinion, unless it be along a few lines, like the suppression of the liquor traffic. Yet this is exactly what all Christian churches must undertake if there is ever to be a Christian world. They must go into the business of creating an effective public conscience regarding all relations of individuals, classes, nations, and races. The cry of the world is for Christian churches to go into this business at once. If the world is to be saved for Christianity, the churches must soon become more effectively organized for the guidance and control of public opinion. Only thus can a Christian environment be created for the nurture of Christian character.

COMMENT AND OUTLOOK

BY E. HERMAN, OUR LONDON CORRESPONDENT

Post-war Reaction Against the Old Testament in Germany

Among the most significant events in the world of Biblical scholarship within the last twenty years or so was the conversion of Professor von Harnack to Sir W. M. Ramsay's view of the early date of Luke and of the historical reliability of Acts. This meant a complete revulsion from a modernized Tübingen School position, and it led simple-minded English readers to rejoice as over the finding of the sheep that was lost. But it takes something more and other than a change of critical front to revolutionize a scholar's outlook, and in the light of Dr. Harnack's latest *tour de force* in his book on Marcion it is abundantly clear that his fundamental *Bibelanschauung* is unchanged. The book is typical of the present-day reaction against the Old Testament which, rooted in the latter half of the eighteenth century, has been brought to a head by the Great War, with its recrudescence of anti-Semitism. The Jews, it is alleged, were the cause of this tragedy; hence let us have no more to do with their sacred book. That sounds crude enough, and Harnack would scarcely admit it. Professor Friedrich Delitzsch, however, frankly avowed anti-Semitism as the reason for his quite widely savage attack on the Old Testament, published at a time when the German public were only too eager to absorb it, and constituting nothing short of a degradation of theological scholarship. Harnack is, of course, cast in a far nobler mold, but he, too, would like to see the Old Testament classed among the Apocrypha. Marcion, he holds, was premature in separating the Old Testament from the New, but Luther missed a great chance of doing so and the omission was fateful to the Church. Ever since then it has been becoming more and more urgent that a radical separation must be effected.

There is no doubt that the Church as a whole has found the Old Testament a dead weight. During the war especially men of good-will were perplexed and harassed by the teaching of certain Christian leaders who defined God in terms of the Old Testament not at its best but at its worst. But the way to get rid of the difficulty is not to cast the Old Testament away—to do so would be to fling away one of the great keys to the gospel—but to interpret it so as to transmute it from a drag into a means of progress. Given the idea of a progressive revelation culminating in Christ, the Old Testament becomes luminous and educative. Harnack's rejection of it is in reality as crass—or shall we say as superstitious?—as the old-fashioned Calvinists' reverence for it. Both defy history and the canons of valid criticism.

Dr. Tagore's Advice to Missionaries

Dr. Rabindranath Tagore lately received a letter from an Englishman who wishes to go out to India as a missionary and asked the poet's advice. Dr. Tagore's letter is being given a wide publicity in India (one wonders how it got that publicity, since the letter was presumably private), and it is characteristic of the great Indian idealist who, as a member of the Brahmo-Somaj, is as near to Christianity as one can get without faith in its central doctrine. The letter, like most of Dr. Tagore's recent work, savors too much of the "superior person" to be quite admirable, but it contains things eminently worth quoting and pondering. "Do not be always trying to preach your doctrine," he writes to the young would-be missionary, "but give yourself in love. Your Western mind is too much obsessed with the idea of conquest. . . . The object of a Christian should be to be like Christ, never to be like a coolie recruiter trying to bring coolies to his master's tea-garden. . . . The real preaching is in being perfect, which is through meekness and love and self-dedication."

There can be no doubt that the besetting temptation of the young missionary is to become a self-conscious apostle. His language is not the unctuous old-fashioned language of his predecessor, but he tends to succumb to the same pitfalls. The missionary who goes to India to-day, however, is immediately plunged into an atmosphere of criticism and attack which, at any rate, ought to keep him humble. The minister at home has the same vigorous counter-irritant applied to him, and one wonders whether Dr. Tagore and those like him will ever realize that to preach the gospel in these days is not, as he describes it, "a luxury," but a constant humiliation and searching of heart.

Baron von Hügel: A Bit of Soul-history

Writing of his much-loved friend, the recently-deceased Mgr. Duchesne (one of the greatest church historians and liturgiologists Rome has produced in recent times), Baron von Hügel has an autobiographical passage which goes far to explain how it was that this acute and liberal thinker, who had so much affinity with the noblest leaders of Roman Catholic modernism, remained an orthodox believer. He tells us of two things which helped to keep his faith and his reason during "those terrible years of 1906-1914"—years which saw the defection of Houtin Hebert and Loisy, the tragedy of Tyrell, and the radical skepticism of Duchesne. One reason is religious, the other philosophical. On the spiritual side his contact with the late Abbé Huvelin—"that truly masculine saint who won and trained so many souls"—saved him. "There sanctity stood before me in the flesh, and this as the genuine deepest effect and reason of the Catholic Church." The other reason was philosophical: he became a thoroughgoing realist. "I believe most earnestly that the future, also in philosophy proper, is away from all skepticisms, subjectivisms, agnosticisms, pragmatisms, to belief in our real knowledge of real objects, distinct from ourselves and from our knowledge of them."

Preachers, whatever their theological or philosophical position, must, to a greater or lesser degree, sympathize with these views. For if recent years have taught us anything, it is that the type of philosophical idealism current for so long is ultimately incompatible with belief in a personal God and his self-revelation, and that sainthood is one of the most powerful arguments (taken singly) for the reality of our faith.

"Not Against Flesh and Blood"

The question of the existence of evil spirits, "the world rulers of this darkness," has for decades past been relegated to the realm of folk-lore and superstition. This was inevitable in days when the doctrine of evolution was prest into the service of materialism on the one hand and rationalism on the other. To-day the pendulum has swung back: both science and philosophy have opened doors to the supernatural and admitted into the realm of possibility things that our fathers banished to the region of mythology. One of the results of this change of front has been the appearance of several books on the spiritual warfare and the spiritual equipment of Christ's Church on earth. One of the writers, the Rev. F. R. Priddie, emphasizes the fact that the apostolic Church was acutely conscious, not only of the supernatural in general, but of the supernatural character of its warfare as being faced with spiritual hosts of wickedness. In view of a devil-ridden world it was endowed with supernatural gifts such as exorcism and miracle-working.

But can this belief in spiritual hosts be maintained? Mr. Priddie argues it can. Vitalism has shown that matter can not be accounted for by natural laws merely—there is a *causa causans* which has still to be taken into account, and this has directed our thought toward new ideas of personal and spiritual elements in the development of human nature. Theologically, the attempt to restate the doctrine of God in terms of the Eastern *pantokrator* rather than of the Western *omnipotens* helps in the same direction. Nor is it possible nowadays to ignore the cumulative testimony of the New Testament itself to the conception of the Church as engaged in a warfare that is "not against flesh and blood."

A nation's life is its men, women, and children, and so its history, philosophy, literature, politics, education, culture, have their origin and their end in the human beings that make up the nation. Simi-

The Human Factor in Education

larly, religious revelation must come through human agents, and to human beings; and thus the Bible, regarded as divine revelation, becomes intelligible and meaningful in the men and women and children that act their parts in the vast drama of the divine and the human unfolded in that book.

A study made some years ago of children's interests in the Bible showed conclusively that at all ages children are interested chiefly in the characters of the Bible. The historic events, the literature, the philosophy, the religious doctrines, and all else are of secondary concern to their minds. In fact, these various factors of divine revelation, as conceived by orthodox Christianity, appear to become meaningful chiefly through the men, women, and children of the Bible. The same doubtless holds true of adults as well as children. Conventional standards of Biblical exegesis and conventional methods of pulpit exposition and religious instruction may often create an apparent interest in the non-human factors of the Bible; but such interest is more or less affected and unreal. What men and women actually seek, in the Bible as elsewhere, is the way of life human beings have journeyed over, the inspiration and example of human characters, the successes and failures, the hopes and disappointments, in the eternal human drama, which past and present records of whatever name do no more than sketch.

It is evident, then, that religious education, the study of the Bible, as well as all other kinds of education, and study of all kinds of books whatsoever, should make liberal use of the human factors. Facts and principles should be taught through the lives of men, women, and children as the living embodiments of all that constitutes knowledge. Purpose and inspiration in life should be fixt in human minds and hearts through the examples of living witnesses in the things that make purpose and inspiration worth while.

✠

The mind creates its own pictures. The picture of to-day may be very different from that of to-morrow.

To-day and To-morrow

The clouds hang dark over to-day, the wind blows harsh and cold, and the precious growths of the human spirit droop and delay. The hearts of men are hopeless and hard. The aftermath of human hatred and destruction

stares us in the face on every side. Life looks gray. Will it be so to-morrow? Not if history and experience and the hope that springs immortal in the human heart are to be trusted.

To-day naturalism, behaviorism, relativism; to-morrow the new idealism. To-day education confused, commercialized, undisciplined; to-morrow education organized, vitalized, spiritualized. To-day literature seduced, cheapened, sensationalized; to-morrow a literature that enlightens and leads and inspires.

To-day Shaw and Galsworthy and a host of lesser exponents of the dark side of life; to-morrow a drama that reveals life in its rich possibilities. To-day *Main Street* and *If Winter Comes;* to-morrow Neighbor Street and When Summer Is Here. To-day H. G. Wells and Van Loon and history shadowed by the low-browed simian; to-morrow a true philosophy of history, pointing the way toward limitless progress. To-day an art aimless, bizarre, impressionistic; to-morrow an art that mirrors eternal beauty and eternal truth. To-day industry paralyzed, embittered, impatient; to-morrow confidence, cooperation, service. To-day prohibition and lawlessness struggling for the mastery; to-morrow a saloonless and law-abiding world. To-day a fever of pleasure, salacity, cheap "movies"; to-morrow pure mirth, the honor of womanhood, wholesome recreation. To-day nationalism, jealousy, distrust; to-morrow internationalism, interchange, brotherhood. To-day America for the Americans; to-morrow America for the world. To-day religious reaction; to-morrow religious advance. To-day fundamentalism, millennialism, literalism; to-morrow the spirit of faith and the theology of experience. To-day denominationalism, division, disunity; to-morrow cooperation, love, unity. To-day the gospel of church and creed; to-morrow the gospel of the living and conquering Christ.

But when is to-morrow? To-morrow is when men come to themselves. And why is to-morrow? To-morrow is because God's in his heaven and his Spirit is in his world.

✠

When the country is confronted with serious problems like the railroad and coal strikes, the minds of those directly concerned with the difficulties involved turn more readily to some kind of adjustment **The Square Deal** where self-interest and expedients of a patchwork nature **In Business** play a large rôle, rather than to the consideration and application of moral principles to industry.

R. H. Tawney in his excellent book on *The Acquisitive Society* says:

An appeal to principles is the condition of any considerable reconstruction of society, because social institutions are the visible expression of the scale of moral values which rules the minds of individuals, and it is impossible to alter institutions without altering that moral valuation.

An industry is in its essence—

nothing more mysterious than a body of men associated, in various degrees of competition and cooperation, to win their living by providing the community with some service which it requires. Organize it as you will, let it be a group of craftsmen laboring with hammer and chisel, or peasants plowing their own fields, or armies of mechanics of a hundred different trades constructing ships which are miracles of complexity with machines which are the climax of centuries of invention, its function is service, its method is association. Because its function is service, an industry as a whole has rights and duties toward the community, the abrogation of which involves privilege. Because its method is association, the different parties within it have rights and duties toward each other; and the neglect or perversion of these involves oppression.

Then he points out that the first condition of a right organization of industry is—

that it should be subordinated to the community in such a way as to render the best service technically possible, that those who render no service should not be paid at all, because it is of the essence of a function that it should find its meaning in the satisfaction, not of itself, but of the end which it serves. The second is that its direction and government should be in the hands of persons who are responsible to those who are directed and governed, because it is the condition of economic freedom that men should not be ruled by an authority which they can not control.

No great advance can ever come in the world of industry until men on all sides are prepared to make the necessary sacrifice.

Those concerns which have experimented in the direction of the Golden Rule are satisfied and convinced that the spirit and practise of the principles of profit-sharing, labor co-partnership, and the elements of sacrifice are all essential to contentment and peace in the industrial world.

In *The Contemporary Review* for May Mr. Theodore Cooke Taylor, writing on the labor crisis, says:

I recommend to all other employers what I have for thirty years past practised myself. As the head of one of the oldest and largest woolen manufacturing concerns in the country [England] I declare without hesitation that our system of sharing with our workers all profits over five per cent is of the utmost moral and material value and never more so than to-day. If all employers had in good times shared their profits with their workers this time of transition from higher to lower prices need not have been as it now is, one long period of bitter struggle, individual suffering, and national loss.

Dr. Tippy's article, on page 190 of this issue, offers some sober reflections on the whole question of sounder economic foundations.

✠

On October fourth of this year will be celebrated by various religious and other bodies the fiftieth anniversary of the first formal meeting of the American Revision Committee. This committee continued **The Significance** its arduous and self-denying labors for thirty years. The **of the American** results were of two kinds: first, the embodiment of many **Standard Version** "American renderings" in the text of the Revised Version and the inclusion of others in the margin or footnotes; second, the issue, after a stipulated time, of the American Standard Version which, as we have often said, is as a whole the greatest advance yet made in concerted effort to have the Bible "understanded of the people." It is the culmination of the long line of English renderings begun by Cædmon and carried by a series that includes Wyclif, Tyndale, Coverdale, and the authors of the "Authorized Version."

The improvements of the future will depend in all probability on studies of the text, particularly of the Old Testament, now being made by many faithful scholars working devotedly in the new light constantly being focused on this problem.

Meanwhile the celebration will honor anew the names of such men as Drs. Philip Schaff, Howard Crosby, William Henry Green, Joseph Henry Thayer, Theodore Dwight Woolsey, and the rest of the noble company of American Revisers, of whose fidelity to their task this celebration again re-minds us. The occasion will give new opportunities to pastors to direct at-tention to the importance of Biblical study, especially to that best of versions, the American Standard.

The Labor Sunday Message for this year will consist of a concise summary of important labor events and court decisions for 1921 and 1922, together with brief introductory observations. The message may be secured for fifteen cents, which includes postage, by writing to the Commission on the Church and Social Service, 105 East 22nd Street, New York City. (*Federal Council of the Churches of Christ in America*.)

Free literature on Christian public education will be furnished to pastors who are planning to preach on some phase of that subject on the day of prayer for public schools, the second or other convenient Sabbath of September. This literature consists of a packet of pamphlets and may be obtained by addressing a postal to the National Reform Association, 209 Ninth Street, Pittsburgh, Pa., and stating where this notice was seen.

TIME-SAVING IDEAS FOR MINISTERS

The Rev. A. W. BLOOMFIELD, Owego, N. Y.

The time factor is one of the greatest problems of the ministry. The modern trend toward specialization in so many of our church activities has compelled the minister to become more like a business executive than a pastor and teacher. If he attempts to "run" all the organizations and activities advocated by our various "movements," he is liable to be overwhelmed by a mass of details and lose the time for that gathering of power, to say nothing of the gathering of ideas, which is essential to the life of his church. Yet he must adopt and oversee many of these new activities, and hence the need for adopting at the same time any idea which will conserve his time, and if possible increase his efficiency.

Organization of time is the secret, but most ministers are nonplussed by the problem. Their duties are so manifold and irregular that it seems impossible to follow any system. Here is a clue to the maze by which whole sections of time can be saved. It lies in a principle which can be stated thus:

Every recurring task can be organized.

Example number one of the application of this principle: Nearly every minister has to find two texts each week; that will be true as long as he is in the active ministry. Many a minister's life is overshadowed by the misery of text hunting, by the feeling that precious time is wasted every week in the task. Yet he never seeks for a text for the coming Sunday without passing by several that would be just the thing for other occasions; as they are not fitted for the day, or would take too much time to prepare, they are passed by and promptly forgotten. If he would sit down in his study for two hours with the purpose of arranging a series of sermons for eight or ten weeks ahead, he would find it a fairly simple thing. He would find his texts and themes for eight weeks in as little time as he usually spends in finding them for one week, with the additional advantage of being able to collect material for all in his reading and experience during the period they cover.

Example number two: Every minister who makes the most of his service spends much time selecting hymns, probably reading over and testing scores in order to find half a dozen. Yet he passes by a number he would like to have for some other sermon. If he had his sermons arranged eight or ten weeks ahead he could select the hymns for them in little more time than he usually spends selecting hymns for a week.

A minister to whom this suggestion was made writes this:

"Thanks for that suggestion about selecting hymns. In a couple of hours yesterday I prepared sermon themes, texts, scripture, psalter, and hymns for both sermons for eight weeks, a great saving of time and energy."

Example number three: Stories

for the children are used every week by many ministers and most of them are selected from books of stories. Selecting by the weeks as they go puts the man in the same position as selecting hymns. Many stories are summer or winter stories, or special-day stories, and have to be passed over by the man seeking for the one day; but the man who is planning ahead can save hours by selecting them all at one time. A minister said, "I was able to select stories for eighteen weeks in less than three hours, and I have spent as much time as that trying to find two good stories."

KINDLING AND INSPIRING THOUGHTS

All wisdom is a divine gift.—CLEMENS ALEXANDRINUS.

Plain industry is more important than cleverness.—WILLIAM FEATHER.

Suffer us not for any pains of death to fall from thee.—ANCIENT LITURGY.

Democracy is fellowship, science is knowledge, religion is love; and these three are friends.—JOSEPH FORT NEWTON.

To sweep a mass of men with spellbinding emotional appeal is not good religion, nor is it true statesmanship.—THE CHRISTIAN CENTURY.

Some missionaries are so deeply religious (in the orthodox sense) that they are constitutionally incapable of conceiving that any one can really be happy unless he has been saved.—STEFANSSON.

When we stop growing morally and intellectually, we ought to be buried, if not in our own interest, at least to protect our fellow men and women from the stench of our decay.—EDWARD HOWARD GRIGGS.

"It is better to have the pain if it brings the pearl. It is better to have a thorn in the one balance if it brings such grace into the opposite balance that one is better off with the thorn than without it.—F. W. BOREHAM.

Simplicity and purity are the two things by which a man is lifted above all earthly things. Simplicity is in the intention, purity in the affection; simplicity tends to God, purity apprehends and tastes him.—THOMAS À KEMPIS.

Labor is the price of life. The tree labors in growth; the field-mouse labors in each search for grain. Man differs from other animals in that he is conscious of his labors and articulate concerning them.—ARTHUR POUND.

Medical science is so definitely based upon and intimately associated with zoology, botany, chemistry, and physics that advance in medical science must naturally wait upon advance in all the sciences just named as fundamental to it.—W. S. HALL, M.D.

Employers tell workingmen not to watch the clock. Employers do not seem to realize that it is just as foolish for them to watch their profits as it is for workingmen to watch the clock.—HENRY FORD.

The curious fact that the human embryo in its successive stages of development is indistinguishable from that of lower forms of life suggests the thought that every human soul must travel life's pathway from the moneron to Christ.—T. C. FOOTE.

The golden hopes of mankind can be realized only by men who have iron in their blood; by men who scorn to do wrong and equally scorn to submit to wrong; by men of gentle souls whose hearts are harder than steel in their readiness to war against brutality and evil.—THEODORE ROOSEVELT.

Work is no grievance and no grief, nor is it a dullard sluggard's story. It is a chime of bells that swing and hearten all who hear. It is a laughter in the skies, a flight among the clouds, a rapture in the sun. When we recollect all we have done, how sweet the perusal!—W. A. QUALE.

We believe, and on the whole justly, that we are much more sensitive to the maladjustments of a world that our fathers were pleased to accept as the best of all possible worlds. We have made a duty of discontent. In a word, where our fathers were smug and dead, we are dissatisfied and alive.—SIMEON STRUNSKY.

ECONOMIC PRINCIPLES IN CHURCH PRACTISE

JOHN F. COWAN, D.D., San Diego, Cal.

It shouldn't make any one blush to admit that "the children of this world are in their generation wiser than the children of light," since Jesus said it. But to come down to specific "cases," at least three almost revolutionary economic principles lately strest give the "children of light" a mouthful.

1. "Regenerative braking" is a suggestive phrase smacking somewhat of evangelism. It is used by Herbert Quick in urging the electrification of steam railroads as their only salvation from bankruptcy.

What is "regenerative braking"? It is braking trains without brakes—simply by reversing the electric motors into generators and thus harnessing to the job of generating power to climb the next grade the momentum that would plunge the train down a grade into a pile of junk.

Here is the way it works: coasting at sixteen miles an hour, the reversed motors charge as much "juice" into the line as they sucked out climbing at fourteen miles. How does this eclipse the steam-drawn train? Why, its engine is burning coal all the way down, and what the company gets out of it is the squeal of the hot brake-shoe wearing out on the wheels. That might be called "degenerative braking."

How may the Church convert its handicaps into positive driving power? What is the spiritual equivalent of "regenerative braking?"

Take this concrete illustration. In the average adolescents' and men's Bible classes the teachers' problem is to head off "hot-air" discussions, to curb restlessness, whispering, and "cutting up," or to draw out rankling prejudices, objections, misunderstandings. The purely didactic method of trying to cram certain truths down unwilling throats doesn't meet any of these problems.

One wide-awake editor of lesson helps has launched a "lesson discussion questionnaire." There are six or eight topics, notes, illustrations, and discussion questions on each lesson, each of which presents two sides of an ethical or moral issue so sharply that discussion is provoked. It is designed to bring out objections, rankling prejudices, and befuddling misunderstandings. In airing these the feeling behind them is expended, and the right side of the problem is strengthened by the very attacks that have spent themselves upon it, as a quartering wind against a ship's sails push the craft ahead. It is the get-together principle of the open forum applied to Sunday-school teaching. It is one kind of "regenerative braking" in the realm of religious education.

It isn't hard to see how mischievous human traits or tendencies may be used as a regenerative brake, socially and morally. For example, a child is afflicted with what we call "prurient curiosity." It eavesdrops at the keyhole to overhear what the servants are saying to one another confidentially, and then "tattles" it to schoolmates. Now there you have the red-hot, creaking, smoking brake-shoe, wasting young vitality.

But suppose the mother or teacher does some regenerative braking? This mischievous trait is turned into a generator and harnessed to—well, say, geography or history lessons by piquing the curiosity of the child concerning strange lands and peoples, just as the servants' low conversation made its ears itch to know what they were saying. Presto! tattling waste is turned into educational gain.

This principle of regenerative braking in ethics and morals is susceptible of many other applications—for instance, eighteenth-amendment enforcement. Here we have an ultra individualism, a prejudice against "Puritan blue laws," a jealousy of personal liberty making the Volstead brake-shoe hum and smoke. Regenerative braking would set at constructive tasks the misspent energies that concoct home brew and engage in bootlegging and smuggling. Tax the bootleg activity in support of prisons, irrigate land instead of throats, and drain swamps instead of bottles. Offer prizes for the best home-brew fuel alcohol so alluring that "Get-Rich - Quick Wallingford's" gilt-edged roads to wealth would look like cow-paths. Put rum-runners to cracking stone for highways over which the illicit traffic now passes. By bold strokes of statesmanship convert the whole force of lawlessness into regenerative braking, instead of frittering energy away in the picayune effort of hunting down the man with a pint flask in his hip pocket. Make the "hair of the dog cure the bite."

2. "Standardizing products" is a second economic principle of vast importance, now being worked out by Secretary Herbert C. Hoover. For example, he found that the brick-

makers were putting out sixty-six styles of paving brick, to meet all the whims of buyers. Some of these sizes were little called for, but had to be kept in stock, and the loss on them was charged to the price of the other sizes. Mr. Hoover saw the waste, and got the manufacturers and buyers into an "open forum" where they agreed to cut the sizes from sixty-six to eleven, which will make a great saving to the public.

Another instance: there were nine different sizes and styles of cast-iron seats for plows, reapers, tractors, etc. None had any special advantage over the others; a farmer was just as tired after riding one all day as another. Mr. Hoover induced the manufacturers to standardize on one seat. It will be a better seat. The farmers will all ride it and be more comfortable, besides saving money and trouble.

Apply this principle to the multiplicity of denominational Sunday-school lesson helps, other publications, missionary societies, colleges, etc. Remember that there are 180 varieties of sectarian Sunday-school publications listed in Ayer's Newspaper Directory, all printed from different type on different presses, and edited by different staffs of salaried workers, and some for relatively small constituencies. One wants to grin sardonically at the huge farce being enacted.

As a beginning, this array of nondescript publications, with sectarian names legion, might be "simplified" (that is the word Mr. Hoover prefers to the more irritating one "standardize") into half a dozen large groups —Methodist, Presbyterian, Baptist, Lutheran, Reformed, etc. A number of years ago an astute man, Rev. Rufus W. Miller, D.D., of the Reformed Church Board of Sunday-school publications, attempted to make a beginning at this by offering syndicated pages to a number of these various periodicals. The same thing was tried by others in the form of syndicated articles for the denominational papers.

More recently the M. E. Church North and the M. E. Church South have been syndicating many pages of matter in *The Sunday-school Journal* and *Sunday-school Magazine,* respectively. And the Congregationalists, Presbyterians, Methodist Protestants, and United Brethren have editions of a young people's weekly paper which are printed from the same plates, with the exception of one page. It is a successful standardization, and a much better paper than any one denomination alone could produce.

In such home mission fields as Alaska and certain of the Northwestern States, also in Maine and some older States, a comity is practised among denominations by which certain territory is allotted to each. This is done in Mexico, China, Hawaii, Korea, and other foreign fields. It is an adaptation of Mr. Hoover's principle of standardizing, or "simplifying," for the sake of economy and efficiency. But the applications of which it is susceptible are so vast and untouched that present achievements are only a drop in the bucket.

3. The Superpower Plant is a third economic principle that the Church must come to use. It is recommended to the railroads in electrifying their lines. Mr. Quick contends for a few great electric-generating plants near the coal mines and water-power sources, under a separate corporation, to sell power to railroads and other users. It will be more economical because, with individual users the "peak load" comes at different intervals and can not be distributed as it can with a corporation that supplies all classes of users whose "peak load" comes at different hours of the day. The loss to capital while plant is partly idle, yet must be able to deliver peak-load requirements, is immense.

Now this principle applies to our preceding Church problem. There is tremendous unvisualized waste in small sectarian plants, whether rival local churches, printing plants, missions, colleges, or what-not. A few superpower plants for educating missionaries and ministers, for training Sunday-school teachers and lay workers, would mean untold gain in quality of equipment and efficiency.

In an increasing number of communities this is being cautiously worked out in the shape of community schools of religious education, for training Sunday-school teachers, and conducting vacation Bible schools. In a few cases, as in the removal of Andover Theological Seminary to Harvard, and the cluster of denominational schools of theology around Chicago University, and other similar instances, an approach of a few inches has been made toward the ideal.

Likewise community combinations to secure religious education in connection with the public schools, like the Malden, Mass., Community Religious Board of Education, are tentative superpower stations.

In a more complete way this ideal is being realized in the organic union of Lutheran bodies, Reformed churches in the United States, and all Protestant bodies in Canada and Australia. There is a hopeful looking forward to union of Methodist bodies, and approaches are being made by Episcopalians.

One great purpose of the Interchurch World Survey, published in two volumes, was to gather data that would open the eyes of the Church to the striking possibilities of economies through cooperation and the strangling of sectarian rivalry, which is the devil's squealing, wasteful, hot brakeshoe.

So far, not much that is practical has been accomplished—just tiny beginnings for which, however, we should "thank God and take courage." It seems timely, therefore, to use these three modern urgent economic principles to prick the lagging Church to action; for the Church of Jesus Christ is as much under the economic law of his kingdom as are the railroads or brickmakers.

Jesus did not mean that his criticism that the children of the world were wiser than the children of light should rest as an everlasting stigma upon us. Let us try to hasten the days of regenerative braking, standardized products, and superpower stations.

"INDEX-LEARNING"

The Rev. WILLIAM S. JEROME, White Pigeon, Mich.

Pope is the author of this word, which he no doubt coined, and a most expressive word it is. In the *Dunciad* he tells us:

How index-learning turns no student pale,
But holds the eel of science by the tail.

The word exactly meets the need of the scholar and the literary worker today. So vast is the growth of human knowledge, and so enormous the accumulation of material, that no one mind can hold it all. "Of making many books there is no end," and even if a pastor's library does not rival the great collections of Washington and London, yet something of index-learning is an absolute necessity if he is to make his books and periodicals practically useful in his work. To know where to find a thing is next best to knowing that thing, and it is of little use to know something and yet not be able to locate it. How often we find ourselves unable to trace the fugitive thought or to give the vague recollection! We have "seen it somewhere," but where? "That's the rub." We say, "I'd give ten dollars to find that story, or sermon," but it has disappeared from our memory. Like the revolver out West, we may not for a long time want a particular thought or fact, but when we do want it, we want it "powerful bad." The remedy for this unfortunate condition is "index-learning." The

wise pastor will take time to note down the striking thought, the apt illustration, to preserve the able sermon and the scholarly discussion, that he may use them again. But it is not enough to "make a note on it," like Captain Cuttle. We must also so arrange these notes and collections that we can promptly lay our hand upon them in time of need.

My system originally included: 1. An interleaved Bible. 2. A series of scrapbooks. 3. An index review. 4. A card catalog.

In the interleaved Bible every book in my library, every periodical on file, and every scrapbook, is represented opposite the book, chapter, or verse treated. In this system, "H. Rev." stands for *The Homiletic Review*, "S. S. T." for the *Sunday School Times*, and so on. Thus opposite Matt. 5:8 is written, "H. Rev., Aug. 10," and Dr. Rush Rhees' fine sermon is available whenever in future I want to study that text. It takes but a few seconds to make the entries, preferably on some one day in the week, or at odd times, and my Bible, representing more than twenty-five years' study and annotation, is now simply invaluable.

The scrap books I do not use much now, preferring to put everything in the way of clippings, illustration, etc., in the card catalog.

This is a home-made affair, and is based upon the well-known principle used in all public libraries. Old envelopes, or similar scraps of paper are used, and they bear written references, printed scraps, or anything likely to prove helpful to the preacher. The slips are arranged alphabetically in narrow boxes, by the first vowel, and can be added to or subtracted from at any time. Envelopes, portfolios, and everything of that sort, are unnecessary and cumbersome. No expensive book is required, and no index, for it indexes itself. All that is necessary is the box and a bundle of slips upon the study table, which when written upon, can be at once put in place, can be easily found, and can be discarded when no longer needed.

I have also largely dropt the use of the index review, for all that it contains can as well be arranged in the card catalog. That and the interleaved Bible are all that are really necessary. Of course, in the process of time, the catalog overflows, and more room must be made for it, but it is room well used. The systematic pastor need never be at a loss for appropriate quotations, references, and arguments on any subject. Nor does that imply "scrapbook sermons," or a mosaic system of homiletics. Neither Bible nor catalog are intended to supersede original study or thorough thinking, but simply to give the preacher prompt access to the results of his own reading and the stimulating productions of other minds.

With the subject of index-learning may properly go some discussion of the minister's "barrel." This is the familiar name for the collection of sermons which accumulates in every pastor's study. Even if we do not fully write our sermons, most of us make use of notes more or less full. These results of our study and thinking should not be lost. If a man is tempted to depend on old sermons, he may perhaps heroically destroy his intellectual offspring on the principle that condemns even the right eye which might cause us to stumble. But for future pastorates and for other purposes and reasons a pastor should preserve his sermons. And my plan is to keep them in a box or case which I had made for the purpose, which consists of sixteen boxes or compartments arranged in four rows. Each compartment is wide enough and deep enough to take in an ordinary sermon. The size of the whole thing is about thirty-three inches in height, and the same in width, looking like a small bookcase. Each compartment bears an appropriate lable, the different books of the Bible being divided among the sixteen compartments. The labels in my case are as follows: Matthew; Mark; Luke; John; Acts; Romans and Galatians; 1 and 2 Corinthians; Ephesians and Philippians; Colossians and Thessalonians; Pastoral Epistles and Hebrews; Catholic Epistles and Revelation; Psalms; Historical Books (O. T.); Poetical Books; Major Prophets; Minor Prophets.

The Old Testament books are placed last, because least used. Of course other arrangements can be made if desired. As fast as preached, the sermons, after being marked with date and place of use, are laid in the appropriate division. When wanted again, they are easily found. And the same compartment will also hold sketches, plans, printed sermons, and anything else that you find suitable to the sermons in that division. When in the course of reading a fine illustration or strong argument is found bearing upon the text of a certain sermon, it is an easy matter to note the reference on a slip of paper, and lay it with the manuscript, and then when you wish to use the sermon again, you have ready the accumulated material and added results of your study, to give it freshness and new life.

Where Preachers Need Advice

Most preachers are easy marks for dishonest promoters, and the recent experience of a well-known New York preacher who had judgment entered against him for more than $24,000 on a note he had endorsed, excited general sympathy. Practically all the clergy are savers, comments the Chicago *Journal of Commerce*, and "a depressingly large percentage of them make unwise investments." The adventurer with a patent announced to be worth millions, the stock salesman whose certificates will double in value in a year, the man who has valuable corner lots to sell, and all other gentry who gabble of get-rich-quick schemes find the penurious pastor a lamb only too ready to be shorn. We are reminded that

Several years ago a bank president in Marietta, Ohio, Mr. W. W. Mills, was so disturbed by the number of preachers whose savings were dissipated by hazardous investments entered into with so much credulity when they were solicited by business adventurers, that he delivered an address to a body of clergymen which was in substance a primary lesson in the care and protection of savings. His audience needed just such a lesson, and no doubt his kindly and intelligent advice saved many of those who heard him from serious losses.

Every ministerial body, at least once a year, should be given instruction in the care and investment of their small savings. With little or no business training, they need this kind of advice to save them from "confidential opportunities" to lose all they have. One word of caution every clergyman should be willing to remember, and that is never to invest with a stranger or with anybody else until the investment has met the approval of a banker or a prudent business man in his congregation.—*The Literary Digest.*

Communion vs. Communication

Communion with Christ will alone safeguard the soul's integrity from all evil influences of the spirit-world. Communion with Christ alone will assure us of permanent and satisfying communion with those we love.

What, after all, is the greatest obstacle between soul and soul? Not the veil of matter hiding the spiritual world. Not time, or space, or the sundering of worlds—not any of these things separate soul from soul with any such impassable gulf as does sin.

A spiritualism, therefore, which ignores that factor, which begins and ends in mere "communication of spirits," without any real interest in a gospel of redemption and the saving grace of Christ, is utterly inadequate to human needs, and, insofar as it absorbs human interest and energy, it is pernicious.

What will it profit me to learn that my loved one lives in that other world unless at the same time I am assured of the "moral fitness" that will bring me at last to her side in a like purity and goodness? And only Christ can bring me there.

So it is faith in him we need rather than any sight or hearing that "mediums" profess to supply. Is there not something forced and artificial in our willingness to hear the testimony of "spiritualistic mediums," whilst we ignore and fail to rest in the testimony of him who said, "In my Father's house are many mansions; if it were not so, I would have told you. Because I live, ye shall live also"?

Let us ask ourselves what, after all, has Sir Oliver Lodge accomplished, if *Raymond* be true? He has proved that his boy lives after death. Is that much? Is that enough?

In the first place, faith plays a big part in it. Sir Oliver Lodge believes in his mediums. In the second place, he only needs to receive a message revealing disaster to Raymond, either moral or physical, to be plunged at once into terrible distress of mind and to realize that "spiritualism" is not enough. Unless the great common element of souls, Christ our Creator and Redeemer, is in possession, there can be no true and satisfying communion.

"Spiritualism," therefore, can never be a substitute for the Christian faith; at most, it represents but a small part of our spiritual interests. It ought never, therefore, to have broken away from the Christian Church as a separate movement.

It reminds one very much of a clever little parable of a caterpillar that was in too great a hurry to be a butterfly. He climbed the stalks of grasses and hurled himself from the top in the belief that the air would support him. He fell ignominiously to the ground; he poked his nose into the delicate cups of flowers, seeking to extract their honey; he only succeeded in spoiling them. Finally, he entered the chrysalis stage, and at length emerged—a butterfly, indeed, but in a rather damaged condition. He had not realized that his first duty was to be a good caterpillar! And many who take an interest in the problem of the future life ignore the insistence of Scripture that the first qualification for reaching and enjoying the fellowship of those high realms is just to be a good man, by the grace of the Lord Jesus Christ.

Let us turn away from the uncertainties and problematical findings of scientific investigators, from practise of intercourse with spirits who may be rogues of the under-world rather than lords of the over-world, unto that one who tolerates no medium between himself and the souls he died to save, and, listening again to him, believe him, and rest in him. For "them also that are asleep in Jesus will God bring with him."

A. D. BELDEN in *The Pilgrim* (London).

MID-WEEK PRAYER MEETING

Sept. 3-9—Real Co-Laborers
(Isa. 41:5.7)

Cooperation in industry is no new thing. Away back in the early days of Israel we find outcroppings of the group spirit which in after years found expression in guilds and trade-unions. But before it began to function in definite ways it manifested itself, as in the instance before us, in a spirit of mutuality. In this interesting historical fragment we see exhibited first of all mutuality of helpfulness. When the exiles who returned from Babylon were seeking to rebuild a ruined civilization, just as the people of Europe are trying to do to-day, it is said that "they helped every one his neighbor." With very little in the way of organization, they cooperated in working out the same ends. They were neighborly and friendly, like the pioneers in a new country; and like them they also found that this spirit of neighborliness gave charm and zest to life.

In his account of the early Church Paul gives a list of the gifts of the Spirit by which it was characterized. One of these gifts which has been strangely overlooked is the gift of "helps" (1 Cor. 12:28). This is a common gift, not spectacular like some others, but one that meets the supreme test of practical usefulness, and hence a gift which is to be earnestly coveted. And unlike many other gifts it is within the reach of all. The Church and society in general are structured upon the principle of mutual helpfulness. One member depends upon another; and it is by each one supplementing the work of the other that the circle of service is compassed and the whole work is done.

Along with the spirit of mutual helpfulness there was also a spirit of mutual encouragement. "They said every one to his brother, Be of good courage." It was a time of deep depression. The work of national restoration was toilsome and slow, and every one needed encouragement; so not finding it from without they encouraged every one his brother, looking together at the bright side of things and assuring one another that the better day for which they were looking would surely dawn.

There is no better work in which one can be engaged than that of being an encourager of others. The hearts of men are hungering for a word of cheer and hopefulness. But for that word to be effective it must be grounded upon encouraging facts. Much of the shallow philosophy of life taught in the present day might be summed up in the counsel, "Keep a stiff upper lip, smile, and go ahead."

That, however, does not reach the bottom of a man's need. He has not only to stir up the gift that is in him, he has also to stir himself up to "lay hold upon God." He needs, in a word, to have his hands "strengthened in God." This is what a true encourager will ever do. He will not utter empty words, merely saying, "Cheer up, brother"; but point him to the true source of help and hope.

Another quality that shines out is mutuality in appreciation of each other's work. It is said that "the carpenter encouraged the goldsmith, and he that smoothed with the hammer him that smote upon the anvil, and the whole group examining the work of the tinsmith joined in a chorus of praise, saying of the soldering, It is good." Then one of the number took nails and fastened it together, that it should not be moved. When the finishing touch was given they surveyed the result of their joint labor with honest pride. In spite of difficulties it was at length done, and well done, because it was the work of real co-laborers. The readiness of every one of the group to praise the part done by his fellow workers was a noble trait which all of us may well imitate. For a master to praise his servant, for a teacher to praise his pupils, for a general to praise his soldiers, is the way to get the best out of them. Many a man has been saved from despair by a word of earned praise. Fulsome flattery is one thing, merited praise is another; the former is always harmful, the latter gives inspiration and hope. Criticism of another's work should be not censorious but creative, putting into the worker a heart of hope. Many children have their lives shadowed because they never received from their parents a single word of commendation, tho they were severely censored for every slip and shortcoming. Our divine Master, who when on earth did not break the bruised reed nor quench the smoking flax, will at last say to every one who has been true to the trust committed to him, "Well done, good and faithful servant, enter thou into the joy of thy Lord." And in the approbation of the Master will be found the highest heavenly bliss. J. M. C.

TYPES OF WOMEN

Sept. 10-16—Deborah

(Judges: Chaps. 4-6)

Deborah, as a woman, belonged to Israel. She was what we would now call "a woman in public life." She was a prophetess, a judge, a patriot, and, incidentally, a militant woman. She was married and her husband, Lapidoth, was presumably living. But there is nothing to indicate that either he or any other domestic impediment interfered with her public work. She was the Biblical prototype of the modern versatile, aggressive woman, more or less detached from the hampering cares of wifehood and motherhood, who prophesies, sits in judgment, and conducts crusades. Deborah sat before her tent, under the palm-tree near Bethel, showing forth as a prophetess the evil condition into which Israel had fallen, and inspiring those who came to her with a vision of better days for her people. She called the warrior, Barak, before her and told him what Jehovah, through her, commanded him to do. She went with Barak to raise the army of ten thousand men which was to execute Jehovah's will and overthrow the forces of Sisera. What her presence with Barak meant for the expedition may be inferred both from Barak's words that he would not go unless she went along and from her own incisive reply that she would surely go. Finally, she composed her song of triumph, which is an epitome of all her qualities and activities as prophetess, judge, patriot, and warrior.

In Deborah we have an illustration of the old truth that there is nothing new under the sun. The modern woman of public affairs is as old as the race. Perhaps there are more of her type in these days than in those of Deborah; and if there are, it may be that it is because the world needs them more, or there are more women so constituted and conditioned that they choose to be prophetesses, judges and the like. If the modern Deborahs prophesy as sanely as did she of Israel, judge as searchingly, act as loyally to their country's interests, and fight as bravely, then many a modern Sisera will be vanquished, and many a Jabin's army will be annihilated.

Sept. 17-23—Hannah

(1 Sam., chaps. 1 and 2)

Hannah was a different type of woman from Deborah. She was what we would now call a "domestic" woman. She was a woman of the heart. She did not prophesy, or judge, or lead a crusade against the enemies of Israel. She was a "home-body." She won her husband's affection and respect, altho she had another woman in the family to compete with, and that woman had done what was dear to every Jewish woman's heart, borne children to her husband, while Hannah had not. Did not Elkanah, her husband, in consoling her for her failure to bear children say unto her: "Why is thy heart grieved? Am not I better to thee than ten sons?" Hannah was a woman of the heart and the home, or she would not thus have endeared herself to Elkanah.

But Hannah was more than a wife. She was a mother. She desired motherhood long before the Lord blessed her with a son. True, the rival woman may have made her desire motherhood more intensely because of her taunts. But everything about Hannah suggests that motherhood was necessary for the fulfilment of her desires. And so Hannah prayed to Jehovah for a child, a son. Herein is revealed another aspect of Hannah's character. She was a deeply religious woman. She not only turned to Jehovah in her eager craving for motherhood, but she also pledged in advance that if she should bear a son, he should be dedicated to the Lord. Subsequent events confirmed her faith and strength of purpose. If ever a mother tried hard to carry out her promise to the God who gives the joys of motherhood, that mother was Hannah. Samuel was brought up before the Lord. All that Hannah had craved in a son, both for herself, her husband, and her religion, was realized in him.

In Hannah, then, we have undoubtedly the typical woman of the home in distinction from the woman of public life, as was Deborah. She was not a prophetess, a judge, a patriot, a warrior; she was a wife, a mother, a woman who prayed and worshiped at the shrine of a household God rather than at the shrine of a nation's God. There have always been many Hannahs in the world, and, probably, there always will be many. It is hard to see how the world could go on very well without its Hannahs. Conjugal affection, with all its tender and humanizing influences; maternal affection, with its stabilizing, creative influences; religious faith and sanctions for the privileges and duties of parenthood—these are personal and social forces that surely make for an orderly and growing race of men. And yet the Hannahs should not boast of their superiority over the Deborahs, any more than should the Deborahs consider their emancipation from the cares of those who make homes and bear children a warrant of distinction. Both types have always existed, and their respective functions have blest civilization.

Sept. 24-30—Martha and Mary

(Luke 10:38-42)

In Martha and Mary we have two women that traditional religious thought has sharply contrasted. Martha has stood in literal truth for those who forget the Master in the rather sordid cares and duties of common life, while Mary has stood for those who choose the better part, and sit at the Master's feet. No doubt something of this contrast has been due to the words of the Master himself. But the Master may have been misinterpreted in this as in some other things. I wonder if he really meant a rebuke, for all time, for the women who get so absorbed in waiting upon their guests that they forget them; or whether he meant to exalt, for all time, the women who become so absorbed in the personal charm and words of their guests that they forget to feed them, or otherwise provide for their wants. Very likely the lesson of the Martha and Mary episode lies in a balance between the extremes. Perhaps the Master meant, rather playfully, to "jolly" Martha for her fussiness, and to help Mary out of her embarrassment due to Martha's scolding her in the Master's presence.

In any event, the writer of this sketch has always felt, as he is sure many others have felt, that Martha has been dealt with too severely and Mary too tenderly. Martha does, indeed, typify for all time the thoughtful, busy, anxious women who are so concerned about doing their duty by their guests, and, incidentally, satisfying their pride, perhaps, in being thrifty housekeepers, that they for-

get, betimes, the guests themselves. While Mary typifies for all time the women who think little, perhaps too little, of the things that worry Martha, and are absorbed in personal attentions to their guests, in giving themselves up to the joys of sitting by their side, talking with them, and profiting by their words of friendliness and instruction. In Martha, perhaps, duty is written large; in Mary, affection. In Martha there may be more facility in doing things; in Mary, more facility in making herself agreeable and surrendering herself to the stimulus of people. All of these are good qualities, but strict virtue does not lie in their exaggeration. Martha should have imitated the traits of Mary, without sacrificing her own merits; and Mary should have imitated the traits of Martha, without sacrificing the qualities that have earned for her the reputation of choosing the better part. Far be it from the writer to question the propriety of the Master's words. It may indeed be that these words were put into his mouth by those who recorded the incident, and reflect not the opinion of the Master himself but the bias of one who heard him. In any case, one could wish that the Master had told Martha to sit down and rest a bit, let things in the kitchen take care of themselves, and talk with him. And one could wish, too, that he had told Mary to go and help Martha betimes, so that she might worry less over her work. Perhaps, the Master did just this in both cases. Certainly such were not a violent supposition in the light of his wisdom, his sympathy with all such human frailties as those of Martha, and his sense of proportion in estimating the entire situation of which he was a part.

G. E. D.

THE EXILE AND THE RESTORATION[1]

Professor JOHN E. MCFADYEN, D.D., Glasgow, Scotland

Sept. 3—Nehemiah Rebuilds the Walls of Jerusalem
(Neh. 3:1—7:4)

The life and, above all, the religion of Judah were in perpetual peril from the heathen nations by which she was surrounded. No permanent national reconstruction, therefore, was possible until Jerusalem was secure—in other words, until the walls were rebuilt. The chapters (3-6) which tell the fascinating story of the reconstruction of the walls may be summarized as follows:

Soon after Nehemiah's arrival and under his inspiration (chap. 2) the building was prosecuted with vigor and speed. All but the nobles of Tekoa lent a helping hand, from the high-priest to the private man, from the nobles to the trade-guilds (chap. 3). Irritated, however, by the progress of the building, their heathen neighbors ridiculed their infatuation and provoked Nehemiah to an earnest prayer for vengeance. The redoubled efforts of the builders, who had now almost succeeded in closing the breaches of the walls, so enraged these foreigners that they determined upon a sudden attack. Nehemiah, however, frustrated their plans by making adequate preparations for this contingency, and strengthened the hearts of the despondent people not only by his own heroic example but also by reminding them that their God, the great and terrible Jehovah, would fight for them (chap. 4).

At this juncture the wrongs of the poorer people found a voice. To procure money for food and for the royal tribute they had been driven to mortgage their property to their wealthier brethren and even to sell their children. At a great public meeting Nehemiah indignantly accused the leading men of their unbrotherly rapacity, contrasted their conduct with his own and that of his friends, and finally induced them to restore the mortgaged property, binding them by an oath and invoking on traitors a solemn curse (5:1-13). Nehemiah's example was as good as his precept. For during the whole period of his governorship (444-432 B.C.) he scrupulously refrained, in spite of precedent to the contrary, from burdening the people with the expenses of his large establishment. Nay, he could appeal to an unusually generous hospitality. Hence the justice of his prayer, "Remember unto me, O my God, for good, all that I have done for this people" (5:14-19).

The walls were now completed. But the enemy, not to be balked, cunningly proposed a personal conference with Nehemiah on non-Jewish soil at a place about twelve miles northwest of Jerusalem. Each invitation he peremptorily refused. Then came a letter with insinuations of rebellion and treason abetted by prophetic intrigue, all of which Nehemiah pointedly denied. As a last resource a prophet backed by members of the

[1] These studies follow the lesson-topics and passages of the International Sunday-school series.

prophetic order was suborned by the enemy to destroy his credit by inducing him to flee for his life to the temple—a proposal which Nehemiah rejected with scorn. So, by the manifest favor of God, the walls were finished in the almost incredibly brief period of seven weeks and a half—to the amazement and humiliation of the enemy, who regarded it as nothing less than a miracle. (chap. 6). Nehemiah then placed the city in charge of two officials, and took vigorous precautions to have it strongly guarded and more thickly peopled (7:1-4).

We, like Nehemiah, are, or should be, engaged in the process of reconstruction, of building a safer and nobler national life. "There is much rubbish" to be cleared away (4:10); many are disheartened and appalled by the task, and "the strength of the bearers of burdens is decayed" (4:10). In this mood and facing this task, we may learn from Nehemiah the need of (1) prayer. Chapter 4, which is full of action, is also full of prayer (cf. 4:9, "we made our prayer unto God and set a watch"). (2) Plans. Nehemiah met the plans of the enemy by plans of his own. He skilfully disposed his forces in such a way that a possible attack should be repelled, but above all that the great work of building should go on. Prayer, planning, work went hand in hand. "We made our prayer and set a watch" (4:9); "remember the Lord and fight" (4:14). (3) There is also need of concentration. The builders were scattered over a wide area, but the sound of a trumpet brought them together to whatever point was threatened, and in union was strength. So must men of different types and persuasions be prepared to unite and concentrate their strength when a great wrong like the drink traffic has to be combated, or an inestimable gain like the peace of

the world has to be achieved. (4) There is need for unremitting perseverance. The city of our dreams will rise at last when we learn to work with such energy as that of Nehemiah and his men, who for days did not put off their clothes (4:23) and stuck to their task "from the rising of the morning till the stars appeared" (4:21). We are all too willing to be deflected from our work by trivial reasons, and we sorely need a larger measure of the devotion which prompted Nehemiah to say, "I am doing a great work, so that I can not come down. Why should the work cease, whilst I leave it and come down to you?" (6-3).

Sept. 10—Teaching the Law of God
(Neh. 8:1-18)

This chapter, in which Nehemiah is hardly mentioned (8:9) and Ezra is a figure of great prominence, probably rests upon the memoirs of Ezra. At a great convocation Ezra was requested by representatives of the people to bring the book of the law, which must have been, if not the whole Pentateuch, at any rate the legislative part of it. The reference in verse 14 to the celebration of the festival of booths is to the legislative portion, in particular to Lev. 23:33-44. Mounted on a pulpit of wood and supported by thirteen, or more probably twelve, prominent men, Ezra, after solemnly unrolling the book, began by offering a prayer of adoration to God, to which the people responded with a double Amen. In his task of presenting the law, he was assisted by a number of Levites who "gave the sense so that the people understood the reading." What is meant is apparently that Ezra read a passage aloud, and then the Levites took it up, possibly in separate groups, and expounded it in detail.

The people were moved to tears, as they listened to the demands of the law and remembered how frequently and how seriously they had transgressed them. But it was no part of Ezra's design to have the people prostrated with grief. Consequently he spoke to them words of cheer, reminding them that it was at once a holy and a glad day—holy, because, being the first of the month, it was the day of the new moon, and glad, because it was the season of the feast of booths, at which the law had ordained a great rejoicing (Deut. 16:14). This festival was held at the the end of the harvest and vintage, it was a merry time, a time for "eating the fat and drinking the sweet," and for making gifts or "portions," especially to the poor. The people took Ezra at his word and made great mirth, now as glad that they had understood the law as formerly they were grieved that they had transgressed it.

Next day a deputation of laymen, Levites, and priests went to Ezra for further instruction in the law, and we may presume it was then their duty to instruct the circles with which they were immediately connected. Considering the season of the year, special attention was naturally devoted to the law regulating the feast of booths (Lev. 23). Booths were erected on the flat roofs, in the courts of houses, and on broad open spaces. The festival was kept for a week, and during the week the law was read daily.

We learn from the passage (1) how important is the teaching of Scripture in the reconstruction of the national life. Ezra took steps to have the Scripture not only read but explained in such a way that all could understand. Nothing is more needed to-day than an intelligent and vital interpretation of Scripture in our churches and Sunday-schools. It must be so expounded that its truth will touch the conscience, create and quicken an interest in religion, and react transformingly upon the social, civic, and political life of our time. The most charitable critic of our churches could not maintain that to their members and adherents the Bible was a familiar book. It is a curious combination—this theoretical admission of the Bible's unique supremacy and the practical neglect of it. Ezra clearly saw how much his nation's welfare depended on knowledge of it. But how much ampler are our Scriptures than were Ezra's! And how stable and fruitful might our national life be, if it were more deeply rooted and grounded in the Scriptures which it is the Church's business to teach—in the social righteousness for which the prophets pleaded so earnestly, and in the love for one another which was urged by Jesus Christ our Lord. (2) We learn also the importance of sacred festivals. The religious spirit must express itself, and a festival is peculiarly appropriate when God has crowned the year with his goodness and the worshiper's heart is filled with joy and gratitude. Religion is a happy experience, and the passage rings throughout with joy (8:10, 12, 17)—a joy which the worshiper helped his poorer brethren to share by sending them "portions." The Christian year, too, furnishes many occasions worthy of public commemoration —the birth of Christ, his resurrection, etc., and the life of the individual is incomparably enriched by associating with his brethren throughout the world in the celebration of such festivals as these.

Sept. 17—The Message of Malachi

(Mal. 3:1—4:3)

A study of the prophet Malachi is appropriate at this point because he was contemporary with Nehemiah and contributed, by his message of rebuke and encouragement, as Nehemiah by his building of the walls, to the reformation and reconstruction of the life of Jerusalem. His book is an eloquent witness to the desperate need for reform. Religion and morals were at a low ebb. The priests were bored by the worship which it was their duty to conduct (1:13): they presented inferior offerings—blind, lame, sick animals—anything was good enough for Jehovah (1:8, 14). The people were defrauding the sanctuary of its dues —the tithes and other offerings (3:8). With this religious apathy went low moral conduct; social life was honeycombed with perjury, immorality, superstition, exploitation of the defenseless (3:5). And the harvests were as bad as the morals were low— to Malachi the two things were most intimately connected. The windows of heaven were closed, no rain had fallen, the fields remained unwatered, unblest, unfruitful (3:10). Good men were driven almost to despair; they began to think that it was useless to serve God, and maintained that life's prizes went to the unscrupulous (3:14f.) and that only those who did evil prospered (2:17). In the bitterness of their heart they could not help asking, "Where is the God of justice?" (2:17).

Now that is the mood which Malachi has to meet in chap. 3 and he meets it by the sublime assurance that the Lord Jehovah is coming. He is not so far away as they think. But before he comes in person, he will send his messenger—perhaps the prophet is thinking of Elijah (4:5) come back to earth—to clear the obstacles out of his way, and thus prepare for his coming. So that coming would be, first, in judgment, for the community must be cleansed of its dross and impurity; only after that stern process could the better day dawn. The judgment was to fall alike on priests and people—on the apathetic priests and the superstitious, immoral, and cruelly unjust people. Hollow worship

found its counterpart in a wicked social life. Very significant is the last clause of 3:5, "and fear not me"; it is this that explains all the crimes that precede it. Disregard of the moral law and of social decency is rooted in disregard of God, the lack of religion accounts for the prevalence of the sins by which society was disgraced and enfeebled.

The prophet clinches his appeal by pointing to the bad harvest, which he interpreted as God's curse upon them for their failure to pay the temple dues. Light is cast upon this passage by Neh. 10:38ff., which tells that the tithe of the produce of the fields which, by an older law, had been given every third year to the Levites scattered throughout the land, was about this time given to the Levites who served in Jerusalem at the sanctuary. But apparently these dues had been inadequately paid, and we learn from Neh. 13:10-12 of the steps which Nehemiah successfully took to secure payment of those dues to the Levites who, through deficient revenue, were compelled to scatter about the country for their livelihood, to the neglect of the temple service. So Malachi's preaching was not without result.

Apparently the fields had been devastated by locusts as well as by drought, and Malachi assured the people that God would respond to their honest efforts to pay their dues by sending his blessed rain to fertilize the fields and by removing the locusts which devoured the crops. The people, however, were unconvinced; they thought God had forgotten them; and Malachi comforts them by assuring them that a book of remembrance was being kept, a book of life in which their names were being written, which would, so to say, keep God in mind of them, and when the judgment fell, it would not fall upon them. The fate of the good and the bad would then be sharply distinguished: the latter would be trodden under foot—such was the vindictive hope even of good men in Malachi's age—while upon the sad and darkened world of the former the sun would arise, from whose beams would stream healing upon their wounded hearts, and, frisking like calves of the stall, their joy would be full.

The passage suggests (1) the nature and source of sin. Perjury, immorality, cruelty, exploitation, injustice—these are the things that the prophet denounces, and they have their origin in the disregard of God (3:5). But Malachi, as a good churchman, also counts it a sin to be remiss in the payment of one's church dues—this is robbery of God, as exploitation was robbery of man. Considering that the Church stands for nothing less than the welfare and redemption of the world, it is not too much to say that a member who contributes to its resources meanly or not at all has failed in his duty and deserves the solemn reprimand and reminder of the prophet. (2) The penalty of sin. In common with all men of insight, Malachi believed in a moral order. Every day, said Emerson, is a judgment day; but there are great crises in history, like that through which the nations have lately passed, when in lurid letters of fire God's judgments are written. (3) The reward of faithfulness. As surely as evil is punished, God is working all things together for good to those that trust him, and he will bring them at the last to peace and victory. The faithful are never forgotten. Jehovah has his book of remembrance. He is mindful of his own.

Sept. 24—Review. The Exile and the Restoration

The lessons of this quarter cover a period of almost exactly a hundred and fifty years, from the call of Ezekiel in 592 B.C. to the building of the walls of Jerusalem by Nehemiah in 444 B.C., and include the enormously important periods of the exile and the restoration—the exile which so deepened and enriched the spiritual life of the Hebrews, and the restoration which enabled them to continue and develop their work for God and the world in their own land, and so prepare the way, in the fulness of the times, for the coming of our Lord.

Many figures of great historical and religious importance have passed before us in the course of our study this quarter—Ezekiel, Ezra, Nehemiah, Daniel, Esther. The first three names show that Hebrew religion was drifting towards the priestly rather than the prophetic type. The motto is no longer, "I will have mercy and not sacrifice" (Hosea 6:6); it is precisely upon sacrifice, and in general, on the rites and ceremonies of the Church, that Ezekiel, Ezra, and Malachi lay predominant, tho of course not exclusive stress. But it is more important for our purpose now to notice (1) that the lives of the people we have studied were marked by a high sense of responsibility and deliberately devoted to the public weal. Ezekiel sought to warn his countrymen of impending danger and, when the blow fell, to inspire them with hope for the days to come. The dead nation, he declared, would rise again to its feet, an exceeding great army (37:10); and the last nine chapters of his book constitute a program of worship for the restored community, when they should be able to re-establish their religious life. Nehemiah was equally devoted to the welfare of his people, and his devotion took a peculiarly practical form. He secured permission from the Persian king, at whose court he served, to return to Palestine, and he immediately took steps to have the walls of Jerusalem rebuilt without which Jewish life could not be secure from assault nor Jewish religion from contamination. Malachi pleaded for a purer worship and a nobler social life. Ezra crossed the desert with the book of the law in his hand (Ezra 7:14) in order to lay in that book the foundation for the future life of the Jewish people. Daniel and his companions risked their lives in Babylon rather than be false to the religious customs and ordinances of their nation. Esther in Persia risked her life to save her people from destruction. All these men and women were patriots, they could all be described in the terms applied by Sanballat to Nehemiah, as governed by the passion "to seek the welfare of the children of Israel" (Neh. 2:10). This, too, should be our ambition, only we must remember that the welfare of our country includes not only material things, but far more the things of the spirit, and also that it can never really clash with, but actually presupposes and demands the welfare of every other country.

We learn (2) the importance of nationality. Each of these great characters was devoted to his country—Nehemiah in one way, Ezra and Ezekiel in another—because he believed that, in the purpose of God, it had a great part to play in world history. As the great writer of Isa. chaps. 40-55 saw so clearly and said so emphatically, it was Israel's privilege and duty to be the servant of Jehovah. At a time like this, when nationality is beginning to count for so much in world politics, it is of the highest importance to grasp the truth which Israel's greatest men understood so well, that a nation's business is not to glorify and serve itself, but to glorify God and to serve the world. What a different world we might have if all the nations could learn to look upon themselves as servants of the Lord and of humanity, each using its gifts and powers consciously to this great end, one serving through its commerce, another through its learning, and so on. Thus the modern emphasis upon nationality, which has been stimulated by the results of the war, may be a blessing to the world; otherwise it may well be again, as it has occasionally been, a menace and a curse.

(3) The importance of the Church. The story of the Jewish nation which we have traversed this quarter has really been the story of the Jewish Church. Everything has centered round Jerusalem, the temple, and the temple services. There were special reasons, of course, which drove the Jews of those days back upon ecclesiastical life and organization as an expression of their national distinctiveness; and perhaps in no modern nation can the Church ever again have the same dominant position as she had in the ancient Jewish world. Yet from that world we have much to learn. The Church exists to emphasize the highest values in human life, and with these values surely every good man and more particularly every church member must deliberately and effectively identify himself. He will share his church's life and worship, take part in her activities, and support her generously in every way he can. Ungenerous and shabby contributions in so great a cause roused Malachi, as we have seen, to a white heat of indignation.

(4) The importance of Scripture. Ezra's presentation of the book of the law to the assembled people and its exposition by the Levites who "gave the sense so that the people understood the reading" form an unforgetable picture. Ezra knew that a national life based upon the Scripture he had offered them would be well and safely built; in point of fact it is hardly too much to say that it is the Old Testament and that alone that has held the Jews together throughout the long centuries in which they have

been scattered throughout the world. Here again is a permanent lesson for us. It is universally admitted that the Bible, taken as a whole, Old and New Testament together, offers the greatest moral dynamic and the profoundest religious inspiration that the world has ever seen. No one denies that if the righteousness for which the prophets plead were realized in the relations of men and nations with one another, and if something of the mind which was in Jesus Christ were also in us, there would be a transformation of human society which would seem a veritable miracle. That is the supreme and sufficient justification for such work as that in which we are now engaged. Preachers who expound the word, teachers who teach it, and scholars who learn it and lay it to heart, are all helping to usher in the day when, with ennobled minds and friendly hearts, men the world over will count it their joy to serve God and one another.

How the Bible Was Written

I want, in passing, to emphasize for you the fact stated by the inspired writers themselves that they wrote their histories of past ages much in the way that Mr. Green or Professor Gardiner or any other historian wrote his history. This is most important to remember in the scare about higher criticism which some of you know about. You would never think of doubting these historians' account of William the Conqueror merely because they wrote their histories 900 years after his death. Of course you would believe that they studied the books of earlier historians and old letters and parchments and inscriptions and monuments. And if all the libraries and museums which contained these should be burned down tomorrow you would surely think it unreasonable if people should say that we have no good grounds for believing that William the Conqueror ever lived.

Yet something of this kind is what makes people uneasy in the statements of what is called "higher criticism." Scholars express the opinion that the Pentateuch in its present completed form was written centuries later than Moses' day. Then somebody suggests that if that be so it can not be trustworthy history, in fact the writer must have been romancing a good deal. It is a steadying thought to keep in mind that the writers keep telling us that their histories were so much made up out of pre-existing documents. On reading Green's *History of the English People* you know that 300 years before him there were several less complete printed histories—and 300 years earlier still there were still less complete manuscript chronicles, and 300 years farther back there were separate uncollected annals, and state papers and letters and documents of various kinds. Thus gradually by successive editing English history grew. And thus also gradually Bible history grew, under the care of that inspired Church whose history it was.— J. PATERSON SMYTH in *The Bible for School and Home.*

SYRIA IN CHRISTIAN ARCHEOLOGY[1]

With the exception of Mesopotamia, no country so well as parts of Syria illustrates the saying, "They made a desert and called it peace." This was accomplished by the Mohammedans of the early seventh and later centuries. For nearly a millennium it was forgotten that in Syria there once lived a large Christian population, dwelling in cities of considerable size and in fine villages, the former of which contained beautiful examples of architecture—churches, monasteries, palatial homes, fine inns, etc. Following upon the Persian wars of the Byzantine empire, the irruptions of the Saracens, Turks, and Mongols and the settlement there of the people of the crescent, depopulation, de-

[1] *Publications of the Princeton University Archeological Expedition to Syria in* 1904-1905. Division II. Ancient Architecture in Syria. By Howard Crosby Butler. Section B. Northern Syria. Part 6. Djebel Sim'an. 12½x10 in., 356, xviii pp.
Division III. Greek and Latin Inscriptions in Syria, by Enno Littmann and David Magie, Jr. Section A. Southern Syria. Part 6. Si' (Seeia). 372 pp.
Division III, Section A, Part 7. The Ledja. 486 pp. Late E. J. Brill, Leyden, 1921.

cay, stagnation ensued, till where once lived and toiled thousands now only small bands of Arabs and the like find scanty shelter and a scantier living. Buildings are in ruins, tho often large parts—arches, walls, pillars, etc.—still stand, mute witnesses of a departed excellence in conception and construction.

The earliest suggestion of what existed there came to the modern world from the travels and books of John Lewis Burckhardt between 1808 and 1816 (his books were published 1819-30). Others—Seetzen, Wetzstein, Porter—spoke of "ghost cities in the wilderness." And then Marquis E. J. M. de Vogüé and Waddington in 1861-62 made an extensive tour and five years afterward called attention to the fact that within a territory of not more than a hundred square miles they had found over a hundred cities which carried the evidences of the same faith—early Christianity—with varied and important inscriptions. As one writer has said, these towns are evidence of a large, opulent, artistic life, displaying itself in roomy dwellings built of heavy hewn stones, perfectly put together on a palatial plan, while inscriptions bring to us voices of a previously unknown "Church triumphant."

But decay works rapidly after it gets under way. These ruins served as quarries out of which later generations got materials for their hovels or huts. The sands of the desert are covering the blocks and inscriptions, while earthquake, winds, and rains are toppling the remains which still stand. The testimony they bear—architectural, inscriptional, etc.—is disappearing. It was therefore a most worthy conception that sent forth the Princeton University Archeological Expedition in 1904-05 and 1909 to investigate, measure and chart, photograph, and record for all time the remains of this extensive Christian population of Syria. And it is a munificent service that enables the results of these investigations and studies to be set forth by text, photograph, plans, copies and interpretations of inscriptions in a splendid series of large quarto volumes.

In the REVIEW for April, 1915, and July, 1916, attention was called to certain parts then recently issued. Those volumes have recently been completed by the issue of the parts named in the footnote. These leave

only the geography and itinerary and the inscriptions in Syriac, Safaitic, and Arabic still to be dealt with.

Possibly the most interesting item in this mass of splendid detail is that which concerns a site known as Der Sim'an (Telanissus or Telneshe). This place owed its celebrity, perhaps its very existence as a city, to the renowned "pillar saint," Simeon Stylites, who lived for nearly forty years on the top of a pillar which he gradually increased in height till it reached sixty feet. The spectacle itself, together with the saint's reputation for sanctity thus gained and for the power to accomplish miraculous cures, made the place, up to the Arabic conquest, a goal of pilgrimage, a busy town, the site of splendid churches, a triumphal arch, important monasteries, and large inns for the entertainment of the pilgrims. There were also bazaars, shops, and smaller hotels, with all the activities involved. "The main body of the ruins covers a space about half a mile long, east and west, and a third of a mile wide."

The place "was entirely a religious center, in which hundreds, perhaps thousands, of pilgrims were housed and fed during the days of their visit to the most renowned shrine in Syria."

Here the two convents, the church of St. Simeon Stylites, two great inns, the "sacred way," and other monuments have been photographed and measured, and drawings made of the buildings as they must once have appeared.

The great value of this Princeton exploration comes more clearly into view when we realize that Der Sim'an is only one site in a previously unexplored region covering 70 square miles where are twenty-five ruined towns of which not more than five appear on any previous map, where none of the monuments had been measured or investigated except those of "Simon's town," as above.

In this set of books is material to keep long employed the student of Christian archeology in Syria, the student of architecture, of inscriptions in Greek, Latin, Nabatæan, Syriac, Safaitic, and Arabic. Professors Butler, Littmann, Magie, and Prentice have reared a splendid and abiding monument to themselves and to the university in the work embodied here.—G. W. G.

⧓Social Christianity⧓

WHAT THE CHURCH IS DOING AT HOME

ALFRED WILLIAMS ANTHONY, D.D., LL.D., Executive Secretary of Home
Missions Council, New York City, N. Y.

Sept. 3—The Mental and Spiritual State of the Church

SCRIPTURE LESSON: Matt. 16:18; Mark 16:15.

1. The Great War left the Church in turmoil, as all the world was left. The Church is a part of the world and must be affected by it. The Church can not pass through mire without getting her garments soiled. But she has recovered herself and cleansed herself more quickly and more extensively than has any other department of human relations and organization. Economics, industry, and politics are not so far along toward "normalcy," to use the newly current word, as is the Church. All men know that neither Christianity nor the Church failed. Never before has the spirit of the Church's faith so thoroughly permeated social institutions and so effectively influenced national and international relations.

2. Intense theological stress was occasioned by the war. Many people regarded the war as an evidence of the "great apostasy," and a token of "the last days." Others saw more manifestly than ever before that the need of the world was a fuller expression of the gospel, not for individuals and between individuals alone, but for groups and between groups, for nations, and between nations. Some men began to declare that Jesus had rejected the world and would speedily come in the flesh to pronounce judgment and destroy it, while others confidently said, "His spirit, already with us, is striving in new forms and in richer measure to express itself for all mankind in every conceivable condition. We must take the challenge of the world's needs and apply the gospel to all human relations." So the controversy arose between "fundamentalists" and "modernists," or "evangelicals," as many of them prefer to be termed. The one believed that the substance of faith was once for all set in definite conceptions and phrases; the other was confident that conception must necessarily be enlarged and phrases be modified as conditions change and comprehension becomes more inclusive of truth.

The controversy is not over, nor can the significance of it be minimized. Practically every denomination has felt the shock. Parties have been formed, passions have been aroused, funds have been withheld from mission treasuries, serious schisms have been threatened. Yet the crisis has been passed, "the peak of the load" carried, and the machinery has not broken down.

A quick review of the attitude of several of the larger denominations will show the stabilizing tendencies now in progress. The Methodist Episcopal Church early passed the word around through the channels of "the system" that controversy over doctrinal questions was not in place, and outspeaking controversy has not appeared. The Protestant Episcopal Church has gone on its way, firm in its historic faith, enlarging its conception of social service and increasing its ministries to all classes and conditions of men. The Presbyterian Church, in all its branches, has raised more money, won more converts, and by great reconstructive movements knit its various parts and organizations more compactly together for efficient service than ever before, and theological controversies have simply been silenced by the onmoving of the work. The Reformed churches have likewise recorded years of solid achievement. The Lutheran Church is steadily standing for its sound doctrine and is unifying slowly, yet surely, its scattered parts. The Congregational churches have experienced somewhat the strain of internal variation and discussion, particularly in the

West, yet have maintained their characteristic fellowship in the midst of freedom. Their record for the year shows that a denominational consciousness, finding expression in a more efficient central council, is seeking and securing results in ministry and work, rather than in opinions and doctrines.

To an observer only two denominations seem seriously threatened by dissension and division over theological views and creeds. The present leaders among Disciples and Baptists have been challenged by groups arising from within, under aggressive leadership and supported by ample funds, as departing from the faith and unworthy longer to administer denominational affairs, and these groups have demanded that the control of missions and schools and benevolent enterprises shall be turned over to them. Attacks and charges have been violent and disruption has seemed to impend; and yet the observer feels assured that the atmosphere will clear, ways of peace will be found, and essential unity will be preserved.

3. The developments of the last few centuries give assurance that denominations will not multiply by partition through strife.

(a) It is sound democracy, as it is essential Christianity, to allow free speech and full discussion. Controversy may stretch the fiber of Christian patience but will not break the strands in this late day, when unity coupled with diversity has been experienced so largely in the national life and in our social structure. The Church will not divide when the men who compose her have learned how to hold together, under similar trials, organizations of lesser moment.

(b) The whole trend of human organizations is toward more intimate relations and closer cooperation. Even great political overturnings can not prevent the movement of men toward common interests and associated action. The war taught this; the after-effects of the war are now disclosing it. As nations became solidified, so all humanity has taken great leaps toward a consciousness of community of interests. Information and knowledge spread everywhere. Men travel and mingle and migrate and fuse; economic conditions reach over boundaries and across seas; ideals and purposes, exprest differently, and frequently at wide variance, nevertheless tend to blend and form a common stock. He who under-

takes to pull men apart is really setting his face against the full flow of human history. There is a basic brotherhood in creation, realized now as never before, because of the unifying devices and the common experiences of men.

(c) The Christian religion in its essential simplicity bulks bigger to-day than ever before. Men know that the mind of Christ is discernible not in dialectic hair-splitting of medieval theologians but in the great motives of love and the sacrificial reach of altruistic service. Jesus did not die for phrases and forms; he gave his life for men. His meaning becomes lost when words are substituted for soul-commitment. In the back of our heads, in the subconscious depths of our beings, are fundamental convictions of an essential unity which we all possess in the redemptive work and the saving power of Jesus Christ, even when we attempt to make definitions which divide us, and seek and crowd for place, in order that we may rule the affairs of the Church according to our own liking.

(d) There is the great Holy Spirit, member of the triune God, as yet but partially known to the best of us, who has been striving with men through the centuries to make known to them the things of God, to give them power, and to reveal their oneness. He is in the world; he holds more of it in his keeping and under his direction than ever before. He will not take freedom of action from men, but he does not mean that they who have learned to know him and who have called each other brethren shall divide and oppose and destroy each other. A divine purpose, resident in a divine Person, rules in the world.

Sept. 10—Growth and Progress of the Church

The substantial gains of the Church are numerous and significant. To enumerate them all would carry us far in detail. It must suffice us to pick out some of the more important.

1. Dr. H. K. Carroll, who has been a long-time, careful statistician of church membership, reports the gain in 1921 of 761,727, bringing the total of all communions up to 43,523,206 members. This includes all bodies, Protestant as well as Roman Catholic, within the United States. In 1919 the increase was

less than 44,000. In 1920 it was reported as 667,007. Several denominations in their annual meetings are rejoicing over larger accessions to their churches and larger attendance in their Sunday-schools than for many years, if not indeed larger than ever.[1] The net gain for ten years has been 7,427,521.

2. Never have Christians contributed, through the channels of individual giving, so large a sum of money for church expenses and for missionary objects as this last year. The national Home Mission boards and societies received and expended $30,128,769.09 in 1921, as compared with $26,306,201.60 in 1920, and $18,502,846.01 in 1919. These figures do not by any means represent all that is spent annually for home missions, as these cover only the national boards, and do not include expenditures by other agencies for church erection, publications, Sunday-schools, social service, and education, and church extensions within the limits of the lesser organizations of the Church, nor the expenditures of interdenominational bodies. The important thing is the gain. This is significant.

It must be remembered also (1) that this is after the bitter disappointments due to the failure of the Interchurch World Movement, with its more than seven millions of dollars of debts, which the churches had to pay; (2) that this is in the midst of a period of curtailment and deflation in all kinds of business the world over; and (3) when denominations, geared up to larger programs, because of reconstruction policies following the war, and of great expectations awakened by the Interchurch World Movement, have been obliged to contract their plans, reduce their staffs, and in some instances face dissension and disloyalty within their natural constituency. The showing is remarkable.

3. The Church has evinced an awakened consciousness of obligations to "new Americans" who come to our shores. Of thirty-two organizations, most of them religious, which have membership in a General Committee of Immigrant Aid at Ellis Island, seventeen maintain regular paid workers on the island. This committee and government officials are cooperating in welfare work more intimately than ever before. On Jan. 22, 1922, a plan of holding religious

[1] See the REVIEW for June, 1922, p. 461.

services Sunday morning, in three groups, for Protestants, Roman Catholics, and Jews, was inaugurated. Plans for following immigrants from Ellis Island to their final destination are now being worked out by Protestant bodies in conjunction. Through the Committee on New Americans of the Home Missions Council and the Council of Women for Home Missions a Bureau of Information is maintained which (1) gathers information respecting all literature published in foreign languages in this country; (2) issues through the foreign language press on special occasions, like Easter, Labor Day, and Christmas, Christian messages prepared by some of the best-known ministers of the country; (3) brings denominations together in publishing religious papers and helps in foreign languages; (4) prepares religious tracts especially fitted to the needs of foreigners, and procures the publication of special books relating to racial groups. It would be an interesting story to tell of successful church enterprises maintained in our American cities for those who speak a strange tongue. They are numerous all over the country.

In this connection it is significant to note that one foreign church, hitherto maintained and controlled by its ecclesiastical parentage in the old world, has severed its connection with the homeland and become affiliated with strictly American denominations. There are approximately 500,000 Hungarians in the United States, who are organized into ninety-two Protestant congregations. During the last year these congregations have severed their connection with the Conventus in Hungary and become identified with American denominations. Forty-five have allied themselves with the Reformed Church in the United States, seven have come under the Episcopal supervision of the Protestant Episcopal Church, and others are working out the question of their final destiny, whether with one of these denominations or with the Presbyterian Church, U. S. A.

4. In the field of race relations more has been attempted and more accomplished this year than ever before. For three years the Home Missions Council has had a special secretary giving most of his time to negro churches and organizations. This last year the Federal Council has created a Commission on the Church and Race Relations. During the war some prominent Christian gentlemen of Atlanta, Georgia, formed a Commit-

tee of race cooperation which has extended its gracious influences into more than 800 communities of the South. For a time the Young Men's Christian Association made generous grants for the support of this Committee. Now it is relying more directly upon support from the churches. The Christian women of the South, notably of the Methodist Episcopal Church South and of the Presbyterian Church in the U. S., have formed an efficient organization for promoting good-will between whites and blacks. The Federal Council, through its Commission on International Justice and Good-will, is doing much to create better conditions on the Pacific Coast for the Japanese, and throughout the country for all races. The Church Peace Union and the World Alliance for International Friendship Through the Churches held a significant congress in Cleveland, May 16-18, 1922, at which influences were given which spread nation-wide. All the churches have upheld the President and the Secretary of State in convening the Conference on Reduction of Armaments and in making its conclusions effective. More than 20,000 clergymen signed a petition addrest to the President urging the calling of this Conference. There is a movement in Christian circles for combating Anti-Semitism and promoting good-will toward the Jews. Church Congregations and individual Christians have prayed, petitioned, worked, and talked for peace and good-will as never before; and the implications of the gospel, for the promotion and preservation of good-will between nations and between races, are recognized now, almost everywhere, as a part of America's Christian program.

5. A sense of American unity and of obligations for all her parts has taken hold of the Church. Alaska, the Hawaiian Islands, Cuba, Porto Rico, Haiti, Santo Domingo, the Canal Zone, and even Mexico have received peculiar attention from the Christian churches of America this past year. In the Canal Zone one Christian church, with congregations and pastors in four places, is receiving grants from several denominations to help erect suitable meeting houses. A special committee appointed by the Federal Council has supervisory charge of this enterprise. In the southern half of the Dominican Republic five boards of three denominations jointly begin missionary work with an initial commitment of $80,000, furnished by

the five treasuries. In Porto Rico cooperation has resulted in (1) respect for each other's territory, (2) the maintenance of one theological seminary, (3) correspondence courses available for all preachers, (4) one common religious paper, and (5) united evangelistic campaigns. A group of churchmen from America has studied religious and social conditions in Haiti and, concerning some of them, has made recommendations to a committee of Congress. All America is conscious of itself in a Christian way as never before.

6. The movement toward unity and efficiency is pronounced in three quite different fields: (a) The first which will be thought of naturally is in the field of interdenominational organizations. The Interchurch World Movement, whatever else it was, was in effect a criticism of existing interdenominational bodies as unsatisfactory and ineffectual in dealing with the whole work of the Church—foreign missions, home missions, education, and philanthropy. Existing organizations specialized in but one phase of the work, and were tied down with agreements and precedents. Men felt this, even when they did not express it. But the Interchurch World Movement sought its goal too rapidly, without due regard to uninformed minds which must be enlightened, to conservative habits which must be altered, a newly created organization which must be seasoned and trusted, and inefficient helpers, who needed more time for experience and coordination. The lesson of the Interchurch Movement was not lost, however, by the other bodies. Never have they consulted together so much, never before cooperated so fully. The Federal Council, the Foreign Missions Conference, the Federation of Women's Boards of Foreign Missions, the Home Missions Council, the Council of Women for Home Missions, the International Young Men's Christian Association, the Young Women's Christian Association, the Council of Church Boards of Education, and the Council of Evangelical Denominations have drawn toward each other, and worked together through subcommittees, and by representation in each other's committees. A Consultative Committee, including them all in its membership, seeks, but has not yet found, ways of dealing with subjects of common interest, such as the dates and places of our annual meetings, publicity methods,

uses of the church year, especially with reference to times of appeal and the proportioning of benevolences, the rise of the community consciousness, and the creation of community trusts, race relations as they reach from this country to other countries and from them to this, the recruiting of young people for the service of the Church, the preservation, the housing, and the use of missionary literature and many other important subjects.

In the meantime the Federal Council has drawn closer to its own constituency, regulating its program more nearly as its constituent parts desire and receiving from them in return more adequate financial support.

A voluntary committee, known as the Committee on Social and Religious Surveys, has come into existence, following the Interchurch World Movement, whose financial supporters prefer to remain anonymous. This committee has made valuable surveys of twenty-four typical counties in different parts of the country, of one city (St. Louis), and of practically all of the Indian fields, and is publishing results of its studies in twelve volumes.

(b) Denominations themselves have been unifying and consolidating their missionary agencies. Practically every one formed a few years ago some kind of central committee, known as an Advance Movement, a New Era Movement, a New World Movement, or something similar. Some have gone further. The Disciples have gathered their

missionary boards into one united missionary society. The Episcopalians have created a Presiding Bishop and Council, superior to all of their national organizations. The Methodists have set up an overhead Board of Benevolence. The Presbyterians of the North have gone the furthest of all, having determined upon consolidating sixteen boards and agencies into but four boards. This movement is impressive. It means that the churches no longer will permit rivalries between their own parts, that they purpose to have a common and well-proportioned plan for all their work, and to use their resources of men and money with economy and efficiency.

(c) A striking movement toward unity is in local communities. Union churches, of the old type, have been tried and found wanting. Federated churches have been proven to be of a temporary usefulness. But the need of maintaining but one church in a one-church sized community has seemed imperative; and the community church has arisen. It is pleading its case and testing its merits now. It maintains a periodical, holds conventions, and has developed a consciousness of individuality and strength. Practically every one sympathizes with the purpose to eliminate duplication, waste, and inefficiency; but many are wondering whence the community church will draw its outside inspiration and oversight, and whither it will direct its missionary impulses, and how it will relate itself to the world.

WHAT THE CHURCH IS DOING ABROAD

Professor HARLAN P. BEACH, D.D., F.R.G.S., Yale University,
New Haven, Conn.

Sept. 17—Japan, Korea, China, India

To describe missionary operations in the seven fields mentioned below with any attempt to cover the leading operations of the various societies is impossible within the limits assigned. What is attempted is to point out a few salient features of the enterprise to-day, leaving unmentioned many other important phases of the program, and omitting entirely work in Latin America and in the papal countries of Europe.

JAPANESE HEGEMONY: This is actual in the rôle which the Japanese empire is playing, and in the attitude of Western powers toward Asia. No nation in history has achieved such large things in so brief a time as has elapsed since she first opened her sea gates to the Occident in 1854. No Asiatic race is so well equipped, so well trained, so ambitious to lead as the Japanese. And Japan does outstrip every nation in that great continent in industrial, educational, governmental, military, and political progress,

But what of her moral and possible religious leadership? Most of the Japanese believe, hazily at least, in the descent from the sun goddess of their emperor, "The Sovran Grandchild," and emperor worship is waxing rather than waning. Shintoism, officially declared not to be a religion two decades since, is increasingly exercising the prerogatives of natural religion. Buddhism's votaries number 45,482,941, worshiping in 70,717 temples and ministered to by 116,510 priests. One of its sects, the Shinshu, having 13,089,890 believers, is the greatest non-Christian missionary body in Asia, with representatives using Christianity's missionary methods in Korea, China, Hawaii, and on our Pacific slope. Japanese Christians also are active. They are sending missionaries to Korea, part of their own empire now, and they are engaging in evangelistic campaigns at home. One venturesome and resourceful evangelist, the Japanese Moody, is conducting an enterprise at Mukden in Manchuria which will weld enemies—Japanese and Koreans—into one through Christ; and his power is such that the government has sent him to their mid-Pacific mandatary to win the natives to a better life. While the foreign missionary becomes less and less necessary because of the higher degree of education and training of Japanese pastors and Christian leaders, and because of their independence and nationalism, these Christians are filling positions of trust and leadership better, perhaps, than missionaries could. Had Japan not alienated the sympathies and incurred the hatred of the Far East, the hegemony would be hers in Christian and other lines of leadership. She sees her past mistakes, and since Washington opened her eyes, her future as to Asiatic influence seems surer than hitherto.

KOREAN RESILIENCE: Tho politically part of the Japanese empire, by race, language, traditions, and choice, Korea is apart and would evermore remain an independent nation, were it possible. In her missionary accomplishment she is vastly more promising than her overlord, ranking with India's mass-movement areas and the African fields of Uganda, Livingstonia, and Kamerun. The Japanese occupation of 1910, the "conspiracy trial" and persecution of leading converts in 1911, and especially the atrocities and wholesale attack upon Christians following the Declaration of Independence of

March 1, 1919, have been extreme tests of the reality of religion in Korean Christian life. Its depth, and especially its marvelous resiliency, have been amply demonstrated. To-day the Korean Church is advancing and proceeds as if there were no bloody yesterday and crippled ranks, with many dead. Devoted Christians are full of evangelistic labors, entered upon after the annual meetings and sectional Bible classes have endued them with Bible knowledge and spiritual power. Because political independence is denied them, their organizing ability is spent in developing the "church in the house" into the village church, a power-house for leagues around. What it means to-day is suggested by Bishop Welch in these words: "There are in all 3,300 employed Korean workers and 3,000 organized churches and groups. The entire Christian community, including members, catechumens or probationers, baptized children, and enrolled inquirers, comprises about 340,000 souls, of whom approximately 220,000 are included in the first two classes. Women constitute about sixty per cent of the Korean Christian body, and it is estimated that nine-tenths of the church membership can read and write." And all this in thirty-seven years!

CHINA CONFERRING: The three most important items to be mentioned are the New Thought movement and the two great conferences. The *Hsin Ssu Ch'ao*, "New Thought Tide," began flowing in Peking University when its chancellor, Ts'ai Yüanpei, assumed his duties in 1916. "The aim of the movement is to spread as widely as possible among the Chinese people a knowledge of the philosophic, scientific, and social conditions in the most highly civilized nations of the world in order to bring China to their level." The six young men who rallied under Chancellor Ts'ai's flag in Peking have become legion in all higher educational centers of China, where it stands as a challenge, or as a coadjutor of Christianity, depending upon its reception, guidance, and advocacy. As long ago as 1919 groups made up of Chinese holding these views and of missionary educators gathered in a week-end retreat near Peking to the mutual enlightenment and well-being of both parties, an experiment deserving frequent repetition.

From April fourth to ninth of this year 126 students and delegates from thirty-three different lands joined 648 Chinese delegates at the Indemnity College near Peking for a World's Student Christian Federation Conference. Their coming had been anticipated by students who were bitterly opposed to Christianity on the grounds that it "is a foreign religion, that it is political, that it is a superstition, that it is an oppressor of mankind, that it is an ally of capitalism, and that it is a dying religion in Europe and America," and they consequently had established The Anti-Christian Movement. While its manifest ignorance and venom—exprest more strongly by its women members than by the young men—indicate its ephemeral nature, that and the New Thought movement are symptoms of crisis. The conference discust topics germane to the leading theme, "Christ in World Reconstruction," while the sectional meetings and familiar intercourse between persons naturally hostile—Koreans and Japanese, e.g., imparted light and harmony to many minds.

The third conferring body was the National Christian Conference, held in Shanghai, May 2-11, reports of which are not available at time of writing. That it made the indigenous church the main issue is evident. The facts that half the delegates were Chinese and that instead of having one English and one American chairman as heretofore, a Chinese, Rev. C. Y. Chêng, D.D., was elected sole chairman, are indicative of the changing status of missions in China. The anticipated conflict between fundamentalists and the liberal wing was averted, and a new national organization was established to replace the China Continuation Committee. This committee's massive valedictory volume, edited by Rev. Milton T. Stauffer, is entitled *The Christian Occupation of China* and easily surpasses any similar production dealing with mission fields.

TUMULTUOUS INDIA: Gandhi's imprisonment has not greatly affected the empire, moved as it had been by his non-cooperative scheme and his theoretically ideal *Satyagraha* movement—literally, "holding to the truth"; "I have also called it love-force, or soulforce," he adds. While this appeals to the pious, his watchword, "The Satanic raj must go; Swaraj must take its place"—the Satanic British rule must give way to self-government—is not bound like its author. The past year has welcomed the future Kaisar-i-Hind; yet the Prince of Wales has

not been free from verbal attack and bodily danger. His coming was an inspiration to all. "Not least will the missionaries thank him, remembering his regular attendance at divine worship, his brave words of good-will, and his sincere desire to identify himself, at all times and in all places, with the actual life, as well as the best ideals of India."

Apropos of China's movement toward an indigenous church is this action of the All-India Christian Conference of last December: "Resolved, that Protestant missions as such should be completely merged in the Indian Church, and that in future all foreign missionaries should be related to it. [At present many missionaries retain membership in their home churches.] That in the meantime "missions should appoint Indians of ability and character on an increasing scale as their lay and ordained missionaries. In view of the complaints made by various missions that educated young Indian Christians of character are not available to take up positions of trust and responsibility, this conference recommends that the policy of finding young men who are suitable from other missions be adopted by all missions, instead of allowing denominational barriers to stand between such young men and responsible positions." Link with this interdenominational declaration the action of the Provincial Council of the Anglican Church in India of last February, when it was agreed to submit to the National Assembly of the Church of England a measure designed to exclude the present jurisdiction in Indian ecclesiastical affairs of both the archbishop of Canterbury and the government, in order to give complete autonomy to the synods and assemblies, diocesan and provincial. The British union of Church and State—is this the rift in the lute? And simultaneously the committees of the Anglican and South Indian United churches, appointed to consider the union of churches in South India, are nearing a consummation that should stimulate the larger similar project in America.

Mass movements have puzzled the 1921 census takers when they found that entire villages, ten years ago animists or Hindus, now report themselves as all Christians. American Baptists immersed 1,000 a week, while all Protestants baptized 15,000 a month. Tho mainly recruited from the lower castes and untouchable outcastes,

Christians are gaining in influence as the more liberal attitude of the Government permits local elections. Thus in the newly constituted Legislative Council of Madras twenty former students of the Madras Christion College are members, one of them of cabinet rank. Three of the under-secretaries are its graduates. In Ceylon seven of the nine members recently elected are Christians, tho ninety per cent of the inhabitants are non-Christians.

"The tumult and the shouting dies;
    The captains and the kings depart."

Sept. 24—Turkey, Persia, Africa

TURK AND CHRISTIAN: The "unspeakable Turk" has become even more so in the last year, as trustworthy reports of atrocities, testified to by Dr. Ward and others in London and Washington and leading to a united investigation, very clearly prove. Hundreds of Christian churches in ruins or appropriated to secular purposes; an estimated million of Christians either slain openly or forced to trek their way to lands of death; missionaries, compelled to leave their stations as *personæ non gratæ* because of their devotion to Armenian and Greek Christians and their protests against massacre and persecution; schools and colleges closed and their native teachers often put to death; hospitals taken possession of and misused; Christian minorities but little considered in the peace terms with the Allies out of fear lest Moslem feelings would be stirred: these are some of the "clouds and thick darkness" of Turkish missions.

The silver lining of these clouds has been thus described in a *Missionary Review of the World* editorial: (1) Christian refugees have entered Russian Armenia, where they and the missionaries are conducting schools and establishing churches, thus influencing Bolshevists. (2) In occupying Smyrna and Saloniki the Greeks have come into direct contact with evangelical missionary work hitherto excluded from Greece, while the new Greek patriarch in Constantinople, recently from America, openly advocates affiliation with the Protestants. (3) The Allied occupation of Constantinople has made it a haven of safety for thousands of refugees who are open to the message of Christian love. The old missionary schools and colleges and others recently opened are meeting the eager desire of the varied elements present in that city. (4) The war has awakened the Turks, especially in Constantinople, to read. Bookshops supply new magazines and newspapers which are very popular. This has led to a survey of existing Christian literature and to plans for additional material suited to the new demands.

PROSTRATE PERSIA: During the recent Armageddon the greedy, avaricious eyes of Turkey, Russia, Germany, Britain, France, were fixt upon Irân, the ancient realm of Cyrus, Darius, and Xerxes. What they saw, however, a Presbyterian missionary there tells us:

"She who once had an army whose tread shook the world now cowers behind a few shabby soldiers with antiquated weapons and overdue wages. The people that once had a glorious literature, now has no poet. Once Persia was the leader in astronomy; now she has no star. With large cotton-growing areas, she is naked; with richly productive land, she is hungry; with God-given coal in her hills, she shivers with cold; with abundance of oil, she has no light; with mountains of minerals, she has no mines; and with eighteen hundred miles of seacoast, she has neither ships nor sailors, fisheries nor navy."

But the star of the Magi has not yet set. From Ararat to Meshed near the Afghan border and southward as far as Shiraz, where are buried the two famous poets, Sa'di and Hafiz, are the flaming or flickering lights of Persia's 66-branched candlestick. Urumiah's flame is quenched, fairest of all the candelabra; the Persian majority is war-weary; the Anglo-Persian agreement of August, 1919, is still unproductive of the development and reconstruction hoped for. Notwithstanding the eager desire for light —not the *mehr Licht!* of Goethe's expiring request, but Western science, history, economics, religion—is strong and hence mission schools are demanded, particularly for hitherto despised girls and young women. In Ispahan several new schools have been opened, one with 1,800 boys, while in Teheran, the capital, a Presbyterian school has 607. Among these are over twenty boys of the most influential classes, from a nephew of the recent regent and the son of the prime minister to the brothers of the leading editor—these sons of princes and potentates sharing in the school's management, government, and service. And Mr.

Allen of Urumiah writes hopefully: "A period of peace under the guidance of British officers will bring a development of the abundant natural resources of the land that will make Persia prosperous. The presence of British officers will insure safety to all, and a democratic spirit may even overcome the fanatical prejudice of Islam against other religions. Oppression will cease and sanitation, education, and development will progress."

ETHIOPIA'S OUTSTRETCHED HANDS: And what can one say of even negro Africa, omitting North Africa and Egypt? With the reassignment of German territory after the war, occupation ends and exploitation in the peaceful sense begins. Problems arise for both government overloads and missionaries, nowhere better set forth briefly than in J. H. Harris's *Africa: Slave or Free?* Climatically much of negro Africa is impossible for permanent white occupation. The African has simple needs and is no more enthusiastic about manual labor than white people. Some means must be found to set him at work, the corvée of feudalism and of Kongo Belge to-day being impracticable; tho had it not been for British missionary influence insisting upon a policy of trusteeship, it would have been followed last year in a modified form in Kenya Colony where possibilities of white residence and the desire to develop the land made the question more acute than in malaria-ridden Nigeria. The investigations and findings of the Phelps-Stokes fund in 1921, aided by the missionaries, will also do much to further the industrial and educational development of Africa. Meanwhile the vigorous methods of Christian social help, led by Ray Phillips in Johannesburg, the present storm-center of industrialism, and his appointment to keep the colored miners amused and contented during the incipient war there last winter, are other indications of the value of missionary influences in black Africa.

The sub-continent—south of the Zambezi and Cunene rivers—is full of negro unrest, due to many causes. Chief of these are a needed rise in wage to enable laborers to live under soaring prices of necessaries; the native land allotment, which is increasingly cramping where populations double in from twenty-five to thirty years, and especially in Orange Free State where recent legislation prevents negroes from buying land; the increased salaries of white teachers, while negro teachers are not similarly favored; and a host of color questions and problems. The war opened the eyes of multitudes of negroes who saw in France a kindlier attitude toward them than is known in Africa. The older Ethiopian movement fostered and led by men educated in America and the rise of Christian separatist movements—thirty-two in Johannesburg and sixty-three in Pretoria, for example—have spurred men on to religious revolts and opposition to white pastors and leaders. Hence our Marcus Garvey's "Black Republic" propaganda attracts attention when it promises the expulsion of the whites and their misrule; negro autonomy, with Garvey as Lord High Potentate; a black star fleet, with powerful armies bringing salvation and bags of grain to relieve poverty; and a motto which has reached backwood hamlets, "Ama Melika ayeza," The Americans are coming!

Kongo Belge had a most helpful conference of 103 delegates at Bolenge last November, when measures were adopted looking toward multiplied cooperative institutions, better and more plentiful literature, and the establishment of one *lingua franca* for the entire colony. The symptomatic craze of the year originated with a Baptist native, neurotic to a degree, who started the "prophet movement," which was stayed with his trial and death sentence, canceled by King Albert. In Kamerun, the Presbyterian work has been affected by the evil influences of the war, necessitating the exclusion of some 3,000; tho the statistics still show a communicant list of 25,883, with 34,500 catechumens and 99,366 adherents, and a single Efulen congregation recently counted, when 6,854 were present. Uganda and Livingstonia are little short of such records, after many years of Pentecostal growth. One of the most inspiring volumes of the year is W. P. Livingstone's account of *Dr Laws of Livingstonia*, one of the greatest records of individual missionary accomplishment ever published.

Sermonic Literature

GOOD NEWS[1]

CHARLES E. JEFFERSON, D.D., New York City

I propose to speak to-night on one little word: "gospel." That is my text, just "gospel." When you open your New Testament, it is about the first word your eyes fall on. The first book in that Testament is called a "gospel." Then, when you turn to the second book, again it is "gospel," only another version. The third book is also a "gospel," from yet another new view-point. The fourth book is called a "gospel," but is a gospel with shifted emphasis. But all the way along it is "gospel."

And when you begin to read these gospels you find that the central character is Jesus of Nazareth, and that he is always talking about the gospel. For instance, he stands up in the little synagog in Nazareth and quotes the passage from Isaiah and says, "The spirit of the Lord is upon me because he hath anointed me to preach the gospel. . . ." By and by John the Baptist sends asking him if he is indeed the Messiah. Jesus says, "You go and tell John the gospel is being preached." On a certain occasion a woman steals behind him and anoints his feet and head with perfume. Jesus' heart is soothed, and he says, "Wheresoever this gospel shall be preached in the whole world, there shall also this that this woman hath done be told for a memorial of her." At the very end of his life, before a cloud received him from men's sight, he said, "Now go and preach the gospel to the whole creation." That word "gospel" was always on his lips.

When you leave the gospels and come to the epistles you can hardly turn a page of Paul's letters without finding the word. "Woe is me," he says, "if I preach not the gospel." To the Romans, people he has never seen, he says, "I am not ashamed of the gospel." To his Galatian friends he says, "Though we, or an angel from heaven, preach any other gospel unto you than that which we have preached unto you, let him be accursed." When he is an old man in prison, owning nothing, he feels himself rich because he possesses the gospel of the Blessed God. Everywhere, then, in the New Testament we find ourselves reading of "the gospel." In the very last book we find an angel in the midst of heaven entrusted with the everlasting gospel which shall be preached to all nations.

But now the question comes: What is meant by "the gospel"? That is a significant thing, is it not?—that a word may become so familiar that it becomes smooth, so smooth that it slips through the mind without scratching the mind, without leaving any mark behind it. It is possible to speak a word so many times that it seems to paralyze the feeling, the nerves of the understanding, so that we do not know what it means. Now every boy in the congregation to-night knows that this word translated "gospel" means good news. I would suggest that it might be well for us just for a month or so to drop the word "gospel" from the New Testament and substitute the words "good news." It would light up many a page. For instance it would do ministers good, I think—at least, some ministers—if they would call themselves not ministers of the gospel, but ministers of the good news. That might save a minister from becoming gloomy. It might prevent him from dwelling too much on the somber side of life. If every Sunday on his way to church he would say to himself, "Now I am a preacher of good news," he might become more radiant in his utterances. I think it would be a good thing for laymen, too, to remember that the gospel means good news and that it is their business in this world to tell the

[1] Preached at the City Temple, London (June), and specially reported for THE HOMILETIC REVIEW.

[231]

good news. In the book of the Acts we are told that the Christians, when they were scattered broadcast from Jerusalem, went everywhere "preaching the gospel." I am very sorry it is so translated, because that makes the task which they performed seem to be something more arduous than anything we could profitably attempt. Preaching the gospel: that is an elaborate sort of business that only experts can engage in. Ah, but simplify it. What did they do? They did not stand in pulpits and give literary dissertations, they did not indulge in heavy theological discussions. No, they went everywhere telling the good news, and that is exactly what every Christian is in this world to do. Everybody can do it. No matter whether a man is educated or not, he can do that. He can tell good news. There is nothing in this world easier than that. Everyone of you knows that if you have been in possession of news that was very good it simply leapt out from your mouth. There was no effort at all. We are in this world to tell the good news. It is the chief business of every Christian.

And is that not, too, the work of the Church? When we come together in great missionary meetings, we are always thinking of how we can perfect our methods of carrying the gospel to distant lands. Yes, and that is the work of the Church in the great city: to tell the city the good news. A church is no church at all if it is gloomy. A church has lost touch with God if it is not radiant.

Now I think we are living in a time when it is specially important that the Church of Jesus Christ should tell good news. The newspapers have a different sort of mission. Their mission is to chronicle the happenings of the passing day and it falls to their lot to tell a good deal of news that is bad. For instance there is a crime of which everybody is talking. A girl is murdered, her body is found under a bush, and you read all about it in one paper, in two, in three, in four—you can hardly help seeing all the tragic details. An accident happens, and it must go into the paper. Was it not last August that a great airship collapsed and tumbled into the Humber, snuffing out forty-four lives? Why our American papers were filled for a week with accounts of that awful catastrophe.

Miseries, too, are reported. A home disintegrates, husband and wife can not live together—that goes into the papers. Hundreds of thousands of people are starving in Russia. That, of course, must go into the papers. So, day after day, we are compelled to read news that is bad. All the more necessary is it therefore that the minister of Jesus Christ, that the Church of the Son of God, should deal in news that is good.

Now the question comes: What is the news about? My answer would be: It is, first of all, about God. In the second place, it is about man. These are the two great subjects of the Bible. I am not going to think with you tonight about the good news concerning God. We may deal with that at some future time. To-night I want to discuss with you the good news concerning man. My reason for choosing this subject first is that we are living in a time when we need good news about man. The Great War lasted for fifteen hundred days, and during that long period we lived in a chamber of horrors. Every day we heard news that was bad; some new atrocity, some new cruelty, some new disaster. Even on the days when news of victory came bad news came too. Yes, there was bad news from the firing of the first gun to the firing of the last. And since the war was ended the news has not become much better. Indeed, in some respects it has even grown worse. During the war there was a certain idealism. Men and women lived at a high level, and dared to dream of beautiful things that were coming to pass with the dawn of peace. So much of that idealism has now passed away. Human nature is showing itself in such ugly forms, there is so much greed, there is so much profiteering in all centuries, that many men have grown pessimistic, and multitudes are saying, Who will show us any good?

Well, it is because that is the prevailing mood in so many circles that I thought it would be profitable for us to-night to think about the good news concerning man. I have five items of news which comprise, I think, on the whole, what the New Testament has to tell us about man.

The first item of good news is this: The deepest thing in man is something fine. The New Testament never blinks the facts.

It does not deal with human nature, as many sentimentalists do, saying that it is altogether beautiful, that everybody is very eager to be good, that everybody would be good if only they had the chance. No, the New Testament never talks in that fashion. Listen to what the Master says. He understood the human heart as no other man has ever understood it. "Out of the heart proceed evil thoughts, murders, adulteries, fornications, thefts, false witness, blasphemies"—you know the list. All that brood of devils comes out of the heart. No, Jesus understood what was in man and he never taught sentimentalism. But he said of a man out of whose heart such devils came that when such a man came to himself he said, "I will arise and go to my father and will say unto him, Father, I have sinned against heaven and before thee." The deepest thing in that man was beautiful. He had acted the fool. Nevertheless, when he came to his true self he said, I am going home. Our Lord, right at the end of his life, knowing that he would soon hang upon the cross, said, "I, if I be lifted up, will draw all men unto me." That is to say, when they see the exhibition of love, they will respond. He knew what was in man. He knew that the deepest thing in human nature is fine. If the deepest thing in man were black, then the future is hopeless; but if the deepest thing in man is white, then all the future is shot through with golden fire. If the deepest thing in man is devil, then we are on the way to the abyss; but if the deepest thing in man is angel then we are on the way to the promised land. That is the first item of good news.

Here is the second: Every man can change himself. There are many people, of course, who are always insisting that it is impossible to change human nature. I have heard even Christians contend that you can not change human nature; that human nature always has been and always is going to be what it is now. Oh, what nonsense! Why, human nature is the very thing that can be changed. Human nature is the very thing our Lord says must be changed. When he talks with Nicodemus, what does he say? "You must be born again." When the old man asks for an explanation he does not get any explanation. He gets only a reaffirmation of what was

said before, "You must be born again. That is the fundamental fact. It is not for you to argue about it. It is for you to accept it. You can be changed, from the very root up. Your life can be changed, from the fountain down." That is the teaching of our religion. Anybody who has any doubt concerning the ability of human nature to change ought to read Mr. Harold Begbie's book, *Twice-born Men*, where he gathers together, as you know, a great number of men, adulterers, drunkards, gamblers, thieves, who by the magical touch of the Son of God have become new men. So, if man is in a rut, he need not stay there. He can get out. If a man has a bad disposition, he can change it. If he has an unruly temper, he can curb it. Is not that good news? That is the gospel. That is the message the Church has to proclaim. Everybody can change.

Then there is a third item. Man can conquer all his enemies. He can defeat them, every one. Nothing can permanently thwart his progress. Within the last fifty years we have heard a good deal about environment and heredity. Environment means surroundings, and, we are told, the surroundings determine the character and fix the destiny. To be sure, environment has its influences. It leaves its mark upon a man. But it is not the determining factor. Why should we be fatalists, we who are the followers of Jesus Christ? Other people are always insisting that heredity is the determining factor, that everything depends upon the blood, upon your ancestors, in regard to what you are, what you are going to be. Of course it counts for much, but it does not count for all. Abraham Lincoln was brought up in a western forest in an environment that was hostile, with a shiftless father and a commonplace mother, with nothing great in the corpuscles of his blood, but he rose to become the great American. Everybody can conquer all the opposing forces.

And the fourth item of good news is this: Nothing can hurt a man but himself. Any man can hurt himself, but nobody else can hurt him. Jesus, when he sent out his disciples to preach, said: They will arrest you, they will whip you, they will put you in jail, some of you will lose your lives. That does not matter. Nobody is going to harm you. Nobody is going to curtail your vitality.

Nobody will put limits to the range and the reach of your personality. Nobody is going to subtract from the sum total of your joy. Go on and do your work, and you will get your reward. Nothing can be done that is fine that does not receive recognition at the hands of the king of heaven. It may be a cup of cold water only, but the heavens will open and God's blessing will come down. That is the fourth item of good news.

And the fifth, and last, is this: Death does not take from us anything that is worth keeping. Death is an incident only in the process of an unfolding life. Death is a shadow that falls athwart the current of a flowing stream. Death is the opening of a door that gives the soul a chance to exhibit its powers on a higher level. O death, where is thy sting? O grave, where is thy victory? Thanks be unto God who hath given us the victory through our Lord Jesus Christ.

Therefore, my beloved brethren, be ye stedfast, unmovable, always abounding in the work of the Lord, forasmuch as your labor is not in vain in the Lord.

IS THE IDEALLY RIGHT POSSIBLE[1]

R. J. CAMPBELL, D.D., London, England

Who knoweth whether thou art called to the kingdom for such a time as this?—Esther 4:14.

A few days ago I received a letter, apparently from a man in middle life. He wrote about the omissions of the pulpit. One of the great omissions, he said, was that we preachers did not give sufficient help in what he called the practical moral difficulties of life. He found himself between the devil and the deep sea. If he did what he felt he would like to do and what conscience would tell him, other things being equal, he ought to do, well, he would be removed from his position and someone would take it who had not the same scruples that he had. So the last state would be worse than the first, and the harm done to his family would be irretrievable.

Answering that letter, I took occasion to point out that there is not a single individual anywhere in the world who is not having to compromise every day he lives with what, in the abstract, he knows to be right and just. It may be a man's bounden duty to do just that. There is no material good we enjoy, any of us, under present conditions, which has not been obtained at the cost of injustice somewhere, yet we can not refuse to partake if we would live at all. There is something like tragedy in the situation. One man's duty to his country may place him in the battle-field face to face with another man who has obeyed a similar mandate. The same thing holds good in

commercial and industrial life, as you know only too well, some of you. A man's duty to his family may compel him to compete with others. As things are, there is no help for it. Cooperation is the ideal, not competition; but while we are on the way to what we may hope will be a better state of things, it is our plain and simple duty perhaps to those dependent upon us to accept a very unideal situation for the time being.

That applies to everybody. Do what we will, while human society remains as it is every member thereof finds himself in the position of having to do (shall I say?) as his task—I will go further and say, as his duty, in the concrete what in the abstract he knows is not of the highest. There is such a thing as a duty of compromise—so long as you do not compromise with your back to the light.

But once we see this clearly, another consideration emerges and thrusts itself upon our view. That is the question when the point may be said to be reached in a man's experience at which he ought to refuse all compromise on some particular issue, and abide the consequences. That there is such a point hardly anybody would dare to deny. No one can fix it for any one else. You must not make me your conscience. I can not fix the point for you. Every man must stand alone in taking the final decision, and reckon only with God. The moment comes when all personal security, all reputation, all in-

[1] Reported for THE HOMILETIC REVIEW.

fluence, has to be staked in the cause of truth. There is nothing then to be done but to venture everything on one simple moral issue which God has shown, or else to stand forever self-condemned. That is the way in which the world's moral advance has always been made. There is a legend of an Indian prince who refused to enter upon a war because he knew he would have to take sides against some who were near and dear to him. According to the story, a divine visitor appeared to this prince and said to him:

If, knowing thy task, thou bidst the
task go by,
That shall be sin in thee.

It is only too easy to compromise from cowardly motives. Life is so hard a struggle for most people that few dare to take more risks than they are obliged. You can not help noticing how few people in these days are willing to shoulder personal responsibility in matters that affect the public good. Something in human nature makes us very unwilling to encounter the hostile opinion of the society to which we belong. It takes a good deal of faith and independence of character to make a man willing to do that and to carry it right through. The world is very cruel to failure, and most pioneer work looks like failure. Men like John Wycliffe who refused compromise were the fore-runners of men like Morris and Kingsley. Wycliffe saw further and deeper than many of the reformers who succeeded where he failed. Without the work of his "poor preachers" Puritanism would never have taken root in our country. There were some heroic pioneers among the Anabaptists who declined resolutely to compromise with the secular power. Four hundred years ago one of these said, "A society which contains rich and poor is not a Christian society." What do you think of that? Another of these old thinkers said, "The nation which fears God ought to have no hungry mouths to feed and should not know lords and vassals, but only brothers." Ah, when the great day of revelation comes, and you and I know as we are known, we shall have to come face to face with very many whose names we never heard who perished because the golden scepters of secular power were not held out to them, whose failure, however, has done more for mankind than all the triumphs of celebrated men.

In one of Mr. Bernard Shaw's plays, Major Barbara (and I must say they are very clever plays, tho I confess Mr. Shaw irritates me about as much as any one in this country), there is an amusing scene in which a milksop son undertakes to lecture his father, a manufacturer of explosives, on right and wrong. The family are scandalized, they say, by the way in which the father makes his money, tho they do not hesitate to benefit by it. "What!" says the father to the son, "you say you have discovered the secret of right and wrong —and at twenty-four! You must be a genius, a god!" The son, you see, did not grasp the fact that there is no absolute right and wrong. They are relative terms. What it is right for you to do to-day, may be wrong in some future day, when society is adjudged differently. It is ideally right that nations should live at peace with each other, that every man should seek to enrich the life of his brother man. Yet, as things are, we know how a Prussian horde was let loose in Belgium, and if a thing like that happened again, nobody could convince me that it was not my duty to defend my child from torture and shame if I could. The ideally right would be impossible.

Yet there comes a point at which you know the ideally right asserts itself and demands at all costs that it be honored and obeyed. We live in a very unideal, a very disappointing time. In 1914 we saw the nation rise to a great height; since then we have suffered a bitter disillusionment. Yet without any of the incentives to high endeavor which you had then, opportunity is waiting at your door. Is this a sordid, a selfish time? Now is your time to play the man!

Under the present system you may feel that the ideally right is not possible; that you must keep your position, tho the ideally right may be that you and those who govern you ought not to be thinking of profit at all, and you should not exploit your brother, but should minister to him. But one day a specific crisis emerges, and you are up against it. You are required to cheat, to lie, to do some foul thing, some mean or cruel thing, to debase your manhood in order that you may keep your position. You must do it or go. You feel your dismissal would not help matters.

Well, my dear lad, it seems a hard thing to say, especially if there are others whom your decision will affect. It is harder to hurt those we love than to take the hurt ourselves. Which mother here would not have gone to Belgium or France willingly to sacrifice herself if she could have spared her boy? That is where the hard part comes. But you will know. God will tell you what to do. The system may crush you; perhaps it will. "Who knoweth whether thou art come to the kingdom for such a time as this?" If no one challenges the cruelty of any particular system which has power to afflict the human race, it will not change by itself. Take your stand. You will know when the moment comes, and what for you is ideally right will not be silenced. Do not fail at that moment. All heaven will be watching what you do.

THE GLORY OF THE CROSS[1]

God forbid that I should glory save in the cross of our Lord Jesus Christ.—Gal. 6:14.

After much discussion and prolonged argument about things not easy to understand, this is the conclusion Paul reaches. Is it a sane conclusion?

Is the apostle level-headed or flighty in his determination to glory in the cross? Is his statement sound sense or a spasm of hysterics? No doubt the great majority of the people of his day thought Paul beside himself. In deference to public opinion, he himself seems to admit it, when he declares: "I have become a fool in glorying."

Then the cross was a badge of shame. It was a stone of stumbling and a rock of offense. The world regarded it very much as we now regard the gallows. It was a mark of infamy, a symbol of the penalty for the worst of crimes. It was the fate society visited on those who were too dangerous to be kept in prison, and too bad to be allowed to live. There is no glory in this sort of thing. We would call the man crazy who would boast of the gallows, who would take pride in suffering the severest penalty the law inflicts on red-handed transgression. If this is what Paul means, he has worse than hysterics. It is not what he means.

He had seen the cross in the light of Calvary, haloed with the love which redeems the world, consecrated by the sufferings not of a criminal, but of a Savior, who makes bad people good, rights wrong, comforts sorrow, and banishes evil from the world. He saw the cross as the symbol of the sufferings of God for his wayward and wandering children. He heard there the call of the Father for his own. He beheld the cross, not as the symbol of the penalty society inflicts on the worst, but as a token of the sufferings of the holiest and best to save the worst. He saw it as Christ had transformed it into a sign of heroic self-sacrifice, and he said: "I glory in that!"

Is this the boast of a crazy man? Is it wild and fanatical? Is it flighty and hysterical? Is it the mood of a man whose emotions have swept him from the moorings of sound judgment and ordinary sanity?

What is more glorious than true heroism and real sacrifice? The world worships heroism. The religion of the people is still hero worship, and it is not a bad religion. It would be a tame, stale world were heroism and sacrifice to go out of fashion, were deeds that are daring, dangerous, and difficult no longer to be applauded.

It is simply the glory of heroism, of dangerous and daring adventure, that the world worships to-day,—now of a man who flies in an airship, now of a crew who cross the ocean in a submarine, again of an explorer who three centuries ago pushed out into the wide, wild, trackless sea in a frail boat, and again of those who fight their way through fields of arctic ice and across perilous leads to the top of the world. The story of Hendrik Hudson is not the story of a man discovering a river. Anybody might do that. The discovery of the North River was a mere incident of Hudson's career. The real story is that of a bold explorer who adventured an unknown world ocean on a tiny craft and died at last on the frozen sea in quest of a northwest passage.

[1] In *The Breaking of the Bread*. By James I. Vance. Fleming Revell Company, New York, 1922.

The glory of the bold explorers who over and again hold the center of the stage as the world listens to their story of hardship and heroism in quest of the earth's poles is not that they have added anything to the world's wealth or happiness. They have opened no new continent whither the downtrodden and opprest of earth may flee for refuge. They have made no valuable contribution to the solution of the great problems of government and trade and social life. The world admires them because they have done or seem to have done a hard thing. They have been daring enough to jeopardize life in a difficult enterprise.

This on a divine scale is the fascination of the cross of Christ. The cross is the world's finest symbol of heroism. It is the highest expression of the life laid down. It is the loftiest standard of unselfish service and sacrifice.

The cross is more than this. It does not stand for mere spectacular sacrifice, for ordinary newspaper heroism, for a barren exploit ending in fireworks and a dinner party. Calvary is not stagy. Its publicity is not intentional but incidental. Jesus did not die just to be dying. He died to bless people, to make the bad good, to heal the open sore of the world and banish evil from mankind. There is no such heroism as that of the Man of Galilee, and the thought of it down the ages has been stirring the sluggish pulses of a dying world, and lifting men to high ideals and noble deeds. Little wonder that one of the greatest and best of men should say: "God forbid that I should glory save in the cross of our Lord Jesus Christ!"

What Christianity needs to-day is a fresh infusion of the heroic. It has grown soft and flabby with success. A cheap religion will never save the world. Ease and self-indulgence can not speak to men in the tones of Calvary. The religion of the future, like the religion of the past, will be hero worship.

The cross stands for the heroism of God, who did not spare himself in the hardest thing ever attempted by God or man. Paul was not glorying in his own cross. He was not proud of crosses, of petty trials, of daily vexations. It was the cross of Christ that held him. It was that cross on the lonely hilltop where hung one who

being God became man, who tho rich became poor, who took the great world up into his heart, who having lived the sweetest, fairest life, died the saddest and the most shameful death just to help people, to comfort them and save them from despair.

Paul says: "This is the thing in which I glory, and God forbid that I should glory in anything else!" I think he had his wits about him. We can afford to be enthusiastic over the cross. If there is anything glorious, it is the cross. If there is anything worth living for and giving to and dying for, it is the cross. If there is aught to which we may proclaim allegiance without a blush, to which we may anchor our eternal hopes without a fear, it is the cross. Glorious cross! "All the light of sacred story gathers round its head sublime!"

The holy communion is the Church's solemn applause of the cross. In the sacrament of the Lord's Supper we commend the sacrificial heroism of the world's Redeemer. If we are sincere as we take the bread and wine, it is just a way we have of saying: "God forbid that I should glory save in the cross of our Lord Jesus Christ!" Save in the heroism and sacrifice of him who died to find me, who gave his life to discover my lost soul amid the barren wilds! Have we made the vow? Are we praying, not for ease or success, but for a soul great enough to appreciate Calvary? The communion is the call to get away from the shop and mart and desk and tools and little time plans, and survey the wondrous cross on which the Savior gave his life. As that cross casts its spell over us, "our richest gains we count but loss, and pour contempt on all our pride."

Let us understand that glorying, to be genuine, must be more than a phrase. For one to say, "I glory," means far more than for him to say, "I approve; I am pleased; I am proud; I boast." It is comparatively easy to do that with Calvary. It is not hard to stand off and gaze at it and say fine things about it, and say it is wonderful, it is great and glorious. But that is not what Paul meant. He meant, "I am ready to be offered; I yearn to experience the cross." Glory is a word for character. When a man says: "God forbid that I should glory save in the cross," he is praying that the cross may become a personal experience.

We are beginning now to see what he meant. He was dead in earnest. He was making a great vow that he could pay only with his life. Am I ready to make it, and in the same great way? God forbid that I should seek a life of ease, of selfishness, of vain pleasures, of worldly fame and gaudy show! God forbid that I should draw back at hardship, or protest at self-denial! There stands the cross. Let me experience it. Let me taste its passions.

Let me be swayed by its power. Let me live it and prove its reality.

It is not easy. It is easy to sing: "In the cross of Christ I glory," but to live that song is not easy. May God grant grace to live it! In the hallowed hush of a mystic communion with him who has made the hated cross the radiant symbol of the world's sublimest heroism and holiest sacrifice, may my halting lips try to make the prayer of the cross! "God forbid that I should glory save in the cross of our Lord Jesus Christ!"

THE MIND OF THE PRODIGAL

The Rev. HARRY PRESCOTT PATTERSON, Granville Ferry, N. S.

The case of the younger son who became "prodigal" should not be prejudiced by the exercise of his natural desire and right to journey to the far country. The far country of itself was not that bad place where only the riotous live and selfish and supercilious pork-growers batten on the misfortunes of their employees. It is not a land cursed by famine and distress and carob-pods.

The far country is the psychologic creation of every normally minded youth. He is bound on that journey if he is to express the truth that is within him. It is the land of his dreams. It is a wonderland he visualizes, and must visit if the powers with which God has endowed him are to function properly.

The far country is a land where the unearned increment of character is realized. Was not the proverb confirmed by our Master: A prophet is not without honor save in his own country and among his own kin? It is where folks accept one at face value and the incentive of their trust makes for laudable enterprise. It is where opportunity is raised to the nth power.

The lure of the far country is markedly an adolescent experience. It occurs at that glorious period when there is the adjustment and amplification of life; when restlessness must have vent in physical, mental, and religious activities, else morbidities of all sorts will follow. Assuredly youth is traveling somewhere in his own consciousness. It is not to be charged to his dis-

credit that he sets his eyes toward the faraway country. He is motivated by the impact of ideals, the urge of ambition, the thrill of new possibilities, a passion for novelty, and the love of adventure. He feels the majesty and mystery of millenniums of subtle racial forces at work within his personality, impelling him to grand achievement. It signifies a personal response to the spirit of progress inherent in the race.

The way the story turns out, it would seem as tho the choice of the younger son in going to the far country was unwise. He became "prodigal," but that was a matter that can not be attributed to the fact of his going. It is not just to impute the loss of visions and ideals and control to the far country. Environment is not a magic word to minimize or extenuate delinquencies. What we should allow is the legitimacy of his choice to journey to the far country. That he acted within his right is evident from the fact that the father made no protest on his going, and on his return did not chide him for having gone; moreover, we may observe that the elder son was not any the better for having remained at home, for he exhibited, if not as gross sins, as deadly sins as the prodigal. The lesson lies in the fact of his moral failure. He set forth as one of King Arthur's knights of the round table, with purity and strength, and with all the signs of a heroic soul on a great and noble quest; but he came back a woful object of pity in dejection and disgrace. He had foolishly thrown to the winds good habits, moral restraints, and discipline that would have ensured him success and respectability; but instead he suffered impoverishment of life and reaped a whirlwind of inanities and tortures of dissipation and broken law.

We deplore the far country experience of the prodigal. It proved to be a sorry experiment in social adjustment. It was also a departure from his true self—a case of arrested development. He put on a mask of self-deception that served to prostitute his fine qualities to ignoble uses. But who has not felt the blight of confounding appearance for reality? And who can measure the immensities of that pregnant phrase for all prodigals. But when he came to himself! It was the prodigal's first step toward self-realization. And here the story takes a happy turn.

It was the dawn of a brighter day when the true self of the prodigal was given a chance of asserting itself. This seems not to have been possible until he had endured a certain degree of distress and discomfort. However this may be, the chief interest of the narrative consists in the endeavor to revive normal interests, feelings, and capacities—to restore the spirit of youth. A realinement of life is essential. All the paraphernalia and devices of a revival must function to accomplish the reconciliation and reclamation of the prodigal. Revivalism is the sort of re-education that should be employed only with prodigals. Let us picture the scene. Beside the swine troughs he framed in his soliloquy a confession that savors of servility—"make me as one of thy hired servants," he says. But the father heaped upon him on his return every evidence of sonship. He gave him the paternal sign of affection, a kiss! He directed the servants to bring the former robe of distinction and dignity, and put on the signet ring of honor, and the shoes which are for sons, not sandals which were for servants. Then followed the feast, the music, and the dance. There was much ado, but it was all as necessary as it was sincere. The purpose was to exorcize the spirit of degradation and servility that now possest the prodigal and to release restorative powers within him. An "instinctive social endowment" had impelled him to seek reinstatement in human society under more favorable conditions. The father encouraged this. The

father saw what no other man saw, viz., the possibilities of a second chance. Certainly his elder brother did not see much good in him. The father took that poor spent life, exhausted by famine and want and sin, with but a fraction of its former beauty and strength, enfolded it, and warmed it with his love, and tended it back to vigor and virtue.

O Love that will not let me go
I rest my weary soul on thee;
I give thee back the life I owe,
That in thine ocean depths its flow
  May richer, fuller be.

To be noted is the value of music and festivity for the reorganization of the individual. The divided self becomes unified and peaceful. It serves to bring him en-rapport with his surroundings. Life expands and is renewed under a joyous experience. The devils of illusionment, servility, and pessimism must be effectually driven out. The prodigal can then sit clothed, and in his right mind. He has been beside himself. He has come to himself. It is manifestly desirable that he should remain so.

I wish there were some wonderful place,
  Called The Land of Beginning Again,
Where all our mistakes, and all our heart-
  aches,
  And all our poor selfish grief
Could be dropt, like a shabby old coat at
  the door,
  And never put on again.

The prodigal has had a sorry time of it, and now enters The Land of Beginning Again with hope and resolution. It is not an easy land to enter. It requires humility, confession, and repentance because of the misdeeds of the past. It also requires courage and perseverance for a man handicapped by a sense of failure and inferiority before a man arrives. A man can not spend his substance in riotous living without paying the penalty of impoverishment of life. The marvel of it all is that God has given unworthy prodigals the privilege of beginning again: therein consists the genius of the gospel.

Memories of home cast a lingering radiance along the pathway of life. A man is reluctant to see his ideals fade away. A man is not liable to yield to despair when there are those at home who believe in him. "It is certain," says Novalis, "my conviction gains infinitely the moment another will believe in it." In dire distress, homesick and heartsick, the prodigal turns his thoughts toward the father. He can surely rely upon the magnanimous trust of the father toward him. It is pertinent to notice that nothing short of the unquestionable support of the father in such an extremity could have accomplished the fixation of conviction necessary, not only for the initiatory stages of a converted life, but also for the later development of that life.

Dr. J. H. Jowett quotes to good purpose, in a brief sketch of the prodigal, the words of another. He says:

I like these human words of Mr. Morrison. "He saw the farm embosomed among the hills, and the weary oxen coming home at eventide, and the happy circle gathered round the fire, and his father crying to heaven for the wanderer. His crown of sorrow was remembering happier things. He came to himself and was homesick." Then, Dr. Jowett adds: And this homesickness of the soul is God-sickness, a longing for reconciliation and communion with the Father—God.

Dr. R. F. Horton, in an article entitled, The Homesickness of the Heart, after drawing attention to two phrases: the first, "the exile of the heart," taken from Kempis' *Imitation of Christ*: the second, a remark of Rothe, namely, that "philosophy is homesickness," proceeds to illustrate the meaning of these phrases by a description of Mr. Swan's painting in the Tate Gallery of the forlorn figure of the prodigal.

If you will spend a little time in contemplating that figure, ragged and weatherstained, which sits with back turned to you by the swine trough, and his eyes presumably lifted to the rift of sky in the heavy heavens, if you will let the forlornness grip your heart, and then the subtle hope steal into it,—the hope which, after all, is the dominant note of it all, you will have a fair sensation if not a full understanding of what is meant by the exile of the heart, and by the homesickness which is designated philosophy—a philosophy that is the mind's protest against the tyranny of sense.

Nothing but a home-reception can cure the nostalgia of the soul. By his return home he hoped to achieve his freedom.

The prominence that confession is given in the conversion of the prodigal is significant. No doubt the very appearance of the prodigal was a confession—the outward and visible sign of an inward struggle toward self-realization. But there must be more than that. The very statement of our complaint and unworthiness and wretchedness results in bringing definitely before our consciousness the heinous nature of our sin, and a clarification of thought and feeling that is wholesome and restorative. Prof. W. E. Hocking of Harvard University says: "This merely formal conceiving of the facts of one's own wretchedness is at the same time a departure from them—placing them in the object." This psychological process is objectified, and conveys an ethical meaning when it is transmuted into action. The process of confession acts as a psycho-therapeutic agency, a catharsis by which tension and strain and conflict are relieved and resolved by bringing to consciousness facts that have been suppressed. Dr. George A. Coe, the well-known psychologist and authority in religious phenomena, ventures the opinion that to bottle up one's experience as merely private is morbid, but he asserts that "there are plenty of occasions when the road to poise, freedom, and joy is that of social sharing," hence, "the prayer of confession, not only because it helps us to see ourselves as we are, but also because it shares our secrets with another, has great value for organizing the self."

We would like to have a complete account of the prodigal, but a Christian theology demands a triumphant conclusion of his life. No doubt, the next ten years were a sustained and consistent effort to regain the untold losses of those prodigal years. It was a loss so difficult of reparation that nothing less could suffice. He was compelled to overcome a feeling of ostracism, and all that dead weight of uncharitable influence that is held against an outcast. The power of divine grace is as truly wonderful as it is spectacular in the case of sudden conversion, but its quiet energy in the ordinary course of the Christian life is equally effective and comforting. It is the heart of Christianity that men can be saved from the power of sin. Thanks be unto God who giveth us the victory through our Lord Jesus Christ.

THE LIFE BEYOND[1]

Death is a very small thing in comparison with what comes after it—that wonderful, wonderful, wonderful world into which death ushers us. Turn away from the face of your dead. Turn away from the house of clay which held him an hour ago. The house is empty, the tenant is gone. He is away already, gasping in the unutterable wonder of the new experience.

"Oh change! stupendous change!
There lies the soulless clod.
The light eternal breaks,
The new immortal wakes,
Wakes with his God!"

Oh, the wonder of it to him at first! Years ago I met with a story in a sermon by Canon Liddon. An old Indian officer was telling of his battles—of the Indian Mutiny, of the most striking events in his professional career; and as he vividly described the skirmishes and battles and sieges and hairbreadth escapes, his audience hung breathless in sympathy and excitement. At last he paused; and to their expressions of wonderment he quietly replied, "I expect to see something much more wonderful than that." As he was over seventy, and retired from the service, his listeners looked up into his face with surprize. There was a pause; and then he said, in a solemn undertone, "I mean in the first five minutes after death."

The story caught on to me instantly. That has been for years my closest feeling. I feel it at every death-bed as the soul passes through. I believe it will be my strongest feeling when my own death-hour comes—eager, intense, glad curiosity about the new, strange world opening before me.

As soon as we try to peer further into the vista beyond we are up against a difficulty. Our thoughts must be confused unless at starting we make clear distinction between:

(i) Those who have died in the fear and love of God; and

(ii) Those for whom we are afraid.

Here we shall assume that our departed one died in Christ's faith and fear. Later we shall think of the others.

What can we know about him? We can know little or nothing about his outward environment. Even if we were told in words, we have no experience to help us in realizing it.

Imagine yourself trying to tell a blind, deaf man about the lovely sunset or the music of the birds. We, shut up in these human bodies, are the blind, deaf men in God's glorious universe. Some of our comrades have moved into the new life beyond, where the eyes of the blind are opened and the ears of the deaf are unstopt. But we have no power of even imagining what their wondrous experience is like.

I suppose that is the reason why we have no description of paradise or heaven except in earthly imagery of golden streets and gates of pearl. I suppose that is why St. Paul could not utter what he saw when in some trance condition he was caught up into paradise. I suppose, too, that was why Lazarus could tell nothing of his marvelous four days in the unseen.

Be content, then, with what you can know. Don't cry for the moon. Follow your departed in thought and realize what Scripture teaches you about him.

What are we taught about him?

First that it is a vivid, conscious life into which he has gone.

There are some passages in Scripture which speak of death as sleep, and which taken alone might suggest a long unconsciousness, a sort of Rip Van Winkle life, sleeping thousands of years and waking up in a moment at the judgment day, feeling as if there had been no interval between. But a little thought will show it is a mere figure of speech taken from the sleeping appearance of the body. "The sleep of death" is a very natural expression to use as one looks on the calm, peaceful face after life's fitful fever and the long pain and sickness of the death-bed. But no one can study the Bible references to the life beyond without seeing that it cannot be a life of sleep or unconsciousness. "Shall we sleep between death and the judgment?" asks Tertullian. "Why souls do not sleep even when men are alive. It is the province of bodies to sleep." This

[1] From *On the Rim of the World*, by J. Paterson-Smyth, Fleming H. Revell Company, New York, 1922.

sleep theory has always been condemned whenever the Church has pronounced on it. Even the Reformers declare it at variance with Holy Scripture, in spite of the strong feeling in its favor in their day.

You who have followed thus far need no proof as to the teaching of Scripture that the waiting life before the judgment into which your dear ones have gone is no unconscious sleep, but a real, vivid, conscious life. So vivid that our Lord's spirit is said to have been quickened, made more alive, as he passed in. So vivid that the men of the old world could listen to his preaching. So vivid that Moses and Elias —those eager, impetuous leaders—in that wondrous life could not be held by its bonds, but broke through to stand on the mountains with Christ a thousand years after their death. So vivid that Lazarus (whom our Lord describes as in Abraham's bosom) is depicted as living a full, clear, intelligent life, and Dives as thinking anxiously about his five brothers on earth.

That was surely no unconscious life which St. Paul saw when he was caught up into paradise and heard unspeakable things, nor was it a blank unconsciousness that he looked for in his desire 'to depart and be with Christ which is far better" (Phil. 1:23).

Or glance again at the story of our Lord and the thief on the cross. "To-day," said Jesus, "thou shalt be with me." To-night, when our dead bodies are hanging upon the cross, you and I will be together. Which surely means we shall be conscious of each other as the two who hung dying together on Calvary.

Beyond all question God has revealed to you plainly enough that your beloved has gone into a full, vivid, conscious life. He is more alive to-day than he ever was on earth.

What follows? This. If I am fully conscious, what am I conscious of? Surely first of all I must be conscious of myself, conscious of the continuity of my personal identity, conscious of the continuity of my personal character. I must feel that I am the same "I," I am still "myself." You remember what our Lord said from the other side of the grave: "Handle me and see, it is I myself."

It is I myself, the very same self. It is they themselves, the very same selves

whom I loved and who loved me so dearly. In that solemn hour after death, believe it, your boy, your wife, your husband, who is experiencing the startling revelations of the new life, is feeling that life is an unbroken continuance of the life begun on earth. Only the environment is changed. He feels himself the same boy or man that he was an hour ago, with the same character, aspirations, desires, the same love and courage and hope. But oh, with what a different view of all things! How clearly he recognizes God's love and holiness! How clearly he sees himself—his whole past life! If he ever cared for Christ and his will, how longingly, wonderingly, he is reaching out to him! If he ever loved you tenderly on earth, how deeply and tenderly he is loving you to-day!

What else have you learned? That he remembers clearly the old life and the old home and the old comrades and the old scenes on earth. There is no conjecturing about that. That goes without saying if "I" am the same "I" in that world. Personal identity, of course, postulates memory which binds into one the old life and the new. And the Bible takes that for granted. We saw that Lazarus remembered Dives, and Dives remembered Lazarus and remembered his old home and the five young brothers who grew up with him. He remembers that they have grown to be selfish men like himself, and is troubled for them. And Abraham assumes it as a matter of course: "My son, remember that thou in thy lifetime," etc. Our Lord comes back from death remembering all the past as if death made no chasm at all in his memory. "Go and meet me in Galilee," he says. "Lo, I have told you" (before I died). The redeemed in the future life are represented as remembering and praising God, who had redeemed them from their sins on earth. So you may be quite sure that your dear one is remembering you and storing up in his memory all your love in the past.

And he has taken with him all the treasures of mind and soul which by God's grace he has won for himself on earth. A man can take nothing of the external things—of gold or lands. Nothing of what he has, but all of what he is—all that he has gained in himself. The treasures of memory, of disciplined powers, of enlarged capacities, of a pure and loving heart. All the enrichment of the mind by study, all the love of man, all the love of God, all the ennobling of character which has come through the struggle after right and duty. These are the true treasures which go on with us into that land where neither rust nor moth doth corrupt.

And he is "with Christ."

The Bible teaches that the faithful who have died in Christ are happy and blessed in paradise, even tho the final heaven and the beatific vision are still but things to be longed for far off in the future. Lazarus is "comforted" after his hard life on earth. "The souls of the righteous are in the hands of God; there shall no torment touch them." "Blessed are the dead which die in the Lord . . . they rest from their labors." But, best of all, it assures us that they are with Christ. "Lord, Jesus, receive my spirit," the dying Stephen prayed as he was passing into the unseen. They are "absent from the body," says St. Paul, "at home with the Lord." They "depart to be with Christ, which is far better."

"With Christ." One has to write carefully here. The full vision of the divine glory and goodness and love is reserved for the final stage of existence in heaven, where nothing that defileth shall enter in,

whereas this intermediate life is one with many imperfections and faults, quite unready for that vision of glory. But, for all that, St. Paul believed that the presence of Christ was vouchsafed in that waiting land, in some such way, we may suppose, as on earth long ago. Only an imperfect revelation of the Son of God. And yet—and yet—oh, how one longs for it! Think of being near him, even in some such relation as were the disciples long ago!

Yes, St. Paul seems to say, you shall be with him, you shall have that longing gratified in some measure even before you go to heaven. So that paradise, poor and imperfect as it is compared with the heaven beyond, is surely to be greatly desired.

I can imagine some mourner shrinking from the thought that paradise, into which which his dear one has gone, is not the final heaven. Nay, shrink not. Paradise means the park of God, and the garden of God, the place of rest and peace and refreshing shade. The park is not the palace, but it is the precincts of the palace. Paradise is not heaven, but it is the court-yard of heaven. And (the dearest, tenderest assurance of all) they are with Christ. Is not that sufficient answer to many questions? At any rate the Bible definitely teaches that.

MUSIC HATH CHARMS

The Rev. ANDREW J. MEYER, Brooklyn, N. Y.

*When the morning stars sang together,
And all the sons of God shouted for joy.*
—Job. 38: 7.

The Christian Church, the wide world over, was, not long ago, pouring forth its glad Easter songs and shouting its loud hallelujahs of joy because of Christ's triumph over death and the grave. It did so because music is one of the most powerful agencies the all-wise Father employs to interpret his divine messages of love and salvation to his earth-born children. The Church sings because, when the heart is full almost to bursting with thankfulness and praise, it must find some outlet for its surcharged emotions, and music offers the most natural and only adequate way of escape. From the beginning of time music has been the chosen me-

dium through which humanity has given expression to its tidal waves of supreme joy or its measureless depths of passion and of wo. Creation itself was ushered in with the most thrilling strains of supernatural music. We are told that when the foundations of the earth were laid "the morning stars sang together and all the sons of God shouted for joy." From that moment in creation when the brooks went singing down the hillsides of Eden and the birds made glad the dawn of time with their thrilling melodies, music has had an indisputable place in the world.

Christianity was born with a song upon its lips. Mary sang in the wonderful measures of the Magnificat; angels sang in their jubilant hallelujah chorus, and the shepherds sang in the strains of a devout ecstasy. The Church of Christ has been singing ever since. Paganism does not sing: it laments. Pagodas and mosques do not lighten their somber interiors with music, but every Christian Church, however humble, is a conservatory of sweetest music. The word music is derived from the Greek term which includes all the learning of the muses. Of all the fine arts, music is the most comprehensive. The majesty of the architect, the pictures of the painter, the rhythm of the poet, and the themes of all these belong to the musician, whether he sits at the instrument or pours out his soul in vocal melodies. A fable tells us that Mercury stretched strings of dried skin across a shell and, striking them with his fingers, invented the lyre. The bow as an instrument was probably first used by the warrior who, as he described his successes in battle, unconsciously twanged the string of his bow. It was later discovered that the bow when drawn across certain hollow objects, produced pleasing sounds—hence the lute and the violin.

Music has been called the universal language, and truly it is a means of communication between all men, whatever clime may have given them birth. It is the most responsive of all arts, the most human. It more nearly breathes and sees and feels. It interprets all the varying emotions of the soul. The music of the siren might attempt to lure a Ulysses to his death, but the monotonous tones of the bell-buoy direct the imperiled mariner to safety. Tumultuous music is the completest expression of happy souls on festal days, and tender, somber strains interpret the language of sad hearts when a nation mourns for its martyred heroes. Glad hallelujahs or penitential psalms express the contrasting emotions of the soul.

When the *Titanic* was slowly sinking into the depths of the ocean and the souls on board were going out into the yet greater darkness of the dread unknown, what nerved them to the final struggle with the pitiless waves, and gave them courage to go through the valley of the shadow of death fearing no evil? As the musicians played steadily the sublime strains of "Nearer, my God, to Thee," who can doubt that he was indeed with them to the very end, that his rod and staff comforted them? When we lay away our own precious dead, why do we call upon those skilled in song to interpret for us those sweet, comforting selections that breathe of hope beyond the grave and the assurance of a blessed reunion in the land where there is no more death, neither sorrow nor sighing, for the former things are passed away?

But music ministers to our joy as well as to our pain. The bride goes to her bridal with every throb of her heart in time and tune with the inspiring music that accompanies her steps. The soldier, eager to do battle for his country, marches forth exultingly to the enlivening strains of the national airs. The sailor, leaving the home port for far-distant lands, raises the anchor with glad merriment and song. Why, then, should not the greatest and most joyous events the world has ever known—the bursting of the bands of death and the resurrection of Christ from the grave—call forth our grandest jubilates of triumph and our loudest hallelujahs of praise unto him who was dead but is alive forevermore? And because he lives we shall live also.

Music has been defined as love in search of a word. There is an inexpressible something in the heart of man which seeks to define itself in speech; but, failing in this, music flies to his relief and in melody man pours out his imprisoned soul. The deeper the soul life the more one is conscious of feeling beyond the limitations of articulate utterance. In the attempt of the finite soul to praise and glorify the infinite, all earthly devices of language utterly fail and music alone enables man to sing what he can not express, his adoration and gratitude to his great God and King. Consequently, wherever religion is the sincerest, music will be the purest, because it is the echo of God's voice in the soul of man.

It is the mission of music to soften and remove the asperities of life. It helps to unify the race and make our sectarianism slink into hiding places of shame as Charles Wesley, a Methodist, sings "Jesus, Lover of my soul," and Toplady, a Calvinist, sings "Rock of ages," and Sarah Adams, a "Unitarian, "Nearer, my God, to thee," and Faber, a Roman Catholic, "There's a wideness in God's mercy like the wideness of the sea," and Doddridge, a Baptist, "O happy day, that fixt my choice on thee." To-day these well-known hymns are sung by all and claimed by all. In spite of controversy and unbelief, the music of the Christian Church is saving this world for Christ. I believe, too, that music refines and ennobles. It brightens life's dark places and soothes the heart in trouble. Many prison doors besides that of Paul and Silas have opened and have burst asunder when troubled hearts have sung songs in the night. In the battle with life many a weary soldier, tired and foot-sore, has leapt on to victory under the magic spell of music.

Schopenhauer says that music is the shower bath of the soul washing away all that is impure. We are all familiar with. the exhilarating effects of the bath and the healthful, invigorating glow that follows its indulgence. Have we not also, when listening to some wonderful production of the great masters, some grand oratorio or sweet soul-stirring symphony, felt a spiritual uplift that has carried us beyond the limits of time and space, even into the realms of immortality, and aroused a longing within us to be as pure in heart and soul as is the body when physically cleansed from its earth stains? That is the way many a prodigal has felt when, wandering in a far country away from God and home, spending his all in riotous living, he has chanced suddenly to hear some familiar but long-forgotten strain of sweet, compelling music, reminding him of the hymns he sang or heard sung by the dear mother in the long ago of his childhood.

What is the real secret of the power that lies in the beautiful gospel hymns to bring comfort to the afflicted, peace to the troubled heart, and repentance to the erring soul? Sometimes when we have gone to the house of God on the Sabbath day, perplexed in mind, deprest with care and anxiety, the choir has chanted some wonderful promise of the Father that has instantly made a rift in the dark clouds, or the soloist has sung in tender, sympathetic tones, "Jesus of Nazareth passeth by," and the weight of care drops off as if by magic as we seem to feel that nail-pierced hand resting in loving sympathy upon our shoulder and meet that glance of comforting assurance that all will yet be well, for the Master himself will work for and with us. We see then that true religion, like true love, is emotional and music is the most adequate expression of the emotional faculty. Faith sings, unbelief never. Music reveals God. When Handel was writing the Hallelujah Chorus he said, "I saw all heaven open before me, and the great God himself appeared." Haydn said: "When I was occupied with the Creation, always before I sat down to the piano I prayed God with earnestness that he would enable me to praise him worthily." The greatest musicians have been good men, and to develop the mighty impulses which they have felt in their souls they have chosen lofty, divine themes. This was true of Jubal and Job, of David and his harp, and Solomon with his sweet songs. It was true of Beethoven, whose soulful sonatas have won for him a genuine priesthood of the emotions. It was true of Mozart, whose thirty-five years gave to the world such treasures from the infinite that he is actually exhaustless; and of Liszt, for during the days of his best work the book, the *Imitation of Christ*, by Thomas à Kempis, was his constant companion.

It is evident then that, like his Maker, man is a spirit. It is also evident that the infinite God is more perfectly worshiped with music than in any other way because it opens up the vistas of faith through which can be seen the King in his beauty. That is the reason why all great revivals of religion have been accompanied with revivals in sacred song. Ay, even as we reach heaven, where the present conclusions of men shall be abandoned for the completer revelation of all the truth of him who is the Way, the Truth, and the Life, we shall find that music, which was never anything but divine in its nature and influence, shall be our old familiar friend, increasing in divinity as our own evolving souls are permitted to comprehend and participate in that divinity in the heaven and through the eternal life that is to come. John, the beloved disciple, had a foretaste of that when, an exile in Patmos in the midst of the boundless sea, there was given him, in his awful loneliness and isolation, a vision of the New Jerusalem such as never before nor since has been granted to living man. After describing the inconceivable glories of that paradise of God, he tells us, "And I heard the voice of harpers harping with their harps, and they sung as it were a new song before the throne; and no man could sing that song but they which are redeemed from earth." So as the curtain rises on creation's dawn to the exultant singing of a choir invisible, it falls in John's beatific vision to the accompaniment of golden harps played by the angelic orchestra.

In music everything depends on tune. It is so also in living. Before we can receive the blessing of the heavenly life our hearts must be made ready, must be in tune with God himself. In wireless telegraphy the receiver must be perfectly attuned to its transmitter or it will not get the message. There may be one thousand stations with their wires and electrical apparatus, but only the receivers which are in tune with the transmitter sending the message can get it.

God's love sweeps out from his heaven over all the earth. It comes to the door of every life. There is not one person anywhere among all earth's families, however far off he may be, whom God does not love. But there are many into whose hearts the consciousness of his love never comes. The message of grace is for all, but only those whose lives are in tune with the life of God hear it. The object of all spiritual training is to bring our lives into tune with God. We begin very far away, and at the best we are only learners. Heaven always keeps above us at our highest. But we are living worthily when we are getting a little more into the heavenly spirit every day. We never can enter heaven until we have brought heaven down into our hearts. We would not be happy there if we had not learned heaven's lessons before we go there. So the great work of life is to come into tune with God, to grow into such trust that we shall rest in God in the silence of love, so to lose our wills in God's that there shall never be any disharmony in our relations with God.

THE CHILDREN'S SERVICE

DEMOCRATIC NATURE [1]

Robert Sparks Walker, Chattanooga, Tenn.

Nature is the author of democracy. None of her creatures were ever bred for serfs. To insure the freedom of plants and animals, her laws are the very essence of democracy, which gives each and every creature an equal chance according to its habits.

Every part of the beautiful blooming ornamental plant known as oleander is dangerously poisonous. Throughout the warm climate it finds a useful place in beautifying the great outdoors, and it is highly valued as an indoor plant in a colder climate. The political, social, or financial standing of a person makes no difference, he who eats its flowers or foliage suffers death from its poisons. Even the camper whose needs call for a skewer for cooking meat must pass the oleander by or take the risk of losing his life.

Democracy in nature knows no favorites and yields to no pulls or party affiliations. Her laws are just and her rains fall on all alike; she gives heat and light to every creature on the same terms. In the forest no trees, no matter how great, can dictate to the infant tree by its side or apportion its allotment of moisture, sunshine, or food. The infant tree growing by the greatest giant of the forest has an equal chance with its brothers and it remains with it to take advantage of the opportunity and acquire its maximum growth. The tadpole and the water-beetle use the water with as much freedom as any other animals that find the ponds favorable for life and growth.

There is an interesting group of plants known by the name of cress, many varieties of which grow throughout the world. This group of plants is very democratic, and for the purpose they serve nature gave them corresponding habits. The common garden cress, when used as a food, is a powerful agent in preventing the disease known as scurvy, and many other species serve the same purpose. The perennial aquatic watercress found growing in the clear streams in the United States is so democratic in its habits that it is a native of practically every part of the world. In furnishing solid and green food to the human family in the winter months when such foods are scarce, it acquires great value. Its habit of growing in the gravelly bottoms of clear running streams gives it few competitors. With all its democratic manners, the watercress does not always monopolize the sandy bottom of the streams, for by its side may often be observed the beautiful flowering lizard's-tail and peppermint.

Every phase of nature condemns in the severest terms any autocratic doctrine, and any nation or individual who wishes to settle the problem as to the propriety of autocracy needs only turn to the first page of nature to find that, in the democracy that she has established, autocracy was doomed from the beginning of the world.

OUTLINES

Jesus' Tastes and Preferences

And when they saw him, they were aston-ished, etc.—Luke, 2: 48, 49.

Jesus' life was full of surprizes. His parents were surprized to find him in the temple. He was more surprized that they should have sought anywhere else for him. So it was all through. The very things he expected which were most evident and characteristic of him to others, came to them as a surprize. Even so late as his last talk with his disciples, he was astonished into saying, "Have I been so long time with you, and yet hast thou not known me, Philip?" They had missed the most significant thing of all.

I. His passion for worship. Not only was he at home in the temple when a boy, but "as his custom was" he entered into the synagog on the Sabbath day. This was the master passion of his life. Whether it took the form of (1) devotion expressing itself in adoration; prayer, in which we are told more than once he continued all night, as more necessary to him than sleep; or praise. Dr. W. Robertson Nicoll has recently said that "the good part" chosen by Mary was "the listening part." So it has been said of Jesus, "he was a listener unto death." (2) Enquiry. Teaching, education, enlightenment, are an essential part of worship, as out of God's treasury "things new and old" are brought forth. Jesus gathered with the worshipers to "enquire in his temple." (3) Service. When Jesus attended the synagog in Nazareth and, as the distinguished stranger present, was handed the Scripture roll, and "all bare him witness, and wondered at the gracious words which proceeded out of his mouth," it was not the first time he had made a contribution to the service. Every synagog service was richer for his presence, his faith, his sense of the divine presence; the outpouring of his soul for others "made their faith strong."

II. His comradeship with the common people. That he should mix with publicans and sinners was not only a surprize, but an offense to many. (1) His choice. He was no associate of intellectuals or the élite of his day either in society or religious circles, tho he was head and shoulders above them. They took counsel how they might entrap him, but he, single-handed, and unprepared, was more than a match for them in subtlety, keenness, and power of repartee. (2) His reason was that he was a physician. He therefore not only dealt with men and women on the side of their weakness and need, but they were stript of their adornments and trappings to which so many people owe much. How differently some would appear without their wealth, their position, their dress. Jesus saw people as they are, and dealt with them along the line of their common human nature. (3) His justification. We are told of "certain which trusted in themselves that they were righteous, and despised others" (Luke 18:9). They did not welcome Jesus. We read of only one church in the New Testament where Jesus was outside at the door knocking for admission, yet it was saying, "I am rich, and increased with goods, and have need of nothing." It is always on the side of their self-sufficiency, and when they lay the emphasis on the things wherein they differ from others—that men shut God out. Jesus was attracted by our common human nature.

III. His love of the children. The "stern

disciples" who "drove back" the mothers who brought their little ones to Jesus, were not the only ones who thought he was too great to be bothered with children. "It's only a child" has been heard in many a church that has forgotten that the Master took them up in his arms and blessed them." How Jesus loved the children! How they were attracted by him! How he watched their games! How he spoke up for them!

We like to think of the old Sunday-school superintendents, on all fours on the grass, surrounded by the tiny mites of the Sunday-school; some on his back, some leading him, he as happy as they. Can we not say "How like Jesus!"

"Around the throne of God in heaven,
Thousands of children stand."

May it be true of us in regard to our tastes and preferences—"as he was so are we in this world."

Significant Voices

There are . . . so many kinds of voices in the world, and no kind is without signification.—1 Cor. 14:10.

"God has something to say to us from the lips of all."

I. Voices from the Church claim our attention—reverent attention. Truth is voiced by Calvin and Wesley, Erasmus and Luther, Bunyan and Thomas à Kempis, Kingsley and Robertson, Channing and Martineau, Spurgeon and Parker; also by a miscellaneous company who may be described as poetic, prosaic, pedantic, pessimistic, or prophetic—each type claiming to convey the mind of God to sinful men.

II. Voices from the wilderness not without signification, also. Poets, a goodly company, the prophets and interpreters of our day; novelists, not a few; scientists, a host; social economists and nondescripts; gentle outlaws, a band of men whose hearts God has touched to good purpose. Many of these lay no claim to godliness, and yet live, move, and have their being in designs for the common weal.

"God has something to say to us from the lips of all."

III. Voices from nature never cease to challenge attention in sensitive minds. Tongues in trees—"wailing like voices of woe," or laughing merrily as doth the corybantic aspen. From the overarching heavens at night, from the bird-frequented grove at morn or dewy eve, one ceaseless anthem rises. The foaming cataract and hidden murmur of the brook alike make music. The fecundity of nature proclaims the fertility of God's mind. "Outdoor sights and sounds provide a gospel to the city-tired spirit. Voices greet him in the quiet haunts of fairy and dryad which may fellowship every mood—voices pathetic, despairing, endearing, bucolic, strident, imperious—and transcending all shall steal into the soul a sense of that presence, which, tho subtle and mystic, will be more real than sight or sound, poetry or fragrance.

IV. Voices from history are clamant for thoughtful attention—uttering notes of warning, instruction, and inspiration. History repeats herself, insisting on the relation of cause and effect, that the curse causeless shall not come, that the solidarity of the race urges, that to injure one is to prejudice all, that to oppose the divine order is to provoke disaster; that all deeds are freighted with consequences, good or ill; that history is but one man's life writ large; that the wheels of God may grind slowly, but the end is not doubtful; and that the fear of God is the beginning of wisdom.

V. Voices from the classic world are worthy of an open ear. They speak significantly of footsteps round and about every mystery of life and death. The ancients have anticipated all speculation. These voices mellowed by time and distance tell of attempts to solve the insoluble; of Hadean researches, of fate and immortality; of personal identity hereafter; of the sentiments of the Elysians; of "the resentments of the dead"; of presumptive reincarnation. Everywhere and when is voiced hopeless despair, and the great need of the divine superman who should speak with a voice that will bring life and immortality to light.

VI. Voices from the mystic world which environs us greet sensitive ears. Deaf adders are the secular multitude, but to those whose nervous antennæ can be pained by an averted look or satirical word, responsive to every mental and moral fluctuation of atmosphere, there are presences "that touch us as lightly as angels' wings," voices more felt than heard, messages that inspire, and for the moment plant the tired soul "quite within the verge of heaven." *Bona fide* spiritualism is theirs, not of the seance order, but approximating to that weird scene on Tabor when Christ the Lord held fellowship with the immortal dead. Happy those who in this day of strain and stress hew the path to the mystic world, where the peace of God passeth all understanding.

Religion Defined

Pure religion is this.—Jas. 1:27.

Religion is the life of God in human personality. It is life in God. It is conformity to the true and godly order of things. I. What religion involves. 1. Belief in God—revealed in (1) nature, (2) Bible, (3) conscience, (4) Christ. Against atheism and against polytheism. 2. Revelation of God's will, in nature, Bible, conscience, Christ. 3. Obligation to obey God. "To obey is better than sacrifice." God (1) made us, (2) redeemed us, (3) preserves us—hence is entitled to obedience. 4. State or condition of rewards and punishment. (1) Heaven for the good, (2) hell for the

evil—justice and mercy require it. "A God all mercy is a God unjust."

II. What religion requires. 1. Godliness of living—(1) following Christ, (2) worship and thanksgiving, (3) observance of Sunday (God's day). 2. Cleanliness and morality—(1) personal purity, (2) avoidance of evil habits, (3) all duties to self and to others. 3. Man's accountability to God. We must give account for (1) every idle word, (2) disobedience, (3) indifference, (4) self-satisfaction and sufficiency.

Religion is both a principle of life and a program of conduct. Religion is a welding together of (1) prayer, (2) thanksgiving, (3) faith, (4) love, (5) service into "life." It is (1) "the revelation of a new life," (2) "the inspiration of a new hope," (3) "the communication of a new strength." It teaches that the "cost of not doing right" is greater than the "cost of doing right." In the former you pay "in the integrity of your manhood, in honor, in truth, in character." Without the Christian religion your "forfeit your soul's content and for a timely gain you barter the infinities."

OUTLINES IN PERSONAL MESSAGES

S. B. Dunn, D.D., New York City

Sitting Down With God

Then went David in and sat before the Lord, etc.—2 Sam. 7:18.

King David goes indoors and sits down with God.

I. Find in God a closet. 1. God is inside of things. 2. Only by being closeted can soul commune.

II. Finds God a looking-glass. 1. To himself. 2. To God (verses 18, 22).

III. Finds God an armory (verse 26; 8:1). A tower of London hung about with war-weapons.

IV. Finds God a ferry, to carry him to success (verses 28, 29). Only by God's fidelity can David attain.

Conclusion: Do we go in and sit down with God?

Sitting Down With Oneself

He sat in the tent door in the heat of the day.—Gen. 18:1.

Snap-shot of Abraham in single posture. 1. Alone. 2. At tent door. 3. At mid-day.

I. Good to get acquainted with oneself. 1. For self-knowledge. 2. Reflection. 3. Rest.

II. Good to sit at tent door of things. 1. Where things go out. 2. Come in. Unroll themselves. Life, every day has its strategic tent doors.

III. Good to have visits from God. 1. When Visitor unveils himself. 2. Unveils his secrets.

Conclusion: World too much with us. The soul has its privacies.

Sitting Down With the Other Man

And I sat down where they sat, etc.—Ezek. 3:15.

Ezekiel in person shared fortunes of captive on Chebar banks. Was broken-hearted as they were. Put himself alongside. Had fine imagination, a feeling heart, and Christian grace.

I. A man is most near to fellow when nearest to God.

II. A man is nearest to God when most near to fellow.

III. The essence of sympathy is sitting down with other man.

IV. Here is solution of social, national, international ills.

Peace conferences are Chebar-bank and Washington–table conferences.

Sitting Down With One's Problem

For which of you, intending to build a tower, sitteth not down first, etc.—Luke 14:28.

What a portrait-painter Jesus is! What a master Jesus was of the merit of contrast: wise, foolish.

I. We are all tower-builders.

II. The finish as important as foundation.

III. The initial thing is counting the cost.

IV. Every problem a matter of mathematics.

Prime factors in success are: 1. Sitting down in deliberation. 2. Foresight that anticipates. 3. Heroic counting and paying the cost.

Sitting Down With Jesus on the Mount

Therefore all things, etc.—Matt. 7:14.

A mountain task in a mountain sermon, which would lift world to sublime heights. The genius of life is mutual service. The Master's rule:

I. Simple. 1. Accurate. 2. Portable. 3. Personal.

II. Benign. 1. To oneself. 2. To society.

Christianity is the art of living together. It is experience plus conduct.

Sitting Down in the Kingdom of God

And they shall come, etc.—Luke 13:29, 30.

Jesus star optimist. Long-sighted. The Man of the universal, eternal soul.

I. Sovereign of four-cornered kingdom. Four-pointed compass of soul. Variegated color of faith and character and service.

II. Host of a royal feast. 1. Nuptial. 2. Commemorative of conquest. 3. Festive in exuberance of hospitality.

III. Discriminating in awards. 1. In position. 2. Order. 3. Felicity.

What an incentive to conservation, patience, and hope!

THEMES AND TEXTS[1]

Abigail Voices. "And when Abigail saw David, she hasted, and alighted from her ass, and fell before David on her face, and bowed herself to the ground," etc.—1 Sam. 25:23 ff.

The City Without a Wall. "And I lifted up mine eyes, and saw, and, behold, a man with a measuring line in his hand," etc.—Zech. 2:1-5.

The Transport Wagon. "And Moses took the bones of Joseph with him: for he had straitly sworn the children of Israel, saying, God will surely visit you; and ye shall carry up my bones away hence with you."—Ex. 13:19.

The Lure of the Wilderness. "And when Balaam saw that it pleased Jehovah to bless Israel, he went not, as at the other times, to meet with enchantments, but he set his face toward the wilderness.'—Num. 24:1.

Void or Voice? "While he was yet speaking, behold, a bright cloud overshadowed them: and behold, a voice out of the cloud, saying, This is my beloved Son, in whom I am well pleased: hear ye him."—Matt. 17:5.

The Danger of Looking Back. "Remember Lot's wife."—Luke 17:32.

Degrees of Spiritual Perception. "The multitude therefore, that stood by, and heard it, said that it had thundered: others said, An angel hath spoken to him."—John 12:29.

His Own Clothes. "And when they had mocked him, they took off from him the robe, and put on him his garments, and led him away to crucify him."—Matt. 27:31.

The Exits of the Soul. ". . . and all their egresses were both according to their fashions, and according to their doors."—Ezek. 42:11b.

The Snare of the South Wind. "And when the south wind blew softly, supposing that they had obtained their purpose, they weighed anchor and sailed along Crete, close in shore."—Acts 27:13.

Cherishing the Dream. "O Jehovah, the God of Abraham, of Isaac, and of Israel, our fathers, keep this for ever in the imagination of the thoughts of the heart of thy people, and prepare their heart unto thee."—1 Chron. 29:18.

Memory and Morning. "And as Peter was beneath in the court, there cometh one of the maids of the high priest," etc.—Mark 14:66-72.

---

[1] From *The Intention of His Soul*, by Hubert L. Simpson.

ILLUSTRATIONS AND ANECDOTES

The Rev. F. C. Hoggarth, Bradford, England.

The Flowers On the Altar

I remember well a little village church in France, over the hills behind the hospital, into which one day I entered. Like the rest of those village churches it was open all day and had about it an air of homeliness and the signs of much use. For there the villagers are not afraid of entering their church in working garb or in soiled boots, straight from the fields. They do not dress for worship. They do not wait to put on finery before they pray. They enter and worship as they are, in homespun. The homeliness of their religion very strongly appealed to me. And tho one may have no room for gilded images, or figures of the Virgin, or candles and crucifixes, one may nevertheless admire what is admirable and learn valuable lessons from folk of different ways from ours. Their religion seemed more natural than ours, a more intimate part of the common day.

That was the thought focused for me in some flowers on the altar. They had not been bought for the purpose, not sent down by some city florist nor even arranged in some so-called artistic way. They were just the flowers of garden and of field—nature's own wild flower children for the most part. There was one huge bouquet, an all inclusive one, such as people in the country made when I was a boy, more homely than artistic and yet, nevertheless, with a certain native artistry. The villagers had gathered with their own hands the simple every-day flowers, their little flower comrades of garden and wayside, to put on Christ's altar. It seemed a parable of what our religion and our service should always be. It is the homely things of life's every day that are to be offered to him.

We are to make a bouquet of simple, loving words and deeds, done for Christ's sake each day, and set that upon our altar. In that spirit Jesus himself lived; he also served in life's homely ways and set his seal on homeliness in worship and in service.

The Tug of Home

Mr. Stephen Graham tells of meeting an aged Russian tramping across America. He had come 250 miles from Minnesota in the empty truck of a freight train. At New York he would buy a ticket for Libau, the port of arrival in Russia, and then once more set out on tramp to his native village.

"Why are you going home? Can't you find work?" asked Stephen Graham. "I am going to pray," he said, "going to my village to see my father's grave and then to a monastery. I would finish my years in Russia and be buried in Russian ground." He then told of a dream that had influenced this pilgrimage. He had in a dream seen his father and his father's guardian angel pointing eastward and that he had taken to be a sign. "I am Russian; Mother Russia! she is mine. They may keep you down and oppress you there, but the land is holy and men are brothers." Even if he died on the way, he felt that his face would be toward home and that his soul would get there just the same.

That solitary pilgrim homeward bound is perhaps the most representative man in the world. On all the earth's great highways, routes of land and sea, there are those who turn again home. It is one of the deepest human instincts, this love and yearning for the motherland and the mother village, for the places sacred by all the ties of kinship.

So after long years in far-off cities men return for the time of sunset and evening star. Death, so they feel, will seem more friendly amid those of familiar scenes. Heaven, it may be, will be nearer in that place where in infancy heaven was all about them and where, in the dreams of youth, there seemed a golden ladder on which the angels came and went. In theory all places are equally sacred. The golden ladder may be let down, the vision may come anywhere, in an alien land no less than in the homeland and in the crowded city no less than in the lonely village.

Yet in the practise the earth has just one or two preeminently sacred places for most men. And it may be that the nearest way to heaven is from the "hills of home."

A Man Who Never Lost Heart

In a book on Q-boat adventures (Q-boats were the mystery ships of the war that hunted submarines) I recently came across the extraordinary story of a man who never lost heart. No matter how black the outlook, his buoyant, unconquerable soul cried cheerio. The actual story concerned the sinking of a mystery ship called *Stonecrop*, far from land. As there were not enough boats for the wrecked survivors, they began to build a raft, swimming about in the water for planks. On the raft were put three officers and twenty men and a share of such supplies as the boats had—namely, three gallons of water and one tin of biscuits. They set up an oar as a mast and a piece of canvas as a sail. The sea rose, swept the raft and carried them all into the sea. They got aboard again, but found a bottle of water and the tin of biscuits lost. A destroyer was sighted after some hours, every one stood up and shouted and waved but in vain. One and another of the men died. One and another of them went mad as night followed day and day followed night on those friendless waters. Not until the sixth day were they picked up by a patrol vessel. The men were so exhausted that they couldn't speak. Only two officers and eight men survived, for after the second day they had no food at all. That any of them ever came through was due to one lieutenant, who never lost heart, tho death stared them in the face. Without his leadership none would have survived.

The story is just one more instance of how vital a part hope plays in all true leadership. Despondency and despair are fatal disqualifications for leaders. It is the man of hope who wins through. The man who never loses heart inspires confidence, courage, and endurance in others. Hope is a Christian virtue, surprisingly rare, considering the central place it occupies in early Christianity. In the New Testament hope is third, along with faith and love. It would seem as tho all

things were possible to the man of deep-founded hope.

Narrow Spires

Stephen Graham, tramping from New York to Chicago, met on the road a Bulgarian and together they came to a village with two severe looking churches. "When I see those narrow spires," said the Bulgarian, "I'm afraid. I should have to wither my soul and make it small to get into one of those churches. I like a church with walls of praise and a spire of yearning. . . . That spire says to me, 'I feared thee, O God, because thou art an austere man.' "

The spires may symbolize something quite different to different hearts. They may indeed be literally spires of yearning; symbols of the worshiping and aspiring soul. Yet the impression made by our churches on those who are not of our way ought to be carefully considered. Until that is done, we shall never discover why it is that the Church fails to appeal to great numbers of our fellows. Our cramped expressions of religion have been a handicap. Men somehow have felt that to come into church fellowship would involve a real narrowing of their lives. Rightly or wrongly many still have that impression.

Yet there ought to be no room in the Church for littleness of any sort. There should be something spacious about our creeds and our conduct. The Church ought to produce great personalities, big-souled people of widest sympathies and generous judgment. When men come to worship they ought to be conscious of amplitude, of the spacious places of the spirit. "After hearing in a church," said Emerson, "a discourse that makes God a partial being and identifies him with a sect, I delight to escape into the open air, and one view of the heavens or any of the great features of nature is enough to scatter the gloom that has gathered over me and to teach me that what has been said is false." Men ought not to feel on coming out of church that they have escaped into a bigger world, or that entering a church they are in a little world. We must see to that and correct what needs to be corrected. The best corrective is to live much with the high and spacious thoughts of God.

A Song that Lived

Recent years have witnessed revived interest in folk songs. Investigators have gone to and fro in quest of primitive melodies. The study is not without its romance and at times quite amazing discoveries are made. A writer in *Outward Bound* recently told the romance of a song that he heard up the Zambesi River from a crowd of natives traveling in canoes or dugouts, who were of a tribe that had no dealings with white men at all, and disappeared into the bush if a stranger appeared. He wrote down the melody and years afterward showed it to an eminent musician, who was specially interested in old music. He was amazed at the song and closely questioned the investigator as to place and circumstance, and then said that he believed it to be a pure bit of fifteenth century music practically intact and that a record of it could be found in a certain museum. On seeking to trace the connection, it was discovered that in 1586 a party of Portuguese missionaries travelled up the Zambesi, and there made a home, seeking to teach the natives. The climate, however, took swift toll of their lives and before long they were all dead and little trace of their work was left. The song was one of the melodies used in their little services, brought by them from Portugal. · It had been handed down from generation to generation literally from ear to mouth for over three hundred years. The missionaries died, but their song lived on, for songs have a strange power of life. When all else is forgotten, they endure. It is not otherwise in our modern day. When almost every other trace of religious work and influence is blotted out, in all too many modern lives, the hymns and melodies learned in childhood remain. There have been not a few instances in which some bairn's song, some prayer of childhood, like "Gentle Jesus," has been the one kindly light to some prodigal's feet. Possibly we never do finer or more enduring or more helpful service than when we teach the little ones about us the songs of Zion.

After Many Days

In his book, *The Saints of Formosa,* Dr. Campbell Moody has a chapter entitled "Loiterers," the subject of which is that of delayed harvest. The problem is not unfamiliar at home. Abroad it is an ever present temptation to despair. So much seed has to be sown for so little results. In hospital, in school, in market-place, the work so unceasing yields so little that can be tabulated. Yet quite wonderful things happen. Not a few loiterers find their way into the kingdom. He tells of one Formosan Christian who first had his curiosity aroused by something that he read in an old church calendar pasted to a wall. The seed lay dormant for twenty years, till a place of worship was built about half a dozen miles from his dwelling. In another case, when speaking in the streets of one of their towns, two young men started a conversation with him. He brought them home and gave them tracts. They returned to their village miles away and nothing more was heard of them. Some four years later misfortune fell on one of them; having spent a good deal on his gods without avail, he bethought himself of the Christian religion and both he and his friend began attending the nearest church.

An even more remarkable case was that of a youth in a wild district who got some knowledge of the gospel from conversation with Christian neighbors. He paid no heed, but plunged deeper into wickedness, finally becoming one of a robber band. At last he was caught and imprisoned for twelve years. In his need he remembered words of hope heard long before from Christian lips. He found a hymn book in prison which deepened these impressions. He became a changed man—and he who had gone into prison a heathen robber, came out a Christian and amazed the nearest Christian church with his story and his desire to join them.

So it is at home and abroad. The word spoken to-day, fruitlessly as it seems, may yield a harvest after many days. Experience is ever proving the truth of the hymn, "Sow in the morn thy seed"—

Beside all waters sow,
 The highway furrows stock,
Drop it where thorns and thistles grow,
 Scatter it on the rock.

The Flowers of Childhood

Younghusband in his recent book *The Heart of Nature* describes a wonderful journey that he made from the Ganges valley up to the Himalayas. He describes the infinite variety of plant life as he passed from the tropical climate of the plains to the arctic climate of the heights. He tells of blooms which in temperate countries are treasured in hot-houses, that there grew in wild profusion, of giant lilies, of some four hundred varieties of orchids, of every conceivable shade of loveliness, of all manner of new and impressive beauty. It was a most spacious revelation of the things of which nature is capable. But he adds significantly, "we shall never be able to give to even the most exquisite orchid, or the most perfect lily, the same affection that we give to the primroses and violets of our native land."

After all, the simple flowers of home, the so unassuming blooms that were about us in our childhood, can more than hold their own against all the flower wealth and display of the tropics.

Sometimes youth grows weary of the flowers of home, and goes in quest of other blooms. Those goings are not seldom revealings. Against the new background the old, simple things stand out in most appealing loveliness. Israel at times grew weary of her narrow and austere life. Israel had no great river like the Nile or the Euphrates. Jerusalem was huddled on a rock and had none of the imposing beauty of Babylon. Israel lusted after that more luxurious life of the East, much as London and New York are lusting after similar things. Yet the day came when exiled Israel cried for the old familiar things, for the "flowers of childhood." "If I forget thee, O Jerusalem, may my right hand forget its cunning and my tongue cleave to the roof of my mouth."

A River's Unseen Resources

Last summer the River Thames suffered from the prolonged drought. There was some risk of it running comparatively dry, for the rainfall had been deficient for something like eighteen months. The *Children's Newspaper* pointed out that old **Father** Thames was not like a river rising in mountains where snow lies and melts eternally. Tho there are rainless days and nights such a river flows tranquil and abundant. "With the Thames it is as in human affairs." The things unseen are greater than the things seen. The rains that fall in the gathering grounds of the Thames do not all come at once to the river. We save up for a rainy day; nature saves up for a dry one.

The bulk of the water descending on our land goes down. It soaks into the earth, through the soil, through the rocks and chalk. The land is as a great, hard, unyielding sponge, soaked with water. Thousands of unseen inlets admit water into the ground, which becomes a concealed storage-basin for the kindly rains from heaven.

Thus the Thames is fed in time of drought, and unless the drought is quite abnormally severe the great river fails not. Unlike the streams in the desert it has its reserves. Any worth-while life should be like that with simple unseen reserves. Too many lives are like streams in a desert, "to use Job's comparison for his friends." The secret of such a life, that fails not and fears not when the drought cometh, is that the life should be open to the rich incomings of God's grace through a thousand tiny inlets.

The article went on to tell of a little and unknown river, the Wandle, not marked on many maps, which once through a practically rainless season of eighteen months over its catchment area nevertheless poured forth its ten million gallons of precious water daily. So wonderful was the reserve of water in the fifty-one square miles of chalk on the South Downs drained by the Wandle.

Some lives are like that little river. Without fame in the noisy world, they quietly do their beneficent work and in the day of testing fail not. Sometimes obscure lives give a deep impression of adequacy. The secret is that they are in vital contact with the unfailing reserves in God. By their adequacy ye shall know them.

Recent Books

THE REIGN OF RELATIVITY[1]

It takes no small courage for a philosopher to go into the field of higher mathematics. But since the law of relativity has been so long known in philosophy, its new application to physics should not be allowed to go as a wholly new discovery as the present tendency seems to be. At the same time full credit ought to be accorded to the keen-minded men who have captured this new field for the old principle of an open universe of qualitative values, which subordinates to itself mere quantitative measurements. This appears to be the conclusion drawn by Viscount Haldane in his weighty but fairly readable book on *The Reign of Relativity*.

Thinking minds need to become familiar with the new concepts which come along, for they are the tools and furniture of the mind. New ideas become familiar only by going back over them again and again. Like all strangers and novelties they are unwelcome to conservative minds, but after a while they make a place for themselves. Relativity is the least understood and the most often referred to subject in scientific philosophy. It is a familiar idea in some of its applications, but the universality of its application had been unthought of until recently, and it leads to some strange conclusions. In the same way light has always been well known to man, and yet when scientists began to talk of light in terms of motion and time, and to use the light-year as a unit for measuring distances, it was not at first easy for some minds to follow the discussion. But soon those ideas became common property, and so it will no doubt be with relativity.

The hill at home looked big to the boy, but when he returns fifty years after to the old threshold the hill looks small; and if it were looked at from the moon or from the north star it would have no size at all. It has no size except relatively to perceiving minds, and to them in varying conditions of light, of distance, of other objects, and of recent associations. In the philosophy of every-day life as well as in art and religion relativity is a familiar fact. It has been recognized in metaphysics all the way from Plato to Bergson.

But it has been the pride of science that its data were objective and absolute. There was no guesswork supposed to vitiate the finality of scientific facts and methods. This assumption has been mostly to blame for the chasm which a generation ago was commonly supposed to separate science from other knowledge. Now the unreality of that difference is well known. Knowledge is the best way we have of apprehending things, but it has its limitations. It is generally recognized to consist of faith somewhat verified, but the verification is relative even at the best. "The distinction between appearance and reality becomes one of degrees toward full comprehension" (p. 36).

Philosophers have abandoned the notion which prevailed in the days of Euclid and Newton that space and time are independent frameworks subsisting as self-contained phenomena regardless of the objects in them. Space and time have no meaning save that which we discover and read into them gradually in our own experience.

"It seems, then, that the new system which we are considering is not that of any merely psychological or intuitional space and time directly and completely given in direct sensation, for this could not be resolved in the way the facts require, but only one of interpreted space and time in which our perceptions are correlated. The psychological data are only the beginning. We construe these into an objective space-time manifold, not merely for the purposes of science, but as a necessity of our daily life. Our space and time may well be real, but reality has now a relative meaning. Apart from construction (construal) there could be no world before us" (p. 46).

This has long been a familiar idea in phi-

[1] By Viscount Haldane. Yale University Press, New Haven, 1921. 430 pp.

losophy, but the men of science have gone farther with their reconstruing of space and time. The two ideas are now found to be inseparable. If there were no time succession we could not distinguish different points in space. If there were no separateness of points in space but only one point there could be no intervals of time in passing from one point to another as on the clock face, and there could be no time. Space and time are each relative to the other and they are not fixt entities, but mean only relations between things. It is a mistake to assume the possibility of absolute rest or absolute motion. There is a fundamental feature of nature called "duration" or "passage" of events, from which both time and space are constructed by our abstractions. This is the space-time continuum called by Bergson the fourth dimension, and by Einstein made the basis of his theory of quantitative relativity in physics.

The so-called force of gravity has long been regarded with suspicion because it implies action at a distance by one body in its supposed pull upon another body. This force has seemed to belong to a class of mythical objective entities which have been eliminated by science.

The physical results of calculation by Newton's law of gravitation remain reliable for all practical purposes, just as the calculation of the calendar was unchanged after Copernicus turned astronomy upside down. But we are assured that another way of computing gravitational motions is now to become approved. The new way dispenses with the idea of force, makes the straight line not necessarily the shortest distance between two points, and introduces "tensors" into the mathematics of physics. "Tensors are expressions which seem to include intrinsic qualities of the continuum, ... They stand for what are qualities more than for definite quantities."

Haldane is one of that modern school of philosophers who recognize the validity of both the realistic and the idealistic points of view, and seek for a working understanding and constructive reconciliation between them. He believes that relativity is now winning its way into the last stronghold of rigid mechanism hitherto defended by physical scientists. It should be a turning-point in scientific philosophy. We should then see how much more we are than we have taken ourselves to be from our particular standpoints. We should be liberated from those particular spots in the space-time continuum, and should begin to see as God sees.

But it will no doubt take some one besides a mathematical physicist to blaze the trail for the new philosophy. Our author has made a good start, and is the type of mind needed for the job. Certainly it will need a mind who can start with faith in the Being of the world as an ethical and dynamic spirit in whom we are all borne forward in our mutual relativity. The professional man who has the determination and self-control to hold himself to a subject and a book like this until he feels somewhat familiar with its terminology and its view-points will always afterward be a larger man. But these are things which a man does not acquire by a casual reading or simply by being told.   —W. J. M.

SCIENCE FOR EVERYBODY[1]

Rarely indeed can it with mature and sound judgment be said of a book, This should be in every home. Concerning this one those words sound too tame, when weighed with the book's worth. Its aim is to give the intelligent student-citizen, otherwise called "the man in the street," a bunch of intellectual keys by which to open doors which have been hitherto shut to him, partly because he got no glimpse of the treasures behind the doors, and partly because the portals were made forbidding by an unnecessary display of technicalities.

Its editor is one of the foremost scientists of our day, and is without a peer as a "popularizer" of scientific achievement, with a score of scientific works to his credit. As a survey of the present state of achievement in science the London *Morning Post* regards it as "so accurate that the expert can not cavil at it, and so simple that the general

[1] *The Outline of Science.* Edited by Professor J. Arthur Thomson. Vols. I. and II. G. P. Putnam's Sons, New York and London, 1922. 10¾ x 8 in., 3-295, 297-564 pp. $4.50.

reader, who has no time for special study, can understand it."

The first volume of four of which the set will be made up is essentially a setting forth of the grounds òf confidence in the doctrine of evolution. Its chapters cover astronomy, the story of evolution, the struggle for existence, the ascent of man, evolution going on, the dawn of mind, and foundations of the universe. By means of the last chapter, which treats of the constitution of matter as made up of protons and electrons, and the first, which shows the presence of the well-known chemical elements in the stars, one really gets a view of orderly progress in the whole universe from the simplest chemical constituent to the mind of a Bacon or a Shakespeare. Could one possibly read this fascinating, absorbing, yet authoritative narrative and follow the opponents of evolution? We trow not. One noteworthy example of its deadly refutation is in its proof of the fact of mutation of species as a constant and present factor. The anti-evolutionists ask—Whoever saw a species develop? Professor Thomson cites Marquis wheat as a new development since 1903! The conclusion of Chapter VI is:

Are we not convinced that evolution is going on? And *why should it stop?* (italics ours).

One thing more should be said here. The real scientist is never a dogmatician. He never overstates his case. So Professor Thomson has the following:

In all this, it may be said, the fact of evolution has been taken for granted, but what are the evidences? Perhaps, it should be frankly answered that the idea of evolution, that the present is the child of the past and the parent of the future, can not be proved as one may prove the law of gravitation. All that can be done is to show that it is a key—a way of looking at things —that fits the facts. There is no lock that it does not open.

Let not the theological dogmatician-antievolutionist take this as basis for an argument. For the following context refers explicitly to facts which are "evidences" of the validity of the evolution hypothesis— facts historical, embryological, physiological, and anatomical.

Volume II might well go under the caption "Natural History"—which is indeed assumed for three of the chapters. The chap-

ters are numbered continuously with the first volume, and the second adds chapters nine to fifteen. These are on The Wonders of Microscopy, The Body-Machine and Its Work, How Darwinism Stands To-day, and then the three under Natural History dealing with Birds, Mammals, and The Insect World. These are capped by the chapter on The Science of the Mind which takes up the New Psychology and Psycho-Analysis.

In chapter nine we find a splendid account of the power and the limitations of the microscope, with suggestions of the extensions of this power still possible. In this is also contained a description of the ultra-microscope, and an almost poetic description of the beauty revealed by this wonderful instrument. So much is quotable here that one hardly knows where to begin or where to stop, but perhaps these two sentences are as revealing as any in the chapter because of their tremendous scope:

Every many-celled creature, which reproduces in the ordinary way, starts on the journey of life as a single cell—the fertilized ovum. As we have made clear in a previous article, the usually microscopic fertilized egg-cell contains, in some way that we can not picture, the initiatives or "factors" for the hereditary characters of the living creature in question.

Professor Thomson begins his description of the human body with this statement: "The most perfect machine in the world is the body of man." Here all the processes which go to make that perfection possible are described, with the inclusion of the latest discovery which is still going on, namely, that of hormones. The question of mutual influence of mind and body is discust, and about two pages contain especially pertinent food for the pastor under the paragraph headings of The Cult of Joy and Healthy-Mindedness. Here for instance is a single sentence quoted from another of Professor Thomson's standard works:

Good tidings will invigorate the flagging energies of a band of explorers; an unexpected visit will change a wearied homesick child, as if by magic, into a dancing gladsome elf; a religious joy enables men and women to transcend the limits of our frail humanity.

What then can be said of Darwinism today? A chapter debates this subject pro and con and closes with the following dictum:

When we use the term Darwinism to mean, not his very words, but the living doctrine legitimately developed from his central ideas of variation, selection, and heredity, we may say that Darwinism stands to-day more firmly than ever. It has changed and is changing, but it is not crumbling away. It is evolving progressively.

The three chapters which follow on "Natural History" are a review of the subjects noted, namely, birds, mammals, and insects. How rich they are and how illuminated by the wonderfully pertinent and numerous illustrations, a review can hardly describe.

The final chapter of this volume on The Science of the Mind is a splendid resumé of the latest discoveries in psychology. The subject of the unconscious or the subconscious with that new term which is already become dominant in psychological discussions, namely, the "complexes," is illuminatingly set forth, brief but crystal clear.
—G. W. G.

The Historical Evidence of the Virgin Birth. By VINCENT TAYLOR. The Clarendon Press, Oxford, 1920. xiii—136 pp.

Belief in the virgin birth rests on two lines of consideration, namely, the accounts of the nativity in the first and third gospels and the dogmatic implications of the incarnation. These are commonly allowed to blend and affect the value each of the other. Mr. Taylor believes that each must be conceded a certain weight in the decision of the question. In fact, he claims that in the end the solution of the problem must depend on "the dogmatic considerations." But in undertaking the investigation of this treatise he has limited himself strictly to the historical evidence. Of the six chapters of the book the first is introductory. It presents the author's findings regarding the virgin birth in the New Testament, exclusive of the first and third gospels. The last chapter deals with the limits and bearings of the evidence. Of the four chapters between the first and sixth, three are given to the examination of the third gospel and its testimony, and one to that of the first gospel. The method of the author is scientific throughout; which means that in examining and estimating the evidence he aims to divest himself of all presuppositions. Of course, this is a very difficult goal to achieve. And if the author betrays in subtle ways his inclination to accept the virgin birth as historical on dogmatic grounds it does not mean that his criticism has been vitiated

by this acceptance. On the whole, it is difficult to see how a more calm and judicial attitude could have been maintained throughout the investigation.

The Teaching of the New Testament on Divorce. By R. H. CHARLES. Williams and Norgate, London, 1921. xiii—127 pp. 6/- net.

The critical study of the New Testament has brought into view a certain interpretation of the words of Jesus on the subject of divorce which Dr. Charles thinks is not justified. This view assumes that the report of Jesus' words given in Mark is the primitive and correct one, and that Matthew's report which includes the additional words "except for fornication" is an unauthorized elaboration. Dr. Charles is not satisfied with this conclusion; and, upon a thorough examination of the subject in the whole New Testament and of the background furnished by the Old Testament and the Jewish thought and practise, he shows that Matthew's report is more nearly expressive of the mind of Jesus. The method of the author is thoroughly scientific and his conclusion commends itself as inevitable.

The Promise of His Coming: A Historical Interpretation and Revolution of the Idea of the Second Advent. By CHESTER CHARLTON McCOWN. The Macmillan Co., New York, 1921. xvi—256 pp.

If the word "revolution" in the subordinate title of this book were changed to "revaluation" it would, in our judgment, quite adequately describe the nature and drift of the author's thought. What he aims to do is to find the spiritual value of the belief in the millennium and of the expectation of a second coming of Christ and to show how that spiritual value may be conserved in the life of a generation that can no longer believe in the literal fulfilment of the Scriptural foreshadowings of the event. The author's method is predominantly historical. He traces the belief in an age of ideal conditions from its beginnings in the earliest stages of human civilization through its Old Testament form, as the hope of a Messianic kingdom, to its final formation into a clear conception of a millennium in the New Testament. The fact that this conception has been so tenaciously held convinces him that it has spiritual value. But he is also convinced that the apocalyptic presentation of it, still clung to by the premillennialists, has lost its power on the modern mind. He offers as a substitute for this presentation the "social spiritual view" of a golden age as the fulfilment of "the promise of his coming." That the offer will be accepted is too much to expect. But if the author's view meets with the interest it deserves and arouses further discussion it will have served a good purpose.

America's Stake in Europe. By CHARLES HARVEY FAHS. Association Press, New York, 1921. 8¾ x 5¾ in., 186 pp. $1.35.

America's part in the foreign affairs of the world is greater than ever before and the need to-day is to get the people interested and informed on all the questions that have been discust at Washington. Hence a book like this one before us will serve a useful purpose. Each chapter has two parts: a list of questions lead to ten points at issue and quotations drawn from many sources throw light on the particular subjects. The nature of the questions may be gleaned from the headings of the first three chapters: What is America's Present Stake in Europe, Should America Reassert Her Former Isolation from European Affairs, How Long Ought America to Share in European Relief.

A Cruise to the Orient. By ANDREW W. ARCHIBALD. The Stratford Company, Boston, 1921. 7¾ x 5½ in., 286 pp. $3.50.

This very attractive and interesting volume has six chapters on what the author is pleased to call "the world's greatest centers of interest," Rome, Athens, Cairo, Karnak, Constantinople, and Jerusalem. In his preface he mentions that he has aimed to produce a volume, which might be considered a satisfactory resumé for those who have been to the Orient, and a sufficient guide, as to the main things to be seen, for those who plan to go, and a succinct yet graphic compendium for those who can not gratify their desire to take the trip, but who still wish for the information that would seem to be essential to any claiming to be at all adequately educated. There is a vivid sketch at the beginning of the volume entitled "Dramatic Ending of the World War" which is very well worth reading, even tho we are three years from the close of the war. The volume has four maps and sixty-four illustrations.

System der Ethik, VON REINHOLD SEEBERG; **Grundriss der Theologischen Ethik,** VON OTTO KIRN; **Grundriss der Symbolik: Konfessionskunde,** VON GUSTAV PLITT. A. Deichartsche Verlagsbuchhandlung, Leipzig.

These books by well-known German writers, two of whom are no longer living but whose works have been edited by competent hands, bear the marks of thoroughness which characterizes German scholarship. One hopes that the time is not far distant when our study tables will again be enriched by works which enshrine the method and results of German learning, which so far at least has not been eclipsed by attainments of scholars in any other part of the world. We can only pray that the day may be hastened when the economic condition of the Fatherland may once more enable its research students and its thinkers to enlarge our facilities for the better interpretation of the meaning of life.

The Psalms as Liturgies, being the Paddock Lectures for 1920. By JOHN P. PETERS. The Macmillan Company, New York, 1921. 494 pp. $4.00.

This book is an elaborate and well-reasoned protest against the prevalent critical attitude to the Psalter, which regards the psalms as occasional poems and attempts with more or less confidence to discover the occasion of them in historical incidents or personal experience. As against this Dr. Peters regards the psalms as essentially ritual or liturgical hymns; in some of these he even finds rubrics (e.g., 118:27b; cf. 68:12₋14) which have hitherto been wrongly regarded as part of the text. Even more striking is his plea for an early date for psalms which much criticism has complacently relegated to the post-exilic period. David, we are told, is "the father of a new liturgical hymnody on the ancient lines," and Psalms 18, 20, 21 and 24 are "indisputable evidence of an early pre-exilic period." More striking still is his view that while books I, IV, and V are in origin Judean, books II and III are in origin Israelitic, and in particular that the Korahitic psalms are connected with the sanctuary of Dan (cf. Pss. 42, 46) and the Asaphic psalms with Bethel. All this is urged with great skill and cogency, and the various points of the argument are illustrated by a detailed investigation of each of the Psalms seriatim. This is a very forceful and independent contribution, which may well prove to be epoch-making, to the criticism of the Psalter; in any case it will have to be seriously reckoned with by critics of every school.

On the Rim of the World. By J. PATERSON-SMYTH. Fleming H. Revell Company, New York, 1922. 7¾ x 5¼ in., 83 pp. 75 cents.

The well-known author describes exactly his aim in the first sentence of his Preface:

The purpose of this little book is to offer assurance and consolation to that wistful crowd who stand, as it were, on the Rim of the World looking out through the earth mists toward that land where their beloved have gone.

By the "rim of the world" he means actual or conceived proximity to death. Death is to him entry upon new life. From a firm faith in this as a certainty proceeds a most alluring and satisfying "book of comfort"—for the living who have long to live or but a brief time, particularly for those who have dear ones the other side of the "rim."

Outside of comforting and fortifying the ministers themselves, this little volume may well prove a welcome source from which to derive real comfort while ministering in public or private to those long ago or recently bereaved by death.

A chapter from the book is reproduced on p. 241 of this issue.

In the Breaking of the Bread. By JAMES I. VANCE. Fleming H. Revell Company, New York, 1922. 7¾ x 5¼ in., 183 pp. $1.25.

Everybody knows that preparation is a necessary part of getting the most out of a thing or putting the most into the things we do. The seven or eight hours' rest every night is a preparation of body and mind for the duties of the day. Likewise a preparation of the spirit, by meditation and prayer, will create an attitude and an atmosphere rich in results. It is in this connection that these communion addresses will be found to be helpful and suggestive.

Our readers are introduced to the volume by one of the addresses (there are twenty-four in all) given in another department of this issue.

Religioses und Kirchliches Leben in England. By OTTO BAUMGARTEN, B. G. Teuber, Berlin, 1922. 8½ x 5¾ in., 122 pp.

One hardly expects from German sources so appreciative an estimate of religious forces in England as this from Professor Baumgarten of Keil. He divides religious life there into eleven types—those represented by the terms state-church, low-church, high-church, evangelical, broad-church, Methodistic, Puritanic, "life-reform" (Baptists and Quakers), millennarian, ecclesiastical-social, and esthetic-religious (Ruskin and his like). The background of each of these types is given and evaluated, and their significance in the present is pointed out. Some shrewd judgments are exprest, e.g., on the great power of the Bible in English life and thought, or as Baumgarten expresses it, the English "biblicity." The author sees many characteristics that might be included in German religion, altho German forms of piety are "purer and truer."

The Study of the New Testament, 1883-1920. By CUTHBERT H. TURNER, Oxford. University Press, Oxford and New York, 1920. 66 pp.

On assuming his official duties the Dean Ireland Professor of Exegesis in the University of Oxford took occasion to speak of the progress achieved in the department of New Testament interpretation from 1883 to 1920. The first of these dates marks the accession to the Dean Ireland professorship of the late Dr. Sanday, the second his own inauguration to the same chair. It is a significant period and Professor Turner gives an interesting sketch of the work done in it. The personality of Dr. Sanday appears conspicuously in the story and adds to its interest. The lecturer follows the line laid down by Sanday in tracing progress first in the study of the Christian literature of the second century, second in New Testament introduction, third in the criticism of the New Testament books, and lastly in the criticism of the text of the New Testament. It is a scholarly production and suggestive as well as informing throughout.

GEORGE HOLLEY GILBERT

Born at Cavendish, Vt., November 4, 1854; son of Oliver C. and Harriet E. G. A.B., Dartmouth, 1878; graduated from Union Theological Seminary, 1883; Ph.D., University of Leipzig, 1885; (D.D., Dartmouth, 1894). Ordained to Congregational ministry, 1886. Acting professor of New Testament literature, 1886-7; professor, 1887-1901, Chicago Theological Seminary. Author: *The Poetry of Job*, 1888; *The Student's Life of Jesus*, 1899; *The Student's Life of Paul*, 1899; *The Revelation of Jesus*, 1900; *The First Interpreters of Jesus*, 1901; *A Primer of the Christian Religion*, 1902; *A Short History of Christianity in the Apostolic Age*, 1906; *History of the Interpretation of the Bible*, 1908; *A Commentary on Acts*, 1908; *Jesus*, 1912; *The Bible and Universal Peace*, 1914; *Jesus for the Men of Today*, 1917.

GEORGE HOLLEY GILBERT, D.D., Pʜ.D.

The HOMILETIC REVIEW

VOL. 84   OCTOBER, 1922   No. 4

JUGGLING WITH THE BIBLE

GEORGE HOLLEY GILBERT, Ph.D., D.D., Dorset, Vt.

History and the modern scientific investigation of religion support with overwhelming force two propositions concerning the Bible: First, that it is the apex of the religious literature of the world, and second, that, when juggled with, it may be one of the greatest hindrances to human progress. There are many other sacred writings, some much older than the Bible and some that have ministered light and comfort to millions of men more in number than the Bible has yet reached; but for a century at least the Bible has had a missionary reception and influence unparalleled in the history of any other sacred book, and it would probably be difficult to find a student of comparative religion, whether Christian or not, who would hesitate to rank some of the Hebrew psalms, portions of the prophets, and the Sermon on the Mount above the most inspiring passages in Confucius, in the Vedas, in Zoroaster, or in the classic poets of Greece and Rome.

Mahatma Gandhi, said to be the best loved man in India to-day, declares that he has found a more potent stimulus and a fuller joy in the words of Jesus than in the Vedas, tho these also he profoundly honors.

It may be true, on the other hand, that we can not find in any of the greater ethnic religions a narrower conception of man's duty, a more ignoble view of God, or a more pessimistic outlook on the future beyond the grave than can be found here and there in our Old Testament. Notwithstanding this admission, the claim is confidently made that the Bible as a whole is the supreme achievement of the religious spirit of man. This is a lofty and a sufficient claim. It is this clear and solid ground that the Church should hold, and not continue to make for the Bible those unprovable claims which have always fostered a juggling method of interpretation, destructive of the historical sense and often seriously militating against human progress. How universal and persistent has been the influence of such claims on the exposition of Scripture one may learn from the literature of the Church, and one must learn this in order to appreciate the vast and unique service rendered to the world by the modern scientific study of the Bible.

We shall make some references to this rich literature of exposition, not to bring any reproach on the authors, who were good men—some of them also great and to be held in high honor—but merely to show how even such men, approaching the Bible as a strictly supernatural product, juggled with it. We begin this brief examination with the second century.

Barnabas, whose epistle was once regarded as a sacred writing, found deep mysteries beneath the literal sense of the Old Testament text. It is said in Genesis, in the epic of creation, that the Lord finished his work in six days. This, says Barnabas, implies that he will finish all things (i. e., close human history) in six thousand years, since it is said in psalms that one day is with him as a thousand years. Again, we are told that Abraham had 318 trained men, born in his house. Barnabas assumed that there must be some deep truth wrapped up in this number, and he labored with it until he discovered therein the doctrine of the cross of Christ! And note how he discovered it. Each letter of the Greek alphabet has a certain numerical value. The letters that correspond to the figures 3, 1, and 8 are the same as the first two letters of the name Jesus in Greek, and the letter T, which by its very form points unmistakably, says Barnabas, to the cross. The historical sense of the statement in Genesis is of course wholly eclipsed by this deep unfolding.

Origen's great ability and voluminous writings helped to make juggling with the Bible a necessity, for he taught that all its words have two senses and the majority of them three. This made the Scriptures a playground for fancy, the only check on the interpreter being this, that he must not bring forth anything that did not square with the traditions of the Church. Let the following instance suggest how Origen extracted the third and profoundest sense of the text. The modest forerunner of Jesus declared himself unworthy to loose the shoe-latchet of his successor. In one narrative he uses the word "shoe" in the singular and in another in the plural. Now the shoe, says the great Father of the third century, is a mysterious reference to Christ's human-

ity, the explanation of which is "tied up." This is the first step in the interpretation. No reason is given why one should hold that the "shoe" means Christ's humanity, because there is no reason. The idea is an absurd fancy. But why does one gospel have the word in the singular and the other in the plural? Origen replies that when the forerunner spoke of one shoe he was in doubt whether Jesus was to descend into Hades, which is the meaning of the second shoe!

Augustine was another master of this art of burying the historical sense of Scripture and of summoning forth high mysteries from the most unpromising soil. He regarded every statement of the Bible as having two meanings, one literal and the other figurative. His chief interest was in the latter meaning, and in determining this he gave free rein to his exuberant fancy. Thus the ark of Noah meant the body of Christ and also the Church. Its very dimensions prefigured the human body, for its length was six times its breadth and ten times its thickness or depth. The door in the side of the ark, says our interpreter, surely signified the wound in the side of the crucified Savior. As for the numbers found throughout the Bible, even those of the most commonplace narratives, under the magic touch of Augustine's fancy they yielded rich meanings. Thus in the number of fish taken one night by a group of the apostles he discovered a double reference to the mystery of the Trinity, and in this manner. The number is 153, and this contains the number fifty three times with a remainder of three, plainly two allusions to the Trinity! And even this is not all that the number teaches. If a man is to be saved, says Augustine, the law must be supplemented by the spirit of grace. Now the number of the law is ten, that of the spirit is seven—seventeen in all, and, wonderful to relate, if we add the numbers from one to seventeen we get 153!

Athanasius, the famous theologian of Alexandria, constructed the "orthodox" doctrine of the person of Christ, not chiefly from the New Testament, not even from the gospels, which one might think a natural and safe thing to do, but out of a vague poetic passage in praise of wisdom in the book of Proverbs! And it was over this doctrine that the Church was split and much blood was shed.

During the chaotic centuries of the medieval period there was no independent study of the Bible, and extremely little study of any sort whatever. Those of the clergy who could read explained the Scriptures as the ancient Fathers had taught. When Boniface VIII wished to prove that the Christian Church is one and that outside of it there is no salvation, he appealed to three texts, all from the Old Testament, all therefore from a time when there was no Christian Church. His demonstration, tho not wholly original, is true to the traditional type. The first of his texts is the words of the lover in the Song of Songs: "My dove, my undefiled, is one." Obviously a cogent proof if we allow the far-fetched fancy that the maiden of this old love song stood for the Church of the future. A natural reading of the text, of course, sees in her simply a maiden and nothing more. The second proof that the Church is one was found in the story of the flood: as there was but one ark, so there is but one Church. It is indeed a little strange that since the Biblical doctrine of one Church is so obvious there should be now about 700 different churches! The third and last proof that Boniface ' offers is found in a couplet of the twenty-second Psalm:

"Deliver my soul from the sword,
  My darling from the power of the
    dog."

"Soul" here means Christ—that, by the way, is taken as self-evident—and "darling" means the Church—one Church. This is all beautifully simple and conclusive if only it can be shown that the author meant Christ when he said "soul" and meant the Church when he said "darling." But we must not be critical over against Boniface or his greater predecessors. They had small use for the plain sense of the Bible and great confidence in their ability to get out of it a mystical sense of far more worth.

We pass from Boniface VIII to Luther without experiencing any serious jolt. Both approached the Bible as a miraculous book in which one has but to penetrate beneath the literal sense in order to reach profound mysteries. Luther, like the early fathers, went to the Old Testament rather than to the New; and with utter disregard for historical development, which Jesus never disregarded, he boldly read into it the traditional theology of the Church. He found more references to Christ and his kingdom in the book of Genesis than in any other book, and there, in the epic of creation (which has its roots far back in Babylonian history), he discovered the doctrine of the Trinity with an "unspeakable and unfathomable" Christ! The poetical designation of the eastern sky, in Ps. 110, as "the womb of the morning" is said to point to the supernatural birth of Jesus. The words of another psalm, "Let God arise, let his enemies be scattered!" which were rightly taken by Cromwell as a prayer and a war-cry when he entered on the battle of Marston Moor, were interpreted by Luther as referring to the resurrection of Jesus. Here is a final illustration of his handling of Scripture. We read in Ps. 3 these words:

"I laid me down and slept;
  I awaked, for Jehovah sustaineth
    me."

The ordinary unsophisticated reader has no more trouble with these words than with the modern rime: "Now I lay me down to sleep"; but Luther, not content with the simple sense of the words and continually looking for proof either of N. T. historical statements, which might be left to take care of themselves, or of the teachings of traditional theology, thus expounds the passage. It would be "absurd," he says, to suppose that it refers to natural sleep, hence it must refer to the resurrection of Jesus, and therefore we are obliged to believe that it was spoken by Jesus! To such desperate logic may one descend who regards the Bible as a miraculous book of mysteries and who is hunting for proof texts.

These illustrations must suffice, tho one might give thousands like them, drawn from nearly all the famous interpreters and theologians down to recent times. The natural historical sense of the Bible has counted for little, the real divine treasure has been obtained by allegorical, anagogical, mystical means. This juggling treatment might be passed over in pity and forgotten had it not deeply colored or even essentially determined the doctrines of the Church.

With the study of Hebrew and Greek in the sixteenth century began the scientific method of Bible interpretation, and the development of this method in the past hundred years forms one of the most instructive and valuable chapters of all Christian history. Yet the old leaven is by no means all purged away out of the life of the Church. How widespread, for instance, is the undiscriminating use of Scripture! Is it not all a garden of the Lord, and can he not be found in every part of it? It is this view which is responsible for a colossal waste of time in the religious training of the young who are taken through the Old Testament as well as the New.

This method usually means a reading of the New Testament back into the Old, which of course is nothing less than an overturning of history and the nullification of the divine law of development; but whether it means this in every case or not, it always means a certain neglect of that element of the Bible which alone is essential, that is, the Christian element.

It is this undiscriminating use of Scripture that gives so keen a pathos to the story of religious persecution. The burning of heretics and the hanging of witches, once not unpopular among our ancestors, were advocated on the ground of clear Biblical texts. Where then was the trouble? Our ancestors were not less merciful than we of the present day, but they were more completely imprisoned in a false view of the Bible. In their saner moods they might feel that there was a conflict between the command to exterminate the Midianites and the teaching of Jesus to love our enemies, but being men they chose the line of least resistance, and when occasion offered they proceeded without scruple to exterminate their Midianites, and did it for the glory of God! Gross indiscriminateness in the use of the Bible in high places has hurt the cause of truth again and again in our own day. For example, there has not been a trial for heresy in which the Scriptures have not been conscientiously tortured in this respect, juggled with as a book of mysteries and their authority with thinking people often undermined.

Another remnant of the old leaven is to be seen in the fact that many regard the Bible as a book of rules, valid for all people of all times. The Old Testament lends itself to this unfortunate view far more readily than does the New. Indeed no footing whatever can be found for it in the authentic teaching of Jesus. His concern was with principles, not with rules. They who regard the Bible as a book of rules juggle with it variously. They take one rule and ignore another. They preach that one should give tithes to the Church, but they eat pork. They teach that no work should be done on the Sabbath, but they do not keep the feast of the new moon. Thus they choose and reject, but always claim Bible authority for that which they choose. Naturally, too, they who find in the Bible rules for the outward life, tho not denying that it contains principles also, sometimes choose a rule given to Israel and thereby neglect a principle laid down in the gospel. As between these two the rule is less exacting than the principle. Thus a certain Jewish rule demands of you a tithe, but a certain Christian principle, working from within, constrains you to give all, yourself included.

And so we come again to the admission that through the traditional handling of the Bible the Christian element is ignored or minimized, while other elements lower and hostile to it are exalted as a divine standard. What now can be done to save the Bible from the indifference which is felt toward it among great masses of educated people in Christian lands? Must we not first of all strip off the false claims made for the Bible and try to look at it naturally and sensibly, in its naked strength or weakness, just as we seek to look at other books which we desire to understand? The temptation to juggle with the Bible would thus be largely removed.

Must we not also—we at least who wish to promote the Christian religion —concentrate our interest and our claims on the Christian element in the Bible? This is but a small fraction of the whole. There are various standards of thought and life in the Bible, but only one Christian standard. One of the greatest needs of the Church to-day seems to be to liberate this standard from the vast heterogeneous literature in which it is contained. It is this alone that really matters: the rest, tho of value for the history of religion, is a burden to Christian faith.

Doubtless there are many preachers who quietly limit their teaching to the gospel, and those other parts of Scripture which they regard as akin to the gospel, but this has never sufficed The Christian element, the unquestionable religious basis of the Christian social structure of the future, must come out and be separate from the Jewish and pagan elements. There is no successful business and no successful government which rests upon such a medley of conflicting standards as we have beneath the historical Christian Church.

And finally, must we not add to our Christian standard those revelations of truth, that is, revelations of the will of God, which have been made in subsequent centuries, especially in the recent scientific period? If Jesus saw religious values in nature—in the dress of lilies, in sunshine and shower, and in the mysterious potencies of the soil beneath his feet—may we not also find religious values there, and especially since through the microscope, the telescope, and the spectroscope wide realms of truth, undreamed of in his day, have been opened before us? The vastness and the unity of the universe, the absoluteness of the reign of law, the conservation of energy, the method of creation, the inexhaustible wonders of organic structures, the mechanisms of plant life, the growth and powers of the human mind—have not the discoveries in these lines of investigation a religious value which binds them up harmoniously with the supreme spiritual revelation in Jesus' person and teaching?

It may sound like a paradox, yet it can not be successfully gainsaid, that the Bible is much too large and is also too small. There is very much in it that does not belong to the Christian standard, and a great deal outside which ought to be reverently associated with that standard as confirming, modernizing and expanding it for the enlarging life of to-day and of the future.

The state of the Church can not be deeply and permanently bettered while its fundamental documentary basis remains vague, shifting, and composed of irreconcilable elements, all protected by the magic shield of a supernal origin.

WHY I SUPPORT MISSIONS

John Archibald MacCallum, D.D., Philadelphia, Pa.

The mere announcement of a missionary sermon is enough to keep a considerable number of people away from church in most Christian congregations and even among those who come there will be not a few whose attitude of mind is indifferent or latently hostile. Sometimes I wish we could find another word for missions, tho I suppose it would soon become worn and weak in its appeal. The important question is why so many people who support missions even in a perfunctory way are not interested in hearing of the results of missionary effort. They say that the subject is dull, but I am sure that this is not the deep underlying reason. The mention of missions is a reminder of those obligations which lie beyond the zone of immediate responsibility, and we naturally prefer to draw the curtains of our minds over them. It is unpleasant to be reminded of duties we have no intention of performing and for the avoidance of which we have built up a formidable breastwork of excuses. But we must be honest with ourselves, and even tho our defenses have been put together at a great cost of time and trouble, we should not be afraid to have them tested. If they can withstand the weight of argument brought against them, well and good. Then we shall have peace in our minds, knowing that we are in an impregnable position. But if our bulwarks yield and

a breach is opened through them, however disconcerting it may be, we shall have the satisfaction of knowing the truth. He who wilfully shuts his mind to truth lives in a fool's paradise.

Let us then divest ourselves as far as possible of all preconceived ideas and traditional opinions and ask whether as Christians we should be supporters of missions. I am not drawing a line between home and foreign missions, for in the realm of moral obligation distance is not a factor. Geographically we can say where our nation ends and other nations begin, but in ideas, motives, and spiritual influences nations overflow their boundaries and interpenetrate one another throughout the world. A thought born in Tokio may lodge forthwith in responsive minds anywhere and everywhere in the world and bear much fruit for good or ill. Altho for practical purposes the Church is organized with home and foreign spheres, so far as obligations and ultimate purposes go there is no distinction between the two.

I. First, as a Christian I am a supporter of missions because of the explicit command of our Lord. "Go ye therefore and teach all nations. . . . Ye shall be witnesses unto me . . . unto the uttermost parts of the earth." In so far as we are loyal to our Master we have the missionary motive, because it is in accordance with his will.

But the divine commands are never arbitrary. They are not the capricious orders of a despotic ruler. Before the decalog was written upon tables of stone its laws were inscribed upon the hearts of men. They were a part of the texture of personality, both in God and man. Thou shalt not kill, or commit adultery, or bear false witness. Why? Not because God has so ordained, but because the personality of our neighbor is sacred and must be honored or there can be no social life. God's laws rise out of our nature and our needs. And this command that we go out and teach all nations is no exception to the rule. There is a reason for it, and that reason is to be found within ourselves.

It is an inherent quality of spiritualized human nature that we should act for the good of others as we have the opportunity. Suppose a child across the street is seriously ill, and I believe I know of a physician who can effect a cure. My impulse is to tell its parents at once. Nor would I check this impulse because they are strangers or Buddhists or Mohammedans. But I believe in the gospel of Christ, and I am confident that when it is proclaimed and understood it saves men from superstition, from inadequate knowledge of God and duty, and above all from sin. If I am ready to act on the lower ground of my neighbor's physical good, surely it is most inconsistent to refrain from action in behalf of his immeasurably higher spiritual good. In a word, that is the genius of missions. The missionary is the man who tells those who do not know Christ that he will give them strength, freedom, peace, illumination, power against evil, and eternal life. Surely we have every reason to shrink from being numbered among those who know a great life-giving truth and refuse to tell it to those who do not know it and allow them to stumble on in superstition.

One of the most glorious things about Christ is this—he never asks his friends to do what he refuses to do himself. We are his friends as well as his disciples and apart from all constraint should rejoice to follow his example. From the beginning of his ministry he was a missionary, a herald of the truth. He called his first disciples and taught them. He gave them a self-respect and sense of worth they never had before when he told them they were the children of God, and that God cared for them; but tho they were his countrymen and co-religionists, he did not restrict his message to them. Once, when the people became too clamorous for signs and wonders, he left Jerusalem for Galilee and passed through Samaria, an alien country, and talked to a woman he met at Jacob's well, and she believed his message. Through her he met several men of her city and they also believed and invited him to remain with them, which he did for two days. Jesus was a foreign missionary before any of his disciples.

II. In the second place I support missions because I myself am a direct fruit of missionary endeavor. We can pay our debt to those who went before us not by singing their praises but by carrying on in their spirit. It was almost overwhelming for the first disciples to grasp the wider meaning of their commission, to go into the outside world and preach, and most of them were incapable of it, even tho they had been close to Jesus for so long. Paul, however, did grasp the purpose of the Lord, and so he and others who saw the same truth went out into Asia Minor along the great highways of the Roman empire planting missions in foreign lands and often in non-Jewish neighborhoods, until at last he reached the zenith of his ambition and preached the gospel in Rome. Through the heroic self-sacrifice, fervor, and wisdom of the first missionaries of the cross, Christianity became rooted in the Roman empire. It would have remained a mere sect in Palestine had it not been for this vision of a redeemed world which has always characterized the leaders of the Church except in time of decadence.

Nor did the impulse stop at Rome. Thence it spread like leaven into the surrounding peoples, and tho the rough men of Northern Europe bore down upon the empire and submerged it, in turn they were at least partially subdued by the chastening and uplifting spirit of the gospel. Charlemagne became a convert, and tho the Christian experience of the multitudes was sadly immature, it contained the germs of a great promise which some day will be fulfilled. Meantime, the missionaries went to England, Ireland, and Scotland, where the forefathers of this republic were dwelling in bogs and fens and worshiping stocks and stones. The Pilgrims and the Puritans and the other adventurers who crossed the Atlantic to establish themselves on this continent were the result of Christian missions, and as their children we share the same inheritance. It is only through ignorance of this essential fact that anyone professing to be a follower of Christ can disavow interest in the very agency by means of which our civilization, culture, and faith were made possible. No wise and kind-hearted man denies to others at the bottom the ladder by which he has climbed out of a pit. The only way for the Christian to repay his debts to those whose heroism and sacrifice created the benefits he enjoys is by working to fulfil their uncompleted tasks.

III. The third reason why I support missions is the value of the investment from a material point of view. I realize that this is to put the matter on a low level, but life is composed of many motives, and it may not be amiss to remind those who have little imagination and idealism that there is a close relationship between business welfare and the evangelization of the world. The truth is that for every dollar that has gone into missions several dollars in actual profits have come back. Take any frontier town with its saloons and gambling houses running day and night at full blast with attendant disregard of law and order, and establish a church in it. Even tho the vicious elements in the community are not transformed, they will soor be unable to ply the worst features of their trade in the open, and gradually but inevitably a better type of citizen will develop and secure at least partial control of affairs. Public opinion will be elevated by the very men who without the church would have conformed to the lowest standards. The teaching of the gospel draws out' and nurtures their better nature and they shake off the rule of violence and passion, and their improved citizenship more than compensates in money for the cost. This is equally true of missions in remote lands. Many years have passed since John Williams was killed by cannibals on a far-off island under the Southern Cross. He was followed by John G. Paton who, undeterred by his tragic death, went in and out among these primal men and by his Christlike patience, wisdom, and love won them to accept his God. In that work he has been followed by many others with the result that to-day British, French, American, and Japanese traders move freely from island to island, buying the rich products of the soil with their cotton and other goods. The missionary made this possible, tho those who profit most by his heroism and sacrifice rarely give him help or credit, and even speak scornfully of his motive and work.

What is true of Polynesia is even more true of China, Japan, and India. Enlightenment brings enlarged personality and enlarged personality again results in increased wants. The growing demand for Western goods in all parts of the Orient is largely due to the intellectual and spiritual expansions of the people brought about directly and indirectly through the efforts of the Christian missionary. Many a manufacturer or merchant who has grown wealthy through foreign trade remains utterly blind to his benefactors and never dreams of expressing his gratitude by supporting the cause from which he has received so much. While this is not an argument that should be emphasized, since the essential purpose of the gospel is not material gain, for the sake of the weaker brethren it is well to keep in mind that Christian enlightenment always pays. If every man in the world were truly Christian our taxes would be lower, our homes safer, and the physical fabric of civilization much more secure.

IV. The fourth reason why I support missions is the type of manhood represented by them. The royalty of human nature at its best is nowhere so well illustrated on a large scale as in the men who have the imagination to hear "the still sad music of humanity," and seek to transpose it from a minor to a major key. They catch the vision of the tears of the uncounted millions of other faiths and races, and because of the depth of their sympathy and their clear understanding of the purpose of God, they renounce every material prize the world affords that they may follow the example of Jesus and do good where the largest opportunity offers. Theirs is the greatest adventure of the spirit, for they go out into hard places and strange lands, not for what they can get but for what they can give. The soldier may be equally

brave and the trader equally ready to face hardship, but in neither case is the sustaining motive so free from the taint of worldly advantage. From God alone comes the strength which enables a man to accept poverty, obscurity, and humiliation for the good of men different in color, traditions, and ideals, who do not ask for his ministry and often reject it when it is offered.

In the light of these considerations it is not surprising that the number of missionaries of majestic proportions forms so imposing a list. While they gave themselves with no thought of earthly reward, fame and reverence have often been their portion. In losing life, they found it. Who is so dull as to fail in appreciation of such a hero as Francis Xavier? He was born in a princely home in feudal Spain, with the assurance of every material gift this world can offer. He was a courtier of distinction and a scholar of wide interests and rare culture. But when Ignatius Loyola, his superior and friend in the Jesuit order, asked him to go to India, he went without hesitation, living on the long voyage out among the common sailors in order to convert them; remaining with them and ministering to their needs during an outbreak of scurvy. Thereafter we find him moving swiftly from place to place through malarial jungles, or traveling on pirate vessels to various islands of the Malay Archipelago, or on the burning sands of the deadly shores of the "Fishery Coast," or hurrying to Japan, his soul aflame with zeal for the conversion of the people. Tho fever racked him, his spirit remained undaunted. Never did he allow an opportunity to pass without trying to kindle in the minds of all whom he met a sense of sin and of the need of salvation. The burden of his message to everyone was this—"What shall it profit a man if he gain the whole world and lose his own soul?" He died at his post, worn out at forty-six.

Equally heroic and inspiring is the record of the service rendered by a multitude of men with a kindred zeal to help and uplift their fellows. Adoniram Judson lay for eleven months heavily fettered in the death prison at Ava in Burma. In this dark and filthy hole which had been unwashed since it was built, crowded close to other prisoners, life was too horrible to describe. His tortures were intensified by fear of the fate of his wife, yet when he gained his freedom he did not turn his back upon his oppressors, but continued his ministry to those who had mis-judged and maltreated him. For sheer determination in the face of difficulty none can surpass William Carey, the first Protestant missionary from England to India, who tho still a shoemaker at twenty-eight, became famous as a scholar and translator of the Bible and a great light in a dark land. In practical achievement David Livingstone is one of the colossal figures of history, for he was great as a pioneer, an empire-builder, a geographer, and "a visioner of a bet-ter day." For romantic, self-sacrific-ing achievement, Pennell of the Afghan frontier stands at the sum-mit of his generation. Tho he in-herited wealth and culture, he chose the most difficult and dangerous field of service, and in the pursuit of duty died an early and glorious death. To mention only one man among the liv-ing who is cast in the same heroic mold, there is Grenfell of Labrador, patrolling its grim coasts through wintry seas that he may heal the neglected fisher-folk of that bleak northern land. We speak of Xavier as a saint only because he was unique in his generation. An extended cata-log of sublime achievements could easily be made from the stern Jesuits

of North America of whom Parkman tells, down to a recent martyr, Dr. Shelton of Tibet, who a short time ago was murdered by bandits in the foothills of the Himalayas. There are thousands of missionaries to-day who with no complaint and no thought of doing anything noteworthy are giving their lives to a cause so vast that its impact upon even a small man makes him large. Sometimes their creeds are narrow, but their motives are so pure and free from self-regard that in action they burst these self-imposed shackles, and their minds move with mighty strides toward a world re-deemed from ignorance, superstition, and sin.

V. The fifth reason why I support missions is their definite results ex-prest in terms of human betterment. The missionary uses as his vehicle of light the school and the hospital, and in these latter days he teaches the people to rise in the scale of well-being by showing them how to use their own resources. The work of Sam Higginbottom in introducing modern methods of agriculture into India marks him as one of the greatest forces for good in this generation, and as much of a pioneer as Carey. For there is a definite relationship between physical and spiritual health. Impoverished men can not have aspi-rations equal to those of men who are strong and self-respecting. Dr. Vin-cent of Siam rendered great service to that nation by teaching the people to tan and manufacture leather and thus better themselves economically. The modern missionary is a teacher who opens a new world of thought to ignorant men, and thus points the way to God. He is a physician who heals their bodies, and shows others how to heal. He is a thinker who sees the virtues of the strange people among whom he works, and he en-larges those virtues by grafting into them the truth of the gospel; and as things true, lovely, pure, and of good report when woven into the fabric of personality become our civilization at its best, as shown in people who are generous, chivalrous, loyal, reverent, and God-fearing, so the missionary works to make a world in which no child will be robbed of his divinely given right to grow up "unto the measure of the stature of the fulness of Christ." And tho this is still a remote ideal, there are many encouraging signs which show that it is not visionary. No man who visits a mission station, whether in Africa among primal peoples, or in India, China, or Japan, will dare deny the great benefits it confers upon the community in many direct and indirect ways, sanitary, economic, intellectual, and spiritual.

VI. The sixth reason why I support missions is my patriotism. Strong tho this nation is, it is not immune from those dangers which injure and threaten other nations. Whatever our politicians attempt, we can not live to ourselves alone. China tried building a wall around herself centuries ago, but it did not keep out foreigners or their ideas. Japan and Korea also tried isolation. There is no absolute quarantine against disease. Our brotherhood with all other peoples was attested and confirmed by the influenza which broke so many of our homes a few years ago, coming from the interior of Russia. If we would escape from such disasters in the future, we must remove the cause at the source. Thus every alert American has a direct interest in the sanitary conditions of the Urals or Mongolia. And there are diseases of the mind and soul as well as of the body. Here quarantine is impossible. The false doctrines of Bolshevism, anarchy, and atheism are always seeking a lodging place in the minds of our people. And while we must adopt such preventive measures as are with-

in our power to destroy their virulence, here again the best strategy is to attack them at their source. If the present leaders of Russia had been Christian, how vastly different, less painful, and less disastrous would have been the course of recent history.

The world has become a neighborhood. In a short time a few powerful radiophones will reach out over the whole earth. Even now the human voice is distinctly heard by wireless anywhere in a circle within a radius of fourteen hundred miles. Little calculation is necessary to show that a very few stations would cover all the populated areas of the globe and most of its waters. Hence our only safety lies in constant watchfulness against false doctrines abroad. Nor can these be destroyed by force. We might as well try to kill microbes with clubs. Truth alone destroys error. If we go with the truth as it is set forth in Christ to those who are the victims of error, in God's own time our light will become their light. Every intelligent and true lover of his country will support the missionary on the remotest field, for he stands guard against evils which if unchecked will injure or destroy the nation.

VII. The seventh reason why I support missions is the welfare of my own soul. Nor is this a selfish motive, since my well-being can not be achieved apart from the well-being of others. Only as I give can I receive fulness of life. A measure of happiness may be realized by those whose one aim is to acquire wealth and to eat, drink, and be merry, but this happiness has no growing or creative content. It is sterile, and as the years flow on the soul becomes increasingly barren and less receptive to those values and interests which widen the range of life and bring peace because they are in harmony with the purpose of God. We are his children and all other men are our brothers. We pass from death to life only as we love them and have faith in them and work for their emancipation from sin. We find our lives by losing them in a holy purpose, and there is no purpose so sacred and ennobling as that of introducing men to Jesus Christ.

VIII. So far I have spoken in positive terms and have taken no account of the various objections that are offered to missions, usually by those who have given the subject little thought. I trust that I am right in the conclusion that most of these objections fade away in the light of the considerations I have set forth and therefore require no further rebuttal. The old missionary motive was to save dying heathen from hell; the modern motive is to give our less fortunate neighbors a more abundant life now in the assurance that this is the best way to immortality hereafter. Our Lord always emphasized the present values of the gospel. "This day is salvation come to this house." And while it is true that some Mohammedans, Buddhists, Zoroastrians, and Confucianists are better than some Christians, the reasons I have given for spreading Christianity are based on the unshakable conviction that it is the noblest of all faiths, and has developed a higher average of virtue and a better civilization than any of its rivals. But if any one believes sincerely that any other religion is nurturing as high a type of manhood, or as just and generous a social order as Christianity, after all its immaturities and shortcomings are admitted, this argument is not for him. My appeal is to those who believe that Christ is the light and hope of the world. Every one who professes allegiance to him and confesses faith in him, must if he is consistent do all within his power to make him known to those who do not know or understand him.

THE NEW CONFORMITY

The Rev. FRED SMITH, Carthage, S. Dak.

Without question the outstanding fact in modern social and religious life is the realization of the significance of the corporate life. Tho we are by no means all socialists, nor ever likely to be, we are all socially minded. The individualist exists no longer save as a left-over from a by-gone day. Many still cling to the name, but the substance is gone. We are all bound together in the bundle of life. Psychologists, sociologists, ethicists, outvie each other in their emphasis of this communal relationship. The theologian also has at last come into the light of this illuminating truth, and under its genial influence his one-time arid abstract science is taking to itself newness of life and meaning. No longer is man to be spoken of as a soul, shadowy and intangible; he now is to be thought of as a *socius*, related always and vitally to the manifold relationships of the environment of life. Out of this has come a new ethic of conversation. The salvation of a man is the salvation of society in him, not merely through him. But that is another story. Meanwhile we can go on to note that the ecclesiastical leader has accepted this fact also, to the upsetting, be it said, of many a tradition and fetish. Current denominational papers give evidence enough that many of these leaders have no small task in explaining the new conformity to some of their churches. We have no doubt that the work is lacking neither in excitement nor enjoyment.

The light of the new knowledge is

sufficient to reveal to the discerning mind the inadequacy of historic Protestantism for our day and age. It is increasingly evident that the "granular independency" fostered by the older Protestantism is not capable of solving the complex problems of our organized industrial life. Protestantism was born in a reaction against an organized church; its continuance depends upon its readjustment to the organized life of society. The mere nonconformist has no adequate remedy for the ills of to-day. The days are opportune for the justification of the new conformity.

By its name rather than by its nature Protestantism from the beginning was committed to a sympathetic attitude towards the prophetic spirit. The seat of authority was shifted from without to within. While nominally subject to the authority of Scripture, in practise it came to pass that each man became a law unto himself, for there were many interpreters. Beginning as a movement that meant "freedom from," it passed by a natural transition into a movement where the emphasis was laid on "freedom to." Freedom, like electricity, has a positive as well as a negative pole. Far be it from us to say that the enunciation of this double-phased truth was not needful. For the Protestant there is no question concerning that matter. Our task, however, is not the evaluation of the past but the examination of the present.

Turning then to our immediate topic, while recognizing the virtues of the past, we have to say that Protestantism is emerging from the "doldrums." She carried her chief virtue to excess, which means that it became a vice. Denominationalism went to seed in sectarianism. What was called Protestantism had often better have been named provinciality. Men gloried in their narrowness and called it liberty! Merely to be different was

thought to carry a measure of divinity. It is not altogether to be wondered at, therefore, that Baron Friedrich von Hügel (whom Dean Inge characterizes as perhaps the greatest of all living theologians in this century) should say of Protestantism that it "is fissiparous." We fear that Protestantism has been victimized by its own name. It is for this day and generation to make. it greater than its name and truer to its nature, and, incidentally to make of none effect the judgment of von Hügel. This is the task before the conformist.

It should not be overlooked in this connection that the effect of a name on a movement seems not to have been overlooked in what is perhaps the most ambitious project for church cooperation in this country as yet. Seeking the federal union of all the Protestant churches of America, asking none "to surrender its historic name or creed," it so happened that when the union was given a name the most historic name of all, that of Protestant, was omitted from its legal title. We venture to say that such a thing was not a mere omission but rather a recognition of a new truth. The omission of the name was an untrumpeted declaration that Protestantism has ceased to be fissiparous. Nonconformity was giving place to conformity. On the other hand, while the clumsy but catholic title of "The Federal Council of the Churches of Christ in America" was chosen, the mistake was not made of using the historic name of "Catholic" in the legal title. That, too, is a word that has been soiled by ignoble associations as well as deeply stained by prejudice in the minds of most Protestants. The fact of importance in this cooperative effort is the desire to give the "catholic" note to Protestantism. We know not whether the Free-churches of England have as yet taken to heart the counsel of P. T. Forsyth that they "need to cultivate a sense of the great Church, if their freedom is not to lose its greatness"; this much we know to be true, that in America, the last refuge of individualism (if Dean Inge speaks truly), this advice was acted upon before it was given.

Lest we should not appreciate the difference between the old nonconformity and the new conformity it will be well to show how far we have moved since the days of the Puritan. Appended is a declaration of the liberties of the Church of that day:

1. All the people of God within this jurisdiction who are not in a church way, and be Orthodox in judgment, and not scandalous in life, shall have full libertie to gather themselves into a Church Estaite. Provided they do it in a Christian way, and with due observation of the rules of Christ revealed in his word.
2. Every Church has full libertie to exercise all the ordinances of God, according to the rules of the Scripture.
3. Every Church hath libertie of Election and ordination of all officers.
4. Every Church hath free libertie of admission, recommendation, dismission, and expulsion.
5. No injunctions are to be put on any church, church officers, or members in point of doctrine, worship, or discipline.
6. Every Church of Christ hath freedome to celebrate dayes of fasting and prayer.
7. The Elders of the Church have free libertie to meete monthly, quarterly, or otherwise.
8. All Churches have libertie to deal with any of their members in a church way that are in the hands of justice.
9. Every Church hath libertie to deal with any magistrate, deputie of court, or other officer.
10. We allowe private meetings for edification in religion amongst the Christians of all sortes of people.

With the coming of a later day came the influence of Emerson to keep alive the nonconforming spirit in the religious life of America, an influence which has not as yet been outgrown. We ourselves are not ungrateful that we are not too young to have felt its impact. We counted that a great day when we first read the words: "Whoso would be a man must be a noncon-

formist." We were not insensible of a certain thrill when we heard the declamation of Patrick Henry: "Give me liberty or give me death," or the statelier words of him who said:

> We must be free or die, who speak the tongue
> That Shakespeare spake; the faith and morals hold
> Which Milton held.

We aspired to that elevation where we should join not the choir invisible but the galaxy of those whose souls were like the stars and dwelt apart.

But the new knowledge came upon us, and our eyes were attracted to other horizons and our hearts were touched with other aspirations. We came to realize that all of life was not contained in liberty. To be forever prating of freedom is to come perilously near being a fanatic. We observed that not always was the prophetic urge productive of the highest good. And current tendencies indicate that others seem to have been of like mind. The five-fold influence of psychology, sociology, ethics, theology, and church cooperation has brought to pass the new conformity of our day. No longer does Protestantism believe that she must "divide to conquer"; rather does she now know that "unity is strength."

The new conformist of to-day recognizes that he is a cellular part of an organism, not a granular atom in an organization. He feels that no church can be true church that does not have and emphasize the note of catholicity. While he is conscious of his rights and jealous of his liberty, he believes it more fundamental to give attention to his duties. Without compromising his conscience he realizes that he must give due regard to a church etiquette as well as proclaim a Christian ethic; that he must give attention to manners as well as to motives. He remembers that folks have idiosyncrasies as well as ideals, prejudices as well as principles, and therefore he must not speak the truth too often to the forgetting of tact. Remembering the counsel of Paul that "the gospel of Christ is the dynamite of God" he acts upon the further counsel of that great apostle and "speaks the truth in love." Counting the Puritan conscience a desirable possession, he yet is wise enough to use it pragmatically. In so doing he neither abrogates his common sense nor denies the faith. For him it is valid that the prophet may sometimes have to be subject to the Church as well as to the spirit of the prophet. And if this seem to some a signing away of our birthright of freedom, we reply that things are not always what they seem. Rather would we draw attention to the fact that the ultra-Protestant has often forgotten to his own defeat the sound words of the Scripture that "no scripture is of private interpretation."

In saying this we recognize that we have come to the age-long problem as to the relation of the Church to the prophet. The long story of this relationship has been a sorry one. Even to-day when it is not a tragedy it is a trial. We find ourselves asking with Richard Roberts:

Is human nature so defective that it can not cohere into a society in some manner which should save it from branding as an outlaw the man who sees visions and dreams dreams? He troubles Israel and therefore must be done away with. Is it impossible to get the good out of him without abusing and maltreating and killing him?

And in the asking of the questions we come across a partial answer. The presence of the new conformist within the Church is an augury of success. For the conformist is not as the conservative, who has ever been the avowed enemy of the prophet. The ultra-conservative, the traditionalist, who worships the God of things as they are, has always hung on to things when the prophet would have overturned them. But the conformist sees the need for progress, and when the prophet goes ahead that he may pull then does the conformist stay "by the stuff" that he may push. And it is not for us to say who does the greater work. We simply affirm that both have work to do. This is the spirit of the new conformity within the Church. On the other hand it should not be overlooked that sometimes the problem has been aggravated by the prophet rather than by the Church. Not seldom has it been found that the prophet, having truth, has also temper and temperament. And that is a combination hard to deal with. When these three things are manifest in full measure, only the future can cure the situation.

This then is the new conformity. To allay any needless fear we hasten to say that it by no means spells a new uniformitarianism. That would be to kill ourselves in the name of progress. If the new conformity means anything, it means a unity of life; it means the sinking of a separatist individualism in the interests of a higher personalism. It conserves the rights of personality since it recognizes that man is more than soul, he is a *socius*. Life comes to realization in felicitous relationships, not in granular · independency. Man was not made to realize himself *in vacuo*. The wilderness is not his home. Man is a conjunct self. The Christian life is the corporate life. The old-time individualist was apt to believe in God and himself. To-day the new conformist believes in God and the people. The new conformist is the new churchman. He dares to say that the Christian who does not feel that he is born into a society is not yet wholly a Christian. To use the words of Royce: "There is a certain universal and divine spiritual community. Membership in that community is necessary to the salvation of man." The balancing truth to the Protestant principle of liberty of conscience is "loyalty to the beloved community."

THE NEW EVANGELISM

Professor Arthur S. Hoyt, D.D., Auburn Theological Seminary, Auburn, N. Y.

Evangelism in America in the last century and a half has largely taken the form of revivals, with their special evangelists and periodic quickenings. Revivals in this sense have not marked the churches of Europe or those of Great Britain, with a few notable exceptions. They have governed and directed the religious life of America to such an extent that many churches have hardly expected to have accessions to membership except from revival seasons.

They grew out of the condition of frontier communities, when churches and ministers were few and special meetings were the easiest way to maintain the religious life and increase the number of Christians. A method especially adapted to frontier life has been taken over bodily for our more settled cities, without regard to differences of conditions, and still is largely the method of churches.

But an increasing number are asking whether there can be a better way. The professional evangelists still go forth for their winter campaigns. But the churches are not open to them as freely as formerly, and the tabernacle campaigns seem a waning force. A recent conference of Methodist bishops—a church noted for its revivalism—sent a pastoral letter to the churches urging the ministers to be their own evangelists and to use their churches for such purposes. A more striking expression of this

Why should there be a new evangelism? Is there not some discredit of the old in this very question? Why not repeat the evangelism of the Wesleys and Whitefield, of Finney and Moody? And there are some who say that we have in Mr. Sunday and his tabernacle evangelism a true succession of the movements of the last century, fitted to the masses of our city populations and the organised methods of modern business. We need, say such persons, no new evangelism, only to restore the old paths, preach the old gospel, and expect the old-time power.

change, and a more thoughtful study of conditions and means, is the last report of the International Convention on Sunday-school Work. It is called "An International Declaration on Evangelism."

It is the sense of the Department of Education of the International Sunday-school Association that evangelism should be considered under two heads: 1. Formative, or training the boys and girls directly in the Sunday-school and church and indirectly in cooperation with the home, so that their lives will always be lived in commitment to Christ and Christian teachings. This can best be done: (a) by using safeguard instead of recovery methods; (b) through the more thorough teaching of the graded lessons; (c) in furthering individual Bible study and prayer; (d) through the fostering of home religious training; (e) in the systematic planning of self-expression; (f) by personal or group instruction leading to church membership; (g) by conducting forward-step campaigns. 2. Reformative or making special effort at stated seasons or days to persuade the uncommitted or unconverted to pledge their individual allegiance to Christ and Christian living. This can best be done: (a) by promoting such carefully planned campaigns of personal work as the win-my-chum effort; (b) by working up to a "decision day"; (c) through graded and grouped Sunday-school evangelistic meetings; (d) by using any period of revival effort as an opportunity to bring the uncommitted and unconverted in touch with the evangelistic message.

I. Why this change of attitude toward evangelism? It must be confessed that there is some distrust of modern evangelism interpreted as revivalism. It has been exprest in a recent English book on evangelism—a symposium by well-known English leaders. Dr. A. S. Peake, the well-known Biblical scholar, writes on "Evangelism and the Intellectual Influences of the Age." The intellectual life of the age is critical of evangelism. Some of it may come from a critical spirit toward Christianity itself, but far more to the method of the professional evangelist. It is not so much the criticism of the essentials of evangelism as of the personal and local defects or eccentricities attached to it and handed on as tho essential to the very system.

Thoughtful men object to the antiquated theology. The view and use of the Bible seems untrue and unreal to modern Biblical students. The common saying of the evangelist, "I believe that every word between the covers of the Bible is from God," gives a false idea of the origin and growth of the books of the Bible. Every word is equally authoritative. They find the gospel in a rite of Leviticus or a verse of Kings equally with a parable of Luke or the spiritual truths of John's gospel. With such a view Biblical theology in the modern sense is impossible. The Bible is a book of magic, not a record of unfolding religious experience.

A second reason for criticism is the atmosphere that frequently attends revival efforts. It seems man-made. The announcement is made that there will be a revival in a certain community or church at a certain time, the date as much fixt as a lecture or a supper. It is the extreme swing of the pendulum from the sovereignty of God in religion—that God changes whom he wills, that periods of religious quickening are not in man's power, but God's gift—and all that man can do is to get ready for them and await the divine will. The swing away from this to man's responsibility and man's part has removed the mystery and much of the solemnity of the new life, and made it as plain

as any business transaction. It is true that the gift of God's Spirit—the life from above—is not an arbitrary matter. "The wind bloweth where it listeth." But there are certain laws of the winds, and science has discovered them; the reports of the weather bureau are of immense help to man, and the work of the Spirit is not lawless. It depends upon certain human conditions. That is clearly pointed out in the New Testament. "Repent ye—turn again that so there may come seasons of refreshment." God works according to great laws of spiritual life, and we can study them, find out something about them, and conform our lives to them.

And the methods of revival are made a business concern. Its advertising rivals that of any business enterprise, even of patent medicines. It lifts up its voice in the streets, it comes with banners and bands and processions; its organization of helpers and means is minute and complete. There is the sound of the money-changers. It is keen on receipts. Now the religious worker must be wise and use every means that can be made into a spiritual help. There are some good discussions on church advertising. But the spiritual temple of God goes up without sound of hammer. The rattle of machinery does not make a silence so that God can speak. And one wonders sometimes if Christ should come again if he would not have a whip of fine cords and drive the money-changers out of his temple. Mr. Moody was a great business man in evangelism; but he was a greater Christian, and the message of his Master was always the supreme impression.

There is a growing feeling that there is peril in evangelism, first to the evangelist himself. The man who is ever facing crowds and passing from place to place is subject to influences that are not altogether helpful to the religious life. It is the same influence that beats upon the actor or the great singer, the fascination of the crowd, the desire to please the crowd, the sense of power over a crowd.

The effect upon the evangelist has often been to make him spiritually proud, overbearing, and censorious toward those who differ from him or hesitate to follow his lead. All churches must yield their own plans and ordered life to the success of his efforts. He is dogmatic in asserting his views of truth as the only Christian view and his method as alone God's way. Few evangelists have entirely escaped from the sins of dogmatism and censoriousness. They have been notoriously critics of their brethren, and while claiming the special guidance of the Spirit have failed to manifest the fruits of the Spirit. It takes a humble, single-hearted, unselfish man to withstand these lower influences that forever beat upon the platform of the evangelist.

Thoughtful Christians often dread the emotional atmosphere of evangelism. The man tries to create an emotional crisis. To secure an immediate decision means are sometimes used that are largely physical, that appeal to the primitive instincts of man, and are no more religious than the snake dance of the Sioux or the repeating of the ninety-nine names of Allah by the howling dervishes. And where men are swept along by crowd psychology, largely physical contagion, without inhibition of reason and conscience—whatever the immediate action, there is the relaxing of the moral fiber. The influence is not only non-ethical, it may be immoral. The revival may be a sensuous stimulus, and when it is removed men yield again to their sensual appetites.

This accounts for the temporary influence of some evangelism. It is not the result of thorough teaching and

wise appeal, and so the converts are unstable. These are the hardest people to reclaim. Their first impressions were shallow, and they can be touched, like an impaired taste, only by a greater sensation. But, worst of all, there are many turned from Christianity by the unreal, theatrical expression of it. There is no doubt, however, that there are marked changes of life even from an unworthy evangelism. This criticism is not against evangelism but against the men who wrongly use it.

Probably the majority of present American church-members have been brought to faith by special revival services. This is the fact found wherever a list has been made. It simply indicates the fact that the increase of the Church in the last half century has been by revival methods. But such evidence is by no means conclusive. The question is not one of outer fact but the deeper one of character and fitness. Has this method produced the best results in character and is it best fitted to the life of our day?

II. What are the demands of a new evangelism? The old evangelism was carried on in communities largely homogeneous, children of the early settlers, who had a common inheritance of Bible training and religious ideas. There are such communities now where mass movements in religious persuasion may still be successful. Recent evangelism has secured its results chiefly from Christian congregations; it has made few conquests from the unchurched masses of men. This was proved by a careful study of the Torrey-Alexander meetings in Great Britain. Now the increased divisions of classes and social conditions and races make unity of impression less possible, make it harder to gather great audiences under one voice, and prevent the rapid contagion of feeling. Other methods must be used in our cities, often more than seventy-five per cent foreign or children of foreigners.

It is plain that there is need of new methods and new devotion if we are to maintain the position of the Christian religion in our land, and certainly if we are to make any decided advance in Christian life. Our home life is threatened in many ways, and we are not sure of Christian nurture even in families active in the Church. Our Bible school is on the way to a better life; but any one familiar with present Bible instruction must confess that it is very imperfectly done. And yet the Bible school is our chief instrument. The public school in a democracy can not teach religion; the home does not do it well enough; multitudes of youth will be untaught in religion unless the Church does it. There is now a great leakage in our church schools. Half of the pupils pass out without decided Christian faith. Only one in three of the youth of the nation is under Christian teaching. Multitudes of men have lapsed from faith or have grown up ignorant and indifferent to religion. The mass of men in great cities, especially those who have cast off old and repressive forms of the Church, care no more for the great questions dear to us than for last year's birds' nests. Miss Jane Addams recently spoke to the Ministers Association of Chicago on the relation of workmen to the Church, and she startled her hearers by saying there was no relation—the workmen of Chicago hardly knew there was a church there. Fifty-six per cent of the people of America are without even nominal church connection.

Could there be a greater challenge to the Church? The evangel has not lost its power—God has not forgotten. But this divine life must be mediated by the Church through a life that witnesses to its power and by ways that shall be convincing and life-giving.

It is the time of seeking and experimenting. But there is a growing feeling among the more thoughtful leaders of the Church that there must be more timeliness, more adaptation, more variety, more intelligent use of the gospel and the laws of the human soul. The greatest possible apologetic is the interpretation of the divine fitness of Christ to the nature of man, and the most persuasive evangelism is in so presenting Christ that he shall have this adaptation to the fullest extent of man's nature and experience.

From all this experiment and from a rapid study of the evangelism of different centuries, what practical suggestions can we make for our own work? The new evangelism will have more regard for the psychology of conversion. It will not violate the moral nature of man in its eagerness for immediate, visible results. It will not put stress upon any superficial action that can be tabulated, but upon the new motive and spirit and on the change of character. It will recognize the unity of life, that vision and conviction, emotion and will, are not separate but are inseparably connected in the one personality. That no life can grow into the Christian image without an increasing knowledge of the Christian truth, that no life can be greatly changed unless it sees and accepts the truths of the new life. This is always at the heart of the most wonderful changes. Saul thought that Jesus was the foe of his nation and their religious hope, that Jesus was dead and buried and that was the end of the delusion. But the knowledge of the living Christ removed his prejudice and reversed his life. And the conviction of the truth is back of all moral change.

So a better evangelism will exalt the teaching function of the Church. It will honor the pulpit and the Bible school and try in every way to recognize their worth and strengthen their influence. All great evangelism has come from great truth. Every new era of spiritual life has come from the rediscovery or reinterpretation of the gospel. The prophets of the Christian centuries have been men who have discovered some latent or forgotten factor of the gospel, or carried the truth into some new field of life. The growing phases of Christ have been adapted to the condition of the age and seen in the light of the new day.

The new evangelism must do something more than repeat the formulas of a past age. It must use the best light the spirit of truth casts upon our own age. It must have reasonable ideas of the Bible, and state its truths so as to command the respect of educated men and women. It will recognize different interpretations of Christianity, and hold its own views in the Christian spirit of tolerance. And it must state its gospel not in archaic terms that limit its appeal and make it impossible to some of the finest spirits of our time, but in speech that all may understand and that conveys the great principles of life to all men.

The new evangelism will have regard for various ages and conditions. The old evangelism did not distinguish sufficiently as to ages and conditions. It was inclined to treat all alike, the children and youth from Christian homes and the hardened sinners—men who had grown up as practical heathen. The new evangelism tries for Pauline adaptation, if by all means it may win some. It is a difference both in doctrine and psychology. It does not hold that we have a right to teach the sharp and fast classification of saints and sinners, that the "white wings of the Holy Ghost" brood over all men, that Christ meant what he said when he called little children subjects of the kingdom of heaven. It uses a psy-

chology that shows that character is the result of the proper awakening and unfolding of life. Therefore it recognizes "Christian nurture" as the first and most important dealing of God with a life and does everything to give significance to child life and to beautify and sanctify the life of the family.

It recognizes that the truest evangelism for youth from Christian homes or brought up under Christian influences is religious education. That it must make the best use of the laws of education in the interest of the Christian life—suggestion and imitation and self-expression. That time and method and personal influence are all-important matters; that it may be a grievous sin against children and youth to subject them to the influences of mass evangelism.

We ought to practise what we know—we ought to refuse to be stampeded into wrong ways by popular clamor or by impatience for immediate success. At the same time we must see to it that the educational agencies and processes of the Church have the evangelistic aim and spirit. The growing religious life should have distinct expression; it should find its loyalty to the Church and its part in the program of Christianity. This means definite decision, frank and sincere stand for the things of Christian faith. There can be no rules for securing this. It is a personal and spiritual matter and should be done in the simplest way with the least outward stress. The Christian home is the best agency; the pastor who is a real friend of children and youth can be a wise guide. The teacher of youth can never be content until there are evidences of a positive Christian life. And the Church by its method and controlling spirit must seek to win and train for the Christian life.

But the matter can not end with religious education, however evange-

listic its aim. Training at best will be imperfect. Some will escape from it. In the changing life of America, while the increase of the Church may have equaled the increase of the people, an increasing number of our people are wholly secular in their interests and habits. Millions are neglected. The heathen are everywhere at our door. They are the toughest problem of our Christianity, the greatest challenge of our Christian faith.

The age calls for a more positive evangelism. It means personal evangelism first of all. This is the method of Jesus himself. He did not depend upon impression upon masses of men. Even where he spoke to many, it was to a smaller group close to him that his word had special meaning. He seemed to have little regard for numbers but supreme regard for individuals. The most significant and distinguished incidents of the gospels are his dealing with persons. He took infinite patience with a chosen few, knowing that a life thoroughly awakened and trained was the greatest force for a new world. And it is so now. The weakness of our Christianity has been its mass movements and lack of personal conversion. A ministry forever seeking the individual as Christ did will be the greatest force for salvation. A church so fully Christian as to have personal interest in the Christian life of friends and neighbors, forever widening its circle and making every human touch spiritual, will be the greatest force for the kingdom of God. In fact, we can hardly expect any marked spiritual advance until the Church itself is thus quickened.

And there is a proper use of group and mass evangelism. A greater use can be made of the natural association of men in work and fraternal relations. Shop meetings and club meetings are suggestive of what can

be done. Laymen may often be of the largest use. The "Men and Religion Movement" shows what can be done to impress a community with the reality and importance of religion.

There are times in every church when special emphasis may be placed upon evangelism. In a busy age, with little pause and meditation, fed on sensations and disinclined to serious thought, the repetition of truth, the constant iteration of a few essential truths, is the law of impression. It fixes thought on religion, it opens the heart to religious impression, it creates conditions for the effective working of the Spirit. The pastor should do this work if possible. He best knows the conditions of his people, he has their confidence, he can best conserve the results. If others are brought in, evangelists or pastors gifted with persuasive appeals, great care should be taken that these be wise, unselfish, spiritually minded men who will strengthen the Church, not lead to an eccentric and divided faith.

Mass evangelism may still have its uses in neglected communities or for the homeless and churchless masses of great cities. Its true use is not for the Church but for those outside. It has a right to use all the means of suggestion—through the power of song; of imitation through testimony and example. It has a right to use any means that shall awaken great enthusiasm that is spontaneous and genuine. It should use all the psychology of the crowd for impression and directed decision. But emotion should be rightly and ethically controlled. There should be strong inhibition of everything tending to physical excitation, the presenting of the gospel in its larger demands, the appeal to the nobler motives, so that Christian faith shall mean the act of the whole man and lead to the largest life.

A word in closing about pastoral

evangelism. The winning of men to faith should be ever on the heart of the true minister, and constantly exprest in his method. He will have lists of people who seem interested in the gospel, who will be constant objects of his prayer and preaching. He must expect their conversion and never give up that hope. He will constantly study the best approach to the modern mind, and of the particular men and women before him. He will increasingly plan his sermons so as to lead to faith and confession. He will always sow, tho the reaping may not be continuous. There are periods of special interest in religion as in human concern. But the man who regards evangelism as the constant duty of the pulpit, as the primary and pressing demand of the gospel, will often have the prophet's word fulfilled that "the reapers shall overtake the sowers." There are possibilities that the pulpit has barely touched in a true evangelism.

COMMENT AND OUTLOOK

By Our London Correspondent

Domesticating the Supernatural

What is wrong with our religion? The Rev. T. J. Hardy supplies a thought-provoking answer. We have domesticated its "winged Eros" into a tame "angel in the house." We have harnessed its elemental forces to moralistic ends. We have reduced it to a humble handmaid of good conduct. Writing in the *Hibbert Journal*, Mr. Hardy castigates the moralistic outlook which culminated in the nineteenth century when the dictum that Conduct (with a capital C) is three-fourths of life was received "by solemn people in Manchester and Birmingham as 'a revelation from Sinai' "; when everybody asked, Who is my neighbor? and only Herbert Spencer, Who is my God? Mr. Hardy thinks that, compared to this, the faith of the ancient Briton was "pure religion and undefiled." At any rate, he did not attend Stonehenge with a view to "getting good," nor did he revere his religion because it kept his neighbor from stealing his coracle. "He was religious because of a certain wild necessity in him . . . . because the universal within him sought the Universal without."

In fact, religion, declares Mr. Hardy boldly, is not only a moral: it is even antagonistic to morality. The moment Christianity is introduced into a primitive community, the morals of that community vanish! "If, for example, our lot had fallen in the Solomon Islands, we should to-day be bemoaning the decline of cannibalism, and financing societies for its preservation. . . . When the apostle warned his readers to 'flee fornication,' he was saying something absolutely eccentric. Nor did he give any reason for such an exhortation, except the mystic reason that these lusts 'war against the soul.' It is not 'morality'; it is the life of the soul that religion rekindles." The principles for which Christ was crucified can not be called "moral." They are not self-regarding; they are not other-regarding; they are God-regarding. They are little understood among us and seldom acted upon. They seek to establish a supernatural claim on the whole of human life.

Mr. Hardy's thought, paradoxical in form as it is, goes very deep. Nietzsche's revolt has a profound significance for the Christian thinker, and the note it struck will vibrate for generations. Mr. Gladstone warned emotional devotees not to let their religion spoil their morality: the time has come for us to beware lest our morality spoil our religion.

The Mystery of the Philistines

Professor Garstang, the well-known archeologist, has returned to Palestine in order to investigate more fully the vexed problem of the Philistines. For the past two years he has been conducting excavations on the sites of Ascalon and Gazi; but so far comparatively little has been unearthed that would throw much light upon the history of that mysterious race. Many theories have been advanced as to the origin of the Philistines, and it is generally believed that they came from the neighborhood of Cyprus. But that is about as far as we have got, and Professor Garstang thinks that the present series of excavations will take nearly twenty years to complete.

Now that we are witnessing a great revival of exploration in Palestine, it is well to ask what precise value for religion these investigations possess. Only an ignorant person could deny that exploration has thrown considerable light upon both the Old and the New Testaments and that it has supplied corroborative evidence of the highest value, which neither the apologist nor the scholar can afford to neglect. But one feels none the less that a certain disproportionate emphasis upon such investigations—an attitude popularized by Professor Ramsay— is in some quarters creating a view of Scripture which is more anti-quarian than vital. True, the explorer and excavator can, even by a single discovery, throw a flood of light upon an obscure text or corroborate a Scriptural statement; but the apologetic value of their discoveries is only subsidiary. After all, the characteristic quality of a really effective apologetic is spiritual; it has always been by spiritual arguments that men are finally convinced and convictions victoriously established. The scholar who will ultimately do more for the interpretation and vindication of, say, St. Paul's epistles, is not the explorer who has been to Iconium, tho he has his own honorable place, but the inter-preter of spiritual insight, and the apologist who is at the same time an apostle.

"The Lazy God Evolution"

There can be no doubt that to-day the "immovable East" is in vigorous motion, and that India especially is discovering the significance of positive, personal energy—destructive energy if need be—in the great battle for right. Whatever view be taken of Mahatma Ghandi, and his non-cooperation movement, it is certain that he has infused a new quality into the soul of India; or rather, that he has liberated a dormant quality. In a recent article in the *Indian Social Reformer* (an anti-Ghandi journal, be it noted) a Syrian Chris-tian criticizes the attitude which says, "Why increase effort and suffering; why not bide God's time? God's in his heaven, all's right with the world!" He contends against such quietism that if it could be said of anyone that he came upon the scene in God's good time it could surely be said of Christ. But if that be so, why was he crucified? If he had waited and allowed the forces of evolution to do their work, might he not have come to an expec-tant world ready to receive him with outstretched arms? And then, using a phrase that suggests the active West rather than the pensive East, he says, "No; it is not such a tardy consummation as the lazy God Evolution brings forth that love regards as 'the fulness of time.' For love the time is fulfilled when its own suffering and sacrifice have a reasonable chance of achieving some good. The harvest to it is already ripe; only the laborers are few. There is an enemy sowing tares in the world, and the mere process of the suns will, therefore, never bring about the millennium." People quote, "First the blade, then the ear, then the full corn in the ear"; and say that the fulness of time is when the next step can be taken without effort. But is this the test in human life? The human child is surely born "in the fulness of time," just as the corn is; but it is born of pain and anguish—not "without effort." Talents are not vegetable seeds. Things do not "turn up" in society, unless someone "turns them up." The writer pleads for non-cooperation with evil. What-ever be true of Ghandi's practical policy and of the errors of his followers, his principle of non-violent non-cooperation with that which we believe to be evil is the only true Christian philosophy.

Brotherhood in Egypt

The World Brotherhood movement has come to stay, and there is scarcely a land in Christendom where it has not some footing. Critics have arisen, of course, and their main contention is that the movement stands for little more than a big talking campaign—that it's an affair of big meetings, popular speeches, rousing sing-songs, and vociferous cheering, and that is about all. There can be no doubt that such movements are beset by the peril of degenerating into a "hot-air machine," but the promoters of world brotherhood are doing their best to inspire the local leaders with a passion for translating their ideals into action. In Egypt a young brotherhood, dating from 1916, has made a record well worth noting. This movement was founded mainly by men in khaki, and from the first British and Egyption members met together in an atmosphere of genuine fellowship. Two years later, in 1918, the cry of the outcast children in the streets of Cairo—the result of easy divorce—knocked upon the heart of the Brotherhood, and immediately the impulse was acted upon. A great feast was prepared for these waifs and strays, and they came in their hundreds and consumed like famished dogs the good things provided, a wild cheer rending the air when cooked meat came upon the scene. There they were, a pitiable mass of degraded childhood, filthy beyond description, and ninety per cent of the boys under twelve the victims of venereal disease. The members of the brotherhood began to investigate the hideous facts, and, in 1920, with the sympathy and concurrence of Mohammedan leaders, they opened an industrial training home for these unfortunate boys—an institution of which any society might be proud. Every boy is given an elementary education and equipped to earn an independent living, and it is scarcely credible, yet happily true, that these children, all under fourteen years of age and hitherto regarded as worse than useless, should today be producing carpets and furniture that can compete with those made by the much older students of the government Arts and Crafts schools. Moreover, these boys are developing into true "little brothers." They have absorbed the spirit of the Home, and are showing great capacity for kindness and self-sacrifice.

EDITORIAL COMMENT

What are the true issues involved in the great strikes that have marked and marred the summer? The mere newspaper reader who tried to define the quarrel of operator and miner, railway executive and shopman, might well have given the problem up in despair. Watching their mutual recrimination, the indifference of the coal operator to the urgent need of the public, the violence and bitterness of the miners, the shameful crime of Herrin, the intractability of the railway executives, the note of triumph with which shopmen proclaimed from time to time the falling off in equipment and the danger of travel, together with the brutal abandonment of trains by members of other brotherhoods in the heat of the western desert, he was tempted to cry "a plague on both your houses." There is no denying the encouragement that such things give to cynicism, bitterness, and malice. But bitterness, cynicism, and malice will never solve our social problems. Nothing can be really settled here until it is settled right.

The Moral Issues of the Strikes

Some things stand out clearly as moral issues. They are too often regarded now as academic and impracticable; but in the end the moral issue will prove to be most intimately bound up with a practical solution of our difficulties.

Chief among these is the fact that great industries exist primarily for the public service. The railway executives have made considerable advance in their understanding of this truth. The greater "brotherhoods" of railway employees show at times a glimmer of it; but it seems to have been nearly absent from the thought of the shopmen. The inconvenience of the public, deepening sometimes into danger and suffering, has proved a handy stick wherewith to beat the enemy—only this and nothing more. The coal operators still seem quite oblivious of this foundation stone of their continued existence; and the miners' unions are in little better case. At least, if the need and anxiety of the public have any influence upon their leaders' action except to serve as a possible weapon in the conflict, the fact has been successfully concealed.

A second moral issue involved in the two great strikes and one that must be recognized before industrial peace can come to stay is that of according to the worker some positive "stake" in industry beyond a bare wage. We are told that this is an exceedingly difficult thing to do. It may be admitted; but it remains no less a necessary thing. Wages have recently been offered in some of the mines that, if they could be earned the year around, would seem to the average man to be extravagant; and from the standpoint of the average preacher the wages paid to the higher classes of railway employees are quite beyond his own expectations. He has, however, certain compensating rewards in that a position of leadership and some opportunity for initiative are accorded him. These can not, of course, be generally distributed through a vast and highly organized industry; but something can be done to convince the worker that he is more than a cog in the machine; that his interests in the way of steady employment, of as good a wage as the industry will bear, and of recognition of any special service or method originating with him will be generously and humanely considered. It is claimed that these things are impossible under a system of private or corporate ownership. We incline to believe that there is larger opportunity for them there, if they are really sought for, than under government control with its tendency to formality and red tape, dry rot and waste. But an option between the two is likely to be eventually forced. The managers of private and corporate industry and the leaders of union labor must somewhere learn the secrets of service and the practise of a higher humanity or both will be dealt with by a patient public whose patience has been at last worn out. The people are greater than any portion of the people; the "stable majesty of the moral order" still reigns.

✠

By these words, in his notable sermon published elsewhere in this issue, Dr. Jowett describes the ministry of the gospel. They are worth the consideration of every preacher as he reviews his choice of a **The Sacred** life work, considers his place in the world, and in particular **Apostolate of** plans his scheme of sermons for the year. He may very **Love and Grace** likely feel that he stands apart from the world's affairs; too much apart, indeed, to exert any material influence upon their direction. It should encourage him to realize that one reason why he seems to stand apart from the surface activities of life is that he is in reality close to its heart. In preaching and practising a gospel of grace he is at the springs of redeeming motive. From that fountain the thirst of restless and striving man must be finally quenched, if quenched at all. What, for example, shall heal the wounds that war has made? What shall establish good relations with our late enemies? Nothing in the world but the spirit of fundamental good-will which was incarnate in Jesus Christ. This will lead us not merely to be formally forgiving as a Christian duty but so to examine all questions at issue as to bring an understanding heart to their solution. Good breeds good nowhere more certainly than in the realm of will, as has been notably manifested in the regions lately hostile to us where representative friends have been at work fighting famine and rescuing the lives of children.

What are the most significant things for America in the anarchy which has afflicted unhappy Ireland this past summer? The manner in which the patience and self-restraint of England have availed to pluck out the sting of bitterness that has so long rankled in the minds of Irishmen, and the degree in which the agitation against Great Britain has died down in the United States. What shall heal the open wound that weakens our whole industrial system and threatens to poison the health of our body politic? What, indeed, as is suggested in the preceding editorial, but a bringing of our industrial problems into the presence of the "stable majesty of the moral order" and a solemn consideration of the moral issues involved in a spirit of sacrificial good-will? The friendly imperative of a voice clearly uttering such truths as these is one of the most haunting things in the world. Christ's message of love and grace is like the voice of God walking in the garden of old. However deep we try to hide ourselves, it seeks us out. It is finally inevitable and will not be gainsaid. The preacher who is its true and whole-hearted organ may be perfectly sure of his mission and his place. He is, we repeat, at the heart of things. His words to-day, even when they seem to have but a careless hearing, are establishing the basis of significant memories to-morrow. The future is with him because his message is one of fundamental good-will; and the problems of the world must wait until the "sacred apostolate of love and grace" shall have thrust the key of good-will into their locks. Nothing else will serve.

This generation is getting a good idea of the sinister meaning of the word diplomacy; it is learning that the stroke of a pen may do more damage and undo more good than a dozen battles. Soldiers are trained to kill, as every child knows; but what about international politicians? Are they still expected to lie and bully and cheat and cajole? Of course, a thinking man knows what to expect from politicians who talk peace with pistols and platitudes in their hip-pockets, and therefore can not be disappointed at the spectacle staged in various countries by their respective champions. But there is danger that the unsophisticated turn cynic when they discover how pitifully low their idols have fallen. And that must be avoided at all events.

Some More Humanity

The United States of Europe is still a beautiful dream. The division of Europe into well-defined economic and political camps has at last been accomplished—a consummation which everybody but blind demagogs foresaw long ago. But we must not put this all into the shoes of the politicians. They are no worse than the folk who support them. Every nation has the representatives it deserves.

Mr. Vanderlip informs us that the world needs a new type of statesmen, men who "actually comprehend the meaning of humanity." This may seem a bit late to some. Some are capable of asking, with tongue in cheek, whether this humanity business was not all settled on the battle-fields and in the bond-raising drives? They remember having heard something about humanity of late. It is not too late for honest people to speak out and to disown these petty politicians who play with empires as a cat plays with a mouse. Once there were preachers who told kings and queens the truth to their faces. We do not hear that the "leaders" are much exercised at the schemes that are grounded upon trickery and fear.

These nations have talked loudly about being saviors of society, champions of humanity. Are they holding their spokesmen to a strict account of their actions in translating the claims into reality? It speaks volumes either for abysmal stupidity or for blithe optimism to have a man expect, after the happenings of the last six years, that statesmen anywhere could be in training for the salvation of humanity. What school of statesmen ever concerned itself about such a program? Let us do what we can, by the grace of heaven, to help bleeding humanity, but let us not conjure up a mirage for credulous people.

Is there then no help for the weak? Assuredly. Any nation that is willing to help itself, if given a chance, will help humanity. This is not so cruel and unscriptural as it sounds—it is the very law of nature. This self-help may come by the way of self-sacrifice, it may come by being a servant, it may come by being healthy and honest and hopeful; it must come through the expression of its natural genius and character. No tribe of professional statesmen can rob the world of the example of true manhood and womanhood. Also, those who are so concerned about having humanity saved may discover that, as usual, the race is not to the swift nor the battle to the strong. By a queer caprice or law of things the crucified always determine the fate of the crucifiers. Any one who remembers that need not get excited at the blindness and the selfishness of—"statesmen."

✠

The Federal Council of Churches is calling attention once more to the gruesome fact implied in the caption. The Nationalist Turks are carrying out ruthlessly and unhindered their proclaimed purpose of

Dire Tragedy In the Near East exterminating Armenian, Greek, Syrian, and other Christians in the Near East. They propose to accomplish the annihilation of Christianity in that entire region.

The Federal Council notes that the Baptist churches, north and south, the Presbyterian Church north, the United Presbyterian Church, the Methodist Episcopal Church South, the Congregational Church, and others have called for governmental intervention by the United States and European countries to save the remnant of the Armenian nation and to intervene in behalf of these other Christian peoples.

For the salving of them from physical extinction through forced migration, starvation, and exposure Americans alone have expended over fifty million dollars. This has gone into the feeding and clothing of children and adults, into building up or creating industry, into restoration of agriculture, and the like. Are all these and other efforts to be lost while Christian nations stand by knowing the facts, witnessing the tragedy, but supinely consenting to it by inaction? Even the investigation once proposed seems to have been abandoned because, forsooth, the perpetrators of the horrors protested and refused opportunity to seek the evidence.

Let us "speak out in meeting." Great Britain and France conquered the Turks in the Near East; they had power then to make terms with the Turk, they now have mandates in the region. Is it not the case that these "Christian" powers refuse to exercise restraint lest their Moslem subjects elsewhere complain that they defend Christians against Moslem ferocity? We urge our own government to make emphatic and outspoken protest to Great Britain and France against this breach of duty as respects both humanity and religion. Christian sentiment should be aroused.

HOMILETIC GAMBITS

The Rev. GEORGE H. HUBBARD, Cambridge, Mass.

Don't be shocked. I am not "making game" of the preacher or his work. I have good precedents for my figure. Paul the apostle filched many a type of Christian life and service from the contests of the arena. Ay, and a greater than Paul drew spiritual lessons from the games of the children in the market-place. Is it any less fitting to point a moral for preachers with a suggestion from the chess board?

For the benefit of the uninitiate let me premise that a "gambit" is an opening in chess, consisting of the first few moves in the game, by means of which the player seeks to secure a favorable grouping of his important pieces for attack and defense, and so prepares the way for final victory. The "homiletic gambit," therefore, implies such an introduction to the sermon or other pulpit exercise as shall ensure an effective result for the entire effort. The success or failure of a sermon often lies in the first three or four sentences. If these be significant, if they secure attention or pique curiosity, it will be an easy matter to "hold one's audience" for a half hour. If, on the other hand, there is no grip in them, the audience may go woolgathering at once, and the sermon will be wasted.

A certain opening in chess is known as "the fool's mate" because it makes possible the defeat of the player in three moves. Another opening bears the more dignified title of "the scholar's mate" because it demands five moves for defeat. There are not a few preachers who invite defeat for their sermons in the first three minutes. Others, perhaps more scholarly, keep up appearances for five minutes. But in either case the preacher is checkmated before he has fairly warmed up to his work.

The "fool's mate," homiletically speaking, may be said to consist in pure conventionalism. The text is announced Sunday after Sunday in precisely the same way. Then there is a brief "exposition," or discussion of the "context," not because these are at all necessary or germane to the topic in hand, but by way of padding. They demand little thought on the part of the preacher and inspire less on the part of his hearers. But they are the proper thing. Who cares whether St. Paul was in Jerusalem or Jericho when he wrote a given verse? Who is interested in the fine shades of meaning conveyed by particular Greek words? Surely not the average layman. A look at the clock, a yawn, or a restless rustle may announce "Checkmate!" within three minutes for such dawdling.

Here is a scholar who has a vital message wrought out with great care. His introduction is fresh and germane. But his first sentence contains a hundred and fifty words, and long ones at that. His second sentence follows with two hundred words, mostly of Latin derivation. And so he goes on. Only trained minds by giving careful attention can follow him through his devious windings of thought and over numerous hurdles of comma and semi-colon. And so he, too, if he have keen ears, may hear the "Checkmate!" before the first five minutes are past.

Epigrams are good materials for the gambit. Only they must be real epigrams, not mere rhetorical sparklers. Pack a vital theme into six Anglo-Saxon words, announce it in a clear, incisive fashion, and the audience will at once sit up and take notice. Then it is easy to hold them for the allotted time and win a victory. If you must expound the text, do it in a crisp fashion. Don't dillydally with it. Get it out of the way as quickly as possible. Exposition is soporific. Sacrifice a few pawns of rhetoric or scholasticism. Get your major pieces where they can rake the board. Play promptly but carefully; and announce "Checkmate!" before your hearers expect it.

So, too, with your pulpit prayers. The average extemporaneous prayer is dull, monotonous, commonplace. In most churches where such prayers are the custom, the intelligent part of the congregation can easily keep several words ahead of the minister, because they know the prayer by heart. How can the ordinary preacher escape this tendency to monotonous expression in prayer? Must he write out and memorize his pulpit prayers for each successive service and so lay upon himself a great extra burden? The answer is in the "gambit."

The "Invocation" may easily be made a gambit for the entire service. This means a fresh, apt and incisive invocation for each Sunday of the year. A brief collect from the Anglican prayer-book will serve for one Sunday, a verse from the psalms for another, a prayerful utterance from one of the epistles for a third, a stanza of a prayer-hymn for a fourth, an original and unhackneyed production for a fifth, and so on. No invocation should consist of more than three or four brief sentences. It is not a general prayer, only a gambit.

For the "pastoral prayer" two or three carefully prepared sentences as an opening gambit will serve to lift the mind out of its conventional ruts and set it off on a fresh track. In this way the preacher will compel his hearers to listen and will checkmate the devil of inattention.

"Applied Christianity"

The First Congregational Church of Mount Vernon, N. Y., has an Automobile Corps whose object is to bring people to church who could not otherwise atttend.

The following letter has been sent to each member of the church and congregation who owns an automobile, and a generous response has been made to it:

There are some fifty members and attendants of the First Congregational Church of whom you are one who own automobiles.

There are a number of people living in Mount Vernon who would be glad to attend our Sunday morning service if means of conveyance were provided them. It has been suggested that a volunteer First Congregational Church Motor Corps be organized whose privilege it will be to do this work. The duties of this corps will be moderately light, providing thirty-six volunteers can be secured and the work divided among them.

To make a beginning three cars each Sunday morning will suffice; as the work grows, six cars should be ample. By this you will see a call would come to you but once in six weeks. Admit that nine cars would be needed, even then you would be called upon once every four weeks.

The program will be for our pastor or any of our members to phone me at my residence giving name and address of those who desire to attend church the following Sunday A. M. In turn I phone a sufficient number of volunteers to perform this service, calling those whose turn it is to serve, avoiding duplication as far as possible.

It seems to me that this is a work "worth while." We make the privilege which is granted us available to those whom age or physical condition deny on account of lack of conveyance.

To me this is practical Christianity properly applied. Will you be one to volunteer? Call me on the phone, Hillcrest 271, and say "yes," or write me to the same effect. "Do it now!"

This is signed by the chairman in charge of the work.

KINDLING AND INSPIRING THOUGHTS

Genius is patience. Sir ISAAC NEWTON.

You can't beat the combination of enthusiasm and common sense. WILLIAM FEATHER.

Life is a pure flame, and we live by an invisible sun within us. Sir THOMAS BROWNE.

Faith must not be inert and alone, but accompanied with investigations. CLEMENT OF ALEXANDRIA.

No silence is possible when once the Everlasting Melody has caught us by the hand and by the heart. W. A. QUAYLE.

A man must be very careful, as Mr. Gladstone once incisively observed, to prevent his religion from damaging his morality. F. W. BOREHAM.

The prophet should have not only range of vision, but penetration as well. He should look far out upon life, and also far into it. DAMON DALRYMPLE.

My imagination would never have served me as it has, but for the habit of commonplace, humble, patient, daily, toiling, drudging attention. CHARLES DICKENS.

Man is not born to solve the problem of the universe, but to find out where the problem begins and then to restrain himself within the limits of the comprehensible. GOETHE.

A mind not wholly wishful to reach the truth, or to rest in it or obey it when found, is to that extent a mind impervious to truth and incapable of unbiased belief. W. L. DAVIDSON.

The absolute things, the last things, the overlapping things, are the truly philosophic concerns; all superior minds feel seriously about them, and the mind with the shortest views is simply the mind of the more shallow men. WILLIAM JAMES.

True religion is rational: if it excludes reason, it is self-condemned. And reason without religion fails of its object; since, if philosophy can find no place for religion, it can not explain man. AUBREY MOORE.

I spoke a kind word, almost thoughtlessly, and a long time afterward one thanked me for it, with tears in his eyes. Then I thought, since kindness costs so little, and helps so much, why am I not always kind? W. E. BARTON.

It is quite as easy to hypnotize oneself into imbecility by repeating in solemn tones, "Progress, Democracy, Corporate Unity," as by the blessed word Mesopotamia, or, like the Indians, by repeating the mystic word "Om" five hundred times in succession. DEAN INGE.

Christianity can be ultimately and comprehensively conceived only in the developmental sense, as the product of actual persons working out their religious problems in immediate contact with their several worlds of reality. SHIRLEY J. CASE.

On one occasion some one, upon hearing Beethoven rendering his great pastoral symphony, said to the musician, "I have never heard sounds like that in the country." "Neither have I," replied the great master, "but that is how I felt when I was in the country." SAMUEL JUDSON PORTER.

Continue to act thus, my dear Lucilius—set yourself free for your own sake; gather and save your time, which till lately has been forced from you, or filched away, or has merely slipt from your hands. Make yourself believe the truth of my words—that certain moments are torn from us, that some are gently removed, and that others glide beyond our reach. The most disgraceful kind of loss, however, is that due to carelessness.—SENECA.

Be on thy guard, not only in the matter of steady judgment and action, but also in the matter of gentleness toward those who try to hinder or otherwise trouble thee. For this also is a weakness, to be vexed at them, as well as to be diverted from thy course of action and to give way through fear; for both are equally deserters from their post, the man who does it through fear, and the man who is alienated from him who is by nature a kinsman and a friend.—MARCUS AURELIUS.

A democracy which has only learned to read, without learning to weigh and to discriminate, is a much greater danger to the world than its illiterate ancestors, for it is much more liable to be misled. Without judgment the man follows his favorite newspaper blindly, hoping all things, believing all things. Now, a man who does that is no whit better than the man who, in the old days, voted according to the directions of his landlord or his priest. LORD BRYCE.

Church and Community

SUGGESTIONS ON PASTORAL CALLING

President PHILIP WENDELL CRANNELL, D.D., Baptist Theological Seminary, Kansas City, Kansas.

So long as human souls are individual, needing individual care, encouragement, and nurture, so long will the "pastoral call" have its legitimate and important place in the church life and the minister's activity. Our increasing modern complexity is making the pastoral call ever more difficult and ever more needed. In metropolitan districts the flat, the apartment house, the family hotel, and the general seething rush of city life raise its difficulties to the nth power, demanding all a pastor's ingenuity, grace, and persistency to get into touch especially with the outer fringes of his "clientele." But as yet, six-sevenths of our people live in the country or in towns less than 500,000 in size, and five-sixths in the country and towns less than 300,000, where a good deal of American home life still lingers, modified though it be by conditions that affect us all.

Pastoral calling implies two things. It implies a real church, small enough for the personal touch among members and between members and pastor; a real church, and not an exaggerated ecclesiastical department store of manifold and largely mechanical activities, almost as impersonal as a modern factory. It implies also a real pastor, a man with the shepherd heart, the shepherd eye and head and hand, not the bustling manager of a great ecclesiastical machine, or the oratorical or sensational or strenuously intellectual pulpiteer who draws his crowds one Sunday and dismisses them and the thought of them, except as open-mouthed hearers, till the next. These great churches at the centers are doubtless a necessity in limited number in our city life, as also may be a great metropolitan pulpit—and pulpit only—for the seer-like utterance of its orator, for its appeal to and supply of the intellectual in Christianity. But the heart of the work of Christ's Church is where one man, with a due number of associates for specialized auxiliary details, undertakes the faithful, particular, blessed "cure of souls."

The ultimate aim of pastoral calling is "the greater glory of God" in the spread of the kingdom, the up-building of the Church, and the care and culture of the individual.

Its "general aim" is the personal touch of Jesus Christ through the personal touch of the pastor upon the local church, its "adherents," its "constituency," the community, in concentric, widening circles. Nothing can take the place of this "hand-press"; not the printing press, not the prophet's staff in the hands of a messenger, paid or voluntary, church missionary, or assistant pastor. These have their valued uses; but no hand can compare in week-day efficiency with the hand the people feel on Sunday, and no hand can touch the people to the highest help on Sunday which has not touched them during the week.

[291]

The "immediate aim" of any pastoral call—and all pastoral calling, in the last analysis, must "get down to the brass tacks" of the single call—will depend on its circumstances and object. Religious it always must be, in its motive, spirit, character, and general aim. What specific use it shall make of prayer, Bible reading, the old-time "catechizing," the personal appeal to the unconverted, the range of subjects, the style of language, the length and frequency, will depend, after the question of habitat and the ideas and expectations of the people dealt with are considered, upon what kind it is.

It may be a *"routine call,"* for systematically keeping touch with the whole force and field. This is the sort which pastors and often people groan over, which is indeed so intolerable to so many of us because so hard to make real and vital. But its need will never pass away. Does not every wholesale business by personal visitation of its traveling men keep its hand on the pulse of its clientage and itself before their minds? It must do this systematically, regularly, never letting a period go by without this individual notice of, and to, the dealer. In no way can our churches hope to succeed without using the same psychological principle of the sustained acquaintance and maintained interest. And surely, as in business, the thought of the ultimate end may "give grace and glory" to the individual detail.

Or this may be a *"consolatory call,"* after death or great misfortune to family or person. There is nothing "routine" or forced or mechanical about this. It usually challenges all the powers of mind and heart, and leaves a real man after it "as weak as a rag," when "the power" of love "proceeding from him has gone forth." A certain preacher of widest fame declined to make many calls like

this. They were too great a strain on his tender emotions. Obviously, he was no pastor.

Very much more effective will be such a call if it is simply following many a *"sympathetic call,"* on lesser occasions, for the daily need, joy, sorrow, on the sick, the tried, the troubled. The foot that has not found its way often to the home in the ordinary times finds itself treading an unfamiliar path in the great strain and stress, when in very truth a pastoral "stranger intermeddleth not with its joy" or bitterness.

But sickness, death, trial—are comparatively infrequent clouds in life's sky, and hence a more common, and most effective, helpful, enjoyable pastoral visit is the *"business call,"* one of the finest; urging to, consulting about, pushing on, "rounding up," some common Christian work, church enterprise, individual task. This has reality in it. It "means business." It enlists, interests, stimulates. It deepens fellowship as almost nothing else can. There is no fellowship quite so vigorous and vital as a fellowship in real work for God and man. Every such call that can be made to take the place of the "routine call" is a marvelous vitalizer.

The *"evangelistic call,"* designed to lead a single soul to Christ, or to work for that same end in the midst of a given family on a given evening, has not been developed by our pastors as it should have been. Its possibilities are boundless. It also calls for tact, persistency, spiritual insight, skill, love, and power in the highest degree. But it is in pastoral contacts of this kind, and not in the great evangelistic meetings, or even in the weekly pulpit work, that the hope of Christ's world-conquest lies. Never, till pastors and people "get busy" in this fashion, will Christianity really capture the world.

The *"shepherd call"* may partake

of the nature of several of these others, but it is inspired by the eye that watches the individual member with his burdens, temptations, peculiar needs, and hastens to his help, comfort, or warning. How absolutely is it needed, and how many great men and great preachers are utterly incompetent to give it, and what a pity that life should grow so complex, or mere church activities so absorbing, that this becomes impossible! It must not be impossible. What is a machine beside a man?

The *"friendly call,"* neighborly or otherwise, just out of pure human and Christian friendliness, just because you like folks and like to be with them—what a luxury that is! The minister's own heart hungers for it. The people's heart hungers for it. But time is short, life exacting, and no one can do as much of this as he ought to want to. And a caution is needed. The minister must control his natural impulse to "selective friendliness" in his calling. "God plays no favorites," and God's man mustn't, being the friend of all, making love supply the lack of congeniality. Some lesser loves must be crucified, or at least curbed, in the interest of the greater.

For efficiency in these, and the many others which present themselves, may we suggest a few catchwords?

Believe in them, every kind. In the full-rounded work of pastor and church not one can be omitted. We can not bring ourselves to believe that some of them are as easy or pleasant as the others. But he who does not heartily believe in them all is no complete pastor. "Without faith it is impossible to please" with a pastoral call. What you groaningly dislike the other folk will, too.

Systematize them, in plan and execution, in campaign and in individual detail. A card index, name directory, street directory, map of your district with salient details of membership and constituency appropriately indicated, is as needed for shepherding as for generalship. Headwork and kneework with the card-index and then footwork on the street.

Individually specialize them, as to which of these various sorts, or a combination of several, each one is. Carry them out on the basis, along the lines, of their particular purposes. This gives point, push, particularity, power. The neighborhood "routine call," for example, can be lifted into life if it be so planned as to "work up" a neighborhood cottage meeting or social, or the like.

Particularize them; the persons in each family, great and small, near and far, church members and nonmembers, the details of their lives being always on the mind before, during, and after each call, and often on the tongue. Particularizing the individual is, in every department of human life, the secret of capturing and holding the individual. The small boy among the mourners whom the minister forgot to pray for at the funeral has never forgotten that. Nor will he ever forget that when another pastor visited the theological seminary where this boy was later studying, the last call that pastor made on the home field was on that student's family, that he might bring to the lonely heart the latest news from home.

Accordingly humanize them. Systematized they must be, or field and work can not be covered, but wo to pastor or church worker who gives the impression, because it is true, that call, and people, and work, are just parts of a "system." That is fatally to mechanicalize them; and machinery is a non-conductor unless there is a real human heart at its center and a real flesh and blood human hand out at the ends of it. The "flirt" succeeds because he or she makes the victim believe that "there is no other person in all the world." There should not be, just then, for the minister. He particularizes, not with ready professional flexibility, but because his heart particularizes; he really has a warm personal interest in these people as "folks." It must be real. Folks may be gullible temporarily; eventually they can tell an incubator from a living breast.

And, since the minister is the human hand at the ends of God's machinery, useless unless the central life flow through him, it is not needless to add: pray them, before, during, and after. He is going to represent God in that household. Shall he? On his manner, spirit, words, acts, depends the effect of the closest touch with personal, "official" Christianity that family will get for three months, six months, a year. What shall it be? Shall goodness appear "awful," or genial, kind, wise, attractive, faithful? Shall Jesus Christ be more honored, loved, obeyed, these souls helped heavenward and in earthly power? Or shall his visit just in a general way indicate his and the church's interest, and otherwise no more than "mark time"? Or shall it distinctly lessen religion's weight, grip, demand, power? Shall some member of that family miss his "portion of meat in due season"? If ever a pastor needs prayer, it is before an afternoon of calling, and after it, and during it.

Over pastoral calling thus believed in, systematized, specialized, particularized, humanized, spiritualized, no minister will ever have to groan.

The Boy Rangers of America

In 1913 Scout Commissioner Gray, of Montclair, N. J., invited the writer to visit a group of younger boys which had been meeting weekly under the leadership of one of the local teachers. Stories were read and they marched, drilled and played games. As a Scout Master and Member of the National Council, my interest in boy work had centered on the prevailing belief that twelve years was the proper age to begin character development. Studying the situation as developed by several visits to the youngsters, I became more and more convinced that the old belief anent the twelve-year age was all wrong, and that the finest of foundation work could be started earlier, provided a plan could be evolved and worked out which would attract and hold the interest of the boy. Deciding that nothing could compare with Indian lore and atmosphere, I resolved to adopt this form of organization.

The Boy Ranger movement was actively launched in January, 1914, at Montclair, N. J., with a total found membership of six boys, their average age being eight years. Over 500 boys have enjoyed the benefits of Ranger membership since then in Montclair alone, many now being Scouts and others in business or at college.

The little nest egg, so to speak, of six boys grew until my Indian lodge had a membership of 151. The boys were organized into four tribes, Sioux, Crows, Blackfeet and Pawnees, with Sachem, Chief, Medicine Man, Wampum Keeper and Indian Runner, each receiving a well-authenticated name borne by a member of one of those tribes. In order not to burden the boys with two lines of expression, the Ranger constitution is built on the twelve Scout laws but does not duplicate them.

The Boy Rangers of America were incorporated in New York State several years ago and have been registered in many states.

Pastors have told me that they would gladly start a lodge of Rangers if they could find a leader, or Guide, as we call him. My answer to that is: "I think your view-point is wrong. Get your group of boys together and put it up to them to pick out the leader they would like to have; then let them lay siege." This applies also to church school-teachers, by the way.

The Ranger headquarters are at 10 West 23rd Street, New York, where a full supply of literature is kept on hand for distribution.

—EMERSON BROOKS.

MID-WEEK PRAYER MEETING

THE CHRISTIAN FAMILY

Oct. 1-7—The Husband and Father

(Eph. 5:22-23; Acts 10:1, 2)

The word family in the English Bible represents original terms in Hebrew and Greek which convey a broader and looser idea than our word carries to-day. The commonest of these original terms is "house"; and it means all persons living under the shelter of the same building, or moved together with the same conveniences in the way of tents and utensils. The Hebrew family, in particular, was much larger than that of to-day. It consisted of all who were dependent on the one man who was at the head of the group. And he was called the father. Modern usage distinguishes between this sort of father, whom it designates as a patriarch, and the father strictly so called.

The ancient usage plainly shows the beginnings of the idea of fatherhood. He was the father who had authority, who could protect his dependents by the use either of superior strength or of superior skill, direct and lead them in their activities, and serve as the center and rallying point for all their common life. Such a father might be, and often was, the husband of many wives and concubines. If he approached the ideal of his type he might win the esteem and loyalty of the household. If he failed to do so he would exercise his authority and demand and enforce obedience even tho arbitrarily.

From this type to that of the New Testament ideal of fatherhood the transition is gradual. But the difference between the two is marked. While the household, as referred to (for example) in Paul's epistles, still contains others than the wife and children, it no longer admits of more than one wife. And what was left to the disposition and temperament of the man is now made the subject of exhortation and voluntary effort. It is no longer a matter of whether a man is naturally endowed with discretion and kindness, but one of obligation to be kind and responsible in the performance of his functions as a father and husband.

This difference was not the result of blind evolution, but the direct insertion into thought of the new ideas by Jesus Christ. Jesus lifted the word "father" from its lower level to the higher one in which it has remained in Christian thought if not always in Christian practise. A father, according to Jesus, is one who begets new lives. But in so doing he assumes responsibilities. Toward his offspring he can not be a mere master. He must provide for them, he must protect them, he must train and guide them until they are able to do all this for themselves; and then he must love them and be interested in them forever. It might cost many an anxious moment and many self-denials, but the true father must do all this.

The husband's relation to the wife in the household is in all respects the counterpart of that of the father to his children. There was much in the ideals current in Jesus' time, both within the Jewish community and in the large Roman world, to encourage other ideals. But Jesus leaves no room for doubt that his own conception was pure and lofty. The husband must cherish his wife as himself. "The two shall become one flesh, so that they are no more two but one flesh." And what Jesus taught his disciples adopted and his followers have held up as the ideal ever since. Thus the Apostle Paul likens the relation between the husband and wife to the mystical union between Christ himself and the Church.

This ideal of husband and father has not been outgrown. It has scarcely become the dominant one, so high and unattainable does it appear at times. And it will not, because it can not, be outgrown. It is rooted in the nature of God himself. Jesus derived his idea of what an earthly father should be from his consciousness of what the heavenly Father is. And the best that any human father can aim to accomplish is so to illustrate in his life the ideal fatherhood that his children may be able to say that they understand in some measure God's fatherhood because they have seen it reflected in their own earthly father.

Oct. 8-14—The Wife and Mother

(Prov. 31:28, 1 Sam. 1:27)

The sphere of parenthood consists of the two hemispheres of fatherhood and motherhood. Therefore it would appear that what has been said of the father and husband from the moral view-point might be easily transferred and applied by a simple substitution of terms to the mother and wife. But the analogy is not quite so perfect as to admit of this. The mother's share in the common responsibilities distinctive of the inner life of the family is by far the larger one. While the father and husband may be called upon to do more toward supplying the means of support and toward shielding the whole group from danger, the mother is in the nature of the case charged with the more arduous and painful functions which build up and conserve the family as such.

Hers, too, is the more sensitive nature. In delicacy of feeling and responsiveness to touch she is far more developed and quick. One of the commonest observations in religious life is that women are vastly in the pre-

ponderance in the membership of the Church. It has raised the question of its cause and meaning. The explanation of the fact is to be found in the higher development of ability to react possest by woman. It does not necessarily indicate a fundamental lack of religious or spiritual faculty in the man; but it shows a nature in woman quicker and readier to respond and express itself.

In non-Christian times this greater refinement of woman's nature issued in great injustice and suffering. The wife and mother was allowed to bear her burden without the sympathy and moral support for which her heart craved. Even within Christendom, in times when brute strength was deemed the greatest of all virtues, her tasks were placed on the lowest level and her contribution to the welfare of common human progress was undervalued; one might say that it was even looked upon with contempt.

But in the Christian ideal this is all set right. In the first place, it is remembered that Jesus himself entertained the most reverent and affectionate heart toward his mother. Next, in his perfectly balanced human nature he held the motherly instinct alongside of the strongly masculine qualities that made him a leader of men. Consequently, the community of his disciples soon felt that motherhood had been ennobled and given a new meaning by his being born of a human mother. Thus it came to pass that in the middle ages his mother was idealized and lifted to a place of unique honor. What was in him of beauty was transferred to her and she was made an object of worship.

This was a healthy and wholesome movement, but sadly misdirected. A saner and more reasonable control of it leads to the clearer definition of the duties and privileges of the wife and mother. In the thoroughly Christian family the wife realizes hers to be the part not of ornament but of self-forgetful ministry. "The heart of her husband trusteth her. . . . She doeth him good and not evil." "She openeth her mouth with wisdom and the law of kindness is on her tongue." And as a mother her chief concern is how to form the lives and characters of her children so that they may be useful men and women and thus enter into the happiness which is the reward of the righteous both in this life and in the life to come.

And for this ideal motherhood the Christian religion, developing the thought of its Lord, inculcates the tenderest appreciation and regard. The Christian ideal made a beginning and some progress in this respect in the days of medieval chivalry. It became the badge of the true Christian to defend women against insult and defamation, to rescue them from danger and distress, and to defer to their desires so far as they are in harmony with the law of Christ. Thus, for the present day the Christian ideal has given a new meaning to the old commandment: "Honor thy father and thy mother." To honor one's mother means to respect and revere her, to shield and support her, and to satisfy her heart by realizing her most cherished ideals for one's own self.

Oct. 15-21—The Children

(Deut. 4:6-9; 2 Tim. 3:14, 15)

Children may make their appearance in a home without any thought on the parents' part of the meaning of the fact to society. They may be accepted as the necessary incident of marriage, with all its other trials and burdens as well as its pleasures and rewards; or they may be viewed from the view-point of the State as a means of perpetuating and increasing national strength. In militaristic countries large families, especially of male children, are much favored. Or,

again, children may be welcomed for the sheer natural pleasure they bring. God has affixt to parenthood an instinctive satisfaction. He has made everything that is healthy about childhood a means of stirring the keenest enjoyment in the heart of the parent.

But Christianity, without in the least degree or particular abating the values of these aspects of child life, adds to them and expands their scope. In the Christian home the child is not only a source of natural pleasure but also of profound gratitude to the Giver of all life. It brings to the individual the experimental realization of how God feels toward himself. Feebly it may be and imperfectly the father, more vividly the mother, come to know what is in their heavenly Father's heart toward them because they feel in their own hearts the throbbings of parenthood. Thus from the natural relationship the Christian ideal develops the spiritual. "A little child shall lead them" is a phrase that has been often used in other senses than the original in the old prophecy of Isaiah; but none of them is fuller of meaning than when the words are applied to the influence exerted by little children on all around them in the Christian home.

Jesus was a lover of children. He saw in them the trustful faith, the innocence and purity, and the possibility of development toward the best which constitute the conditions of membership in the kingdom of God. And to judge from the few data available in the record, Jesus was a child in his mother's home in all respects conformable to his own ideal of the child character. Christians can never forget what their Master said about children and how he lived the child's life. And as he said about the ointment which seemed to be wasted: "Wheresoever this gospel shall be preached in the whole world, there shall also this be told." And we may add there shall also child life be respected and provided with safeguards and helps such as it deserves.

From what children bring to a home of blessing we may pass to what they demand of care and provision for their preparation for the kingdom of God. Parental privilege, like all other privilege, brings its peculiar responsibility. So far as this responsibility concerns the preservation of the new life brought into the world, God has made ample provision for its adequate, tho unconscious, discharge as a responsibility through those laws of nature which govern the lives of all animals. An unerring and irresistible instinct guides the parent animal to provide food and protection for its young until such time as the young is able to go out and find its own food.

But for the child of human parents there is something more than mere preservation of physical life. "The kingdom of God is not eating and drinking." The eternal, which is personality, must be developed and brought to full conscious functioning. Consequently, throughout Scripture large stress is laid on the duty of instructing and training children in and toward understanding the realities of the spiritual life and assuming upon themselves the vows of loyalty to God their Creator and Christ their Savior.

Almost the only provision made for the children in the old Mosaic law is that they shall be taught the will of God and reminded of his wonderful favor to Israel. In the New Testament the experience above all others that Paul takes pains to recall to the mind of Timothy is that he had a faithful mother, herself the daughter of another faithful mother, who took pains to instruct him in the Scriptures.

To bring children to know God and Christ is the supreme work of life in its ideal. All other needs may be conceived as ceasing or losing their importance, but this one, never!

Oct. 22-28—The Home Atmosphere
(Eph. 6:1-9)

Not every house is a real home. The difference is not easy to point out or define in brief and clear terms. But this may be safely taken for granted, that the house whose human denizens are controlled by a moral atmosphere is a home. It may be a good home or a bad home, an ideal or an unideal home; but it is a home as distinguished from a house.

It is one of the distinctive achievements and the chief glory of the Christian religion that it has produced the Christian home. It has produced it by creating an atmosphere for it producible in no other way. From the mere, and one might add, coldly scientific view-point, as a sociological study the Christian home and the atmosphere which gives it its distinctiveness are worthy of the closest and most careful examination.

The physical atmosphere is constituted of oxygen and nitrogen and in very small quantities of other elements. It varies in different localities according as it contains and retains in it carbonic acid or other noxious gases, or ozone with other health-giving elements. Of what does the atmosphere of the Christian home consist? The question obviously answers itself. If it deserve the name at all, the Christian atmosphere must be pervaded by the spirit of Christ? Certainly not the mere outward imitation of Christ, no matter how literally.

The spirit of Christ can exist only where he is himself loved with a passionate but reverent love. That social group every member of which holds Christ as his supreme object of affectionate devotion is Christian. But since the home, like every other social group, is made up of individuals, and since every individual allows himself to be possest and constrained by the love of Christ in a different degree from every other, it follows that the spirit of Christ manifests itself in different groups in varying degrees of power.

The question is sometimes asked whether a nation can ever be Christian as such, and why it is that the so-called Christian nations show so little regard for the exprest will of Christ. The only answer possible to such a question is that no nation can be more Christian than the degree in which the individual members of it taken together are controlled by the love of Christ. The atmosphere of a community is created by the moral principles and convictions cherished by the membership of the community. And a home is the smallest kind of a community.

Hence the importance of cultivating the love of Christ in the household, first by making him more and more fully known. The love of Christ is a fire that needs the fuel of knowledge to feed it. But more effective even than the spreading of his knowledge is the living out of his life. If the father and mother consistently and continually live out their love to Christ, the children in the home will not fail to catch the contagion. If the fire on the family altar is kept alive, and the daily meeting around it reminds every member of the household of him who has loved us all unto the uttermost, the incense burned on that altar will not fail to pervade with its fragrance and its health the atmosphere of that home.

Practically in such a home there will be mutual forbearance and helpfulness. Criticism of each other will be always constructive. Murmurings and complaints will be conspicuous by their absence. Sweet words of greeting will be used not as a matter of custom, but because they express genuine affection among the members. Endearing terms of address will mean what they appear to say. And in one word, natural affection and pride in each other will be sanctified and ennobled because they will conform to the pattern of Christ's own mind and heart.

Where this atmosphere exists in its perfect constituency and distinctiveness, there will be a happy place not only for the parents and children but also for the servants. For in such an atmosphere no pride of social position can survive. Nor, on the other hand, can suspicion and distrust on the part of those who occupy the humbler place of servants thrive there. For masters will deal with servants as with brothers and sisters and servants will remember that Christ himself assumed the place of the "servant in the house," and will endeavor to perform their part as he did.

Oct. 29-Nov. 4—The Family and the Community

(John 12:1-9; Luke 10:38, 39; Mark 12:17)

What the individual is to society that the family is to the community. Just as society as a whole takes up and integrates into a large unity the characteristics of many individuals and expresses them in one common life, so the community, which is a section of society, concretely developed, takes up and organizes the lives of many families. The unit in the community is not the individual but the household. The unit in society abstractly considered can be none other than the individual.

When this fundamental principle is fully realized it will enable us to see that the strength of the community depends on the strength of the families constituting it. The community in which each constituent family is sharply defined from the rest and lives a life of its own, where the members of each family are knit together by ties regarded as sacred, is the community which develops character and vitality. Such a community was that of primitive Rome before the corrupting influences of the outside world loosened the bonds holding its families together as single and separate units. On the contrary, wherever the family has existed as a loosely joined group with vague and variable lines around it, the community has been weak and ready to disintegrate at any moment. Rome again in the late imperial period may furnish an illustration of the condition.

It is obvious, however, that the vitality of the family depends on the theory and practise of marriage. It is not necessary that marriage should be held to be a sacrament, but something of sacramental indelibility and a consequent inviolableness of it must be assumed before the strength of the family life can reach its maximum. If it be said that this makes the relation of husband and wife in the family the only condition of its vigor and totally ignores the other members, the answer is that the relations of husband and wife as constituted by the marriage bond are determinative of all others. All others become hopelessly confused as soon as these primary ones are relaxed or annulled.

All this is nothing more than a repetition of what Jesus told his followers in terms intelligible in their day and generation. It was a time when the spirit of laxity had made its appearance in Jewish family life. By adopting a liberal interpretation of the Deuteronomic law the rabbis had come to advocate loose ideas of the marriage tie. Jesus taught that the home is a divine institution. "He who made them from the beginning, made them male and female, and said, For this cause shall a man leave his father and mother, and shall cleave unto his wife; and the two shall become one flesh." The family is an integral part of God's plan for the human race since God planned it "from the beginning." In other connections Jesus taught that the tie is indissoluble. Wherever he appears to make an exception in favor of divorce it is because he recognizes the power (tho not the right) of men to break the tie by sinning.

And Jesus' teaching is vindicated by a study of human nature. Such study shows that marriage is neither an artificial overgrowth nor a conventional construction which may be changed with changing times. It is due to an inherent necessity, a law of man's nature. Every effort, by experiment or otherwise, to escape this necessity or evade this law ends disastrously. All the utopias from Plato's republic to the Bolshevik Constitution of Soviet Russia have dashed themselves to pieces on this eternal rock.

In the ideal, *i.e.*, Christian family, then, lies the hope of the community. All tendencies away from this ideal, like the present-day tendencies toward easy divorce and refusal to assume parental responsibilities or to yield honor to parents, must sooner or later defeat themselves. All forces that work toward the increase of the purity, the stability, and the full invigoration of the family are means toward advancing the community toward its supreme development and permanent vigor and life. The nation of ideal homes will be, in the future as it has always been in the past, the strong, healthy nation which enjoys God's blessing.   A. C. Z.

The Book

JESUS THE WORLD'S SAVIOR—STUDIES IN LUKE[1]

Professor ANDREW C. ZENOS, D.D., LL.D., McCormick Theological Seminary, Chicago, Ill.

Oct. 1—The Birth of John the Baptist

(Luke chap. 1)

When, after a silence of many generations, the voice of prophecy was again heard it was in the wilderness of Judea through the mouth of John the Baptizer. The importance of this man for the New Testament has always been appreciated. But even in his own day, and before his true relation to the new age could become clearly visible, it was felt that his was a figure of sufficient magnitude to elicit inquiry about his parentage and antecedents. And the information gathered in answer to such questions has been brought together by Luke in a story whose charm is felt to this day.

The new prophet's father was a priest, Zacharias, of the course of Abijah. The name was, no doubt, taken as an omen, for it means Jehovah has remembered. After such a long interval of silence the God of Israel gave a sign that he had not forgotten his people. Zacharias' wife, Elisabeth, was also of priestly ancestry. Like the parents of Samuel, the founder of the prophetic line, Zacharias and Elisabeth were devout but childless. To be childless for a husband and wife among the Hebrews was a great affliction, and by many even regarded as a sign of the divine displeasure, therefore a "reproach."

There were at this time about 20,000 priests. To minister in the service of the temple was not possible for all. The selection of those who should do so was a subject of careful and elaborate regulation. The privilege could not be accorded to the same individual for more than one day. The whole priesthood was divided into twenty-four courses, and each course was assigned one week for its service. From among the men in the course those who were to serve in various capacities were chosen by lot. It may be imagined, therefore, with what feelings Zacharias began the memorable day on which the lot indicated that he was to "burn incense in the temple of the Lord." For this act was especially honorable; it signified the offering of the prayers of the people.

When the moment arrived for the performance of this service at the altar of incense, the people stood without the Holy Place bowed in silent prayer. This was the very moment at which Zacharias received the assurance that his prayers had been heard, and that a son should be born to him. In spite of his habitual attitude of trustfulness Zacharias was filled with fear and perplexity. He dared to question the messenger of God and ask for a sign of the truth of the message. The sign given him was the temporary loss of speech.

[1] These studies follow the lesson-topics and passages of the International Sunday-school series.

The mind of Zacharias was especially imprest by the work assigned to the son to be given him. Repeating the thought of the angel who foreshadowed this work to him, in a song of thanksgiving after the birth of the child, he says that the child was "to go before the face of the Lord to make ready his ways, to give knowledge of salvation unto his people in the remission of their sins." These were great words whose import no one at the time could understand fully.

Another point dwelt upon in the angel's address was that the promised child should be trained in the strictest mode of life, to abstain from intoxicants and thus to keep himself clean for the full operation of the Holy Spirit through his healthy body. "He shall be filled with the Holy Spirit from his mother's womb." That all this was realized in the life of the child John appears when later the evangelist records (verses 66, 80) that "the hand of the Lord was upon him," and that "the child grew and waxed strong in the spirit."

Whether John was affected either in his manner of life or his message to his generation by the ascetic community of Essenes, who lived in the same general region, has been discust by scholars. The question is purely academical. If John ever came in touch with this community the traces of its influence on him have certainly been practically obliterated. They lived in a community; he lived alone. They glorified asceticism for its own sake; he practised a form of it simply as a means toward doing a special work under God's guidance.

Oct. 8—The Birth and Childhood of Jesus (Luke chap. 2)

Luke's account of the birth of Jesus is more extensive than that of Matthew. Matthew records the visit of the wise men from the East and the adoration of the wonderful Child by them. Luke mentions the song of the angels in heaven, the visit to the manger by the shepherds, the presentation of the Babe in the temple and the greetings of the aged Simeon and Anna as they realize the character and destiny of the infant. Both accounts are restrained and reticent concerning the childhood and youth of Jesus. Considering the natural tendency to inquiry in such matters, and the ease with which stories are built up to satisfy curiosity, this silence of the evangelists is significant. It shows that the gospels were produced while as yet the whole interest in the life of Jesus was centered in his wonderful ministry. It was later, when this interest lost some of its fervor and edge, that men began to ask about the details of his childhood. It was then that the apocryphal stories of the infancy were woven together. It is a sign of the very early date of the first three gospels that they do not include any of the quaint, fantastic, and in some respects repulsive, stories so common in the apocryphal writings.

It is also a sign of the sanity and sobriety of the canonical evangelists that they abstain from gratifying mere curiosity in telling of Jesus. In collecting their materials they were evidently governed by the desire to get and give only such facts about Christ as would lead men to understand his mind and to accept him as their Master and Savior. John takes his readers into his confidence on this point when he tells them that he had written "that they (ye) might believe that Jesus is the Christ, the Son of God." This sanity of mind is nothing less than evidence of the inspiration of the evangelists.

But if the omissions of the evangelic narrative are significant, so are the items given. The childhood of Jesus is not altogether passed in silence. A single incident is incorporated into the account; and thereby the fact that Jesus, as a child, had a normal human experience is brought into view. Thereby, also, the sympathy of Jesus for child life, which so frequently crops out during the course of his ministry, is shown to be rooted in the remembrance of his own childhood days.

And more significant than the mere fact of the inclusion of the incident in the gospel story is its subject matter. In the first place, it gives us a glimpse of the household atmosphere within which Jesus grew up. The spirit of loyalty to God ruled in that home. His parents faithfully observed the law regarding going up "to Jerusalem every year at the feast of the passover." In these days, when places of worship are within easy reach of every one, it may be difficult to realize that to make the trip from Nazareth to Jerusalem every year cost some effort and planning; but the love of Joseph and Mary for the house of God was strong enough to lead them to this sacrifice.

In the next place Jesus' mind was full of the thought of God and of all that concerned the relations of men to God. When in Jerusalem he knew how to find those who were, or were supposed to be, expert in matters of religion; and he entered into earnest conversation with them. Considering how reluctant old and wise men sometimes are to enter into serious discussion with children regarding the difficult matters of the inner life, and how prone to postpone such talk to a later time, one is forced to think that there was something about Jesus which challenged and invited the wise men of Jerusalem to open their minds to him.

From the astonishment of his parents at his words to Mary that he "must be about his Father's business" it is clear that the home influences and parental instructions were only the atmosphere and environment within which the mysterious and unique element in the personality of Jesus was beginning to make its power known.

And yet, Jesus was a normal child. "He went down with them to Nazareth and was subject to them." "And he increased in wisdom and stature, and in favor with God and man." In all that makes the whole man, *i.e.*, body ("stature"), mind ("wisdom"), social qualities ("favor with man"), and religious life ("favor with God") the child Jesus advanced toward maturity and perfection.

Oct. 15—The Ministry of John the Baptist (Luke chap. 3)

In many respects the character and work of John the Baptist resemble those of Elijah. The resemblances are so close that both in the Bible and in Christian lore the coming of John is spoken of figuratively as the reappearance of Elijah. At least in one particular, however, the careers of the two prophets are different from one another. Elijah flashed into the skies like a meteor, unheralded and unexpected. No word is spoken of his parentage or even of his remote ancestry. John's birth was announced to his parents and is recorded in detail. We can imagine his parents telling him of the life which was foreshadowed for him and of the type of his ministry. We can imagine, too, the ready acceptance by him as a boy of the austere life prescribed and of the task outlined. Whether on account of the teaching of his parents or because of an inborn disposition, John was early distinguished for sobriety of mind and devotion to the spiritual life. "The hand of the Lord was with him, and he waxed strong in spirit, and was in the deserts till the day of his showing to Israel."

That day came when John attained the age designated in the law for the priest's entrance upon his official work, namely, in the fifteenth year of the reign of Tiberius, he being at that time about thirty years old. John chose for the scene of his ministry the wilderness of Judea. When a messenger of God has a message to deliver he usually goes to find the persons to whom it is to be delivered. There are times, however, when he can perform his duty as a messenger by challenging the audience to come to him. John chose this latter method; and the event proved that it was an effective one. His picturesque appearance, his sincere self-denial, and his vehement earnestness, when they became known in the centers of population, pricked the conscience of the easy-going multitude and brought them to the usually dreaded wilderness to hear him.

John's message was direct and personal. He charged his hearers with grossly sinful conduct and warned them of imminent judgment and retribution. "The axe lieth at the root of the trees; every tree therefore that bringeth not forth good fruit is hewn down and cast into the fire." The only escape from doom was through repentance; and when requested to prescribe constructively the way of repentance to each class, he showed the multitudes the excellence of charity, to the publicans the necessity of justice and fairness, and to the soldiers the duty of restraint and honesty in the use of the power vested in them.

These are crude, elementary, and obvious instructions. They indicate on the one hand the moral bankruptcy of the times, and on the other the unassuming character of John as a religious teacher. He was not aiming at a great revolution of thought. He was attempting, by the reiteration of a few fundamentals in morality, to break open the path for the great Reconstructor.

John's chief task, after all, was not to found a new religion, but to point out him who was to usher the kingdom of God. Of the presence of his august successor in the world already he was aware. Therefore, when asked of his own mission and person, he made it clear that he was not the Messiah, nor a prophet returned from the tomb, but the herald of the coming of the Lord.

John symbolized his spiritual work through the ceremony of baptism. The ceremony was well known among the Jews. It was practised in welcoming proselytes from the Gentile world into the commonwealth of Israel, and it was administered as a sign of the putting away of Gentile uncleanness. So when John practised it, it meant the putting away of sin as a preparation for the coming of the kingdom of God.

The resemblance between John and Elijah reaches its clearest form in the act of denouncing Herod for his sinful relation with Herodias, his brother's wife. Elijah, too, had denounced Jezebel and Ahab. But Elijah escaped the wrath of the angry queen and her good-natured husband. He lived to see his denunciation of wrath realized. John the Baptist was imprisoned and suffered martyrdom. Both prophets had their reward in a clear conscience, even tho their outward experiences were diametrically opposite.

Oct. 22—Jesus Tempted [1]
(Luke 4:1-30)

At his baptism Jesus accepted the call to the messiahship. For nothing else can be meant by the words he heard on the occasion: "This is my well beloved Son." He had, no doubt, thought of the work of the Messiah before, and often seriously. But now he must think of it again, and in a direct and personal way. This is the meaning and intention of his with-

[1] We would like to refer the reader to the article on "The Battle of the Wilderness" in THE HOMILETIC REVIEW for August, 1916.

drawal into the wilderness. There, far from the distractions of busy streets, and also from the attractions of the countryside, he could face the task and think of the ways and means to be used in accomplishing it. Undoubtedly there is a right conception of the fulness and import of any task and some wrong conceptions. There is also a right conception of the means to be used in accomplishing it and many wrong conceptions.

It is when considered from this view-point that the temptations of Jesus disclose their full meaning. The consciousness that he had been called to be the Messiah brought to Jesus the assurance that he possest supernatural powers. To what end and upon what principles was he to use these powers?

The first temptation brought into view the possibility of subordinating the chief end in view to other and intermediary ends. Supernatural power might be used in satisfying personal and bodily needs. Jesus had voluntarily placed himself far from the ordinary ways of getting the necessary means for keeping up his bodily strength. Might he not properly use his privilege as the Messiah in changing the dead stones of the wilderness into life-giving loaves of bread and thus reviving his strength? The Messiah must live, and at first glance, it would appear that he might use his supernatural endowment in supernaturally creating the means of perpetuating his life.

But Jesus felt, first, that to do this was unnecessary, and, secondly, that it established a barrier between him and his people. It was unnecessary because, as it had been set down in the Scripture, "man shall not live by bread alone." The bread question is important; but to make it the only question is to narrow life down to its mere animal proportions. As the parallel account in Matthew has it, man shall live "by every word that proceedeth out of the mouth of God." Man has powers in him which can hold in abeyance his bodily cravings until they may be satisfied in normal ways. But to use this power in supplying food upon the appearance of every one of his personal needs would establish a gulf between him and those who belong to him. And if he undertook to bridge this gulf and provide bread for them in the same way, it would degrade the messiahship into a means of material comfort.

In the second temptation as recorded in the third gospel Jesus was called upon to achieve his messianic lordship over the whole world by the way of compromise. A medieval pope purchased the papacy out of the pure and laudable motive of reforming and dignifying it. It had fallen into a state of decay and corruption. If he could only get the authority into his own hands he would restore to the office its spiritual power. The motive was good, but the method of achieving the end was that of compromise. Jesus' temptation was similar. The messiahship meant the rule of the world. Once achieved it would furnish an opportunity for unlimited good. But could the good so done be called good? Jesus' answer is, "Thou shalt worship the Lord thy God, and him only shalt thou serve."

The third temptation was to achieve the messiahship by an appeal to a non-moral display of power. Later in his ministry Jesus was challenged to prove his claim by performing some sign. He declined, just as he put away the temptation to cast himself from the pinnacle of the temple in presence of the people. Moral ends must be morally attained. He who violates this law "makes trial" of his God.

Temptation is a means of testing moral strength. As such, in the case of Jesus it proved his ability to resist all wrong and unworthy ideas and methods of approaching and undertaking his work. But for the very reason that he had set aside these unworthy conceptions, temptation became a means of equipment. He was ready to enter upon his task, and as the same insidious suggestions of doing it in less than the most perfect form came to him he was able to set them aside and the more easily. Furthermore, his temptation became a help to all his followers first because they are assured of his sympathy in all their temptations, and then because they learn from him how to resist and overcome temptation.

Oct. 29—World-wide Prohibition— World's Temperance Sunday

(Isa. 61:1-9)

Prohibition, either national or world-wide, was far from the thoughts of the Biblical writers. No method of exegesis usable by the self-respecting interpreter can be made to show that any prophet or apostle of old time entertained the idea that the manufacture and sale of alcoholic beverages should be forbidden by the State. The whole problem of intoxicants is viewed from the standpoint of its moral aspects. Drunkenness is severely and without qualification condemned as degrading and therefore as a sin in the sight of God.

It would be a mistake, however, to suppose that the question of indulgence in intoxicants is left to the preference or the judgment of the individual altogether. There is no such principle in the Bible as "personal liberty" in the sense commonly given to that phrase. The Old Testament in particular presents all moral questions from the view-point of their bearings on the community. Intoxication is a sin not only against God and the individual self, but against the social unit whether it be the city (Zion, Samaria) or the nation (Israel, Judah).

Looked at from this point of view, the whole matter is placed in the class of problems of public policy. Neither the Jews nor any other ancient people had developed a social theory according to which the drink question could be made the subject of national laws. But the ethical system of the Bible includes the two fundamental principles upon which State regulation and prohibition rest. These are, first, the essential harmfulness of intoxicants, and, second, the right of the community to control the practise of the individual when it conflicts with its own interests.

Prohibition is, therefore, after all, rooted and grounded in sound Biblical principles. The prophecy in Isaiah, which Jesus quoted in his speech in the synagog of Nazareth and applied to himself, represents the faithful messenger of God, the preacher of good tidings, as announcing a great day of world-wide reconstruction. Broadly this reconstruction involves everything that pertains both to the spiritual and temporal welfare of the whole world.

The trend of affairs in recent years has reduced the whole race of mankind to a single life. The world is practically one body. The welfare or distress of one part of it can not be segregated and limited to that part. Upon this showing, which is coming to be realized more and more fully, the day is coming when world-wide prohibition will cease to be a mere ideal entertained by high-minded prophets alone, and will become a program for practical statesmen.

But for the Christian, world-wide prohibition should remain always a goal to be attained by brotherly love. Its motive is the missionary one of sharing with all men a blessing that one has realized for himself, and its method will be that of persuading men to accept the blessing by their own decision rather than of coercing them to it.

"Caste" at Work

Observation shows that the "caste system," that bed-rock of tho Hindu religion, is the fundamental cause of India's poverty, in that it is the greatest factor in limiting production. It does this in a number of ways. For instance—I employed a sweeper whose work kept him occupied for less than two hours a day. His wages were two dollars a month. Indian servants feed themselves. He had a wife and six children. When I paid him his wages he held it in his hand and looked at it. He said, "Sahib, it is very hard to feed eight people on such a small sum." I answered that I did not see how he did it. I said, "I would like to pay you more money if you earned it. The gardener has asked for help to dig in the garden. If you will go and help him I will gladly pay you." He replied that he would go and dig in the garden. He started in to work. In a few minutes the gardener came to me and asked for his pay. I said, "What is the matter? Are you not satisfied with your work? Do I not treat you fairly?" He replied, "O yes, Sahib, you treat me all right and the work is all right, but I must leave." "Why? What is the matter that you can not work?" "Well, Sahib, you have sent that sweeper to work in the garden. If he stays I go." "But you asked me for aid and I sent him to help you. He has a wife and six children and gets two dollars a month. You have a wife and four children and get two and a half dollars a month. Yet, you complain of the difficulty. How much harder then for him. So I thought if he were willing to work extra, I would pay him for it, and you would get your digging done and he would have more food for his family." "Yes, Sahib, that is all true, but you see he is not of my caste and so can not work in the garden with me. If he stays, I go. If I stay while he works in the garden my castefellows will not drink water or smoke the hooka with me, and I can not suffer the disgrace of this just for a sweeper. So I must leave." I call the sweeper away from the garden and explain the trouble to him. He understands perfectly well the reason. We both know that if the gardener leaves, I can not get another. They would boycott me if I allowed my gardener to leave for such a reason. So the sweeper must look otherwhere to sell his labor, and always with the same result, so with sad, resigned air he accepts his fate. Not the oppression of the Indian by the foreigner, but the oppression of the Indian by the system of caste which is the heart and essence of the religion of the Hindus. —*The Gospel and the Plow*, by Sam Higginbottom.

The American Schools of Oriental Research

The exclusion of the Turk from the Holy Land accomplished by the war is showing already far-reaching consequences for archeology. One of these is the security of Christian interests in property and investigation. An illustration of this may be found in the favorable conditions which now loom up for the American School in Jerusalem. The ground had long been paid for, but the title rested in the Turkish Kavass or guard. This provided no assurance that the grant or sale would not at some time be cancelled. Mrs. Nies bequeathed $50,000 for a building, but required as a preliminary condition the vesting of the title in the school or its trustees and some degree of assurance of permanence in the institution itself. Under the mandate to the British the school has been incorporated, its board of trustees appointed, and the title to the grounds secured in fee simple. Plans for the building have been drawn, and study of their suitability to the location will be completed this spring. Materials will be collected during the summer, and erection will probably start in the autumn. The library of the late Professor Jastrow has been given to the school, and will be shipped as soon as room has been provided for it.

The opening of the American School in Bagdad is also provided for. It is for the present to be given a place in the home of the American consul at Bagdad. The splendid library of the late Dr. William Hayes Ward was bequeathed to this school on condition that the institution get under way within ten years, and the bequest is available. The service this school so located will do for Babylonian, Assyrian, and Hittite archeological research is beyond calculation. It is strategically placed, and may become the clearing house for scholarship in the subjects named.

THE MORAL EFFECTS OF WASTE

Professor RUDOLPH M. BINDER, Ph.D., New York University

Oct. 1—Waste Reprehensible

SCRIPTURE LESSON: John 6:12; Luke 15:13, 16:1ff; Prov. 18:9; 1 Kings 12:11.

INTRODUCTION: The problem of waste is two-fold—the doing of things which are not worth while, and the uneconomical doing of things worth while. The former may be called social waste, the latter economic.

Anything which does not contribute to the improvement of man and the betterment of society may be considered wasteful from the social point of view. Such things may be produced economically, that is, the quality and quantity of output may be large in proportion to the means and effort employed. There may not be any waste of materials, and scientific standards may be used in production. The products should, nevertheless, be considered waste from the social point of view, because they do not help man or society by improving the former and creating better relations in the latter. They are, indeed, harmful to both. Luxuries, as a class, belong in this category.

Articles which are necessary for helpful relations between men may, on the other hand, be produced by such wasteful methods in regard to men and materials employed that their cost becomes disproportionately high, and the development of man is thus hindered, if not prevented.

Whether waste be of the social or the industrial kind, it is reprehensible from every point of view, and should be avoided.

SOCIAL WASTE: The one object for which society and business, as indeed all social institutions, exist is the creation of a higher type of man—more self-reliant, moral, spiritual, and intelligent. This test must be applied to all human activities, because we do not live primarily to become richer or happier, but to become more helpful and efficient. Measured by this standard, there has been much waste in production from the social point of view. A few illustrations will make this clear.

The brewing and distilling of alcoholic beverages had been brought to a high state of perfection before the Eighteenth Amendment to our federal Constitution was passed. All the aids which the sciences of chemistry, mechanics, and management could render to the business were utilized to reduce the cost of production and to increase the profits of the brewers and distillers. It was rumored that in some breweries hops and malt were kept in show-cases only, since chemistry had, under the guidance of highly paid specialists, furnished means to produce beer without these natural ingredients. Whether literally true or not, the rumor had a solid foundation in the utilization of many chemicals even in the best breweries, and the very large wealth of many brewers, acquired within a comparatively few years, furnished ample evidence of very large profits. The business was, then, a success from the purely economic point of view; it was not wasting materials.

What about the social waste? The fact that evils accumulated in immorality, politics, the family, and other social institutions and finally compelled the people to proscribe this business is sufficient testimony. We are still suffering from its effects, of which a large amount of lawlessness is one.

Take another case. After a journey when you get off the train the porter takes down your bag, another porter takes it to the sidewalk, then you take it yourself and carry it for three or four blocks to a hotel without apparent discomfort. The moment you enter the hotel, your strength seems suddenly to leave you, and you gratefully hand over your bag to a little fellow one-half your own size, who carries it to the registration desk, and from there to the near-by elevator. This work may be done precisely as it should be done, but—practically all the work of the "fronts" and "bell-hops" is waste from the social point of view. There are thousands upon thousands of men, women, boys and girls who perform similarly useless tasks for the support of whom society has to pay.

Take one more case. Thousands of people have gazed at the pyramids in Egypt with awe and wonder, and admired the lofty pillars of stone. Egyptologists and travelers have told us in books and articles by the thousand what great builders and geniuses the Egyptians were. Yet it seems to have struck few of these writers that those buildings were monuments of folly and of phenomenal social and economic waste. They had slight practical value—to aid the surveyors to re-locate the property of different individuals after the annual floods. A block of stones, built square and topping the highest flood by a few feet, would have served the purpose better. What were the pyramids for, then? For royal tombs. What a vast amount of labor was spent on these tombs may be guessed by the pyramid of Gizeh, which was 480 feet high and is supposed to have required the labor of 100,000 men for from twenty to thirty years. Perhaps 20,000 died owing to hardships and lack of food. But kings must have tombs befitting their rank as demi-gods! Even animals had gigantic monuments built for them—the so-called Serapeum is a huge building; it contains the embalmed bodies of the bulls Apis, worshiped during their lives as gods. The villages of Karnak and Luxor, about a mile distant from each other, are united by a double row of sphinxes, of which more than a thousand are supposed to have existed before time and greed destroyed or removed them. How many worked on these sphinxes and the pedestals it is impossible to tell. That the labor was socially useless is certain. That the work of these men would have been better employed in their fields is equally certain.

THE MORAL EFFECT: Very little needs to be said about the destructive influence of such waste. Men had always great difficulty making "ends meet" in the past. The numerous famines are ample proof, and whole tribes have passed away for sheer inability to procure necessary food. The only alternative was war. It was resorted to almost constantly owing to the need for food. But once the habit was acquired, wars were waged out of sheer greed. It was much easier to let others till the soil and then take the harvest than himself to till the soil.

In face of this difficulty in making a living the effects of the deliberate misdirection of human efforts could have been none other than degrading. All waste is morally reprehensible because it diverts human energy from what should be constructive to that which is destructive. Man has an instinctive love for achieving something useful—not necessarily in the economic sense but in giving joy and happiness. The wasting of his labor lowers morale; it gives stone for bread.

Oct. 8—Waste in Government

Government waste will be considered only from two angles—federal and municipal. Only specific cases will be given with little comment, since they tell their own story.

FEDERAL: The United States Post-office has been a conspicuous example of the "pork barrel" method of appropriation. This method means that wholesale appropriations are made for sites, buildings, and maintenance to certain villages, towns, and cities, irrespective of the merits of the particular cases. This method has always been employed by Congress; it became, however, particularly conspicuous in December, 1916, and aroused wide-spread attention and condemnation. From a choice lot of cases the following give good illustrations of wastefulness. The appropriations are for both site and building:

City and Amount	Population[1]	Receipts 1915	Annual Rent
Athens, Ala.			
$35,000	1,715	$9,393.82	$508
Clare, Mich.			
$35,000	1,850	$8,596.91	$509
Corning, Ia.			
$35,000	1,702	$7,188.25	$660
De Ridder, Ga.			
$30,000	2,100	$8,854.54	$300
Hazard, Ky.			
$40,000	537	$4,488.43	$250
Lewisburg, West Va.			
$82,000	803	$8,017.37	$540

[1]It should be remembered that a post-office in a rural community may supply the needs of a population two or three times that of the town.

The specific loss to the Government may be shown in the case of Hazard, Ky. The rental for ample post-office accommodation in 1916 was $250. The Government invested $40,000 in a building; invested at 5 per cent that would bring $2,000; the maintenance charges are at least 10 per cent or $4,000, making a total of $6,000. Subtracting $250 for rental, leaves a clear loss annually of $5,750. A total appropriation of $28,000,000 was made in 1916 and 1917 for post-offices chiefly in places where the sage-brush or the swamp was skirting the new building. One village in Florida had an appropriation for a post-office sufficiently large to house the whole population; one village in Oregon was so liberally provided for that the people were scandalized and declined the offer.

The franking system is another source of governmental waste. In 1912 more than 300,000,000 pieces of mail, weighing in the aggregate about 61,000,000 pounds, were carried free of charge under the franks of Congressmen and of the various government establishments. The total loss to the post-office was $20,000,000. It may, of course, be debatable whether the federal government should charge itself with postage in one department to pay another department; but the free paper, envelopes, and franking privilege of the members of Congress might certainly be curtailed with decided advantage to the public.

A still further source of waste is our pension system. From July 1, 1790, to July 1, 1916, the federal government has paid for pensions $5,054,630,727. During the same period the total war bill of the government was $7,657,322,205, and the naval bill $3,233,862,-654. Reasonable pensions should, of course, be paid. In 1916 there were still 115 widows of soldiers of the war of 1812 on the pension list; and of the Mexican War 513 soldiers and 3,785 widows still draw pensions.

Only a few comparatively small items have been mentioned here, because the harbor bills, levee bills, and those of other purposes are too numerous even to be referred to. Their amounts run into hundreds of millions. During the World War money was spent lavishly, much of which went to waste, and only recently (May, 1922) an appropriation of $500,000 was asked for by Attorney General Daugherty for an investigation into war frauds. He claims that in 275 cases pending the federal government stands to recover $192,000,000; and 135,000 cases are yet to be investigated. Not a little sensation was created a few years ago when the news leaked out that the only tangible result of an appropriation of $600,-000,000 for experiments in airplanes was the so-called "liberty motor."

MUNICIPAL: Waste in cities takes the form chiefly of corruption. It is exceedingly difficult in a given case to prove that an appropriation is not needed, because at least a good excuse can be made for it.

Hence waste consists primarily in paying too much for a schoolhouse site, for instance, or accepting the bid of a man who is in league with the "bosses" under the pretext that he is the more dependable party. It is likewise difficult to prove that a number of clerks are not needed in a municipal office, because no one has ever been able to run it any other way. When Mr. Franklin D. Roosevelt was Assistant Secretary of the Navy, he said in an address at Harvard: "I have no hesitation in saying that if I were given a free hand in the Navy in the matter of pay to employees I would increase the actual number of dollars paid to them by $5,000,000 a year, but at the same time, through increased efficiency, I would save the government at least $15,000,000 gross, a net saving of $10,000,000." If he were a czar or kaiser, he might do it, but in a republic with a representative government he would never get the opportunity. It is the same way in municipalities; the payrolls can be padded considerably and much money wasted before the taxpayer can prove the waste.

There has been a vast amount of corruption in all our municipal governments; it seems to be a peculiarly American shortcoming. There is not a single large city in our country, perhaps not a smaller one, which has not been defrauded of vast sums by corrupt methods. Attempts at reform have been made time and again; they have usually failed after a few successful spurts.

From 1867 to 1872 Tweed and his ring plundered New York City of more than $100,000,000; the boss of Tammany sold some of the valuable franchises and privileges to the highest bidder, and some of the largest private fortunes of New York City are based on these purchases.

In the spring of 1922 the question of enlarging the city's transit facilities became extremely urgent after having been debated for several years. Certain bids for extensions were rejected, the new bids were less than $4,000 lower than the old ones; but the delay cost the city $42,000. Meanwhile the people are dependent on inadequate transit facilities and the companies are making money by having at least 50 per cent of the passengers stand.

For whatever the city buys it has to pay more than the business man or smaller cities. A recent example is found in the voting machines sold to Syracuse, N. Y., at

$750 in 1918, but offered to New York at $940. These are only some of the more flagrant cases. What is wasted through inefficiency or connivance with contractors and building corporations passes scrutiny and runs into much larger sums.

Nor is New York alone in this respect. Boston, Philadelphia, Pittsburg, Cincinnati, Chicago, St. Paul, San Francisco—these and other cities have a similar record. The taxpayers are not organized and have to pay.

MORAL EFFECTS: If, as stated above, some of the largest private fortunes in New York are the result of fraudulent purchase of valuable franchises from corrupt bosses, the effects on the people can readily be imagined. There would be no bosses to corrupt if there were no corrupt business men to bribe them. These men often give largely to philanthropies, churches, colleges, and for other purposes. The people look at the large donations but—do not praise the donors. They begin to realize why it is so difficult to throw off the rule of the political rings when they find politics and business morganatically married with the purpose of robbing the people. Apathy steals over them, since as soon as they have cast out one master they find the new one to be little, if any, better. The corporations are always with the winning side—they can afford to throw bribes both ways, and the politicians of both parties manifest a perpetual hunger for the loaves and the fishes. The people may have their ideals as long as they are willing to foot the bills for their masters. Ours is a "free government"; one man has the right to dream and work, the other man seems to have the right to exploit and get rich!

Oct. 15—Waste in Industry

There is perhaps nothing of which Americans are more proud than their efficiency. For the last twenty-five years that word has been rung up and down the scale in every possible variation. From the large corporation down to the smallest business man the word "efficiency" was used as if it were a magic charm. The man in the street used a humble synonym—"live wire," or "near-live wire," since the more highly sounding term was left to the intellectuals or the "highbrows." But we were proud of our achievements. Even during the World War the

professor of a famous Eastern university was readily quoted far and wide as the exponent of true Americanism when, after the briefest possible visit to a European port, he declared his countrymen the most efficient people on earth, notwithstanding the incredible waste referred to in the preceding lesson!

APPROACHES: As early as 1873 the American Association for the Advancement of Science had called attention to the rapid depletion of our natural resources. The statement and proofs were not heeded. A repeated call for the conservation of these resources finally brought some action during the presidency of the late Theodore Roosevelt.

In 1913 *The Price of Inefficiency*—a book by Frank Koester—appeared. The author is an engineer and knows the methods of production and distribution well. His astonishing conclusion was that out of every dollar we earn forty cents goes for nothing; or differently, the out-and-out waste of this country amounted to ten billion dollars. This was previous to the high prices.

In November, 1920, Herbert Hoover, the first president of Federated American Engineering Societies—representing about 200,000 engineers in every branch—appointed a committee of fifteen to investigate waste in industry. On June 3, 1921, the committee made its report, which was published later in the same year under the title *Waste in Industry*.

In England a book, *Poverty and Waste* by Hartley Withers, appeared in 1914; and in 1920 *Millions from Waste* by Frederick A. Talbot. Each of the authors mentioned attacks the problem of waste from a particular angle, and the findings are in most cases extremely interesting.

THE FACTS: The first item in *Waste in Industry* is low production. The loss from waiting for material and for work amounts to 35 per cent in the shoe industry. In the printing trades the standardization of newspaper columns to one size would make possible an annual saving of from $3,000,000 to $5,000,000 on composition and plates alone. In the clothing industry—men's ready-made alone—$750,000 could be saved per day by better management of employment; the efficiency of the plants could thus be increased by 40 per cent. What loss may be incurred by lack of management may be inferred from the following instances given on page 12:

A shoe factory having a capacity of 2,400 pairs of shoes a day could turn out for a considerable period only 1,900 pairs because of shortage of needed racks. Another factory had 50,000 pairs of shoes tied up in the fitting room instead of the normal 15,000 because of congestion of operations. In another case a factory producing 700 pairs of shoes a day had 36,000 pairs in its fitting rooms, or ten times the normal supply. An entire factory was held up for several days waiting for leather heels.

The shoe industry has a capacity of 1,-750,000 pairs of shoes per day, and produces but little more than half that number. This means idle capital, plants, and men. Labor unions are in many cases responsible for waste through restricted production. The following case is quoted from page 20:

Hoisting engineers claim the right to run all types of engines, including small gas-driven pumps which require no skill. On one job a contractor had to hire a union engineer at $8.00 per day simply to start a pump in the morning, oil it occasionally, and stop it at night.

Lost production, due to poor health and accidents, is another source of waste. The 42,000,000 persons gainfully employed lose about 350,000,000 days of work per year. Including medical care, special diet, etc., this means a loss of $1,800,000,000 of which at least $1,000,000,000 could be saved by better attention to health. Industrial accidents of various degrees cause an annual loss of about 286,000,000 working days, causing in 1919 alone a money loss to workers of about $853,000,000; additional expenses for care, surgical aid, and hospital bills, etc., brought the total loss due to accidents up to $1,014,-000,000, of which $349,000,000 was borne by employers and $665,000,000 by employees and their dependents.

The engineers came to the conclusion that even in the so-called standardized industries there is a great lack of efficiency, viz., the building industry was 60 per cent efficient, shoe industry 65 per cent, clothing industry 60 per cent. The responsibility for this inefficiency was placed as follows: management 50 per cent, labor 25 per cent, other conditions 25 per cent.

Strikes and lockouts caused a loss of about $2,000,000,000 in 1919—$725,000,000 to labor, and $1,250,000,000 to capital.

Mr. Talbot proceeds in a different manner. He shows that the material thrown away in manufacturing may often be very valuable, for instance in the burning of coal. One single item of great economy may be referred to. The soap trade of Great Britain is now saving $1,750,000 in paper alone, due to more scientific cutting.

Mr. Withers claims that with more economical production and better methods of saving, poverty could be, if not eliminated, at least greatly reduced. He is of the opinion that it is a crime to have men starve in the midst of plenty, and believes that the time must soon come when all waste will be stopt, and more useful economic goods produced. Our system of distribution with its middlemen, hangers-on, and other intermediaries, is perhaps as much to blame as uneconomical production. It is a well-known fact that in our own country the farmer gets only around 40 cents for every dollar the consumer pays.

MORAL EFFECTS: When a person becomes accustomed to being careless in regard to methods and materials in his work, he soon loses respect for human labor and its products. This is only a short step from negligence to sabotage, or the destruction of property through indifference and intention. As was shown above, the management is accused by the Committee of Engineers of twice as much inefficiency as the workers. The workers are shrewd enough to notice slipshod procedures on the part of their superiors, and they naturally fall into similar habits. If a worker gets irritated or angry, he will readily resort to methods of destruction deliberately, and go undetected because destruction has been a general practise. If so, it will be exceedingly difficult to prove carelessness in one case and deliberation in another.

Every right-minded person is anxious to see poverty abolished. It can be done only with the greatest thrift and economy in the utilization of all available resources of wealth. These qualities may no longer figure among the greatest virtues, but they are important for the elimination of many social evils. Poverty may not be a crime, but it is a great handicap in the endeavor to develop a full personality. And a society which manages its industries so badly that fully one-half of its work is wasted is certainly not in a position to assist in the development of larger personalities among its workers. One may admit that the problem is complex; that is, however, the most urgent reason why much thought should be devoted to it, since a solution must be found if we are not to perish.

Oct. 22—Waste in Families

Waste in the family means two things— the careless use of things useful, and the acquisition of things not needed for existence and comfort; briefly, lack of thrift and luxury. The dividing line between the two is not easy to draw; nor should it be drawn between the poor and the rich. Both classes are guilty in each respect. While it is true that chiefly the rich are guilty of indulging in luxury, it is true also that in proportion to their means the poor are just as culpable. Both waste things necessary for maintenance of life. The line, if it can be drawn at all, should be drawn from a different point of view. Whatsoever contributes to the enlargement of personality may be a need or a comfort; whatsoever tends to gratify a mere whim and caprice is a luxury and, socially considered, waste.

A FEW FACTS: The statement has been made repeatedly that the population of France could live comfortably on what we throw into the garbage-pail. Whether literally true or not, the statement is significant; our wastefulness has become an international by-word. A washwoman was recently reported from Detroit to have boasted that they had five kinds of meat at the family meal; every member worked at good wages, so "we can afford it." What will happen when work stops no one knows. Perhaps the government will be accused of not caring for the poor workingman, or the capitalist will be charged with grinding him down. In August, 1920, an Italian cobbler in Newark, New Jersey, spent $400 for the burial of a pet canary. The coffin alone cost $25; it was borne in a white hearse, followed by two coaches, a fifteen-piece band which played funeral dirges, and 500 people on foot.

The rich in many cases spend lavishly. In September, 1913, the Dressmakers' Club reported 10,000 women in our country to be spending $5,000 per year on personal adornment, 100 social leaders going as high as $50,000, and a few needing $75,000 to be properly drest. That was before the high prices had come in.

A decade ago, first-class opera-glasses could be bought at $20. Yet $75,000 was paid for a pair with no better lenses, but richly adorned with precious stones.

A certain rich man bought the home of a deceased friend for $2,000,000, which had originally cost $4,000,000. Then he spent $500,000 on a tiny garden, $200,000 on a bedstead, $65,000 on wall decorations, $20,-000 for ten pairs of curtains, $150,000 for the wardrobe in his bedroom, $65,000 for a dressing table, $38,000 for a washstand, $8,000 for a mantel, $10,000 for four doors.

Modern emotional refinement demands that we should be kind to animals. But why a pet monkey should cost a woman between $10,000 and $11,000 a year, requiring the constant attention of three human beings, having a bed of solid ivory, a private trotter of his own, and eating the choicest food out of solid silver plates, is difficult to explain on this basis.

These are but a few cases of extravagant waste previous to 1913, when prices had not yet risen mountain high. What happens to-day may be illustrated by three cases. A pork packer from Chicago recently had his picture taken with his $10,000 German shepherd dog. An opera star in Paris appeared in a mantle of finest Russian ermine, which could not have cost less than $50,000. The widow of an automobile maker is reported to be wearing a necklace worth $1,-500,000; private policemen are always with her when she goes out. The New York press frequently reports the loss of jewels costing anywhere from $5,000 to $100,000.

According to figures furnished by Mr. Houston, then Secretary of the Treasury, we spent in 1919 nearly $23,000,000,000 for luxuries—or over one-third of our total national income. Two of the largest items were, luxurious food $5,000,000,000, and luxurious services $3,000,000,000.

THE EXCUSE: Many people justify this extravagance on three grounds—it gives them pleasure, it makes the money circulate, they have a right to do with their own as they please.

Such expenditure for luxuries certainly gives pleasure; but what kind? Merely that you can outdo somebody else. There is no virtue in it, except the gratification that your purse is larger than your neighbor's. True satisfaction can come only from the development of one's powers. Anything else is spurious and feeds a sense of vanity and a false idea of superiority.

The economists have long ago exploded the notion that any kind of employment for which wages are paid is justified. Every dollar paid for luxuries and every hour of work employed in their manufacture raise the price of necessaries. These men must live, have food, clothes, houses; the fewer the men employed in the production of necessaries the higher the prices must rise, because the supply gets smaller and the demand greater. It is still true that eventually the producers of raw materials and the men who get them ready for consumption support the whole economic fabric of society, while the workers in luxuries produce things which satisfy whims and caprices.

No person living in a civilized society has a right to do what he pleases with his property; he may not set fire to his house without facing prison. He may legally have the right to spend his money for luxuries, but morally he has not. The legal right is based on the now exploded economic theory mentioned above. As we come to understand our interdependence better, the moral obligation for judicious spending, now recognized by a few men only, will be put in the form of law and become the duty of the many. Society must protect itself against injurious production and consumption; and the Eighteenth Amendment to the Constitution proves its power to do so.

MORAL EFFECTS: A few lavish expenditures have been referred to in this lesson. There is a vast amount of discontent among the poor and the working classes. Is it any wonder? Thousands of fathers have hardly bread for their children; one woman spends over $10,000 on a pet monkey. Many children come to school poorly clad and shivering; one woman spends over a million dollars on a useless necklace. One man commands the living of thousands by raising prices, maintains an expensive lobby in the state and federal legislatures in order to get protection for his products, and then—spends $10,000 of his vast wealth on a dog.

These statements do not imply a condemnation of wealth, because, as we saw, supposedly poor people waste as much proportionately. It is rather an indictment of our whole moral and social attitude. We value people in proportion to what they spend instead of what they produce; what they have, instead of what they are; what they get, instead of what they give in service.

Oct. 29—Remedies

GREATER REGARD FOR LABOR: Whatsoever has been produced by human labor partakes of human values. It may have little social value, but a part of man has gone into its making, and it should not be destroyed ruthlessly. The mud-pies and the sand-bridges of our children are of no earthly use; what patience, ingenuity, and pleasure have gone, however, into their making. The children have exprest their personality in their creation, and only a human brute will destroy them.

When socially useful things are wasted, the damage is much greater. A certain amount of capital, social knowledge, and enterprise have gone into their making, and of these we never can have too much. Even the waste of things for which man has not labored is reprehensible, because it shows a disregard for the rights of others. The wholesale destruction of wild flowers is a case in point. These tender plants are beautiful only in their natural environment; if picked, they soon wilt. But thoughtless people pick them, uproot them for the temporary satisfaction of carrying them home; other people who pass through the woods are deprived of the pleasure of seeing and enjoying them. The disturbance of the economy of nature is a more important matter which has already cost our farmers millions of dollars that a little consideration for others and for the beauties of nature could have saved.

LESS CARELESSNESS: We are apt to accuse the government of carelessness but fail to see our own defects in this matter. One instance will illustrate this point. In New York City alone the work of correcting faulty addresses costs about $500 per day, and even after this expensive work has been done, 20,000,000 letters find their grave in the "Dead Letter Office" in Washington. That makes an annual loss of $182,500 for New York City alone. The work necessitated in other cities, towns, and villages for similar defects must cost the United States Post-Office a considerable sum. Then comes the additional outlay for forwarding the undecipherable letters to Washington and for the new attempts to locate the addressee. A large percentage of the letters mailed without street and number are so mailed through the laziness or carelessness of stenographers and clerks.

A similar attitude of negligence is maintained by the people toward other departments of the government. No figures are available as to the extra cost which the carelessness and the intent to defraud impose upon the Treasury in collecting income taxes.

GREATER INTEREST IN GOVERNMENT: The majority of voters feel very virtuous when they go to the polls on election day instead of taking a ride in their automobiles or going fishing. They have discharged their duty. The issue is as a rule simple for them—the Democratic or the Republican party must win. Events may then take their course. They do! The person elected feels that he has *carte blanche* for the tenure of his term. He looks out for opportunities to supplement his salary. Generally he does not need to do even that; they come to him. The lobbyists of large corporations and special interests are busy to get favorable or to defeat unfavorable legislation. There need not be direct or even indirect corruption, altho there often is; votes are necessary to pass the bill. And our representative remembers when a bill comes up to which he may be opposed that he has a pet bill, an appropriation let us say, for his own district, which will assure his reelection. So he votes favorably, and insures votes for his bill. This dickering for votes in our legislative halls is one of the worst features of our government. The voter at home seldom follows the ins and outs of his representative, and votes for him again. "Didn't he get us our new post-office?" That settles the question. How many extra dollars that post-office costs the voter he never realizes, since his representative may have voted for hundreds of bills to secure it.

And here lies the trouble. Most of our taxation is indirect. Our friend would object to the new post-office if he were taxed five dollars directly. Since it comes as an apparent gift from a generous government and an astute representative, he never realizes that it may cost him ten dollars, owing to the many bills for which the representative had to vote. The Bonus Bill, now before Congress, is a conspicuous example. So many Congressmen were willing to vote any amount of money for this purpose in order to secure the votes of the soldiers that they did not stop to find out how the money was to be provided. Hap-

pily the direct income tax of the last few years has taught the voter a lesson. No indirect way could be found to pay the bonus, and the voters realized that it would mean further direct taxation. So they spoke wherever they had a chance in 1922.

Indirect taxation, *e.g.*, through import duties, has been a source of vast evil. It permitted the avoidance of responsibility under the guise of protecting American industries. Appropriations to any extent could thus be made with a patriotic motive, and few people understood that the maintenance of the government cost them, through the raising of the prices of every article consumed, from three to five times what a direct tax would have cost them. The income tax has justified its existence as an educational measure, if for no other reason.

STRICTER SUPERVISION OF THE CORPORATIONS: A vast amount of waste is imposed upon the country by spurious and fraudulent corporations. For several years this country has paid about $500,000,000 to all kinds of firms whose only assets were glib-talking salesmen, fine office furniture (payable on the instalment plan), and the credulity of the public.

We often read about a large company "scrapping" a practically new plant or machinery, because more expensive and, supposedly, more productive machinery is to be introduced. We always admire that procedure, not realizing that we have to pay for it by increased prices for the product. This is the parallel of indirect taxation; it does not "come home" directly, so we applaud the enterprise of these men. The stockholders should watch their directors more carefully.

Public service corporations were formerly run for the benefit of the directors who gambled in the stock on the exchange and let the "service" look after itself. New York City is not alone in the shameful exploitation of her local transportation system. A few men became multi-millionaires; but the New Yorkers are handicapped to this day owing to the financial depletion of the transportation lines. Supervision is a little stricter now, but juggling with figures and bookkeeping is still too common. Much of the public's money is wasted in these transactions, and the loss due to inadequate transportation is greater still.

THE CALL TO THE MODERN MATTHEW[1]

J. H. JOWETT, D.D., London, England

He saw a publican . . . and said, Follow me.—Luke 5:27.

This is an extraordinarily brief and pregnant biography. All that we know about this man is packed within the stingy limits of three short verses. I remember once George Meredith said that he always sought to endow his poetry with the two qualities of concentration and suggestiveness. Both of these qualities are here. The main happening in this man's life is described in thirty words, and the only other incident in his life which is named is dismissed in twenty. In fifty words his life is told.

But then there are some single words which have histories in them. There are some words which when you look at them are like long roads crowded with traffic. There are some single words which reveal characters. They reveal not only characters, but the processes by which character has been made. So it is with this little paragraph, this fragment which I have read to you. It is a very, very brief paragraph, but when you have read it there is a man there; you can form some idea of his stature, his caliber, his quality.

Little is written, yet much is said. For instance, we are told that he was a publican. That word is one of what I call highway roads, which lead you across great stretches of landscape. In the first place, who ever heard of a publican who was poor? The very name publican, as we now read it, is primarily associated with money-getting. Every Jew seems to be peculiarly gifted with powers of monetary acquisition. The publican was always studying how to get money. In whatever else he failed, he always succeeded here. Whether he was popular or unpopular, he was always the moneyed man of the district, and sometimes, perhaps frequently, he made a somewhat loud and garish parade of his wealth. The publican was what we would call a great success.

Now, what kind of gifts does it take to make money? I would prefer that that question should be answered by somebody who has made it! Therefore, I turn to a book recently published by a very prominent public man, who professes to tell the secret. What, he asks, are the qualities that make for success? They are three—judgment, industry, and health; and, perhaps, the greatest of these is judgment. These are the three pillars on which we can build the golden pinnacles of success. A little later in the book this wealthy guide tells us that the art of making money implies these qualities: resolution, concentration, economy, and self-control. He goes on to give certain definite rules for success: "The trading instinct, which is a knowledge of the real value of things; the practise of economy, and the ability to read the minds of men." I take up another book, in which the writer invokes mystical forces and harnesses them to the chariot of the man who is on the road pursuing money. The particular chapter to which I turn has the very attractive head-line: "How to get what you want." That sounds very hopeful! I will quote only one passage: Nothing can attract prosperity but that which has an affinity for it; the prosperous thought, the prosperous faith, the prosperous ambition. That is to say, if you harness pessimism to your wagon, your wagon will stick in the ruts. If you put despondency in the shafts, you will never arrive at the treasures which are housed in the town of Vanity Fair.

Now, let me take both analyses and combine them. I am told that the successful money-maker must be a man of shrewd judgment, a lover of work, with power to concentrate upon his task. I am told he must have a discriminating sense of values and

[1] Specially reported for THE HOMILETIC REVIEW.

he must have the forward-looking faculties of faith and hope. These are the things you must have if you would make money. Well, here is a man who made it—piles of it. He had a big house, big enough to entertain a host of friends in great festivity. Then he must have had some of these faculties, some of these gifts. I may infer—for conditions have not changed essentially in two thousand years—that Matthew had business ability, great powers of discrimination. He had sagacity, tenacity, audacity. He had more than this. A publican was beset by social hatred. Everybody disliked him. Doors were always being shut in his face. He would never win anything easily. He would have to fight for every inch. Such could be no meager man, no fool, no weakling. Jesus sees him, and recognizes his gifts, and covets them. So he got to know him—I do not know how. Little by little, with infinite tact and grace and delicacy, he loosed the man's spirit from its bondage, until one momentous day, when Matthew was bound to his old world by but a single fragile thread, Jesus said, Follow me, and the big man rose and followed him. Come, said Jesus, and transfer your business ability to my side, transfer your courage, your splendid independence, your majestic will, your powers of industry and self-control, your faculties of imagination and vision, to my side. In answer to that authoritative word Matthew rose and followed.

Now, I am saying all this because I want to declare that Christ is on the lookout for big men. He is on the lookout for disciplined gifts and accomplishments. He yearns to enlist these men in his kingdom. I am proclaiming that Christ is out on the road seeking fine faculties, vigorous minds, lusty wills. I confess to you, I think this side of the Master's call has been sometimes overlooked. We have remembered that he calls the man with the one talent, and we have sometimes forgotten that he calls the man with the five or the ten. We have pointed out that he will glorify the meager gift, but we have ignored the larger one. We have never forgotten the widow's mite —and we ought not to forget it—but our Lord wants the millions, as well as the mites; he wants the superb gifts as well as the slender endowments. We have almost proudly counted the five loaves and the three small fishes. Is that all we have got?

Are there bursting granaries somewhere? Are there larders well stocked with loaves? We have to bring our bigger resources to our King and put them in his hands for his wise and discriminating control. Christ wants not only the little man and the little woman with their lesser gifts. He wants the man or the woman who is fit for the bigger tasks. Standing absolutely on my text I say he wants the Matthews, the men who can cut their way through the big difficulties just as a plowshare cuts a furrow through a stiff and reluctant sod.

Now, bring it to a practical issue. There are many men in this congregation this morning who are, no doubt, gifted with special business ability. They have been gifted from their earliest days. Their talent began to blossom quite early. It has been disciplined by the work and experience of subsequent years. Yet what is Christ getting out of it? They are like Matthew; they have made money and have a reputation for success, but what is Christ getting out of their success? What gain accrues to his kingdom and the proclamation of his truth and grace? If our Lord were to become reincarnate in London to-day, and were to go along the streets and meet these men, he would surely covet their gifts and they would surely hear the word heard spoken in olden days: Follow me! There are women in this congregation, specially gifted women, who have enjoyed rare advantages of birth and training. They have refined their discernments, they have acquired stores of scholarship and learning. They have social gifts. They are rich in insight and in intuition and in sympathy. Well, what is Jesus getting out of it? What contribution do they make to the cause of his kingdom? What gain accrues to him through the wealth of their gifts and accomplishments. The Savior sees their gifts and covets them, and if only we could once again hear his voice as they heard it in olden time, these richly gifted women would hear him say, Follow me.

You see, I am using this old-world incident to suggest that in our own time the Lord is on the lookout for gifted men and gifted women who will invest their gifts in the cause of his kingdom. I am perfectly sure I am speaking to quite a number of young people who are face to face with a momentous decision: the choice of a career. They have finished with school and college. They have all their faculties well in hand. They are full of life. They are strong in nerve. The day is before them. They are looking around, and all sorts of roads stretch from their center like the radiating spokes of a vast wheel. There is law, there is medicine, there is surgery, there is teaching, there is art, there is literature. There are a dozen mechanical sciences. There are a hundred different avenues of industry and trade. Have you ever thought of the ministry? I mean the ministry of the gospel—have you ever thought of that? I mean the sacred apostolate of love and grace—will you look down that road and listen? Amid all your thinking have you once thought of that? It may be that Christ is summoning you along that road and you have not thought of it; you are not listening. At any rate, I am very strongly led to suggest it this morning because sometimes when men are standing at the cross-ways of choice a hint may help to determine a destiny.

Perhaps you will allow me to relate my own personal experience—a thing I very rarely do. When I stood at the cross-roads in my early life and chose my career, I decided for the bar. My father had made or was making all the necessary arrangements for my being articled in a solicitor's office that I might have all the elementary discipline from the earliest stages to my coveted profession. Then, when everything was nearly ready and I was just about to begin, an old Sunday-school teacher of mine met me. I can remember just where we met. It was on the North Bridge in the town of Halifax. He asked me what I was going to do with myself. I told him I was going to the bar. He quietly answered: "I always hoped and prayed that you would go into the ministry." It was a momentous word. It threw all my life into confusion. I went exploring down another road and I found my destiny. Found my what? No, destiny is a blind word, without eyes, a heartless, comfortless abstraction. I did not meet that ghostly jailer whose name is destiny. I met the great Companion whose name is Christ. I heard him say in tones I could not misunderstand, Follow me. In reverence I followed him. At the end of thirty-five years I have to say that never once have I regretted my choice. So I say to young men, Have you thought of the ministry?

You say, What is there in it? What is there in it? There are privileges in it which can not be shared by any other calling. For instance, there is the privilege of spending half your life, and more, in exploring the mind and heart of God as revealed in the unsearchable riches of Christ. There is the wonderful privilege of bringing your findings to your fellow men, God's truth to their minds, God's holiness to their consciences, God's grace and love to their hearts. There is the privilege of telling the good news of God's salvation to people who have made a mess of their lives and would like to live them all over again. There is the privilege of ministering to them that are bruised, of speaking to men who are faint in heart—who have been defeated, who have failed—and of pointing out to them new lands of possibility where they can see only moor and fen and crag and torrent and fearsome night. There is the privilege of dwelling on the New Jerusalem and of impressing its fair lines upon people's aspirations and hopes. Privileges?—no end of them! And when Jesus says, Follow me, they are all included in the fellowship.

Ah, you say, that is only one side of it. Well, what is the other side? Well, you say, what chances are there? Chances of what? Well, look at the bar. Fabulous riches, if only you can get there. Look at medicine and surgery; you have a chance of getting to the top of the ladder and if you do get to the top wealth is assured. If you are lucky in trade you may win a fortune in a year.

All these roads are like shining streets. They are like Broadway at night. But the ministry is very dimly lit. The gay flash seems to be altogether wanting. There does not seem to be much money in it. Still I hear him say, Follow me! See how many folks you have to please; how many queer ones there are amongst them. Churches, you say, are like caves of Adullam; all sorts of crotchetty, angular people get together in superficial and ineffective and almost mean fellowship. Still I hear him say: Follow me! But go on. Well, look at your disappointments. Not many people care to hear you, and when they hear you, they still less care to heed you. You are like a voice in the wilderness. Your message comes and goes with no more effect than the hooting of an owl in the indifferent night. Still I hear him say, Follow me! But go on, go on! Well, you live and you move in very ill-ventilated mental rooms. You are imprisoned within the thick walls of venerable creeds. There are such tiny windows that you can not see out. If you can see out you can not get out, because you are locked in and the warder who holds the keys is that grim presence named tradition.

My brother, I have heard all this before. Some of it is true, some of it is untrue. But look here, my young brother. When you have said all you can say, when you have placed the advantages on one side and the disadvantages on the other and hold the scales with a firm hand, you will find the disadvantages are only as dust in the balance. I proclaim the ministry as a calling which offers an exceedingly broad road for the finest service. It will take all your gifts, every faculty you have got, and every accomplishment; then there will still be room. But what am I, that I should make comparisons? Who am I, that I should say, Here is the bar and here is the ministry, and which shall it be? Who am I that I should compare the ministry with medicine, or medicine with the ministry? It is mine to listen down every road, and to listen for one all-commanding and final voice and when I hear him say, Follow me, to rise up and obey. You are settling your career. You are wondering which road to take. What about the foreign field? You have thought of the bar, medicine, surgery, engineering. Have you once thought of the foreign field? That will take all your gifts, and more. If I were just beginning instead of closing I would like to say, my Savior is calling for big men and big women for the task of the foreign field, the biggest people we can send, the Matthews, with their prepared gifts and blades. Twenty-five years ago I remember hearing Henry Drummond when he came back from Japan and brought a message from the Japanese. Here is what Drummond said:

I had the privilege of addressing some thirty or forty Japanese Christian pastors in Tokyo. At the close of my address I asked if there was any message I might take home to the churches in England and America. They appointed a spokesman who stood up and told me there were two things they would like to say. One was this: Tell them to send us one six-thousand-dollar missionary rather than ten two-thousand-dollar missionaries. The other was: Send us no more doctrines. Japan wants Christ.

It is the first word that I want to emphasize. One six-thousand-dollar missionary. What they say is this: Big men, big women, for a big job; men and women of superlative minds, fine gifts, fine discernments. Listen to the breathings of India. I do not refer to riot, to mob violence, or anything of that kind. I think of the spirit that can get into the hearts of the people and can lead because it can interpret. If you want adventure, there it is. If you want chivalry, there you can get it. Is it your job? Do not listen to me. Spend a large part of to-day in listening for his voice. Put your ear to that road. Perhaps you may hear the Savior say, My child, follow me. With all my heart I pray that you may arise and obey. For my Lord is calling for big men and big women for the big tasks of the modern world.

CAN WE BELIEVE IN GOD THE FATHER

WALTER EVERETT BURNETT, D.D., Columbus, Ohio

Like as a father pitieth his children.—Ps. 103:13.
When ye pray say, Our Father.—Matt. 6:9.

There is a large number of men and women to whom the question I have propounded means nothing at all. "Of course we can believe in God the Father," they would at once reply, and if one should say that there are serious difficulties that make faith hard, they would answer that we must believe regardless of the difficulties and that is all there is to it. One must admire this simple and thoroughgoing faith and at times is tempted to covet the serenity that it brings—unless indeed the law of the mind is to struggle, and by fighting hard battles with doubt to win one's way to larger truth. Those who thus consider the matter closed before it is ever opened will perhaps be patient while I say a few words to the men and women who have real difficulties about believing in God as a Father.

I have in mind particularly just now the practical difficulties that stand in the way of belief—the terrible misfortunes and cruel accidents that make men shudder and that seem irreconcilable with the notion of a protecting providence. Surely an all-wise and all-loving God would put out his hand to stay such crushing blows as sometimes fall upon his children, and that he doesn't do so makes it very hard to believe that there is a God, or if there is, that he is the kind of God in whom we have been taught to believe.

THE MORAL DUTY OF BEING INTELLIGENT: At the outset we may well justify the necessity of thinking this matter of religion through just as clearly as possible. It is very hard to call any cherished belief in question, but if we are confronted by hard facts that do not fit in with the belief, there is only one thing to do and that is to subject the belief to a searching reexamination. We may be sure that, however keen our reluctance, nature will approve such a course and that life as a whole will profit by it. For these facts are a part of nature and we fall short of a complete understanding if we leave them out. It is by just such methods that larger truth has always been won. Facts are imperious things that simply must be reckoned with. However grim and destructive they may seem at first sight, they will soften into friendliness and beauty when men get better acquainted with them, and the outcome will always be a larger, richer view than men possess before. Nothing is to be gained, therefore, by ignoring a fact, however inconvenient and disturbing it may be. We must be honest before we can be religious, and if our religion ever stands in the way of sheer intellectual honesty we would better move out, lest our house of religion come tumbling down when we are unprepared and crush us.

Here then are the facts. Life is hard for many folk. Terrible things occur that shatter human happiness. So far as we can see, desolating catastrophies fall upon good and bad alike. Just here is where the strain upon faith arises. How can a powerful and loving God allow such things to be?

LET US CEASE BLAMING GOD: Suppose we begin by saying that God has little to do with most of these things. I am aware how strange and perhaps shocking this will sound to some people, but in the end it will lead us to a view of divine providence that will stand the strain of life. It is helpful to recall that the Master dealt specifically with this very problem and took a long step toward the explanation that we shall here propose. "Do you think," he said, "that those men upon whom the tower of Siloam fell were sinners above other men? I tell you nay." He thus demolished at a stroke the easy way of explaining misfortunes that assumed an immediate divine judgment in them. Of course if they are empty of direct moral meaning the older view of Providence collapses.

The Master's denial of God's immediate action in the fall of the tower of Siloam, and that as a swift and direct judgment upon the men who were hurt, does not go to the length of saying that he was not involved in the event in a larger way. That he is involved in everything is of course the foundation truth of the Christian religion. But the question as to a satisfying faith in Providence hinges upon how he is involved, and we are emphasizing now that he is not involved in the little, immediate way that men had supposed. Probably some of the men upon whom the tower fell were good, but along with the bad men they were seriously hurt. The question of individual moral merit did not enter at all.

HUMANITY IS AT SCHOOL: The large way in which God is concerned in such matters appears when we consider the natural laws which determine whether towers shall stand or fall; and the need of such a degree of knowledge and oversight that such accidents shall not happen. In the goodness of God these laws are firmly established; we can depend upon them. This is not a happy-go-lucky world in which natural laws operate one way to-day but some other way to-morrow. It is inconceivable that the laws of chemistry were ever a particle different than they are to-day. It is an orderly, dependable universe. It is all-important that men learn how these laws work. Civilization depends upon such knowledge. I suppose we would say that civilization is to be measured by the degree in which human beings understand the laws of nature and use them for ideal ends. If in the course of learning how natural laws work a poorly built tower has to fall and kill some men, the accident is unfortunate, but the big lesson is so important as to shrink the individual aspects of the affair into incredible smallness. The question as to whether a few persons suffer becomes almost inconsequential in the presence of the huge insistent fact that men must simply learn how to manage such matters intelligently or civilized life on the planet would be impossible. When a ship goes down at sea, it is not a question whether the passengers are good or bad, or even whether or not the captain is a praying man, it is a question of skilful seamanship; and if a ship is lost now and then, the price is not too great if human knowledge and skill are thereby furthered, for upon these depend the happiness of unborn generations. When a plague sweeps through a city it is not a question of the moral tone of the city or the spirituality of the churches, it is a question of hygienic sanitation, and if ten thousand, good and bad alike, shall suffer because of carelessness or ignorance, the price is not too great in view of the fact that the happiness of ten thousand times ten thousand of unborn men depends upon a clearer knowledge of these laws that have in this specific case manifestly been ignored. God is in it, you see, he is in all these things, but mainly in the large way of being very determined that mankind shall learn to understand natural laws and use them more intelligently.

THE SINE QUA NON OF HUMAN PROGRESS: It is perfectly clear that the one big matter is that the universe should be utterly dependable. Human intelligence would be impossible otherwise. A student would never master mathematics if two plus two equaled four to-day and five to-morrow. But natural laws are mighty forces. If he is ignorant they will hurt him, if he is careless they may destroy him. That is the price that the race must pay for its schooling. The price seems hard at times, but the result is glorious. A race of intelligent human beings that has gathered ample stores of exact knowledge which it puts to humane uses is so obvious and sublime an expression of a beneficent purpose guiding human affairs, as to justify any price of loss and pain that men through ignorance may have to pay along this arduous climb to the mastering heights.

THE WORLD'S VICARIOUS SUFFERERS: There is then no satisfactory explanation of the huge dead weight of human suffering except to say that it is vicarious. It is borne by individuals because the race has not grown wise enough to lift it off. Under the costly stimulus of suffering humanity will grow wiser and will attain to that finer degree of organization that will eliminate a great deal of this unnecessary wo. An epidemic of typhoid fever in a community is a serious indictment of the intelligence of that community. The collapse of a theater roof is an indictment of the intelligence of the community. The collision of a locomotive with an automobile with no signals to warn of danger which could not be perceived by ordinary caution is an indictment of the community. These events simply indicate how far we have to travel before we arrive at intelligent cooperative living. That individuals by the thousands must suffer from such causes is appalling; but it is unavoidable by any wisdom that these human individuals can exercise for themselves; only social control can regulate these matters; it seems likely that mainly through suffering and loss will the social mind be stimulated to finer efficiency.

THE NEGATIVE SIDE OF A POSITIVE TRUTH: And so we find ourselves talking almost without being aware of it about the kingdom of God. For that was Jesus' term for this finely organized and fine-spirited cooperative society which shines like a bright ideal upon the heights toward which the race is moving. Only our approach to the kingdom in this case is from a new direction. We approach it now from the direction of the rank and terrible failures of men to achieve well-being and happiness. We approach it from the dark aspect of the terrible burden of misery, that is actually crushing human society from its very lack of the kingdom insight and the kingdom spirit. Who can make such a survey without a quickened sense of the immense urgency for the development of the social virtues. Society is a great seething mass of human life, none too finely organized, formless and amorphous. It is about in the state of the overgrown boy who has grown arms and legs faster than he has developed the nervous system finely to coordinate these bodily expansions. He feels gawky, and looks it. So society is clumsy, oh, so clumsy and ignorant! And yet not so ignorant as uncontrolled and uncoordinated. Every thinking person ought to be able to read in such dire calamities as I have mentioned, as in huge blazing letters bigger than were ever printed upon a page, the need of finer social understanding and more effective cooperation. Surely, surely, the kingdom is the urgent message of the hour.

THE CREATIVE POWER OF THE CHRISTIAN MIND: Now it is not too hard a challenge to man's intelligence that he lay hold upon the materials that life offers and shape them finely for human welfare as a whole. We have had far too much talk depreciative of human power and the effectiveness of human energy. What men need to understand is that the most important matters concerning human well-being will never be attended to unless they themselves do it. Man is largely his own providence over a very large range of vital affairs. Granted two things, we could expect an immensely better world: first, clearer thinking; second, more sympathy and finer cooperation.

We may well ask if we are not sinning grievously against the Holy Spirit in failing to face actual conditions dauntlessly and to claim our right as spiritual creators. For that is what we are. We all know that Christianity cherishes precious traditions, and enshrines deathless chapters of history within its glowing heart, but it is none the less true that our religion glorifies the free creative spirit. In a real sense the incarnation is forever incomplete, for "the spirit shall lead you into all truth," and "greater things than these shall you do, because I go unto my Father." We have not yet caught the thrill and the power of our sublime investment by the free creative spirit of the living God, "throwing off the golden spray" of new and wondrous deeds, wrought out by the wisdom and enterprise of Christian men and women.

FOR INSTANCE, WHAT ABOUT WAR: The nearest example that occurs to one is this terrible holocaust of war, that humanity tolerates despite our ample knowledge of its costliness, its beastliness, and its futility. Like a fascinating serpent-eye this grim and monstrous thing has fixt its gaze upon humanity and well-nigh paralyzed us, so that many people are found thinking and saying that we can not abolish war, or find a rational way of settling international disputes. Surely we have reached an age when we shall be able to thrust away this devil's-brew of sophistry and break the bloody shackles of our jungle-past, and deal as intelligent humans with one another. Without undertaking to present a complete plan forthwith, a Christian minister may be pardoned for saying that conciliation by butchery seems a ghastly joke in an age of Christian enlightenment and the extension of rational inquiry, and that we are due to have a revulsion that will sweep the world clean of it. We are not organizing human thought to this end as fast as many of us would like, but the attainment of sanity in this regard is inevitable. Faith in war will go the way of other hoary superstitions, and the race will stand forth in the majesty of a new and splendid triumph of reason and cooperation.

THE PRESENCE AMID THE PROCESSES: Well then, some one may ask, is this what we must come to think about Providence—that God keeps his hands off human affairs and sits a distant Spectator while his children bunglingly and with many a bruise slowly attain mastery over the forces of life? Far from it. He does not interfere with the life processes in the way we used to think, being already in those very processes, and operating all the while to build up strong, fine intelligences that will be worthy of his sons and daughters. He does not thrust himself into the regular on-going of his laws, because he is already in them in a far more vital and intimate way, namely, as the immanent Spirit that is directing them and that is always at work from the inside to urge mankind to the diviner things.

We must learn to think of God as present in this living inward way in man's ineradicable impulses of sympathy and humanness. The keen revulsion from unnecessary human suffering and loss which has found expression in these paragraphs, together with the urgent call that we stand together and make an end once for all to such crass folly and unnecessary waste, is a sign and a witness of the presence of the spirit of love in the human mind that will not rest content until the new and finer order of truth and love is builded in the earth.

I BELIEVE IN GOD THE FATHER ALMIGHTY, MAKER OF——: Can we believe in God the Father? Rather let us say, "can we disbelieve in him whose living creative presence alone can account for this ineradicable human impulse to establish society in friendliness and helpfulness, and who will quicken and urge the human spirit until in full strength of wisdom and love the sons of God shall rise and build the fair city 'that cometh down out of heaven' to shine resplendently upon the earth!"

> Ah, earlier shall the roses blow
> In after years, those happier years,
> And children weep when we lie low
> Far fewer tears, far softer tears.

It would seem that the truly thoughtful mind surveying this scene of human suffering, yet noting the presence of sympathy and a brave purpose that burns like a flame in man's mind to build a finer order of society, is fairly driven to the confession "I believe in God the Father Almighty, Inspirer of wisdom and brotherhood, the Maker of Christly men and through them of the radiant kingdom of truth and love."

SHALL WE MIX RELIGION AND POLITICS

The Rev. A. E. Cooke, Vancouver, B. C.

Curse ye Meroz, saith the angel of the Lord, curse ye bitterly the inhabitants thereof; because they came not to the help of the Lord, to the help of the Lord against the mighty.—Judges 5:23.

Thy kingdom come. Thy will be done on earth, as it is in heaven.—Matt. 6:10.

Meroz was a city of "slackers." This was a day of war in Israel—red war. The river Kishon ran crimson with blood. The plain of Esdraelon was strewn with the slain. Mount Tabor looked down on the wreck of Sisera's army fleeing before the men of Barak. The invader had been routed, Israel delivered from foreign oppression, and Deborah's war-song sounded across the field of blood. But back in some sheltered valley, just out of reach of the shock and clash of the conflict, the town of Meroz lay hidden, sheltered, supine. The call of patriotism had sounded down its streets and into its homes, but it paid no heed. It was in no immediate danger. While the heroes of Zebulon and Naphtali hurled themselves on the spears of the oppressor, "the men of Meroz skulked, sullen and craven, behind their walls." Others shared the horror and the glory of the fight; they hung back in the hour of desperate need. They hid behind the courage of the gallant men who risked their all for national liberty. They were the "slackers" of ancient Israel, and when Deborah's triumph-song had chanted the praise of the victors, it changed to a flood of corrosive scorn for the cowards who skulked in the day of battle. "Curse ye Meroz, saith the angel of the Lord, curse ye bitterly the inhabitants thereof; because they came not to the help of the Lord against the mighty."

Meroz has gone. It and its people have utterly disappeared from the face of the earth. But the curse remains. The violent outburst of contempt for the shirker which burst from the lips of a heroic woman still stands to express the condemnation of the men who fight and suffer and bleed in a great cause for those who shirk the conflict but afterward share in the victory they have done nothing to win. These cowardly and idle people had not come "to the help of the Lord" when the cause of his people was in greatest danger, and they stand forever pilloried in shame, as the type of those who keep out of the battle for God and his kingdom in every age.

The "slacker" is found not only in the day of great military struggles; not only where men bleed and die upon fields of blood, but everywhere that a great moral conflict is waged; everywhere that men struggle by voice or pen or vote against the forces of evil in the name of humanity and the name of God—there we find the "slacker" who shirks the fight, ready with some glib excuse for his refusal to get into the fray. If a reform is urged in any community there are always some afraid of getting into trouble. If a labor-union goes on strike against some industrial tyranny, there are usually some who are willing to "scab." If a board of trade would denounce some business dishonesty, there are certain members afraid of their "profits." If a political party seeks to get rid of "graft," there are always some cowards to hang back and let the crooked element escape with the spoils. We even find the "shirker" in the pew and the "slacker" in the pulpit—men who are scared to speak the truth, because it might disturb the soul of some heavy subscriber to the funds.

Some men are so sensitive of soul, so timid in judgment, so flabby in principle, so spineless in their Christianity, that they seem to live in mortal dread of the preacher speaking unpleasant truths above a whisper. They almost sweat when he chooses a text from an ancient prophet of righteousness like Isaiah or Amos. To use the word "politics" inside a church is nothing short of desecration to them. They believe in the separation of Church and State, but they make it complete enough to separate the Church from the whole of society. They would perpetuate forever the old, false distinction between things sacred and secular. But Christ never made any such distinction. All life was sacred to him. No human question was foreign to Jesus. So I make no apology for the theme I discuss to-night. Like everything else that interests men, it comes within the sweep of the kingdom of God. If politics have a rightful place in the life of man, then moral agitation which determines the moral quality of politics can not be wrong.

Besides, I must take my instructions in the matter of preaching from the God who rules in the realms of conscience. As one of our ablest preachers has said, "I must take my instructions, not from the man on the street, nor from the man on the board, nor from the man on the newspaper, nor from the man in the club, nor from the man in the pew, but from the Man in the skies—the Man of Galilee." It is my business to preach the gospel as Christ gives me to see it in its application to all the affairs of human life.

I. Shall we mix religion and politics? I answer, first, that neither the Christian man nor the Christian Church can avoid political questions, because it is their business to establish the kingdom of God upon earth.

The kingdom of God is the central theme of the Bible from cover to cover. Old Testament prophets and New Testament apostles were alike commissioned of God to proclaim the kingdom, in which God should rule over men. Christ himself came preaching, not what some of us have called "the old gospel," but what he called "the good news of the kingdom." He declared that kingdom to be at hand, already amongst

those to whom he spoke. It was the theme of the Sermon on the Mount, it breathed in the prayer "Thy kingdom come"; and the commandment, "Seek first the kingdom of God and his righteousness," summed up the duties of his followers in all ages.

But what did he mean by the kingdom of God? In briefest definition it means simply the reign of God in the hearts of men and in all their affairs. It means Christ's laws of love, service, and sacrifice applied to all human institutions—the family, the school, the store, the factory, the Church, and the State. It is social as well as religious, political as well as moral, collective as well as individual, present as well as future, earthly as well as heavenly. Those who became subjects of this kingdom were to form a common brotherhood bound together by cords of love, obeying the law of service, and inspired by the spirit of sacrifice. To accomplish the building of this world-wide kingdom of God amongst men, the Scripture shows that the work of Christ was a two-fold work. "Thou shalt call his name Jesus, for he shall save his people from their sins." That is one aspect of his work, but the other is equally important. "He was manifested to destroy the works of the devil." Unfortunately, many men forget, or else have never learned, the latter text, hence we hear a lot of nonsense about preachers sticking to "the simple gospel" and letting other issues alone. If some men only knew as much of their Bibles as they do of party politics and the partizan newspapers, they would be much more careful of exposing the vast depths of their theological ignorance when they lecture the clergy on the meaning of the gospel.

Christ spoke of his gospel as "the gospel of the kingdom," which means a gospel of regeneration, not only for the individual soul, but for all society and all the relationships of human life. This means things political controlled by the spirit of Christ just as much as the prayer-meeting or the Sunday-school. A man's work for his church is only a part of his work for the kingdom of God. The progress of the Church and the home, the conditions of both and their happiness, depend largely upon civic and political conditions. What revival of religion can we expect where the people have shared in other men's sins by placing the scepter in the hands of corrupt politicians?

A political house-cleaning followed by a crusade against social evils is a splendid preparation for a work of grace. While corruption sits in the high places the King of kings is dethroned. While men are forced into starvation because a political machine slams every door of employment in their face, and church-members and Christian preachers stand like dumb dogs looking on, you can't expect these men to listen meekly to flowery sermons on the providence of God and love to our neighbors.

One of the strongest reasons why the mass of working-men has so little use for the Church of to-day is because preachers and churches have so largely failed to testify against social injustice and political iniquities, and gone on talking about the world-to-come while this world was becoming more and more like hell for thousands of their fellows. "This pretense," said Henry Ward Beecher, "this pretense that a man is to preach the gospel and not touch a single one of the things which the gospel is meant to heal—a wayfaring man, tho a fool, would understand the fallacy of that; but there be many fools that are not wayfarers, who do not seem to understand it."

The trouble with some men who talk so much about the need of "gospel preaching" is that they don't know the gospel when they hear it. What they are looking for is a one-sided, emasculated fraction of the gospel which never touches the common affairs of daily life. They will hire a man to preach the gospel and promptly fire him when he does so. The gospel of Christ's kingdom is, "not a gospel for disembodied spirits, but one for men in the flesh; not a gospel for a fraction of the man, but for the whole man; not a gospel for isolated individuals, but one for men in an organized society—a kingdom coming in the earth."

II. Again, we must deal with political issues because every Christian is responsible for the condition of the community and country in which he lives.

Every man is a member of the society in which he finds himself, a unit in the nation, and as such he has certain God-given duties which he can not shirk and be guiltless. "No man has attained unto the measure of the stature of Christian character till he has learned to honor and fulfil all the relationships which he sustains to his fellows." John Pym, the great Commonwealth leader,

was right when he said, "I hold it to be part of a man's religion to see that his country is well-governed." Lord Bryce declares that modern citizenship in Europe and America has failed because of three great evils—indolence, selfishness, and party spirit. Bishop Potter was speaking straight truth when, discussing the evils of modern society, he said, "At such a time for the Church of God to sit still and be content with theories of its duty outlawed by time, and long ago demonstrated to be grotesquely inadequate to the demands of a living situation, this is to deserve the scorn of men and the curse of God."

In a certain city two men were up for election. One was a clean, upright, honorable man; the other a scalawag ward-politician. For the one the strongest, cleanest men in the city spoke and wrote and worked. Behind the other, the liquor element, the vice element, and all the forces of corruption lined up. The issue was squarely between decency and indecency, between character and hoodlumism. The workers on each side did their utmost. Election day came, and that night the rum candidate celebrated his victory over the forces of righteousness with a free-for-all debauch. There was to be a "wide-open town" for another year. A visitor asked one of the Christian men of that city a few days later, "Why in the name of all that is righteous in this pious town of yours wasn't the decent man elected?" "Because," said the other, "just about sixty of the pious church-members stayed at home or let their sons neglect to vote. We have the names of that many who didn't vote. We tried our best to get them out; telephoned, and sent for them, but no good. They were 'too busy,' or they 'weren't needed,' or they 'didn't believe in mixing in politics.' The other side got out every man; so we lost by forty-one votes." "But," said the visitor, "do not these pious men go to prayer-meeting?" "Yes! But I'd rather have one good cross after Smith's name on that ballot than ten years of prayer-meeting eloquence without it." And that man was right.

Religion can be much better exprest to-day at the ballot-box than in the prayer-meeting. The prayer-meeting is the power-house where we get the energy of the spirit of God, but the polling-booth is about the best place to let it loose. To pray "Thy kingdom come. Thy will be done on earth, as it is in heaven," and to refuse to lift a finger or cast a vote to bring that kingdom nearer is a poor compliment to the intelligence of the Almighty. It is nothing short of an insult to God.

Is it the will of God that wrongs should be righted; that laws should be made which are just and humane; that parliaments be composed of God-fearing men instead of swindlers; that righteousness shall permeate the whole life of the nation? Then if that is his will it is your business and mine to see that it goes into effect.

I maintain that a large share of responsibility for the evils that curse humanity to-day lies at the door of the men who have too much "religion" to help God establish his kingdom on earth. God will not thank you for sitting with idle hands lamenting the social evils and political frauds that are thick about you, or for making the Bible an excuse why you should refuse to clean up the city you live in. One day he will ask you why you didn't throw off your coat and set to work for the overthrow of all these iniquities. He will want to know why you didn't see that the Bible called you to get out and help Christ destroy the works of the devil in public affairs. No man who professes to be a Christian, and least of all the Christian minister, has any right to stand aloof from the great issues that have to do with the morals and destiny of the nation.

III. But I go further, and say that he who neglects his political duties is guilty of sin against God and man.

"Curse ye Meroz, saith the angel of the Lord, curse ye bitterly the inhabitants thereof." What for? "Because they came not to the help of the Lord against the mighty." But people are not cursed except for sin. And that was the trouble with the "slackers" of Meroz. They were sinning against their heroic brethren and against the God who was leading Israel toward enlightenment 'and liberty. They were traitors to the cause of righteousness, just as the so-called Christians of to-day are traitors to the cause of Christ when they refuse to strike a blow for his kingdom in public life. It is Dr. Washington Gladden who frankly states that "refusal to take part in the government of the city and the State and the nation is nothing other than a flagrant

breach of trust . . . 'Too busy!' a man might as well say, 'I am too busy to pay my note at the bank, or to provide food for my household.' No moral obligation can outrank our duty to the commonwealth, for on the maintenance of good government everything that we hold dear in the world depends—our lives, our property, the security of our homes, the possibility of sound manhood and womanhood for our children. Here, if anywhere, is the central obligation of social morality, and the man who shirks it must be made to feel that his defalcation exposes him to the wrath of God and the scorn of man." That is sound theology as well as sound common sense.

A man's duty to the State is just as sacred, just as God-given as his duty to his family and his church. For a man to say that any part of human life is something to which Christianity can not be made to apply is to declare that Christ is not a sufficient Savior for the world. It is to take the position of the American Senator Ingalls when he asserted, "The Decalog and the Sermon on the Mount have nothing to do with a political campaign." That is a damnable philosophy of national life. It is the philosophy of the saloon-man, the white-slaver, the ward-heeler, and political grafter. It is the evil philosophy which has cursed the public life of this whole continent. Yet it is the identical philosophy upon which a great many Christian people unconsciously base their idea that religion has nothing to do with public affairs and that politics have no place in the pulpit.

The whole history of modern democracy proves that the worst enemies of national life and the kingdom of God are not the corrupt, grafting politicians who swarm about the spoils of office, but the careless, indifferent electors who don't care what happens in political circles so long as their own interests are not disturbed. They think it is Christianity keeps them out of politics, but it is simply a purblind selfishness masquerading in the garb of religion.

Charles Stelzle tells how he heard a prominent Presbyterian layman get up on the platform at a Men and Religion Conference in Chicago and say, "I believe in the evangelistic message, and I believe in the Bible message, but I haven't any use for this message on social service; we have already too many sociables in our churches."

That was all the benighted heathen could see in a social message. But Stelzle went into a tenement house, and in a little bit of a room he saw a four-year-old child sitting on a pile of white coats which her mother was making for a department store. Ill with disease—"hasty consumption," her mother called it—she was sitting pulling the basting-threads out of those coats. And when he came back to the house a little later she had died—toppled over, her mother said—on that pile of coats. Yet some men who go to church and talk about the "simple gospel" don't believe in a message or a gospel to set such things right. Are they going to set them right with ice-cream festivals and oyster suppers? Or are they going to wake up and put men in Parliament who will make such conditions impossible by putting the Sermon on the Mount on the statute books of the land?

Why is it that all over this Dominion the big corporations can ride roughshod over the will of the people and corrupt parliaments to do their bidding whenever they will? Why can railroads and express companies fleece the public with impunity? Why has the "whisky ring" been allowed to damn men and women, and work its helleries from ocean to ocean, and from Mexico to the Yukon for the past century? Why are the streets of many of our cities paved and lighted with money that partly comes from the prostitution of the souls and bodies of the "white slaves" of modern civilization? Why have world wars desolated the nations, and graft scandals covered even the righteous cause with burning shame? Because men have shut God out of their political life. They have said to Christ, "You may stay in the Church and Sunday-school, but we will not allow you to touch our business life or public affairs." And I say, again, the professing Christians who preach the false doctrine that religion and the Church have nothing to do with politics must share the blame. If there had been more politics in the pulpit and more religion in politics there would have been much less corruption and scandal throughout the land.

IV. I say, again, religion and politics must intermingle, because there is no other way to purify the national life.

Some poor, simple souls tell us that Christians can not mix in political matters because politics are so dirty. God knows they have been dirty enough to disgust some of us to almost despair. These sickening revelations of private graft and public plunder and exploitation of national resources that make us ashamed of the country we live in—we smell the stench of them from ocean to ocean. But why are they possible? Why can't we wipe out the whole noisome business once and for all? Just for the same reason that the war in Europe dragged on so slowly. Because the shirkers and "slackers" did not enlist in the fight for righteousness and the kingdom of God in the national life. Politics are dirty because clean men have stood back and let the devil and his angels get a mortgage on the whole business. And till clean, strong, Christian men take hold and do their duty to God and man in public life, politics will stay dirty.

Dr. Jowett has said, "There is a type of piety abroad which says, 'Have nothing to do with politics, stand aside from embroilments of civic strife.' Who, then, is to have the shaping of the unclean things? It gives the whole world away to the devil. I prefer to pay heed to the word which is in the old Book. 'The kingdoms of this world shall become the kingdoms of our Christ!' Wo to the city and nation if the affairs of that city and nation are in the hands of men who approached them from beneath."

Arthur James Balfour once spoke in Ottawa of the dangers of democracy. But the greatest danger of democracy is that the best citizenship should keep aloof and allow the public business to fall into the hands of men of the lowest type. Let the ground-hogs and grafters of public life get into control and democracy is doomed. If democracy is ever to succeed it demands that you do your share to make it a success.

As society is organized to-day, the only effective means of putting down iniquity and bringing about reform are the ballot-box and the legislative assembly. The ballot is the sword of democracy, the "greatest weapon ever placed in human hands for the defense of common rights and for striking down common enemies." It is the duty of every Christian to use this sword in the great battle for Christ and his kingdom. The time must come when the destiny of our cities and our country will not be settled in dens of iniquity. We ought to have enough Christianity and common sense to prevent saloon-keepers, thieves, gamblers, jail-birds, and machine politicians from dominating our civic policies and our national affairs.

V. Of course, all this means that the earnest Christian will sometimes get into trouble.

Like Daniel, he may get into the den of lions. When a man will heed the voice of God more than the voice of men he will need to be a man of courage. The man in the pew whose breath is foul with whisky naturally thinks the church no place for prohibition sermons. The deacon who owns a tenement in the red-light district will not approve of the brother who enthuses over a social survey. The alderman who has grabbed more land than the law allows him will rise in wrath if any one suggests an investigation. The ward-politician who has grown fat on "rake-offs" will raise all sorts of trouble for the honest reformer. The "forty thieves" of modern industry will wax indignant if any one dare to expose their extortionate profits or their soulless oppression of their workers. When the devil is hit, he first raises a howl, then he rouses hell.

When Henry Ward Beecher took the pulpit and platform against the curse of slavery, he was execrated and howled at by the mob. When Dr. Parkhurst went after Tammany Hall, he was denounced and abused by thousands of reputable citizens, as well as by all the crowd of grafters. Gladstone was ridiculed and hated because he took his religion into British politics. Luther was opposed by all the political powers and ecclesiastical councils of Europe. Daniel was flung in the den of lions. Jeremiah into the slimy pit. John the Baptist lost his head, and Jesus Christ was nailed to the cross, because they all denounced the national leaders and demanded righteousness in public affairs. But they were not intimidated into silence. Their courage never faltered; their message was delivered in scorn of consequences, and to-day the world worships at their feet.

The need of the age is men of courage in public office and Christian pulpit. The demand of the hour is the fighting saint. Every man who sees a wrong is thereby called of God to fight for the right and put down the wrong. Dr. J. L. Gordon declared from his Winnipeg pulpit, "I have one question to ask of every person who professes to walk in the footsteps of Jesus Christ: 'What are you willing to stand for?' These are the rules of the battle: first, have a conviction; second, take a stand; third, have a hand in the fight!" Beecher asserted in Plymouth Church pulpit: "He who goes through life with an unbeating heart and an unhelping hand, refusing to take sides for the ignorant, the poor, the despoiled, the suffering, is fighting against God, because he is fighting against his fellow men, having taken sides against them." Dr. Jowett declared to the students at Yale, "I must not be an alien to the commonwealth, living remote and alien from its travails and throes. My strength must be enlisted in the vital, actual forces which, through tremendous obstacles, are seeking the enthronement of justice and truth." Moody asked an evangelist before an election what was the political outlook, but the man replied, "I don't know. I am not concerned about it. My citizenship is in heaven." And Moody retorted, "Better get it down to earth for the next six weeks." These men were fighters for the kingdom of God. They remembered that Christ was "manifested to destroy the works of the devil," and that he had said, "He that is not with me is against me." They were in the real apostolic succession. They were in the ancient prophetic line.

I am astounded at some men in our Churches talking about preachers "interfering" in public affairs. What have they done with their Bibles? Moses dealt with political problems all his days. He fought an iron despotism in the interests of freedom and the people. Samuel was the creator of the two dynasties. Nathan and Gad were the political advisers of David. Elisha conspired with Jehu to overthrow the corrupt house of Omri. Elijah roused the whole kingdom against Ahab and Jezebel. Isaiah saved Judah from international strife for thirty years, in spite of the folly of King Ahaz. Amos and Jeremiah scored the iniquities of corrupt kings and courtiers. Daniel guided the destinies of Babylon's empire for many years. John the Baptist died because he exposed the immoralities of Herod. And Jesus was murdered because he denounced the devourers of widows' houses and oppressors of the poor in the person of the national leaders. These all realized that public iniquity must be denounced as well as private, and that righteousness must be preached in scorn of consequences.

Politics no sphere for the Christian! I tell you the man who believes in God and fights for the right can never get out of his sphere, for it is wide as the whole range of human activities. The Christian Church must have a voice in every great moral discussion. She must rally men to the flag of the kingdom, the banner of the cross. She must cry in louder tones than Carlyle, "Are there not in this nation enough to venture forward and do battle for God's truth versus the devil's falsehood?" She must never repeat the tragic mistake of her earlier history, when her sons crowded into monasteries and hermits' cells, shutting themselves off from the life of humanity. It was then that she denied her Lord and the power of his gospel. It was then that irreparable mischief was done, for then the devil and his angels laid hold of political affairs, and they have a mortgage on them yet. It was a wholesale desertion of the cause of humanity. It was the great refusal of the Christian leaders to face their responsibilities. It was a gigantic betrayal of the interests of the kingdom of God.

The blind delusion of the monastic idea, the cold, clammy shadow of religious Buddhism, are with us yet in some quarters; but, thank God! Christian civilization and the Christian Church are breaking away from all such narrowness. Men are coming to see that the party which tries to ignore a great moral issue, the newspaper which tries to straddle the fence on great public questions, the pulpit which fears to proclaim a whole gospel, and the Christian who refuses to march against the citadels of corruption where the foes of our nation are seeking to destroy its very life—men are coming to see that these are guilty of treason against God and his kingdom.

Thank God! we can see the dawn of a new day in the public life of this Dominion. The number of men who are bringing conscience to bear on public questions is steadily growing. But it must grow much more rapidly. The religion of Christ must claim the field. If ever the kingdom of God is to come upon earth the Christian men and

women must rise in his name and go forth to wage war with the powers of evil at the polls.

While you hold back, hell rushes on; while you sleep, the devil pads the voters' list and stuffs the ballot-box.

Are you men studying the great questions of our public life in the light of the teaching of Jesus Christ? Are you calling on God to free you from the shackles of partyism and to guide you in the highest interests of the national life? Did you ever get down on your knees to ask God to show you how to vote at the next election? Some of you smile at the thought, but why? Is it too ridiculous a proposition that the Almighty has any interests at stake in this country? Was Daniel acting ridiculously when three times a day he left the presidential chair of Babylon's empire to consult with God? Was Abraham Lincoln playing the fool when in the crisis of America's history he spent long nights in prayer? Was Gladstone a fool when he made the Most High his confidant in the great affairs of the British empire?

Men, listen! The kingdom of God is above all the kingdoms of men. Its interests are supreme above all policies of men. Its sway shall endure all down the eternal ages when the kingdoms of earth shall have vanished forever. Remember that every word, every act, every vote of yours is either helping on or holding back the coming of that kingdom of righteousness, peace, and joy. "Seek first the kingdom of God and his righteousness" and all other things shall be added unto you.

Oh! that every man and woman in this country would realize that the right to vote is a gift from God, a weapon with which to hew out a path for their country's advance to the heights of eternal triumph! Then might the low, grovelling, unclean politics of mere party be purified by the elevating, firm grasp of men ̧ who take counsel with Christ in the heavenly places. Then would bitterness, strife, and faction disappear, and this nation become one mighty brotherhood of purity and love, working onward and upward toward the dawn of that glorious day when "He shall have dominion from sea to sea, and from the river unto the ends of the earth."

THE HEART OF A FATHER

The Rev. C. E. MEAD, Chatfield, Minn.

And he arose, and came to his father. But while he was yet afar off, his father saw him, and was moved with compassion, and ran, and fell on his neck, and kissed him.
—Luke 15:20.

I do not wonder that the world has lost its heart to mother. Her place in the world's affection is secure forever. When the last word of appreciation and praise of mother has been said we are conscious of our inability to give her what is justly her due. She has appealed to the world's imagination with her mother-love for her children, her almost unlimited capacity for sacrifice and service, her tenderness, her gentleness, her brooding care, her lovely eyes so often tear-dimmed, her cheerfulness amid disappointments, pain, suffering, toil, and sacrifice, her strength to bear such wearying burdens, cares, anxieties, to answer numberless calls for care and love and service. Father has not so appealed to the world's imagination—father, stern, ready for life's battles, out in the world of actual conflict, toiling, struggling with his burdens, striving to do his best for those he loves and for whom he would die if need be; father, with his heart of gold—often tarnished to human sight; father taking life's buffetings with never a word nor a tear, smiling, fighting his battles, grimly, steadily "carrying on," even when he knows he wages a losing fight, but hoping, fighting, toiling, taking reproaches and praise with the same smiling face, failing often to attain the highest things in life; rough and ready, grim and fighting, forgiving and kind, father has not appealed to the world's imagination, and so has not been enshrined in the world's heart as has mother.

As we study the parable of the Prodigal Son we are apt to overlook the fact that Jesus uses a real, an earthly, father to show to us our heavenly Father. Not all human fathers would qualify for the place of the father in this loveliest of parables, but there are more of them who quite nearly approach the standard of this father than many are aware.

In America, where the home has had such wonderful development, the place of mother has been high, secure, and her character has been exalted. In perhaps no other country has this been true to the same limit as in our own land. And father has suffered by comparison. Father is not measured in terms of his life and character, but in terms of mother's life and service and character. He has been compared with mother instead of being compared among his own fellows. The result has been distinctly to father's discredit. Because he has not been gentle, tender, tearful, of unwearied and exhaustless patience, of the same introspective and devotional spirit, he has been condemned as hard, unspiritual, wooden; believed to be of the earth, earthy; and therefore earthy in his thoughts and tendencies. I am not making a plea for a double standard. Let us have a single standard for both sexes. I am pleading for an understanding of the fundamental differences between the sexes. This is a plea that father be measured by the things which are of his own world.

The heart of a father is seen in the parable.

First, a true father is ready to minister to the happiness of his household. He went out of his way, beyond what law and custom required, that he might hold the good-will of this wayward son. He shrank from the ordeal of the son's departure from the home, and would go to the utmost that he might not break with him.

Second, his love did not fail. Tho absent, the son was still dear to the father's heart. Knowing the waywardness of his son, now a wanderer from home, he loved him with undying love; others might scorn him, but to the father he was still "son." Words can not express what the father suffered through the long months of the son's absence, but in it all there was only compassion and longing for his return.

Third, the father's forgiveness of the son reveals the high quality of his manliness. How full, how ready, the forgiveness recorded. How blessed the son's reception. Only a real man could forget all he had suffered, all his heartache, all the shame he had endured, while the son squandered his money in the evil life to which he had gone, all the anxiety which had tortured his heart, all the fears that had shadowed his waking hours—only a real man could so forget and open heart and hand and door in so glad a welcome, so complete a forgiveness. Forgiving is the acid test of a man.

"It is godlike to forgive."

Fourth, father is often misunderstood. Where the mother sheds tears, the father's heart bleeds. He rarely weeps; his heart aches with a pain too deep for tears. Because he smiles as he bears his burden he is judged to be hard, unfeeling, indifferent. Nothing could be further from the truth. He laughs that he may not cry, like Lincoln, criticized because he smiled at Richmond on the day he viewed the desolated city, made answer: "I laugh because I must not cry to-day." He smiles as he bears his burden that his strength be not spent in unavailing tears. With steady faith in God he goes on life's way. If he weeps, none but God knows the agony that wrung tears from his eyes.

Fifth, father is sometimes basely slandered. The rigors of his daily tasks make heavy drafts upon his vitality. A demand for food is created, and he delights in satisfying the cravings of his appetite, a delight that has been misunderstood, until a proverb has become current among wives: "The way to a man's heart is through his stomach."

It is a base slander. He appreciates appreciation and responds ⁻to kind treatment. He is often gruff and brusk when words of thanks are given him, but he is glad with great joy when he knows his efforts in behalf of his loved ones are recognized and appreciated. Some things we learn from father—

He taught us industry by his fidelity to the tasks which fell to his lot in daily life. He taught us patient endurance by his stedfastness under the exactions of daily life. He taught us justice, for he sought to be just. He taught us faith by his dependence upon God and his trust in God's love and care. He taught us faith, in our fellows by his readiness to forgive and forget, his cheerful companionship with, neighbor and friend.

THERE IS A LAD HERE

The Rev. ALBERT E. BEEBE, Brooklyn, N. Y.

There is a lad here.—John 6: 9.

This lad, with his five loaves and two fishes, was the solution to Jesus' problem of feeding the multitude. His supply was not very large, but distributed by the hand of the Master, it became food sufficient for the multitude. The lad was undoubtedly surprized to see his small stock of provisions so wonderfully multiplied. The disciples were surprized. In answer to the question as to where food might be obtained Andrew answered: "There is a lad here with five barley loaves and two small fishes, but what are these among so many?" On that day, in a moment of emergency, it was a boy who saved the situation.

To-day, realizing the importance of the boy for the emergencies of to-morrow, scholars are out in search of the secrets of boydom. Men are giving their lives to a study of the boy and how to appeal to him. Some have tried to tell us how much a boy is worth to society. Having given us various estimates as to the costs of feeding, clothing, and educating a lad, they say, "Now this is what he costs. How much is he worth?" There is no man who can tell how much a boy is worth. We measure various commodities by various standards. We measure wheat by the bushel, silk by the yard, milk by the quart, gold by the pennyweight, and coal by the ton. We measure music by the ear, argument by the laws of logic, deeds by conscience. But we have no standard by which we may measure the value of a boy. Booker T. Washington went back to the old plantation on which he was reared and found that on the books as a slave he was valued at $400, but as a freeman he organized an institution at Tuskegee that now has an annual income of more than a half million dollars. And through his work hundreds of young men and young women of his race have been trained for service.

There is a lad here. What sort is he?

He may be a little Lord Fauntleroy wearing a velvet suit with a big starched collar, with new shoes and white hands, but he may otherwise be a bare-footed, red-headed, freckle-faced lad with grimy hands, a soiled blouse, and patched knickerbockers. But of whatever sort he is, there is nothing in the community so important unless it is the girl.

He is probably a busy lad, a bundle of nerves and muscles, bubbling over with enthusiasm and always on the jump. Sometimes you hear some one whine at the boy, "Can't you keep still?" Of course he can not. And if you could keep him still he would not be worth keeping. He is a practical lad who wants to own things, to manage a business, and to have some practical purpose in life. The acquisitive instinct is strong within him. The student of adolescence declares that it is a good thing to encourage boys to become collectors of stamps, coins, or curios, and that the boy is often saved from becoming a thief by being made a collector. He is an adventurous lad. For him life is a glorious field for struggle and adventure. He loves the daring and the heroic. He is a growing lad. The early adolescent period is one of remarkable growth. The boy of thirteen or fourteen sometimes increases his height by four or five inches in a single year. The physical surpasses the mental in development. Consequently he often appears stupid and awkward. If you give him something to carry he drops it and trips when he attempts to pick up the pieces. Meanwhile he is cuffed and scolded and ridiculed and looked upon as a pest and a nuisance. It is a period of turmoil and confusion. New interests are appealing to his mind, new emotions are welling up within his heart, new ideals are appearing upon his horizon. What can we do for the boy?

Theodore Roosevelt once said: "If you are going to do anything permanent for the average man you must begin before he is a man." I believe that the Church should offer to every adolescent boy the opportunity to become a member of some good club where the gang instinct might have a chance for expression under intelligent Christian leadership. It is not enough that we shall provide schools for the boy. There is a training due him which can not be gotten within the schoolroom. Then, too, every man is under obligation to the boy to give him recognition and encouragement. In speaking of his native State, Daniel Webster said: "Our soil is poor; we can not produce great crops, but we plant schools and churches and raise men." And that is the greatest achievement of all. You may not be wealthy; you may not occupy the most conspicuous place in a social or industrial world, but if by example or suggestion you help some lad to come to himself, yours will be a service the very nature of which shall be immortal. Are you able to make some boy see the importance of doing some one thing and doing it well? Can you hold up before him some one task and urge him to work while it is the day? Can you make him realize that the ship never comes in for the lad who simply sits on the dock and waits? Can you teach him that altho all boys can not become famous, every boy can be successful in that the successful man is the one who makes the most of his talent and ability? Can you bring some lad into touch with noble ideals and reveal to him the importance of starting right, keeping right and to the right? If you are able to do this one thing you may easily take your place among those noble souls whose names are written in the record of truth.

There is a lad here in the Sunday-school. He is probably not very pious, but he is inherently religious, and the religious instinct is as fundamental as the play instinct. Upon the Sunday-school rests the responsibility of teaching the Bible, and that book full of the stories of adventure can be made wondrously attractive to the adolescent boy. The school must bring God near to him. And the lad is keyed in advance to love truth and beauty and sincerity. The lad loves to do things, and the story of that hero who could do all things through Christ who strengthened him makes a natural appeal. One leader of boys said: "Boys enter the religious life in at least as many ways as they enter the water for swimming. Some plunge in—a definite decision which settles once and for all what their attitude toward right and wrong shall be, what their relation to their God shall be. Some wade in—deliberately, cautiously, step by step, each step revealing that another step is desirable. Some run in a little way and out again, but continue to run in a little further each time, till at last they swim off—a number of changes of mind. Some are forced in. They may, finding themselves in, decide to remain or they may make frantic struggles to get out. Some sit down on the beach and simply let the tide come up about them till it floats them off; by not resisting the tide about them they practically accept the situation. A boy enters the religious life by deliberate, comprehensive decision, by an accumulation of little decisions, by non-resistance to influences about him, which is decision."

Now it is the task of the Sunday-school to present to the boy a brand of religion that is so attractive that he will recognize the Christian as one who lives a natural, normal, full-rounded, wholesome life, and, in the manner and according to the method which most appeals to his own peculiar nature, he will accept Christ as his Savior, unite with the Church, and join hands with

others who have pledged themselves to the advancement of the kingdom of God.

There is nothing that will do more for the boy than the intimate fellowship of his father. Happy is that lad whose father is his most intimate friend, the one to whom he naturally turns at every new crisis in his physical and mental development. Nor is there anything nobler for the father than to be the companion of the boy. Abraham Lincoln's greatness was no more clearly manifested when he stood before Congress as a statesman than in the hour when as a father in the home he was down upon the floor playing with the boy, Tad. It is a great thing for the father to be a boy with the boy, to begin where he finds the boy and to lead him, day by day, in a strong, manly companionship until he has inspired him with the noble ideals of Christian manhood.

THE CHILDREN'S SERVICE

TREASURE TROVE[1]

Seek first the kingdom of God and his righteousness.—Matt. 6:33.

Those who have much money to-day usually put it into a bank. It is much more difficult for burglars to steal it there than in a private house, and the bankers use it as long as it is not wanted, and have so much from many people that they are always ready to pay it out again when it is wanted. Others who have valuable jewels and costly things made of gold generally give them into the charge of those who make it their business to keep such articles in strongly made places, where someone is always on guard. But these are for the most part quite modern ways. In the old days, and especially in countries where enemies were likely to come taking all they could lay their hands on, it was not at all uncommon for treasure to be buried in the ground, where other people who did not know would hardly think of looking.

But, of course, if anything happened to those who had buried it, if they were killed

or taken away as slaves into another country and never came back, the treasure would remain hidden, and nobody would know anything about it.

It was about a hidden treasure such as this that Jesus told one of his stories. He said that the kingdom of God was like treasure, lying hidden in a field. The man to whom the field belonged had never heard of it, apparently. I suppose he had bought the field or got it in some way after the people to whom the treasure belonged had died or been carried off.

But a man was walking in that field one day, gathering berries or something of the kind, when he caught a gleam of gold, perhaps a flash from a beautiful jewel. How it came to be uncovered Jesus does not say. You know that heavy rains sometimes wash the earth away, and part of the ground may slip from its place. It may be that the man pulled up a plant and found part of the treasure where the roots came away. The point is that somehow or other he stumbled

[1] From *Stories of the Kingdom*. By WILL REASON. Published by George H. Doran Co., New York, 1921.

on it, and guessed that there was more there than he had seen. He meant to have that treasure; but before he could take it out, he must have the field. So he thought of the value of the gold, jewels, and precious things, and also reckoned up how much he had himself. Then he decided that the treasure was so much more valuable that it would be well worth his while to sell what he had already, so as to be able to buy the land. The treasure would pay him over and over again.

Some people have wondered why Jesus made the man act like this, because they do not think that it was a very Christian thing to buy the field from its owner without telling him what was in it. Well, I do not know that the owner deserved to have the treasure any more than the one who had found it; he had not paid anything for it, and if we had to argue about it I think a very good case might be made for the honesty, if not the kindness, of the finder. But it really has nothing to do with Jesus' meaning. What the man did was what men in such a position generally do. If anyone gets knowledge that there is probably a valuable coal-seam or oil-spring below any land, his one business is to make it his, even if he has to get the money by selling everything else he has.

Sometimes in other ways people give all they have for something better. When the great artist in metal, Benvenuto Cellini, was casting a beautiful piece of his work, his fuel gave out before the metal was properly melted, so as to run into the mold he had made, and he had no money to get more. He valued the statue-that-was-to-be so highly that he just burned up all his furniture to keep the furnace going, until the metal ran out, and the beautiful thing was made. What Jesus teaches is that the kingdom of God is so beautiful and worth so much to a man, that if he really catches sight of it, he too will be ready to give up everything else for it. That is, to have one's life ordered by God, to do what he wants done, and to be what he wants us to be is ever so much better than going on doing just as what we want to do for our own little selves.

This, however, is hidden from most of us. It is buried by the rubbish of our selfish-ness, our pride, and our greed. We think that of course it must be much better and nicer to choose our pleasures and to heap up things for ourselves. So the commands of God seem very stern to us when they tell us not to do the things we are so fond of, and to ask that we shall always think of what he wants done, without thought of ourselves, looks to be very hard indeed.

Yet there is plenty to show that the things we choose for ourselves and think so nice make us weaker instead of stronger, and lose their niceness very soon. Doing what we like makes slaves of us to our own desires. Then sometimes we see that doing what God wants really makes us stronger, nobler, and better in every way. Because God is himself love, everything he wants is for the good of his children. The chief thing he asks of us is to do the things that are good for others, instead of what we like ourselves, while it hurts others. If we do that, he will take care of ourselves, and it is much better to have him doing it, for he is wise and knows all about it, while we are silly and make mistakes as to what is good for us.

But there is something more to be thought of than what happens to ourselves, and sometimes this flashes upon men. They see of course the things that God wants are ever so much more important and finer than the things we want for ourselves alone, and to be allowed to share in them makes our concern with ourselves a very small and mean thing. You have admired those who, when their country was in danger, left all they had and went to risk their lives, often to lose them, for the bigger thing. If you were told of a man who had the choice of saving his own skin or his own purse or of saving a hundred others, you would think him very mean and small if he chose himself. Well, the kingdom of God is a bigger thing even than one's country, and it is very small and mean of us to choose our own pleasures and likes instead of it.

But we can not come into the kingdom of God unless we are ready to give up all we have; that is, to hold everything, including ourselves, for God's purposes. If we do, he will set us free from those terrible likes that make us selfish, and teach us to like the "things that are more excellent."

SIDE-LIGHTS ON THEMES AND TEXTS

The Rev. EDWARD H. EPPENS, Ann Arbor, Mich.

The Intimate God

But will God, in very deed, dwell on the earth?—1 Kings 8:27.

It is false that this Platonist says Plato said: "God hath no commerce with man," and makes this absolute separation the most perfect note of their glory and height.—AUGUSTINE, *The City of God*.

Amid the weak, one strong,
Amid the false, one true,
Amid all change, one changing not—
One hope we ne'er shall rue,
In whose sight all is now,
In whose love all is best:
The things of this world pass away—
Come, let us in him rest.
—FRANK SEWALL.

It was not a new idea that divine wisdom might be a quasi-personal emanation from God, and live in intimate fellowship with man; but Jesus saw that this Spirit was God and cared with creative purpose for despised field flowers and sparrows, for the body of man as well as the soul. He saw that this divine Spirit was at the same time the emotion that surges up into the practise of parental kindness, the instinctive wit of all true love, and also the eternal source and goal of all.—LILY DOUGALL, *The Spirit: God in Action*.

I learned by experience that in falling over precipices, in sinking in swamps, in tumbling into pits, in drowning in seas, I did but find God at the bottom—
Thus does thy hospitable greatness lie
Outside us like a boundless sea;
We can not lose ourselves where all is home,
Nor drift away from thee.
—EDWARD CLIFFORD, *Father Damien*.

God and religion and art: so these are all one and the same. They are the fiery love for all creating and all creation.—G. FRENSSEN, *Meditations*.

Life—a Family Affair

I bow my knees unto the Father from whom every family in heaven and on earth is named.—Eph. 3:14, 15.

When thou art most alone thou must still, if thou wouldest pray, be in the midst of a family; thou must call upon a Father; thou must not dare to say, my, but our.—MAURICE, *The Kingdom of God*.

No man has come to true greatness who has not felt in some degree that his life belongs to his race, that what God gives him he gives him for mankind.—PHILLIPS BROOKS.

Perpetual devotion to what a man calls his business is only to be sustained by perpetual neglect of many other things. And it is not by any means certain that a man's business is the most important thing he has to do.—ROBERT LOUIS STEVENSON.

It has taught me this great lesson of morality, perhaps the only one that can have any conspicuous influence on our actions, that we should ever carefully avoid putting our interest in competition with our duty, or promise ourselves felicity from the misfortunes of others, certain that in such circumstances, however sincere our love of virtue may be, sooner or later it will give way, and we shall imperceptibly become unjust and wicked in fact, however upright in our intentions.—ROUSSEAU, *Confessions*.

There are no virtues which are merely personal or private. Self-love must be organized with the love of others.—E. W. HIRST, *Self and Neighbor*.

Not Roberts, he of Kandahar,
Not Cronje with his scar-seamed men,
Not any man of noisy war,
Nor boastful man with blood-dipt pen!

No, no, the hero of the strife
Is he who deals not death but life;
I count this man the coming man,
The rounding glory of God's plan.
—MILLER.

Following the Gleam

We grope for the wall like the blind.—Isa. 59:10.

To see truly is to see dimly.—E. RENAN.

It must be the work of wiser generations than ours to work out a complete and consistent theistic evolutionary philosophy.—WM. N. RICE, *The Return to Faith*.

Man never has known what he wants; but he won't be happy till he gets it.—W. J. ALLEN, *Politics*.

Heresy is truth in the making, and doubt is the prelude of knowledge.—DRUMMOND, *How to Learn How*.

Religion lives through conflict, and the Christian religion more than any other has from the beginning been engaged in a ceaseless warfare for its rights to exist.—W. R. MATTHEWS, *Studies in Christian Philosophy.*

The whole end, for which God made and thus governs the world, may be utterly beyond the reach of our faculties; there may be somewhat in it as impossible for us to have any conception of as for a blind man to have a conception of colors.—BUTLER, *Analogy of Religion.*

All three might have sat with advantage at the feet of that gifted Swiss maiden, Mlle. Alice de Chambrier, whose thoughts incessantly tended to the immortality to which she was so early called away, and who felt so deeply that the life of man on earth is but a slender gleam of light between immensities of darkness.—FLINT, *Philosophy of History.*

The pretended separation between that which lies within nature and that which lies beyond nature is a dismemberment of the truth.—THE DUKE OF ARGYLL, *The Reign of Law.*

Fuel for the Fire

For if they do these things in the green tree, what shall be done in the dry?— Luke 23:31.

Those who profess Christianity . . . find themselves almost inevitably driven into a position of revolutionists. For those teachings, if they be fully accepted and fairly interpreted, must be seen to be incompatible with the whole structure of your society. . . . It may be held that force is essential to the preservation of society; that without it there could be no security, no order, no peace. But one who holds this view can not be a Christian, in the proper sense of a follower of Christ.—G. L. DICKINSON, *Letters from a Chinese Official.*

The third evil spirit which is corrupting the Church does not disguise itself as an angel of light, for it well knows it can not deceive; it is satisfied with the garb of common human honesty. This is the spirit of avarice.—FOGAZZARO, *The Saint.*

The failure so unfortunately charged against Christianity to discriminate between established wrong and manifest right is not wholly unconnected with an incapacity it has sometimes shown of discerning between error and truth. Unconsciousness of right and wrong, of justice, of the elementary moral values, is the inevitable correlative of unconsciousness of intellectual values.—ROBERT BRIFFAULT, *The Making of Humanity.*

Legend and parable and drama: they are the natural vehicles of dogma; but wo to the churches and rulers who substitute the legend for the dogma, the parable for the history, the drama for the religion! Better by far declare the throne of God empty than set a liar and a fool on it.—G. B. SHAW, *Back to Methuselah.*

There remains as a stand-by for the coming days of the oppression and the decline of freedom the religious metaphysic of freedom and of a faith based on personal conviction. Let us jealously preserve that principle . . . otherwise the cause of freedom and personality may well be lost at the very moment when we are boasting most loudly of our allegiance to it, and of our progress in this direction—TROELTSCH, *Protestantism and Progress.*

The Heart of the Whole Matter

*Love taketh not account of evil.—*1 Cor. 13:5.

I can not admit that any theologian, or church, or council, has ever drawn a larger base of doctrine, or more rich, than Christ himself has given us in his threefold stock of gospel outfit. Here, in fact, is the whole Christian system, without any pretense of system; and the doctrine of the Spirit given by Christ himself.—HORACE BUSHNELL, *Forgiveness and Law.*

It seemed to him that we begin to love when we cease to judge. . . . There is no judgment where there is perfect sympathy. —GEORGE MOORE, *The Lake.*

All bodies put together, and all spirits put together, and all their various productions, are not worth as much as the least movement of charity.—PASCAL, *The Mission and the Grandeur of Jesus Christ.*

The true Christian is the perfect lover, and those whom it helps to associate their lives with moving names may without usurpation assume the honorable style of a Christian, tho they can not sign the thirty-nine articles, so that they love. It is strange to reflect that up till recently the name of Christian has been denied to such, and has been allowed only to those who subscribe to the mistakes rather than the verities of Christianity.—RICHARD LEGALLIENNE, *The Religion of a Literary Man.*

If we could read the secret history of our enemies, we should find in each man's life sorrow and suffering enough to disarm all hostility.—LONGFELLOW.

Ignorance is always abusive; the man who does not know is full of violent affirmations and malign interpretations—FABRE, *Social Life in the Insect World.*

The Heights and the Depths of Religion

I perceive that ye are very religious.—Acts 17:22.

The world by professing Christianity is so far from being a less dangerous enemy than it was before that it has by its favors destroyed more Christians than ever it did by the most violent persecution.—WILLIAM LAW, *Serious Call.*

Religion also hath become a set of opinions and party distinctions separated from high endowments and herding with cheap popular accomplishments—a mere serving maid of every-day life, instead of being the mistress of all earthly, and the preceptress of all heavenly, sentiments—the very queen of all high gifts, graces, and perfections, in every walk of life.—EDWARD IRVING, *The Word of God.*

They met the next year where the cross-roads meet,
Four men from the four winds come;
And it chanced as they met that they talked of God,
And never a man was dumb.
One imaged God in the shape of a man,
A spirit, did one insist;
One said that nature itself was God,
One said that he didn't exist.

But they lasht each other with tongues that stung,
That smote as with a rod.
Each glared in the face of his fellow man,
And wrathfully talked of God.
Then each man parted and went his way,
As their different courses ran:
And each man journeyed with war in his heart,
And hating his fellow man.
—SAM WALTER FOSS, *Odium Theologicum.*

The goal of religion is the fulfilment of the moral duties and opportunities of life as we experience it, with sympathy and idealism and passionately unselfish devotion.—E. S. AMES, *The New Orthodoxy.*

One holy church of God appears
Through every age and race,
Unwasted by the lapse of years,
Unchanged by changing place.

Her priests are all God's faithful ones,
To serve the world raised up;
The pure in heart her baptized ones;
Love, her communion-cup.
—SAMUEL LONGFELLOW.

THEMES AND TEXTS[1]

Sensation or Sacrifice? "Cast thyself down. . . ."—Matt. 4:6.
" . . . Come down from the cross."—Matt. 27:40.

Kings in a Cave. "And these five kings fled, and hid themselves in the cave at Makkedah," etc.—Josh. 10:16-18.

The Rush for the Door. " . . . they wearied themselves to find the door."—Gen. 19:11.

"Confessions of an Adventurous Soul." "And I applied my heart to seek and to search out by wisdom concerning all that is done under heaven."—Eccles. 1:13a.

Abner's Peace Offensive. "Shall the sword devour for ever? knowest thou not that it will be bitterness in the latter end? . . ."—2 Sam. 2:26.

Castles in Spain. "Whensoever I go unto Spain. . . ."—Rom. 15:24.

The Sighting of Cyprus. "And when we had come in sight of Cyprus, leaving it on the left hand . . ."—Acts 21:3.
"And putting to sea from thence, we sailed under the lee of Cyprus, because the winds were contrary."—Acts 27:4.

The Greatest Love-Story in the World. "Jehovah did not set his love upon you, nor choose you, because . . . but because Jehovah loveth you. . . ."—Deut. 7:7, 8.

A Shining Epitaph. "He built the upper gate of the house of Jehovah."—2 Kings 15:35b.

An Acid Test. "The high priests therefore asked Jesus of his disciples. . . ."—John 18:19.

The Syrian Sneer. " . . . Because the Syrians have said, Jehovah is a god. . . ."—1 Kings 20:28.

Jeremiah's Bet. "And I bought the field that was in Anathoth of Hanamel, mine uncle's son, and weighed him the money, even seventeen shekels of silver."—Jer. 32:9.

The Credentials of a Leader. "And Moses said unto God, Who am I, that I should go unto Pharaoh, and that I should bring forth the children of Israel out of Egypt? . . . And God said unto Moses, I AM THAT I AM; and he said, Thus shalt thou say unto the children of Israel, I AM hath sent me unto you."—Ex. 11, 14.

[1] *From The Intention of His Soul, by Hubert L. Simpson.*

ILLUSTRATIONS AND ANECDOTES

The Spiritual House Secure

I came across the following a few years ago: "When John Quincy Adams was eighty years of age, he met in the streets of Boston an old friend, who shook his trembling hand and said, 'Good morning, and how is John Quincy Adams to-day?'

" 'Thank you,' was the ex-president's answer, 'John Quincy Adams himself is well, quite well, I thank you. But the house in which he lives at present is becoming dilapidated. It is tottering upon its foundation. Time and seasons have nearly destroyed it. Its roof is pretty well worn out. Its walls are much shattered, and it trembles with every wind. The old tenement is becoming almost uninhabitable, and I think John Quincy Adams will have to move out of it soon. But he himself is quite well, quite well!' "

It is good to see old people with an unconquerable spirit. When their earthly course is almost run how often they fearlessly look into the future. It is well when they have such vital faith in God that they think of the worn body, shaken by every wind, as only becoming "uninhabitable," that soon they must "move out of it," as exprest by the venerable ex-president of the United States.

Fun with a Thousand Dollars

Last Christmas, John D. Rockefeller sent Mr. Conwell a check for one thousand dollars. And this is what he did with it: "When I opened the envelope and found it, I said to myself: 'Here's a thousand dollars that I hadn't expected at all. How can I have the most fun with it? Well, I went over to the dean of Temple University and asked him for the names of six boys who had been forced to drop out for lack of money; I gave a hundred to each, and they were able to finish the year. Then I thought of a poor old widow out on the edge of the city who had been sick, and was not able to pay even the pitiful little rent for her tiny cottage. So I rode out there and paid her rent for two years in advance—$200 a year—and took the receipt and gave it to her as a Christmas gift. Talk about satisfaction! Why, I sang all the way back to my home. You asked me whether money can help to make old age happy, and I tell you with all my heart that it can—provided you don't keep it, provided you don't hold on to it for your children to quarrel about after you are dead, or covet and scheme for even before you are dead! What a fool a man is to leave a great fortune to his children! Of the 4,043 millionaires whose lives I have studied, 3,807 began life without a dollar. Some statistics compiled years ago in Massachusetts show that not one rich man's son out of 117 ever dies rich. The money you hoard impoverishes you, but the money you give away—it blesses old age like the cool shade of a tree.''—RUSSELL H. CONWELL, in American Magazine.

Building for Others

Recently there appeared in the New York Times "Book Review" a report of the poem called "Building the Bridge for Him." The story is of an old man who had safely crossed a "chasm vast and deep and wide," but who paused on the other side and "built a bridge to span the tide." A fellow pilgrim remonstrated with him for wasting his time, stating that his journey was done and he would never again pass that way, therefore the folly of building the bridge "at evening tide."

"The builder lifted his old gray head.
'Good friend, in the path I have come,' he said,
'There followeth after me to-day
A youth whose feet must pass this way.
This chasm that has been naught to me,
To that fair-haired youth may a pitfall be:
He too must cross in the twilight dim.
Good friend, I am building this bridge for him.'

This poem is an epitome of the Christian life. It is a parable of our expected ministry and service. The true Christian is a builder not only for his own age and safety, but for the safety of generations yet unborn. The follower of Jesus Christ, gospel preacher, Sunday-school teacher, missionary of the kingdom, whatever his sphere, entertains not only ideas for the perfection of his own age, but ideals for the perpetuation of the values that make for perfection in every age. An ideal differs from an idea in that it has a tendency. It has going strength. The kingdom of God is not only an idea of realization, but an ideal of becoming. Idealism is the science of hope, and hope is what men live by. The story of Christian progress and righteous civilization is simply the record of the high hopes of the upward-striving souls that have wrought faithfully and toiled heroically for those who would follow after them. The idealists of the Church are not only brilliant talkers about the kingdom, but they are also passionate workers at its establishment. With them as with the Christ they follow, the vision and the task are one.

Christian Advocate—Nashville, Tenn.

Choosing and Emotions

It was a summer evening by the seaside, and a group of us were sitting on the porch, having a sort of heart-to-heart talk about psychology—which means, of course, that we were talking about ourselves. One by one the different members of the family spoke out the questions that had been troubling them, or brought up their various problems of character or of health. At length a splendid Red Cross nurse who had won medals for distinguished service in the early days of the war, broke out with the question: ''Doctor, how can I get rid of my terrible temper? Sometimes it is very bad, and always it has been one of the trials of my life.'' She spoke earnestly and sincerely, but this was my answer: ''You like your temper. Something in you enjoys it, else you would give it up.'' Her face was a study in astonishment. ''I don't like it,'' she stammered; ''always after I have had an outburst of anger I am in the depths of remorse. Many a time I have cried my eyes out over this very thing.'' ''And you like that, too,'' I answered. ''You are having an emotional spree, indulging yourself first in one kind of emotion and then in another. If you really hated it as much as you say you do, you would never allow yourself the indulgence, much less speak of it afterward.'' Her astonishment was still further increased when several of the group said they, too, had sensed her satisfaction with her moods.

Hard as it is to believe, we do choose our emotions. We like emotion as we do salt in our food, and too often we choose it because something in us likes the savor,

and not because it leads to the character of the conduct that we know to be good.— JOSEPHINE A. JACKSON in *Outwitting Our Nerves.*

A Sterling Quality

In an appreciation of John Foord, one of the founders and for some time secretary of the American Asiatic Association, the following paragraph is given:

A little incident connected with his recent journey to the East brings out one of John Foord's finest qualities, his unwillingness ever to appear under false colors. When he was about to sail for home, some of his old Japanese friends came to see him off at Yokohama and exprest their regret that a pair of silver vases, which were being especially made for him as a testimonial of appreciation and a mark of personal friendship, were not quite finished and would have to be sent on afterward to America. Mr. Foord knew that he was planning to say some things in the articles he expected to write on his way home which might not be considered altogether complimentary to Japan. Under such circumstances, he felt embarrassed at the idea of accepting a gift. So he took care to send back copies of his articles to Japan as soon as he had written them, that his Japanese friends might have the opportunity to change their minds about making him a present. But John Foord's friends knew him too well and admired him too much to change their attitude. In a few weeks, the vases found their way to New York and became one of Mr. Foord's appreciated gifts.—*Asia.*

Keep to the Right

As I stepped out of the church study a few days ago I saw an automobile backing around the large circle that occupies the center of the square. In front of the car walked a policeman, who was telling the occupants, to their great embarrassment and disgust, how dangerous it is to go to the left. He said there would be few accidents if every one followed the signs and kept to the right.

As I stood listening, I found myself nodding assent. If every one were to keep to the right in life, there would be few accidents. There are "keep to the right" signs of health all about us but we swing to the left and before we know it, we are ditched by a procession of disorders, germs and diseases, and our car must be completely overhauled. We follow our selfish desires to the left in the home and we smash into pathetic bits the happiness of other members of the household and lose control of our own steering-wheel. There are those who secretly go joy-riding to the left in their moral lives, but sooner or later their character is buried beneath an avalanche of shattered debris; for the laws of God driving right will not be denied. And some there are who know that the left hand leads to collision with sensitive souls, but they callously ride rough-shod the wrong way around the circle, leaving in their wake open sores and mangled lives stabbed and broken by unjust criticism and stinging sarcasm. It is humiliating to retrace our steps around the circle, but when we have run amuck in our individual lives by obstructing the traffic there is only one way out: to back up and follow the sign, "Keep Right." —For grown-up children.—CARL S. WEIST.

Pride of Caste

In the face of the debasing beggary one meets with at every turn in India, the inviolate pride of caste offers constant surprizes. A man who would beg *bakshish* from you with whining servility would scorn to accept food polluted by your touch. He would throw it away if your shadow had contaminated it. I remember a wonderful morning at Benares when I was being rowed up and down the Ganges at that early hour when thousands of pilgrims from all over India crowd the steps leading down to the river, singing religious songs as they cast garlands of orange flowers out upon the breast of Mother Ganga, and descend and immerse themselves in her sacred waters. As our boat glided along close to the bank, I saw a holy man with Ganges mud smeared over his face, sitting cross-legged in a little temple and eating rice out of a brass bowl. He happened to glance up, and with an expression of startled horror seized his bowl and jumped back to the farther end of his narrow stone shelf. It was only then that

I noticed the shadows of the rowers and myself passing horizontally across the floor where he had been sitting.—GERTRUDE EMERSON in *Asia*.

Transmitting Disease

What right has a man crippled by a lifelong disease to transmit to half a dozen children a corrupt strain of blood? What wide-branching misery develops! Despite the statement of some scientists, it seems certain that men transmit their acquired qualities as well as their physical peculiarities. In general, the children of educated parents are the more easily educated, while the children of untaught parents are slow to learn. Lying men tend to have lying children, is a proverb. Thieves breed thieves, drunkards breed drunkards, insane men breed insanity, and vicious parents hand their vice on to their children. Men who sin against their own bodies, and develop disease, may obtain a certificate from the physician that they have been entirely cured, but oftentimes their short-lived delirium of pleasure will send its curse on to the second and the third generation. Some historians have claimed that Columbus' sailors took back to Spain a certain disease found among the Indians, and that this black taint rolled like a wave all over Europe. There was a certain queen in Great Britain, born in sorrow and nurtured in treachery, who lived for a time under the influence of the basest family in France. That woman handed on through her son a legacy of treachery, cruelty and lust that destroyed her grandson and devastated the whole land of England—NEWELL DWIGHT HILLIS.

Truth

Truth only needs to be for once spoke out,
And there's such music in her, such strange rhythm,
As makes men's memories her joyous slaves,
And clings around the soul, as the sky clings
Round the mute earth, forever beautiful,
And, if o'erclouded, only to burst forth
More all-embracingly divine and clear:
Get but the truth once uttered, and 'tis like
A star new-born, that drops into its place,
And which once circling in its placid round,
Not all the tumult of the world can shake.
          —JAMES RUSSELL LOWELL.

Recent Books

PREACHING IN LONDON[1]

A diary of Anglo-American friendship by an American who filled the pulpit of the historic City Temple in London for over three years and a half forms the substance of this book. It is not often that we have one's observations and impressions and reflections of men, women, and movements given in such an interesting way. Dr. Newton is particularly happy in all this. While there is the critical there is always the appreciative and sympathetic mind. His ministry at the City Temple was never intended to be permanent. It was "undertaken as a kind of unofficial ambassadorship of good-will from the churches of America to the churches of Britain, and as an adventure in Anglo-American friendship."

Naturally the readers of a homiletic magazine would be interested in reading what one leading American preacher has to say about one of the strongest of English preachers. In referring to the time when Dr. Jowett began his ministry at Westminster Chapel, he goes on to say:

Somehow, while Dr. Jowett always kindles my imagination, he never gives me that sense of reality which is the greatest thing in preaching. One enjoys his musical voice, his exquisite elocution, his mastery of the art of illustration, and his fastidious style; but the substance of his sermons is incredibly thin. Of course, this is due, in large part, to the theory of popular preaching on which he works. His method is to take a single idea—large or small—and turn it over and over, like a gem, revealing all its facets, on the ground that one idea is all that the average audience is equal to. Of this method Dr. Jowett is a consummate master, and it is a joy to see him make use of it, tho at times it leads to a tedious repetition of the text. Often, too, he seems to be laboring under the handicap of a brilliant novelist, who must needs make up in scenery what is lacking in plot.

Since his return to London he has been less given to filigree rhetoric, and he has struck almost for the first time a social note, to the extent, at any rate, of touching upon public affairs—altho no one would claim that Dr. Jowett has a social message, in the real meaning of that phrase. No, his forte is personal religious experience of a mild evangelical type; and to a convinced Christian audience of that tradition and training he has a ministry of edification and comfort. But for the typical man of modern mind, caught in the currents and alive to the agitations of our day, Dr. Jowett has no message. However, we must not expect everything from any one servant of God, and the painter is needed as well as the prophet.

Some of our readers will recall the article which appeared in the REVIEW (December, 1921) entitled "A Preacher to the New Age." (See also p. 354, May issue.) This preacher was none other than the Rev. G. A. Studdert Kennedy, and Dr. Newton has this to say about him:

Studdert Kennedy—"Woodbine Willie," as the Tommies called him—is undoubtedly the greatest preacher to me which the war discovered and developed; and one has only to hear him to understand why. He loves it, knows the knack of it, and it was a great sight to see him addressing a vast khaki-clad audience, using the direct speech of the soldier—even his slang —to discuss profound issues of faith, as well as intimate personal problems. What he called "Rough Talks of a Padre" were in fact great sermons, and when to their forthright and vivid style one adds a rich Irish accent and a personality as virile as it is winsome, it is easy to know the secret of his power. It would be difficult for any one to forget his address entitled, "Why Aren't All the Best Chaps Christians?" The last time I heard him the sermon had to do with the truth that God limits himself to make room for man—giving us a tiny province within his divine providence. It was a very striking sermon, but I thought he should have distinguished more clearly between the truth of the reticence, the restraint, the august humility of God, and the idea of a finite God fumbling his way through time, not knowing his own mind, as proclaimed by our novelist-theologians. The one is Christian gospel; the other a camouflaged atheism.

[1] By JOSEPH FORT NEWTON. George H. Doran Company, New York, 1922. 7⅛ x 5¼ in., 140 pp. $1.50.

Another observation, altho along a different line, is worth mentioning. The author had spent an afternoon and evening at the country house of Lord and Lady M———. The gathering was composed of "journalists, labor leaders, socialists, radicals, conservatives, moderates, and what-not." The freedom of discussion, the frankness with which everything was said, came as a revelation to Dr. Newton, and this is what his diary on that day records:

There is more freedom of thought in England than in America. Liberty, in fact, means a different thing in England from what it does with us. In England it signifies the right to think, feel, and act differently from other people; with us it is the right to develop according to a standardized attitude of thought or conduct. If one deviates from that standard, he is scourged into line by the lash of opinion. We think in a kind of lock-step movement. Nor is this conformity imposed from without. It is inherent in our social growth and habit. An average American knows ten times as many people as the average Englishman, and talks ten times as much. We are gregarious; we gossip; and because everyone knows the affairs of everyone else, we are afraid of one another. For that reason, even in time of peace, public opinion moves with a regimented ruthlessness unknown in England where the majority has no such arrogant tyranny as it has with us.

There are five chapters, all of which are extremely interesting. They are as follows: A Pulpit Romance, Joseph Parker, The City Temple, War and Preaching, Peace and Chaos.

The Evolution of the New Testament. By JOHN ELLIOTSON SYMES. E. P. Dutton and Company, New York, 1922. xviii—353 pp. $7.00.

That the science of New Testament Introduction can be made readable is demonstrated by this charming volume. Beginning with a survey of the conditions and events which led up to the writing of the New Testament books separately, the author tells in a clear and consecutive story how each of these books came into being, what it contains, and how it fitted into the special setting that evoked it. Yet in order to make his story simple and interesting he never for a moment sacrifices accuracy and proper regard for scientific method. Perplexing problems of authorship and literary composition such as emerge in the study of the Pastoral Epistles, of the Synoptics, or of

the Fourth Gospel and the Apocalypse are given their proper consideration in a series of "Notes" appended to the successive chapters. But even these "Notes" are free from pedantry and padding and may be read without abatement of interest. In fact, many of them will be read with a relish aroused by the text of the chapters they follow. The author's tendency is to keep well within the bounds of the conservative camp of scholarship. But he never neglects to do full justice to the views of the so-called "advanced" or radical critics. Altogether it is an ideal work not only for the layman, but also for the student who wishes to know the latest findings of history on the origin, composition and collection of the New Testament writings.

Landmarks in the History of Early Christianity. By KIRSOPP LAKE. The Macmillan Company, New York, 1922. x—113 pp. $1.25.

The core of Dr. Kirsopp Lake's theory regarding the origin and nature of the Christian religion is that some original and fresh impulses and thoughts contributed by Jesus to the general stream of religious development have been intermingled with others already in course of movement in the world, thus giving rise to a complex whose subsequent great power has given it the appearance of a preternatural insertion into history. Upon this theory Dr. Lake traces the gospel from Galilee through Jerusalem, Antioch, Corinth, Rome, and Ephesus, and notes the elements so far as discoverable introduced into it and assimilated by it. It is a suggestive study, which, however, must submit to a searching criticism and testing as far as its separate propositions are concerned. That Christianity has taken into its form of thought and organization many elements from its original environment can scarcely be questioned.

An Introduction to the History of Christianity, A.D. 590–1314. By F. J. FOAKES-JACKSON. The Macmillan Company, New York, 1921. xi—390 pp. $3.50.

This book would have been more accurately entitled if it had been called "A History of Christianity in the Middle Ages." The word "introduction" has been adopted in the title evidently in order to signify the author's intention to suggest the outline of interest rather than to narrate the full content of the story of the period. He treats his subject not as a record of facts but as an interpretation and estimate of their meaning and value. The historians of the Medieval Church have not, as a rule, pursued this course, and the consequence has been a rather discouraging loss of interest in this portion of the story of Christianity. Dr. Foakes-Jackson has rendered a valuable service to the study of church history, and it may be confidently anticipated that his work will, as it deserves to, be used extensively and will contribute to the revival of interest in its subject.

The Pilgrim. Essays on Religion. By T. R. GLOVER. George H. Doran Company, New York, 1922. 7¾x5¼ in., 272 pp. $1.75.

The author of these thirteen essays has by his several books (e.g., The Jesus of History, see our REVIEW for November, 1917, p. 429) effectively introduced himself to our readers. The contribution which in this collection stands out above the rest is on The Holy Spirit. It is a discussion that goes to the basis of things in both primitive and advanced thinking, thoroughly vital and essentially historical. We may mention also the essay on The Statue of the Good Shepherd discovered at Akhmin in Egypt. The story of this noted piece of sculpture and the reason for its particular form, etc., are imagined, but on the basis of works left by Tertullian and Clement of Alexandria. Finally we may note the chapter on Study of the Bible. We wonder what kind of a preacher he is who can not get at least one sermon out of this essay.

For many reasons one just has to read this virile writer.

The Septuagint and Jewish Worship. A Study in Origins. The Schweich Lectures, 1920. By H. ST. JOHN THACKERAY. Oxford University Press, London and New York, 1921. 9¾x6¼ in., 143 pp.

Appointment to the Schweich lectureship is in the gift of the British Academy. It is intended always to go to an eminent scholar, master of his subject. The present appointment met this provision. Since the death of Dr. Swete, probably no student is better qualified to speak of the Greek versions of the Old Testament than Mr. Thackeray. In these lectures he has made expected notable contributions in four directions: (1) elucidation of Old Testament teaching;

(2) clarifying of practise in Jewish institutions; (3) notations on the text both of the Septuagint and the Hebrew; (4) a fine discussion of the (apocryphal) Book of Baruch.

This is a book for scholars. It requires a fair knowledge of Hebrew, Greek, and Aramaic. Its reading will amply repay the diligent student.

The Religion of the Psalms. By J. M. P. SMITH. University of Chicago Press, Chicago, 1922. 170 pp. $1.75.

So much toil and ingenuity have been expended upon the criticism of the Psalter that one gratefully welcomes this little book, dealing with various aspects of its religion, such as its idea of God, its attitude to immortality, to suffering, etc. The writer has the art of teaching, without being "preachy." Careful scholarship underlies the whole discussion, but he keeps his eye steadily upon the things that matter.

The Biblical History of the Hebrews to the Christian Era. By F. T. FOAKES-JACKSON. George H. Doran Company, New York, 1921. 492 pp. $3.00.

This deservedly popular history by a scholar who is equally at home in the problems of the New Testament and the Old, now enters upon its fourth edition, and brings the Hebrew story down to the period where the New Testament begins. It is written with complete command of the often perplexing material, and offers a fine combination of scientific thoroughness with religious reverence. The sane and cautious temper of the book is best seen in the writer's treatment of the historicity of the patriarchal stories. While fully recognizing that tribal and national movements are frequently described in terms of personal experiences, he yet leaves open the possibility that the traditions about Joseph, e.g., rest upon a solid substratum of fact.

Problems in Pan-Americanism. By SAMUEL GUY INMAN. George H. Doran Company, New York, 1921. 8 x 5½ in., 415 pp. $2.00.

This volume is an effort to help the man in North America to better understand the man in Latin America. The contents are: Assets of Latin America, Problems of Latin America, Early Efforts Toward Pan Americanism, Early Efforts of the United States Toward American Friendship, The Monroe

Doctrine and Latin America, Pan American Conferences, Latin America and the World War, Problems of the Caribbean Countries, Pan Americanism vs. Pan Latinism, Next Steps in Inter-American Friendship.

To those interested in the racial and political relations between the United States and the twenty Latin-American Republics we commend a reading of this work.

The Ruin of the Ancient Civilization and the Triumph of Christianity. By GUGLI LMO FERRERO. G. P. Putnam's Sons, New York, 1921, 210 pp.

The famous Italian author has comprest a number of ideas in this short volume; the publishers might have comprest it into a pamphlet of fifty pages if they had been less generous with thickness of paper, size of print, and margins. Such a procedure might have made the contents available to a larger number of men who cannot afford to pay two or three dollars for what they should get for fifty cents. The number of these men should be large, because few men are able to get the larger works of this author, and they would welcome a cheaper edition.

The author takes up the following five topics: The internal decomposition; the crisis of the third century; Diocletian and the reform of the empire; Constantine and the triumph of Christianity; in the third and twentieth century.

Encyclopaedia of Religion and Ethics. Volume XII. Edited by JAMES HASTINGS. Charles Scribner's Sons, New York, 1922. 11½x8½ in., 876 pp. $8.00.

While the place of knowledge is not the first consideration in life it is an auxiliary of the greatest importance. And to no body of men is it more necessary than to ministers of the gospel.

Many of us justly take great pride in the work of the past. We are profoundly grateful to the intellectuals, to the moral and spiritual leaders of other days. And yet we must remember that we are also the heirs of many fears, superstitions and irrational ideas that only time and wisdom can correct.

It is right here where the value of a new and great encyclopedia like the one before us has its justification. The amazing amount of knowledge found in the twelve bulky volumes that comprise the set is now at the service of every seeker after the truth.

Dictionaries and encyclopedias of a specialized character have had considerable vogue during the last twenty-five years or so. Nothing, however, has matched the dimensions of this one and in this particular field no work is as authoritative.

As announced in the preface to the first volume the words "Religion" and "Ethics" are both used in their most comprehensive meaning. The encyclopedia contains articles on all the religions of the world, and on the great systems of ethics, on religious beliefs, customs, and of "such persons and places as are famous in the history of religion and morals."

The first volume bore the date of 1908 and this one, covering from Suffering to Zwingli, is dated 1922. The Great World War interrupted the progress of the work but now that the undertaking has been completed so satisfactorily the editors, the hundreds of contributors, and the publishers are to be congratulated.

Stories of the Kingdom. By WILL REASON. George H. Doran Company, New York, 1922. 8x5½ in., 175 pp. $1.00.

In the introduction to this volume the author says that the most important qualification for talking to boys and girls is to be a boy or girl oneself. Such a one, he says, "will never make the fatal mistake of talking down to his hearers; they resent it very much, and quite rightly." In these twenty-five talks on the parables, the author adapts his vocabulary, but credits his hearers with the capacity to understand the truths he wants to drive home. We give one of the talks in another department of the magazine, as a sample of one of the best collections of this kind.

The Wisdom of the Beasts. By CHARLES AUGUSTUS STRONG. Houghton Mifflin Company, Boston, 1922. 8x5 in., viii—76 pp. $1.50.

The professor of psychology in Columbia University here presents a series of fables quizzically caricaturing the theories of Einstein, Bergson, James, the monists, the realists, and other modern schools of philosophy. One can skim this extremely clever little book in twenty minutes, but he will spend several hours in going over it several times in order to see just where, in each case, the "catch" of the theory is.

·PREACHERS EXCHANGING VIEWS

[Editors are not, as a rule, in as good a position for taking care of the overflow as lecturers and preachers. If the main hall in a town is inadequate for the multitude recourse can often be had to a smaller audience room. Not so with editors. When their correspondence bulks large, as was the case with letters address to the editor during the last month or so, we had but two courses open to us. One was to condense, the other to postpone. The former seemed the wiser. Several communications have, nevertheless, to wait over for our next number.—Eds.]

Christian Cooperation

The Rev. W. H. Chambers, Clarkston, Mich., quoting the following from Dr. Macfarland's article (July) on "Christian Cooperation the Call of the Age"—

A few years ago the Committee on Home Missions of the Federal Council of Churches of Christ in America investigated the State of Colorado. One hundred and thirty-three communities were found ranging in population from one hundred and fifty to one hundred thousand souls, without Protestant churches of any kind, one hundred of them being also without a Roman Catholic Church.

makes this comment:

There is but one city in the State to-day with a population of one hundred thousand or over, and that is Denver. Pueblo comes next with about sixty-five thousand. I was director of Religious Education and Music there and was quite familiar with general conditions. Colorado Springs was well churched. Salida and Boulder were churched. I question if there is a place in the State with a population of one thousand which does not have a church. Pueblo has 29 churches.

Dr. R. K. Massie, Lexington, Ky., also writes on the same subject as follows:

With the exception of Denver there is no city in Colorado that approaches anything like one hundred thousand. In fact, there are only two or three more than ten thousand in the census of 1910; and furthermore, every town in Colorado as large as five thousand has at least one Episcopal Church to my certain knowledge as our official records show.

Meaning of "Destroy," "Perish"

The Rev. J. W. Patterson, Pavo, Ga., has this to say concerning the above article, which appeared in the July number:

Are words capable of such analysis that one may say with finality that this is the primary meaning of this or that word and no other interpretation is possible? Was language built up scientifically of so many prescribed elements of exactly prescribed values or is it not rather a living thing adjusting its powers of expression to every emergency of thought? Every word is sub-

ject to the law of relativity. Every word not only imparts to but takes color from the whole theme in which we may find it imbedded.

Suppose a word, taken as a word, or even taken as used in certain sentences had a limited meaning, suppose the word translated here "destroy" can be reduced to the one meaning, "to take life," in these given instances of its use, does that limit also, within the same bounds, other very plain and more far-reaching teachings of scripture? In other words, if our Lord has declared very forcibly and plainly a doctrine of eternal punishment, is this declaration to be set aside because a word sometimes elsewhere used to describe that punishment may be reduced to a meaning more in keeping with the "consummation devoutly to be wished" by them that oppose him?

In striving about this one word "apollumi" the author has overlooked whole discourses that the Master himself has given to explain and enforce it. After all, the Great Teacher is the final authority on all matters scriptural. What does he say? He describes very vividly the condition of the man who in hell lifted up his eyes being in torments —who was there forever, because the gulf was fixt—and there was no passing over. It may refresh the memory of the author to read this account in Luke 16:19-31.

In Matthew 25:46 our Lord says of the wicked in closing his description of the judgment, "And these shall go away into everlasting punishment: but the righteous into life eternal." And after he was raised from the dead he gave us these words of warning through John the Apostle. See also Rev. 14:11.

The Rev. A. R. Empie, Cobleskill, N. Y., says:

To me the article conveyed the idea that the soul as well as the body of the wicked is killed, dies, past feeling, absolutely dead, no more in existence. If this be what the Bible teaches, then what are we to do with such passages as the following: Dan. 12:2; Matt. 25:46; Rev. 14:11; Matt. 25:41; Rev. 20:10? -

The soul can not be killed. It does not absolutely die, perish nor is destroyed. The body perishes, but out of this perishable body comes an immortal body, and together with the soul has an everlasting existence. From God's view the spirit of all mankind has always had an existence, and always will have. And that spirit, being a part of the divine Being can not die or be killed.

Is Human Nature Good or Bad

The Rev. R. J. Dodds, Walden, New.York, writes concerning the above article (July):

By the term "total depravity" Calvinists only design to signify that the tendency of human nature, since the fall of Adam, is to evil and that it is tainted throughout with depravity. In the development, however, of the theory in this discussion, Professor Wells shows that it differs much more widely from the view of Calvin, Augustine and Jonathan Edwards than from that of Rousseau. . . .

Instead of the theory of innate good tendencies the unrestrained expression of which results in the furthering of personal and social interests and a consequent increase in happiness, the Calvinist holds the more hopeful and comforting view of divine grace and an ever-watchful, interested, overruling Providence. Professor Wells' statement that the modern scientific view can not accept the Calvinistic theory of depravity is perhaps a little vague. It seems, however, to mean that the modern scientist can not accept the Calvinistic view. The division, however, between scientists and those who are not to be so classed is not clear. Certainly many scientific persons do accept the Calvinistic view and hold it tenaciously. This possibly led Professor Wells to employ the term "the modern scientific view" rather than the modern scientist, as signifying that group of modern scientists who hold the evolutionary view and think they find some good traits in the natural man. . . .

After a careful study of what Professor Wells has written, the unavoidable conclusion is that Calvin, Augustine, Edwards, and the Church were right. The Scriptural doctrine of the total depravity of the race as a result of Adam's fall stands forth unimpeached. Men's hammers break; God's anvil stands.

Women and the Ministry

Belle Reid Yates, Grenola, Kan., makes this comment on the letter written by the Rev. O. J. Roberts in our July number. She cites the following texts: Joel 2:28; Acts 2:17, 18; 21:8, 9.

The first preacher of Christ in the temple was a woman (Luke 2:38): "And Anna spake of him to all them that looked for redemption in Jerusalem." Mary was the first traveling evangelist under orders from Christ himself, "Go,"—"Then she runneth and cometh unto Peter and the other disciples," etc. Dorcas was a disciple of Christ, so is any good woman who does his will. Acts 8:3: Saul made havoc of the church, hailing men and women, committed them to prison, therefore they (both men and women) went everywhere preaching the word. Paul took Aquila and Priscilla with him on his missionary journeys, left them in charge of a church (Acts 18:26) where Apollos was converted under them. See also Gal. 5:15.

The Minister's Side Line

The Rev. H. Russell Clem, Greensboro, N., C., writes concerning the above (July):

I would like to give my commendation and endorsement to the good un-"common" sense in it. Few ministers can follow their profession or calling exclusively and lay up a competence for the years when the churches will not accept their services. And as long as we have our church boards and denominational leaders insisting upon the minister giving his entire time to his calling, without insisting likewise that he be paid sufficiently, he is likely to continue to have his side line, or leave the ministry altogether.

Facing the Facts on Christian Unity

The Rev. M. S. McGee, Parlier, Cal., makes the following comments on a letter on the above subject (see June number, page 518):

If I understand Brother Barrow aright he wants us to unite on what appeals to him to be the right interpretation of Acts 11:26; 2 Pet. 4:16; Mark 16:16; Acts 2:38; Col. 1:8, and Matt. 28:18-20. I am wondering if Brother Barrow means that he would be willing to unite with the Quakers, the Salvation Army, the Seventh Day Adventists, if all other churches would be willing to unite on the terms which these people believe the Bible teaches. . . . I am interested in a real Christian union but not for a minute on what any other man or set of men tell me one thing the Bible teaches.

Approval of Long Contributions

The Rev. H. Newton Smith, Palermo, Ont., Canada, writes approvingly of the long articles and sermons, but not so of the outlines and word texts.

Evolution, the Bible, and Religion

The Rev. F. J. Dodd, La Grange, Ga., writes as follows on the above question:

I too am a subscriber of your interesting preacher's journal and have been most of the time for twenty-five or more years, and as such I suggest, as was recently done by an evolutionist (see August number, page 103), that some one who believes that the Bible is true be asked for an article in reply to the one in this issue (August) by Frederic Gurney. I would be glad to see a reply by William J. Bryan, J. W. Porter, or George McCready.

"The Southern Methodists are reaching out boldly for a community program, both rural and urban, and are holding numerous summer institutes to train their pastors for the new type of service which combines religious education and community service with evangelism. The Board of Missions of this church is devoting large sums of money to demonstration parishes, and is subsidizing churches in downtown and industrial neighborhoods. It is making use of the survey in establishing these new enterprises and in reorganizing long-established parishes.

"The most significant of these new enterprises is the Broad Street Church of Richmond, Virginia, which has just completed a new $250,000 community house, toward which the Board of Missions appropriated $150,000."

BROAD STREET METHODIST EPISCOPAL CHURCH SOUTH, AND PARISH HOUSE
RICHMOND, VIRGINIA

[See page 353]

The HOMILETIC REVIEW

VOL. 84   NOVEMBER, 1922   No. 5

THE GREAT BECOMING

The Rev. J. E. WARD, Amherst, Mass.

Down across the years St. John sees the universal life as a wondrous "becoming." It has for him "a continuous history which runs out of an unmeasured past." Far as his piercing vision can discern, and illimitably farther, he feels the meaning of that pulsing surge which is the energizing principle of all that is.

"In the beginning," place it where you may, describe it as you will, out beyond the utmost bound of thought, back through the million years, that life principle, that creative force in nature, the reason of order in the world, was there. In the beginning was mind and in that mind was a divine idea. It was through that i d e a that all things became. There was no development, no progress, no creation, except in the light of that idea. It was to work out that idea that all things are.

Try to grasp the meaning of this. The simple profundity of the thought of this man is astoundingly attractive to the modern student. In the be-

> There is something very wonderful about the thought of St. John. It is so simple, so beautiful, yet so profound. It is born of a clearer vision than that of St. Paul, or at any rate finds a clearer expression, and withal it is so modern in its import and so intimately true. Far from the prolog of his gospel being a sort of afterthought, as has been suggested, it contains the very kernel of this old seer's life philosophy. It might well be taken as an introduction to a treatise on "Evolution in the New Testament."

ginning was mind and mind was with God and mind was God.

Mind and the expression of that mind is all that we have and are. Behind all, in all, through all, is the absolute, the infinite mind, expressing itself here in the form which has become a habit of thought, the form of law; or there in the freedom of another and a higher law of love.

The old Hebrew had tried to think through to the meaning of this divine expression, and he spoke in his naïveté of the "angel of the Lord." His confrère had puzzled it out too and used for it the term "the wisdom of God." Later someone else had called it "the word of Yahweh," and someone later still "the expression [*logos*] of God." They were all of them trying to put into words that which no vocabulary can express or contain, that which can alone find meaning in terms of life itself.

Would that we could read it all in the very speech of the beloved disciple's tongue. Our English is a clumsy sort of vehicle for expressing these deep thoughts.

This divine idea "tarried" in the divine mind ("the Word was with God"). That is what he says. It is the same word as Paul uses—"I went up to Jerusalem to become acquainted with Cephas and tarried with him fifteen days" (Gal. 1:18), a personal dwelling of mind with mind. The old English is not so bad after all if it only be given a chance. There was intercourse in the tarrying. Think of the infinite spirit-mind dwelling upon the idea of finite expression. Think of the great Absolute couning over the idea of relative expression. And the idea tarried in the infinite mind—the divine idea in the divine mind.

Of course the two were inseparable. Mind must think, and infinite must think within infinity. It must think of itself. It has no other of whom to think. It must think of a relative image of itself. And it did, so the old Book tells us.

It is all so simple. Just through that idea, the idea that the infinite must find relative expression, all things came. They came because, like all ideas thus dwelt upon, this idea must realize itself. It was and is inseparable from the mind that conceived it. Our own ideas are that. Stored up somewhere with this weirdly mysterious entity we call our self, they are all there, every one of them that we have ever entertained. They are a part of us, we are their life. The expression, the idea, was the mind and yet the idea was not the whole mind. One can easily see this, and it is not very difficult to understand that there never was a time when this relationship did not exist.

Yet it is eminently necessary to grasp the meaning of the disciple's thought or so easily we miss the whole purport of his teaching.

So the great process of realization began. And we have to understand that it is the self-realization of the infinite Being. The infinite mind is working out its thought, is expressing its thought. The infinite Spirit is realizing his life. The nature of both these—the infinite and the relative, the infinite consciousness and the individual idea—was the same. Both are divine. The word was God, but was in a sense "not God." The idea was not the whole mind, yet was the expression of the mind, and was one with the mind.

Self-realization meant relativity. The absolute Being must pass through a process to a goal. In order to reach that goal all things came about. As the disciple puts it, it is a great process of development—evolution, if you will. All things became or were becoming through him. The process has no meaning apart from the goal. Consciousness seeks relative consciousness. Personality seeks relative personality. And just because the divine life must find self-realization, all things which are necessary in process to the attainment of the goal must come into being.

This is not so profound or difficult after all. The nearest we have to creation is invention. The inventor has an idea, a complete visualization of that which he yearns to visualize. He goes into his shop and gathers round him a mass of material, a seeming chaos apart from the intention in the inventor's mind. The idea in his mind is the cause of all this collection, and of the ultimate process through which it passes and the form which it takes. The whole process in reality takes place within the inventor's mind, the idea is the cause of it all and guides its development. It is all from the idea, and through it and unto it. It is no less truly from and through and unto the mind in which the idea originates.

A nearer analogy in a human way would be the development, within, not without the human being, of some form caused by thought. In reality this takes place more often than we know. It is true, scientifically true. that within the individual self an idea will realize itself in physical form. Should a man become obsessed with the idea that he has a certain physical disability he is almost certain to develop that disability—physically develop it. It comes through the idea; it is caused by the idea. If this is so in a human being, need we quibble about the possibility of it all within the divine infinite self?

James expresses it in another way. He says, "Of his own will he brought us forth by the word of truth, that we should be a kind of firstfruits of his creatures." It is a very strong expression which he uses, the same that is used in the Greek for human birth.

Paul applies this same idea of travail, but with it is also exprest that of a great development through an evolutionary discipline. "The earnest expectation of the creation waiteth for the revealing of the sons of God. For the creation was subjected not of its own will (i.e., we must get outside and beyond the process of evolution to find the meaning of it), but by reason of him who subjected it, in hope; because the creation itself shall be delivered from the bondage of corruption into the liberty of the glory of the children of God. For we know that the whole creation groaneth and travaileth in pain with us until now. And not only so, but ourselves also, which have the firstfruits of the Spirit, even we ourselves groan within ourselves, waiting for our adoption, to wit, the redemption of our body." And the goal of this vast evolutionary process, in which the indwelling "Spirit himself maketh intercession for us with groanings that

can not be uttered," is that we should be "conformed to the image of his Son, that he might be the firstborn among many brethren" (Rom. 8:29).

So we do not wonder that Paul (Rom. 11:36) speaks thus in referring to God, the infinite Being—"of him, and through him, and unto him are all things." Again in his letter to the Colossians (1:13ff. he gives thanks to God: "Who hath delivered us from the power of darkness, and hath translated us into the kingdom of the Son of his love; . . . who is the image of the invisible God, the firstborn of all creation; . . . for in (through) him were all things created, in the heavens and upon the earth, things visible and invisible, whether thrones or dominions or principalities, or powers; all things have been created by him, and unto him; . . . and he is before all things, and in (through) him all things consist (hold together)."

It is an evolution from darkness to light, to the light of the conscious freedom of personality—just what John says also.

So we have a process working toward a goal, inspired and sustained by the idea of that goal. The goal is the idea in the infinite mind, the idea of a relative image of its own being, and within its own being, and the goal is responsible for the process.

In terms of plain, every-day, modern thought, John says in effect: The initial cause of evolution is to be found in an infinite activity of the divine mind. Evolution is God realizing his idea. The cause of evolution is the search of the infinite life for relative expression. Its meaning is to be found only in a perfect personality which is conscious, as perfect personality must be conscious, of its absolute spirit of the whole. Through all the years, the millions of years, the vast process has gone on seeking its goal. In one sense the goal has been attained in Jesus. He is the initial image, the first fruits not only of redemption but of evolution. His nature and consciousness, which is to say his personality, images relatively the infinite nature and consciousness. In dealing with Jesus' mind we know what the infinite mind is like when functioning in the dimensions of time and space. When we find Jesus condemning hypocrisy, we know that hypocrisy is against the eternal order of things. When we find him urging men to love, we know that the eternal Spirit is a Spirit of harmony. When we see him girding himself with a towel and showing forth the meaning of service, we know that the infinite Being demands cooperation and fellowship and union of heart with heart.

Jesus didn't go out as a sort of celestial carpenter and pull the worlds together any more than the idea of the modern inventor goes into the workshop and makes a gramophone. There never was a workshop in heaven, so far as God is concerned, and there never will be. Nor was God ever a great Architect in any literal sense. Nor does he stand yonder (and the world revolve here) and look on and direct; he doesn't even do it by wireless, so to speak. Literally all things are either directly or indirectly an expression of his thought activity.

It isn't all so impossible as may seem. Sir Oliver Lodge can sit down quietly as a great scientist and say:

Of our own knowledge we are unable to realize the meaning of origination or of maintenance; all that we ourselves can accomplish in the physical world is to move things into desired positions and leave them to act on each other. Nevertheless our effective movements are all inspired by thought, and so we conceive that there must be some intelligence immanent in all the processes of nature, for they are not random or purposeless, but organized and beautiful.

There are those who think that in the last resort the ultimate reality will be found to be of the nature of spirit, consciousness, and mind. It may be so—it probably is so—but that is a teaching of philosophy, not at present of science.

Mental faculties seem intimately associated with, and are displayed by, our bodily mechanism; but in themselves they belong to a different order of being, an order which employs and dominates the material, while immersed or immanent in it. Every purposed movement is preceded and inspired by thought.[1]

Another scientist addressing not some little group of crank enthusiasts on the scent of a new idea but a staid British association can say without fear of ridicule: "In its ultimate essence energy may be incomprehensible by us except as an exhibition of the direct operation of that which we call mind or will"—this not in a religious address, but in a lecture on "Waves in Water, Air and Ether" delivered at the Royal Institution by J. A. Fleming in 1902.

Even on relative and individual grounds there have been such things demonstrated and photographed as the materialization of thought. The world is very loath to believe the truth of such phenomena, but there they are. Psychology does say that "an idea tends to realize itself"—a man's idea—physically realize itself. Negatively this is recognized by the whole medical profession. Man's physical health depends upon his thought. It has even been demonstrated that such emotional states as fear, hatred, and love are accompanied by physical changes within the body.

More than this the whole trend of science is toward a fuller recognition of man's physical being as truly an expression of his indwelling mind. The subconscious, or perhaps more correctly the unconscious, control of the body is a marvelously powerful and effective control. Moreover the body's activities are measured by a certain degree of self-recognized power. For this very reason Jesus never attempted to heal without belief on the part of the subject. He

[1] Lodge, *The Substance of Faith.*

could do no more for a man than a man could believe possible of himself. Jesus knew that he was reaching the man's physical nature through the man's own indwelling mind. The same is true to-day. There is a reason for it all which lies in the very heart of the infinite Being himself.

Let us grasp firmly one other thought, that the universe including man is within the being of God. It might seem a mere platitude to say that we can not very easily get outside infinity. Yet folk are assuming every day that they can. But there is more in it than that. We have so become accustomed to thinking in terms of matter and spirit, and as such cut off and distinct from each other, that it is nearly impossible to get anyone to think in any other terms.

We are not trying to make John and Paul square with Darwin. No, twenty-five years before *The Origin of Species* was penned, Browning set forth that eloquent passage in *Paracelsus:*

> Thus He dwells in all,
> From life's minute beginnings, up at last
> To man—the consummation of this scheme
> Of being, the completion of this sphere
> Of life: whose attributes had here and there
> Been scattered o'er the visible world before,
> Asking to be combined, dim fragments
>   meant
> To be united in some wondrous whole,
> Imperfect qualities throughout creation,
> Suggesting some one creature yet to make,
> Some point where all those scattered rays
>   should meet
> Convergent in the faculties of man.

Tennyson, presenting his wonderful offering of a full heart in memory of his friend writes in *In Memoriam* published in 1850:

> They say
> The solid earth whereon we tread,
> In tracts of fluent heat began,
> And grew to seeming rounded forms,
> The seeming prey of cyclic storms,
> Till at the last arose the man.

Well may one ask how came this clash between the teaching of religion and of an evolutionary idea in science.

There is nothing in the New Testament to demand such a disagreement. Surely it was just that men of faith did not allow for that leading into all truth by the Spirit of truth through the ages. They looked upon revelation as a deposit given to guard inviolate rather than a seed given to plant and tend so that in the end they might enjoy the fruits thereof. And to this idea of a complete faith, "once for all delivered to the saints," they added the impossible theory (for it could be nothing but a theory) that God, so to speak, dictated to his stenographer Moses a geological message to be typed and delivered say to the Geological Society some 6000 years hence. However, that ground has long since been covered and with an amount of bitterness on both sides which it seems difficult now to understand.

It is a very striking fact, that the basis of our modern methods of studying the evolution problem was established not by the early naturalists, nor by the speculative writers, but by the philosophers. . . . They alone were upon the main track of modern thought. It is evident that they were groping in the dark for a working theory of the evolution of life, and it is remarkable that they clearly perceived from the outset that the point to which observation should be directed was not the past but the present mutability of species, and further, that this mutability was simply the variation of individuals on an extended scale.

Indeed what is there in this idea of evolution that has so often seemed to conflict with religious teaching (rather one should say theological teaching)? Is not life as John and Paul and James and Darwin and Christ have said, "A great 'Becoming'"? Was Aristotle more or less Christian because he said: "Nature produces those things which, being continually moved by a certain principle contained in themselves, arrive at a certain end."

Is there any conflict between the belief in a "principle contained in themselves" and a "divine indwelling"? Is there any clash in the statement "arrive at a certain end" and "growth unto the fulness of the stature of Christ"?

Again if it is said by the scientist quite reasonably:

It must be borne in mind that the general idea of organic evolution—that the present is the child of the past—is in great part just the idea of human history projected upon the natural world, differentiated by the qualification that the continuous "becoming" has been wrought out by forces inherent in the organisms themselves and in their environment,

need one, being a believer in the indwelling spirit and mind of the divine Originator—need one, we repeat, find any fault with a scientific assumption of "forces inherent in the organisms and in their environment"?

What if a vast unity of progress covering millions of years is shown to exist; is such a unity not just what we would expect? Would that men would be less prone to *apologia* in the sphere of the infinite, and more given to care for the right lines of their own responsibility for the little universe of the individual self, for which daily they must answer. Through millions of years the infinite Spirit would seem to have been well able to write his own *apologia* in the stars alike with mother earth.

Building truth on truth we have both faith and hope that the years to come will lead us, on to even higher and higher planes of knowledge and life, in the great fathering Spirit's home of many dwelling places. That we have come a little on the upward path need not be a source of disagreement but of joy. Has Moses learned no more, think you, in his years between, in the unseen country whither he has gone on pilgrimage? Is there no joy in reaching across the ages in a firm hand-clasp to the Hebrew and the Greek, in gratitude for comradeship of interest and community of faith? The theologian no less than the scientist can only ever stand upon

one small spot in the great pilgrimage of truth; may ever look both backward and forward with joy; and may well be grateful if the small spot be a vantage point.

Thus, down across the ages, philosophy and science alike have pictured for us a great becoming and a great unity. It is a unity of purpose. Circles there are within nature, but the one vast circling, which must comprehend them all and give them meaning, is that from consciousness through unconsciousness back to consciousness. Evolution, as a process, can truly be viewed only as a vast progress from the unconscious to the conscious; but the process is not all. The inventor's paraphernalia means not overmuch until we read his mind and know the idea which forms his mental image toward which he works. The process has no meaning as such apart from his thought, except as an interim expression of that thought. It has no meaning except as interpreted by its goal.

How easy it is, in the illimitable grandeur of nature's wondrous being, to lose oneself in the great pilgrimage and forget to ask whence coming, whither going. How human, immersed in present interest, to cease all thought of human destiny! Not so St. Paul. He sees the source in the mind of the great Absolute. "To us there is one God, the Father, of whom are all things, and we unto him." He sees the reason of the vast creation in him who was conceived in the mind of that holy fathering Spirit. "To us there is one Lord, Jesus Christ, through whom are all things, and we through him." We are still in the wider process moving toward the goal of the fuller incarnation of the race.

If evolution has found its culmination in one being more truly than in any other, then that being is unique. His position is assured, while his nature may be shared. If the infinite Mind has found perfect expression in relative and finite consciousness, then that expression is divine. This was the claim of the Master and of his followers. The divine idea was realized, the fullest expression of the thought of the Deity in finite terms; not all of God but the relative image of God, the Son of God. Because the idea is likewise a true human ideal, man's true self, so he is the Son of man. Moreover, as an idea and an ideal do not bring to us any sense of conflict or contradiction in terms, so these two great titles do but point to that further development of the great process in which man shall accept the initial presentation of his evolutionary destiny, and grow in consciousness unto the fulness of the stature of the divine ideal.

A MODERN SOUTHERN CHURCH ESTABLISHMENT

Worth M. Tippy, D.D., New York City

The South has entered upon a phenomenal period of church building—new churches, new parish houses, new adjustments to the community. It is spending large sums of money in these enterprises, much of it well spent, but some of it badly spent because of inexperienced architects, and because many churches see as yet only the house of worship and the Sunday-school, with the result that seven-day work, neighborhood service, and club organization for age groups will find inadequate facilities when in the course of a few years these churches reach the stage of community service. There is no escape from an ugly and badly conceived building but to make the best of it or finally to tear it down.

The South goes to church and is overwhelmingly Protestant, and the churches have great influence upon public life. These facts combine to give the religious spirit in that area a great opportunity. Will the churches see and grasp the opportunity? There are many indications that they will, for there is everywhere in the South intense religious activity. The greatest danger is the impossibility as yet of the denominations working effectively together, due to the fact that the Southern Baptists stand almost solidly against cooperation. The churches can not do their great work until they act concertedly in their general strategy and eliminate the economic and spiritual waste of unnecessary competition.

The Southern Methodists are reaching out boldly for a community program, both rural and urban, and are holding numerous summer institutes to train their pastors for the new type of service which combines religious education and community service with evangelism. The Board of Missions of this church is devoting large sums of money to demonstration parishes, and is subsidizing churches in downtown and industrial neighborhoods. It is making use of the survey in establishing these new enterprises and in reorganizing long-established parishes.

The most significant of these new enterprises is the Broad Street Church of Richmond, Virginia, which has just completed a new $250,000 community house, toward which the Board of Missions appropriated $150,000. This combination Sunday-school building and neighborhood house is not only one of the best of its kind in the South, but will rank with the great parish houses of the country.

That which adds fascination to the Broad Street Church is that it has a history reaching back to the great days of the Civil War. The church was erected in 1858, on the corner of Tenth and Broad Streets, in the immediate vicinity of the State Capitol, the governor's mansion, and the City Hall. Its pastor was the Reverend James O. Duncan, D.D., one of the great preachers of the South, who was reassigned to the pulpit in 1863. During the eventful years of his pastorate thousands flocked to hear him. His influence widened and deepened until it is probable that no minister in the city accomplished more for the cause of Christ in his day. President Davis and General Lee, altho communicants of St. Paul's Episcopal Church, were frequent worshipers at Broad Street Church, due to the influence and popularity of Mr. Duncan, and when the city was evacuated, he was invited with Mrs. Duncan to a seat in the President's carriage. He remained in the city, however, to strengthen his people in their hour of adversity.

Broad Street Church had years of notable service after the Civil War, but finally the movement of population westward and the enlargement of the business district slowly emptied its pews. Seven years ago it was decided to abandon the site and to bring the eventful history of the church to an end.

But wiser councils finally prevailed. It was decided to undertake to reintrench the church in its historic parish. Rev. Fred R. Chenault was called to the pulpit from Los Angeles, and the Board of Missions made a survey of the parish under the direction of Dr. A. C. Zumbrunnen of Nashville, preparatory to the reorganization of the church's program.

The survey revealed greater opportunities of service: thousands of young people in boarding houses; a large hotel population; great numbers of women in stores, offices, and tobacco factories; near-by districts populated by families of industrial workers. In addition, the church keeps its old commanding place in the monumental center of Richmond, alongside its stately neighbor, St. Paul's Episcopal Church, which is three blocks away, and one of the general group which includes the State House, City Hall, and the former President's residence.

The new community house adjoins the church on the east. Fortunately the old church with its imposing lines, attractive auditorium and historic associations has been kept, and it is to be hoped that it will never be torn down until the years force its demolition. The community house is three stories high, with basement and roof garden additional. It contains suites of rooms for each department of the Sunday-school, an auditorium seating 700 with stage, church and Sunday-school offices, two gymnasiums with showers and lockers—one for boys and men, one for women and girls—a large and attractive roof garden for athletics, socials, and open-air meetings, rest rooms for women, club room for men, an elaborate kitchen, serving-room, and combination dining-room and social hall, a day nursery, a library. Each Sunday-school department has an assembly-room, cloak-room, wash-room, storage room, and a surrounding series of individual classrooms. These rooms are light, airy, attractively decorated, and completely and expensively furnished.

On the whole it is a wonderful plant. That which most impresses the visitor is its completeness, its solidity and attractiveness, and the success with which it combines a modern equipment for religious education with the essential features of a community house.

Since the building will be studied and copied, it is advisable to offer a few minor criticisms and suggestions. The church offices should be larger and more accessible. Instead of two, one gymnasium with separate showers and lockers would meet the needs of the parish and would allow a larger and better appointed gymnasium and equipment. The women's rest rooms are admirable, but do not provide a suitable work room and meeting room for the women's societies. Club rooms for the boys and girls and men have been sacrificed to the educational equipment, when they might have been secured by a more careful study of multiple uses of rooms. A club room or parlor, by the use of movable screens, makes a good class or department room, whereas, a classroom seldom makes a good social room. The elaborate Sunday-school equipment has forced a sacrifice of parlors and of the young people's department.

It is possible, however, to provide for almost any kind of work by the present arrangement of rooms. One notes the absence of swimming-pool and bowling alleys, but with approval, since they are expensive luxuries in churches. They require trained supervision, which few churches are able to afford. The roof garden has splendid possibilities, since it covers the space of the building and can be used two-thirds of the year.

The pastor of the Broad Street Church holds positive theories as to the lines along which the church should be developed. He is not sensational, but depends rather upon religious education, pastoral evangelism, visitation, and organized activities. He gives careful attention to the music, to public worship, and to publicity, and is developing a staff of specialists. Dr. Chenault's theory of religious education is a distinct departure from accepted methods. Instead of one director of religious education he plans two, each with recreational assistants, one for girls and women, one for boys and men. All the women's work of the church is under the direction of one woman. This sex differentiation runs through the entire work of the church and explains the two gymnasiums. All the women's work of the church is under the direction of one woman, who is responsible not only for the women's side of the Sunday-school, but for work with business women, with young women who work in factories and stores. A like director for boys and men will be provided as soon as he can be financed. One would approve of this except for the Sunday-school. A sounder educational theory would seem to be to have one director of religious education, with recreational and club assistants for the sexes, treating the educational work as a unity.

The church under the new methods has grown rapidly and has become again one of the commanding churches of Richmond and of the Methodist Episcopal Church South. Its membership has increased from a few hundred to above a thousand, and is growing steadily and rapidly. Finances have increased eightfold in a period of seven years. Another inspiring example has been given in a new Broad Street Church of what can be done in the readjustment of a church to its neighborhood. While under Methodist control, Broad Street community house is a true social center in that it is open to all and aims to serve the entire neighborhood, regardless of religious affiliations. Its development will be watched with sympathetic interest in the South and should be followed also in the North.

CHRIST AND CHRISTIANITY CREATIVE[1]

Professor C. A. BECKWITH, D.D., Chicago Theological Seminary, Chicago, Ill.

The two works which are the subject of this review could hardly have been better planned for our purpose if the authors of them had agreed upon their task, each assuming a different portion of the common aim. Each is preliminary to the other, just as the other is supplementary to the one. The reader of both feels that each is incomplete without the other. It would have served an admirable purpose if the two courses of lectures had been given in due sequence the same year to the same group of students. They are bracketed here by reason of their kinship and individual incompleteness; they belong together.

In 1921 Professor Drown of the Episcopal School in Cambridge, Massachusetts, delivered the Bohlen Lectures in Philadelphia for that year on The Creative Christ. He suggests what is required for the Christ of to-day, defines divine and human, and then inquires, What is the Incarnation. This is followed by two lectures on the Uniqueness of Christ and the Incarnate Life. The Christ for to-day must be interpreted, after the manner of the New Testament, in moral rather than in metaphysical terms. God is not a metaphysical substance but a moral being whose essence is love. Every truth about him is capable of expression in man's life. The essential reality of

> **STATIC OR DYNAMIC**
>
> The term "creative" which appears in both these titles arrests attention. It discloses a notable characteristic of present-day approach to the highest realities of the Christian religion. Not in vain did Bergson entitle his great work *Creative Evolution*. The title carries irresistible persuasion. The static is being rapidly replaced by the dynamic conception of reality. This is true of the world of scientific observation and experiment, of the social order, of all forms of the ideal; but it is nowhere more valid than with reference to Christ and Christianity.

Christ is his moral nature. God is revealed as Father, that is, as creative, and man as his son. The difference between God and man is not in the so-called attributes but in the source of them. As self-existent God is the Creator and Giver, man the creature and recipient. All other differences between God and man may be swept aside and the possibility of perfect moral unity of God and man assumed. The incarnation consists in the actualizing of that unity in Jesus Christ. This does not mean that two metaphysical natures were joined in his person, but that in him was the manifestation of the ideal unity of God and man. What relation then does Christ bear to men? His uniqueness is affirmed and that in three respects. (1) The unity of God and man is in him perfectly, in others only imperfectly, realized. (2) His origin is immediately, the origin of others is mediately, from God. (3) He alone has the power to create a new humanity in his image. The incarnation is to be conceived of not as a momentary act but as a moral process, involving the entire development of Jesus, which may be regarded from two aspects—his knowledge and his righteousness. Altho his knowledge was a growth, it was characterized by such moral and spiritual insight that it became a revelation of God. His

[1] *The Creative Christ. A Study of the Incarnation in Terms of Modern Thought.* By EDWARD S. DROWN. 5 x 7 in., 167 pp. *Creative Christianity.* By GEORGE CROSS. 5 x 7 in., 164 pp. Both published by Macmillan Company, New York, 1922.

righteousness in relation to temptation, sin, and suffering was an achievement and therefore real and progressive, and found its complete expression in the sacrifice of the cross.

In the course of the presentation many subsidiary questions are disposed of: the influence of Greek thought on the development of the doctrine of Christ; Christianity as idea rather than historical; the notion of substance as applied to God; the two natures of Christ; miracle; the kenosis. His main contention is that every truth about God is capable of application to the life of man. The meaning of Christ is therefore, first, that he has perfectly embodied all the moral values of God; and, secondly, that because these values are moral they become creative in the individual and social life of man, even as they were creative in the life of Christ.

The Nathaniel W. Taylor lectures, delivered at the 1921 convocation of Yale Divinity School, fall into four sections: the method of study; the discovery of the perfect personality; the making of the better world; and the power of cosmic interpretation. In the first section Professor Cross shows that the genius of Christianity is to be sought not in any exact teaching of the New Testament, not even in a few possibly authentic words of Jesus, but in the worth of that which is conveyed to us in the New Testament. Our interest in Jesus' words and doings is primarily not that of scientific knowledge or even reports of eye and ear witnesses, but in the impression which Jesus made upon the early Christian community as declared in the New Testament writings. If we seek further for the creative force of the Christian religion we shall find it outside of the great creeds and confessions, the liturgies, and the organized activities of the Church, in a study of the whole career of Christian people in its great general characters.

The subtle suggestion is made that the Christian religion may be just "the native inner power of the human spirit coming into action in a distinctive way"; the coming of Jesus may have "released hidden energies." Christianity, which has no existence apart from people, and especially experiences of the common people, is continuously reorganizing the forces resident in them.

This creative activity has taken three directions. (1) The progressive discovery of the perfect personality. As a historic movement the coming of Jesus Christ into the world is creative both of a new experience and of a new estimate of the meaning and value of human life. There was also originated a new communion and a new appreciation of the members of this fellowship which was destined to create a final unity of men in a higher order of experience. It has also introduced a juster valuation of man as man, so that even for the lowest there exists the potentiality of the perfect life. All of this is to be referred to Christ's inexhaustible impact upon his followers as the one who incarnated the most precious hopes of the race. In this capacity for infinite moral and spiritual transformation we have the revelation of perfect personality.

(2) After describing the background of mythology, the fact of death, and the natural feeling about the future life, the lecturer shows how the idea of the better world arose. Profound moral dissatisfaction with things as they are gave birth to a longing for a better world, whether elsewhere or here below. From the Jewish source has come the apocalyptic hope, the Christian catastrophic view of death; from the Greek conception of the spiritual as the alone real has come the renunciation of earthly good; from the Christian point of view, however, the meaning of this hope takes on a different form.

The spirit of Jesus, as it seeks to fulfil itself not in a self-contained sufficiency but in the lives of men, lays hold of the natural forms of the common life, in order, first, that it may progressively realize itself; secondly, that it may find in others the necessary organs for its self expression, and finally, that it may eventually bring about the unity of the human race. The genius of Christianity lies in its creation of an increasingly better social order determined by the personality disclosed in Jesus Christ.

(3) In the final chapter—on the power of cosmic interpretation—the exposition is carried forward by the use of an illustration which outlines substantially human progress, culminating in Christian experience. The primitive man who turned a rough stone into a tool initiated a process in which, making his tool beautiful as well as useful, he passed from artizan to artist, put a new interpretation on nature, and introduced morality and the social complex to his fellow men. In addition to these creative achievements, when religion is united with science the world takes on a religious meaning in which a cosmic philosophy originates. This cosmic philosophy, having its roots in the idea of Christian personality perfected in sacrificial self-giving, shows the universe as a sphere for the realization of personalities after this highest vicarious type which becomes creative from Jesus Christ.

Unusual space is here devoted to a synopsis of these courses of lectures which have so much in common, partly by reason of their intrinsic worth, and partly because they are symptomatic of tendencies which promise much for the future of Christianity.

At no moment in the life of Jesus was his spirit a fixed and final quantity—not at his birth, not at his baptism, not at the transfiguration, not in the garden of Gethsemane, not even on the cross. At the time of his death neither his intellectual nor his spiritual development had reached its limit. It would be idle to speculate how with a lengthened earthly experience his spirit would have still further unfolded. It is enough to be assured that it would have continued according to the same type and on the same general lines as the life which we know of. We can, however, conceive of what it might have become if prolonged toward the end of the first century: his ministry like that of St. Paul would necessarily have been thrust out of the immediate Jewish circle into the world of Greek and Roman culture and ideals. But, however extended his years and widened the circle of his activity, the development of his consciousness would never have reached its climax, for it contained a principle of perpetual growth.

The hope of the continuance of this type of life lay in its power of initiating a never-to-be-completed development in the community which Jesus founded, to be referred to the creative spirit resident in him. This is one reason why it has been so difficult to define Christ and Christianity, why no wholly satisfactory life of Jesus has been or can be written, and why those who undertake to describe historical Christianity never fully satisfy the reader: there is always a plus or elusive element which escapes the writer. We have the synoptic Jesus and the Johannine Christ, the historical Jesus and the essential Christ, the Christ of history and the Christ of faith. And with reference to Christianity, a definition of it which answers for the apostolic age, the Scholastic period, or the Reformation of the sixteenth century is inadequate for to-day. When we have described Christ and Christianity in the most comprehensive possible terms, we are aware that we have left much, perhaps the best, unspoken; both of these are puissant and prophetic of far greater achievements and of

"something evermore about to be."

This view of Christ and Christianity as creative has several decided advantages. One is that it relieves us from that minute exegetical study of the New Testament which has been both a feature of the curricula of theological seminaries and an oppressive ideal in ministerial study. As these writers point out, the essential reality for us in the words and deeds of Jesus is the moral values. This is not to discredit scholarship but to set for it a different task. The present writer recalls having spent the chief part of a seminary year in the New Testament department in an exhaustive study of the first letter to the Corinthians, wherein the object was not so much to acquire knowledge of the contents and meaning of the experience of these people in relation to Jesus Christ and the development of Christianity as by the comparison of MSS and by careful and prolonged exegesis, aided by lexicon and grammar, to decide upon the authentic text and to hunt down every shade of meaning which had ever been put upon it by scholars ancient and modern. This is indeed for some scholars a legitimate task, but it should never take the place of the far more vital inquiry as to what moral and spiritual values first transcendently real in Jesus' own consciousness were communicated by him to his followers, as disclosed in the gospels, the Acts, and the epistles of the New Testament. More than this the procedure inculcates upon the minister about-to-be a mistaken ideal.

Another long period covering two hours a week was devoted to an investigation of the New Testament evidence concerning the divinity or deity of Jesus Christ. In this course each of the outstanding texts of the New Testament was separately investigated with a thoroughness which left no stone unturned. The judgment respecting each text was that the evidence slightly preponderated for or against, and when the whole was summed up the conclusion took the same indecisive form; one felt, what later years only served to confirm, that if the divinity of Christ rested on so insecure a basis as the citation of proof texts, however well authenticated, then one must assume either a waiting or else an indifferent attitude until something capable of creating conviction became available. Indeed there is not a single truth of the Christian religion which is valid for the sole reason that it depends upon statements of the New Testament for its proof. If it is not true for other reasons than that proof texts may be cited in its behalf, then it is not true at all.

This general point of view provides relief in another direction; that is, in defining Christianity. Many attempts have been made along this line, in the belief that its essential nature can be thus adequately set forth. As one of the world-religions, it is felt that like Buddhism and Mohammedanism it lends itself to accurate definition. But when the undertaking is completed, the result provokes a further effort. It is presented from the point of view of dogmatic content, as a type of religious experience, as a social movement, or as an eschatological program. Some have sought to determine its nature by a study of its earliest history, with a view of returning to the apostolic order. Others have believed that it could better be described by consideration of its final form; but this expectation is doomed to disappointment, for since it is a development it can be subject to no end. There is indeed finality to it;

but this means not that "Finis" will mark the end of its progress but that in its essential nature and in the spirit of its Founder it possesses a principle of unlimited purposive unfolding. As implied by Professor Cross we can define Christianity neither by Jesus' words and deeds which his followers ascribed to him nor even by the words and deeds which are supposed to be authentic as his very own. We have also seen that we can not define Christianity by any historical cross-section of it.

Christianity appears to be a very simple thing, if we go back to about A.D. 30 and think not merely of the words and deeds of Jesus but as "he wrote himself down in the hearts of men around him." If we confine our attention to that bright dawn, it seems comparatively easy to decide just what Christianity is, but in this very apparent ease lies the danger of a serious misunderstanding. At first it may have been chiefly an eschatological hope with strict ethical precepts for the brief interim. Later it was concentrated in a powerful missionary impulse with the same insistence on the ethical ideal. But it did not long hold to the simple program of either its Founder or his earliest followers. As a spirit of life it soon called to its aid the Greek ideals of beauty, of ethics, and of speculative reason. As it pushed on into the West it availed itself of the Roman administrative program. It found in the desert ideals of life which sharpened its impulse to renunciation and world-flight. This appropriation of elements in the existing social order has been the continual characteristic of Christianity. Once these have been appropriated they are regarded as an integral part of it. Perhaps a supreme instance of this is seen in the dogmas and administration and many customs of the Roman Catholic Church.

This fact need occasion no surprise. For first, no spirit of life can function without a body; again, as a developing entity Christianity could not remain in the embryonic form of its earliest period; finally, since it is not alien to the human spirit but is its most natural and therefore inevitable expression, it may be regarded as the fuller awakening of the human spirit in a definite moment of its development to an aspect of life of which it has hitherto been only in part aware. It will not, however, remain an isolated experience, out of relation to the whole of life, but tends to permeate the entire consciousness and transmute it into its own law and end. When we speak of the personal Christian life or of the social consciousness, we mean not that these exist apart from the world they live in or are already perfected, but that they are at home in a world where their creative power may be active.

A suggestion of Professor Drown respecting the two-nature doctrine of the person of Christ will bring relief to many preachers who ever since their seminary days have been troubled with this doctrine. Coming as it does from a source unquestionably orthodóx, it will carry the greater weight. The dogma of two metaphysical natures in Christ arose at a time when these natures were differently conceived of from what is at present understood by "nature." There was then no other form in which the men of that day could so state it that it would conserve the interests of faith. Because the metaphysics which underlay this conception changed but little for fifteen hundred years, during all that time the statement itself remained in force. And to-day, in quarters where the same metaphysics is in force the two-nature doctrine continues not only unchallenged but defended with the utmost vigor and rigor.

Another type of thought has, however, arisen. Values which it was supposed could exist only if enshrined in a particular setting are now seen to be capable of a very different connection. "Substance" sustains no essential relation to ethical and redemptive action. Success has never crowned the attempt to find a reasonable relation between the two substances divine and human, radically different in nature, and between the two substances and the one personal consciousness of Jesus, so that the person thus resulting shall be real and capable of real love and self-giving. This relation has therefore been declared a "mystery"; men have been required to accept the dogma on the authority of the Church, by which it was originated and imposed. But the mystery was of man's devising, its elements speculative and imaginary. Accordingly, when its place is taken by a simple reality which is at home in the common life of men, nothing is lost, but on the other hand great gains are possible. It is always to be remembered that the consciousness of value precedes the interpretation of value, and that in the interpretation of value the reigning philosophy is adopted as the vehicle by which the interpretation gets expression. Value is permanent, interpretation transient; one is creative, the other a product of the creative activity. Since value arose first in experience and is the essential thing, its existence is not destroyed even if no interpretation is found to be adequate or if an interpretation once acceptable is changed for another. What philosophy can not give, philosophy can not take away. So much needed to be said in justification of Professor Drown's position and to allay a very natural feeling that in surrendering the two-nature doctrine of Christ and substituting for it love as the essential reality in him one is disloyal to his faith. In doing so, however, one is not disloyal but merely disowns a certain type of Greek thought.

If the interpretation of the creative Christ offered by Professor Drown could have been suggested at the beginning of the nineteenth century, it would have provided a way out of the controversy which caused bitter feeling and a split in one of the historic denominations of New England. I do not mean that the two parties would necessarily have accepted his conception of Christ, but something like it would have marked out a common path which both could have embroidered to suit their individual fancy, and they could have agreed to walk together as Christian brethren. Even now it is not perhaps too late for some platform on which they could harmoniously cooperate.

The emphasis upon the moral rather than the metaphysical in the interpretation of Jesus Christ is destined to draw denominations into agreement and ultimately perhaps into vital union. When it is seen not only that nothing has to be surrendered which is real in the Savior but that all the values which feed loyalty to him have been conserved, the way will have been paved for a sympathetic cooperation among Christian forces now divided, which will enable Christ and Christianity to be more effectually creative.

An attempt is made in the works to which attention is now directed to ascertain and redefine the genius of Christ and Christianity. This might well be called the central aim of both courses of lectures. On this point Professor Cross has two suggestive statements. According to the first the genius of Christianity lies in the worth of the New Testament message; according to the second it lies in creating a social order increasingly determined by the personality disclosed in Jesus Christ. This double statement points to several very interesting conditions. The fact that he offers two descriptions of the genius of Christianity shows that he approaches the matter by the way not of abstract interest but of living Christian experience. Here definition gives place to description and description singles out particular aspects, now one, now another, to serve a practical need. It therefore never aims at exhaustive completeness, but at a partial, vivid, and pragmatic presentation of material. Accordingly, at one time the genius of Christ and Christianity is seen to be ethical and redemptive, at another centered in the individual, at yet another aiming at social regeneration. It is thought of as finding its highest expression in dogma or in administrative organization. It is conceived as adapted primarily, if not exclusively, to this world, or on the other hand it is proclaimed as other-worldliness for which the earthly life is a period of probation and expectancy.

These and many other diverse aspects of Christianity are indeed tantalizing to one who seeks the genius of Christianity in a single aspect, but to one who discovers these to be revelations of its inexhaustible richness it is full of comfort and inspiration. For the discovery of the genius of any organism and particularly of one of great complexity of structure and function is always difficult, if not impossible. Even so common and apparently so simple a fact as life escapes scientific analysis. Whether it is a purely physico-chemical combination, or whether there is truth in vitalism, or what its real nature is, no one appears to be wise enough to tell. Ever since democracy threw its spell over human hopes men have sought to ascertain its exact genius. And now the Bolshevist in Russia, the Socialist in Germany, the Labor Unionist in America, and a hundred other groups, renouncing all other historical experiments, believe they have discovered the ultimate principle of social well-being. That can not, however, be a complete democracy which suppresses or ignores so many precious social values; it can never be complete until every interest of human life is recognized, developed, and harmonized. And the genius of democracy is ever pressing on, with frequent mistakes indeed, toward this flying goal.

The genius of Christianity also, just because it is creative, urges to an infinite variety of developing forms, some appearing to be contrary to one another, others agreeing and sympathetic. It manifests itself in revivals of religion as well as in Christian nurture. It is at home in the wayside shrine, in the simple country church "far from the madding crowd," and in the stately cathedral in the heart of the great city. It is in the song of the mother crooning to her baby in arms, in the deed of the soldier laying down his life on the battle-field, in the mart of commerce where the world's business is transacted, in the mind of the judge arriving at a decision which shall become a binding precedent for a thousand years. It steadies the soul of the youth meeting his first great temptation, it gives to the scholar sincerity and poise as he searches for truth amidst the fierce rivalry of conflicting philosophies. It is with the monk in his solitary cell, with the social worker in the city slum, with the pioneer pushing westward to subjugate new lands, with the missionary losing himself in darkest Africa, with the union labor leader, the capitalist, and the arbiter seeking a just solution of their problem.

It is the genius of Christianity to enter into every form of life as a creative spirit, rearranging, transforming, renewing every element of it,— like nature, everywhere present, active, expressing itself in infinite profusion and manifoldness. If, as Professor Cross intimates, it should turn out to be true that Christianity is the native capacity of the human spirit acting in a distinctive way, releasing energies which were otherwise latent, then there is no field of experience alien to it, nor can any limit be set to its possible development. And because it is nature acting in a distinctive way, it can not be imposed from without; the secret of it lies in the inner awakening to the ideal as that which may progressively pass into the actual in the common life of men.

THE PREACHER AND THE OLD TESTAMENT

I. THE HISTORICAL NARRATIVE

Professor ALEXANDER REID GORDON, D.D., Litt.D., Presbyterian College, Montreal, Canada

There was a time when the Old Testament was the preacher's favorite text-book. As a moral and religious standard it enjoyed equal influence with the New. It had the advantage of setting forth the things of faith in a concrete, pictorial fashion that appealed strongly to the imagination. Apart from its spiritual interest, it was the recognized authority in the domain of scientific and historical knowledge. Equipped from this arsenal, then, the preacher was furnished completely "for teaching, for reproof, for correction, for instruction in righteousness."

In recent years the situation has strangely altered. Science has demonstrated the unscientific character of the accounts of creation in Genesis. Archeology has thrown back the history of the race thousands of years before the supposed origin of man. Criticism has called in question much of the Old Testament narrative. The higher ethical consciousness of our age has challenged the primitive morality of Israel. Distracted by so many cross currents, the preacher is tempted to steer clear of the Old Testament, and to seek a safer channel in the pure waters of the New.

The reaction is healthy, in so far as it sets the perspective aright. We are Christians, not Jews. The norm of faith is "the truth as it is in Jesus." And this truth is mirrored to us in the gospels and epistles of the New Testament. Yet the preacher will lose much by undue neglect of the older Scriptures. Through them plays the broadening light of revelation. In this light we may still see light. In this light we may still lead others to the light. Only we must view the light steadily, and view it whole, as it shines "more and more unto the perfect day."

In the first of these articles we deal with the Old Testament narrative in the light of modern criticism. Afterwards we shall discuss the poetry of religion and the problem of moral and religious development.

For a full generation the storm center of criticism has been the hexateuch, the first six books of the Bible. As the result of incessant inquiry and discussion the books have been analyzed into four main elements: two popular documents, the Jahwistic and Elohistic (J and E), embodying the primitive traditions of Israel as they took shape respectively in Judah and

Ephraim, the former belonging to the middle of the ninth century B.C. (about the time of Jehoshaphat), the latter to the first half of the following century (probably during the reign of Jeroboam II); a prophetic revision of the old law of Moses in the book of Deuteronomy (D), dating from the time of fiery persecution under Manasseh, or the bright dawn of Josiah's reign (the close of the eighth, or beginning of the seventh century); and the priestly revision of both history and law in the Priestly Code (P), compiled not long before Ezra's epoch-making visit to Jerusalem (444 B.C.).

While the fires played round the hexateuch, a quieter process has been at work on the other historical books. But the result has been essentially the same. The books of Judges, Samuel, and Kings are now seen to consist of popular narratives of Jahwistic and Elohistic quality and origin, interspersed with fragments of ancient poetry on the one hand, and extracts from civic and priestly records on the other, set in a Deuteronomic or prophetic framework. With the latter element may be classed the stories of prophetic activity incorporated in the books of Amos, Hosea, Isaiah, Jeremiah, and Ezekiel. The priestly revision of the history is found in Chronicles, with its supplement in the memoirs of Ezra and Nehemiah. In addition, the books of Ruth, Esther, Jonah, and the narrative parts of Daniel are fine examples of the parabolic literature which was so much used by the teachers of later Judaism, and notably by Jesus Christ, for the purpose of illustrating or enforcing spiritual truth.

As a whole, then, the historical books of the Old Testament are composed of popular, prophetic, priestly, and parabolic elements.

In popular narratives the idealizing influence must always be reckoned with. Primitive peoples delight to weave around their traditions a garland of simple poetry. From this impulse arise the wondrous creations of myth and legend. If Israel had a history like other nations, we can hardly deny them a share in these creations. And, indeed, the tone and color of the narratives in Genesis (chaps. 1-11) bring them into the closest possible relation with the myths of ancient Babylonia. The stories of the patriarchs, Abraham, Isaac, Jacob, and Joseph, are as clearly national legends. Even when we enter the world of sober history—with Moses and the exodus—the horizon is still lit up by the glowing rays of popular imagination. All through the period of the judges, and as late at least as the heroic age of Elijah and Elisha, the legendary impulse remains at work. Prose melts into poetry, fact into fancy.

For many serious minds the use of the terms myth and legend is sufficient to condemn them. But this is an unwarranted prejudice. Myths and legends are neither empty fables nor "pious frauds." They are both natural products of the human intelligence at certain stages of its development. Myths are the concrete molds in which nations embody their early thoughts about religion, as well as their first attempts to understand the nature of the world and man. We may perhaps describe them as "primitive philosophies of religion." As such, they are the purest revelation of the genius of peoples just passing from infancy to adolescence, the mirror of their religious and moral thoughts, feelings, and aspirations. Legend, on its part, is "primitive history," the history of the nation arrayed in the poetic dress it receives through centuries of contact with the fresh, creative national spirit. As the deposit of popular tradition, it always clusters round a solid nucleus of historical fact. And this nucleus is probably much larger than the Western mind is often inclined to allow. But the value of legend is not so much in the body of fact which it yields as in the ideals which it enshrines. For through the instinctive play of national imagination the heroes of the prehistoric age become ideal types of character, immortal expressions of the people's will to do and to be.

If this be so, the attitude of the preacher to the earlier chapters of the Bible is evident. He will not treat them as scientific explanations of the origin of things, or as exact historical records of human development. But he will cherish them as the morning beams of revelation, the heralds of the perfect day. And he will seek to elucidate the spiritual truth that underlies them. With the authors of the creation stories he will trace the presence of God behind the outward movements of nature and life. While recognizing that many of their ideas about God are crude and childish, he will show that the God who inspired them is the good and gracious Father of our Lord Jesus Christ, who made man in his image, loves to have fellowship with him, seeks his highest welfare, and helps him to reach the end of his being. The story of the fall he will treat as a profound analysis of the workings of sin in every man. At the same time he will show from the story how God seasons justice with mercy, punishment with pardon. The gospel of forgiving love he will see shining with equal radiance through the tragedy of Cain and the colossal judgment of the flood. But he will find a still more congenial field in the stories of the patriarchs. As studies of human character these stories are unsurpassed. As Schultz says, "Abraham is the peerless type of the faithful man of God, for Old Testament revelation a more instructive figure than all the kings of Israel from Saul

to Zedekiah, while in Jacob-Israel the Israelite is more truly delineated than in any personage mentioned in Kings or Chronicles." Isaac is the model of simple goodness. And Joseph is the knightly figure, "without fear and without reproach," of commanding ability and resource, yet of scrupulous faith and honor, the very soul of purity, straightforwardness, and generosity.

Conscientious preachers are often sensitive about using Biblical materials of whose historical character they are in doubt. Their scruples are worthy of all respect. They rest, however, on an outworn theory of inspiration. We do not shrink from quoting Shakespeare, Milton, and Tennyson, even when they deviate as far as possible from prosaic fact. It is, indeed, when they soar the highest that we value them most. If we had only a due sense of the greatness of God's ways with man, and of the "divers portions and divers manners" in which he reveals himself, we should not stumble at the presence of poetic elements in the Biblical narrative. We should rather welcome them, as we welcome the expressions of fine art in every form. And we should make a real effort to render them intelligible to our people. I do not mean that we should lightly brandish the words "myth" and legend." But we should seize what opportunities we have of explaining the manifold, human, and progressive side of revelation. When this side of revelation is clearly understood, the bogies raised by science and archeology cease to trouble.

A personal testimony may not be out of place. When the writer was an arts student, introduced for the first time to modern historical methods, he was sorely puzzled by these old stories in Genesis. Fortunately he attended a Bible class conducted by one who is now a distinguished Scottish principal. In this class the problem of the Old Testament was treated from the critical point of view. At once his difficulties were removed, and he felt free to study for the ministry with an honest mind. Later on, as pastor of a small country charge, he discust the same questions with his young men and women to the mutual benefit of himself and them. At present he enjoys the ministry of an able representative of the modern school, who every winter gives a series of lectures on aspects of faith in the light of present-day thought. Among other subjects he has dealt with the inspiration of the Bible, stating the critical position as frankly and fairly as possible. The interest awakened by these lectures was remarkable. And the result has been wholly for the good.

In the more strictly historical parts of the narrative a large field lies before the preacher. As a rule he will find that the field is richest where it is illumined most freely by the divine light of poetic feeling and imagination. And this light is never absent from the popular page. Even when we are in touch with almost contemporary records—as in the story of David—the narrative is set in strong dramatic outline, with a full play of light and shade, which makes it singularly effective as a source of moral and religious instruction.

The prophetic element offers another very fruitful field to the preacher. This field is one that has been thoroughly cultivated by recent critical scholarship. We can now see the heroic figures of the prophets as they stood out on the background of their age, bringing home to the conscience alike of king and of commoner the word of the Lord that burned so fiercely in their own hearts. No true preacher can breathe the atmosphere in which they lived without being braced and strengthened for his work. He will find in the story of their

words and deeds, too, themes of unusual interest and importance for the modern mind.

The application of prophetic principles in the book of Deuteronomy is a real mine of precious metal for the preacher. Much of the legislative material, no doubt, belongs to primitive times. But the spirit that suffuses the book—love to God because of the love with which he has loved us—is the motive power of every true life. Its constant appeal to humanity as the fulfilling of the law brings it into vital relation with the New Testament. It is significant that Jesus drew from Deuteronomy the first great commandment: "Thou shalt love the Lord thy God with all thy heart, and with all thy soul, and with all thy mind." While he found the second commandment in another part of the Pentateuch, he turned instinctively to Deuteronomy for illustrations of its working. The book was never far from his heart and lips. And where he led, his disciples will be wise to follow.

The priestly element yields, in comparison, very barren soil. Nuggets of pure gold are, it is true, to be found even here. As has just been suggested, the second commandment of Jesus— "Thou shalt love thy neighbor as thyself"—is drawn from Lev. 19:18. One or two fine stories, like the repentance and conversion of Manasseh, appear in the books of Chronicles. In addition, the memoirs of Nehemiah introduce us to one of the most attractive characters in the Old Testament. But as a whole the priestly narrative is a mass of hard, dry rules which are wholly at variance with the spirit of Christian freedom. It need hardly be said that the modern preacher cannot translate the paraphernalia of Levitical worship into symbols of Christian truth. The days when one could preach on "Christ in Leviticus" are gone beyond recall. For this we should be thankful. The Christ we exalt as Friend and Savior is to be sought, not in the "weak and beggarly elements" from which he set us free, but in the gospels where he reveals himself "with open face."

The parabolic literature recalls us afresh to the waters of life. Ruth is a charming idyll of simple faith and life, from which the preacher may draw lessons even for the vastly more complex life of the present. The narrative parts of Daniel are a rich source of inspiration to Christian heroes of every age. Esther stands on a much lower level. The undisguisedly secular tone of the book, its crude nationalism, and its strongly vindictive spirit remove it poles apart from the warm and spacious atmosphere of Ruth and Daniel. So far as we can trace, Jesus Christ made no allusion whatever to Esther. Apparently he reacted against the whole temper of the book. And the modern preacher will doubtless feel much as he did regarding it.

The book of Jonah, on the other hand, reaches the high-water mark of Old Testament inspiration. Unhappily the question of its historical character has largely blinded men to its true value. Once we grasp the parabolic quality of the book, we can do justice to its spirit and purpose.

Jonah is the typical Israelite of his day, jealous of his spiritual prerogatives, and eager for the annihilation of the heathen nations rather than their reception into the kingdom of God.

The object of the book is to bring the people to a better mind: to make them realize their responsibilities to the world lying in darkness about them, and inspire them with something of God's passion for humanity. The conception of God is singularly pure and lofty. He is the God of all men. His ears are ever open to the prayer of sincerity, while his heart flows out in sympathy to the weak and helpless, the little children, and even the cattle, doomed to die for no wrong that they have done. And they are God's true people who have most of his heart of love. We can understand, then, how the book appealed to the imagination of Jesus, how he pored over its gracious message, and found in Jonah the "sign" of his own ministry. The preacher who has learned at his school will not lose himself in the mere details of the story, but will lead his hearers into the living heart of it. Thus he will impress them with the sweep of God's redeeming grace. And he will bear them along the channel of that grace till it reaches its ocean fulness in Christ.

COMMENT AND OUTLOOK

By Our London Correspondent

The Aramaic Origin of the Fourth Gospel

Since Grotius first noticed what Dr. Lightfoot referred to as the "Hebræo-Aramaic mold" in which the language of that gospel was cast, nothing has been done to verify that thesis until the recent appearance of an important volume by Dr. C. F. Burney, in which that eminent scholar makes a good case for concluding that the character of the language of St. John's gospel is due to the fact that it is a translation from an Aramaic original. He parts company with Bishop Lightfoot in refusing to accept a Hebrew element. There are Hebraisms in St. Luke, he points out; that is, reminiscences of the Hebrew

Old Testament *via* the Septuagint. In St. Mark, however, and still more in the Fourth Gospel, there are distinctly Aramaic traits, not due to Old Testament influences but to the fact that we have here a translation of an original Aramaic document.

If Dr. Burney's thesis can be proved—and he has gone some way toward proving it—then "the figment of Alexandrine influence upon the author" must be held to be finally exploded. In other words, the Logos doctrine of St. John is Palestinian and not derived from Philo. The bearing of this upon the Johannine problem is obvious, and conservative scholars will doubtless exploit it in the interests of the Johannine authorship. Dr. Burney himself leans toward the hypothesis which would make it the work of John the Presbyter, but possibly the scholarship of to-morrow will tend to revert to the traditional view. I have lately come across a circle of brilliant young scholars of a distinctly advanced type and was struck by the fact that two-thirds of them, while holding radical views on many New Testament problems, were wholeheartedly convinced of the Johannine authorship. One looks forward with interest to the books of these young explorers in a difficult field.

The Pillar of Cloud—What Was It?

After centuries of Biblical study and investigation the symbolism of the Old Testament still remains largely unelucidated. Theories there are in plenty, and a few well-established interpretations; but a great deal of ritual and symbol remains to the cautious student a veritable pillar of cloud. In this nebulous region must be included that actual pillar of cloud which went before the children of Israel by day as they marched through the wilderness. Where did that symbol originate? To what cult can it be traced? Lieut.-Colonel L. A. Waddell, writing in the *Expository Times*, says it is derived from An, Anna, or Anu, the father-god of the Semitic Chaldees, a lunar deity, such as Sayce and others think that Abraham's God was also. That An was a lunar god we learn from the official Akkadian rituals for his service, which have been preserved in cuneiform tablets. There we are told that when, at the solar festival, the images of the solar divinities are brought into the temple, the images of An and his lunar satellites are to be veiled. Hence the "cloud." Dr. Waddell thinks it not improbable that we have here the source of the title of *anan* applied in the Old Testament to the pillar of cloud and the appearance of *An* or *Ann* in Hebrew personal names. He also thinks that the Sin or Moon-cloud title for the residence of the lunar god An may supply us with the key to the lost source and meaning of the names applied by the early Hebrews to their several chief residences in company with their divine cloud—Sin, Sinai, Zin and finally Zion, the interchange of "z" and "s" being a common dialectic change. According to Dr. Waddell, then, it would appear probable that the early Israelites worshiped the lunar father-god An in their "pillar of cloud" and named their sacred abodes after his residence. In time, however, they forgot his identity, just as Abraham's god, *El Shaddai*, was forgotten by the time of Moses.

Blurring the Frontier Lines

It still remains one of the characteristics of the present day that certain quasi-mystical Christian writers seek to demonstrate their breadth of outlook by blurring the frontiers between Christianity and the religions of the East, and presenting us with a Buddhacized or Brahmanized Christianity which, attractive enough to men of undogmatic mind, is exceedingly irritating to those with any sense of history or of logic. The theosophical movement began after this manner; where it finally landed, unbiased students of the development of Mrs. Besant and Mr. Leadbeater may easily ascertain. Outside the theosophical circle, we have among us a veteran writer who, beginning as an old-fashioned evangelical Christian of the "Mildmay" type, is to-day somewhat difficult to locate religiously. I refer to Mrs. E. A. Gordon, the author of several remarkable books on popular comparative religion, among them a critically vulnerable, but none the less deeply suggestive, book on *The Temples of the Orient*. Mrs. Gordon has taken up her abode in Tokyo and become immersed in Japanese Mahayana Buddhism, which, so she tells us in her latest book on "Asian Christology," is identical with Christian doctrine. In this she has followed that interesting man, the Buddhist abbot of Chioin, who had traveled in Western lands and come to the conclusion that the early Christian symbolism was identical with that found in Korean and Japanese temples. His dictum that "Buddha and Christ are one, only one Great Way," is endorsed by Mrs. Gordon, and, one imagines, by a growing proportion of the half-educated Christian public in revolt against narrowness. In our reaction against the old-time missionary apologetic which sought to exalt Christianity by vilifying other religions, we are tending to forget that our only justification for missionary work is not the superiority of Christianity over other religions—one agrees with Mrs. Gordon that this boasting about the superiority of our religion is the reverse of admirable—but its uniqueness. To restate the grounds of that uniqueness is a desideratum of the hour.

Professor Peake and the Traditionalists

Professor Peake has been breaking a lance with certain obscurantists who have attacked his position on the question of Old Testament criticism. At a recent meeting of that most reactionary of associations, the Victoria Institute, Dr. St. Clair Tisdall discussed the bearing on the date of Daniel of the new linguistic evidence derived from the Aramaic papyri of Elephantine. Col. Mackinlay, a leading member of the Bible League, in opening the discussion accused Professor Peake, and incidently Dr. Driver, of being ignorant of these discoveries; and, indeed, when Dr. Tisdall's paper appeared in print, it was patent that he ignored the fact that in the ninth edition of his "Introduction" Dr. Driver had entered fully into the evidence of the papyri. This, however, is only a side issue. What has put Dr. Peake on the war-path is the claim of another champion of the traditional position (Rev. John Thomas) who declares that there are hundreds of competent English scholars who repudiate the Grafian criticism and will have none of Wellhausen. To this Professor Peake makes the pertinent reply that if such is the case, why do not these scholars produce a volume of work to strengthen the traditional position? It is surely very strange that, while those they call the destructive critics are so hectically busy, they should content themselves with issuing a few popular books and Bible dictionaries, and leave the vast field covered in England by such works as the *International Critical Commentary* to the enemy? Where can the student or the intelligent layman get a really up-to-date view of the traditional position reenforced by the new archeological discoveries? Dr. Peake is quite merciless on the point. Either you are wrong, he says in effect, or the hundreds of competent scholars of whom you speak exist only in your imagination; or, if you are right, then the more shame on them for so flagrantly neglecting their duty and leaving the field to the destructive critics.

Dr. Jowett on Peace through the Churches

The recent International Conference of the World Alliance at Copenhagen has impressed it upon many of our religious leaders that if we are to have peace on earth it will come not through the diplomatists but through the ambassadors of the cross. Dr. Jowett, who for some time past has been advocating a common organization of churches, Catholic and Protestant, in the interests of peace, has returned from Copenhagen more firmly convinced than ever that the world will once more be plunged into war, and that perhaps more speedily than we think, unless the churches can "fashion some sort of instrument which can effectively express to governments the convictions of those who claim to live under the sway of the highest moral ideal. . . . The Church does not believe half enough in her power to direct the course of governments. There is not the slightest doubt that the decision of the United States government to join with representatives of Great Britain, France, and Italy in making an investigation into the atrocities against Christian minorities in the East is an illustration of the power of Christian public sentiment when clearly focused and expressed."

This badly needed saying. But in estimating the difficulties in the way of such organization one must not forget that in the past the individual churches have been culpably remiss in creating a right opinion among their own members. Peace talk of a kind there has always been, and also a considerable amount of support of peace measures from purely utilitarian motives. Any movement for effecting international friendship through the churches must include as an integral part of its policy an educational campaign among the rank and file of church membership. We need a popular Christian peace literature in which the plea for international peace is based, not upon political and economic benefit, but upon fundamental spiritual principles. In the last resort, our "will to peace" will be determined by our will to Christian faith. We need more than enthusiastic leadership at peace conferences: we need an informed Christian conviction among the "common folk" within the churches.

Bolshevism and the Church in Russia

Attention has been called in these columns recently to the plight of the Russian Church,[1] and if I return to the subject now, it is in order to report on recent developments, and also to appeal to American readers to agitate on behalf of the persecuted Christians in that tragic country. Matters have now come to a crisis. It was clear from the beginning that behind the Bolshevist persecution of the church lay the conviction on the part of the Bolshevist leaders that their materialist psychology had proved fallacious, and that their appeal to purely economic motives had failed. The Russian people had remained spiritual at heart, and the government was afraid. A wild but justified alarm lies behind the present intensifying of persecution. Bolshevism is afraid of the people, afraid of a revived and spiritualized church which is fast winning back, not only the peasantry and many of the soldiers, but also

---

[1] See The Homiletic Review for August, p. 112.

leading intellectuals. When "red" soldiery begins openly to make the sign of the cross and to go to confession, there is every reason for the revolutionaries to tremble in their shoes. Lenine and his advisers were far too shrewd not to realize that the only chance of overcoming a religious force is by quasi-religious weapons; and so a self-appointed "Supreme Church Administration" composed of clerical "creatures" of Bolshevism has been called into being, and its first act, as is well known, has been to force the Patriarch Tikhon into retirement. It is now dismissing, and frequently arresting and "trying," all priests who don't belong to the "New Church" party. The people, however, are in ever-increasing opposition, and wherever the Bolshevist Bishop Antonin and his clergy conduct services there are disturbances. This will inevitably evoke a new bout of bitter persecution, and we who realize that the salvation of Russia depends upon a revival of her ancient national church and Christian faith must not leave our brethren in Christ without the most effective support we can give.

"A Beam in Darkness"

The phrase was used by an English artist on his return from Oberammergau. Germany, he said, is not beyond spiritual renewal as long as Oberammergau is possible. He contrasted the exquisite spiritual beauty—so homely and yet so exalted—of Anton Lang's "Christus" with the pictures of the crucifixion by new German artists which disfigure the galleries of Berlin, Dresden, and Leipzig. At Oberammergau not even the presence of the ubiquitous non-religious tourist can take away from the depth and reverence of the religious feeling which makes the Passion Play an act of worship. As for the "common people," they live so vividly in the scenes of the great drama of redemption that on one occasion when "Judas" inadvertently left the theater in his stage dress he narrowly escaped being roughly handled by the peasantry.

But even apart from Oberammergau there are signs of religious awakening among the hitherto hostile or indifferent masses, both in Germany and in France. An English visitor to Leipzig was wandering through the art gallery and paused before a beautiful picture by Uhde, showing a very sweet and patient Savior surrounded by some very stolid and typically German children. As he stood there a little girl in rags came in dragging by the hand her small brother. Dirty and unkempt, with somewhat coarse, dull faces, these children stood in front of the picture. Then suddenly there broke from the girl's lips the half-smothered cry *Wunderschön!* ("amazingly beautiful") and the children stood in silence as if they meant to stand there forever totally absorbed in the vision of the Christ. This reminds one of the story of a recent traveler in France, who also watched some children before a picture of the crucifixion. "Poor wretch!" one exclaimed. "He looks as if he were crying. Who is he, and why is he treated so disgracefully? It makes my blood boil to look at it." Not one of these children had heard the story of Jesus—all they knew was the *République* and *à bas les prêtres!* But as long as there are sacred pictures and plays, the door to knowledge and vision will remain open, and hearts no preacher can reach will be touched and purified.

Editorial Comment

In closing his recent rectorial address on "Courage" Sir J. M. Barrie said:

The Best University

> Mighty are the universities of Scotland and they will prevail; but in your highest exultations never forget that there are not four but five. The greatest of them is the poor, proud homes you come out of, which said so long ago, There shall be education in this land.

This striking testimony concerning one of our institutions accords with the facts and the history of the home in all lands.

One can scarcely venture to write on home life without experiencing anew an uprush of long-ago memories and affections more precious than rubies and more lasting than the hills.

Our age is afflicted with new cults and new organizations of one kind and another. Would that the force so often misspent on them were concentrated on the strengthening and the establishing of home life.

Whatever comes in the way of new things we must hold fast to the home, for nothing can take its place as a character-forming institution.

There is much that stands in the way of fostering proper home life. First of all, back of the home is the house and back of the house is a non-living wage. Further, there is the steady drift of population city-ward; there are the congested tenement sections with their miserable and inadequate accommodation for family life. These are all factors and tendencies that should be forever on the hearts and minds of Christian people.

✠

An editor who is in touch with preachers remarked the other day that he was struck with the intellectual laziness of too many of them. This is a hard saying, but we fear that it is a true one. The minister who ceases to love God with his mind may continue to live an innocent and negatively blameless life. Too many good men are satisfied with mere innocence on the one hand or mere bustling activity on the other. Under either type of ministry the hungry sheep look up and are not fed. Preachers of the word are set to declare the whole counsel of God so far as they can perceive it; and then to help in the translation of its truth into goodness. This very fact implies that truth is dynamic rather than static. It is to be rediscovered, restated, and reapplied to life in every generation. The man who maintains that the terms in which great doctrine was formulated one hundred years ago will meet the needs of to-day is as much mistaken as he who fancies that the doctrine itself has no significance because the old terms seem outgrown. The greater doctrines of the Church have eternal significance. The minds of men who are to apply them to the problems of their own generation must be alert and disciplined; alert because they have been constantly exercised upon great truths; disciplined, not merely by residence in college or seminary, but self-disciplined by honest study in maturer years. It is the intellectually lazy man who has just cause to dread the dead-line of fifty. The intellectually alert preacher for whom the past still lives because he is in touch with its great

"School Still Keeps"

souls, and who is equally alive to the problems and the men of to-day, will generally find, keep, and magnify his place.

We are, we venture to prophesy, upon the verge of a revival of the teaching function of the Church. There is no better teacher than the one who is old in experience but young in the play and vigor of his mind. Such men do not happen. They develop through self-discipline. They keep themselves at school. The intellectually lazy are truants. So in their public ministry as in their private thinking old tags of phrase, illustration, and formula, the rusty baggage of early student days, are still forced to do duty. Congregations are sure to see their dinginess, to hear the creaking of their joints, and to perceive the intellectual sloth that has permitted vital things to slip away, leaving only these outworn puppets to fill the gap.

Yet for a multitude of men who have thought themselves to be too lazy or who know themselves to be too lazy to study a way of escape is open. There were never so many good books on big themes, never so many or so available teachers. School still keeps.

✠

Some months after the close of the Great War a little German girl, poor but happy, was asked how she was being fed. "Oh!" she quaintly replied, "I am being Quakered." An eloquent tribute this to the gra-

Quakered   cious ministrations of the Friends! She meant, "My need is sore. I have been poor and hungry. But the Quakers heard of me, and they came to me; they fed me and cared for me; and it is well with me now." Doubtless the Quakers were not the only Christians who lavished their practical love upon the needy; that would indeed have been an indelible reproach to others who bear the name of Christ, had they not cared too. But it is the simple truth that the Quakers, as a body, won an imperishable place in the hearts of the needy by the swiftness and the devotedness of their response to all the manifold distress and sorrow created by the War. One who watched their work reported that "no more intelligent and valuable relief work was being done anywhere: they were Friends in deed."

Friends in deed! They were just exhibiting Christianity in practise; and Christianity is nothing unless as it affects practise, and affects it throughout. "Every one of them out there," another reporter of their work in Belgium has written, was there "actually to do things, and not to supervise some one else. They took hammers and nails and saws and built houses for people to live in. The girls baked and stewed and washed and visited the people in their homes." The spirit of him who said, "I am among you as he that doth serve," was shining through those eager but unobtrusive servants of his—shining through their radiant eyes and happy faces and through their every act of unstinting help. Here was a religion in whose beauty and power every one was constrained to believe, for it was expressed not in formulæ, but in deeds of love. For the needy to know that they were in the hands of the Quakers was to them a source of inexpressible comfort and strength. Why should not every Christian, in just the same way, be radiating comfort and strength and help? And what greater need is there than that which exists in the present Near East crisis?

This is our business as Christian men. It is a thoroughly fair, but terribly revealing test of the quality of our religion, to ask ourselves what we are doing to meet the desperate need—the hunger, the misery, the destitution, the sorrow—of which we all know only too well. It is a fair test, because it is Jesus' own test. In his wonderful picture of the great judgment he represents the King as honoring certain people with a place at his right hand, inasmuch as they did something. Did what?—inasmuch as they gave food and clothing and shelter to those who needed them. Simple enough things these! Yet by doing them or neglecting them men reveal their inner quality and determine their place now and in the world to come.

✠

Professor Gilbert Murray, in his volume on *Tradition and Progress*, throws some light on a question which betimes baffles even intelligent persons. He says:

Are You Focusing Aright? When I am disposed, as I suppose all of us sometimes are, to despair of modern civilization and to think that the world has gone mad, I always counteract the impression in one way. I turn from contemplating vast masses of life, which one can not fully survey and can not possibly divide into elements and add up into totals, and take some one particular branch of human activity. Ask the various specialists and they will generally tell you that, tho the world as a whole is very likely going to the dogs, the particular part they know about has improved. Ask the engineer, he will tell you of the enormous advance made in engineering; the schoolmaster, he may complain that education does not advance faster, but he has no doubt that it is advancing; the doctor, he thinks the world is in a very poor state because it does not attend sufficiently to medical men, but medicine itself is improving hand over hand; the sociologist or social reformer, he will denounce the present state of things as heartily as any one could wish, but he will generally admit that in detail everything that has been worked at has been made rather better.

Aside from this excellent point of view, the fact is: the human mind is incapable of assessing the whole stretch of human activity. It is not an entity by and of itself. From its earliest formation on to its highest development, it is dependent on other minds and environment.

The practise of evaluating one particular branch of activity enables one not only to see the prospect of peace and prosperity ultimately emerge from despairing situations, but it also serves to keep alive the graces of faith, hope, and love.

A concrete case may suffice to bring home what Professor Murray has pointed out in the paragraph above. For years the gaze of the world has been turned on the struggles, the agitation, and the crime going on in Ireland. Almost every conceivable outrage has been perpetrated. If ever a country had dark and discouraging days, it surely has been the Emerald Isle. People in their sober moments have asked, "Can any good come out of Ireland?"

Now that is one way, but not the only way, of looking at Ireland. Suppose we pass from "contemplating vast masses of life" to one particular activity, what do we see? Look for a moment at Trinity College, Dublin. How many know, for example, that Samuel Mather, Increase Mather, and John Winthrop, the younger, all very prominent figures in the history of New England, claim Trinity as their Alma Mater? And how many know that among the famous names connected with this age-long institution, the following may be mentioned: Archbishop Ussher, Burke, Sheridan, Swift, Goldsmith, Berkeley, and Sir William Hamilton?

Such knowledge and light from a particular sphere of activity does help to counteract wrong impressions.

LOOKING FROM THE PULPIT

The Rev. WM. J. MAY, Wellingborough, England

What am I preaching for? I stand in my pulpit on a Sunday morning and look at my people wondering what it is they need that I can give them; what I can effectively do for them. No task in the world is as hard as the preacher's. He must be an entertainer. He must interest men and women who have come jaded and weary and want to go away renewed and refreshed. They want to be taken out of themselves; they want to taste, if only for an hour, the fare of happiness. For many of them it is the only hour in the week in which they can escape from the besetting worries of every-day life, from the cramping environment of over-heated kitchens and dingy offices. If the preacher fails to appeal to fagged interest and to stimulate tired minds, many of them will go home with a sense of disappointment and failure, feeling that the preacher has not done for them nearly all he should have done.

The preacher must do more. He must be an educator. His people are looking to him for guidance on all manner of questions. He is a specialist, set apart that he may search out and understand: My people are saying to me, We know that these things that you are dealing with are important. Often we feel they are all- important. We are up against the moral basis of life continually. The problems we are facing in our relation with our employees are moral problems; our problems of home and family life, the social problems of our community, are moral problems; we want guidance and light and education about them. There are problems we are seeking to work out in our own lives, the problem of living decently and cleanly, the problem of knowing the right thing and doing it; and we want help to see our way through them. How can a man adjust the conflicting claims of home life and business? How can a man be fair to his employees and give the community a square deal and at the same time be just to himself? What are the principles by which the solution of these problems has to be worked out? It is a full-sized man's job to undertake to educate men in such problems as these. Yet I know every time I face my people that if I fail to help them in these problems they will feel that the time spent at church has been wasted.

These tasks, great as they are in their scope, exacting as they are in their demands, are still but the least of the tasks committed to me. Primarily, I am not in my pulpit to entertain or even to educate, but to elevate. My real work is not to be an entertainer or a lecturer but a transformer. I know that even the worst man in my congregation knows far more of his duty than the best man ever performs, and even the best man often despises himself for the things he allows himself to do and hates himself for the things he shirks.

Somehow I have to get these men

and women in front of me into contact with some power which will come into their lives and make them the men and women they ought to be, the men and women that in their secret hearts they are longing to be. That is the difference I believe religion is to make in their lives. That is why I am there.

In front of me are young men and young women at the cross-roads of life, trying to decide which way to take. They are full of all manner of wonderful possibilities, and the peril is that they may choose the wrong road and spend their strength for nought and vanity. Their peril is my opportunity. If I can but speak the right word with the right accent I shall lead them to see possibilities and make decisions which make all life good and glad. How can I speak it?

Can you measure my task? Most of these people in front of me are just ordinary church members; neither very good nor specially unsatisfactory. They are good neighbors, decent citizens; people who will be found busy on relief committees and at Red Cross working parties, but mostly lacking in vivid imagination or deep enthusiasm. How can I make them see that religion is something more than a privilege to be enjoyed. They enjoy the comfort and peace and ease it brings to them. But they do not see that to be Christian is to feel as Jesus feels, to be as concerned over the physical and spiritual welfare of the people as he is; to see that the well-being of one of the untidy foreigners down at the Flats is as important as the well-being of Mrs. Amberson of Amberson Avenue; that to be a Christian is to believe the best of every man; to see every man not as he is, but as he would be if he gave Jesus a chance. How can I make them see that to be a Christian is not merely to be saved from immorality and swearing but from bad-temper,

the love of scandal, and from narrow-minded prejudice? These are the needs I see in men's faces as I look at them from the pulpit. I have to accomplish that before I can feel that I have really done a preacher's work. When you look back upon the work you have tried to do and see how little you have really done and feel that preaching is but wasted time and that your ministry is an utter failure, do you wonder that preachers are subject to a complaint known among the cloth as blue Monday?

Each congregation has an atmosphere and a personality of its own, and the man in the pulpit develops a capacity to sense the distinctive personality of the people before him, even if the congregation is a strange one. But to the man who knows his people the interest centers in the individuals who make up the congregation. Inevitably there are some people who make a stronger appeal to him than do others. There are faces to which he will look for understanding and encouragement and there are others to which he will appeal with all his skill and force just because he feels that they are the least likely to understand and respond.

Stand with me behind the pulpit desk and look at my people. Listen to the appeal they make to me as I hear it.

There are two or three rows of free seats yonder at the back, sparsely occupied, and most of those who sit there are people who are more keen for the material things the Church has to offer than for spiritual things. But we catch sight of the pinched face of Widow Tomlinson, shrinking into her corner, with the two youngest of her many children shuffling impatiently on the seat beside her. She is putting up a big fight with poverty and sickness and is finding it almost more than she can do to keep her head above the rising waters of the high cost of living. I have simply got to say something, read something, get her to sing something that will put new heart and new hope into her and help her to fight her fight a trifle more hopefully and bear her burden a little more bravely. I have to restore the morale of that woman and of many another man and woman like her who have come to church feeling that the struggle nought availeth and the fight is not worth while. You can see the story of the hopeless fight and the lost courage written in their faces as you look at them from the pulpit.

Across the aisle, in the block of pews we know as Quality Square, my eye is caught by the twinkling eyes of young Marjorie Benson. She is just twelve, as full of life as a bunch of kittens, as full of movement as quicksilver. She smiles as her eye meets mine and I know that at the back of her mind she is going over again the romp we had together on the porch the other night. She's a girl who is going to count, is Marjorie. The mischief of to-day will be energy to-morrow and she will lead movements as to-day she leads games.

My task is to plant so deeply in her heart faith in the power of my gospel, love for the things which are true and good, and enthusiasm for service that none of the experiences which will come to her in the future will be able to pluck it out or destroy it. I want to give her a faith that will stand the test of college days and help her to solve the problems that will come with the years. I want to make her see that religion will not injure her happiness but will establish it. Hers is not quite the same sort of problem as Widow Tomlinson's across the aisle, but I have to make the same service helpful to both. I have to speak a message which will appeal to both.

Half way down the center aisle your attention is arrested by the fine head and the clear-cut features of young Stewart Robson. He is home from college on vacation and comes to church out of respect for his father's wishes. He has not cut loose from the church, but he told me frankly the other day that he can not see that there is much good in it. He plays for Merrimac in the ball team. He has taken honors in more than one examination this year. After next term he will be coming home to enter his father's business. He will count in this town for fifty years to come. I shall be gone in five. It is my faith —that is why I am a preacher—that what he will count for depends largely on what religion counts for to him. There he sits looking at me with great, questioning eyes and is asking all the time, "What's the good of it all?" In his mind he challenges almost every statement I make before he lets it pass. What will it mean if only I can make him see that the thing that really matters is not that he does well for himself and for his father's firm here in Eastville but that he does well for God and for the things for which religion stands in the world.

Such as these are the people to whom all your soul goes out in a great passion to help. Because they are typical of scores of others who are there I feel that preaching is just the finest man's job in the world.

They do not make up all my congregation. If they did my problem would be far simpler than it is. My real problem is the people who are armored with conventionality and self-satisfaction. Lawyer Appleby spreads himself in state in a prominent place. I know that he is obviously bored by the whole service. He feels that the Almighty ought to be very much obliged to him for putting off his motor trip till the afternoon and coming to church. A couple of pews in front of him is Mrs. Grayling in a new gown which drew the wondering eyes of most of the congregation as she swept down the aisle in it just now. She would have been fearfully disappointed if it had not. I have never yet discovered that religion has made the least difference in their lives. They have cased themselves in armor of proof; the heaviest shots never seem to dent it, and it seems to have no chinks where a rapier point might enter. Yet these people, and the great host of whom they are typical, are the people who need such help as I can offer them most of all. The tragedy is, the tragedy that baffles me constantly, that when I say to them: "You need Christ. I am here to give him to you"; they only lift surprized eyebrows and say, "Is that so, pastor? But what about the church aid supper?" These are the people who send me home in fits of black despair.

Thus I see the need of my people. How can I meet it? A doctor can deal with his patients one by one. No school teacher is asked to teach a class which contains all ages from seven to seventy and all grades of education from corner-boy to college graduate.

I am set to minister to minds diseased and to souls that are sick, but I have to deal with my patients in the mass. Even if I think in my heart: This is what that man needs and this will cure the sickness of the other's soul, I dare not stop to say, "This is for Carol Kennacott from Main Street," or "That home thrust is for the Widow Boggart." I am dealing with people in public and it would be unpardonable to chasten and admonish individuals. All I can do is to proclaim the truth as I see it; tell of life as I know it, and knowing the need of the souls of men, endeavor to meet it.

So life looks from the pulpit. The man who is there is passionately eager to help you. He knows your problem. He tries to look at life from your level, he tries to see life and the world with your eyes. He is out to help you make the best of things as they are; and if sometimes he fails to reach you, well, you are not the only man in the church and the word that seemed a stone to you may have been living bread to some other hungry soul.

FOR THE BENEFIT OF MY CREDITORS[1]

JOHN H. WILLEY, D.D., Montclair, N. J.

This book by Professor Mitchell is somewhat unequal in interest, yet it contains matter of absorbing moment to every clergyman and scholar in America. *Zion's Herald* says "Every minister in Methodism should purchase and read" the book. But why limit the venue? The laymen of Methodism have as much at stake in the future of Methodism as the ministers. Moreover, "Tarquin had his Brutus, and Charles I had his Cromwell"—and there are George IIIs in other than the Methodist commonalty.

Zion's Herald is right, however, in its implication, for as a commentary upon the policy and polity of the Methodist Church this little book has no rival to date.

There are those who declare that Methodism is a democracy. It is safe, and profitable withal, thus to unbosom oneself. But these artless declaimers might gainfully read and inwardly digest this brochure before resuming their declamation.

The first part of the volume is given to autobiography. In a style as limpid in

[1] By Hinckley O. Mitchell. The Beacon Press, Boston, 1922. 8vo., 336 pp. $2.25. Professor Mitchell will be remembered as the author of two splendid essays in Biblical exegesis, entitled respectively *Amos*, and *Isaiah*, a *Study of Chapters I-XII*, as well as of other contributions to Old Testament scholarship. He was professor of Hebrew and Old Testament exegesis in Boston University 1883-1905, in the latter year being "refused confirmation by the Board of Bishops of the M. E. Church for denying the historicity of the early chapters of Genesis." This episode is referred to in the above review of Professor Mitchell's autobiography and set forth somewhat at large in the book itself.

places as Stevenson, otherwhere more or less involved, and bearing witness to his German studies, he prepares himself and his readers for the climax. It is a winsome, wholesome narrative, and we wonder how this simple ingenuous young student can be the stormy petrel of the most turbulent days of Methodist history.

Most gracefully does he account for the title of the book. "As I look back . . . I see that I owe the world much more than it owes me. . . . I have been moved to (write) by gratitude for the helpful influences brought to bear upon my life, I can not repay, but I can confess judgment." Hence the title, "For the Benefit of My Creditors." The unconscious irony of this title may be appreciated when we remember that his debtors, and they were many and pitiless, will more likely draw the subtle fire of his simple story.

This amiable introduction, following so close upon the (entirely justified) *guerre à mort* of Dallas Lore Sharp in the Foreword, is humanizing and saintly. The simplicity of the writer is shown again and again. In glimpses of his home life, in the account of his conversion, in his naïve reference to the young woman who so largely influenced his early years, in the humility with which he waited his first appointment at Conference, in his sense of the sacredness of the hour and the occasion, which was not diminished by his discovering the bishop in the midst of the preliminary prayer taking a pencil out of his pocket and making a change in the list of appointments, and was not discounted later by his work under an elder who loudly boasted his lack of theological training—all this is Mid-Victorian and might have been written by James Martineau or Charles Kingsley.

Of course the paramount issue is reached in the trial and verdict that banished him from the work he was doing and the university he was honoring to find a place in another school whose views were not so narrow, or whose sponsors had larger vision. It is an illuminating page in church history. The late General Convention of the Protestant Episcopal Church solemnly and ponderously decides that "Esthetic infallibility does not inhere in a bishop." Passing strange and wonderful that it should ever be thought that theological infallibility inheres in a board of bishops! And passing

stranger yet the verdict of that board. According to that finding the professor is innocent of attack upon the deity of Christ —the only sphere in which his influence has been in any degree unwholesome—and is outlawed because he does not accept the absolute authenticity and historicity of the Pentateuch! *O tempora! O mores!*

According to Bergson those types of animal life have made the greatest advances that have taken the greatest risks. The shell-fish must forsake the protection of the shell and the safety of the sea, and venture upon land before it could be beast or bird. Evolution is not yet a finished chapter, and clam-shells are not the "more noble mansions" of the human nautilus. If, therefore, there be fellow crustaceans who persist in going ashore, let us who cling to our low-vaulted past, before the next high tide submerges us in the ooze of paludal protoplasm—let us bid them Godspeed, for thitherway lie the hills.

Money Raised by Denominations

In a recent bulletin from the Federal Council of Churches, it appears that the churches of America raised during their last respective fiscal years at least a half billion dollars.

Of the total raised, the combined Methodist bodies lead with $130,730,479. The Roman Catholic Church is second with $75,368,294. The combined Baptists are third with $60,798,534.

The standing of the leading denominations according to the official figures of each is:

Methodist Episcopal (North)..$85,934,000
Roman Catholic 75,368,294
Presbyterian (North) 47,036,442
Southern Baptist Convention... 34,881,032
Protestant Episcopal 34,873,221
Methodist Episcopal (South)... 33,859,832
Northern Baptist Convention... 21,926,143
Congregationalists 21,233,412

These figures show that each of the 46,242,130 church-members of the country gives at least $10 per year to the support of his church and its work.

A Correction

In the Rev. William S. Jerome's article entitled "Index-Learning" in the September number, the words "index review" on page 208, second paragraph, should read "index rerum."

KINDLING AND INSPIRING THOUGHTS

Humility reaps advantage; pride invites loss.—CHINESE PROVERB.

Experience of actual fact either teaches fools or abolishes them.—CARLYLE.

A plant may be born a weed, but it need not remain one.—BURBANK.

Do what you can where you are with what you have.—ROOSEVELT.

He that knows only how to enjoy and not endure is ill-fitted to go down the stream of life through such a world as this.—HENRY VAN DYKE.

Plants, animals, and humans all seem to need a set-back now and then for vigorous life.—WILLIAM FEATHER.

Socialism will only be possible when we are all perfect, and then it will not be needed.—DEAN INGE.

All that pertained to his art had for him a significance approaching religion.
—MR. BERTRAND (ON FLAUBERT).

The truth in one sphere does not contradict the truth in another sphere. Truth is one and in harmony with itself.—A. E. TRUXAL.

It was Charles Kingsley, was it not, who in his dying hour was heard quietly to murmur to himself, "How beautiful God is! How beautiful God is!"—SAMUEL JUDSON PORTER.

The past is a bank where an unlimited number of ideas have been deposited to our credit.—LYNN H. HOUGH.

All truth is a shadow except the last. But every truth is substance in its own place, tho it be but a shadow in another place. And the shadow is a true shadow, as the substance is a true substance.—ISAAC PENINGTON.

Badness can be got easily and in shoals: the road to her is smooth, and she lives very near us. But between us and Goodness the gods have placed the sweat of our brows: long and steep is the path that leads to her, and it is rough at the first; but when a man has reached the top, then indeed she is easy, tho otherwise hard to reach.—HESIOD.

School justice ought to be, as it nearly always is, a stage ahead of the justice of the world. Children are being prepared in the schools not to accept the world's justice as they find it, but to bring a new and more intelligent conception of justice into a world that has to be remolded by the activities of their generation.—KENNETH RICHMOND.

The human race progresses because and when the strongest human powers and the highest human faculties lead it; such powers and faculties are embodied in and monopolized by a minority of exceptional men; these men enable the majority to progress, only on condition that the majority submit themselves to their control.—WILLIAM HURRELL MALLOCK.

The reality of God for us rests on the necessity to explain the time-transcending and space-transcending features of our own experience, the junction of the finite and the infinite, of time and eternity, within ourselves, and upon the fact that we can not interpret any of our supreme values of life, like beauty, truth, love, and goodness, without relating ourselves to a God in whom we live, the life of our lives.—RUFUS JONES.

To-day we are in the midst of a religious revolution, which is going on so quietly that many do not notice it, altho it is a greater and more fundamental revolution than any since the early years of the Christian era. . . . Can Christianity become the religion of reason and science as well as of emotion and faith, and be made the power for individual and social progress which its founder intended?—E. G. CONKLIN.

Say of him what you please, but I know my child's failings.
I do not love him because he is good, but because he is my little child.
How should you know how dear he can be, when you try to weigh his merits against his faults?
When I must punish him, he becomes all the more a part of my being.
When I cause his tears to come, my heart weeps with him.
I alone have a right to blame and punish, for he only may chastise who loves.
—RABINDRANATH TAGORE.

Church and Community

HAS THE CHURCH STOPPED

A Russian writer has recently said that it is idle to look to the Church for the regeneration of society, for the Church has "stopped." If this is true, it is terrible, for the Church should be the incarnate conscience of the world, affecting and inspiring its manifold life to all fine issues. But is it true?

Yes, in part. Whether we look at the social world with its pursuit of money, sport, and amusement, or at the industrial world with its strife between class and class, or at the political world with its often unscrupulous hunt for place and power, or at the international world with its animosities and antagonisms, it is difficult to believe that there is in the midst of us an institution whose business is to diffuse sweetness and light and harmony through all human relationships, an institution which is clothed with power and authority to do this very thing, and which counts her membership by the million. Doubtless, she has done something, even much; but our unhappy world is sadly eloquent proof that she is far from having done all that, in the purpose of God, she was intended to do.

So, if it is not quite fair to say that the Church has stopped, it is fair enough to say that many of her members have stopped, if indeed they can be said ever to have begun. The Church is just the body of Christian people, and if she is ineffective, it is just because some of them—rather let us say some of us—are ineffective. We call ourselves members of the Church, and we forget that a member is literally a limb. The body—alike the physical body and the Church—needs its limbs, every one of them; and any one of them which is not functioning weakens the general effectiveness of the body and exposes it to the charge of inefficiency. What is the use of an eye which is blind, of an ear which is deaf, of a foot which is lame?

To those of us who glibly arrogate to ourselves the honorable title of church "member," it would be a searching and illuminating experience to drop the word "member"—a foreign word which tends to obscure the facts—and describe ourselves as "limbs," limbs of the Church which is the body of Christ, limbs through which the mind of Christ is to act upon the world. Plainly the Church needs all her "limbs" as much as the body, and is as gravely weakened by the incapacity or the paralysis of any one of them.

Let each of us then say to our hearts: "I have solemnly professed to be a member, that is, a limb, of the Church of Christ, and very particularly of the congregation to which I belong. What am I doing for this body to which I am thus intimately attached? What is my function in it? What have I undertaken to do? What am I capable of doing? Am I doing it? Or am I neglecting it? Am I moving? Or have I stopped? If so, God helping me, I will now begin to move. I will be a 'member' in deed as well as in name." If all of us who name the name of Christ did this, no critic could accuse the Church of having stopped.   J. E. McF.

[381]

The Conference on Relief for the European Churches

At the Bethesda Church in Copenhagen, Denmark, August 10th and 12th, official representatives of the Churches of Europe came together for what is believed to be the first event of its kind in modern history. It marks the beginning of a cooperative movement within European Protestantism.

The Conference had its origin in a meeting held on November 3rd of last year, under the auspices of the Federal Council, to consider the responsibility of the American Churches to their sister Churches in Europe. The official invitation to the Conference was issued by the Swiss Federation of Churches, in association with the Churches of Sweden, Norway, Denmark, and Holland.

During the Conference reports were presented from the Churches of the various nations as to their present conditions and needs. A statement was also made by the American representatives as to what had been done already in the way of relief for the European Churches.

The reports from the continental Churches indicated the danger of a great weakening of European Protestantism, through the present economic difficulties, unless help is given quickly ?

The chief practical outcome of the Conference was the unanimous decision to establish a central bureau for cooperation in the relief of the European Churches, to be organized by the Swiss Federation of Churches and to have its headquarters in Switzerland.

An Appeal for a Council of Peace

An appeal to religious leaders and Christian congregations to form a peace council of churches is contained in an article by Dr. J. H. Jowett in this week's *British Weekly* (September 6):

Politicians, he writes, have failed in establishing a righteous peace, and men everywhere are feeling the need of some power which shall lift all political relationships out of the rut and groove in which they are fallen and create the possibility of national and international fraternity. On some appointed day let believers in Jesus Christ go to their churches, as they went in the early days of the war, and by some simultaneous act let them proclaim their desire and purpose for a sacred peace and their belief in a common brotherhood of mankind. Let them assert their determination to have peace on earth and good will among men.

In every nation I would have representative leaders of the Christian Church meeting together, not in councils of war, but in councils of peace, to express the luminous principles of our Lord on some of the grave matters which are now plunging the world into confusion and strife.

As far as our own country is concerned, let us have a council of peace in London, with delegates from every part of the Empire. Let the delegates be distinguished Christian men, not merely drawn from the ranks of ecclesiastics, but also from the wider realms of commerce and art and literature and labor. Let them be broadminded, deep-hearted men, with a personal loyalty to Christ and a passion for the kingdom of God. Let us have a three days' council here at the heart of the Empire, not merely to make speeches, but visualize and demonstrate the existence of a corporate body which has in its custody the high ideals of Jesus Christ and which intends to give them their purposed divinity in the construction of the world.

If the national leaders of the Roman Church regard the proposed step as a serious departure from traditional ways, and if they lack authority for this kind of cooperative service, let them seek the needful authority from the Vatican. The present pope is a man of liberal instincts; he has already given proof of it."—*The New York Times.*

MID-WEEK PRAYER MEETING

Nov. 5-11—The Tragedy of Civic Sins

(Micah 6:9-15)

The above passage will serve as an excellent background for bringing before our readers a matter of the gravest concern to all Americans. First of all let us chronicle a few of the words which the writer of this passage uses to describe the social conditions existing in the time of Micah: "Treasures of wickedness," "scant measure that is abominable," "wicked balances," "deceitful weights," "rich

... full of violence," "inhabitants ... have spoken lies," "their tongue is deceitful."

In the face of such a catalog of iniquities one would imagine there was little hope for a better civic order. But what actually happened then? Out of this miasmic life "the voice of God crieth unto the city" (verse 1). This is a striking instance of a religious fact that even in the most despairing times God is not without his witnesses. That voice is unceasingly reminding us that we belong to a moral order and that those who violate the principles of that order—by living selfishly and uncivically—are but courting dishonor, distress, and defeat. Now what about the year nineteen twenty-two in the homeland?

We deem it of the first importance to bring home to our readers—what many of them know—one of the most inhuman acts in the annals of American life. And we do so in the hope that the voice of God speaking through the preachers of America may cry out against the horrible massacre of innocent men "in a wooded grove midway between the mining towns of Herrin and Marion in Williamson Co., Illinois, on June 22nd."

Nearly fifty men—the exact number is uncertain—who shortly before had been taken out under a flag of truce from the strip mine of the Southern Illinois Coal Company a few miles away and who had been promised that they would be furnished safe escort to the railroad station whence they could entrain for their homes, were lined up in front of a barbed wire fence, and hemmed in by union miners in military formation.

Scarcely before a plea of mercy could be made, shotguns, rifles, and revolvers in the hands of 500 men arrayed in a semi-circle about the miserable group poured a storm of lead into the bodies of the captives. Many fell at the first volley. Some got through the fence only to be shot down in flight. Others escaped the fusillade to fall victims later to a savage man hunt that harried the fugitives for hours through the surrounding countryside. Some of the dead were mutilated, the dying were kicked and beaten, the captured were tortured and then slain.

When the ghastly work was over, nineteen of those who were working in the mine were dead, several died later of the 34 who were wounded and a number are still unaccounted for.

We have space for only a few citations from the press:

The *okeka* of the Bolsheviki has nothing to its shame any blacker than this vengeful assassination of workers by workers.—The Chicago *Evening Post*. Nothing we have ever read of the Russian pogroms, of the Turkish massacres of Christians, nor of the midnight descents of the Red Indians on settlements of the American pioneers surpasses this Illinois horror in unfeeling ferocity and gloating cruelty.—The Knoxville *Sentinel*. Deeds as hideous have been done in this country, but never in the name of labor.—The New York *Globe*. Until the coal-mine butchery is legally avenged, how can America look another nation in the eye and speak the word "civilization"?—The New York *Herald*. Herrin's heinous crime is a challenge to America, the Mother of us all—of the newcomer to her household no less than of the native-born. It is a challenge that must be met standing.—Boston (Mass.) *Transcript*.

The Illinois Chamber of Commerce has made an appeal for funds to enable the state's Attorney-General to make a thorough investigation.

The President of this influential body writes as follows:

The State of Illinois is on trial. Our citizens visiting elsewhere have been compelled to hang their heads in shame. The world is asking us, "What are you going to do about it?"

Is there any question as to this being a matter of the deepest concern to every citizen?

The tragedy of civic sins is the irresponsibleness of citizens and the disrespect for law. R. S.

Nov. 12-18—How Shall We Regard Ourselves?

(Luke 19:41-44; 18:9-14)

In the second reference given above we are introduced to two religious types. Both men possessed the same religious faith, both worshiped in the same sanctuary; both engaged in the same act of prayer. But there the parallel ends. In their spiritual attitude and in all the essential elements of character they were as the poles asunder.

The first of these two men was a Pharisee. As a member of that sect he was no doubt accustomed to be looked to as a model saint, around whom gathered the odor of sanctity. True to type he stood all day in the temple, with eyes and hands uplifted to heaven and prayed thus "with himself"; or to God: "I thank thee that I am not as the rest of men, extortioners, unjust, adulterers, or even as this publican. I fast twice in the week, I give tithes of all that I get." This so-called prayer is really a soliloquy; a catalog of virtues rather than a list of petitions. Nothing was asked for, nothing received. An old New England church was being repaired. One of the workmen found up among the rafters a parcel which he held out in his hand. "What have you there?" shouted out a workmate from below. "I do not know," he replied, "unless it is a bundle of the dominie's prayers that never got above the roof." The prayers of this Pharisee got no farther.

The other worshiper was a publican or tax-gatherer, the representative of a despised and ostracized class. He, too, knew his place, and stood afar off. In his deep self-abasement he would not so much as lift up his eyes unto heaven, but smote upon his breast saying, "God be merciful to me the sinner." He regarded himself as the greatest sinner in the world. There is no self-gratulation or self-glorification, but a humble acknowledgment of personal unworthiness. For such a one there was nothing left but to cast himself into the arms of the All-Merciful. The contrast has been summed up thus: "The Pharisee justified himself, but God condemned him; the publican condemned himself, but God justified him." It was a case in which the first was last and the last first.

In the light of this parable let us consider the question, How shall we regard ourselves?

1. With humility. We are not to think of ourselves more highly than we ought to think, but to think soberly. Self-complacency and undue self-depreciation are equally to be avoided.

2. With self-distrust. We may be mistaken in our estimate of ourselves just as the Pharisee was. This parable was directed "to certain that trusted in themselves that they were righteous and set all others at naught." Their vain self-confidence was misplaced. They were not as good as they imagined themselves to be. Such self-deception was by no means uncommon.

3. With an honest desire to see ourselves as God sees us. Had the vote been taken in the temple that day as to which of these two worshipers would go down to his house justified in the sight of heaven, it would no doubt have been overwhelmingly in favor of the Pharisee. But God seeth not as man seeth, for man seeth according to outward appearance, but God looketh upon the heart. In the two recent clever books, *Mirrors of Downing Street* and *Mirrors of Washington*, certain British and American statesmen may see themselves as others see them.

In the mirror of God's word every person may see himself as God sees him.

4. With a recognition of personal singleness. Old time divines were wont to address their hearers as "fellow-sinners." The phrase has dropped out of use, but the attitude which it expressed ought to be retained. We all sail in the same ship; we are all under the same condemnation. Differences are only skin-deep. We are all sinners and as sinners must come to God on the ground of mercy and not on the ground of merit.　J. C.

Nov. 19-25—The Christian's Appreciation of Confucianism (Missions)

This topic is the fourth in the series of mission studies for this year. See February number for introductory remarks to the series.

The basal characteristic of Confucianism is its emphasis on the moral nature of man. It assumes the inborn existence of the moral virtues of justice and benevolence (kindness), and insists on their application under the stimulus of conscience. It ascribes this moral nature to "Heaven," which is one Chinese way of saying "God." "That is divine which is both wise and upright," says a Chinese proverb.

A second characteristic is that it applies this moral nature to political, social, and family relationships. It sets down specifically the five mutual duties existing between governed and rulers, friend and friend, husband and wife, parent and children, and among brothers. The relationship between ruler and people is regarded as like that between parent and children, and so down the line. And all is founded upon excellence of character. "The five constant virtues are benevolence, righteousness, propriety, knowledge, and truth."

This suggests a third characteristic, namely, a search for the foundations or springs of action or being. If the "root" is good, the stem, branches, and fruit will be good. If the heart is pure, the thoughts right, the action will be beneficent. This religion finds the root of good in the nature of "Heaven" (God) and the nature he implants and encourages in man. "Nourish the vital principle, the soul," is a familiar maxim in China.

In these teachings the Chinese point also to the fact that the great founders and leaders of Confucianism themselves led lives of excellence. The ideal of these men was the betterment and perfection of character, and this they earnestly endeavored to live out. So that Confucius and his chief disciples and apostles stand to-day as the "holy men" of China.

A mistake frequently made is to regard Confucianism as a system for the learned, not for the "common folk." This is due in part to the fact that the avenue of promotion to office formerly lay through a knowledge of the Confucian sacred books. But the essentials of the religion hinge on the common relationships, as mentioned above—those of family life, social life, and citizenship. And these are simple and known to all. Even the extreme to which regard for ancestors is carried is expressible as the apotheosis of the family. It continues filial and family regard and oneness into the next life.

A note of especial value is the character of the Confucian "bible" (the "Classics" and "the Books"). These, of all sacred books without exception, are "absolutely free from suggestion or narrative that is immoral, and may be read through from beginning to end without even a remote prompting to thoughts or reminder of manners that fall short of the highest ethical standard" (Geden, *Religions of the East*, p. 659). It is true that one of the Classics is employed for magical purposes; but we may recall that our own Bible has been laid on the doorstep to keep out witches, and it is still used as a means of casting a lot or foretelling the future. This is misuse, not use.

This purity of their sacred literature has wonderfully impressed itself upon the Chinese people. Nowhere is there a finer ingrained ethical sense, a more diffused chasteness, than is found in China. Could the principle "love one another" be superimposed upon the maxim "be benevolent," with the acceptance of Christ as Master while still recognizing the excellence of Confucius and Mencius, the redemption of China would be near.

G. W. G.

Nov. 26-Dec. 2—The Constancy of the Divine Care

(Ps. 138)

The words, "The Lord will perfect that which concerneth me," may be taken as the key-note of this psalm. The writer had come to see that his life was in the making; that it was being fashioned by the hand of God according to a predestined plan; that the good work which God had begun in him would be carried to completion, however long the process might take. He had come also to discern that life has a spiritual meaning, and that its true end is not comfort or prosperity, but character. He saw that the things concerning him that the Lord sought to bring to perfection were not his worldly but his spiritual interests, and that to these higher interests everything was made subsidiary. To see these things is to find the key that unlocks the mysteries of divine providence.

We are often greatly baffled in attempting to prove, in the face of certain seemingly untoward circumstances, that God really cares for his children. Things happen in the outward life which seem to conflict with what is written in the Bible touching the constancy of the Divine care.

In a world like this, a world disordered by sin, a world in which sickness and disaster have a place, a world in which the loving purpose of God is still unfinished, in which perfection of character can be attained only through suffering, we should expect to find mysteries which the plummet line of human reason can never fathom; but for the explanation of which we can well afford to wait. Yet even now the rainbow of divine propitiousness overarches every life; and there may be found "a soul of goodness in things evil if men would but observingly distil it out." There is no absolute evil but sin; all other evils may be relatively good. All things are not good, but all things work together for good to those who love God and live in harmony with his will. Behind a frowning providence he hides a smiling face and at the heart of every sorrow he hides a loving purpose.

In spite of every difficulty in the way of faith in God's supernal goodness, devout souls in all ages have believed in a loving providence, particular as well as general; and when unbelief has asked, "If God be for us, why then hath all this evil befallen us?" they have asked the further question, "If God be not for us, why then hath all this good come to us?" But it was left to Jesus to scatter the last cloud of doubt, and to teach every man to look up into God's face and say,

Yes for me, for me he careth,
With a Father's tender care.

An aged saint when dying requested that there might be inscribed upon his tombstone the words, "Here lies one of the cares of divine providence."

No more suitable inscription for the tomb of any Christian could be found. Every life is crammed with evidence of God's fatherly care.

But the supreme evidence of God's care for man is Calvary. If he cared for us as much as that, there is nothing in these little lives of ours that can be to him a matter of unconcern. This argument from the greater to the less we have in the lines:

Dear Lord, my heart shall no more doubt
That thou dost compass me about
    With sympathy divine;
The love for me once crucified
Is not the love to leave my side,
But waiteth ever to divide
    Each smallest care of mine.

J. C.

JESUS THE WORLD'S SAVIOR—STUDIES IN LUKE[1]

Professor ANDREW C. ZENOS, D.D., LL.D., Chicago, Ill.

Nov. 5—Jesus the Great Physician
(Luke 4:31—5:39)

Much difference of opinion has developed about what the Messiahship meant to the Jews of Jesus' time. According to some the Messiah was to be a military man, a great general and conqueror; according to others he was to be a ruler. When Jesus was asked by the emissaries of John the Baptist whether he was the Messiah, the signs of the Messiahship which he bade the messengers to report to John in his prison were wonderful works of healing and good-will—"the blind receive their sight, the lame walk, the lepers are cleansed, and the deaf hear, the dead are raised up, the poor have the gospel preached to them." From this it appears that Jesus' own conception of the Messiah was that of a universal benefactor. He was to make God known as the great source of all good.

There are good reasons for thinking that this was more in harmony with the popular ideals of the Messiahship than the narrower ones of a conqueror or ruler. The Jews were trained under the Old Testament to regard human nature as one. The political needs of men were not separated in their minds by a very sharp line from the personal needs, the physical from the spiritual. He who had the knowledge and the power to help men out of one class of evils had it to help them out of another. This is the general attitude of the ancient and primitive mind. The "medicine man" is the religious leader; the priest is the physician. Altho the Jews had grown out of this crude stage of thought, the art of healing was not differentiated among them sufficiently to be detached from that of spiritual leadership.

The first characteristic of Jesus as a healer was that he rejected no cases. "All they that had any sick with divers diseases brought them unto him." And he never shook his head sadly and sent any away without helping them. In the early days of the nineteenth century as the scientific attitude and temper began to prevail the tendency appeared to deny the truth of all miraculous records. The healing of the sick by Jesus was indiscriminately set aside as a mythical element in the gospels. With the more careful study of the human constitution it has transpired that at least some diseases are amenable to control and total removal by influencing the mind of the patient. Men of all shades of belief are now ready to admit that Jesus healed the mentally and nervously deranged. But the record does not discriminate between these and other diseases. Jesus healed all sickness.

Another characteristic of the healing work of the Great Physician was that he saw moral evil interlinked

[1] These studies follow the lesson-topics and passages of the International Sunday-school series.

[387]

with sickness and uprooted it. Indeed, he viewed sin as more fatal to man than bodily ailments. To the paralyzed man laid before him in the crowded room he said, "Man, thy sins are forgiven thee." Neither the man nor his friends had asked for forgiveness. But Jesus saw that the healing of his paralysis would be a small matter unless his soul was freed from the virus of sin eating into it.

And as the Pharisees were much offended at his language he showed them by the efficacy of his word in healing the physical ailment that he had the power of inward cleansing and healing.

But Jesus evidently viewed both sin and bodily disease in the light of their social bearings and results. Accordingly, he accepted and at times required the cooperation of others in his healing work. In the healing of the paralytic the preparatory steps were taken by four persons whose actions up to the time of the presentation of the patient to Jesus were absolutely necessary for the recovery of the man. It was just as much their faith as the faith of the man himself that served as the ground, so to speak, on which Jesus had to stand in performing the miracle. In other cases Jesus depended upon the cooperation of the sick persons themselves. When faith was "wanting he could there do no mighty works because of their unbelief."

Finally, Jesus in his healing work did not mean to contravene or supersede existing methods of dealing with disease. While the use of ordinary curative means is not mentioned in the great majority of the cases that were brought to him, there were enough such to show that he did not mean to be taken as a magician who would dispense with all ordinarily used means of medicine. It must be admitted that these means, viewed

from the point of view of modern art of healing, were futile, but such as they were, Jesus did not spurn or ridicule them. He used saliva and clay for healing the blind man. He sent the leper to the priest to have his cure completed according to the recognized rules of the ritual provided for that type of diseases. The fact that he did not use medicines is no ground why medicines should be despised.

To the Christian of to-day Jesus' healing of disease is both the evidence of his sympathy with all human suffering and the symbol of his saving work.

"Himself took our infirmities and bore our sicknesses."

Nov. 12—Jesus the Great Teacher

(Luke 6:1-49)

In his own lifetime and by his immediate followers Jesus was uniformly called Teacher (*Rabbi, Rabboni*). It was only after the Church realized his divine nature and understood more clearly the meaning of his work that men began to speak of him as "the Lord," "the Savior," and even "Christ." It was as a teacher, too, that he was known throughout his ministry to all outside the circle of his followers. Teaching was his business just as the trade of the fisherman was Peter's and that of tax-gatherer, or publican, was Matthew's. Evidently between his boyhood and his ministry he had made the change from the carpenter's occupation to that of the rabbi.

We do not know enough about the customs of the day to say positively by what procedure or method he assumed his place among the teachers of the time; but we do know that the teaching profession was a well defined and jealously guarded one and that his recognition as a member of it meant that the community saw in him the qualities of intellectual as well as spiritual leadership associated with the work of teacher.

It is significant that the other teachers of the day never challenged his right to take his place among them, even tho his method and the substance of his teaching were radically different from theirs. They placed themselves on the platform of tradition. The law was indeed their ultimate text-book; but in interpreting the law they attributed authority to the opinions of "the Fathers." What the meaning of any prescription in the law was had been decided for them by some rabbi of an older generation, and their work was to transmit (teach) this. Jesus saw no finality in any decision of the Fathers.

This difference between him and the teachers of the day came into view in the matter of Sabbath observance. His disciples, with his apparent approval, were seen doing that which had been declared to be unlawful on the Sabbath day—plucking ears of corn, rubbing them in their hands, and eating. This way of extracting nourishment from growing grain was defined as work. Jesus ignored the definition. He did not denounce it in the abstract; he simply treated it as if it did not exist. He broke away from the tradition and made his appeal to the inner intent and meaning of the Sabbath law.

Similarly in the incident of the man with the withered right hand, Jesus gave a fresh and startling teaching regarding the purpose of the Sabbath law. The law was given in order to augment and maintain vitality at the full. Men must rest one day in seven in order that they may have health and vigor. To give vigor to a man whose full life had been diminished by the withering of his hand was not a violation but a fulfilment of the Sabbath law.

In form Jesus' teaching was no doubt couched in the customary parallelistic "sayings," and in parables which were also used by the rabbis of the day. But both sayings and parables have become more intimately associated with his teaching than with any other. This is due to the uniqueness of the content he poured both into sayings and parables.

In the "Sermon on the Plain"—so much of which is identical with the Sermon on the Mount as reported by Matthew—Jesus put before his followers some thoughts which must have startled them by their unusual import, as for example when he called the poor, the hungry, the persecuted, and the despised "blessed"; or when he exhorted his disciples to love their enemies, to do good to them that hated them, to bless them who cursed them, to give freely, to lend freely, to be merciful. These were teachings diametrically opposed to the temper of prevalent literalistic legalism controlling the teaching of the schools at the time.

This teaching was made vital by the irresistible conviction it aroused that the Teacher was not imparting it as something outside of himself, but that it represented his own personality as a whole. He lived it in thought, feeling, and action before he spoke it. When a teacher identifies himself with his teaching, or rather when the teaching springs from the teacher's inner life, it can not fail to become powerful and effective. The blind can not guide the blind. He who is living contrary to his own precepts —with a beam in his eye—can not pull out the mote from his brother's eye.

Again an unmistakable trait of Jesus' teaching was that it had as a definite goal the building of character. It was not academic or theoretical. It was vital teaching issuing in the fruit of righteousness. He who adopted it sincerely was bound to live by it. And to live by it meant and always does mean to build on solid foundations. Against such building the storm and stress of life have no power.

Nov. 19—Jesus the Friend of Sinners

(Luke chap. 7)

One of the most astonishing things about Jesus to his contemporaries was his free association with a certain class of people whom decent society ostracized and called "sinners." It is to be borne in mind that the term "sinner" upon the lips of the Pharisees in Jesus' day did not convey the deep spiritual significance imparted to it chiefly, if not solely, by Jesus himself. It means every open violator of the conventional way of living prescribed by the interpreters of the Old Testament law.

A Gentile was a "sinner" by the very fact that he was born without the law and lived without any regard to its provisions. Those who oppressed their brethren contrary to the injunction of kindness and mercy given in the law, and especially those who infringed upon the seventh commandment of the Decalog, were regarded and called "sinners"; and they accepted the designation. On the contrary, those who lived punctiliously in harmony with the prescriptions governing the outward life had a right to deny that they were "sinners."

And not only did they claim that they were not "sinners," but they declined to have any relations with those who were classed as "sinners." This they did in self-defense. They properly judged that sin is diffusive and contagious. To mingle indiscriminately and freely with sinners, to breathe the same atmosphere and come in touch with them was to ex-

pose themselves to its contagion. What they forgot or did not know was that the opposite of sin is also contagious; that the atmosphere of health is also diffusive. They did not know that there is a certain way of touching sin which makes one immune against its power.

Jesus knew this, and he endeavored to teach it to the world. The proper attitude toward the sinner must be such as will help to save him while it annuls and destroys the power of the sin. Jesus' efforts to teach them the lesson display infinite patience and tact. It would have been easy to break out in direct invective. And whenever it was necessary Jesus did not shrink from bringing the peculiar sins of the proud and loveless Pharisees and Sadducees to them. But he preferred to lead men rather than drive, to stir them to think out the lesson for themselves rather than to dictate it in his own words.

All this is illustrated in the incident of the sinful woman who followed him into the house of the Pharisee and out of the alabaster cruse poured ointment on his feet, weeping meanwhile and showing by every outward sign that her heart was touched and turned from its sin to the beauty of holiness which she knew Jesus was urging upon men everywhere. The orientalism of the scene only intensifies the psychological and moral aspects of it. Under more restrained forms of life perhaps the woman would not have been permitted to express her mind and feeling as she did. As it was, it became evident that what hard treatment and scorn had failed to accomplish the gentleness and friendliness of Jesus had achieved.

What is more surprising than Jesus' conduct or that of the woman is the purblindness of the Pharisee to the real situation. Until his eyes were opened through the parable of the Two Debtors and its application to his case directly, he does not seem to have perceived anything more in the conduct of Jesus than a violation of the conventionalities due to ignorance. "This man, if he were a prophet, would have perceived "who and what manner of woman this is." But it was precisely because Jesus had perceived not only "who and what manner of woman" she was but "who and what manner of woman" she might become that Jesus showed his friendliness to her. What the Pharisee surmised to be the weakness of Jesus was his great strength.

Furthermore, Jesus carried the warfare into the enemy's camp. He turned his defense into an attack. The woman was a sinner, no doubt. But her sin was that of excess of love. The Pharisee also had sinned by way of defect of love. His conduct, tho socially correct, had lacked the whole-souled devotion which the conditions demanded. Jesus drove this fact to his consciousness, pointing out at the same time that sins of defective love are harder to forgive and overcome.

Nov. 26—Jesus the Great Missionary

(Luke chap. 8)

Jesus not only called some men to follow him but invited all to come to him in order that they might receive the blessing that was in store for them. He not only invited men to himself, he went out to find them. "He went about through cities and villages preaching and bringing the good tidings of the kingdom of God." The chief difference between the preacher and the missionary is that the first addresses those who come to hear him, whereas the second goes out to find his audiences. And Jesus was preeminently a missionary.

There is another sense of the word in which Jesus was the Great Mis-

sionary. He presents himself in this light when he says to his disciples, "I must preach the kingdom of God to other cities also; for therefore am I sent." A missionary is sent to proclaim a message and to win men to a cause through its acceptance. In the words just quoted Jesus views himself as a missionary of heaven to earth. He has come to proclaim the love of God and to entreat men to accept him and his kingdom upon earth.

However, Luke's account of the tour through the towns of Judea looks upon his missionary work from the point of view of the principles and methods underlying it. In the first place, it appears that the substance of his message was "the good tidings of the kingdom of God." Whatever the interpretation of the phrase "kingdom of God" and whatever its history, there is no question at all that upon the lips of Jesus its use is designed to bring men into harmony with God by leading them to recognize his love and to respond with their love and loyalty.

But with the delivery of his message the Great Missionary called attention to the fact that he was placing a responsibility on his hearers. This is the teaching of the parable of the Sower. "Take heed therefore how ye hear." The results of preaching are very different in different cases. This is partly due to the manner of the preacher, but partly also to the manner of the listener. And it is a part of the preacher's task to remind the hearer of his responsibility as a listener.

Another responsibility which the ideal missionary lays upon his hearers is that of communicating what they have received as soon as they come to realize its meaning. "No man when he hath lighted a lamp covereth it with a vessel, or putteth it under a bed." The blessing which the missionary brings is meant to enrich the lives of many. It is a test of his success if those who get the blessing immediately desire and endeavor to impart it to others.

Furthermore, when the missionary has done his work successfully he creates new relationships which, without canceling the old ones, become preeminent. On being told of the desire of his mother and brothers to see him, Jesus pointed to his disciples and followers as bearing to himself relations as close and intimate as those of mother and brothers. On this principle the new community of his followers became a genuine brotherhood; and its members lavished upon one another the affection natural among members of the same household.

The breadth of the range of Jesus' missionary labors is given in the incident of the Gerasene demoniac. Here first of all it transpires that Jesus passes into a country which was foreign from the point of view of the Jews. Here there were herders of swine, an occupation not permitted within Judaism. Here, too, Jesus came across that typical class in which profits even on illicit (perhaps immoral) business are preferred to the ennobling and saving of human life. The missionary must expect to encounter this class in the course of his labors. The only way he can deal with the type is to reach some of its victims as individuals and withdraw himself from it as a class.

Finally, Jesus as a missionary did not disregard the physical and social needs of men. The woman with the issue of blood was healed by touching "the border of his garment." The daughter of Jairus was directly restored to life and the affectionate relations of her father's home during this missionary tour. Sometimes directly and sometimes indirectly the chief concern of the missionary will lead him to engage in philanthropic, social, and medical labors all destined to build up and perfect life after the type of Jesus Christ.

The Book of Job [1]

In sheer erudition this commentary has never been surpassed. Its pages are sprinkled not only with Hebrew and Greek, but with Arabic, Syriac, and transliterated cuneiform. The writer is a phenomenally well-equipped Semitic scholar, and he brings his vast learning, in the most fruitful way, to the interpretation of this difficult book, and incidentally he makes many suggestive contributions to the Semitic philology. Of course he is also keenly interested in the problems raised by the book itself, and his exegesis is illuminated with many a flash of insight. His general view of the book is succinctly stated in the Introduction, one very valuable feature of which is the text and translation of the "Babylonian Job." To the average reader one of the most important features of Dr. Ball's discussion is his conclusion that "the poet's outlook did not extend beyond the present life." The famous passage in 19:25-27 on which so much depends, Dr. Ball renders as follows:

For I, I know my Avenger;
At last He will come forward on earth!
I shall see, yet living, El's revenges,
And in my flesh gaze on Eloah!

I myself shall behold Him, not Another—
Mine eyes will look on Him and no Stranger!
My vitals are wasted with waiting
Until my hope shall come.

This is held to imply no more than that "the God of righteous retribution will appear to right Job's lamentable wrongs in the present life, before his disease has run its fatal course." Whether his views in detail be accepted or not, Dr. Ball must be conceded the honor of having made an independent contribution of great value to the elucidation of this difficult but endlessly fascinating book.

[1] A Revised Text and Version. By C. J. Ball, with Preface by C. F. Burney. The Clarendon Press, Oxford (Oxford University Press, New York), 1921. 479 pp.

THE GATEWAY TO INDUSTRIAL PEACE

[In his new book on *The Quest of Industrial Peace* [1] Professor W. M. Clow has made a timely and excellent contribution to this intricate problem. In the fourteen lectures which make up the contents of the book almost every phase of the industrial situation is discussed from the Christian standpoint. The author deals with the causes of industrial unrest, makes a keen analysis of capitalism and collectivism (used as an inclusive term for such systems as Communism, Syndicalism, Nationalization, Cooperation, or any modification of National Guilds), and ends a searching inquiry with two constructive chapters entitled "The Gateway to Peace" and "An Industrial Covenant."

By the kind permission of the publishers (George H. Doran Company, New York), we are able to give our readers the first of the two chapters just mentioned.]

Nov. 5—Christ's Values

THE FAILURE OF THE QUEST FOR PEACE: The quest of industrial peace has been in vain. From the earliest visionary Utopia to the latest idealistic and sometimes fantastic theory of social order, the record is dark with disappointment and almost tragic with a costly enlightenment. The experiments which have been actually made have been condemned by the judgment of history. As Carlyle wrote to Spedding, "Experience of actual fact either teaches fools, or else abolishes them." The more recent theories set forth by confident advocates have not secured the consent of the conscience or the reason of men. The feverish advocacy of violence by so many of their sponsors is the mark and counsel of despair. Even among nations with a universal franchise, their advocates discern that they can not convince the minds of those who recognize the wrongs of our social order and make protest against them, and can not enlist the sympathies of those who are eager to welcome any method which is according to justice and truth. Yet it can be safely set down that whatsoever of justice and truth lies in the heart of these experiments and ideals, will be fulfilled, sooner or later, in some wiser, honester and

> ### THE NEW SOCIAL ORDER
>
> Every sincere experiment to realize a new social order has failed because it has not succeeded in taming the beast in man. The truth may be expressed more simply by saying that it is only a new spirit which can create a new social order. That new spirit, so far as men yet know or need to know, is the spirit of Christ. He alone has shown men the way of peace.

more reasonable way, and that fulfilment may be wrought out through sacrifices which some are not yet willing to face.

The foregoing chapters [2] are an attempt to set down the causes of the failure of the past experiments and the rejection of the present theories. Among these causes five stand out as cooperant and preeminent. To begin with they have been economically unsound. Economic law is as absolute as any other. Unlike moral law, it keeps time by the clock, because it deals with material things. It is not prophecy but arithmetic which forecasts the hour of a wastrel's poverty. They have also been politically oppressive. Both social and personal freedom have been denied. They have had low or insufficient motives. They have made an appeal to the interests, the greed, or even the sloth, of a class, and have ignored the incentives which meet the whole round of human desire. Still more fatal has been their inaccurate draft of human nature. They have not remembered

[1] 7¾ x 5¼ in., 300 pp. $1.75.
[2] Which deal with The Elements of the Industrial Strife; The Economic Justification of Capitalism; The Moral Values of Capitalism; The Indictment Against Capitalism; The Crimes of the Capitalist—and of Other Men; Utopian Communism; The Cooperative Movement; Marxian Socialism; Anarchism, Syndicalism and Guild Socialism; The Nationalization of Industry.

[393]

that man is "a being of large discourse, looking before and after." The culminating error has been, either by intention or by unthinking blunder, their materialism. They have been based on the conception that in things seen and temporal are to be found the true, full, and all-sufficing satisfactions of life.

The position maintained here is that there is only one gateway to peace, and that is not economic, or political, but ethical. The solution of all social problems and the end of all industrial strife are reached by an obedience to the supreme moralities. Righteousness must be the controlling aim, the master of the method, and the test of the motives. As a Hebrew poet has written in immortal words, "Righteousness and peace have kissed each other; truth shall spring out of the earth, and righteousness shall look down from heaven. Yea, the Lord shall give it, and our land shall yield her increase."

The supreme teacher of righteousness in our modern civilization is Jesus Christ. There are many who protest against some of the claims which are made for him, and these claims are not to be pressed here and now. But there are few voices raised against his moral ideal. By almost universal consent it is agreed that were his teaching and his life rightly understood and unfalteringly followed, there would be, as was promised at his coming, peace on earth to men of good will. It is significant that his last bequest was peace. It is no daring claim to make that the gateway of peace is to be found in the understanding of his mind and the following of his method.

Christ's ethical ideal of the social order has been set in the term—the kingdom of God. In the Sermon on the Mount he explained it to be righteousness; or the doing unto others what men would that others should do to them; or more inwardly, the doing of the will of the Father. One of his disciples, in a fine interpretation, declared this kingdom to be "righteousness, and peace, and joy in the Holy Ghost." It was analyzed in an appeal to Western minds as a moral condition of being true, honorable, just, pure, expressed in words and deeds of loveliness and good report. It may be defined broadly as the rule and realm of God in the hearts and lives of men, wrought out and expressed in their agencies, institutions, and governments. Christ's imperative coun-sel follows, "Seek ye first the kingdom of God, and all other things shall be added unto you." When this righteousness is sought and found and obeyed, we shall be standing at the gateway of peace, and that joy, for which men hunger, will be greeting them on the way.

This ethical idea alters all life. The alteration it makes can be set down in definite notes. The first of these notes touches the values in life. A man's values are the disclosure of his inner mind. They reveal his supreme desire, that gain or achievement which is the prize of life, his summum bonum, or chief good. It is in his values that Christ stands out in contrast and in correction to the minds of our time. On one point he was in agreement with many of the nobler thinkers who have been captivated by the prospect of a new social order. Indeed their inspiration is one of his legacies. That is his intense compassion for the disadvantaged, the outcast, the publican, and the harlot--the man who is down. Christ set a supreme value on manhood, and had a moving passion for human well-being. But when men labored for the meat that perisheth, when they sought him for the sake of the loaves and fishes, when they were eager to make him a king that they might bring in a social order with an earthly content, he declined at once. For those who believed that a man's life consisted in the abundance of his possessions, who craved ease and idle leisure and sense-gratifying enjoyment, who contested with others for authority and power and the chief seats of honor, he had nothing but condemnation. He was not overcome by the temptation of "the kingdoms of this world." He did not crave a share of the purple and fine linen and sumptuous fare of the rich. His passion was for righteousness. For that he lived and for that he died. "Let this mind be in you which was also in Christ Jesus, who being in the form of God thought it not a prize to be equal with God, but made himself of no reputation and took-upon him the form of a servant, and was made in the likeness of men."

Because of Christ's values he had only a spiritual evaluation of the meaning and purpose and work of life. He did not concern himself about a new environment, but about new inward impulses. He did not talk about wages; he talked about hearts.

He strove to make men discontented with themselves and their moral condition, but to be content with whatsoever state they were in. To Christ the world was not a stage where a man may play a high part before men's eyes; not a feast at which he may sate himself with the delights of appetite; not a garden in whose paths he may walk and gather fruits for which he has not labored. The world is a school where a man may learn righteousness; a battle-field whereon he must fight the good fight of faith; a wilderness through which he is a pilgrim to a spiritual destiny. It is not too much to say that did every man, whether richer or poorer, master or servant, hold Christ's estimate of values, the gateway of industrial peace would not be hard to find.

This note of values is in accord with, and an interpretation of, the place of wealth. Christ did not condemn wealth, but he placed no high value upon it. "The Son of man hath not where to lay his head." He was content to be homeless, and to be dependent on the gifts of others, without a grudging glance or an envious throb. He taught that wealth was a peril and a peril greater than poverty. "How hardly shall they that have riches enter into the kingdom of God!" On the rich man who did not see the beggar at his gate; on that successful worldling who proposed to pull down his barns and build greater; on that young ruler who turned back from the narrow way because of his possessions, he passed a withering judgment. He had none of the modern bitterness against the rich. But his ruling thought about wealth is that its only value lies in its stewardship. He taught that no man should count his wealth his own—he was simply a steward who was dealing with the possessions which belonged to another. A great and high life could be lived without it, and, therefore, he did not set that value upon wealth, and upon what wealth can give and attain and achieve, which is one of the obsessions of our modern mind.

It should go without saying that, were wealth regarded as a stewardship, and were its possessions realized to be perilous on the one hand and so impotent on the other, there would not be such a hunger for it or such a corroding envy of those who own it, and spend it so often to their own undoing.

Nov. 12—Christ's Attitude Toward Systems of Industry

A second note to be drawn from Christ's ethical ideal is his attitude toward systems and institutions and organizations. Christ did not advocate the adoption of any articulated social order. The Utopian communists, from Plato to the last founder of a brand-new South American settlement, the fiercer Marxian socialist with his lust for revolution, the syndicalists, Guild socialists, and nationalizers all put their faith in new systems. Some organized environment, they seem to believe, will reorder human life, and lead or compel men into a stable equilibrium, if not to a fellowship and brotherhood. But Christ did not propose schemes of economic, or social, or political order. He made no attempt to express in a constitution and work out into an organization any method of carrying on industry. He did not teach that one social order should be stereotyped and imposed on east and west, on north and south. He left such a detail, as he left many other details, to be one of the other things, "added unto you" when the righteousness of the kingdom had been accepted and obeyed. Let men be willing to do to others as they desire others to do to them. Let them be true and honorable, just and pure. Let them look not only on their own things, but also on the things of others. Then systems, and methods, and social orders would all grow in accordance with the inner spirit and outer methods of righteous men. All systems depend largely on racial characteristics, climatic conditions, geographical distribution, and ineradicable tastes. But if men are just and pure, they will be co-operative and sympathetic. If they submit themselves to the sovereignty of a righteousness whose highest grace is love, all petty ambitions, all self-interest, all base indulgence, all oppression of man by man will cease, even tho it be at the high price of sacrifices such as only righteousness and love are willing to pay.

For that reason it can be said that Christ had no concern with any system of the possession, or any method of the control, of wealth. Whether men should adopt capitalism, or collectivism, or work out some compromise between them, had no interest to him. His teaching distinctly denies that the wrongs from which men suffer are bred by systems or by methods. The wrong method and the wrong system are bred by the evil men. From his teaching it is quite evident that it was of no interest to him as to whether a man should reap his own corn, or get some other one to use the sickle and receive a wage for his service. In his day capitalism was the unquestioned method, and it may be said that he was compelled to use the accepted facts of the time without thereby approving of capitalism. But against such an inference it must be remembered that there is no hint of condemnation of capitalism, and that his counsels assume not only the righteousness of capitalism, but its values as a means of moral discipline. In such parables as the laborers in the vineyard, the treasure hid in a field, the pearl of great price, the talents, the shepherd and the sheep, he emphasizes the fact that the possession of private property and the use of wealth as capital are just and inevitable conditions of industry, fidelity, and loyalty to high ideals. In the parable of the laborers in the vineyard he draws a pen portrait of the capitalist, and it is most evident that were all capitalists as just, as wise, as solicitous for the well-being of those who serve them, we would be already passing through the gateway of industrial peace.

Nov. 19—The Method of a Better Social Order

A third and most distinctive note in the application of Christ's ethical ideal deals with the method of the realization of a better social order. All the wiser advocates of any system of collectivism realize that more is needed than a skilfully devised plan. They have all been on the margin, at least, of demanding a new spirit and a new character. But they have differed as to the creation of that spirit and as to its source. All the wiser thinkers understand that it is vain to draw plans for a temple when there are no worshipers to enter its walls, and foolish to imagine a new social order without men changed in heart to become its citizens. But Christ stands on the other side from those who are prosecuting the socialistic movement. Some of these postulate the inherent goodness of human nature. Others believe that a class war would generate a new spirit. Others maintain that a high ideal would react upon the mind and

will of men. Others believe that an environment of liberty, or ease, or self-willed independence would, as a miracle, change the inner heart of humanity. Jesus set all these shallow sophistries aside. Not only by his stern denunciations, not only by his protests, not only by his demands, but by his express statement he taught the truth which all men know, by the witness of their own actions, to be the truth. "Out of the heart proceed evil thoughts, murders, adulteries, fornications, thefts, false witness, blasphemies; these are the things which defile a man." Because they defile the man they corrupt his life. They degrade his ideals. They make a mock of all system and method.

The most convincing proof of this simple and indubitable truth is to be found in the recantation of Robert Owen in an address at New Harmony, his American commune, delivered in the autumn of 1837.

I have tried Socialism, tried it patiently and thoroughly, and it has failed; failed utterly and miserably as the basis to run a colony or community upon. It has failed because it omitted to take into account the differences between the characters and constitutions of men, failed because it omits to supply an incentive for developing the best out of an individual. We have had a healthy climate, a fruitful land, no rent charges, no interest on capital, no rates, no taxes, unlimited resources, our own laws to make, and only adults to provide for, and yet it has failed. I have been grievously educated in the human being. There are some men who will receive everything and yield nothing. All men receive greedily and yield grudgingly. (*New Harmony Gazette*, vol. iii.)

There was the high ideal, the inspiring endeavor, the ideal conditions of life, the most appealing environment. Yet it failed, and Owen was "grievously educated in the human being." He found what every other has found, that the way into a better social order is by a change of heart.

Christ said that this change of heart and this newness of spirit must come "from above." With such a declaration, if interpreted liberally, all men will agree. Even Sorel is standing before that truth. Only spirit can quicken spirit. Every man who has been moved to a passion for higher things has himself been enkindled by some other, perhaps the mother who bore him, or some simple man who taught him righteousness. Never has it been by a prospect of gain, or a new social order, or a high ideal. It has always been by some personality whose spirit touched the heart and will of a man predestined to leadership and action. It would not be just to Christ to leave this brief statement of his first demand without remembering that for him the statement "from above" meant the power of the Spirit of God. That determines not only the method by which social betterment can be introduced, but the dynamic by which it can be perfected. Only the man born again can "see the kingdom of God." Only the man born of the spirit and wholly devoted to its righteousness can enter into it. Only the man who accepts its laws can receive the potent dynamic. Social service, the service of man, the enthusiasm of humanity, name it as you will, has its own value. But that is not the distinctively Christian motive. The most noted Christian servant of man set the supreme Christian motive in a single sentence, "For we preach, not ourselves, but Christ Jesus as Lord: and ourselves, your servants, for Jesus' sake." When men accept his ideal of righteousness and enter into his mind, estimate life with his values, and keep his open mind as to systems, with his inexorable demand for a change of heart, they will be, at the least, not far from the gateway of industrial peace.

Nov. 26—Apostolic Counsels to Industry

In any brief exposition of the mind and method of Christ there are two difficulties in its application to modern life. One is that Christ's teaching, most naturally, was in the Eastern or Oriental fashion, not by thesis and argument as the Western mind appreciates, but by figure and symbol and aphorism. The second difficulty is that, as we have seen, Jesus assumed and accepted the method of capitalism, and, to a remarkable extent, his counsels imply the possession and use of personal property. It is for that reason, chiefly, that modern socialism has not only thrown over the Christ of the gospels, but sometimes blasphemes him. But in the epistles these two difficulties disappear. The Church of Christ made its way into the West, and the epistles, with the book of Acts, were written almost entirely by men of Western birth and train-ing. Beyond that fact the members of the Church were drawn largely from the ranks of the poor—from the laboring classes. Therefore we turn to inquire into the teaching of the Acts and epistles, and to see how these Western writers, thinking of poor men, sometimes slaves, counseled labor, and in their counsels, conveyed the mind and method of Christ. As we shall see, they faced the same problems as we face to-day, and their quest was also the quest of industrial peace.

If one were to collate all their teaching upon the relationships of capital, and labor, and the social order, most men would be amazed at its weight and directness. Warnings and admonitions abound. Injunctions to masters and to servants are distinctive. The use and misuse of wealth and the sins of the rich and the poor are all noted. But one sentence gives a most detailed message, and this sentence, tho addressed to labor, had its application to all men. It is a golden sentence packed with appeal. "Let him that stole steal no more; but rather let him labor, working with his hands the thing which is good, that he may have to distribute to him that needeth." Examine the five counsels in that appeal.

The first is the counsel of moral integrity. "Let him that stole steal no more." Moral integrity, righteousness, as Christ taught, is the basis of any stable society. You can not build an A1 empire with C3 men physically, and you can not build an A1 social and industrial order with C3 men morally. The criminal, the man who is wilfully dishonest, who gives short measure, uses unjust weights, mocks at the moral commandments, can not be a stone in the walls of an enduring State. No skilfully planned system or shrewd regulations which control hours and wages and reward, not even ideal conditions, are of any avail, if those who are called to live under them, or by them, are thieves. It is difficult to write with patience of the profiteer whose selfish use of his opportunities was a scandalous sin against society and against God. Every penny he extracted shall yet be taken from him. But we must pass an equal condemnation on the shirker and slacker, on the man who did not give a full day's honest work for a full day's wage, who adopted the "ca' canny" policy under a miserable delusion as to its economic results. We need waste no time with these and similar offenders. They are all thieves, and the writer in this passage is repeating the mind of Christ when he cries, "Steal no more." Moral integrity, that is the changed heart and right spirit, is the first necessity.

The second is the counsel to diligence in labor. "Rather let him labor." The dignity of labor was at one time an assured truth. The praises of the village blacksmith and of the hardy fisherman were recited by the children, and Carlyle's tribute to "the toil-worn craftsman, that with earth-made implement laboriously conquers the earth and makes her man's" was read with a thrill of admiration. But to-day it does not seem to be so honorable to earn one's bread in the sweat of one's face. The envied are "the idle rich," the most immoral and most pitiable of creatures, mere cumberers of the ground. The idle poor are not higher in the moral scale. Yet the cry is heard for few hours of work, and many hours of idle leisure. Proposals are made whereby men shall fulfil their calling and discharge their obligation to the community in four days a week, and three hours a day, that they may spend the rest in an ease which is likely to be after the fashion of the animal. There are some confident teachers who would not call on men to labor at all, unless that happened to be their mind, but would give them a dole, and make them the idle paupers of the State. The economic madness of any such method would quickly appear. The law that if a man will not work he shall not eat, and the truth that a man shall not eat what his neighbor has earned, are simply honesty in action. By the lack of stedfast diligence in labor it is always the poor, the disadvantaged, the weaker who suffer. The moral issues are even more disastrous. "Satan finds some mischief still for idle hands to do" enshrines a neglected truth. "Idleness is chief mistress of vices all." To fill one's day with labor is to find health of body, strength of mind, cheerfulness of spirit, and to be ennobled by the discipline of the soul. No man need be called upon, or shall be called upon, to a limiting and burdening toil, but the path of noble living demands a stedfast diligence in labor.

The third is the counsel of production. "Working with his hands the thing that is good." A man may be busy enough. He may allow his vocation to engross his ener-gies and dominate his mind and heart so that his higher aptitudes wither and his tendered affections die. Or, he may busy himself in an occupation which is evil. A good man will not keep his goodness if he works at a bad trade. In Paul's day, as in our own, there are some industries which are base in themselves. The bookmaker, the betting tout, the keepers of houses and of clubs which shelter vice, are making gain out of evil passions of men. Others are busy laboring at work which is base in its purpose. When men print indecent books, or publish papers which live by reporting the scandals of society, or when they produce goods which are not honest but are faked so as to deceive the unwary, or when they minister to the tastes and habits of an immoral class, they are not working at that which is good. One flag-rant instance is to be found in the trade of intoxicating liquors. Its prohibition or restriction may seem to some to be an intrusion on liberty and a limitation of the good cheer of life. But its sadly evident issues, as every man finds his conscience condemning, prove the liquor traffic to be a thing that is not good. Whatever ministers to the pure necessities of body and mind, of flesh and spirit, whatever makes it easier for the weaker to stand in truth, and the poorer to be brought into a more gracious realm of life, whatever will lift men's heart above that pitiful materialism which is the moral drug of our time—these are the things which are good.

The fourth is the counsel of private property. "That he may have." Here there is the vindication of personal property without qualification or stint. And here, with equal simplicity, there is set down the possession of property as a motive to labor. This motive has the consent of both the Hebrew and the Christian scriptures. A Hebrew dare not and could not alienate his inheritance. In the New Testament a mistaken and short-lived attempt to have all things in common broke down. It was never accepted by the community, and it is never supported by the teaching either of Jesus or his disciples. Peter's reproach to Ananias gives the theory an express denial. "While it remained was it not thine own? And after it was sold was it not in thine own power?" His words are an echo of his Master's, who rebuked the envy of the laborers in the vineyard and their complaint against the capitalist by the question, "Is it not lawful for me to do what I will with mine own?" Private property, with the right to dispose of it as one will, is a true incentive, for it provides for the use of a man's talents, the exercise of his powers, and the moral discipline of his will. A strong, free, reliant character is not possible apart from the possession of private property.

The fifth counsel is the unselfish use of possessions. "To distribute to him that needeth." Here we reach the deepest source of the discontent and strife of our time. No one can condemn too strongly the basely selfish use of the possessions of life. We all mark the extravagant and wasteful eating and drinking, the regardless life of frivolous and flippant pleasure, the rich and gaudy apparel of the richer classes, sometimes, in the case of their women, as shameless as it is ridiculous. To turn the pages of a society paper and to mark the entirely self-centered and frivolous life which so many lead is to realize how sternly this apostolic rebuke falls upon them. We need not wonder that certain types of minds are filled with envy, and that hate begins to poison their hearts, and the cry for equality is heard upon their lips. It must not be forgotten that these same transgressions are evident among wage-earners, and that all classes fail in this distribution to him that needeth. If only men used their possessions unselfishly, not simply by way of charity, but with a nobler interpretation of human need, for the interest and well-being of their fellow men and their country and for the uplift of universal humanity, much of the clamor against the possession of private property would be heard no more.

There is one instance in which the writer is convinced a signal and ennobling gain might be made. Proposals have been mooted to confiscate a large portion of our impoverishing national debt. The softer-sounding method of a capital levy has its advocates. Both of these are dishonest and dishonorable. If adopted they would shake our national credit so that men would no longer trust the State or trust each other, and industry would wither at its root, and destitution stalk through the land. But this Christian counsel commends a better way. It would be noble and ennobling,

it would be wise and the teaching of wisdom, it would be economically sound and politically prudent, were every holder of the War loan, from the depositor in the savings bank to the richest investor, to make some surrender of a portion of what he has invested in the national debt, and thereby reduce it and its exacting burden of interest by a notable amount. That would be an application of the fine saying, "from each according to his ability—to each according to his need." That is not a complete or a sufficient maxim for distribution. "To each according to his dessert" is the primary and complemental truth. But there are occasions when there ought to be shining examples of self-sacrifice, and this would be after the example of Christ. The whole world would be thrilled and quickened to faith and hope by such a distribution "to him that needeth."

This gateway to peace may seem too strait. There are minds which may mock at this claim for righteousness as the source of peace. Others may consider it only as a dream. But there is a time to dream, for the vision comes at the hour of the dawn of a better day.

Dreamer of dreams! We take the taunt
    with gladness,
  Knowing that God, beyond the years we
    see,
Has wrought the dream that counts with
    you for madness
  Into the texture of the world to be.

This supreme truth is no idle dream, for it has been "wrought into the texture of the world" that has been. Even in those hapless experiments and impossible theories which we have considered the one appealing note has been the endeavor after righteousness, as that was conceived by their advocates. The renewal of a distraught and disordered society has always been attained through a return to the gateway of justice and truth. Mr. F. B. Lecky, in his *History of Europe in the Eighteenth Century*, has given a vivid description of the condition during its closing years:

Millions of fierce and ardent natures were intoxicated by dreams of an impossible equality and of a complete social and political reorganization. A tone of thought and feeling was introduced into European life which could lead only to anarchy and at length to despotism, and was fatal to that measured and ordered freedom which can alone endure. Its chief characteristics were a hatred of all constituted authority, a habit of regarding rebellion as the normal, as well as the noblest form of political self-sacrifice, a disdain for all compromise, a contempt for tradition, a desire to level all ranks and subvert all establishments, a determination to seek progress, not by the slow and cautious amelioration of existing institutions, but by sudden, violent, and revolutionary change. Religion, property, civil authority and domestic life were all assailed, and doctrines incompatible with the very existence of government were embraced with the fervor of a religion."

Bitter experience of the inevitable issues educated the thinking mind of those who, as in the case of Wordsworth, had been carried away by unfounded hopes. But it was the revival of evangelical religion which brought men of all ranks and classes back to the gateway of righteousness as taught by Christ and saved the community. The enthusiasm for the religious life extirpated the base passions of greed and hate and the lust for power. There is no other way. "The work of righteousness shall be peace, and the effect of righteousness quietness and confidence forever."

Science and Human Affairs [1]

This book is one of a class of scientific works, at present much needed and much in demand as well, which are written to give a humanistic interpretation of biological facts. If science had been at fault hitherto in being too exclusive, it is now certainly making amends. Books are pouring from the press on all sorts of problems, making applications of scientific facts and theories toward their solution. The author of the present volume believes that the future belongs to the scientific frame of mind, and

[1] By Winterton C. Curtis, Professor of Zoölogy in the University of Missouri. Harcourt, Brace & Company, New York, 1922. 330 pp. $4.00.

he seeks to create such a frame of mind in his readers by showing that science is the product of human reason as applied to the understanding of the processes and laws of nature, and the control of these processes for the well-being of men. The scope of the work is indicated in the following chapter-headings: The Meaning of Science to Mankind, The Origin of Science in the Ancient World, The Decline of Ancient Learning, The Emergence of Modern Science, The Further Growth of Science, The Biological Science of the Modern Period (The Cell-Doctrine), The Biological Science of the Modern Period (The Theory of Organic Evolution), Current Problems and Methods of Zoölogical Science, Philosophical and Psychological Aspects of Science, The Nature and Meaning of Scientific Research, The Rôle of Science in the Solution of Social Problems, The Higher Values of Science, and Mankind and the Further Progress of Science.

The author's spirit and the larger intent of his effort are suggested in the closing sentences of the book:

The future of mankind seems likely to be a scientific future. Modern culture has come into being through science and through the control of natural phenomena, which is bred of scientific knowledge. The rationalistic scientific spirit is the spirit of the modern world. Any thinking man can comprehend the relation of science to human affairs, altho comprehension may involve reversal of mental orientation. Science is the product of human reason applied to the phenomena of nature, human nature included. Its course has not been run. The future is bright with a promise that stands at the threshold of realization. Ignoring a science by one generation bars the doors of progress, and the next generation suffers accordingly. Understanding of science is the greatest legacy we can bequeath to posterity.

Sermonic Literature

INDIVIDUALITY AND THE SOCIAL IDEAL

GEORGE A. GORDON, D.D., Boston, Mass.

For each man shall bear his own burden.—
Gal. 6:5.

The social ideal, as well it may, appears to our time with wondrous beauty and attractiveness. Never since Jesus preached the gospel of the kingdom of God on the hillsides of Judea, by the river Jordan, by the sea of Tiberias, and in the fields of Galilee has the social ideal exercised more fascination over mankind than it does to-day. The whole of Palestine came out to hear Jesus, the prophet of a regenerated Israel and of a regenerated humanity. And if he were here to-day this part of his teaching would instantly inflame the mind of the better portion of the world. And all this is well. It is something for which we may and should give thanks,—the responsiveness of the higher mind of the world and the higher sentiment of the world to the glory of the social ideal. We may well give thanks over the selection which the devotees of the social ideal have made in claiming Jesus as their great prophet. "Bear ye one another's burdens, and so fulfil the law of Christ": so Paul renders the social ideal of Jesus.

We must add that men fail to take account of the presence in the teaching of Jesus of two programs, the social program and the personal program. The one is absolutely essential to the other, and it is this fact of individuality, so seldom emphasized to-day, that we find emphasized in the text. I believe that there is everywhere an over-emphasis upon the social ideal in our generation and an under-emphasis upon the personal, individual ideal.

I. In the first place, however mighty environment may be, it is never almighty, which the social gospel, exclusive of the individual gospel, always tends to assume.

The story of Lucifer, who fell from heaven, illustrates the fact that the best conceivable environment, heaven itself, could not keep the spirit that wanted to break out from breaking out.

The story of the garden of Eden illustrates the same idea. Here is an environment of charm and wonder, with only one possibility of transgression in it, and even that environment, mighty as it was, was not compulsory.

Here is the environment created by the personality of Jesus. Tho filled by his mind, irradiated by his heart, and dominated by his will, it had its limitations as environment. It could not prevent Judas from becoming a traitor. It was the best environment in the world, it was mighty, but it was not almighty.

Look at it on the other side, on the side of the bad environment.

There is the belief of certain of the early Christians that Jesus after his death descended into hades and preached his gospel to the lost souls there. That is a pretty bad environment for Jesus to enter; you can not conceive of a more powerful evil environment than hell. Bad as it was, it did not convert him from goodness to wickedness.

Those of you who know the history of Israel will recall the story of the court of Jezebel, in the ninth century before Christ. It was one of the most corrupt. There it was with the four hundred prophets of Baal, and corruption of every kind. What a mighty environment! And yet the great prophet Elijah stood out against it. He thought he was the only one, and had to be reminded that there were seven thousand who had not bowed the knee to Baal. Here was this crushing evil environment, and souls living a clean, honorable, righteous life in it.

The court of Herod is another example. Herod was one of the wickedest and foulest of monarchs. In that court was John the Baptist, prophet of righteousness and clean living, rebuking the king. He lost his life

[401]

for it, yet while he lived, he lived in that evil environment a noble life.

The court of Mary Queen of Scots is another example. Here was a fascinating woman, one of the most beautiful women that ever lived. Everything that she did was so beautifully done that people wanted to say it was good even when it was bad. She was a woman whose beauty and charm abolished moral distinctions and almost took away the power of criticism. Her court and her practises and her devices were all against the good of her people. Even that environment did not prevent John Knox from standing up like a mountain of the Lord. It did not prevent others from gathering under his banner. It could not silence the voice that was like a trumpet, that was worth ten thousand men.

These are examples of what I mean. Environment is never almighty, either for good or for evil. If the social ideal is the only ideal, all I have to do is to put a man in a good environment and he will be made good. Goodness by its nature can not be manufactured from without; we should all be rogues at heart, however much under law, if we did not have personal insight, personal appreciation, personal love, personal devotion. This is fundamental. The gospel that what you and I need is to be in a good environment is one-sided; its one-sidedness is disastrous to you and me. The gospel that all the evil we have in our lives is to be laid on the back of the environment is again one-sided, and is nothing short of a calamity to the wrongdoer.

I admit at once the very great power of environment; that we all know. But I contend that environment is never able to make good those who want to be bad; it is never able to make those bad who want to be good. I beseech you, look at this business. I have seen all sorts of young men in my life, I have been in all sorts of environments, and I have never yet seen an environment that compelled a man to be good who wanted to be bad, or that compelled a man to be bad who wanted to be good; never. I regard it as an insult to a man's character, if he has any, to say that he owes it all to environment; that is a fundamental lie. And again I regard it as the comfort of a sneak to a sneak when men are excused for the evil that they have done because of their "circumstances."

There is no meaner gospel preached than that anywhere in the world.

II. Turn to the next point. It is essential that the social ideal shall be complemented by the personal ideal.

Take our Lord's parable of the lost son. He was in a most excellent environment, his father's home; but he broke out into the wide world. Why did he? Because he wanted to. He thought the better good was out there. His home was stale, flat, unprofitable. He wanted to see the world, he was eager for a good time, he desired to manage his own life. You say that he was foolish. But when he started out he thought he was wise, and he followed what he regarded as his wisdom. The discipline of his life made him see in retrospect that he had been foolish. Very well; but he broke out from the good environment into what he later called the bad environment, and when his discipline had opened his eyes, what was the first thing that he said? "I will arise and go to my father." There was the good environment waiting for him, hospitable, tender, sympathetic, with a welcome back; but it could not compel him to come back. It was the assertion of his own indestructible freedom that brought him back.

There is the temptation of Jesus. What preserved his integrity all through that great trial? You reply, his early education. He was brought up in the most beautiful way by his mother; he loved his mother, and she steeped him in the noblest traditions of his race. No doubt. Then as a young man he had a great many wondrous thoughts about good and in revolt against evil. Again no doubt. And there was his belief in God and the contact between the Infinite and his spirit. No doubt. All that is true, but all that together does not explain the business that he kept his integrity sound and true through trial after trial and appeal after appeal of the wicked world. It was the will applying early training, youthful ideals, all helps of every sort from man and from God, from contemporary life and from history; his creative will was essential, and the issue was a personal issue.

No parent can make a son good against his will. He may be given the best early training, and be surrounded with the best books, and be provided with the best friends, and still there is something in that boy that is his, that is he. He can break out of it all, and all that you can say of the environment is that it reduces the probability of moral disaster. But we must say again, no father can make his son good; if he could, the goodness, it must be added, that is compulsion would not be good. Free choice, free devotion to the eternal good; otherwise there is no good. No teacher, no friend, can compel goodness, the one in his pupil, the other in his friend. No, no; there is a personal equation, there is a personal power; that deep accountability of the soul, the creative source of all character, lies within.

Looking back over life I should repudiate, and I should repudiate in the name of every struggler for an honest manhood I have ever known, the gospel that without personal initiative, sustained, often agonized, character can be won in this world. "Ye have not resisted unto blood, striving against sin"; there is the heroic, the divine, appeal. Here are reality and life as we know them.

The social gospel gives you a great glamor. What we want is triumph over lust, dishonor, and shame of every kind now; we want to win fairness, reasonableness, integrity, fidelity, a useful life now. Bring the universe to help, if you can, but do not cloud the issue. It is yours and it is mine, and our failure is finally a personal failure, our victory is a personal victory. Let no social "Glory hallelujah" cloud the solemn personal issue; society can not do for me what I was made to do for myself. Let there be no substitution of a new heaven and a new earth a thousand years hence for the interior harmony, the honor, and nobility that I, through personal exertion, aided by the universe, may win here and now.

Jesus unites both gospels with incomparable power. He is a supreme socialist; the kingdom of heaven is a redeemed society, with all its powers flung round the individual life. Then again, Jesus cries, "Save yourselves from this untoward generation." The kingdom of heaven suffereth violence, and you have to fight your way into it. It is the second side that I think needs the emphasis to-day. I sometimes listen to speakers who seem to think that if we only had a social apparatus which evened everything up, we should all be just, all love the right things, all be sweet-hearted brothers, and everything would be lovely. I do not say that distribution is right as it is to-day; but I do say this, that you can never make character by machinery. Suppose that degrees were granted to college men, that summa cum laude were given to every one, no matter what his standing or his rank; how long would that kind of civilization stand in competition with another that encourages the winning of merit, of power of every variety, that endeavors to push development to the highest pitch?

III. Jesus said the way to the social gospel is through the individual. Redeemed men individually, working together, bring on the kingdom. If a man is faithful and serviceable, honest, efficient, clean within, true without, is he not the best kind of a social servant?

I hope I need not say that I am in profoundest sympathy with all efforts of a religious character to help the community, but there is one thing that I distinctly do not like to hear: I do not like to hear these efforts called "religious" at the expense of others. A good father, a good conductor, a good brakeman, a good sailor, a man in office of any kind, with a definite opportunity to do the world a service, who does it like a man, puts character into it, and makes it elevate his soul in the doing of it, that man is to me an apostle of religion. Whoever standing at his task, man or woman, anywhere in the world, does it well, does it honorably, puts conscience into it, gets character from it, that individual is in my judgment a great social servant.

When I was in Athens I went, as all travelers do, to the Acropolis. I looked at the marvelous Parthenon, and saw a little temple nearby called the Erechtheum. The roof of that beautiful temple is supported by a line of Caryatids running round the temple, majestic female figures, draped, each standing solemnly under the burden placed upon her own head. Every Caryatid bears her own burden. There she stands, solemn, under the weight placed upon her head as her duty; on either side another is doing the same thing. Thus they run round the temple, and the individual burden multiplied has for its result that the roof of the temple is sustained.

The way in which to support a Christian

civilization is for each individual to stand under and bear up his own burden. Nothing can be done if we drop out of the place that is ours. Each individual in his own place, under his own burden, all together supporting the temple of God, every individual service a sure contribution to a social service; that is my social gospel. Any other way into light is hidden from me. I can see no other way of bringing on the kingdom of God than this: every individual must resolve to stand under evermore, in all solemnity, in silent majesty, and with sublime content, his own burden.

THE INESCAPABLE NATURE OF SIN

The Rev. E. B. DAVIDSON, Mechanicsburg, Pa.

My sin is ever before me.—Ps. 51:3.

Divine forgiveness of sin does not produce human forgetfulness of sin. Twelve months had passed since David committed his crimes against Bathsheba and Uriah. What a year it must have been! Had he been accustomed to commit such deeds he would probably have been very little disturbed. But David had a sensitive soul. He could speak great words in praise of purity. He practised, in a manner which few perhaps have followed, forbearance toward his great enemy. He loved the Lord; he talked to the Lord; he sang about the Lord. When he finally poured out his prayer of penitence he acknowledged that his sins had been committed against the Lord. And so, loving purity, loving his fellows, loving God as he did, what agonies of mind he must have experienced during that year in which he expressed no repentance for what he had done! The thirty-second psalm will furnish an insight into his feelings. "When I kept silence, my bones waxed old through my roaring all the day long. For day and night thy hand was heavy upon me; my moisture is turned into the drought of summer." Terrible, indeed, is the grief which can not express itself in tears.

"And the Lord sent Nathan unto David." Not merely does the Lord require repentance; he also provides the instrument through which we shall be brought to repentance. So Nathan came with his pronouncements of guilt and punishment. "Thou art the man . . . therefore the sword shall never depart from thy house . . . I will raise up evil against thee out of thine own house . . . the child also that is born unto thee shall surely die." The steeled heart of the sinner broke. "I have sinned against the Lord," he said. "The Lord also hath put away thy sin," replied Nathan. "And the Lord struck the child . . . and it came to pass on the seventh day that the child died." Then it was, after all these events, that the king poured out his heart in this great penitential psalm from which our text is taken. He finds himself forgiven, but he also finds he can not forget. "My sin is ever before me."

Our memories are eternal. God blots out our transgressions, but he does not blot out our recollections. He "remembers our sins against us no more," but we remember them. "Son, remember," said Abraham to Dives, calling attention to things which had transpired while the latter had lived in this world. And in eternity Dives could recall the things of time.

Our national and our state governments have what they call "conscience funds," representing sums of money which have been sent to them from erstwhile defaulters, who in this manner desire to relieve their consciences of the stain of robbery. Usually these sums are anonymously sent, indicating that the repentance is not thoroughly genuine, but one thing is clearly indicated—the sinner has not forgotten his sin. We know of a man who traveled from the city of Denver to an obscure town in an Eastern State that he might repay two business firms from whom he had stolen a few articles more than twenty years before when passing through the town with a "show." He stated that he had been converted and desired to make restitution. He need not have feared the "clutches of the law," for both business houses had ceased to exist, and none of the members of the families concerned knew anything about the matter. But he could not escape the memories of his past sins.

He was forgiven, but he could not forget. How necessary to keep the present clean for the sake of our mental and moral comfort in the days which are yet to come!

When Macbeth was seeking to bring himself to the proper mental attitude necessary to the slaying of Duncan he said that it would be well to do it quickly if the assassination "could trammel up the consequence." If the blow which killed his kinsman would be the end of the matter in this life he would be willing to "jump the life to come." "But in these cases," he adds, "we still have judgment here." If we teach bloody instructions, they but return to "plague the inventor." "Even-handed justice commends the ingredients of our poison'd chalice to our own lips." And the mental tortures which were always with him after the deed was done are sufficient indication that he knew whereof he spoke.

There is a great deal of truth in the statement that we "have our heaven or our hell on earth," tho that is only a partial statement of truth. Someone has said, "Of our pleasant sins God makes whips to scourge us." Sometimes we think of sins' punishments as tho they were haphazard. Punishment is a very logical thing, being the natural outcome of the sin. It is the "wages of sin." It is not meted out as are the sentences imposed by a court upon culprits before the law, to whom there is given a definite punishment prescribed by law for each offense committed. Sin's punishment is an ever-present torment, and, while it may lose something of its poignancy with the lapse of time, the knowledge of it will be always with us, and, if our souls be at all sensitive, will even at the last "bite like a serpent, and sting like an adder."

Those who cry out against what they call the "inconsistency" of the thought of punishment and the thought of a God of love have overlooked the fact that sin is its own punisher. God hath no "pleasure in the death of the wicked." It is "evil that shall slay the wicked."

What punishment it is to have always the consciousness of our sins! There are persons who want to live in environments far more pleasant than those which are theirs; who want to enter the sanctuaries of God; who desire to worship the Lord in the beauty of holiness; who wish to mingle with the redeemed of earth; yet they are excluded, not by Divine decree nor by human exclusion, and are held aloof by the ever-present knowledge of their sins. "Shame hath covered their faces." A man whom I know stood by the outside of a church window one evening listening to the words of the preacher speaking within. The man was a member of that church; the preacher was a former pastor, who had returned for a brief visit with his former parishioners. The man on the outside, during this pastor's residence in that community, had not been associated with the church, but had lived a careless, debauched life. But the grace of God had reached him in the interim. Yet he did not go into the church that night. Why? He acknowledged afterwards that he was ashamed to go in because the speaker had known him only in his evil days. God had forgiven, but the man still remembered. His sins were "ever before" him.

The punishment meted out to the "ancient mariner" who killed the albatross, the bird which the sailors looked upon as the bringer of favorable winds, was that he should wear the dead bird about his neck. So sin hangs its carrion upon us, and "instead of sweet smell there shall be stink." Upon the marble monument erected to the memory of Dr. Samuel Johnson there is represented a touching scene. When he was a lad he was asked by his sick father to take some books to Uttoxeter, and sell them in the market-place. He refused to go. When he was at the peak of his fame, fifty years later, he journeyed to Uttoxeter, and with head uncovered, stood for an hour in a pouring rain upon the very spot where the old book-stall had stood. This is the scene portrayed upon his monument. Penitence procured pardon, but could not remove the memory of his sin.

The Rev. Arthur Dimmesdale, in Hawthorne's tale, The Scarlet Letter, who is the father of the illegitimate child Pearl, born to Hester Prynne, after seven years of mental and spiritual torture at last undertakes to declare his guilt. He mounts the pillory in the market-place, the same upon which Hester had stood with the great scarlet letter "A" upon her clothing, thus proclaiming her an adulteress. He summons Hester and the child to his side. He cries to the throng, "At last I stand upon the spot where, seven years since, I should have stood." He calls upon them to behold the scarlet letter which Hester wears. He reminds them that they have shuddered at it. "But," he says," there stood one in the midst of you, at whose brand of sin and infamy ye have not shuddered! It was on him! God's eye beheld it! The angels were forever pointing at it! The devil knew it well . . . But he (himself) hid it cunningly from men . . . Now, at the death hour he stands up before you! He bids you look again at Hester's letter! He tells you that with all its mysterious horror, it is but the shadow of what he bears on his own breast. . . . Stand any here that question God's judgment on a sinner? Behold!—behold a dreadful witness of it!" Tearing away the ministerial band from his breast he reveals to the people upon his own breast, burned into its very flesh, a great scarlet letter "A." Then the people knew the partner in Hester's sin—their own minister. What a testimony to the truth of our text that sin is its own punisher!

Is there any remedy for such a condition? Is there "balm in Gilead?" Is there "a physician there?" Thanks be unto God, there is balm; there is a physician. Get your sins under the grace of God; under the blood of Christ! This is the only remedy. Even then you can not forget them, but their keenness will be lost in the overwhelming joy of deliverance. "Beauty for ashes; the oil of joy for mourning; the garment of praise for the spirit of heaviness"; these all shall be given. Yet the ashes may still be seen—but in their rightful place upon the rubbish heap! "Saved at last," says the sinner as he feels the father's arms about him, and looks into the joyful faces of the welcoming neighbors. But he does not forget the experiences of the far-off land. Yet, thank God, it is a "far country!" The branch from the tree of love thrown into the waters of bitterness does not remove the waters; it merely makes them sweet.

Over the mantelpiece in the study of John Newton, who had spent so many wild, sinful years, and who had sunk so low in life as to seem to be beyond redemption, but whom the grace of God could, and did, reach, there hung, placed there by himself, a framed text: "Thou shalt remember that thou wast a bondman in the land of Egypt, and the Lord thy God redeemed thee." You see its double significance—remembrance of sin, yet redemption from sin. "I was before a blasphemer, and a persecutor, and injurious," said Paul, "but I obtained mercy, because I did it ignorantly in unbelief." With him let us shout, "Thanks be unto God for his unspeakable gift!"

THE GLASS OF FASHION[1]

Ye shall conceive chaff; ye shall bring forth stubble!—Isa. 33:11.
And wisdom and knowledge shall be the stability of thy times!—Isa. 33:6.
Woe unto them that go down to Egypt for help; and stay on horses and trust in chariots because they are many; and in horsemen because they are very strong; but they look not unto the Holy One of Israel, neither seek the Lord!—Isa. 31:1.

Who is not concerned, like Isaiah of old, about the drifting tendency of this age? What preacher has not known the loose moorings in his particular harbor? The tide is going out and the old anchors are breaking loose. "The ancient, outworn Puritanic traditions of right and wrong" are being scrapped along with many things, since the war. "It is a drift age," the *Glass of Fashion* says.

We find the same thing in this great book as we find in *Modern Tendencies in Sculpture*, only in different fields. Where Mr. Taft is concerned alone with his own art, this book is concerned with the world of morals and spiritualities.

The world of painting is finding its "drift age" expression in the cubist school; the world of poetry in its *vers libre* school; the world of sculpture in bizarre work which has forgotten the "hint of eternity"; the social world in its "flappers" and its Margot Asquith and its Colonel Reppington's Diary; and the political world in its Bolshevism.

It is exactly like the age when Isaiah thundered his denunciations against sin. He used different figures of speech in his warnings. He talked of a people who had gotten to trusting in horses' legs and chariots;

[1] From *There Are Sermons in Books*. By WILLIAM L. STIDGER. George H. Doran Company, New York, 1922. *The Glass of Fashion* was reviewed in the August number of THE HOMILETIC REVIEW.

and what he was denouncing was an age that was trusting in materialism.

That is the spirit of the present age which this unknown author so strongly designates as a "drift age." He sets forth the spirit of the present age first as the result of Darwinism:

Darwinism not only justifies the sensualist at the trough and fashion at her glass; it justifies Prussianism at the cannon, and Bolshevism at the prison door.

It is clear to this writer that the explanation for the present "drift age" is that it has sold its soul to a materialistic conception of life. Anything goes with this kind of a philosophy.

The second way in which this writer sets forth the spirit of the age is in a group of stinging phrases.

The first phrase that he uses, as I have said, is that the age is "a drift age." We are like derelicts on the sea of life. We have no moral harbors; no anchors to God; no moorings to morality even. This phrase can be applied to every phase of life in a modern city. It can be applied to young life, to business life, to international life, and to religious and church life. No age but a "drift age" could produce a Fatty Arbuckle orgy, a Stillman divorce case, and a Kennedy murder all in the same month. Something has been thrown away. The pilot has been dismissed and we are near the rocks. Such is the spirit of the book and its warning.

The second phrase that is used to burn this danger into our hearts is a phrase that reads, "We are talking nonsense on the edge of an abyss." To bolster up his statement he uses a quotation from Alfred Noyes which shoots the matter into the souls of an audience as a thousand words of prose will never do. It is Isaianic in its strength and simplicity:

The cymbals crash
And the dancers walk
With long, silk stockings
And arms of chalk;
Butterfly skirts
And white breasts bare
And shadows of dead men
Watching them there!

It is an awful picture that these two writers set before us but it is an accurate picture. Only Isaiah could have made it stronger.

One of the most awful indictments the book makes is that this is an age when love is degraded. He quotes from Mrs. Asquith's *Diary* and Colonel Reppington's *Diary*, to which I shall refer more specifically later, to prove that love means little, any more, in life especially among certain social groups. Old-fashioned love and loyalty of man to woman is sneered at and laughed out of court.

Almost the whole tendency of fashion in this matter is toward the degradation of love. Almost every influence it possesses, so far as I am able to judge, is brought to bear on love with the sole purpose of degrading what the sentimentalists only profaned.

Then he explains the cause of the widely prevalent domestic unhappiness of the world:

"Domestic unhappiness is a consequence of wrong thinking in society. Wrong thinking is fatal to right living." "The woman who knocks about," he says, has superseded "the particular woman," and this is danger to love and home. "There can be no time," says Lord Jeffrey, "in which the purity of female character can fail to be of the first importance to every community."

And so this flaming mind sees the age as an age of "the degradation of love," an age that is a "drift age"; an age that is "talking nonsense on the edge of an abyss."

In addition to these virile phrases, the author tries to make us see the age in which we are living through printing extracts from two diaries, one of which is that of Colonel Reppington and another that of Margot Asquith. Colonel Reppington's *Diary* is filled with the trivial, if not the vulgar and lewd. It is supposed to be a diary of the great World War, but to read it one would hardly know that men were killed by millions and human destinies were at stake and that men were fighting for home, children, country, honor, and the world's hope for democratic life.

Colonel Reppington seems to see nothing that happens save the manner in which a certain widow's bodice is dressed and how late she stayed up at night and how many "rags" they attended together. One critic called Colonel Reppington's *Diary* "A Worm's Eye View of the War" and that about sums it all up. However, the fact remains that there is an educated man alive in the world who could actually write such a diary and who could find an audience for it and a publisher to publish it. This is the great indictment of the age.

The other diary that he uses to illustrate the tendency of the day is that of Margot Asquith. This diary appeared first in the *Metropolitan Magazine* in America. It is the frank, open story of a woman who holds back nothing from the public gaze. Even the pangs of motherhood are not held too sacred to lay out before the brazen gaze of all who may wish to see. Her escapades, her licenses, which are said to have caused the downfall of the Asquith ministry, are brazenly set before all the world to see. The author of this book calls her "The Grandmother of the Flapper," which is a hard saying but a true one; a saying that cuts its way straight to the heart of the matter. These phrases and these two diaries are used to set forth the degradation of the age.

It is a tremendous indictment of materialism and sin.

With these phrases and these two diaries in his hands as bludgeons, the preacher who can not flay sin and knock its head in and leave it a battered and broken ruin ought to quit preaching. These tremendous phrases and these two licentious diaries full of slime and crawling things give him a new vehicle to show on what "treacherous ground" the world is living to-day.

One can preach a thousand sermons and not find so vivid a way to set forth the need of an age or of an individual as through the striking illustrations and pictures and characters of this wonderful book.

The first need of the age is respect for home and love.

Then the author makes a vivid contrast between Mrs. Asquith and Mrs. Gladstone. He tells how Mrs. Gladstone was just as vivacious as Mrs. Asquith; just as charming personally; just as beautiful physically; but what a quiet reserve and dignity she had; what a deep sense of God there was in her heart; and what a strength she was to Gladstone in his public life!

One of the most beautiful incidents set forth was the habit of the Gladstones of going each morning to a little church to start the day off with worship. The author tells how Mr. and Mrs. Gladstone did this for years, walking a mile to the church each morning before he went to Parliament.

Then the author tells of that beautiful custom the Gladstones had of rescuing fallen women and taking them into their home in order to rehabilitate the lives of these modern Magdalenes. One night Gladstone was out on such an errand alone. A friend saw him with a harlot. He begged him to let her go, fearing that if he were seen his enemies might use it against him politically. Gladstone refused to listen. Then the friend said, "What will Mrs. Gladstone say about her?" Gladstone answered, "It is to Mrs. Gladstone that I am taking her."

In contrasting the Gladstones with the Asquiths the author shows that one of the needs of this age, which is deeper than all other needs, is the need of good homes and a deeper reverence for love in home life.

Then he contrasts Colonel Reppington with Goethe the poet. He tells how Goethe started off in a frivolous way of living but how something happened in his young life, and he found that, while he was frivolous at the circumference, he was good at the heart of him. He uses a phrase with reference to Goethe which sums up all that he wants to set forth in his contrast of Goethe and Reppington and that is that "Goethe had an inner earnestness."

That is what this age needs. It needs an "inner earnestness," which it can not have with a materialistic conception of life and living.

But these things are not enough according to this writer. It is necessary to have a new regard for home; and it is necessary to have an "inner earnestness" about life and things in general. The world can not live without these changes. But there is something else needed to save the age.

Edith Cavell said when they were about to kill her, "Patriotism is not enough." And so this author comes to the conclusion that to save this age "morality is not enough." There must be something higher and deeper than morality. There must be God. He says:

Man is a creature most dear to God. He is a citizen of a universe that is infinite. He is the child of a duration that is eternal. He can not be dislodged from infinity and eternity any more than a day can be dislodged from a year. Loyalty to his moral nature is necessary to the understanding of his destiny, but his true happiness lies in the exercise of his spiritual faculties. Until he comprehends the greatness of his glory and the unimaginable splendors of his inheritance, he must be a creature of unrest and ever greater confusion.

Now in this is the excellency of man, that he is made capable of a communion with his Maker, and, because capable of it, is unsatisfied without it!

Linking this book up with prophecies of Isaiah; with his denunciation of sin and materialism; with his thunderings against the Margot Asquiths and the Colonel Reppingtons of his day, the preacher has a dramatic book presentation of sin and materialism, and the remedy for the "drift age" is religion and Christ and God.

I have seldom attempted a book sermon that has so gripped the hearts of my people as the sermon on this great book *The Glass of Fashion* with its vivid picture of the sin of the day and its remedy for that sin; with its cutting and its biting phrases; "a drift age," "an age of the degradation of love," an "age when we are talking nonsense on the edge of an abyss"; and its age of "the woman about town." And then its powerful phrases which suggest the cure for the sins of the age, such as the "inner earnestness" and a "consciousness of God." These are flaming phrases.

These indictments of materialism shall never die. These flames of faith shall burn brighter and brighter unto the perfect day.

This book is a great heart cry for righteousness and he who passes it on through private word or sermon is handing on a lighted torch of hope and love.

THE MEN OF THE HALF-MOON

DAVID JAMES BURRELL, D.D., LL.D., New York City

The conies are but a feeble folk, yet make they their houses in the rocks.—Prov. 30:26.

The original Thanksgiving proclamation by Governor Bradford of Plymouth was accompanied by the words, "after the laudable custom of Holland." It would thus appear that Thanksgiving Day was an institution in Holland before the Pilgrim Fathers thought of it. And thereby hangs a tale.

In 1574 the city of Leyden was besieged by the Spanish army and reduced to the last extremity of suffering. On October first the Duke of Alva called for a surrender and received this answer, "We will eat the flesh of our left arms to keep our right arms strong for the defense of our liberties." On October second a carrier pigeon flew into the city with the news that William the Silent had cut the dikes and ship-loads of provisions were on their way. On October third the "water beggars" of Zeeland with half-moons in their hats came dragging their boats across the flooded fields with bread and dried herring which they threw over the walls. On October fourth the Spanish army withdrew, and the grateful people set apart the day to be observed thereafter in thanksgiving to God.

And now the sequel. One day when the south winds blew softly and the storks were building their summer nests on the house-tops, a ship sailed out from Delfshaven with her prow toward the west. At her masthead floated the name *Half-Moon*, a grateful tribute to the courage of the water-beggars. She was manned by veterans of the Protestant wars. In due course of time she reached America and other vessels of the line came trooping after her. A settlement was presently effected on the island of Manhattan, and the voyagers with their families began to address themselves to the usual pursuits of village life. They were, indeed, a feeble folk; but like the conies they "made their houses among the rocks."

A recent writer says, "The Dutch forefathers had a preemption right to Manhattan Island, but they frittered it away: their influence has vanished into thin air." Neither of these points is well taken. The Dutch possession of Manhattan Island ended with the English occupation in 1664, when there were only 300 houses and less than 1,500 people in the town. Not a very formidable basis for a "preemption right!" That brief period of the Dutch occupation is fallow-ground as yet. The Dutch settlers wrote no poems or chronicles to commemorate their own valiant deeds: but it is a far cry from the truth to say that their influence has "vanished into thin air."

The influence of some of the racial factors in our population is as obvious as the track of the trade-winds over the land or of the gulf stream in the sea. But efficiency is not to be measured by rams-horns or banners on the outer walls. There are others who make their influence felt as quietly and unostentatiously as the pleasant water-courses:

You may trace them through the meadows
By the rushing in the springtime,
By the alders in the summer,
By the white fog in the autumn,
By the black line in the winter:

or as the falling of the dew, of which no note is taken save by the refreshing of the fields and clearing of the air.

I. To begin with, the Dutch strain in our American blood has impressed its character-istic features very clearly on our social life.

The sweet simplicity of the homes of Hol-land is proverbial, and it was early trans-ported to New Amsterdam. At the c'ose of a church service in Michigan the clergyman invited me to the parsonage. The *frau pastorin* was there with her children about her, a happy group where faces shone and eyes were bright with filial love. But the central figure was the grandmother with her white cap and bangles, seated on a throne of state like a queen in gracious dignity. It was all like a foregleam of the Father's house. Was this an exceptional case? I have never seen it otherwise. Measure, if you can, the radiating light of a thousand such homes!

II. Not less potent and pervasive has been the influence of these Dutch forefathers on our industrial life.

We sometimes speak of capital and labor as if they were mutually at odds, when, in fact, they are as closely related as thrift and industry, the twin virtues that enter into the problem of national prosperity. Be it remembered that those Manhattaners were not refugees. They had not fled from either poverty or persecution. Thrift walked at their right hand and industry at their left. They were well-to-do but frankly desired to be better off.

When Henry Hudson, skipper of the *Half-Moon*, returned from his first voyage with a report of "a lordly river flowing through a fertile country and abounding in fur-bearing animals and naked redmen," the fur and the fertile fields suggested a ma-terial profit which moved these Hollanders scarcely less than the possibility of doing something for the souls of the naked red-men.

Nor have their children been suspected of lacking an eye to the main chance. Rare-ly will you find a Hollander going over the hills to the poor house. Their industry keeps them at work until their thrift makes them capitalists; and then watch them go forg-ing to the front. The Vans and the Van-ders, though feebler than the conies in the numerical ratio of our population, have always been leaders in the great enterprises that make us—whether to our shame or glory—the richest nation on earth.

The most important bargain in the early history of our country was Peter Minuit's purchase of the island of Manhattan for sixty florins. A picture of that transaction hangs in our City Hall; a company of In-dians seated on the ground, the chief in the center receiving from the Dutch patroon the paltry sum of twenty-five dollars for a parcel of real estate now worth a hundred times as many millions. A sharp bargain, do you say? Surely: but one that shines "like a good deed in a naughty world" when compared with the customary mode of deal-ing with the Indians in those days, namely, "the good old plan that they may take who have the power and they may keep who can."

III. Let us now inquire as to the in-fluence of this numerically small contingent of our population on our educational life.

In the sixteenth century Holland was the center of universal learning. The youth of all nations came flocking to her universities. Froude says, "Holland stood like Greece among the nations of the ancient world." As a tribute to the heroism of the people of Leyden in resisting the siege of the Spanish armies a university was erected which pres-ently had an attendance of above two thous-and. And there were other institutions where the truth-seeker could pursue his quest under the guidance of expert masters to the utmost limit of his laudable desire.

But the far-seeing wisdom of these peo-ple was exhibited more particularly in their system of public schools. It was obvious to them that in a land where every man was measurably a sovereign in his own right the youthful prince must needs be educated for his place. It is for this reason that the ratio of illiteracy in Holland has always been inconsiderable as compared with that of other nations. The schools there were practically free and the three R's were com-pulsory. Such was the educational system which the men of the *Half-Moon* brought over with them: and it made them the pioneer school-masters of America. In every village or trading settlement which they established along the Hudson they were required, by order of the States-General, to place two deacons or "Zieken-troosters" for the instruction of the young.

The school laws of Massachusetts, requiring that a master should be employed for every fifty families, were enacted in the year 1655; but the same laws were in practical operation on Manhattan Island more than a quarter of a century before. Honor to whom honor is due. In 1633 Adam Roelantsen was made headmaster of the principal school on the island, and that school still exists. It may be visited on West End Avenue and Seventy-seventh Street in this city.

IV. But how about the political influence of these men?

In 1608, the year before the sailing of the Half-Moon, an armistice was declared by Philip III, which closed a weary century of war. In that war Holland, with her insignificant three millions had stood unswervingly against Spain for the inalienable rights of men. Liberty, equality, fraternity, were inscribed upon her banners two centuries before France wrote them in blood upon her dead walls or America sounded them forth in the clear notes of independence bell.

And the men of Holland had fought their campaign to a finish. In one of Carlyle's essays he says:

The Dutch are a strong people. They raised their land out of a marsh and went on, for a long period of time, breeding cows and making cheese; and might have gone on with their cows and cheese until doomsday. But Spain came over and said, "We want you to believe in Saint Ignatius." "Very sorry," replied the Dutch, but we can't." "Aye, but you must," said Spain. And they went about it with guns and swords to make them believe in Saint Ignatius. Never made them believe in him, but did succeed in breaking their own vertebral column and raising the Dutch into a great nation.

In a casual view of our country's history three names emerge above all others as representative of the broad and vital principles on which the republic rests: to wit, Washington, Lincoln, and Roosevelt. Let Americans of English blood be proud of Washington; let those who trace their lineage to Scotland speak reverently of Lincoln; the sons and daughters of Holland on their part will ever be thanking God for their kinship with Theodore Roosevelt. His name alone, were there none other to show for the influence of the Dutch forefathers, would be ample proof that it had not "vanished into thin air."

V. It remains to speak of the religious influence of these men.

The Dutch have ever been a religious people. It is recorded to the honor of the Protestants of England that during the long struggle of the Reformation in that country no less than two hundred and seventy martyrs gave their lives as a willing sacrifice for the truth; what then shall be said of Holland, with her less than three million souls, that in the same conflict under the administration of William the Silent los' more than one hundred thousand?

Not a few of those who came over in the Half-Moon and other ships that followed bore on their bodies the scars of their devotion to the righteous cause. Had they been disposed to leave their religion behind them they would have found it impossible, since by enactment of the States-General, they were required to place religious teachers in every settlement.

In 1628 Jonas Michaelius was sent over by the Classis of Amsterdam to minister in holy things. The deacons who were there before him had already assembled the nucleus of a church; but Domine Michaelius was the first minister installed in America. The Church in the Fort, which was fully organized in that memorable year, is now The Collegiate Church of New York.

We may imagine the welcome of this minister, who had long been looked and prayed for: how at the landing he was met with pomp and circumstance by men with wide-skirted coats and queues tied up with eel-skins, and by women in white caps and voluminous petticoats; how, passing along the narrow street of the village with its scalloped gables, he entered some hospitable home whose sanded floor had been marked with quaint figures by the house-wife's broom; and how he was there entertained at a generous table spread with bread and buttermilk and oely-koeks.

We have a brief account of the communion service held on the following Sabbath in the loft above the horse-mill. In a letter, now to be seen among the historic treasures of our Public Library, the Domine says: "Our voyage was long, of storm and tempest, we had no lack—Our coming was agreeable to all.—The first administration of the Lord's Supper was observed not without great joy and comfort to many." It must have been, indeed, a happy day.

We are left in no possible doubt as to the stalwart faith of these men. They never swerved from the great verities of the Reformation for which they had adventured their lives in the motherland. Christ was the sole arbiter of their conscience, whom they received as King over all and blessed forever. *Pro Christo* was their countersign, as *Oranje Boven* was their rallying cry.

As to their view of Scripture, here it is:

We receive the books of the Old and New Testament, and these only, as holy and canonical, for the regulation, foundation and confirmation of our faith; believing without any doubt all things contained in them; not so much because the Church receives and approves them as such, but more especially because the Holy Ghost witnesses in our hearts that they are from God.

Such were the early settlers of New Amsterdam. A feeble folk like the conies; but the storehouse of their possessions in faith and character was built among the rocks. No slackers they, nor waverers, nor loiterers in the middle of the road. Like Gideon's three hundred they would not bend their knees to satisfy their thirst, but dipped up the waters of freedom with their own hands and drank while standing on their feet like men.

The Italians have a legend of an abbey that long ago was overwhelmed by a landslide in which the monks all perished; but once a year, if you listen, they say you can hear the muffled notes of an organ and the low chanting of prayers. So do the spirits of these ancient worthies speak from afar to us, evoking what response? Shall it be this?

Faith of our fathers, holy faith,
We will be true to thee till death!

For what shall a noble lineage profit us if we do not live up to it? Our mills grind nothing with the waters gone by. When Napoleon was questioned as to his birthright he answered, "My only title of nobility was won at Montenotte." Our standing in the great day will be determined not by the question who were your forebears? but who are you? Let us so live, therefore, that when we met those ancient worthies—as by God's grace we shall one of these bright days—we may be able to say with pardonable pride, "I, too, have kept the faith!"

THANKSGIVING SACRIFICE[1]

Let them sacrifice the sacrifices of thanksgiving,
And declare his works with singing.
                                        —Ps. 107:22.

The sacrifice of thanksgiving under the Old Testament dispensation was an offering of something that was valuable to the owner. It was a sheep or a bullock that would have brought a high price in the market. And the thanksgiving offerings made in those days were made from the very best, and were voluntary offerings, or free will, and, unlike many other offerings, they were not required to be made at stated seasons. The thank offering was made whenever a man felt disposed to do it. It was a freewill offering, of the giver's own accord, made at a time when he felt especially thankful to the Lord. Then he brought the best of his flocks and offered it unto the Lord.

Other offerings were systematic and were made at stated intervals throughout the year in the temple; this was an offering made just before a feast. If a man had occasion to give a great feast; if his family had been well married; if a son had been born in the family; if a great blessing in the way of business prosperity had reached him—then he gave a feast and invited his friends. But before he sat down at the feast he carried, or sent, to the temple a thank offering, being unwilling to feast himself until he had first thanked God for the blessing which led to the feast.

Now the text, which I can not present today as it should be presented, has within it a spiritual idea which Christ evidently sought to evolve from it. When Jesus abolished the Old Testament system, he did not do away with the spirit of the law. He

[1] From *Sermons for the Great Days of the Year.* By RUSSELL H. CONWELL. George H. Doran Company, New York, 1922.

discontinued these thank offerings in the form of sheep or bullocks, but he came to fulfil in the spirit what was done before in the letter. He did not abolish our thanksgiving offering; on the contrary, he enforced the spirit of it. You remember how he told his disciples that when they brought their gifts to the altar, if they remembered that they had aught against another, or he against them, they were to go first and be reconciled with that brother, and then offer the gift. It enforced the same spirit as was supposed to be behind the Old Testament provision.

Then, when Jesus was describing the final judgment, he said, "Inasmuch as ye have done it unto the least of these, my brethren, ye have done it unto me." We were still to worship God and to make thank offerings, but the way we were to express our thanksgiving was to do some deed of helpfulness to these, his brethren, on the earth. He simply changed the form and not the spirit of the thanksgiving offering.

We have come to this Thanksgiving week in the history of our lives, and we ask ourselves, "What is it to be religiously thankful? What ought we to do?" In this text we have this express command, "Let them sacrifice the sacrifice of thanksgiving." If we are to sacrifice, let us do it now, before we feast.

One of the dear old Quakers of your own State, of whom I read with interest years ago, always went to his Thanksgiving dinner by the way of a little side room, where he knelt for a few moments in prayerful thanksgiving and put in a small box the amount to a cent which the Thanksgiving dinner had cost him and his family. Then was his conscience clear; then was he comforted by the thought that he had made his sacrifice offering to God; and he went to the simple, plain feast of the Friends with a delight, and a joy of soul, peace of mind, and rest of body such as another could not have known. Jesus taught the principle that it was right to feast, but that we were to go to that feast by the way of sacrifice.

O my friends, how few people thank the Lord! How few really good men there are in this world! There are half-good ones! There are half-hearted ones! There are half-learned ones, but how few come up to the utmost standard of what Christ sets here as possible! How few true offerings there

are, and how sacred are these few! It is a very curious thing that the Lord makes ten thousand millions of seeds for every one tree that grows from the seed, and so he makes ten thousand human beings in order to get one real man. It seems a very curious thing that he should have wasted (apparently to us, but not to him) his strength, that there should be so few sacrifices made, so few real men, full men, complete men, out of all the millions that the Lord brings into being.

How many trees there are! If any of you own a farm, you have found out how many trees grow there which bear no fruit. You have about six trees to one apple, as a rule, nowadays. The trees grow where you don't want them, all around, by the fence and on the roads. You have the trees, but when you go out in the fall season and ought to find fruit, you find only here and there an apple, only here and there a tree that bears fruit. So many men there are in the world who are supposed to bear fruit, but so few actually bear the fruit for which they are intended. How many of us have prayed and prayed that we might be counted among those who are worthy to be esteemed Christ's disciples, and yet there are only a sacred few. Christ himself said to his disciples, "Pray the Lord of the harvest that he send laborers into his vineyard." "The harvest surely is plentiful, but the laborers are few," Jesus said to them. When there were already hundreds of Christian human beings on the earth, Jesus said to them, "The laborers indeed are few."

How few make the sacrifice of thanksgiving during this Thanksgiving week in its best form! How many express their gratitude to God beyond words and prayers! Now, this is Thanksgiving week. We profess to be thankful! We praise God and thank him for his mercies untold, but what fruit do we bear? Why, we grow up in the spring, we put on our green leaves, and we spread forth our blossoms of thanksgiving, but when this week is gone and God asks us, "Where is the fruit?" we must answer, "There is no fruit!" All the flowers blasted! Nothing but words! Nothing but form! No offerings, no real sacrifice to God!

Once in a while I hear of some heroic deed in connection with my life work in educating or helping to educate young men. I heard of one who gave me a high opinion of a young man's gratitude. An old farmer in New Hampshire assisted this young man to go to Harvard College, and when he had finished his course in Harvard he desired to go to Europe. He secured a scholarship which would have paid his tuition in one of the great universities of Europe. His goods were packed and he had procured his ticket to sail, when he heard that the dear old farmer was very sick and his crops were ready for the harvest. When he heard the facts, that the farmer was sick and that the harvest was ready on that farm in New Hampshire, where it was so difficult to obtain help, he returned his ticket, at a discount, and took a train for the farm. Altho he had been a student all his life, he went right out in the clothes of a farmer and harvested the crops during that season. When the next springtime came he had an opportunity again, for they always come to such men as these, and he went to Europe with a brighter view, a lighter heart, and an ambition purified and blessed indeed by the offering he made to that old benefactor. This young man was sufficiently appreciative of what his benefactor had done for him to go there and actually to gather his crops under the heated sun, exposing himself for the benefactor. We all honor a man who will do that. Of course that man will go to the highest places! He will be honored and loved on every hand. Now, that was an excellent disposition. But suppose when he heard that the man's harvest was going to be lost he had written a beautiful letter of condolence! Suppose with all his college training and rhetorical discipline he had composed a poem and sent it to the old farmer, wishing him all manner of prosperity and even praying for it! Suppose he had done all that, he would have been like many of us Christians—we have done the same thing toward God. God blessed us; we know it and feel it, and we are very thankful to-day, so that we are ready to offer up our wordy thanksgiving, but not the sacrifice!

How many persons now say "thank you," altho some are so stingy in their words that they leave off the "you" and simply say "thanks"! But what is that in the sight of God but an unfruitful tree!

I was told last Wednesday night about a leading pastor of the country. He was born in Scotland, of poor parentage, and had but little opportunity to secure an education. He came to this country as a young man, and went to work in a livery stable, trying to earn an honest living. He drove out to a small pond near New York with an old gentleman who ventured out on the ice to see the skaters. The ice gave way, and many of the skaters were precipitated into the cold water. The old gentleman was also overturned in the water and exposed to the dangers of death. The driver left his horse and waded as far as he could, and then, pushing aside the ice, swam out and saved the old gentleman, with two or three others. When he placed the man in the carriage, he wrapped him in his own overcoat and then he wrapped him in the robes, and drove hastily to a house nearby where the gentleman was acquainted. The saved man said, "What shall I give you?" "The driver replied, "Nothing." The gentleman said, "What is your name?" "No matter," he replied, "I have only done my duty in the matter, and I don't want to be known. I am glad you are saved." He went back to the livery stable. It was more than two years after that when the old gentleman saw him again down at Castle Garden and recognized him as the youth that had saved him. He ran and called after him and said, "Won't you come to my house? I want to see you." He gave the young man his card, and, after considerable hesitation, the young man presented himself at the door and was ushered in by the servant. He was taken right into the open parlors and dining-room, in the midst of a great party. There were assembled the richest, the wealthiest, the most fashionable people in New York. The ladies were dressed in the completeness of fine drapery. Their eyes were bright, their cheeks flushed, their voices happy. The scene was fascinating, and completely overwhelmed the mind of the young man, who had never seen such bright lights and such flashing eyes. The daughter of the owner of the mansion said, "Who is that?" The servant said, "He is the one that your father sent for." "Oh!" she said, "that is the young man that saved my father." She rushed forward to him in the midst of all that company, with all her array of fashionable attire and brilliant diamonds, and expressed to him her joy that she had found him. She brought him right up to the table and introduced him to the people, to his great dismay, terror and pain. "Certainly, bring him in here! Of course he is not dressed for a party, as he knew nothing of it, but bring him right in here and give him a seat at the table!" One of the wealthiest men of New York said, "You must have this place," and then asked the servant to bring in again the course that had already passed. At last, in his confusion, the young man managed to get out and he begged them to let him go. But this daughter of the millionaire bade him good-by and said, "We will always be glad to see you. You will always be welcome in this house." Oh! how many a fashionable girl, even if all her relations had been saved, would on a fashionable occasion like that have scorned to speak to the ordinary young man. But this daughter's gratitude went further. She asked her father to help that young man secure an education, and he obtained it. First he went to a preparatory school in New York, and then to Princeton University, and afterward he married the young lady, and they now live in a magnificent mansion and last Wednesday night I was introduced to the family of this successful preacher, whose benefactions are so extensive and who has the assistance of that lovely and noble wife in all his work. I thought of that story, and considered how many thousands of young ladies there are who in the midst of their fashionable gatherings would have thought it a social disgrace to have welcomed any man not attired in a "dress suit." God makes a thousand human females to one real woman.

But it is just as true of churches as it is of individuals. I was interested yesterday in meeting the Methodist brethren in Baltimore as they assembled to consult over their missionary work. How many churches they have, as we have, in this country which, like the trees on my farm, grow green and blossom, but they have no fruit. We gather so few final results. That is the history of our churches all over the land.

There is a man near Westfield, Mass., who, in memory of his father, keeps the old sawmill just as it was when his father died. The buzz-saw is polished every day, and the dam is kept complete, and the gate is complete, and the wheel is repaired—everything ready to run. It has been there I know not how long, but for quite a number of years; it has not been through a single log in all those years, yet it has been polished and kept in complete condition to do the work it never does.

Like a woman who makes up dresses and never wears them, it is the disposition of the Church to spend all its strength in preparing to do something. We have our prayer-meetings. What for? What is the purpose? Jesus Christ said he came into this world to save the world, and the Apostle Paul, representing the highest aim of Christianity, said, "This is a faithful saying and worthy of all acceptation, that Jesus Christ came into the world to save sinners." That is the chief purpose of the Church, and yet you will find churches in this country where they hold the prayer-meeting for a whole year without one attempt to save anybody—without a thought that they are there to save any soul. They come together and make their prayers and their short speeches, and prepare themselves for a work they never think of doing. It never occurs to them that it can be done!

How many societies we have in this church in which they are going through the same polishing of the saw; just the same repairing of the wheel; just the same keeping of the dam and reservoir in order! What is the Christian Endeavor Society for? It is to save sinners. That is the aim! That is the whole of it! But the Christian Endeavor Society says, "We wish to be trained in prayer, in Christian work." If the Christian Endeavor Society has been preparing itself for five years, why don't the members do actual Christian work now? Why does it not gather some sinners? Why does it not go after some lost soul and thus bring forth the fruit for which it has been preparing? Why is not that the harvest of all the different societies of this church.

We have a great church! We have prepared this institution! We have gotten it ready for the great harvest, and the harvest is as fully prepared as we; yet we will go and hear Mr. Conwell preach, and the chorus sing, and then we will go home and think we have done the whole, when we are only just getting ready for work, when we have only just come to the point where we can do something. We go out of this church with the idea that we wish to do better. Those of you who have witnessed this baptism this morning have a wish that you might reconsecrate yourselves to the Lord, and yet when you get out into the rain it will dampen the whole purpose, and you will come next Sunday the same. It has all been wasted because you do not carry out the purpose for which Christ died and for which his Church was instituted.

There was a man in Pennsylvania whom I always delighted to meet, who always found his way to his Thanksgiving dinner by way of his old mother's home. He took his mother something good and then went to his own Thanksgiving feast. Let no man who wants to serve God go to his Thanksgiving dinner this year without doing something for those whom Christ loves. It is the way to keep Thanksgiving. If a man this week, having in mind the hospital work for the good of those suffering poor for whom Christ died—if a man say, "I will do something for that hospital before I eat my Thanksgiving dinner," and do it, O! then he will make the "sacrifice of thanksgiving."

A man is not sincerely thankful until he is ready to make some positive sacrifice. Not far from here a man belonging to another church never eats his Thanksgiving dinner without hanging up in sight a turkey which he is going to give to somebody else. While it is a peculiar way of expressing it, it does express the great truth that I am trying to evolve this morning: that we, in order to be really thankful, need be thankful enough to express it in charitable deeds.

All who believe in the Lord Jesus Christ have everlasting life, but baptism is the test of that belief. If one believes in Jesus Christ enough to be baptized, then he is sure that he has believed enough to be saved. If a man is thankful enough to Christ for his blessings to his family so as to express it in some deed before his fellow men, then he makes the true "sacrifice of thanksgiving"; then he goes to God with an offering that will be acceptable.

When Christ sat at that well at Samaria, waiting for his disciples to bring him something to eat, a soul came that way. He came into the world to save souls, and when that woman of Samaria came, he talked with her until he was refreshed. He had meat to eat that they knew not of.

You can eat a Thanksgiving dinner for yourself after you have carried one to some poor people. Then you, too, can make your Thanksgiving dinner a spiritual feast. If you have made some one else happier or better in the name of Jesus Christ, you won't need all the luxuries heaped on your table. Christ talked to that soul at the well and pointed her to the Lord. Then he did not care for his dinner. It was of no more value to him, because no feast could add to his exultant joy.

We ought to be thankful enough to bear fruit indeed. As a church we ought to be a saving people. As a society we ought to be a saving people. As individual Christians we ought to be saving souls. As lovers of God, and grateful for his goodness, we ought to worship him by positive open sacrifice of something of value to us. The sacrifice should be real, practical, personal—the giving up of something for the good of some one else—and such a "sacrifice of thanksgiving" will make your Thanksgiving Day the happiest you have ever seen, unless you have practised this often before.

BENEDICTION

O Lord! we know that, whether we have little or much ourselves on Thanksgiving Day, it will be a completely happy day if we have made some sacrifice for thy sake, and for the sake of our fellow man, as an "offering of thanksgiving." O Jesus! inspire us with a sense of our obligation as sinners to rise higher than mere words into the realm of deeds, where we bring of the best of that which we love most, and sacrifice it gladly for thy service and as an expression of our obligation to thee. Now may mercy and peace from God the Father, the Son and the Holy Spirit abide with us as through this week we try to make some distinct offering in his name. Amen.

THE CHILDREN'S SERVICE

THE SUNBEAM [1]

"Isn't it time we had a holiday?" asked the sunbeams one morning in their home high above the world. "We have been on duty long enough," said one, "and now that the flowers are over and the harvests in, I don't see why we should be always at it."

"Quite right!" chimed in the others. "We won't shine again till we feel like it. People don't think enough about what we do, so let them miss us a while."

"I don't want to be disagreeable," said one little beam that had been standing apart, "but I think you are wrong. People do appreciate what we do. I know they are glad to see us, and if the flowers are over that is all the more reason why we should try to brighten up the world. No holiday for me!"

"All right," said the rest. "Off you go! We'll see who has the best time."

Like an airman making for earth, Sunbeam came swiftly traveling through clouds and smoke till he reached a gray and gloomy city. It was quite early, but the people who were going to the mills seemed glad to see him, and he thought one of them nodded in quite a friendly way.

"Now that I've come, what am I going to do with myself?" thought he. "I haven't got very long, and I want to do some one a good turn to-day."

As he looked about, he noticed that right opposite stood a number of houses that had once seen better days. The street was shabby and the people that passed looked poor.

"Wonder if there's any one about here who wants cheering up?" He peered through a window, and there on a wretched bed lay a little fellow with such pale cheeks. Sunbeam saw that the room was bare and comfortless and he felt very sorry for the sick boy, so he hopped on the bed.

The little chap's face brightened up at once, and they had a fine game together, for the boy's wasted fingers were trying to get hold of Sunbeam, as tho he wanted to keep the golden bar of light forever. And the beam danced and dodged till the boy laughed right out at his antics. No matter how swiftly the hand moved, the beam was always too clever and it escaped.

At last it was time for Sunbeam to say good-by. You know, sunbeams can never stay very long in the same place. But it made the beam's heart glad to see the color in the boy's thin cheeks, and to hear his merry laugh.

"Well, good-by for the present," he said to the boy. And as he got out into the street, he said to himself, "That is a good beginning for my day. Now I wonder what's next?"

After a time, Sunbeam found himself before a lot of warehouses and offices. They looked as tho they had never seen the sun, for they were so dark and gray, but that was all the more reason why Sunbeam should spend a little time there if he could do any good. But could he? That was the question.

Looking through a key-hole, Sunbeam saw a man sitting at a desk and looking very unhappy. He was resting his head on his hand, and he said to himself, "Things seem to be going from bad to worse."

Something must have been troubling him. What it was I do not know, but that was enough for Sunbeam. With a bit of wriggle, he found that he could get through the key-hole, and he mounted the desk, looking up into the man's face, and waiting for him to notice.

"I wish I could cheer him up," said Sunbeam. And just that moment, the man opened his eyes, and leaping off his stool, he said, "What's the use of looking on the dark side like this? Why, I declare, the sun's shining. I must pull myself together and have another try!"

He started hurrying about his office, and got out his ledgers, while Sunbeam sat there enjoying the fun. Before he left, the do you will hardly believe it, the man was humming a tune.

"Good turn No. 2," chuckled Sunbeam, slipping out into the street. "Say, I'm having a great time to-day! I'm jolly glad I came. What's next, I wonder?"

While he was making up his mind which

[1] *Parables for Little People.* By J. W. G. WARD. George H. Doran Company, New York, 1921.

way to go, he heard some boys shouting, and there a dog came tearing along the street like mad. Its tongue was hanging out, while its tail was so far between its legs with fright that it was almost tripping him. And these lads were chasing him with stones and shouting till he was scared out of his wits.

"What should be done?" Sunbeam suddenly thought of a plan. He hid round the corner where the dog had run, and just as the first boy came up, out flashed the beam into his eyes. He was dazzled. He stopped. The others stopped, too, to see what was the matter—and the dog had got away!

"Cheerio!" cried Sunbeam. "I never guessed there was such fun in doing good turns. I wish I could stay here forever."

That was impossible. It was getting late. People were now going home from work, and Sunbeam had to get back too. Yet as he danced along the pavement he noticed how the tired faces lighted up at the sight of him. And when he met his friends after sunset he said, "Well, what kind of a day have you all had? I've had the time of my life!"

OUTLINES

The City in a Wilderness

And he built Tadmor in the wilderness.—
2 Chron. 8:4a; 1 Kings 9:17, 18.

Five days' journey northeast from Damascus into the wilderness of Syria brings the traveler upon a modern village of a few mud huts, where he finds thirty or forty families living within the spacious enclosure of a magnificent ancient temple. Its lofty arch and rows of noble columns, once 390, still attest its original grandeur. Once a city of a half million population (it sent 80,000 soldiers to assist the Assyrian army), the city of Zenobia who opposed the Romans, it has disappeared from the face of the earth all but the gorgeous ruins which now lie, "lonely and forsaken like bleached bones on a long-neglected battle-field."

Like travelers, then, who find it worth while to visit this ruin, let us go to Tadmor for a space and learn what the Spirit of God may tell us there by the "City in the Wilderness."

I. Why was it built? 1. To put an oasis to use. 2. For the rest and refreshment of travelers. 3. To satisfy the ambition of its founder, Solomon the wise, the master builder. 4. Why should he exhaust his resources and skill upon such a task? Wisdom and skill are not exhausted upon great tasks, but increased. 5. What gain could come from this enterprise? Here was established an outpost of empire, to push it farther into unoccupied wastes, to ward off the enemy, lest the territory be approached, to make trade safe and protect the king's caravans, to show the munificence and power of the king.

II. Tadmor witnesses to the grandeur of human achievement. 1. As we walk in thought amid these ruins, how they speak to us of the boldness and greatness of human attainment! The vast splendors of Tadmor are eloquent of human glory and endeavor. What a daring being man is! That is God's wish. "Subdue the earth," "Have dominion over it!" Lay an unsubdued spirit upon him. In answer to this command man has established governments, founded empires, builded cities, measured the distances of the stars, weighed the sun and the earth, and still attempts the seemingly impossible. 2. Tadmor pictures all human achievement in organizing society, subduing continents, and overcoming obstacles, and stands for the tasks which yet remain in response to the conviction, "I can do all things through Christ which strengtheneth me."

III. But Tadmor to-day speaks as eloquently of the vanity of all human splendor. 1. How empty it all seems, as we walk here! Ruins and sands. Palmyra the mighty fallen into dust and ashes. What is it, all this human striving, after all? Is it anything more than the activity of an ant-heap busy amid a summer's sunshine? How are we to think of the boasts and tasks of the sons of men? 2. How soon it all seems to pass away and fall to dust! Here only the palms remain to remind us of the greatness and glory of Palmyra! How vain that the Emperor Hadrian once added his name to this city which is no more! Adrianopolis has followed the emperor to dust.

IV. What then is the significance of all this endeavor? 1. There is reward in the very joy of overcoming difficulties. Christians are "overcomers." 2. The graces and virtues we admire are born of great tasks. 3. The reflex action upon the worker is his best reward. 4. The Christ, building his kingdom of more hopeless materials than entered into the walls of Tadmor, wrought in a drearier desert and under more desperate conditions. 5. As this labor of Soloman's was well worth while, so is your task and mine, for

V. This is our task, also. 1. We are invited to become fellow-laborers, not of a Solomon, whose handiwork perishes, but "fellow-laborers with Christ." 2. If you have been disheartened with your lot and dispirited with your task, recall this Tadmor in the wilderness. If you have sometimes desired to give over the struggle, gather courage by assuming an even more difficult endeavor. The picture of an Elijah asking that he may die in the hour of his disappointment is enervating. The glory of Tadmor lay in the fact that it was built in a desert amid difficulties, and such may be the glory of your life and mine. 3. Heroism and the Christian graces do not ooze forth from a life of ease, but triumph through the bread of difficulties. 4. No one may enter into the best, into his best, except through the "strait and narrow way" of tasks which test his every energy. If you have been set to a hard task, it is God's compliment to you. He seeks to place the best within your reach, and this is his method. What will be your grades after the testing-time has passed? The task of building a Tadmor was extreme, but each worker who had a part in rearing that city came where he was glad to say, "I was one of the workmen upon those walls. That city is mine in part." Such may be your experience, when the toils and hard passages of time are over. Will not that be reward enough?

The Mirror of the Soul

But whoso looketh . . . being not a forgetful hearer . . . shall be blessed in his deed.—James 1: 23-25.

One of the essentials of our present civilization is the mirror. Soldier, astronomer, valet, need it every day. Provision has been made by supreme wisdom for mirror of the soul—"perfect law."

I. Not merely a revealer of virtues; only vain souls use mirror to see beauty. Yet some want that kind of religion; which commends, but never corrects.

II. Shows defects—thoughtful hearers here get blessing. "Law of liberty" no misnomer—law guarantees liberty. "Had not known sin except through law" (Rom. 7:7). Enlightens, so that choice for better can always be made.

III. Progress—by "remembering his precepts to do them." Impartial looking. Not a glance, but looking with care: with a view to application. Mirror shows right course. Resolution makes the consistent "doer." Blessing comes in fuller life.

Dethronement By Enthronment

And let Zadok the priest and Nathan the prophet anoint him there king over Israel; and blow ye the trumpet, and say, Long live King Solomon. Then ye shall come up after him, and he shall come and sit upon my throne; for he shall be king in my stead; and I have appointed him to be prince over Israel and over Judah.— 1 Kings 1:34. 35.

David, the warrior king, was old and near his end. God had revealed to him that Solomon his son should succeed him. But Adonijah, a younger son, conspired to usurp the throne. By a clever and quick action David had Solomon crowned before Adonijah. Thus Adonijah was defeated. Adonijah dethroned by enthroning Solomon.

I. This has been God's method from the first. 1. This world designed to be Christ's kingdom. "All things were made by him and for him." Absolute right as Son of God. 2. God had announced his coming to possess it. "I will establish the throne of his kingdom forever." 3. But Satan attempted to usurp the throne by flattery and deceit, and seemed to succeed. God did not send his hosts against Satan and destroy him. But (4) in due time God declared him king. "This is my beloved Son, hear ye him."

King Jesus is now winning the world to himself. Satan's power is waning as Christ's increases. "Now there was long war between the house of Saul and the house of David. But David waxed stronger and the house of Saul waxed weaker and weaker."

II. This is God's method for his Church. 1. Defeat false gods not by armed force, but by crowning Christ in their place. 2. Destroy vice by enthroning virtue. Preach, practise Christian principles. Apply this method to politics, business, social customs.

III. This is God's method for the individual. 1. Man finds himself under power of evil. Tastes perverted, judgment darkened, will weakened, wrong habits formed. "When I would do good, evil is present, etc." "A strong man armed is keeping the palace." 2. Man's only hope is in enthroning Christ. He does this by surrendering to Christ. Then Christ as the "stronger than the strong man overcomes him." And so Satan is dethroned by the enthronement of Christ.

By this method "the kingdoms of this world are to become the kingdom of our Lord and of his Christ; and he shall reign forever and ever."

"What Is Man that Thou Art Mindful of Him?"

When I consider thy heavens, the work of thy fingers,
The moon and the stars, which thou hast ordained;
What is man, that thou art mindful of him?
And the son of man, that thou visitest him?
    —Ps. 8:3, 4; Heb. 2:6.

Question of perennial interest. Asked by the psalmist, by writer of Hebrews, by every thoughtful man. Answer depends upon the view we take of him. In one aspect he seems very insignificant. In another aspect very significant.

I. First, very insignificant. 1. As to size. Compare him with the horse, whale, California trees, mountains, earth, universe. "When I consider the heavens, etc." 2. As to duration. Cf. pyramids, "everlasting hills," geologic ages.

II. But second, how significant. 1. As originally created. (1) In ability. Think God's thoughts after him. Trace God's handiworks. Conquer and harness nature. Determine his own actions. (2) In his purity. Innocent, upright, fellowship with God. Tho fallen, sinful, guilty, yet significant. 2. As God esteems him. Loves him tho sinful. Made infinite sacrifice for him. 3. As seen in the perfect man, Christ Jesus. Gentle, strong, courageous, sinless. Second Adam unfallen. 4. As represented in redeemed state. Purified, glorified, like Christ. Eternally with God.

What an incentive to strive to attain "unto a perfect man, unto the measure of the stature of the fulness of Christ."

What Waiting on the Lord Will Do

But they that wait upon the Lord shall renew their strength; they shall mount up with wings as eagles; they shall run and not be weary; they shall walk and not faint.—Isa. 40:31.

Introduction: Contrast in verses 28, 29 and 30. Isaiah lifted up. The coal of fire and his lips. The great Old Testament gospeler.

I. What is it to wait on the Lord? 1. Take the waiter on some notable, or valet, or maid. Secretary to the President. Hindenberg yields to Ludendorff: "What do you say?" The Christian looks up to a greater. 2. Not mere waiting, as the virgins. Active obedient servants. Nehemiah, Joseph, Daniel, on kings, on God. 3. Christ our King. What should we do but wait on him? "Study to be approved." Prayers to and through him. Appeals and worship. Serve him in Christian fellowship. Through the means of grace and the Church. 4. On "eagles" here, see HOMILETIC REVIEW for May, 1922, page 421.

II. The effect of worship and spiritual service. 1. Mount up, run, walk, according to circumstances. The descending series merely formal, we should think. To walk may require more grace than to run. Errands for Christ and the kingdom. 2. Again. "Mount up with wings"; allows reasonable rein to the feelings. "Rise my soul and stretch thy wings," etc. The feelings and emotions have their proper evaluation in the Christian life. The merely emotional man and the merely formal church-member would better look out here! 3. Let us stress the effect of waiting on the Lord. Renewed strength given; spiritual life quickened. Heart's horizon enlarged. Reconstruction in holy purposes assured and more satisfaction and joy given in religious service.

Three Accents

One thing I know.—John 9:25.

In this expression are three accents.

I. The accent of experience. It was not the accent of intellect so much as that of experience. The man had received the light-giving touch, and because of this, "he knew." How foolish to gainsay knowledge based on such experience. It is the last word of knowledge. Experience is the attestation of theory. Argument is very unreliable; in fact, Renan says that "the best causes are usually won by bad reasoning." The most potent word is the word of experience.

II. The accent of authority. Of all these critics and cavilers only one could speak with authority, and that was a man who had been blind. Others might discuss the question, but he could tell with certainty. Where is the authority of the man who doesn't know? He only can speak with authority who knows. "Why not bleed him?" said a layman to a medical man, as if a layman could speak with authority on the matter. Authority can come only of real experience and knowledge. (Apply to non-Christians criticizing Jesus Christ, the Church and Christianity. What do they really know about it? Have they, to begin with, the inward knowledge qualifying them to speak?)

III. Accent of finality. The man to speak the last word as to whether Jesus had really imparted the gift of sight was the once blind man. If he couldn't tell whether he could see or not, nobody else was better fitted. The man who can give finality to the argument as to whether Christ has saved him is the saved man himself.

"Let the redeemed say so," for theirs is assuredly the last word that can be given.

America's Special Thanksgiving Notes

Thou hast not dealt so with any nation.—Ps. 147:20.

This singer seems to have discovered some special reasons for national thanksgiving. Perhaps the time is right for America to take an inventory.

I. Her very aloofness—set apart by wide seas; also by precedents of "no entangling alliances"—"Free from dead hand of a bygone civilization" (Roosevelt). Free to cultivate lofty ideals, "America cultivates ideals in difficult places" (London *Spectator*), e. g., Boxer indemnity; Mexico; Philippines; Church's foreign mission policy.

II. Statutes and ordinances of Almighty have had their influences. "Ardor for peace" more commendable than militarism. Church's influence more direct. "Home mission week" recognizes this function.

III. Need of appreciation for deeper blessings—not material. Times are "not so good," but many are supporting the institutions that impoverish homes and souls—automobiles; cheap amusements; ward politics. Need fuller comprehension of the meaning of life; catch higher leadings which Church endeavors to impart.

There is love that stirs the heart, and love that gives it rest.
But the love that leads life upward is the noblest and the best. (Van Dyke.)

THEMES AND TEXTS

From the Rev. E. BEAL, Somerville, South Africa

The Gospel of the Incidental. "As they went, they were healed."—Luke 17:5-15.

Christ's Reversals. "I am come to make the sightless see and to make the seeing blind."—John 9:39.

Captain or Calf? ". . . they have made them a molten calf, and have worshiped it, and have sacrificed unto it, and said, These are thy gods, O Israel, which brought thee up out of the land of Egypt."—Ex. 32:8.
"And they said one to another, Let us make a captain, and let us return into Egypt."—Num. 14:4.

The Far View. "Let thine eye look right on."—Prov. 43:5.

Christianity the Best Religion. "What nation is there who hath a God so nigh unto them, as the Lord our God is in all things that we call upon him for?"—Deut. 4:7.

The Architect of Character. "The bricks are fallen down, but we will build with hewn stone."—Isa. 9:10.
"Except the Lord build the house, they labor in vain who build it."—Psalm 127:1.

Polarisation. "I, if I be lifted up, will draw all men unto me."—John 12:32.
"Depart from me, ye workers of iniquity."—Luke 13:27.

ILLUSTRATIONS AND ANECDOTES

God's Oneness With Humanity

Once there was brought home to me in a very beautiful and unexpected manner the Christian truth about God's essential oneness with humanity. Weary from my afternoon calls, I had just returned home. Entering the side hall that was already dark, I saw through the door, slightly ajar, my little son and daughter at play. Philip, eight years old, was building up blocks on the floor, while Esther, two years younger, was standing under the electric light with both arms raised as high as she could stretch them over her head. Seeing her dramatic position, and the unusual look on her face, I remained silent in the hall, knowing that something was coming. With intense feeling she said:

"Oh, Philip! of course we would kiss God!" To which Philip replied:

"Oh, you couldn't kiss God. He is a spirit. Why, God is in you,—and in me."

Still standing in her dramatic position with the light shining full on her face, she began lowering her arms slowly, and as her expression of comprehension deepened she said:

"Oh, well then, Philip, if God is in you and in me, if we were to kiss each other we would kiss God."

"Yes, that is right, you would," was his response. Then said she:

"Let us kiss God." He arose promptly, and the children, throwing their arms tightly around each other, kissed God.

If ever there was a glad father I was one. Standing there in the dark hall, I thought:

"God bless the dear children, they have the evangel. That is the very essence of the Christian religion, 'Inasmuch as ye did it unto the least of these ye did it unto me.' "

Of course we all realize that there are certain proprieties which adults must observe, but what could be more beautiful than for a little brother and sister so to recognize God in each other as to be able to kiss him? The idea here involved, if carried out in every relation of life, would be the kingdom of God realized. Furthermore, there is no other way of making the kingdom of God a reality, either on earth or in the life beyond. Doubtless God never will be seen outside the bodies which he provides for himself and his children to use in common.—RICHARD LABUE SWAIN in *What and Where Is God?*

Flowers for the Living

Many times since the days of Columbus has it been necessary for genius combined with special inspiration to demonstrate the simplest possible proposition. Here, for instance, we go on lavishing flowers upon the dead, and leaving in dismal rooms—often with not a single daisy to look at—the old, crippled, the sick, the merely neglected and shut-in living persons to whom the beauty and cheer of a few blossoms, embodying a message of kindliness and fellowship, would make much difference. The Irene Kaufman Settlement of Pittsburgh, in initiating an annual Flower Day for the Living, has carried into many homes the gladness of the Christian Easter holiday and of the Jewish Purim or Passover. Here are some of the results as recorded by those who took part in the round of visits:

"Mrs. Goldberg, an old lady, crippled with rheumatism, when she received her plant said, 'Long shall you live, and many passovers shall you have.' She bowed and thanked me several times, and placed the flower on the center of the table so the woman who lives in the next room could also enjoy it. Mrs. Goldberg explained that they both use the same sink and spigot and the woman in the next room would have to pass the table and see the flower when she went for water."

"Our Italian mother lives in a dingy court-yard. She beamed with happiness when she received a cineraria, and exclaimed that the flower was a bit of sunshine for the whole court. The rest of the family—ten children and the father, a street-cleaner—were consulted and agreed with her that the whole court must share in their gift. So, with much pride, they placed their 'bit of sunshine' on a little shelf right outside of their second-floor window, which faces the court. Little Tony declared they 'wuz the sweetest folks in the court.' "

"Our colored man of fifty is a patient sufferer. For eight months he has been bedridden and has excruciating pains. When the nurse walked into his room with the flower, the smile on his face confirmed his statement as to his joy in getting such an Easter greeting. 'Lan' sakes, chile, I's not too sick to 'preciate flowers. I's kinda got the feelin' of bein' young in me now. God bless you!' "—*Survey.*

What Is Disease?

It is told of one of the great French chemists, Chevreul, that when he was interviewed in his hundredth year and asked: "Have you always had a good digestion?" he answered out of the fulness of his vigor: "I really can not say, for I have never noticed." This is quite ideal; it indicated a great harmony of internal processes. The antipathy which unsophisticated people have to learning about the works of the living engine, is, in a way, quite sound. For we really should not know anything about organs like the stomach and liver—hardworking structures quite unobtrusive when well used. The body is a great laboratory in which up-buildings and down-breakings, combustions and fermentations, dissolvings and filterings go on in crowded order. They are all summed up in the word metabolism, which means change. We may speak of them as vital processes. And the idea we must grasp is that health spells harmony of vital processes, while disease means metabolism out of place, out of time, and out of tune. What is disease in one animal may be normal in another. What would be ominous at one time of life may be natural at another.

Disease is a disturbance of the body's wholesome routine, and there is progress simply in realizing this. Our forefathers thought of disease as a mysterious potency, stalking out from the unknown, and seizing a man by the throat. There may be a truth in thinking of disease as a visitation or a judgment, but a great part of the value of the truth is lost if we do not understand that disease is often an inevitable consequence of our carelessness, or ignorance, or sluggishness, or foolhardiness. When the disciples asked Christ about the man blind from his birth, "For whose sin—for his own or for his parents'—was he born blind?" they were not thinking about heredity or about transmission of acquired characters,

or about blindness due to infection before birth, they were thinking of the blindness as a judgment imposed from without. That idea of disease must be given up.— J. Arthur Thomson, *The Control of Life.*

The Gospel Rainbow

A friend asked me once: "Is it possible to make the sunbeam more beautiful?" I innocently answered: "No. The sunbeam is God's finished work." I thought that was conclusive. My friend took me to a triangular prism, and ran a sunbeam through it; lo, in an instant it sparkled out into all the beauties of the rainbow. It entered the crystal one miracle and it came out of the crystal seven other miracles. It is possible to increase the beauty of the sunbeams sevenfold. A fine Christian personality is one of God's prisms. Be such a prism and you will be a sevenfold power for good. In this way you can give the truth a sevenfold power among men. Love, courage, purity, optimism, sympathy, conscientiousness, and self-sacrifice, these are the beauties of the gospel rainbow and they are the sevenfold colors of the divine light.—David Gregg in *A Book of Remembrance.*

"Rattling the Pitcher"

I remember an anecdote which illustrates the way in which a man may use opportunities and try to read the character or to obtain an obvious advantage when dealing with a Foreign Minister. I do not vouch for the truth of the story, but tell it as I heard it in Berlin. One of the admirers of Prince Bismarck had presented to him as a gift a large and powerful dog. It was, I think, a wolfhound, or something between a wolfhound and a mastiff; a big animal of formidable appearance. It had a habit of growling and sometimes even of snapping when it found reason to suspect that any one displeased its master. Bismarck frequently kept this dog, which was known in Berlin as the *Reichshund*, the "Hound of the Empire," by his side when he received foreign ambassadors. The story went that the dog would now and then growl and show its teeth in a threatening way at the foreign ambassador, who was seated hard by, not far from the creature's fangs. Bismarck seemed to relish the uneasiness which the ambassador could not help showing at the behavior of the dog, and he derived from his visitor's embarrassment an advantage in his negotiations similar to that which is, I believe, sought in the game of baseball by the practise of what you call "rattling the pitcher."—JAMES BRYCE in *International Relations*.

I Shall Not Pass Again This Way

[*The Baptist* makes this comment on this poem: "Much worn, it was found in the desk of Mr. Daniel S. Ford, the proprietor and editor of the *Youth's Companion*, after his death when his desk was cleared by loving hands. It explains much of Mr. Ford's wide and generous benefactions."]

The bread that giveth strength I want to give:
The water pure that bids the thirsty live;
I want to help the fainting day by day:
I'm sure I shall not pass again this way.

I want to give the oil of joy for tears,
The faith to conquer cruel doubts and fears.
Beauty for ashes may I give alway:
I'm sure I shall not pass again this way.

I want to give good measure running o'er,
And into angry hearts I want to pour
The answer soft that turneth wrath away:
I'm sure I shall not pass again this way.

I want to give to others hope and faith;
I want to do all that the Master saith;
I want to live aright from day to day;
I'm sure I shall not pass again this way.

A Wrong Use of the Bible

A factory owner in the East was undecided whether or not he should put up a cottage by the lake as a summer home for his family. He determined to let the Bible answer, and, letting it fall open as it would, his eye lighted on Ps. 127:1, "Except the Lord build the house, they labor in vain that build it." This he took to be an intimation that he should not build the cottage. A few trials, however, if nothing else, will convince almost anyone that it is only occasionally that the verse found will have any possible bearing on the matter in hand, and that when it does, it is purely accidental. Its only value is that it sometimes helps irresolute

persons to reach a decision, just as flipping a coin does. Tho the Bible has frequently been used in a magical way, it is obvious that such a use belongs in the same class with the ouija and planchette boards, and the telling of fortunes by cards.—A. WAKEFIELD SLATEN in *What Jesus Taught*.

"I Will," "I Will Not"

1. I will not permit myself to speak while angry. And I will not make a bitter retort to another person who speaks to me in anger.

2. I will neither gossip about the failings of another, nor will I permit any person to speak such gossip to me. Gossip will die when it cannot find a listener.

3. I will respect weakness and defer to it on the street car, in the department store and in the home, whether it be displayed by man or woman.

4. I will always express gratitude for any favor or service rendered to me. If prevented from doing it on the spot, then I will seek an early opportunity to give utterance to it in the most gracious way within my power.

5. I will not fail to express sympathy with another's sorrow, or to give hearty utterance to my appreciation of good works by another, whether the party be friendly to me or not.

6. I will not talk about my personal ailments or misfortunes. They shall be the subjects on which I am silent.

7. I will look on the bright side of the circumstances of my daily life, and I will seek to carry a cheerful face and speak hopefully to all whom I meet.

8. I will not eat or drink what I know will detract from my ability to do my best.

9. I will speak and act truthfully, living with sincerity toward God and man.

10. I will strive to be always prepared for the very best that can happen to me. I will seek to be ready to seize the highest opportunity, to do the noblest work, to rise to the loftiest place which God and my abilities permit.—*The Continent*.

All-weather Friends

Pitt once said of Dundas, one of the statesmen of his day: "Dundas is not an orator, not much of a speaker; but Dundas will, without hesitation, go out with you in any weather." That is a strong and perfectly lovely compliment; it puts a crown upon a man which can never lose its luster. This man will go out with you in any weather! And without hesitation! "The sun is a bit hot to-day." "All right," says Dundas, "I'm glad for it." "It looks as tho we shall have a storm; there are some ugly clouds on the horizon." "All right," says Dundas, "I'm ready." "There's a pelting rain outside, and a fierce wind is shrieking around the corner. I think you had better stay in and keep the fire company." "No," says Dundas, "I'll go with you." He is a type of those priceless friends whose feet are always "shod with readiness" for roads of service—ready for a footpath across a sweet meadow, or ready for a mountain path which is overrun with desolating floods. They are all-weather friends. They will sit with us when life is a feast and a festival; they will sit with us when we are wearing a chain.—J. H. JOWETT.

PREACHERS EXCHANGING VIEWS

Will the Homiletic Review Start at the Start

As a subscriber to and reader of THE HOMILETIC REVIEW I am enjoying the articles on the Biblical creation narrative and the naturalistic disquisitions that deal with evolution. The article in the August issue is very fine. So were the two in a previous issue. But none of these touch the real seat of the difficulty. Evolution is made out to be a mode, a process. But how began the process of evolution of life forms, if for argument's sake we accept it as the process of life's unfolding in the universe. Bryan says it puts God too far away from us, by interposing between God and man the prolonged evolutionary process. He would sweep it away as Luther and Calvin swept the hierarchy away, the one by man attaching savingly to God by faith, the latter by attaching God savingly to man by the divine act of election. But how and what or who started the evolutionary process the other writers do not distinctly state. Professor Huxley is on record as to his belief about it. He said by a species of scientific faith he thought the point in the recession of our thoughtful tracing of evolution would be reached where, spontaneously, minute life-forms sprang from the inanimate matter of the earth. This has been elaborated later by the experimentation with colloids. Professor Huxley, therefore, was inclined to use faith to satisfy the mind as to the origin of life at the initiation of the evolutionary unfolding. But this faith attaches itself not to a Supreme Being but to the latent diffused life principle resident as he opined in matter. Here is the place precisely where knowledge can not reach and faith must step in. And here that mysterious inner inclination of a man's higher life gives the impulse that urges him on one or the other side of the point of the wedge in his conclusion. Huxley said, my faith clings to the lower face of the wedge. Life comes from matter. He called it scientific faith. Another mind says, my faith rises on the upper side of the wedge. Life comes from the divine First Cause who is a personality. In neither case does knowledge of a fact decide the issue. Hence it can not be scientific as Huxley claimed. For science searches for facts. It is the religious impulse of each reasoning human whose mind dwells on this proposition that drives him to his decision. And I am quite convinced it will always be so.

I have always felt within me a certainty, before I was familiar by education with these matters, that God is before all and the First Cause. I felt it as a little lad. We discussed it in the grade school as boys and I always clung to that conclusion and never denied it, no matter what was said to the contrary. But other minds as surely make or choose the opposite conclusion. I never can and I never will. On page 355, the second column, of last May's HOMILETIC REVIEW, there is some such final cleaving apart of different human innerisms. The Rev. G. Studdert Kennedy there writes: "There is something deep down within me that when you put your argument before me cries: No, it is a lie!" And of course the other man claims it is truth. There lies the point of the wedge that cleaves the inner life of men into two classes.

If THE HOMILETIC REVIEW is to place the details of evolutionary proofs before us as it purposes in the August number, I for one greatly desire it should begin at this point. If minds can not agree here the wedge's planes will only carry them further, yes, eternally further apart. I little care what position in the learned world or in the church a man may occupy, if he decides to attach his faith not to God but to dirt I must part company with him. And further consideration with him about an evolutionary process is of no value. I have a book here by me by an English naturalist who claims that new life-forms are all the time arising out of the matter here on earth that is in a colloidal state. In the final stage of the analysis the question is atheism or theism. We but strike the identical point the Master stressed: I am from above. Ye are from beneath. If we recede this point beyond the electrons its force is the same.

J. DYKE.

Fairton, N. J.

"Evolution, the Bible and Religion"

EDITOR OF THE HOMILETIC REVIEW:

This article appeared in the August number of THE HOMILETIC REVIEW and was pronounced "fair and constructive." I second the motion that some one with first-hand knowledge of evolution be invited to write on that subject for this magazine. The article under the above caption complicates rather than clarifies the issue. We are sorely in need of definitions which will state the attitude of the natural sciences to the whole subject of the supernatural. Herein lies the whole crux of the present scientific situation. We need a standardization of scientific fact and opinion which will differentiate between the two. It is not necessary that there shall be absolute agreement among individuals as to detail. When such is forthcoming we may be able to frame a really constructive program and clasp hands with our scientific and theological friends alike across the dividing line. To write of "reconstruction" before we are furnished with an up-to-date expression of scientific attitude is but to waste time and strength.

Let science state what it expects of theology and religion and the leaders in religious thought will not be slow in countering with a declaration of intentions as to science. I have no sort of doubt that they will take their stand with the Christ of the New Testament which can never mean a break with the supernatural. Will natural science admit the fact or necessity of the supernatural anywhere? If so, how and where?

From the article which has called out this rejoinder, I quote these words: "We need not raise the question as to the origin of all things. That is a philosophical question and may be left to the philosophers." And who are the philosophers? We can not raise it much more than it has been raised in all the traditions and literature of the ages. Genesis opens with it and Jesus Christ states the great principle of absolute religion when he says "God is spirit." It is at once non-science and nonsense to write of adjustments, reconciliations and reconstructions while the issue involved is in a state of fog and flux. We ought to be able to reach a common ground of agreement in the interest of education. This can only be had by a candid "show down" all around. The assumption is common that bigots are all found in the religious folds. The bitterest bigots I have known during a long ministry devoted largely to men have been found among atheists and agnostics. Let us have new definitions of evolution and science framed by the laws of logic, definitions which will hold water, and we shall have made a long step toward the end of the so-called conflict of science and religion.

CEPHAS C. BATEMAN,
Chaplain, U. S. Army, Retired.
San Antonio, Texas.

[Our esteemed correspondent is anxious for more light on the subject of evolution and the Bible. We hope to give in an early number of the magazine several articles on "Man's Place in Nature"—scientific and religious interpretations by Professor J. Arthur Thomson, author of The Outline of Science. Should these not meet the question at issue Professor Thomson will be invited to write directly on the subject of "Evolution, the Bible, and Religion."—EDS.]

Recent Books

The Sepulchre of Christ in Art and Liturgy. With Special Reference to the Liturgic Drama. By NEIL C. BROOKS. University of Illinois, 1921. 10½x7 in., 110 pp. $1.50.

The Foundations of Æsthetics. By C. K. OGDEN, I. A. RICHARDS, and JAMES WOOD. With Seventeen Illustrations. Allen and Unwin, London, 1922. 8½x5½ in., 88 pp. 7s. 6d. net.

The Gospel of Beauty. By SAMUEL JUDSON PORTER. George H. Doran Company, New York, 1922. 7¾x5¼ in., 118 pp. $1.25.

Much more attention is now directed to the subject of art in its relation to religion, especially to worship, than has been done in recent years. This is especially the case in architecture, church ornament, music, and the liturgical part of church services. It would be difficult to bring together three books that present more widely separated phases of the general subject than these. Yet each makes its special appeal to the cultured minister. The subject of the first is well expressed in its title. It is a painstaking and minute investigation of the way in which the crucifixion has been used East and West in church ornament to induce a worshipful and reverent mood, on sarcophagi, etc. It traces the three commemorative rites at the altar or "sepulchre" in the churches—the *Depositio* (on Good Friday), the *Elevatio* (early Easter morning), and (later on the same morning) the *Visitatio sepulchri*. These ceremonies are followed with diligence in literature and portrayal. To the art employed on the continent and in England especial attention is given. The exposition seems to be exhaustive. At the end the texts of the three ceremonies are given. It is a fine example of patient investigation and lucid explanation. The second work will make less urgent appeal to all except art critics. It is a setting forth of the basis of criticism of art as represented in at least sixteen schools of art exegesis. The fundamental thesis of these different schools is set forth and carefully examined. Treatment really amounts to a brief summary of the philosophy of art.

The third book named above is preeminently for preachers. Its six chapters are on: An Eye for the Beautiful, Christ the Norm of Beauty, Transfigurations, The Principles of Beauty, Beauty Released, Spiritual Beauty Triumphant. Chapter IV presents as "principles of beauty," individuality, simplicity, naturalness, and freedom. The supreme pattern in each of these characteristics was Jesus himself. A splendid section in chapter V is that on Utility and the Gospel of Beauty. In the last chapter is a fine description of the art of mosaic, really traceable to the Romans, tho Greeks and Egyptians knew it. The following paragraph is interesting in this relation:

In the suburbs of Rome is the little church of Santa Costanza, in which, according to art critics, are the first mosaics of Christianity. Two things are noticed. These mosaics are not on the floor beneath our feet but over our head in the ceiling. The change of position permitted the change of materials and so we find glass instead of the squares of marble. Artists tell us that this change from floor to ceiling is a veritable emancipation. Most of the objects pictured in the design suggest little of Christianity, but in a tiny niche there is discovered a figure which we identify as Christ. The birds, the grapes, and other fruit, the cups and water pitchers are superb in design and color, but the picture of the Savior is very small and may be called a failure. A sorry beginning this is of Christian art, but it was not unlike the beginning men were making of a Christian world.

We commend this volume heartily and earnestly to our readers. Dr. Porter is a born aphorist. Meaty thoughts and sentences abound. He has produced a quickening little book that sets the blood coursing in richer, more vital currents.

Modernism in Religion. By J. MACBRIDE STERRETT. The Macmillan Company, New York, 1922. 7¾ x 5¼ in., 186 pp. $1.50.

A man born and bred in traditional orthodoxy, who in the course of hard study and the lapse of many years becomes a doughty

exponent of modernism, has certainly encountered experiences which the standpatter
can not claim. The wisdom and test of
these experiences will be very differently
evaluated by the different ones belonging to
both sides. The author·was at one time a
profesor of philosophy of the George Washington University, and is now associate rector of All Souls' Memorial Church, Washington, D. C.

The appeal that he makes is
to all the churches to recognize, retain, and
seek to gain modernists; to give them a
welcome as a much-needed dynamic element
in their own ultra-conservative life, where
mere traditionalism is a drag on vitality
and progress.

He does not claim that Christianity has
failed, but that the Church as the chief
propagandist of Jesus has failed. He says
her failure
has come largely from her swathing herself
in the outgrown wrappings of ecclesiastical
traditions which are obsolete for the modern
mind.

This is how he defines modernism:
The modernist is a religious man who is
the grateful heir of past ages, but the slave
of none.

Then he quotes from two well-known
writers:

Modernism is not a system or a new synthesis: it is an orientation (Sabatier).
By a modernist I mean a churchman of
any sort who believes in the possibility of
a synthesis between the essential truth of
his religion and the essential truth of
modernity. I think that the best description of modernism is that it is the desire
and effort to find a new theological synthesis, consistent with the data of historico-
critical research (Father Tyrrell).

In the chapter on doctrine he says:
We must think out again what we believe
and why we believe it, so as to be able to
teach afresh, and in such a way as to interest men's minds, and to win their hearts,
the old truth about God and Christ and the
Spirit.

Some perhaps would like to know what
kind of message this thoroughgoing modernist has for his flock on Sunday. Here is
the answer:

When after thirty years of academical
life and after a new and real evangelical
sort of conversion, I reentered the active
work of the ministry, I took this text: "Let
this mind be in you, which was also in Jesus
Christ." Phil. 2:5. And that has been
the burden of my message ever since. The

same mind, the mind of the Master in us,
his spirit motiving all our conduct—that is
the only salvation of soul, here or hereafter.
We are saved just so far as we are thus
saved by him.

The chapters cover the following topics:
Modernism, Polity, Doctrine, A Personal
Confession, What Is God Like, Modern
Biblical Criticism, Cult, Modernism in the
Church of England, Modernism in the Roman Catholic Church, The Roman Catholic
and the Protestant Conscience, Father Tyrrell and Abbé Loisy.

Hellenism and Christianity. By EDWYN
BEVAN, Honorary Fellow of New College,
Oxford. Geo. H. Doran Co., New York.
8½ x 5½ in., 275 pp. $3.00 net.

This book consists of a series of essays
written at different times and for different
occasions, yet with a thread of continuity
running through them. Most of the essays
discuss some important aspect of the Christian religion, and form a powerful contribution to the apologetic of Christianity. Mr.
Bevan is equally at home in the realms of
classical literature, philosophy, and theology;
and he is master of an English style as
graceful as it is lucid. His power of acute
criticism is seen at its best in his analysis
of some of the common catchwords that
work such mischief, such as that "East is
East and West is West," or the popular
antithesis between reason and dogma. In
connection with the former he points out
that what we mean by "the West" is "rationalistic civilization," and that there really
is no intellectual or spiritual entity that can
be described as "the East." Those who
deny that "the West" can have any vital
or permanent influence on "the East" rely
mainly on the historical argument that in
the past Western influence on the Orient
has been so evanescent; on the fatalistic
argument that the future must resemble the
past; and on the personal experience of observers. Mr. Bevan shows how much ignorance or sophistry is involved in each of
these lines of thought.

In the characteristic essay on Dirt the
author discusses the sentiment that attaches
to various kinds of "uncleanness," and has
some illuminating things to say to those who
"speak and write as if the relation of the
sexes were something that could not be put
on a plain, scientific, common sense basis,
without any mystery or sentiment, or hocus.

poems of that sort." This versatile pen can discuss with equal ease Bacchylides, and Augustine as the prophet of personality. Among the more purely religious subjects on which Mr. Bevan sheds a welcome light are, the first contact of Christianity with that amalgam of strange religions and superstitions known as "Hellenistic theology," the relation of Christ to the Gnostic redeemer, sorrow or joy as the deeper note in Christianity, the question whether the movement of the world is toward progress, the permanent validity of Christian eschatology, the meaning and place of miracle, and the position of the Christian religion as affected by the philosophic and scientific progress of the last two generations. Every reader of these pages will find the intellectual stimulus as great as the moral inspiration.

English and American Philosophy Since 1800. A Critical Survey. By ARTHUR KENYON ROGERS. The Macmillan Company, New York, 1922. xiv—452 pp.

Professor Rogers proved himself an exceptional interpreter of philosophy by his *Students' History of Philosophy*. In this volume, with larger freedom and range of treatment, he has produced a review of modern philosophy descriptively clear, critically discriminating, comprehensive, and contributive. Its value as interpretation is rather heightened than lessened by the frank and forceful presentation of the author's own point of view as a background for appraisal and criticism. A convinced idealist, it is his conclusion that "the business of philosophy is to clarify and bring into harmony, but also in the end to substantially justify, the fundamental beliefs that are implicated in our normal human interests." With this clue in hand he moves through the labyrinth of English and American thought of the past century and the beginnings of our own with unfailing sanity and perspicacity of judgment.

It is an evidence of the breadth of his purview and the clarity of his insight that he includes in his treatment not only the technical philosophers but three of the profounder poets—Wordsworth, Tennyson, and Browning—and also a number of the more influential theologians, such as Frederick D. Maurice and Cardinal Newman. The proportion of attention given to British, as contrasted with American think-

ers, is doubtless on the whole just, but the student of American philosophy will hardly be satisfied with the bare mention of such philosophers as W. T. Harris, Bowne and Ladd and with no mention whatever of Noah Porter, G. S. Morris or G. H. Palmer, or such theologians as Elisha Mulford and Horace Bushnell.

The criticism of John Dewey's Instrumentalism is particularly cogent.

The conclusion of the volume is a pertinent recognition of the fact that "the philosophical atmosphere is still sharply controversial rather than cooperative," and the recommendation of a more comprehensive and tolerant attitude in place of this exclusive particularism. At the same time the author's evident lack of confidence in the success of philosophy in reaching any finality leaves the way open for religion to exercise its office of faith.

Christ and International Life. By EDITH PICTON-TURBERVILL. George H. Doran Company, New York, 1922. 7½x5 in., 150 pp. $1.50.

Jesus lives to-day and he will live in all the to-morrows that are to come. Even tho his teaching comes out of the long ago it is not only as fresh as May dew, but it is also far in advance of the practise of modern nations. Jesus lives because he is the Great Revealer of the Father's universal love.

The constructive movements of the ages are spiritual. What is actually at the basis of nationalism and internationalism is profoundly spiritual—the betterment of all nations. It is becoming more and more evident that if we are to live together we must work and prosper together. Only the whole can preserve the whole.

We must admit it looks like a huge task to work for the betterment of all peoples when there are so many things in our own villages, towns, and cities that need attention. The two, however, are not incompatible, nor separable. The broad outlook may easily prove a stimulus to the work done at home.

The author of this creditable production gives an illustration that may serve to show what a difference time and education make, so far as looking at nations in their proper relations is concerned.

Some six hundred years ago, which after all is not a long time in human history, citizens of the towns would have laughed at the idea that a man of York, or a man of Winchester, would ever think of the common good of all England. To a citizen of York a man from another city, let alone far-away Winchester, was a foreigner. Towns levied taxes in those days on "foreign" goods which came in from other English towns, in just the same way as nations tax "foreign" goods from other nations to-day. The welfare of the city to which he belonged was the one concern of every citizen in medieval times. A man who put the interests of his whole country before the interests of his city, was no true man in those days. The idea that he should concern himself with the welfare of the whole country to which he belonged was as preposterous and unpatriotic a suggestion to him as the idea that the welfare of all nations should be our genuine care and concern appears to many people to-day.

In the main the brief chapters set forth the idea that Christian morality must under all circumstances be the guide in national conduct.

There is an introduction by the Right Honorable Lord Robert Cecil.

International Relations. By JAMES BRYCE (VISCOUNT BRYCE). The Macmillan Company, New York, 1922. 8¼x5¾ in., 275 pp. $2.50.

When the late James Bryce (Viscount) wrote or spoke on governmental matters one was quite sure of something more than the ordinary. His thorough education and long experience in statecraft enabled him to see further and go deeper than most writers. This volume, completed just before his death, is the last of his notable contributions. Any one who is desirous of getting an insight into international affairs can not do better than peruse this work.

The author begins with a discussion of International Relations in the Past, a discussion absolutely necessary to an understanding of the facts—the one thing he is intent on laying before his readers. Take this fact, for example, from the first chapter:

Altho in civilized countries every individual man is now under law and not in a State of Nature toward his fellow men, every political community, whatever its form, be it republican or monarchical, is in a State of Nature toward every other community; that is to say, an independent community stands quite outside law, each community owning no control but its own, recognizing no legal rights to other communities and owing to them no legal duties.

An independent community is, in fact, in that very condition in which savage men were before they were gathered together into communities legally organized.

Nature and law, the wolf and the lamb, war and peace, these conflicting elements abide in us. There is no hope for improved relations among individuals or nations until the baser element is mastered.

Human nature will advance no further in communities taken as wholes than the members of the communities themselves advance.

The eight lectures which form the contents were delivered at Williams College in August, 1921. They are as follows: The Earlier Relations of Tribes and States to One Another, The Great War and Its Effects in the Old World, Non-Political Influences Affecting International Relations, The Causes of War, Diplomacy and International Law, Popular Control of Foreign Policy and the Morality of States, Methods Proposed for Settling International Controversies, Other Possible Methods for Averting War.

A Short History of Christian Theophagy. By PRESERVED SMITH. The Open Court Publishing Company, Chicago, 1922. 9 x 6 in., 223 pp.

This title, translated, sounds ugly—"A Short History of Christian God-eating." Of course, it is taken from the practise of the "sacrifice of the mass," and from the dogma that in the eucharist the body of Christ is eaten—the same body "as that once born of a virgin." This practise (and dogma), Dr. Smith notes, "is the most striking of the many instances of the conservatism of religion, . . . the most ancient survival from a hoary antiquity."

A brief review of tribal and ethnic "god-eating" is given in the first chapter under the satiric title of Præparatio Evangelica! The second chapter opens with the broad statement that "the most excellent of the sacraments was borrowed by the Christians from the older mystery religions." This chapter attempts to recover the immediate pre-Pauline idea of the rite, and considers the Pauline "founding of the eucharist," which form became regulative in the Church. The rise and progress of the doctrines of transubstantiation and consubstantiation are next followed, and finally the doctrines of the principal Reformers, the British Reformers. "The Last Phase" states the present state of doctrine concerning the eucharist in the principal communions.

The author evidently favors abandonment of the eucharist as one of a "repetition of outworn survivals from a primeval state." This is the one book which carries back the genealogy of the high-church doctrine of the eucharist to its primitive prototype.

Immortality and the Modern Mind. By KIRSOPP LAKE. Harvard University Press, Cambridge, 1922. 7 x 4½ in., 5¹ pp. $1.00.

It was fitting that Professor Lake, whose early fame rested largely on his book on *The Resurrection of Christ*, should be asked to deliver the Ingersoll Lecture on the Immortality of Man. On this subject Professor Lake's position is hardly distinguishable from pantheism. He insists that the modern tendency to emphasize the resurrection of the "body" (in a sense almost equal to "personality") rather than of the "flesh" is not an explanation but a contradiction of the historic Christian creed. He fully accepts the arguments of those who make the survival of consciousness dependent on the survival of the physical body, a survival which obviously does not take place. The author heartily believes in the permanence of the immaterial, but of thought rather than of thinking, of life rather than of living, of the community rather than of the individual. If we say we do not find much comfort in this, Professor Lake apparently would reply that he does not feel any particular need of comfort.

The Problem of the Pastoral Epistles. By P. N. HARRISON. Oxford University Press, London and New York, 1921. x—200 pp.

Of the various classes of facts, upon the basis of which the alleged Pauline authorship of the Epistles to Timothy and Titus must be tested and proved, Dr. Harrison singles out the linguistic data and makes them in this treatise the field of a most searching investigation. In order to do this effectively he must, of course, explain the problem and some of its more general historical aspects. But in the main the work is occupied with a comparison of the language of the Pastoral with that of the generally accepted Pauline writings. The conclusion reached is that the Pastorals "received their present shape at the hands, not of Paul, but

of a Paulinist living in the early years of the second century." The author's investigation of the field is thorough to the point of exhaustiveness, if such a thing is possible. He has apparently neglected nothing which bears upon the problem either positively or negatively. Proceeding with methodical precision, he notes the resemblances of the diction of the epistles in question with that of Paul on the one side and with that of second century Greek documents on the other, and comes to believe that tho there are genuinely Pauline elements in these writings their present form is the result of work done two generations later than Paul. Other aspects of the problem may offer subject for investigation in the future, but so far as language is concerned this essay will be the new basis for further work.

Language. By EDWARD SOPIR. Harcourt Brace and Co., New York, 1921, 258 pp.

The author of this book attempts to introduce the reader to the study of oral and written speech. Most people take their language for granted, and never get even a glimpse of the slow process which was necessary for its development. It is to be feared that even ministers who have had some elocution in their seminary course are not cognizant of the close relation between speech and thought. Yet they are the ones who should be most interested in a work of this kind.

The work of Mr. Sopir is very well done and deserves wide study. The topics taken up are: Definition of language; elements of speech; sounds of language; grammatical processes and concepts; types of linguistic structure; language as a historical product; drift and phonetic law; how languages influence each other; language, race and culture; language and literature.

The Home of the Indo-Europeans. By HAROLD H. BENDER. Princeton University Press, Princeton, N. J., 1922. 8¼ x 5½ in., 57 pp.

By "Indo-Europeans" is meant a group of peoples whose languages seem to go back to a common origin. They are represented by Hindus, Persians, Greeks, Italians, Slavs, Teutons, and Celts. The indications that all these peoples sprang from a single group living in a single locality have been gathering for several decades and are ac-

cepted as decisive. But where was that
locality? The earliest hypothesis placed it
somewhere in Central Asia, but point after
point has been made against this conclusion,
and the ancestral home has gradually been
shifted westward. Now Dr. Bender of
Princeton University reviews the evidence
and the various hypotheses, states the conclusion that now, after at least seventy
years of study, the present home of the
Lithuanians (it seems most probable) was
the center from which Persians and Hindus
traveled southeast, and the Greeks, Romans,
Teutons, and Celts west and southwest,
while the Lithuanians (Slavs) have remained where they were for 5,000 years.

This little book (it can be read in an
hour) is as clear, logical, and conclusive as
the more or less elusive data permit.

Teaching the Teacher. A First Book in
Teacher Training. Presbyterian Board
of Publication (The Westminster Press),
Philadelphia, 1921. 7¼ x 5 in., 214 pp.
Paper 60c, cloth 85c.

Sunday-school teachers would be greatly
helped in their work in the Sunday-school
by reading a book such as this. It has four
separate sections, each one dealing with
material of the first importance to teachers.
The sections are as follows: I. The Development of the Church in Old Testament Times,
by James Oscar Boyd, Ph.D., D.D.; II. The
Life of Christ and the Development of the
Church in Apostolic Times and in Post
Apostolic Times, by John Gresham Machen,
D.D.; III. An Introduction to the Study of
the Mind, by Walter Scott Athearn; IV. The
Church as a Teaching Institution, by Harold
McA. Robinson, D.D.

There Are Sermons in Books. By
WILLIAM L. STIDGER. George H. Doran
Company, New York, 1922. 7¾ x 5½
in., 232 pp. $1.50.

Out of what people are most concerned or
most interested in preachers may make their
most effective sermons. Most people are
interested in books. Mr. Stidger shows in
these eleven sermons how out of books of
various sorts preachments have been made
that "worked," and were effective in several
ways. And he adds the titles of 500 sources
of material for other "book sermons."

One of Mr. Stidger's sermons on a book
noticed in our columns is given on another
page.

Parables for Little People. By J. W. G.
WARD. George H. Doran Company, New
York, 1921. 7¾x5¼ in., 219 pp. $1.50.

This collection of children's talks is above
the average. The stories contain much of
the romantic or "fairy tale" element, which
is particularly appealing. Some of them
would have to be adapted for American
children, as they employ terms not much in
use in this country. We give one of the
talks in another department of the magazine.

Sermons for the Great Days of the Year.
By RUSSELL H. CONWELL. George H.
Doran Company, New York, 1922. 7¾ x
5½ in., 226 pp. $1.50.

Dr. Conwell stands high among the best-
known preachers of America. This selection of fifteen sermons covers the principal
occasions on the calendar of the Church, of
national celebration and of social life—including St. Valentine's Day. There are suggestions of the way in which many of the
church services can be made to contribute
to every-day inspiration. His Thanksgiving
sermon is given on another page of this
issue.

Books Received

Thinking Through the New Testament.
An Outline Study of Every Book in the
New Testament. By J. J. ROSS. Fleming
H. Revell Company, New York, 1921.
7¾x5¼ in., 254 pp. $1.75.
**The Importance and Value of Proper
Bible Study.** By R. A. TORREY. George
H. Doran Company, New York, 1921.
7½x5 in., 113 pp. $1.00.
**A Manual of Bible History in connection
with The General History of the World.**
By WILLIAM G. BLAIKIE. Thomas Nelson
and Sons, Ltd., London and New York,
1920. 7½x5¼ in., 504 pp.
The Jew and the World. By H. G. ENE-
LOW. Bloch Publishing Company, New
York, 1921. 7½x5 in., 116 pp.
The Modern Theory of the Bible. By
SAMUEL A. STEEL. Fleming H. Revell
Company, New York, 1921. 7½x5 in.,
146 pp. $1.25.
Jesus and Life. By JOSEPH F. McFADYEN.
Second edition. George H. Doran Com-
pany, New York, 1921. 7½x5 in., 277 pp.
$2.00.
**An English Translation of The Teaching
of the Twelve Apostles.** S. P. C. K.,
London (The Macmillan Company, New
York), 1921. 7½x4¾ in., 15 pp.
**Yesterday, A Chronicle of Early Life in
the West.** By CHARLES E. WELLER.
Published by the author, 206 Masonic
Temple, La Porte, Ind. 8x5¼ in., 208
pp. $1.50.

DEBAT-PONSON'S CHRIST ON THE MOUNTAIN: "LOVE ONE ANOTHER"

HACKER: THE ANNUNCIATION

One of the most successful attempts to link ideal beauty with the mystery
of motherhood. As long as there are lovers and mothers and a feeling that
in a child somehow God and man meet, painters will continue to paint
Annunciations and Madonnas.

The HOMILETIC REVIEW

VOL. 84   DECEMBER, 1922   No. 6

RECENT FICTION TOUCHING BIBLE LANDS AND TIMES

The Rev. CLAYTON HAVERSTICK RANCK, Harrisburg, Pa.

NOTE—About fifteen years ago the writer began to read works of prose fiction touching the scenes and times of the Bible, and to make a bibliography covering the better of his findings. The purposes were to review the details of life in Bible-lands, and to help the younger folk of his congregation to orient themselves when reading the Bible. The results of that study were issued in THE HOMILETIC REVIEW (see issues of January, 1914, page 53; January, 1915, page 19; and January, 1916, page 17). This article is an attempt to cover the works which have appeared since that time.

During the last decade, works of this sort have come from the press in greater numbers and in finer quality. In the former articles we reported many volumes from a host of well-intentioned but nevertheless quite ordinary writers, with an occasional oasis; but to-day such well-known names as Bennett, Shaw, Coningsby Dawson, Haggard, Kate Trask, and Hillis appear among the workers on Scriptural soil. Unfortunately not all of them have given us productions suitable for our purposes, for in this work art alone is as impotent as noble purposes alone.

But the larger place Biblical stories now hold is not due entirely to the prominence of those who are laboring in this field, nor to the excellency of their work. The subjects of the Bible and of Biblical characters have a new place in the life of to-day. In her introduction to that splendid little anthology, *Christ in (American) Poetry To-day*, Mrs. Crow says:

First I ran through some fifty volumes of poems, of about 1890. I found few or no poems about Jesus. Then I plunged in again at 1895 and found but a lonely one here and there. At 1900 there were more, distinctly more. At 1905 there was a still brighter dawn. But when I came to 1910 and thereabouts, times were changed. Something had verily happened. The fascinating theme of Jesus, the dramatic quality of his human career, and the miracle of his personality had been discovered.

Not only has the bibliography grown in size and power, but a new use for such works is recognized in the "Book Sermon," *i. e.*, a sermon that discusses a book or tells its story. Not that such sermons had not been preached for many generations, but the homiletic value of well-constructed stories, *e. g.*, *The Other Wise Man*, *In His Steps*, and others, is now undisputed.

Longer stories are now used by the moving-picture artists by following the abbreviated style of the Old Testament prophets and of the modern sacred oratorio, even if they do not always imitate their ethics, so why not abbreviate them for homiletic

[433]

uses? Some books, not at all suited for young people's inspirational reading, are quite excellent materials when treated in this way. A splendid example of the use to which a story with little inspirational value can be put is Geoffrey Whitworth's *Father Noah*. As the title suggests, this work is very light and approaches the irreverent when read carelessly. But when its powerful lesson in selfishness is dissected out of it, we have a forceful sermon.

In a previous article, we made a favorable comment on the *Egyptian Tales* compiled by Flinders-Petrie, recommending them as an excellent commentary on Egyptian life in the days of Israel's bondage. The fact that Delitzsch has since made a similar statement ought to encourage more students of the Bible to read these— the oldest prose stories of which we have any knowledge.

For the Exodus period, H. Rider Haggard's novel, *The Moon of Israel*, is superior to anything that has appeared thus far. His local color is excellent. *When the Sun Stood Still*, by Cyrus Townsend Brady, covers the times suggested by its title, and altho not closely built, is nevertheless a fascinating and helpful story for younger readers. Its author's wide experience in moving-picture work is supposed by some critics to have spoiled his art as a novelist, but not for our present purposes.

"Was she a witch or a vamp, or are they the same?" is the question that will not down as one reads Norwood's *The Witch of Endor*. The work is very mildly exciting and moves too slowly; but as it slightly antedates the time of David, it covers a period which has been hitherto neglected by producers of fiction.

One of the best Old Testament stories to be noted at this time, is *The Court of Belshazzar*, by Earl Williams. In this tale the reader is taken from the quiet Hebrew Shepherd life in Palestine to the noisy court and trading life of Babylon and back again, and there is not an uninteresting page. The description of the practical use of a city of refuge in the civilization of that day is splendid and suggests our lynching problem. Occasionally one feels that social morals to-day are losing their cutting edge. Williams' contrast between the ethics and morals of Israel and Babylon should be both a warning and a challenge to us. Great things do not just happen in moral and religious education. They must be built into the lives of our young people. He calls the gap between Israel and Babylon three thousand years. What of the gap between some of the component elements in our American civilization? We shall not try to state it in years, but it would help to solve our problem if a capable student would do so.

We have one good story written in dramatic form on the times between the Testaments in Arnold Bennett's *Judith and Holofernes*. It is short and interesting and follows the apocryphal book Judith almost to the smallest detail. Unfortunately for the relative value of Bennett's work, we have the story in the Apocrypha and Aldrich's poetic rendering of it, both of which reach spiritual heights to which Bennett's work does not rise.

As we turn to the fiction about the New Testament, may we quote a dear teacher on the Old Testament: "Unfortunately, very few students of the Scriptures are sufficiently poetic to be able to give the world the benefits of their study in adequate language." How great is this artistic need in every department of Christian knowledge and service. Music must be of the finest, architecture must be true to the canons of its art, in fact, all of the arts at their best are but inadequate media for expressing the feelings of the human soul toward its God. In Coningsby Dawson we have a splendid combination of the needed gifts and training, and his little story, *The Seventh Christmas*, is superb. From the pen of so young a writer it gives promise of still greater things. Another story, this one relating to the ministry of Jesus, charms one—*The Little Hunchback of Zia*, by Frances Hodgson Burnett. It has little to tell us except a simple little story of the trials of the sick and afflicted of that time and their pathetic eagerness to come under the healing influences of Jesus, but that is enough.

There are two stories relating to the closing days of the ministry of Jesus, *The Man of Kerioth*, by Norwood, and *Without the Walls*, by the late Kate Trask. The former approaches the Christ through his weakest disciple, the latter through the Pharisees. The power in a moderate use of superlatives is finely illustrated in the last named.

About two years ago a work appeared that was unfortunately advertised in terms of the *Ben-Hur* story. It is not so strong a work as *Ben-Hur* and as a result it failed to get either the recognition it aspired to, or that which it deserved. For *The Princess Salome*, by Jenkins, is a fine story. Its descriptions of the life of the times in Asia Minor and Palestine are done with a masterful hand. It takes a great many liberties with history, e. g., accounting for the character of Salome by making her a noble woman until crossed in a beautiful love by her unscrupulous mother. Should any one desire a more realistic story about the same character, the one by the French writer Flaubert is available in an English translation.

It is difficult to consider seriously the fiction from the men and women famous because of other forms of literary work, for the simple reason that for the most part it is not well done.

The Story of Phœdrus, by Dr. Hillis, is the exception that proves the rule, however, and is valuable for any one desiring to know the trials through which faithful men went in gathering what has now become the New Testament. That the author omitted the almost ubiquitous love-story and yet gave us a most interesting tale is in itself noteworthy.

Another work with a very special value is McGregor's *Rob Roy on the Jordan*. Smith's *Historical Geography of the Holy Land* credits this book with the best description of the Jordan River. After searching for this work for twelve years it was a pleasant surprise to find it in the Pennsylvania State Library. It is not fiction, however, at least not chiefly so, "Rob Roy" being the canoe in which the author explored a number of streams in the Near East. The book is very worth while, but being issued in 1870 and available in so few libraries, its republication, at least in part, is desirable.

For modern Jerusalem the second volume of Lagerlöf's *Jerusalem* is very good. The first volume is the local story of a Scandinavian sect, which makes a crusade to Jerusalem in the second one. The portrayal of the social and racial groups in modern Jerusalem, together with their clashings, is well made.

BIBLIOGRAPHY

Arnold Bennett, *Judith and Holofernes*. Doran, New York, 1919. 96 pp.

Cyrus Townsend Brady, *When the Sun Stood Still*. Revell, New York, 1917, 308 pp.

Frances Hodgson Burnett, *The Hunchback of Zia*. Stokes, New York, 1916. 55 pp.

Martha Foote Crow, *Christ in the Poetry of Today*. Woman's Press, 1918. 227 pp.

Coningsby Dawson, *The Seventh Christmas*. Lane, New York, 1917.

Sir H. Rider Haggard, *The Moon of Israel*. Longman's, Green, New York, 1918. 302 pp.

Newell Dwight Hillis, *The Story of Phœdrus*. Macmillan, New York, 1918. 311 pp.

Burris Jenkins, *The Princess Salome*. Lippincott, Philadelphia, 1921. 352 pp.

Selma Lagerlöf, *Jerusalem*. Doubleday,

Page, Garden City. Vol. I, 342 pp; Vol.
II, 348 pp.
    John McGregor, *Bob Boy on the Jordan.*
Harper, New York, 1870. 464 pp.
    Robert W. Norwood, *The Witch of Endor.*
Doran, 1916. 121 pp.; *The Man of Kerioth.*
Doran, 1919. 138 pp.

Kate Trask, *Without the Walls.* Macmillan, 1919. 196 pp.
    Geoffrey Whitworth, *Father Noah.* McBride, New York, 1919. 76 pp.
    Earl Willoughby Williams, *The Court of Belshazzar.* Bobbs-Merrill, New York, 1918. 352 pp.

HINTS ON CHURCH DESIGN

(FIRST ARTICLE)

Earl B. Hurlburt, East Cleveland, Ohio

I. The Importance of Good Design: A few years ago a writer for an influential architectural journal published a scathing criticism of .the buildings belonging to a university under the control of a great denomination. It is hard to believe that the assault did not do the university and the church supporting it some harm. For instance, he scored the structure of the College of Fine Arts so severely that it is doubtful whether any young draftsman who had considered taking up the course in architecture taught in this building would have had the courage to attend the school after reading that article. He would have argued, and with some reason, that a college of fine arts should be artistic in itself, or else it would lay open to suspicion the value of the instruction given within its walls.

In somewhat the same way an outsider might reason regarding an ugly, barn-like church building. What value, he might ask, should be placed on the teaching in such a place? How could the highest culture be urged when the surroundings are of the opposite description? If beauty of life and character is enjoined, why should it not find expression in the very structure in which the truth is proclaimed? If the glories of the hereafter are preached, should there be no reflected glory in the things of earth? Should not Christianity and the Church stand for the best in all things.

These are not idle questions, for, to come down to facts, who has not known people who have been so repelled by an ugly church building that they could not be induced to attend the services? And these same people very likely have been attracted to some other church than their own because the surroundings there were more pleasant. It will not do to dismiss all consideration of such persons with the assertion that attendance at divine service is not for looking at or admiring external beauty, but for spiritual communion with God and the hearing of his truth. In the first place, these beauty-lovers, for all their exhibition of estheticism, may be as good Christians as those who scoff at externals, and so should have their opinions treated with respect. Secondly, if the argument that visible surroundings are of small consequence in the church is tenable, the same reasoning holds good in the home. But here we find an inconsistency, for many men, living in carefully designed homes, in a cultured atmosphere, affect to believe that beauty of the church home is not of so much importance, as the thought there should be spiritual only. Do these men really believe that spiritual thought does not exist in the home likewise? Do they not perceive that beauty in the home gives insight into the greater beauties of heaven? It does not seem reasonable or right that men should themselves live in homes of the highest type of design, and yet should permit the house of their Maker to be put together with little or no regard for beauty.

To the majority of building committees the problem of church construction appears to be solved when a building is planned with proper seating capacity, with the required number of rooms, with heating, ventilating, and lighting provided for, and with up-to-dateness in social service equipment. As to whether the building will result ·in a thing of beauty or an eyesore little thought is given. The architect is supposed to look out for the finished appearance. In fact, the committee members consider the architect's taste superior to theirs, and so they try to fit their ideas to his, regardless of what he produces. Sometimes this is the highest wisdom and sometimes it is not. There are architects and architects. Some are competent in church design and some are not.

Then there are building committees in which are certain members who insist on the architect's making changes in the design to suit their own ideas. Unless such persons have had architectural training, it is obvious that the results of such meddling must be fatal to good work. Happily, the realization of the horrors that may ensue keeps most committees from interference with the artistic end of a building enterprise. But still occasionally the architect finds a refractory committee to deal with.

It seems, in order to assist in solving the problem of designing a church, as tho the minister should be able to render almost expert assistance. This may seem a good deal to expect from a man burdened with the details of a building enterprise in addition to his regular pastoral work, but it surely pays in the long run. As witness to this it should be noted that there are certain denominations in which the ministers, during the theological course, are given such thorough training in church architecture that these denominations rarely go far wrong in their church, school, or college buildings. Their leaders have been trained to a point where they can discriminate between the crude and the cultured, between the bad and the good. It would seem as if something of this kind might be worked out in the theological seminaries of all the churches, so that such mistakes as those which brought down the scorching criticism mentioned in our opening paragraph could be avoided. For it seems certain that if ministerial training in good architecture had prevailed in the past, it would have prevented some of the other atrocities which positively disfigure our cities and towns, and which must continue to stand, as substantial buildings do continue to stand, in their ugliness for many decades to come.

II. WHAT CONSTITUTES GOOD DE-SIGN: Granted that good design is important, even essential, in church building, why is it that some work is good and some is bad? What is it that gives one building beauty and distinction, while another, where as much or more money is spent, never gives satisfaction to the eye? Why does a person almost instinctively admire one design, but turn from another which may be more showy?

There are many answers to these questions, dependent on just what conditions are found. Then there are some points which are elusive when one tries to explain them, they are so subtle. It seems as if one must have sufficient training to know intuitively when a thing is right or wrong, so far as the finer points are considered. But speaking broadly, possibly nothing is of more importance in design than harmony and unity. Perhaps we should add proportion next, and then

					COLOGNE CATHEDRAL

correct detail. All these should be
guided by good taste, which is cultivated by study of the best examples
of architecture of the past and the
present.

And speaking of the study of the
architecture of the past, one should
not permit himself to get on a wrong
track here, because not all of the ancient architecture was good. To copy
an entire building of a past age is not
necessarily a sign of good taste. The
building may have been the worst of
its class. To repeat a window, or a
doorway, or something else from an
ancient cathedral with a famous name
may be a great mistake, as the feature
may have been the one bad thing in
the structure. As a matter of fact,
there are few, if any, buildings, ancient or modern, which are perfectly
satisfactory to the keen critic. This
teaches us that we should be discriminating enough to separate the wheat
from the chaff when we study old or
new work. That is, we may learn
something from the study of all
architecture; but this study is like
many others in that it shows us some
things to imitate and some to avoid.
And we may not expect perfection in
our own work. What should be aimed
at is the elimination of as much bad
as possible and the appropriation of
as much good as we can find. But
here again we must be careful that
we do not use even a good piece of
design in the wrong place.

Harmony in design implies that a
building should agree with itself. It
means that there is a plan back of it,
that certain lines are followed out
here and there, each harmonious with
other lines and all contributing to the
completed work.

Take a picture of Cologne Cathedral
and look it over carefully. Where are
the lines? They are in the buttresses,

the arches, the pinnacles; and they are perpendicular. They begin low and point up, and up, and up again. The arched windows of the side aisles point to the arched windows of the clearstory above; the lower buttresses rise to the upper ones, which rise again as the flying buttresses spring out; and the eye travels on and up once more until everything seems to break into pinnacles which still point up as they terminate. Study the towers. There are pinnacles all the way in their height, and see how at each line of pinnacles the towers diminish in size until the spires proper begin. Note that this diminishing from bottom to top extends throughout the structure. It adds an effect of height and hence greater accent to those perpendicular lines, of which we now see there are myriads. Any one can see the harmony which here exists, both as a whole and in detail. And at the same time that we note the harmony, we likewise note the unity of this structure. One part fits in with every other part, and we feel that no portion could be omitted without loss. Hence the unity of this wonderful masterpiece compels our admiration as we study the beauty in these upspringing arches, these myriads of pinnacles, ever pointing up and up, and higher and higher—yes, pointing the beholder to heaven itself. It is proper that this style of architecture should be known as the pointed, tho more frequently, perhaps, as the Gothic; but could we not call it the style of aspiration likewise?

Gothic architecture is peculiarly Christian. It developed and flourished in the Christian era and was brought to its greatest beauty and perfection in the cathedrals of Europe. The style is still as appropriate for church buildings as it ever was in the past, for no one can mistake a Gothic church for anything than a Christian house of worship. This fact is so recognized that the Hebrew shuns the Gothic in designing his temples, the Mohammedan and the Mormon will have none of it. It is the style of which ancient Greece and Rome knew nothing. It arose, as did Christianity itself, on the ruins of those heathen civilizations, and marks the old era from the new.

And now we should note the other style in which churches are usually built, the Classic. In this are grouped the so-called orders of the Greeks and Romans, including the Doric, Ionic, Corinthian, Composite, and Tuscan. A little study will show that all these orders are the same in essentials.

Take a picture of our Capitol at Washington and one of St. Peter's in Rome and certain things will be noted at once. There are the columns and the domes, for instance. But now see the direction of the lines here, and it is evident that instead of being perpendicular, as in the Gothic, they are horizontal. The buildings considered in their entirety show much greater breadth than height; and in detail one perceives the long, level lines of entablature and cornice, these lines continuing in parallel rows up the domes at each offset or molded course. The rows of columns will now be seen to accent these horizontal lines, as their purpose, looking at them in relation to the general effect, appears chiefly to separate the long lines below them from the long lines above. Study further, and one perceives that these low, level lines give to a building a surpassing dignity. Strength and power are indicated by this style, which is especially suitable for government buildings, but is, nevertheless, used for Christian edifices likewise.

Strictly speaking, doubtless such churches as St. Peter's in Rome and St. Paul's in London should be classed as Renaissance in style; but as the Renaissance is merely the renaissance or revival of the Classic orders after the Gothic interval, the difference is not material as to whether we consider these buildings under the name of Classic or Renaissance. So-called colonial is another form of Classic, but this is usually simpler in detail.

Romanesque architecture is peculiar in that it combines some of the features of both the classic and the Gothic orders. Its round Roman arches and breadth of outline suggest the classic; but the imposing height often found in structures built in this style, the vaulted ceilings, and many other points both in general effect and detail, suggest the Gothic.

Romanesque is not so popular for the building of Protestant churches as it was twenty years ago. Byzantine is occasionally used by Roman Catholic churches, almost never by Protestant. Moorish and Egyptian probably are never used for Christian houses of worship.

III. WHAT CONSTITUTES BAD DESIGN: An examination of a structure built so as to be characteristic of any

THE CAPITOL, WASHINGTON, D. C.

of the orders considered will convince the observer that each style is consistent within itself, and that the different parts of the building unite to make a harmonious and complete edifice. It follows, then, that anything which destroys this harmony must be wrong—discordant, in fact—and so bad architecture.

Discord in architecture is like dissonance in music. Sit at your piano and press down the sustaining pedal. Then strike the tonic chord of C major—C, E, G. Without removing the foot from the pedal strike the dominant chord B, D. G. The result is to the ear what bad architecture is to the eye. As the crude pianist holding the sustaining pedal causes his chords to jumble together and create jangling discord, so the uncultured architect, by mingling styles which are contradictory, by neglecting proper proportion, by wrong detail, makes confusion and becomes guilty of bad taste. Or perhaps we can call it by some worse name when a person perpetrates, for everyone to see, an enormity which will last for many years.

Examples of bad architecture in church work are plentiful, but the reason why a piece of work is bad is not always understood. Indeed, the wrong cause is sometimes assigned and an attempted improvement makes matters little or no better. For instance, a few years ago there stood a church built with strong stone walls pierced with pointed windows. But there was a low-pitched roof with cornice of classic detail above those walls, and a tower loomed upward which was of a difficult type to analyze, being more classic than Gothic, but not quite the former either. That the building was architecturally wrong was realized, but just why it was wrong was not understood; for when remodeling was undertaken, instead of simply changing the roof lines, removing the tower, and then building anew in a harmonious design such parts as were needed, using the same kind of stone that was in the old walls, a pretentious front was built on of brick and terra cotta in an attempt to modernize the edifice. But the result was that the new front lacked good proportions, and, worst of all, the beautiful old stone walls were hidden from view by the cheaper brick.

Imagine, if you can, after studying as suggested the pictures of Cologne Cathedral and the Capitol at Washingon, what the effect would be if the towers of the cathedral were added to the Capitol. It would be like the proverbial attempt to mix oil and water, which are both good in themselves but will not unite.

Now consider the inside of a church. A structure built after the Classic order may have a simple and chaste design for the interior, keeping to broad, low lines, and even almost devoid of decoration. But if the interior of a building of Gothic design is stripped of those features which make it distinctive, such as its vaulting, columns, and the like, so that the perpendicular lines are lost, we are pretty sure to find a cold, cheerless, barnlike room where it seems almost impossible to preach or listen to a sermon of warmth and power.

It is a curious fact that many churches have good exteriors and poor interiors, and *vice versa*. To the observer of such paradoxes it looks as if the bad portion of a building simply represented ill-advised economy at that point, but this may not have been the case after all. Possibly the architect was untaught, or he may have designed correctly and some member of the building committee caused a good edifice to be ruined because he thought his taste superior to the architect's, and so insisted on the removal of what to him seemed superfluities.

ST. PETER'S, ROME

And possibly the same man, or maybe some other, caused certain decorative features to be omitted, claiming they were "too much gingerbread." And that brings us to another point.

IV. THE DIFFERENCE BETWEEN DECORATION AND "GINGERBREAD": Many, doubtless, looking at that picture of Cologne Cathedral would say it had "too much gingerbread." But the instructed man revels in the beauties of its refined decoration, he gloats over its wonderful detail. Why this difference in ideas?

Speaking broadly, so-called "gingerbread" is useless decoration. It is good decoration in the wrong place, poor decoration in the right place, or, what is possibly more common, poor decoration in the wrong place. To illustrate one of these phases, a church was built recently which was consistently Gothic except near the top of the front gable, where a niche was built supported by a shelf whose corbeling was decorated with Classic egg-and-dart moulding. That was gingerbread because, while the egg-and-dart was good ornament in itself, it was in the wrong place when in a structure of the Gothic order. Another church, a beautiful Gothic structure, holds a baptismal font of exquisite pattern; but the font is of Renaissance design, and there is discord.

Then there is an expensive Gothic church in a large city which at a distance looks good, but closer inspection shows it covered with flat, meaningless ornament, which has no connection with itself nor with the general style of the building. It looks as if some draftsman, in designing the structure, found certain places which needed decoration, and so, without any regard for the fitness of things, he filled in with circles, squares, and triangles as quickly as possible. That is an example of poor ornament in, possibly, the right place, and so is gingerbread without question. The interior of this church is even worse than the outside, for the attempt at vaulting is a failure because the ribs at the intersection of the vaults are simply boards stuck upon edge and sawed into the most torturing curves imaginable. Then there is turned work here and there to make bad matters worse—spindles, balls, and the like. Such work fairly reeks of gingerbread.

There is a large church in another city which has the wrong thing in the wrong place, architecturally speaking. On this building, in stone letters so enormous that they reach the whole length of the front and form the most conspicuous feature therein, is the church's name, which we shall here call, because it is not the real name, "First Avenue Methodist Catholic Church." There are other features about the edifice that are objectionable, but this sign-board is so much worse than the others that they are dwarfed by the greater evil. Why a church should make the commanding feature of the front a sign which should by right be placed unobtrusively on the corner-stone is hard to see. The sign-board makes this church resemble a theater or a business building, but it is doubtful if either a designer of a playhouse or of a mercantile structure would have quite the requisite amount of poor taste to subordinate all the possibilities of beauty in his building to the mechanical lines of a panel of letters. Perhaps the congregation worshiping in this church is very proud of its distinctive locational and denominational sign; but forgetting one's just pride in the denomination or the local church for a moment, can any one think of any building, ancient or modern, which is renowned for its beauty, and which at the same time has a sign for the biggest thing in it? Surely not Cologne Cathedral, our Capitol at Washington, St. Peter's at Rome, or Trinity or Grace Churches in New York.

WILL CHILDREN READ THE BIBLE

Henry F. Cope, D.D., General Secretary, The Religious Education Association, Chicago, Ill.

One difficulty with that question is that it is much like the Bible itself, subject to a great variety of interpretations. There is also a similarity in the fact that many of the interpretations ought rather to be known as assumptions. There is the assumption of the ideality of the picture evoked by the title, the picture of the good boy or girl, seated under the rays of the evening lamp, with the morocco-bound Bible open before him. He may be diligently preparing his Sunday-school lesson—and that would indicate the time as Saturday night—or he may be engaged in the long task of reading the Bible through. There is another assumption: that once upon a time, in those good old days before jazz and newspapers entered the Puritan garden of Eden, all children loved to read the Bible, and now in these dark days no children really read the Book. It is assumed that once in all respectable families the family Bible was actually used, was well-worn all the way through, and that children dog-eared its pages.

We have no way of getting scientific data regarding those good old days; but a recent study of children of junior high-school years, in city and in country, leads to the revision of one of our assumptions. It indicates that, whether they should or not, children of these years do read the Bible a great deal, and that this reading is quite independent of Sunday-school tasks and relationships. The children are at the early exploratory period in literature. The Bible is a book; it is a marked book, and they dip into it. Apparently the most potent stimulus comes not, as we might expect, from parents or from teachers, but from the example of others of their own age or social group. Many are now found attempting the journey from Genesis to Revelation because they have a friend who is doing this or has already accomplished the task. Others are reading because they find so many incidental references to the Bible in their general reading, especially in school; others simply because, just at this stage, they will read everything available.

One single study is inadequate to prove anything, but when it is accomplished by long and wide observation, it at least suggests probabilities. It is safe to say that, under the general stimulus afforded by the teaching of literature, by libraries, and by their own mental appetites, it is probable that any normal child will read the readable parts of the Bible, that there should be little difficulty, so far as the child is concerned, and that the difficulties lie with ourselves.

The first difficulty lies in the fact that family reading customs have changed. The evening lamp is no longer focal; the family disintegrates itself into the community; its members are all seeking for somewhere to go and something to do outside the home. The family is to-day far from being a book-reading group, and many children are likely to receive few incentives to any kind of solid reading.

The Sunday-school has not helped to develop the habit of reading the Bible because it has succeeded in making its own people think of the book as a collection of lessons; it has moved it from the area of pleasure and interest to that of tasks. Its lesson plans have chopped the books into little, disconnected blocks. Few children read lesson books; they only study them.

Somehow, if the Bible is to be a part of the child's spiritual heritage we must make it a part of the life the children are to-day living. It must, first of all, make its own appeal to them on the basis of its interest. Children should not read the Bible with the feeling that they are doing blindly a duty which formal religion requires. That sort of duty once done is done with. So long as the Bible is presented to them in its common formal, peculiarly ecclesiastical binding and make-up, they will think of it as one of those conventions that adults mysteriously impose on life's blind routine. Children should not be encouraged to the block treatment of the Bible, to the attempt to read it all the way through as tho it were a unit. Children should not read the Bible as a task, nor should they be limited to the contacts that Sunday-school lessons make with it. Children should not read all the Bible —tho we have little need to worry on that point as to the passages that modern taste would expurgate; but it is a pity to drag them through Numbers and Leviticus, just as it would be a pity to create an aversion for Browning by forcing a child through *The Ring and The Book*. And, just one more negative: children should not read the Bibles that they carry to Sunday-school, nor any of the popular small-type affairs; their eyesight is too valuable. One might say, then, if in the question, Will children read the Bible? you refer to "The Bible," the standard, specially bound, unitary affair commonly known by that name, we would change the question and ask, "Should they read the Bible?" Then we would answer, No. But we would add, with equal emphasis, that no child should miss what the Bible has for them. And we believe that they do get the essential and appreciable parts of the books when we give them opportunity and make suitable provision for their interests and needs.

This is precisely what *The Children's Bible*[1] does. In the first place, to state that which first impresses one, here is a book which will attract any child by its appearance. It is the peer, in beauty, of any of his treasured volumes. The cover design, the type, the format, and the excellent illustrations, all depart from the traditional in Biblical reprints and present a new and simple translation in thoroughly modern and artistic form. Thus some of our difficulties are met, and we have the material of the Bible for children in a physical form that integrates it into the normal experience of a child's reading life. And this is true, to a large extent of the material in the book. Most of the selections are obviously those of interest to young life or of direct helpfulness to children. It seems strange that over two-thirds of the book is given to the Old Testament until we realize that there is a very large amount of narrative in the early Hebrew stories, and there is a large amount of didactic material in the New Testament. Perhaps the compilers have been influenced by their own interests; it is to be doubted

whether children will enjoy much of the Wisdom literature. This attempt at inclusiveness results in a serious difficulty; the volume is too bulky, too heavy for children to handle with pleasure and ease. That is not a fatal defect; but it is to be hoped that some day we may have the same care and skill devoted to several smaller books, one of which might include the early narratives, another the story of Jesus, and another the apostolic stories.

While the text offers a new translation it does not offend by any attempt to imitate our sporadic newspaper affectations. On the contrary one is sometimes moved to question whether it might not have been modernized just a little more, whether we might not entirely discard archaic forms and still preserve good style. This has been done to a goodly extent in the narrative portions, and the question of its application to poetry is a part of the question of the inclusion of the wisdom and poetic material. Do children read the Psalms? Possibly not more than four or five. Some find pleasure in listening to the sonorous phrases and the elemental word pictures of nature; but the personal experiences and the mystical, as here expressed, lie far beyond them.

However, this book will enable us to answer our question in a practical manner; simply place this book where they may easily find it—and the rest will take care of itself. There are just about four factors in any successful promotion of good reading in the family: that the reading be there, selected, ample, and easily accessible; that it be in suitable, attractive, physically efficient form; that facilities of space and light for reading be provided, and that we hold to a loving and intelligent faith that children will do the rest. Parents, then, may well be grateful that *The Children's Bible* offers the first two of these factors; it is for us to provide the others.

[1] *The Children's Bible*, compiled by Henry A. Sherman and Charles F. Kent. Scribner's Sons, New York City.

Saying these things to a friend he asked, "But what advantage has this over the many similar collections of Biblical material for children?" Well, there are few similar collections; few, if any, that so well meet the conditions we have been suggesting. There is a world of difference between the vigorous use of shears and paste and old plates for making a book for the trade, and the painstaking, sympathetic, discriminate selection, with the original work and artistic sense, that have gone into this new book.

Of course, every man would, for himself or for his children, make a different collection; he would include and exclude. But, since we can not do this, what can we do better than place ready to the hands of our children this rich and inviting treasury of the great literature of the spirit?

THE HISTORIC RELATIONSHIP OF ART TO CHRISTIANITY

Professor ALBERT E. BAILEY, Boston University, Boston, Mass.

A brief survey of the progress of Christian art through the centuries will show how it has throughout been conditioned by Christian thought.

When Christianity began, the only art that Christians knew was Greek. Judaism, for practical reasons at first and for esthetic reasons later, had absolutely proscribed plastic and pictorial art; its creative impulse had manifested itself in ritual and music. Not only did Christians inherit the Jewish prejudice, but they associated all art with pagan worship, which at its worst was immoral and at its best glorified the earthly on which the Christian might not set his affections. The Christian religion was expressed in love for the brethren, missionary activity, literature, philosophy, but not in the fine arts. Bishop Westcott writes (*Epistles of St. John*, essay, p. 319):

Greek art retained to the last the gift of physical beauty, but in the apostolic age it had become the servant of the luxury of the empire. Starting from a human ideal, it became enslaved to man. So far as it had a place in popular worship it brought down the divine to the level of a corrupt life. This being so, the antagonism of early Christianity to contemporary art was necessarily essential and absolute.

In the time of Origen no religious use was publicly made of imitative art; and Eusebius of Cæsarea writes in the early fourth century that "images of Christ are not found among us, that we may not seem like idolaters to carry our God about in an image." Persecution also forced the Christians at times to become a secret organization, and this necessitated the use of disguise. In the West this triple repression of Judaic tradition, Greek immorality, and Roman persecution did not indeed stamp out the artistic impulse but drove it into crass and unesthetic symbolism. In the catacombs and on sarcophagi one finds precisely what one would expect, a disguise absolutely complete except for the initiated. First there are wholly conventional signs such as would be likely to recall to the faithful the beliefs and traditions of the faith: a dove, an olive branch, a star, a fish, a pastoral staff, an anchor, dolphins, palms, a cross. Or where imitative art is employed the subjects are still symbolic, as if the Alexandrian school of Old Testament interpretation had turned artists: Jonah, Daniel, Noah and the ark, Abraham offering Isaac, became similes for Christ and his salvation; so the Good

A CHRISTIAN SARCOPHAGUS

This is a symbolic confession of faith. The side of the sarcophagus represents a temple façade with three gables—possibly suggestive of the Trinity. There are four direct representations of scenes from the passion: right center, Christ guarded by a Roman soldier at the trial before Pilate; extreme right, in front of the pretorium a servant brings water and basin for Pilate to wash his hands; left center, Christ crowned with thorns by a soldier; extreme left, Simon bearing the cross.

In the central section, two sleeping soldiers before the tomb. The person of the Redeemer is suggested by a Latin cross surmounted by the imperial wreath that contains the monogram of Christ (XP). Two doves—the souls of believers—stand upon the arms of the cross and feed upon the leaves of the tree of life that compose the wreath.

CATHEDRAL OF ST. MARK, VENICE:

Detail of the archivolts of the main portal (13th cent.)

The cathedral is the symbolic embodiment of the whole life of man—his activities, his thought, his feeling, his laughter, his tears.

1. Right band: The cycle of the year, each month having a double presentation, one a figure engaged in an occupation appropriate to the month, the other a zodiacal sign or symbol. Beginning at the bottom: *December:* a man killing a pig for the Christmas cheer; above to the right, the sign Capricornus. *November:* a man catching birds with bird lime; above to the left, Sagittarius. *October:* a farmer spading up the soil for the winter rains; above to the left, Scorpio. On the keystone of this archivolt sits Christ, the author and controller of time, in whose service man should spend his days.

2. Left band: The ruin by the fall, and the redemption by Christ. Beginning at the bottom: a half-naked woman with unkempt hair, sitting on a dragon which fastens its fangs in her breast—life brutalized by sin. Above, a child seated on a fallen lion and forcing its jaws open—"Thou shalt tread upon the lion and the adder." Above, two birds struggling to eat grapes. On the keystone of this archivolt also is Christ, whose spirit tames the savage and brings the blessings of civilization.

COSIMO ROSSELLI (?): THE HOLY TRINITY

A representation of the transcendental truths of Christianity.

1. The Trinity: God the Father, an elderly man, supports Christ on the cross; between the two persons hovers a dove. The heavenly nature of the vision is suggested by cherub heads, tongues of fire, and radiating light.

2. The Atonement: Christ is placed in the center of the picture to indicate that the atonement is the central doctrine of the Church.

3. The efficacy and scope of the Atonement are suggested by the skull (Adam's) at the foot of the cross.

4. The blessed Trinity and the salvation it has effected are objects of the Church's adoration. Two worshiping figures stand for the Church: on the right, Catharine of Sienna with her wheel and crown of martyrdom, and on the left, Mary of Egypt in penitential garb to indicate her life of shame. The picture is an endeavor to arouse imagery and feeling in the mind of the worshiper that shall lead to penitence and to adoration of the mystery of redemption.

TITIAN: THE DEPOSITION

Painted by Titian when he was ninety-nine years old in payment to the monks of the Frari for the artist's burial. It was Titian's last work.

The architectural background stands for the Church, the mosaic pelican on the semi-dome reminds us of the central place in Christianity of self-sacrifice. The law and the prophets are schoolmasters to bring us to Christ. Human love holds the dead Savior in a last embrace, while Titian in penitential garb, disguised as Joseph of Arimathca, creeps up to offer his adoration and to beg of Christ his portion of eternal life.

Shepherd, Orpheus, Psyche, the Dioscuri, and even Odysseus and the Sirens. The models were Greek, the methods whether of painting or sculpture were Greek, but the significance was absolutely un-Greek. The Greeks portrayed, the Christian symbolized. And with a poverty of invention that betokens elementary personal development, he repeated the same round of symbols generation after generation. But the break with Greek tradition was absolute; finite forms had begun to express the infinite.

In the age of Constantine the Christian spirit began to come out of the ground and express itself openly; it began to build. It found to hand for a model the Roman basilica, and with a lavishness that betokens a sudden release from repression, the Eastern Church clothed itself in beauty: the beauty of marbles and of mosaic, as in the churches of the Martyrion and the Anastasis at Jerusalem, and in Justinian's Sancta Sophia at Constantinople. But mark how dogma set its dead hand on art. As Hellenic thought had well-nigh squeezed the humanity out of Jesus, so art might not represent him with the sensuous beauty of this world upon him; he must still be a symbol tho in human form, with a conventional face and pose, with conventionalized designs to represent the speculative relations to the universe that theology had charted out for him. And iconoclasm nearly annihilated even so inadequate a representation as that. Throughout the Byzantine period till the fall of the Eastern empire in 1453, Christian art in the East remained static, mechanical, empty of present significance, lacking in inspiration, tho indicative of superficial pomp and splendor. Byzantine art represents the danger of symbolism: it is all thought and no feeling. The key to its meaning is intellectual; the uninitiated find it a blank.

What Christian art might have become in the West we hardly know, for the deluge of the barbarians submerged art and the arts alike, and the Roman world "reeled back into the beast." A crude people living only for the present squatted in the towns where Christian civilization had reared its monuments, threw its marbles into the lime-kiln, and quarried in its temples for material for its fortress walls. Charlemagne made a brave stand for peace and light; but not till the eleventh century dawned was there enough peace and enough intelligence and enough Christianity for Christian art. Then we find the astonishing spectacle of the Church seated on the throne of the Cæsars. She had become the one hope of the world, the great unifier, the great civilizer. Her authority, her organization, her doctrine that all men are equal in God's sight, her championship of the weak against the strong, her claim of holding the keys of heaven and hell, all lifted her into a position of unapproachable power. Doubt had not yet arisen to disunite; "the very community of ignorance tended to produce community of sentiment"; and to the Church the hearts of all were turned as to an ark of safety. The effect of this state of mind upon art might almost be predicted: art was wholly religious, and wholly subservient to the dictates of the Church; and art had practically one manifestation—the building of churches and monasteries. First came the Romanesque churches (from the time of Charlemagne), which by their solidity, their almost fortress-like gloom were a symbol of the majesty and conscious strength of the Holy Catholic Church. Then as the fateful year 1000 passed and men dared to look once more at the world, as the warring spirit was shunted off from domestic fields to the Holy Land, and as various impulses flowed back upon the West from the East, the spirit of man flamed up with an ardor of faith never equaled before or since. The middle age had arrived, and with it the Gothic church, epitome of its aspiring faith.

Reinach says of the Gothic church (*Apollo*, pp. 124-5):

It is a perfect encyclopedia of human knowledge. . . . The first aim of its art is not to please but to instruct. . . . The Church dominated every detail of it, and the Church of the thirteenth century was dominated by the logic of Thomas Aquinas.

Norton characterizes the spirit of this age somewhat as follows (condensed from *Church Building in the Middle Age*, chap. 1):

In the Church the faith of the community took visible form; in it were united religion and local affection and pride. It was a work of piety in which all could share, a work for the glory of God and his mother, for the honor of the saints, for the credit of the community, and for the eternal benefit of every individual who labored on it. The hearts and the imaginations of all men were engaged in it; capacities long unused were evoked and a vivid and earnest faith found its just and characteristic expression. From 1150 to 1300 A. D. came the supreme flowering of emotion and sentiment. Poetic inspiration now entered into Church construction. The sense of beauty, so weak during the earlier age, now became strong; love of beauty became the controlling motive of expression, tho somewhat narrowed and perverted by ascetic ideals and superstition. Men began anew to feeling delight in nature, grace in the human form, joy in color, light, and shade. The artist became the interpreter to itself of his own generation. No wonder his art touched and excited the susceptible feelings of simple beholders, moving them to penitence and tears, or to unwonted gladness and hope.

Walafrid Strabo writes in the ninth century what was even more true at this age, concerning the effect of noble art upon the worshipers:

Et videmus aliquando simplices et idiotas qui verbis vix ad fidem gestorum possunt perduci, ex pictura passionis Dominicæ vel aliorum mirabilium ita compungi, ut lachrymis 'testentur exteriores figuras cordi suo impressas.

("We sometimes see lowly men in private station who by words can scarcely be led to faith in deeds, but by a picture of the Lord's passion, or of other marvels, are so affected as tearfully to show that each one's heart bears an impression corresponding to that of the pictures they view.")

Before the thirteen century had passed, Italy at least had found another language of expression. Duccio of Sienna (1255-1319) began to paint, followed by Giotto of Florence (d. 1336) and then Fra Angelico (1387-1451), with whom the medieval age ended. These all died in the faith—the faith of the middle age, which held religion to be utterly true, the Church to be the all-powerful representative of God on earth, man's vocation to shun hell, win heaven, and enjoy in bliss the beatitude of angels. Never has the art of any age more completely reflected contemporary theology, and never has theology been so sure of itself. One has only to contemplate the frescos on the Campo Santo at Pisa, the church of St. Francis at Assisi, or the walls of San Marco in Florence, or to stand among the soaring vaults and prismatic glooms of Strassburg or Notre Dame, to realize all the glory, all the assurance, all the other-worldliness, and, alas, all the aloofness from world-problems that this art embodies.

With the fifteenth century comes subtly the ebb-tide of faith; and one can

hear
Its melancholy long-withdrawing roar,
Retreating, to the breath
Of the night wind, down the vast edges drear
And naked shingles of the world.

This ebb is caused by the flow of a new spirit, the spirit of discovery, of commerce, of invention. The human heart is no longer satisfied with yearning for the other world alone, it feels itself at home here. Artists, to be sure, still go on painting madonnas and saints, but there creeps in gradually the charm of the earthly, while steadily the angels fold their wings and retire to heaven. Gaily-costumed pageants instead of solitary worshipers, portraits of contemporaries instead of ideal saints, landscape backgrounds instead of plain gold, all proclaim that in the fifteenth century the

Italians have become realists. In the sixteenth century, humanism comes in like a flood; and popes more pagan than Marcus Aurelius adorn their palaces and churches with all the glories of the flesh, with the lust of the eyes and the pride of life. The artistic impulse, while mastering more perfectly its technique, centers its affection on the cult of the outwardly idealized human form. Great souls like Raphael and Michelangelo could still freight these forms with a wealth of religious meaning, but for the ordinary beauty-worshiping artist the transcendental had largely evaporated. Precise composition there was, skilful draping, beautiful color, noble architectural setting, but little religion. Art was still a mirror of the ideals of men, but the ideals were not religious. The seventeenth century saw feeble imitations of the art of the Renaissance, except where, as in Spain, the Jesuit Counter-reformation galvanized art into "passionate fervor and a flush of extravagant sensuousness"; or, as in Jesuit Flanders, where Rubens glorified flesh with a pomp and power never surpassed. The eighteenth century saw the complete annihilation of other-worldliness, and the centering of the esthetic affect about nature and the frivolities of the court. Eighteenth century "Rococo" is the art of play: "The king played with his crown, the priest with his religion, the philosopher with his wits, the poet with his art of rime." Painting became charming and elegant, but frivolous and artificial. The ebb-tide of faith uncovered at last all the shallows.

The tremendous outburst of faith that we call the Reformation embodied itself at first in other forms than art. It had doctrines to shatter and reconstruct, abuses to rectify, persecutions to live through; it had its wars, and above all it had an intellectual life to create in the great middle class whose spirit the Reformation had liberated. This was indeed a hard time for art. As the Christians had once smashed the art of the old world because it was pagan, so the Puritans smashed the art of the middle age because it was "popish." And we look on with a heavy heart while Cromwell's Ironsides shiver the beautiful windows of the cathedrals and melt down the organ pipes for metal. The center of gravity of the world is changing. Power is flowing down and outward. Aristocracies and divine rights and hierarchies are on the wane, while democracy and brotherhood are becoming conscious of their power. The center of gravity of art likewise changes: it is no longer the reflection of a court, of an aristocracy of culture, of a pageant-loving church; it begins to be a reflection of the life and feelings of the common man. Plebeian at first, then moral and didactic; it catches the breath of piety from the Nazarenes of Germany (Wachenrode, 1797, Schlegel, Overbeck, Cornelius, et al., up to 1828), it sees the vision of sincerity with the English Pre-Raphaelites. And to-day, purged of dogma in the crucibles of the Reformation, of rationalism, and modern science, inspired by romanticism and the feeling for common life that the social interpretation of Christianity has engendered, art stands once more as a possible handmaid of religion, ready to embody more powerfully and convincingly than ever has been possible the ideals of a divine life in the soul of man, of a world redeemed from within through what Tolstoi proclaims to be the heart of the gospel, "the love-union of all men and of men with God."

Thus has art followed the fluctuations of faith through the ages and registered in its symbols of beauty the dominant desire of man's soul.

THE RENUNCIATORY ELEMENT IN SELF-REALIZATION IN THE NON-SYNOPTIC GOSPEL

The Rev. Fred Smith, Carthage, S. Dak.

When used for the purpose of conveying instruction with respect to the necessity of the renunciatory principle in the religious life the Johannine gospel ceases to be *"the Fourth Gospel."* Just as Paul speaks of "my gospel," so the author of this gospel could (if he so desired) speak in the same terms regarding his presentation of the renunciatory principle in Christianity. His approach to and his explanation of the place and function of this principle in Christian practise are characteristically different from, without being contradictory to, that which is presented in the synoptic gospels. Hence our title and this present study.

The importance of the principle of renunciation in the practise of Christianity is a point which needs no elaboration for the readers of this Review. Churchgoing Christians, in particular, find its importance conveyed to them through the various avenues of song, sermon and proverb. History is interpreted so as to enforce the value of this principle. As Christians we come into the unquestioned belief that "the blood of the martyrs is the seed of the Church." We accept as an axiom of faith that where there is "no cross" there can be "no crown." *Via crucis, via lucis.* The martyrologies of the Church are its choicest heritage. For the Christian there can be no genuine religion that has not in it the practise of the renunciatory principle. Yet in phrasing this essential truth in this popular way it should not be overlooked that we have come very close to stating it in the form of an error. For in stating this axiom of our faith without due qualification we are within a step of the heresy of advocating "renunciation for renunciation's sake," which is equally abhorrent in religion as "art for art's sake" is in art. Unless we keep in view the goal to which renunciation is a stepping-stone, our Christianity may become a tragedy instead of a triumph. To follow up this statement with a list of unimpeachable facts would lead us far away from our present topic into the fields of monachism and asceticism. Here strange and weird things have been done in the name of renunciation, and, while it is not relevant to our theme to discuss them here, it is necessary that mention be made of them, since it indicates in what strange ways the doctrine of renunciation has been interpreted.

In seeking to ascertain the source of the renunciatory practises which have been condoned, favored, and sometimes fostered by the Church, we find that they root back to the synoptic gospels rather than to the Johannine gospel. In saying this we do not overlook the fact that Paul, using as he does the vocabulary of renunciation and witnessing a good confession thereto, has had some influence on Christian thought and practise in this respect. Nevertheless the chief directive influence must undoubtedly be sought in the synoptic gospels. The imitation of Christ has been peculiarly the ideal of the Christian renunciant, and in the realizing of this ideal the renunciant naturally turned to those Scriptures which gave the facts of the life of Christ rather than those which are more doctrinal in content. The more intent the renunciant was in following literally the life of Jesus the more important would be the synoptic gospels to such a one. Even when we come to modern times, when men pride themselves that they have emancipated themselves from the mechanical idea of literally following the example of Jesus, and speak increasingly of "possessing the spirit of Jesus," we still find that the synoptic gospels are the ones which have directive influence in the interpretation of the renunciatory principle. The reasons for this are worth noting.

There has been in the past a potent but now diminishing influence which has tended to turn the thoughts of men to the synoptic gospels for their interpretation of the renunciatory principle, and that is the strange bias of men generally to interpret religion in terms of renunciation rather than of realization. We have already made reference to this so far as regards hymnody and preaching. We find the same trait in many ethicists and philosophers. One or two typical sentences taken from Paulsen's work on *A System of Ethics* will indicate our meaning with regard to the former. This prominent writer tells us that "the ancient Christians are absolutely convinced that this temporal life is perishable and vain and worthless." [1] Again: "The gospels as they have come down to us, breathe the spirit of world-denial rather than that of earthly joy." [2] And again: "The word happiness or its equivalent does not even occur in the writings of the New Testament." [3] For an illustration from some philosopher one could easily quote from the works of Eucken were it not for the fact that a greater than he lends himself to

illustration here, for does not Kant himself sponsor the idea that action done from inclination can have no moral value! By all these suffering has been capitalized at a high valuation, until the average Christian has come to believe that he who suffers not can be no good. It is therefore no matter for surprize that the synoptic gospels should have had prime place in the interpretation of the renunciatory principle in Christian practise. The main thought of these gospels is renunciatory. Herein we have a definite insistence upon the necessity of self-denial and cross-bearing. The offending hand must be cut off, the offending eye must be plucked out, and, if occasion so demands, father and mother must be hated.

The second reason is more nearly related to our time in particular, and, while not so important as the first, it is perhaps more unexpected. The tendency of Biblical criticism during the nineteenth century was to emphasize the importance of the synoptic gospels. The synoptic problem was the major problem of criticism. The historico-critical school judged the Fourth Gospel rashly rather than rationally. It was relegated to the middle of the second century. So far as the Tübingen school was concerned the value of the Fourth Gospel with regard to Christ and his teaching was incidental rather than primal. The synoptics were "historical." The essential teaching of Christ was to be found solely in the Sermon on the Mount and in the parabolic discourses of the first three gospels. Incidental titbits of fact strung sequentially along a thread of experience was accounted history. This was the medium of truth. In this day it is pathetic to read how that the "apologists" for "John" counter-attacked by showing how "John" was fully acquainted with all the facts concerning the earthly life of Jesus. The study

[1] p. 87.
[2] p. 91.
[3] p. 95.

became microscopic, both by apologist and critic. Now that we breathe an ampler air and have a better view of the Fourth Gospel and its meaning, we can afford to say that the mystical gospel of John was not built to stand that sort of thing, whether it be done by friend or foe. A mystical gospel can not be understood through a microscope. An accumulation of facts may be useful as history, but an interpretation of those facts may be even more useful for truth. This seems to have been largely overlooked in the past century. On the other hand, one is glad to note that during the past twenty-five years there has been a most welcome change on the part of the critics in their attitude to the Fourth Gospel. It is now generally admitted that even a non-historical" gospel can have a rich value for truth. The trend of modern thought has been such also as to enable men to realize increasingly the value of the Fourth Gospel for the new ethic of renunciation which is finding favor in this day. Men to-day are not thinking in terms of renunciation so much as they are thinking in terms of realization. While the renunciatory principle can not and ought not to be denied in the practise of Christianity, there is a strong feeling among many that it needs to be restated, and in the doing of this we suggest that a study of the Fourth Gospel will be of no small help.

A careful reading of this gospel indicates that, while the renunciatory principle is not denied nor compromised, it is given a different emphasis to that which obtains in the synoptic gospels. While revealing his belief in the principle of renunciation, the author seems careful to avoid the language familiar to the renunciant. He has nothing to say of cross-bearing for the individual, nor does he stress the fact of self-denial. Tho he makes little mention of these things, it is

evident that he intends them to have definite place in the Christian economy. He prefers to state this eternal principle of a true religion in another way. And for this reason: to this author the value of Christianity lies in the fact that it imparts life. It spells realization, not, of course according to the Hellenic view-point, but according to Christ; and for the fourth evangelist this is far better. It was to prove this thesis that the gospel was written. Christianity does call for renunciation, but for our author it is of more fundamental importance to show that it confers rights and privileges. Through Christ men are made children of the Eternal (1:12, 16); they are enfranchised in the kingdom of freedom (8:31, 32). Later in his ministry Jesus tells men that he came that "they might have life, and have it abundantly (10:10). If it be necessary to state the renunciatory principle of Christianity in bald realistic terms our author seems to be unaware of the necessity. Nevertheless, he does convey the need for the necessity of this practise, but he does it by recognizing and acting upon the principle that the actions of men are often determined through the inferences they draw as well as by the commands which they receive.

The Fourth Gospel is often spoken of as "the gospel of the incarnation," and while this is a true descriptive statement, we must not let our eyes be blinded to the fact that the shadow of Calvary falls even across the opening pages. From the beginning of his ministry Christ stands before men as "the Lamb of God, which taketh away the sin of the world" (1:29). Before a word is said about the need of renunciation on the part of the believer, it is revealed as a fact in the experience of Christ. But our author goes deeper than that; it is a fact in the heart of God also, for "God so loved the world that he gave his only begotten Son, that whosoever believeth in him should not perish, but have eternal life" (3:16). The inference is unavoidable; nay, it is a challenge: that which is a fact in the life of God and Christ should be a necessity in the experience of the Christian also. But the fourth evangelist does not say so! That is for the reader to infer.

Having brought this cardinal fact to the attention of the reader, the evangelist proceeds to its amplification as he proceeds with his narrative. We have little need to follow in detail this amplification. Certain portions do call for specific mention, however. In the not too easily understood sacramental discourse concerning the bread of life (6:26-60) and in the allegory of the Good Shepherd who gives his life for the sheep (10:11-18) we have the why and wherefore stated of the principle of sacrifice. Very interesting is the fact that the fourth evangelist reveals Christ as expressing the fact of renunciation under the veil of symbol and metaphor. His sense of psychological values, as well as the fact that this gospel was written for Greeks, evidently led the fourth evangelist to state the renunciatory principle of Christianity in such a manner as to contain a challenge rather than to state it as a bald command. For we have good authority for knowing that to the Greeks the cross was foolishness. Therefore did this evangelist accommodate himself to the Greeks without compromising the gospel of his Lord. A metaphor may energize a motive into action where "truth in closest words shall fail."

On the other hand attention should be drawn to the fact that on one specific occasion the fourth evangelist does express the renunciatory principle in terms that have the directness and bluntness characteristic of the synoptic gospels. Significantly

enough, this was when the delegation of Greeks came to interview Jesus as he was coming near to the time of his death. Then it is that Jesus speaks in no uncertain way concerning the principle of sacrifice in his religion. It will be a fact in the life of the believer as well as in his own life. The "troubling of the soul" of Jesus indicates that for him the cross was more than an act of consecration, it was also an act of renunciation. Yet this thought is but as a cloud passing across the sun; his hour of shame was to be his hour of glory and the revealing of the Father. Jerusalem, and not Athens, must be his goal. In this illuminating incident we have positive and direct proof (if such were needed) to show that the fourth evangelist realized the eternal value of renunciation for Christianity.

Yet, having said all this, we still can say that this evangelist is not interested in renunciation as such. As we have already said, he preferred to think of Christianity in terms of realization. He does not emphasize the stern necessity of renunciation as do the synoptists, and for a profound reason which reveals itself in the conversation of Jesus in the chamber with his disciples. In those sacred and solemn hours Jesus created an atmosphere in which renunciation could not live. "Henceforth," he says to the eleven, "ye are my friends, if ye do the things which I command you" (15:14). The synoptists thought of Christianity in terms of discipleship; here it is spoken of in terms of friendship. Disciples think in terms of renunciation; but friends think in the richer terms of consecration. One is loyal, the other is loving. And love does not think of sacrifice, for its very giving is a form of living. Realizing this we can understand why Jesus in these hours when he was standing in the solemn shadow of the cross should also speak of the untroubled heart, the rejoicing soul, and abiding peace. In the words of Jesus himself we have stated for us the Johannine ethic of renunciation: "A woman when she is in travail hath sorrow, because her hour is come: but when she is delivered of the child, she remembereth no more the anguish, for the joy that a man is born into the world. And ye therefore now have sorrow: but I will see you again, and your heart shall rejoice, and your joy no man taketh away from you" (16:21-23).

We believe that such a conception of the renunciatory principle in Christianity has rich value for our day and age. We submit that Chris-tian teachers have been in error in thinking that the sum of the matter was contained wholly within the synoptic gospels. To think this is to mistake the part for the whole. Taking a hint from Scripture in coming to this phase of Christianity it will be well for us to read the last gospel first. In the past the tendency has been, with respect to the renunciatory principle, to forget the end in the means. To correct this unfortunate error is one of the many tasks facing the ministry to-day. The task is by no means an impossible one. The solution lies in a diligent study of the Fourth Gospel, and in the restating of the renunciatory principle with a Johannine emphasis.

A PERPETUAL ADVENT

The Rev. JOHN MOORE, Amesbury, Mass.

The associations of Christmas are so poetically tender and so winsomely beautiful that it is the sweetest festival in the ecclesiastical calendar, and easily holds the foremost place among annual holidays. It speaks of things that cling to the heart: reunion, brotherhood, fellowship, companionship, gladness, and above all else a sense of the nearness of God. Now, if ever, our prevailing secularity of temper is penetrated and possessed by the intrusions of the transcendental. The transcendental realm is continually breaking through into the disordered world which we occupy, and in some degree is perpetually present with us. As George Herbert has it, "Man is one world and has another to attend him." But not always are we as conscious of it as we are at Christmas. We live, indeed, in a world of "perpetual becoming" where "out of the boundless ocean of ether, which forms its basis, solar systems continually arise, evolve, pursue their course for an indefinite number of ages, disintegrate and sink back into their primordial elements, only to begin the same process all over again" without cessation. Hence it is a legitimate assumption that the drama of life is a perpetual advent of God. Christmas stands for a merry, brandy-sauced, benevolent, roistering mid-winter holiday; but it also stands for the birthday of Jesus, the festival of sacrificial joy, of the dawn of life. Father Manning called it the festival of the father. It celebrates the coming of the Christ. He came down from the skies with a message for humanity, to rescue mankind from the obscurantism of theological teachers who were blindly hiding the light of God from his children! A gifted preacher said once, "Every special incoming of God into human experience is prepared in the unseen before it appears in the seen. . . . It is in the highest degree probable, nay, inevitable, that everything worth calling a divine advent, every spiritual uplift which our sunken race receives, is celebrated with joy in heaven before we know anything of it on earth." This is possible, credible. But it is a certainty and ineffaceably true, that we mortals on earth must prepare to receive the divine advent. "Prepare to meet thy God" is an exhortation for all time; not at death alone, but in life, every golden moment of it. God is perpetually coming to mankind, and always his advent is to give life more abundantly. God is always coming, always coming; but so often he finds us unprepared, and therefore unable to recognize him when he comes. Give God a chance, then, to be heard above the tumult and the shout of merry-making; prepare to receive divine impressions and intimations; be ready to make experiments. Take a look at the holy Child and learn afresh from him apart from any previous ideas.

Let every heart prepare a throne
And every voice a song.

Prepare to meet God in the perpetual marvels of existence.

(1) Prepare to meet him in the marvels of development. The ancient inspired poet saw a God who worked with amazing celerity, when the poet after plunging into depths of speculation that must have made his head whirl, finally decided to begin his account of creation with an unchallengeable sentence, and then went on to tell how it all rose from the vast void in six short days. Now we have a longer view of the universe, and we see a God who requires incredible eternities for creation's workings. Infinite space is crowded with unnumbered worlds; infinite time is peopled with unnumbered existences; infinite organisms are filled full of peerless loveliness. To intellect and imagination the world is indisputably larger. The telescope and camera have pushed back the boundaries of space, the microscope has revealed the infinitely little, the chemist has exhibited matter as centers of whirlpools of force. Astronomical discovery and chemical analysis of molecular physics have shoved us shivering into a tremendous world. Some people have become very uncomfortable, the world has become to them a terrifying place, their cozy cosmogony says God came, but does not admit that he comes. How completely unprepared they are who go on as tho the state of things to which they are accustomed will last forever, who can see God in the haze of history but fail to find tokens of him in the pregnant present! The clearest revelation we have is that God comes—this is the message of Christmas. Slowly, infinitely slowly, God comes in the evolution that leads to the development of more complex forms of animal life and finally to man. What a story of the marvels of existence is that!

A fire mist and a planet,
A crystal and a cell,
A jellyfish and a saurian,
And a cave where the cavemen dwell;

Then a sense of law and beauty,
And a face turned from the clod—
Some call it Evolution, and others call it
God.

It needs the preparation of heart and mind to see God marching out of cosmic spaces, vague nebulæ, molecular instabilities, and dancing atoms—marching to meet mankind! Science does not lead to materialism, philosophy to atheism, nor need religion degenerate to a gesture of defiance at a universe that has broken away from God. "God for me," says George Tyrrell, "is the creative Power that pushes everything on to its higher development; the principle of life and health and growth and truth and goodness." Science and philosophy show us these things, but also lead us to think of him who wrought them: "The invisible things of him from the creation of the world are clearly seen, being understood by the things which are made, even his eternal power and Godhead." Religion is just the great adventure of seeing his advent on these dizzy heights and in these whelming depths.

(2) Prepare to meet God in the twin marvel of dawn and eve. It is early dawn, palest primrose of morning, the gray light is breaking tender and fragile, painting a bloom upon the earth as soft and frail as that which sleeps on the wings of June butterflies. Spray-white mists enfold the woods, sleep-closed flowers are wrapped in silver lace, earth scintillates with jewels of transparent crystal pearl-dew as the sun flushes forth in strength and flings the dawn's flimsy veil of shadow from the full light of day, and genial rays are poured through the bedroom window till your baby lies sleeping in the sunbeams! The planet like a garment wears the beauty of the morning! It was the tremulant beauty of the morning that an inspired writer captured and imprisoned in glowing metaphor when he described the incarnation. "The day-spring from on high hath visited us, to give light to them that sit in darkness and in the shadow of death, to guide our feet into the way of peace."

It is night and the time of stars. Subtly, silently, almost imperceptibly, steal in twilight's dusk and the depth of night. The sun sinks thinly veiled behind the purple bar of the west, the delicate sculptured, alabaster clouds, with rounded luster, roll gaily along the blue heavens, between the deep masses of shadow the twilight trembles hesitantly a while, the stars peer faintly through the haze, and lo! the heavens are gemmed with glittering fire. Stars flame out white, topaz, misty-red, and a strange mysterious sense of distance broods over it all, and most of all the solemn silence!

O the silence of the heavens,
How they speak to me of God!

"If the stars should appear one night in a thousand years," says Emerson, "how men would believe and adore and preserve for many generations the memory of the City of God which had been shown." The silver-sprinkled heavens are truly an astonishing achievement.

The heavens declare the glory of God in bewildering contrasts: purity and blackness; mystery and revelation and expansiveness are written there. There is something inexpressibly exciting in looking into such an infinity of space. Yet life's cares and desires shrink and the oppressive weight of reality is lifted by "womanly witching night!" "Watcher, what of the night?" asks one; "Work while it is day, for the night cometh when no man can work," says another; and a third warns, "Beware! the Lord cometh as a thief in the night." Yes, God comes to us in the darkness; subtly, silently, dominantly the night falls, but love's advent lights the skies!

(3) Prepare to meet God in the fourfold marvel of the seasons. Mark the timid approach of springtime that quickens into joyous dance as he pierces through winter's shroud of white and kisses the slumbrous eyelids of earth as he goes till there is bud, leaf, beauty, song. The grass green as emeralds, patches of daffodils that prick out their yellow skirts, and those heralds of April, spear-shaped hyacinths; the pink beauty of almond trees, delicate green beeches, the filmy laciness of gleaming horse-chestnuts, and the deeper green of embroidered hedges; anemones, wild cherry, and white blackthorn blossom, ruddy elms, pendant catkins, and the pale primrose, queen of the wood. And look at the hills in dress of green with bracken-heather-whortle-berry embroidery, broadly flounced with golden gorse, hat of richest russet brown—nature's goddesses bewitchingly beautiful. And how the meadows are flecked with gold and white and sown with the dust of rainbows, the orchards appareled in pink and white, the whole countryside a vast sea of colored brightness! Wonderful spring, the annual illuminated miracle! What is this but God coming in swelling bud and bursting blossom and nature's throb of passion and power? How the heart leaps in the face of it all and sings with Septimus Sutton,

How beautiful it is to be alive!
For lo! the winter is past, the rain is over and gone; the flowers appear on the earth, the time of the singing of the birds is come and the voice of the turtle is heard in our land; the fig-tree ripeneth her green figs, and the vines are in blossom; they give forth their fragrance. Arise, my love, my fair one, and come away.

Such was the love-song of a poet-seer whose religious training taught him to look for the hand of God in every event.

The spacious afternoon of summer is hot, gentle zephyrs carol around as one walks forth, the ripe fruits and golden grain wave in the wind, the land is all aglow with maddening sunlight. The dull non-reflecting surface of summer's leaves lull the wearied eyelids as they hang on oak, elm, ash, and beech; they shade us from the glare of the sun as its heat penetrates and cuts through the nerves and sinews of action and drugs the enervated spirit. A riot of flashing colors waves upon the hillsides, and God comes in the redness and ripeness of flower, fruits, and the gorgeous harvests of summer. A herdsman of Tekoa saw God coming in a basket of summer fruit, the symbol, revelation, and inspiration of a better day.

And the Lord Jehovah showed me: and behold a basket of summer fruit. And he said, Amos, what seest thou? And I said, A basket of summer fruit. Then said Jehovah unto me, the end is come upon my people Israel. I will not again pass them by any more.

The green of spring has changed to the brown of summer, the brown changes now to amber and russet tints, the landscape spreads out like a vast leopard's skin. The planets die down, the wild flowers are gone, and scents of decay are everywhere. It is autumn, and nature is falling asleep amid a blaze of yellow-red-orange glory. Earth flames like molten fire and imperial sunsets blaze along the hills; the saffron stubble transmutes to brown and red, and finally the landscape to buff, as the sun sinks below the horizon. Autumn's sunlight is soft and mellow, but autumn's breezes lash the summer-drugged spirit and "bugle up the laggard self" like the vigorous hand-grip of an intellectual friend. Truly this is God coming!

And the voice said cry! And I said, What shall I cry? All flesh is grass and all the goodliness thereof is as the flower of the field. The grass withereth, the flower fadeth . . . but the word of God abideth forever.

A haze on the far horizon, the infinite tender sky,
The ripe rich tints of the corn-fields,
And the wild geese sailing high,
And all over upland and lowland
The charm of the goldenrod (God's glowing smile!),
Some of us call it Autumn, and others call it God.

And it is God, coming in the burning leaves, and the iridescent splendors of decay! The hoar frost scatters itself abroad, leaves with pearls encrusted lie upon the frozen ground, the snow begins to drift into piles driven by windy gusts, ice covers street and road, pond and lake, and icicles hang fantastically from every building and fence. It is winter! Holly and ivy reflect the light to make the days brighter and more beautiful. The great Geometrician has arrayed himself in the jeweled splendor of a world of sparkling crystals, cubes, triangles, and parallelograms, for as Plato says, "God geometrizes."

"He giveth snow like wool," said one; "He scattereth the hoar frost like ashes," said another; "He giveth his ice like morsels," said a third; and a fourth saw spiritual implications, and said with an inspired declaration of experience, "Tho your sins be red like crimson they shall be as white as snow."

And so winter marches on till once again there is a golden brightness in the air, the cities are washed with gold and mercury, and things begin to stand out crocus-colored. Nature heaves a waking sigh, and we say, "Winter leaves to-morrow!" And the succeeding days are full of nature's rapture throbs, and piping voices. What an advent of God it all is! Human experience watched these spectacular phenomena, this wonderful mechanism, till God was revealed in it, and taking up a pen somebody wrote,

While the earth remaineth, seed-time and harvest, cold and heat, summer and winter, day and night shall not cease.

You may look at the wonder and beauty of things till you are a mere dot in the mystery of earth and sky, you are in the presence of something nameless, incomprehensible, but ineffably real—God! Yes, that is God coming, coming, coming! The first feeling is one of insignificance as the mighty massiveness of nature overwhelms one; but not for long. There rises the feeling of the majesty of man, the sense that bigness is not greatness, that mightier than lake and forest, plain and mountain and sea, is man. The soul transcends all these nether things; it can turn a luminous eye to absorb their beauty, and stretch to the bounds of being in sheer delight at their contemplation. Well, even that is God coming in intolerable craving, shivering through the foundation and framework of being like a bugle blast; it is Christ walking on the waters, which resilient, resurgent, wash the shore of human existence.

Like tides on a crescent sea beach
When the moon is new and thin,
Into our hearts high yearnings
Come welling and surging in:
Come from that mystic ocean whose rim no foot hath trod—
Some people call it Longing, and others call it God.

It is the high prerogative of man to ensoul all nature. It was thus that primitive folk peopled space with fairies, and personified rivers, trees, lakes. The mythology of ancient races teaches the marvelous truth that mountains and forests, clouds and streams, sky and ocean, are ruled and guarded by deities. Such was their awe of the Eternal. "Christianity," says Novalis, "is the capability of everything to become the bread and wine of a divine life." And when the holy Child had grown to manhood, he showed a poet's delight in sky and landscape, in every touch of natural beauty; ay, and he thrilled to the warmth and magnetism of a world of men! Methinks if we could only emulate his example we should do more than "keep" Christmas, it would be to us a veritable advent of God. Peace and good-will would not come in with the dressing of holly and mistletoe and pass out with the withered leaves and dead berries. We should have a perpetual Christmas. Oh! the thrill and glow that steals over one with the carols and the bells! The soft touch of gentleness that holds us in a spell! Hands and pockets fly open, hearts turn golden, God comes!

Think of it—a perpetual Christmas! No wretchedness, no complaining on the streets, the iron bands of coercion broken, poverty and misery abolished, harsh tyranny swallowed up in love, peace among men of good-will!

Men through all time have girded up the loins of their hope as they have realized the presence of God. Comrades in the temple beautiful, the greatest secret of nature is not for the scientist, the philosopher, but for the religious spirit. God lives! God reigns! God comes!

Peace be unto all!

COMMENT AND OUTLOOK

By E. HERMAN, OUR LONDON CORRESPONDENT

Haeckel Redivivus

At this year's meeting of the British Association at Hull we have had a recrudescence of materialism in Sir Charles Sherrington's presidential address. Man, he said, is merely a mechanism. Mind, as hitherto understood, simply does not exist; it is merely the highest point in the development of the nervous system: hence it follows that science can claim the theoretical power to create man.

But this is little more than Haeckel plus the knowledge of to-day. And, like Haeckel, Sir Charles does nothing toward bridging over the gulf that yawns between the ability to understand a mechanism and the power to reconstruct it. Science can take any mechanical model apart and reconstruct it quite satisfactorily, provided—always provided—no part is missing. But common sense assures us that if science tried to reconstruct the human machine, there would be everything missing!

Indeed, in the end Sir Charles had to confess that he is no nearer solving the old enigma as to "the how" of the connection between the nerves and the mind than Haeckel was; and it is precisely that "how" that matters. Until the mechanical theory can expound that baffling mystery, men will look for a solution, not to science—indeed, most of us are convinced that its elucidation is not the function of science at all—but to revelation and to the facts of religious experience.

Dean Inge on Industrialized Religion

Among those who preached special sermons to the British Association at Hull was Dean Inge, who gave his satirical bent free rein in castigating our tendency to worship anything big, or the owner of anything big; to think of God in terms of ownership.

And what does it really mean, this exhortation to worship the hypothetical Creator and Sustainer of the starry heaven? Is it not a characteristic tendency of an industrial civilization to think of everything in terms of ownership? Is it really a valid argument from theism to ask why so eligible a property as the universe can possibly belong to nobody? Do we ever unconsciously argue that because we bow respectfully to a duke who owns 100,000 acres we ought to pay infinitely greater respect to the largest of all landed proprietors who possesses millions of estates, each a million miles in diameter, and whose title deeds are millions of years old?

The dean certainly lays his finger upon a common weakness of Western religion. We speak of "having" a religion, an experience, a God, just as we speak of "having" a summer house or a first edition of Ruskin. We are slow in realizing what our Hindoo mother realizes instinctively that God possesses us rather than we him, that the test of life is not to possess the truth but to be possessed and transformed by it.

Christianity as a World Religion

This year's Conference of Modern Churchmen has not had the *succès de scandale* which its predecessor enjoyed. The press gave it only a moderate prominence, and, since no heresy hunter has raised his vengeful head, it is not likely that it will be made a subject of debate in convocation. On the face of it, such a subject as "Christ and the Creeds" gave far more scope for aggressive heterodoxy than a symposium on "Christianity as a World Religion." Still, certain storm-petrels of the movement—not Mr. Mayor this time, but the even less guarded Mr. Cyril Emmet and Professor Soothill—have let themselves go in somewhat irresponsible fashion. Mr. Emmet, for instance, while admitting that Christianity possessed "distinctive features," warned his hearers that they must not "jump lightly" to the conclusion that it is the best religion to-day because it was the best for an earlier age. Professor Soothill, going on the same lines, suggested that the day might come when "the best men in Christianity and in Buddhism might meet to discuss the possibility of working together for the salvation of the world through love."

Quite apart from the question of the finality of the Christian religion, it is an ominous spectacle to see the vowed representatives of a church whose faith is grounded in that finality and whose formularies presuppose it calmly making the finality and uniqueness of Christianity a subject of doubt at a public conference. Men of good-will and common sense outside organized religion comment upon it as poor ethics, and charge the speakers with a lack of honor which, in a business man, would be swiftly punished by ostracism.

Dr. Jowett on World Peace

Perhaps the most notable result of the recent Copenhagen Conference convened by the World Alliance for Promoting International Friendship through the churches has been Dr. Jowett's impassioned plea for united testimony and action by the churches in the cause of international peace. Dr. Jowett urged that the time had come when the whole Church of Christ upon earth, sinking denominational and party differences, should "give visibility to its existence" by bearing united testimony and embarking upon united action in the cause of world-wide peace. He asks for a central representative body through which the Church would be able to speak and act—a body which might be constituted from members of existing kindred societies, such as the Archbishop's Committee, the National Council of the Free Churches, the League of Nations' Union and the Students' Christian Movement.

Dr. Jowett's manifesto has evoked considerable response, and the Federal Council of the Free Churches lost no time in appointing a sub-committee to take steps to convene a meeting attended by representatives not only of the societies enumerated, but also of the Church of England as such, and of the Roman Catholic and the Greek Orthodox churches—the object of such meeting being "to consider the most effective means of giving corporate expression to the churches' convictions concerning international peace and good will."

What will come of this is uncertain, but there are thoughtful churchmen who feel that churches which can remain corporately indifferent to the wrongs of the Christian minorities in the East at the hands of Kemal Pasha are not ideal advocates of peace on earth, good will toward men. That it is high time for the Church to stand solidly for peace is certain; but she must first be able to "wash her hands in innocency."

The City of David

When Josephus wrote his "Jewish Archæology," he little dreamt of the new and specialized meaning in which a later age would come to use that term. To-day, under the happy auspices of international cooperation, much has already been done, but far more is going to be done, in the entrancing field of archeology in Palestine. For popular interest nothing can rival the announcement of the project for opening up the site of the ancient city of Jerusalem, the City of David. Not even the site of Troy, nor that of the Mycenæ of Agamemnon, can compete in wealth of human interest with those ten acres of Holy Land. Originally within the walls of Jerusalem, they lie to-day just outside the existing walls, immediately to the south, and include practically the whole of the stronghold of the Jebusites, who were there before David and thought "David can not come in hither"; the palace of David to build which Hiram, King of Tyre, sent "cedar-trees and carpenters and masons"; and, very probably, the tombs, of a later date, of all the Kings of Judah.

No one can fail to be moved by the prospect of such discoveries, and happily the opportunity is now open to the whole world of archeologists. Each society will receive its separate concession and will be master of its own investigations. Should the discoveries justify such a course, it is proposed that the ancient city and all that may be found in it shall be laid bare, and be preserved as a historical feature of Jerusalem.

Among other interesting excavations is that of the Franciscan Order at Capernaum, where the extensive ruins of a fine synagog in Jewish classical style of the early centuries of our era are being gradually laid bare.

Australian Democracy and the Church

The problem of the lusty democracies of young nations is one of the most fascinating, alike for the historian, the psychologist, and the minister of religion. In Australia, a large element of the population is not only anti-socialist and anti-church, but frankly anti-religious. "Salvation wanted—no God need apply," which appeared as a head-line in one of the Australian Labor organs, is characteristic of the attitude of this type of Australian. The Rev. J. P. Perkins, who has recently visited Australia, and gives his impressions in *The Christian World,* says there are fewer working folk to be found in church in Australia than in England. There are outstanding preachers who draw big congregations, but on the whole the situation is difficult. The Roman Church struck Mr. Perkins as having a very strong hold upon its members. He speaks of "the ominous triumvirate of Rome, labor, and the saloon," and states that Roman Catholics are in the majority in the labor governments of Queensland and New South Wales. The Protestant Churches, on the other hand, are, he thinks, too closely allied with Orangeism, which, in its bigotry, repels sensible folk. Mr. Perkins tells an amazing story of a church-member of the artizan class visiting a fashionable suburban church. An official accosted him at the close of the service and asked if he was a workingman. On getting an affirmative reply, he was summarily told that that church was not for him. This story sounds almost incredibly Victorian, yet it could possibly be matched somewhere in England. What amazes one is that in a country with blue skies and long summer months open air services are so rare.

Editorial Comment

As the autumn wore on the western world saw with a sinking heart the return of the crescent to Europe. It was another post-war disillusionment.

Christmas: the Cross and the Crescent

We thought the Turk was gone for good; and we beheld him flushed with victory, grasping eagerly after something of his old power in Thrace, and possibly planning by a reentrance into Constantinople before Christmas a makeweight to General Allenby's entrance into Jerusalem five years ago. Meanwhile Smyrna is in ruins, the material results of missionary endeavor on many fields seem wasted, and hordes of refugees look to the western nations for relief. "How long, O Lord! How long!" has been the renewed cry of Christendom.

We do not know how long. But we do know that the message of Christmas is a *"sursum corda,"* a "lift up your hearts" which the Turk is powerless to gainsay. The cross proves its ascendency by the very fact that in the world's deepest sorrow it is to the soldier of the cross that the outcasts look for protection and relief. We do not mean the armed soldier of the Greek type. His part in the problem of the Near East has only rendered confusion worse confounded. He has invited a reaction of the most calamitous sort. This, despite its terrible consequences to the multitude of refugees, may have been a needed reminder that the crescent can never be overthrown by the sword. The cross is the only weapon that can win that victory. The material evidences of its advance in any given field may disappear for a time; its buildings may be burned, its congregations scattered; but so far as the work done was in the spirit and manner of Jesus it does not die. If it have rooted itself in the hearts of men through the presence and endeavor of good will, it lives.

America, for instance, never made a more advantageous investment in the Far East than when she devoted the Boxer indemnity to the cultured advantage of China. It is one of the wonders of the present crisis that the students of Robert College in Constantinople, representing so many different and often conflicting national elements, are reported to be going about their work in reasonable agreement and very much as usual. Where the Quaker has been in Bolshevik Russia, there, it may be safely said, will remain a testimony to the reality of Christian faith which no atheistic propaganda of the government can ever overthrow. These things are so because in each instance the fundamental truth of the Christmas message was translated into goodness that vast sections of needy men could use.

That is the cross in action. It stands for invincible good will, spending itself for the spiritual and physical blessing of men. In no such measure or degree has the crescent ever translated its faith into goodness; nor can it except it go to school to Jesus. No ousting of missions and of relief workers from Asiatic Turkey can be more than temporary; nor can the Turk ever eradicate the influence of what has been done in other years. The fact that among the Turks themselves there has been revulsion against wholesale massacre, and many instances of private protection of those threatened by it,

goes to show that there is human nature to work upon, and that where the Turk
has come into first-hand and continuous contact with genuine Christian influence even he has been moved by it.

The weapons of the cross that must finally prevail to bring peace to the
distracted East are fair international dealing, which may involve in some
cases an international police, but must be free from underhanded scheming
for a monopoly of markets or of raw materials; persistent but good-tempered
and patient missionary endeavor for the material and spiritual advance of
Christian and Moslem alike; and a generous spending of men and means in
meeting the present distress whether due to Turk or Greek. The Christmas
promise is to men of good will; and the good will of the cross is the most indomitable thing in the world.

✠

We seldom intrude our personal affairs or experiences on the patience and
indulgence of our readers. But is there any sufficient reason for withholding
something that is attractable, likable, yes, and lovable,
Correspondence because it happens to note what is not by any means a
That Charms little thing in the editor's morning mail.

There is the bunch of letters on the desk all ready to
be opened. One may surmise what one after the other contains, but nothing
is positively known of the contents until the paper-cutter does its unsealing
work. Letter number one of the batch is of the usual kind, stereotyped and
commonplace. Number two, however, is different, very different. There is
something unusual about the phraseology and the spirit. It begins graciously
and ends thus:

If you do not publish it (the manuscript) please return it in the enclosed envelop
and I will love you just the same.
I am, dear friend, with high regard for yourself personally,
Thoroughly yours,
JAMES L. ————————

Our first observation concerning this kind of correspondence is that it
reveals a spirit that is of unquestioned value in the making of personality.
The love mentioned is not dependent on what the editors do with the manuscript. The love here exemplified is what we find in Paul's classic, "Rejoiceth
with the truth."

It has been said that "The true order of going . . . is to use the beauties
of earth as steps toward celestial beauty." And this is profoundly true of life
as a whole, for we only carry into the to-morrows the beauty we possess to-day.

Another observation is the absence of the beauty of graciousness and
courtesy from much of the correspondence in the commercial life of to-day.
Recently one large American surety company announced through the daily
press that they had started honesty courses, believing that it is good philanthropy and good business. A similar opportunity presents itself to all commercial houses to enter the educational field in the interest of courtesy. Certainly a higher grade of correspondence would add much of pleasantness and
satisfaction to the day's work.

There is no better place than the home and the school for the exercise
and development of this much neglected and important quality.

In the book-review section of this issue one of our scientific reviewers notices a recent volume entitled *Smell, Taste, and Allied Senses in the Vertebrates.* What interest has such a book for the religious or theological mind? We think this simple quotation answers the question:

Homiletics and the Sense Organs

Sense organs have always excited general interest, for they are the means of approach to the human mind. Without them our intellectual life would be a blank. The deaf and blind show how serious is the loss of even a single set of these organs.

Here is a fact of outstanding importance to the preacher, one that can never be overlooked.

Take a passage like the following, for example:

But blessed are your eyes, for they see; and your ears, for they hear (Matt. 13:16).

The Master was moved to say this to his disciples because they had discerned the mysteries of the kingdom but the great multitude had not.

Aside from the immediate lesson in the parable there is a physiological as well as a psychological question involved. It is obvious that if there were no hearers there would be no need for churches. And it is just as obvious that if good hearing is essential preachers should stress the need for keeping the organs of the body in prime condition.

Again, one might describe the wonderful beauties in our national parks to a blind man, but no description, however accurate, would ever convey the same meaning or as much to that man as seeing with the natural eye. If, then, there is a reaction from the deficiency of a sense organ different from that of a normal organ, and if it is a fact that it is always more difficult to move, convince, and educate the deaf, the dumb, and the blind, surely it is worth while to attack the evil of imperfect and diseased organs at its source.

Physiological treatment of this text offers an ideal starting point, inasmuch as it leads up to and has a direct bearing on the intellectual and spiritual side of life.

The area and scope of most men's activities are usually broader than they realize. Most messages from the pulpit would gain immensely by a broader vision of the particular subject treated, as in the passage cited above.

LIGHT FROM MANY QUARTERS

What can not be understood can not be managed intelligently. JOHN DEWEY.

Real wealth is poverty adjusted to the law of Nature. EPICURUS.

The production of men, not commodities, must be the aim of sound social religion. CHARLES A. ELLWOOD.

The pursuit of religious truth is the noblest, as it is the most important pursuit in which any human being can be engaged. WHATELY.

Men must regard themselves not as the owners of rights, but as trustees for the discharge of functions and the instruments of social purpose. R. H. TAWNEY.

Only an eye for beauty can properly discern beauty; only the beautiful heart is able to apprehend the beautiful. SAMUEL JUDSON PORTER.

No one can learn to assume responsibility unless he is made to assume the consequences of his acts. WILLIAM FEATHER.

There is in fact only one thing to live for, for those who see clearly, and that is the great cause of human brotherhood. FREDERICK W. NORWOOD.

Friendship is the nearest thing we know to what religion is. God is love. And to make religion akin to friendship is simply to give it the highest expression conceivable by man. . . . The beauty of friendship is its infinity. HENRY DRUMMOND.

THE CHARMS OF ENGLISH SPEECH

Dr. FRANK H. VIZETELLY, Editor of the Practical Standard Dictionary

If our words are to be audible, intelligible and agreeable our enunciation must be melodious. We are often told that English is a harsh language, and yet it contains the same vowel sounds as Italian, French, and Spanish. The blame for this harshness should not be put upon the language, but upon those who misinterpret and abuse it. Do justice to the vowel element of English speech and you will find that speech full of beauty and melody of sound. Why are we told that Italian is preeminently the language of song? Because of the abundance of its vowel-sounds. Why is Italian speech more euphonious than English to the American ear? Not because it has more vowel-sounds, but because the Italian forms' his vowels more carefully and utters them more sonorously than we utter ours. The vowels are preeminently the music of standardized speech, just as the consonants are its noises. As the consonants are suppressed or imperfectly uttered, articulation becomes proportionately indistinct, but to neglect the vowels is to divest one's speech of its beauty as a means of expression; for, as Dr. Harold Ford has expressed it, "the vowel is the flesh and blood of words, without which the consonants are but the dry bones." By the vowels alone do we develop intensity, purity, and sweetness of voice. They are the musical sounds of speech, the soul elements that admit of modulation. Some of us have acquired the habit of speaking with the teeth compressed or with the mouth almost shut. Such of us as follow this practise reduce to a minimum the sonority of the vowels, impair the quality of the voice, reduce its power, and lessen the extent of its reach. A man may possess the voice of a Stentor, but it will be of little use to him if his enunciation be defective. A clear, crisp articulation of words constitutes that charm in speech which fascinates and frequently holds us spellbound. Actors and singers inflate the chest to deepen, strengthen, and prolong their tones, for the notes or sounds which the chest gives are much deeper, more reverberant, and more affecting than any other. Having both a head voice and a chest voice, there are times when each can be used to advantage. The change from one tone to another, or from one speech level to another—from the lower register to the higher, or vice versa—is often influenced by the character of our utterances.

Variations of tone depend upon the rapidity of the sound vibration. Tone changes may proceed by leaps or glides. As we speak, the voice frequently dwells on one note, but it may move upward or downward from one note to another, so that the different notes merely become points between which the voice is constantly gliding. In attempting to estimate the beauty or ugliness of varieties of spoken English, the impressions arrived at invariably are the result of association which it is generally unwise to discuss. Unity of spoken English is still imperfect, even tho there be a standard. To an educated Englishman, cockney English is very ugly; but what the cockneys think of standard English not one of them has yet told us. The North Briton reproaches the Londoner for mincing words. The New-Zealander finds marbles wabbling in the throats of the university-bred Newnham College women. The London pronunciation of to-day is no longer the mincing pronunciation against which Swift directed his shafts of satire, and, in common with us, the Londoner has learned to give all its value to the full, round word.

Pronunciation is the product of certain silent forces acting on the living language. The genius of our speech is constantly at work but sometimes neglects for years to

[464]

improve existing forms. Seventy years ago the Londoner said "a feller broke the winder and hit Isabeller on the elber as she was playing a sonater on the pianer." Then certain of the gentlemen who adorned the bench addressed the jury as follows: "The conduct of the prisnah and his general character render it propah that he should no longah be a membah of this community." In those days "k" frequently took the place of "g," and "Won't you take somethink?" was equivalent to an invitation to a glass of grog.

It may be hard to believe, but we have it on the authority of Lowell that there is death in the dictionary, for there, said he, "the language is too strictly limited by convention, so that the means of expression are restricted to the point that we get from its pages only a potted literature!" "No one man's pronunciation," says Dr. Edwin Bowen, "accords altogether with the dictionary he claims to follow." Ellis in proof of this suggested a test. Said he: "I do not remember ever meeting a person of general education, or even literary habits, who could read off without hesitation such a list of words as 'bourgeois,' 'demy,' 'actinism,' 'velleity,' 'batman,' 'beaufin,' 'brevier,' 'rowlock,' 'fusil,' 'flugelman,' 'vase,' 'tassel,' 'buoy,' 'oboe,' 'archimandrite,' etc., and give them in each case the same pronunciation as is assigned in any given pronouncing dictionary now in use."

No orthoepist can possibly record all the pronunciations sanctioned by good usage everywhere. Therefore, none can positively affirm that a given pronunciation of a word may not be warranted by reputable usage somewhere where English is spoken. Vowel values are constantly shifting.

Only a few years ago the Board of Education of the City of New York issued a circular directing attention to the more common errors of pronunciation among high-school pupils, and requiring a standardization of sounds. In this circular the pronunciation of the vowel "u" in "Tuesday" received particular attention, as did also the sounds heard in "join," "oil," "oyster," "third," "girl," "turn," and "lurch." In connection with these the board pointed out that "u" was often incorrectly rendered "oo"; that "oi" was far too frequently rendered "er," and that "ir" and "ur" were far too often pronounced "oi." Thus, "Tuesday" and "duty" became "Toosday" and "dooty," and "oil," "join," "oyster" became "earl," "jern," "erster," while "third," "girl," "turn," and "lurch" became "thoid," "goil," "toin," and "loich." The board drew attention to nine classes of mispronunciation which it required teachers to normalize. Normalizing, be it understood, is the only remedy for this confusion, but it has nothing to do with the fixing of orthography. It merely brings out the sound values of standardized speech.

As a rule the people, like spoiled children, need to be reminded rather than chided for their lapses, to which even the greatest of phoneticists sometimes inadvertently contribute. We have but to look up the pronunciation of "the" as indicated by certain of our dictionaries to learn that at one time "dhe" was used to indicate its sound. Is it to be wondered at that the German to whom "the" is "der," "die," and "das" should corrupt the English word to what it sometimes (alas, too often) becomes, der—the corruption noted above? Need we wonder that the Frenchman meets with difficulty when he tries to explain this thing, "th," as bereft of reason and an insult to his intelligence, for it differs in sound when used before the same vowel?

There are very few of us who realize the great debt we owe to the telephone companies for the vigorous campaigns they have been, and are still, conducting on behalf of standardized speech, and to secure the standardization of human voice-sounds. To them and to the phonograph companies, whose vociculturists have aided in the work, we are under an obligation that none of us can ever repay, for it is owing almost as much to their efforts as it is to the increased facilities of travel that standard English has spread, and that we are rapidly marching toward that uniformity of vocal sounds which will ultimately bring English into the same class as Italian as the language song. But before we attain this distinction we must learn to give our vowels their full force, and to use our consonants with proper discretion. Then, wherever the English language is used in accordance with its best traditions, there standardized English will be found, no matter in what quarter of the globe this may be.

Churches' Duty to Near East

To more than 100,000 Protestant churches throughout the United States the Federal Council of Churches is sending this call for concerted action on the Near East.

This appeal to the Christian people of our land is sent because of the deep and widespread conviction that the crisis in the Near East calls for immediate concerted action by those who belong to the 100,000 churches of the United States, both for the provision of relief and also for the exercise of the full moral influence of our nation in behalf of a righteous and permanent peace in the Near East.

THERE IS SOMETHING FOR EVERY CHURCH TO SAY: From every church in the land let the earnest declaration be sent out that America has a responsibility in the present critical situation in the Near East. The Secretary of State has said that we are deeply concerned about the protection of racial and religious minorities and the great interests of humanity which are at stake.

While it may not be the business of the Church to urge special forms of political action or influence to be used by our government, it is the Church's business to give expression to its conviction that our government will have the complete support of the people of this land in using its full moral influence to secure the protection of the oppressed peoples of the Near East and the establishment of peace and justice. Without the positive exercise of this influence the Christian conscience of America cannot be at rest.

THERE IS SOMETHING FOR THE MEMBERS OF EVERY CHURCH TO DO: They can show their representatives at Washington that the people of America do not desire their nation to pursue a policy of inaction toward the Near East. They can declare their belief that the great humane and righteous ends which they seek can be secured by the fearless and adequate use of our moral influence, and they can at once convince the government in Washington that they want that influence exerted to the uttermost in every just and wise way.

By such concerted action from Christian people all over the land we may help the government to discern and to fulfil our country's duty in behalf of the afflicted people who look to us for present relief and for some hope and security for the future.

THERE IS SOMETHING FOR EVERY CHURCH TO GIVE: The incredible disaster at Smyrna has left hundreds of thousands destitute. Immediately following the disaster, Near East Relief emptied its orphanage relief warehouses in Constantinople of all reserve supplies and rushed them to Smyrna. Thousands of lives were thus saved. But these orphanage supplies must be replaced and large quantities of additional provisions sent to care for the homeless, shelterless, foodless refugees.

Preaching and Life

Preaching at the present time is primarily a process of thinking aloud about life. It takes its start with the life of our own time, men's perplexities and needs. We have been told recently that the war discovered a vast fund of "inarticulate religion" in the rank and file of human life. Inarticulate religion is religion which has never really become conscious of itself, found itself, and got itself stated out in the open. The case for preaching at the present time rests on the inarticulate religion of the average man. A surgeon friend once said to me of his minister, "What really interests and helps me in that man is his ability to put into words what I have always wanted to say and have always felt ought to be said, and yet have never been able to say by myself. And that is a very great gift." That, after all, is what all art and every classic does for us. It says what we want to say and know ought to be said, and yet can not say ourselves. That is why pictures and music and plays have a power over us. They help us to find ourselves. And this is the first thing the modern preacher has to do, to help dumb and perplexed men say out what is in them. It is told of William James that the student came out of his classroom feeling not, What a great man Jesus is, but, How great I might be if I only knew myself and found myself. That was a fine tribute to a great teacher. Now good preaching gets just that reaction. In this fallen world the preacher can not always be the voice of God twice every week. But he can always be the voice of the people, trying to find and express themselves.

In the next place the preacher is trying to change men's point of view. And there is confessedly no hope for the future of civilization to-day, unless men's points of view are changed. There is no contribution which a man can possibly make to this generation so important and so absolutely essential as to help, even in the slightest way, to change men's way of thinking about the values of human life and the organization of human society. If our world is to be saved from suicidal disintegration, it must discover afresh its communities of interest. And of all possible bonds of human union the thought of God is the surest and the strongest. Nothing so much needs to be said to the modern world as this, "One is your Father, and all ye are brethren."— W. L. SPERRY, in *Harvard Theological Review*.

The Good in All of Us

In the *Copper Streak Trail*,[1] by Eugene M. Rhodes, a splendid novel of adventure in West and East of the United States, an elderly multi-millionaire of Scotch birth and American activity is talking to a Western rancher of mature mind, keen perception, and kindly instincts, named Peter Johnson. The old millionaire speaks:

There is a hard question I would spier of you. I thought but ill of my kind in my younger days. Now, being old, I see with a thankful heart how many verra fine people inhabit here. 'Tis a rale bonny world. And lookin' back, I see too often where I have made harsh judgings of my fellows. There are more excuses for ill-doings to my old eyes. Was't so with you?

Yes, said Pete. We're not such a poor lot after all—not when we stop to think or when we're forced to see. In fire or flood, or sickness, we're all eager to bear a hand— for we see, then. Our purses and our hearts are open to any great disaster. Why, take two cases—the telephone girls and the elevator boys. Don't sound heroic much, do they? But . . . when the floods come, the telephone girls die at their desks, still sendin' out warnings! And when a big fire comes and there are lives to save, them triflin' cigarette-smoking, sassy, no-account boys run the elevators through hell and back as long as the cables hold! Every time!

The old man's eyes kindled.

Look ye there, now! Man, and have ye noticed that too? . . . Ye have e'en the secret of it. We're good in emairgencies, the now; when the time comes when we get

a glimmer that all life is emairgency and tremblin' peril, that every turn may be the wrong turn—when we can see that our petty system of suns and all is nobbut a wee darkling cockle boat, driftin' and tossed abune the waves in the outmost seas of an onrushing universe—hap-chance we'll no loom so grandlike in our own een; and we'll tak' hands for comfort in the dark. 'Tis good theology, yon wise saying of the silly street: "We are all in the same boat. Don't rock the boat."

An Art Reference Library

The creation of a great reference library to supplement the art collection left to this city by Henry C. Frick is under way at the Frick home, Fifth Avenue and Seventieth Street. The plan includes the collection, arrangement, and indexing of photographic reproductions of all the paintings and drawings of the last eight centuries of western civilization. The task is almost inconceivably great. An art biographical reference work planned in Germany before the war listed more than 100,000 artists, and of many artists' work there is almost no end. The greatest of all, Michelangelo, left nearly 1,000 paintings and sketches. The Library of Congress, whose collection makes no pretense at completeness in any direction, contains 330,000 prints. America at present has nothing which at all fills the need of the great collection planned, and it will doubtless be a great help to all who are interested academically in professions or business with which art is linked. As the New York *Herald* points out, "the historian, the novelist, the playwright, the decorator, the theatrical producer, the costumer, the furniture maker—all will have at their command, when given to the public, the most complete collection of its kind ever assembled."—*The Publishers' Weekly*.

A Jewish Community Prayer

Bless our children, O God, and help us so to fashion their souls, by precept and example, that they shall ever love the good, flee from sin, revere thy word, and honor thy name. May they, planted in the house of the Lord, flourish in the courts of our God; may they guard for future ages the truths revealed to their forefathers.—W. K. WRIGHT.

---

[1] Houghton Mifflin Co., Boston and New York.

Church and Community

CHRISTMAS EVE IN PARIS

WILLIAM C. CARL, Mus. Doc., New York City

Christmas eve in Paris for centuries past has been a magic word. When the night arrives the boulevards are always filled with gaily decorated booths extending from the Place de la République to the Church of La Madeleine. Happy children in great numbers find what please them best at the Yuletide season, and wander from one booth to the next buying tempting articles. All Paris mingles with the throngs in brilliantly lighted thoroughfares until the time for the midnight mass. Then the churches are crowded with worshipers, offering tribute to the Babe of Bethelehem.

The organ preludes are selected from the old Noëls, many of which were arranged by Guilmant when he played at La Trinité; there in the organ gallery the great master, surrounded by his pupils and friends, would play as if inspired, for Guilmant loved these old carols and played them with a rare charm. First he would choose his Fantasie on two Christmas hymns, then in succession his Noël Brabançon, Noël Languedocien, Noël Ecossais, and Noël Saboly. Next the choir would sing one from Brittany, then one from Normandy, and again one from Alsace, so dear to all French hearts. It did not take many minutes for the people to catch the Christmas spirit, for everyone sings. Who in France does not know the charming Noëls? No one who has attended can forget these services, for the people sing with rare enthusiasm and from the heart, producing a wonderful effect.

At St. Eustache, with Joseph Bonnet at the grand organ; Notre Dame Cathedral, with Louis Vierne; The Madeleine, with Henri Dallier; St. Sulpice, with Charles Marie Widor, the old Noëls, such as "Le Petit Jésus," "Le Message des Anges," "Le Sommeil de l'enfant Jésus," "Les Rois Magnes," "Le Bel Ange du Ciel," are sung until the midnight hour approaches and mass begins. At its conclusion, the organ is again heard in another Noël as the people slowly leave the church to join the happy crowds in the boulevards—for is it not Christmas and a feast of great joy? Surely the French understand and appreciate the spirit of Christmas!

Playing the Good Samaritan in Russia

Dr. John Sheridan Zelie recently returned from Russia where he spent the summer as a special representative of the Federal Council of the Churches in administering relief, especially to the Russian clergy and their dependents. In his story of the help the American churches rendered he cites this incident:

One day in Petrograd I was asked to go in and see for a moment the 126 Russian women who were directoresses of the child feeding work in that city. These women went every day from their homes in distant parts of the city to work for hours and over-hours in these kitchens. For themselves they received nothing. As I heard of their work I could not sit there and do nothing. So I just interpreted the commission entrusted to me by the Federal Council of the Churches in my own way and said to myself, in the words which college presidents used to employ in granting diplomas—"By virtue of authority in

[468]

me vested" by the Federal Council every one of those women is going to have a food package this winter. And they had it. This company was about the equivalent, as nearly as anything could be, of the groups of religious and philanthropic women who in our own towns and cities at home are at the center of our most merciful undertakings. They vibrated with excitement when I rose to tell them just exactly who they were that had sent the gifts. "Knowledge that others in far-off America, separated from us by thousands of miles continually think of us, makes our stormy path less difficult. Life feels less hard and less ugly. We feel we are not alone and have more courage for our work"—they said afterward when they presented their response.

Ku Klux Klan Disowned by the Churches

The Federal Council of the Churches of Christ in America declares Christianity and patriotism need no mask. The mistaken impression that the Ku Klux Klan deserves, and is receiving the support of the Protestant churches has led the Federal Council of the churches to make its position clear and unmistakable. A full statement was made by the Administrative Committee of the Council at its last meeting.

While not mentioning the Ku Klux Klan by name, the Council's action declares that any organization whose membership is secret, oath-bound, and disguised, and which tends to foster racial or class prejudice, has no real right to speak in the name of the Christian Church.

Card Suggestion

The Rev. C. E. Turley, pastor of the Methodist Episcopal Church, Oxford, Ohio, sends us a card containing the following on one side:

A SERIES OF SUNDAY EVENING SERMONS

GENERAL THEME: *Builders of the Kingdom.*

Jan. 9. "John Wyclif—The Herald of the Dawn."

Jan. 23. "Savonarola—Prophet of Florence."

Jan. 30. "Martin Luther—The Reformer."

Feb. 6. "John Wesley—The Methodist."

Feb. 13. "Roger Williams—A Plea for Tolerance in Religion."

Feb. 27. "David Livingstone—Christian Missionary and Explorer."

Mar. 6. "Lord Shaftesbury—Friend of the Unfortunate."

Mar. 13. "Peter Cartwright—Pioneer Preacher."

On the reverse side of the card is a picture of the church and notice of regular church services and meetings.

MID-WEEK PRAYER MEETING

JAMES M. CAMPBELL, D.D., Claremont, California

Dec. 3-9—A Heart to Heart Talk
(1 Sam. 23:15-18)

The story of the friendship between David and Jonathan is one of perennial interest and charm. The time when this friendship was born was just after David had slain with his shepherd's sling the Philistine giant Goliath. When David returned in triumph Saul asked him, "Whose son art thou, young man?" and he answered, "I am the son of thy servant Jesse, the Bethlehemite." And it is said that "it came to pass when he had made an end of speaking unto Saul, that the soul of Jonathan was knit with the soul of David, and Jonathan loved him as his own soul."

This sudden friendship was not a thing of blind impulse, but was founded upon mutual confidence and affection. They had known each other slightly before, now they saw into each other's hearts. Jonathan discovered David first. As he witnessed his modesty and manly bearing, and listened to the simple story of his life, told with frankness and winning grace, his heart was taken captive. Nor was David slow to read the language of Jonathan's love-lit eyes, and to let his heart go out toward him. From that hour the two youths, who were nearly of an age but were at the opposite social poles, became sworn friends and entered together into a solemn covenant. Henceforth they were like—

Two berries molded on one stem,
So, with two seeming bodies, but one heart.

The time of testing soon came. Saul, who at first had showered honors upon David because of his victory over Goliath, could not forget that when the men of war returned from the slaughter of the Philistines the women who met them chanted the words—

Saul has slain his thousand,
And David his ten thousand.

These indiscreet words kept rankling within his breast, filling him with insane jealousy and murderous hate, and leading him to seek to compass the destruction of David. So the time came at last when his safety lay in flight.

Through all the bitter days that followed when David was a fugitive, the friendship of Jonathan never wavered. He must have known of the annointing of David to the kingship by Samuel the prophet, and this was to him the seal of divine acceptance. He knew also that since the slaying of Goliath, David had become the idol of the people and the object of their hope for the future. That Jonathan was willing to have it so showed the depth of his affection. He was ready to renounce his royal prerogatives and take the second place, like John the Baptist, who said of Jesus, "He must increase, but I must decrease."

It was during this dark period, when David and the band of fellow outlaws who had gathered round him were being hunted from cover to cover, that the incident referred to above took place. In the simple language of the ancient chronicler it is said that "Jonathan went to David in the word, and strengthened his heart in God." The fellowship of the two young men in that hour of sacred heart-to-heart communion was upon the loftiest plane. What they said to one another we are not told. The record is eloquent in its silence. For such high communion of soul many words were not needed. To David in his despondency the human became the door to the divine; his faith was reenforced, and he parted from his friend braced up for whatever might come by having his heart strengthened in God.

The fondly cherished plans of these two young men were not to be realized. An evil day came when Jonathan was slain in battle. When the word reached David that his friend was no more, he poured out the grief in his soul in that touching lament called "The Song of the Bow," which every rightly instructed Hebrew youth was taught:

How are the mighty fallen in the midst of
    the battle!
O Jonathan, slain upon the high places,
I am distressed for thee, my brother
    Jonathan;
Very pleasant hast thou been to me,
Thy love to me was wonderful,
Passing the love of woman.

Never until his dying hour did he cease to cherish the memory of the friend of his youth; and to lavish favors upon his kith and kin, because by his pure and unselfish love his life had been enriched and his heart strengthened in God.

Dec. 10-16—God's Time Scale

(2 Peter 3:8)

The old threadbare illustration which represented eternity by a bird coming to a mountain every hundred years, and taking away a grain of sand, until the whole mountain was removed, after which eternity had only begun, presented a dreary, doleful outlook from which many shudderingly recoiled. All such mechanical measurements have been discarded. We have come to see that length of time is relative; that an eternity of bliss or of wo may be compressed into a single day, and a single day of bliss or of wo may be expanded into an eternity. This is in accordance with the divine time scale that "one day is with the Lord as a thousand years, and a thousand years as one day."

The true measurement of time is spiritual; the eternal life is not prolonged existence, but life with an unfading spiritual quality. The poet Bailey has said:

We live in deeds, not years; in thoughts, not breaths;
In feelings, not in figures on a dial.
We should count time by heart-throbs;
He most lives who thinks most, feels the noblest, acts the best.

We are impressed with the brevity of life. It seems to us a drop from a measureless sea, a point in an unending line, "a vapor which appeareth for a little time, and then vanisheth away." We know the flight of time only by its loss; we speak of it as past, as present, and as future, but with God there are no such distinctions. With him all time is an eternal now; and may not the poet Petrarch be justified in prophesying the same for us, as he does in the lines:

The time will come when every change will cease,
This quick revolving wheel shall rest in peace;
No summer then shall glow, nor winter freeze,
Nothing shall be to come, and nothing past.
But an eternal now shall ever last.

The divine time scale is set forth in our text to curb the impatience of those who seek to hurry up the millennium. They can not understand why God should delay in bringing the affairs of his kingdom to a speedy consummation. They need to be reminded that God does not reckon time as man does. He is never in a hurry, and he has refractory material with which to work.

If it took the growth and decay of a succession of forests in the carboniferous period to produce one thin layer of coal, need we wonder that it should take uncounted ages to work out the divine purposes in the moral development of man? Think of the countless years it has often taken for God to get a single creative idea to dominate the thought and life of the world! Take for instance the idea of universal brotherhood and see how slowly it has developed. When man first began to function socially they frankly followed—

the simple plan
That they should take who have the power
And they should keep who can.

While this "good old rule" has at length come to be disavowed it is still very practically adopted; and general recognition of brotherhood with its recognition of the equality of human rights and responsibilities is still a long way off. But it is surely coming.

The outstanding lesson in the conception here given of God's great time scale is that we should be patient with him as he is with us. "He is not slack concerning his promise as some men count slackness, but is long-suffering toward us, not willing that any should perish, but that all should come to repentance."

His purposes ripen slowly; but he moves on without pause, nor is he ever tempted to exchange compulsion for persuasion, eternal force for moral power, as many impatient mortals fain would do. He keeps hands off and seeks our free cooperation alike in the matters of personal salvation and of the redemption of the world.

Dec. 17-23—The Greater Things to Come

(John 1:50)

It is the divine purpose that the Christian life should be marked by continual enlargement. When Jesus said to Nathanael, "Greater things than these shalt thou see," he intended that in his religious experience he was to keep moving upon the upward path, from great to still greater things. Very naturally we are led to ask, "What great things did Nathanael already see?" Jesus makes this clear in the words, "Because I said, When thou wast under the fig-tree I saw thee, believest thou? Thou shalt see greater things than these." The crowning proof to Nathanael that Jesus was the Messiah was that he knew all about him. His case was parallel to that of the Samaritan woman with whom Jesus conversed by Jacob's well, who returned to her home in Sychar saying, "Come and see a man who told me all things that ever I did. Is not this the Christ?"

Regarding the soul struggle through which Nathanael passed under that fig-tree, of which Jesus was an unseen witness, nothing is told; but the simple fact that Jesus knew all about it brought Nathanael to bow adoringly at his feet. The great thing that Nathanael had seen was a vision of Jesus as the eternal Christ whose haunting presence men had always felt and for whose advent in the flesh the world was now waiting. The greater things he was yet to see were the things which constitute a still larger vision of Christ, and of his mission to humanity. This is made plain from the words which follow: "Henceforth thou shalt see heaven opened, and the angels of God ascending and descending upon the Son of man."

The two things here promised were that there was to be a new opening of heaven, and a new means of communication with it. Heaven was to be made known and brought near as never before. The figure which Jesus employs to foreshadow the work he had come to accomplish is taken from Jacob's dream; when lying on a pillow of stone under the open skies Jacob saw a mystic "ladder set up on the earth, and the top of it reached to heaven; and behold the angels of God ascended and descended upon it" (Gen. 28:12). The idea which Jesus evidently meant to convey was that from that time on he was to be the medium of conversation between earth and heaven and between man and God; and that by him earth and heaven were to be brought into closer relationship, so that the life of the one would flow in and out of the life of the other.

These larger things which Nathanael saw are to be seen by us in still larger measure. We live in an ever enlarging universe. In the physical world, science is widening our world with a rapidity which is bewildering. The line between the spiritual and the material is being wiped out, space is being obliterated, and communication with places remote is being established. In view of such a recent invention as the radio wireless telephone Sir Conan Doyle hazards the prediction that before many years the wall between the seen and the unseen realm will be broken through, and departed friends will be able to communicate with us. But he is confounding things that differ. The spiritual realm can not be touched by the senses. Between the earth and Mars there might be physical communication, but not between earth and heaven, for they belong to separate zones. To reach the spiritual realm we have to use spiritual means. These we already have. By faith we can see the invisible. By prayer we can send our wishes up and bring heaven's blessings down. The heaven that bends over us is not closed, but open wide. Through Christ we can reach it and enter into fellowship with those who are within, and from that fellowship return to bring some of the heavenly glory into the earthly life around us.

Dec. 24-30—The Humanization of God (Christmas)
(John 1:14)

In the synoptical gospels it is said of Christ that "he came." He came from above; he came from heaven to earth. In the Fourth Gospel it is said that "he became." "The Word became flesh"—the Christ of eternity became the Jesus of history; God became man. In the advent there are three stages, namely—promise, preparation, and fulfilment. Here the later stage is said to have been at length reached.

Christ is called the Word because by him and in him God finds expression. In him we have the humanization of God in the sense that in him God is expressed in human terms. In becoming man Christ incorporated himself into our common human life; making himself one of us; joining his fortune with ours, and saving us from moral bankruptcy by putting his unsearchable riches at our disposal. Humanity with Christ in it and as a part of it is different from what it was before. It is now not on the way to ruin, but is on the way to the glorious end for which Christ took possession of it.

The incarnation was a divine necessity. It provided a new and larger outlet for the rising tide of divine love which could no longer be restrained. In Jesus God came a little closer to man so as to make his influence more powerfully felt and his help more available. This aspect of the advent is well brought out in the following confession of faith:

I believe the blessed Jesus lived divinely,
    suffered much
That God might reach his children
With a closer human touch;
Drawing us with cords so tender, up the
    pathway where he trod
Till we fall like weeping children, in the
    loving arms of God.

A leper in Madagascar was seen hobbling along the road. People shouted to him to get out of the way. A missionary in whose heart was a spark of divine pity stopped and put his hand upon him, and spoke a few kind words. As soon as the leper recovered from his amazement he turned away sobbing, exclaiming, "A human has touched me! A human has touched me!" This is what the incarnation does directly and indirectly — it touches the heart of man with the pitying love of God. And what was Jesus in the totality of his human life but the visible hand of the invisible God reaching down from heaven and laid upon man in blessing?

Another object for which God by the incarnation came within the little horizon of our earthly vision was that he might be known and loved. In Jesus the Father made himself known in a tangible and adequate way. When Jesus speaks it is the Father who speaks through human lips; when Jesus weeps the Father weeps through human eyes. Jesus was Immanuel, God with us, and for us; God by our side and on our side. His incarnation was the temporary outshowing of an eternal reality; it showed what the eternal God is like. The incarnation gives us a Christlike God, attractive and loving, one "to love and be loved forever."

The supreme end of this approach of God to man is redemptive. God stooped to raise man up; he became flesh to make man Godlike. Christ was born that man might be reborn. The mystics do well to remind us that

Tho Christ in Bethlehem a thousand times
    be born,
If he's not born in thee thy soul is still
    forlorn.

And the birth of the Christ-spirit in the heart of the individual man has for its ultimate end the birth of the Christ-spirit in the whole of human kind; for as Christ was the incarnation of God, the whole world is yet to become the incarnation of Christ.

Dec. 31-Jan. 6—Measuring Day
(2 Cor. 10:13-18)

A celebrated writer had a dream, which was not all a dream. He dreamed that it was measuring day when every person's growth in grace must be measured. An angel stood beside a golden rod, which rested on the ground, and over which was a scroll with the words, "The measure of the stature of a perfect man." People came up as their names were called, and their measurements were written down. And the strange thing was that while their measurements were being taken each one shrank or expanded to his proper dimension.

Nothing short of the measure of the stature of a perfect man must be taken as the standard of moral measurement. We are bound to follow the best and to test ourselves by the supreme. Among the standards generally adopted some are faulty, others are utterly false. First there is the standard of self-judgment. Paul describes those who adopt this standard as measuring themselves by themselves, and he adds that in doing this they are not wise. For an artist to measure one of his paintings by another is not wise. He ought to measure its worth by the highest standards of excellence. We counsel our children to take the best models in everything; and we read the biographies of great men and of great saints so that we may be inspired to higher endeavor. Those who measure themselves by themselves are apt to survey themselves with pride and self-complacency. Like the boy who measures his growth year by year by the notches in the door-post, they are apt to think of themselves as taller than they really are. A man's opinion about his own conduct is sure to be biased. He needs something outside of himself to which he is to measure up. Unless he can erect himself above himself, How mean a thing is man!

Then there is the standard of average human excellence. Paul describes those who follow this standard as "comparing themselves among themselves." They are those who measure themselves with those on the same level with themselves. They are swayed by popular opinion and by custom; they know no higher rule than that of their own class or party. In the graveyard of a western mining town is to be found the epitaph: "He averaged well for this community." A doubtful compliment surely! Regarding this class Paul also remarks that they are not wise. Their standard is too low, and hence is misleading. They are prone to think of themselves more highly than they ought to think, and to be rated too high by others. "The one-eyed man is king among the blind." One who could read a primer might be counted a Solon among the Hottentots. A boy at a village school might be looked upon as a prodigy of learning, but when he goes to college he discovers how little he knows.

Character should be measured by the highest standard obtainable. Given two persons equal in attainment, let the one follow a standard in advance of him and the other a standard behind him, and the one will mark progress while the other will retrograde. The decisive question in moral action is not, What are others doing? but, What ought I to do? A church was taking an offering for missions. The parish was divided into two districts. In one the subscription was started at a dollar, in the other at twenty-five cents; and both kept up their ratio, altho equal in wealth.

Is there a perfect standard of conduct to which every one is bound to conform, just as the people of any nation have to conform to the standard of weights and measures adopted by their government? If so, where is it to be found? It is to be found in Christ. In him we have a perfect model, fixed and infallible; one which we can safely imitate in every possible condition.

The Book

JESUS THE WORLD'S SAVIOR—STUDIES IN LUKE[1]

Professor ANDREW C. ZENOS, D.D., LL.D., Chicago, Ill.

Dec. 3—Jesus Sending Out Missionaries

(Luke 9:1—10:24)

Many were attracted to the side of Jesus by his teaching and personality. In accordance with the custom of the time and in analogy with the groups gathered around other teachers, these were called his disciples. Out of their number Jesus chose twelve to enter into a more intimate relationship with himself. Sometimes these are designated as his "disciples." More commonly in the New Testament they are called the twelve. Jesus himself, it appears from a section common to all the synoptics, and therefore belonging to the most ancient tradition, gave them the name of apostles (Mark 2:14; Matt. 10:2; Luke 6:13). The word is significant. It indicates the desire and purpose of the Master to spread the knowledge of his gospel. An apostle is one sent upon a mission. And the special mission of the twelve was to tell the "good news" of the kingdom of God to the world. From this view-point they were missionaries in the strictest sense of the term.

As the twelve performed the task assigned them to the extent of their ability and of their opportunities, Jesus found it necessary to increase the number of his missionaries to seventy. It is a good sign when a good cause is embarrassed because of the enlargement of its opportunities beyond the means at its command to meet them. There was something of satisfaction in the heart of Jesus, as well as something of sadness, when he looked at the field before him and said, "The harvest indeed is plenteous, but the laborers are few." It was a far more hopeful situation than if the harvest had been scanty and the laborers more than sufficient. A plenteous harvest has an inherent tendency, in the wise administration by the world, to call out for increasing numbers of laborers.

Jesus' object in sending the apostles was to make known the coming of the kingdom of God. But this was to be done in such a way as to include his part in the great event. He sent them into every city and place, "whither he himself was about to come." Jesus can not be separated from the gospel. In the ultimate analysis, he is found at the center of his own message to the world. That message loses its vital interest and power as soon as his personality is eliminated from it. The missionary always prepares the way for the coming of Jesus.

While Jesus gave the apostles large freedom in determining the method of their work, he was at the same time anxious that their bearing and attitude as his representatives should be in harmony with his own mission and message. He therefore gave some in-

[1] These studies follow the lesson-topics and passages of the International Sunday-school series.

[475]

structions. The first and foremost of these was that they must be free from resentment against those who would reject their message. They were sent "as lambs among wolves." They must not equip themselves as if for an aggressive imposition of their mission on unwilling subjects. They must let the inward charm of the gospel attract and conquer the world. Jesus was confident that no matter what outward appearances might indicate for the time being, in the long run, in the conflict between the lambs and the wolves, the lambs would win the victory. This is his teaching of so-called "non-resistance."

The apostles found by experience, limited as it was in their case, that the mission on which they were sent was a success. They were inclined to measure their success, as men are always tempted to do, by outward results. Jesus warned them that tho they were right about the possession of power their true success was to be spiritual achievement. Over this type of success Jesus' own soul was and always is stirred to exultation. It moved him to realize his own inner and transcendent relation to God the Father and his supreme task of making the Father known to all men.

Dec. 10—Story of the Good Samaritan

(Luke 10:25-37)

The parable, so called, of the Good Samaritan was called forth by the sincere desire of a certain lawyer to understand the new way of life pointed out by Jesus. This lawyer had evidently studied the old ways with care, but was either not entirely satisfied with them, or he saw in Jesus a personality of force capable of giving new light on an old subject. In either case his question, "What shall I do to inherit eternal life?" was not meant, as some questions put to Jesus by others were, to ensnare him, but to get light.

Jesus' answer suggests in the first place his attitude toward progress in the knowledge of the truth. He sent the lawyer back to the law. Progress was to be made by taking firm hold of some fundamentals given from the very beginning. The lawyer was familiar with the outwardness of these. But he halted at the interpretation of them; and in particular with the meaning of the term "neighbor." Here, too, his question was not captious. The term neighbor had a definite meaning in the earlier days of the simple life. But with the changing of society it became vague. The lawyer could not be sure that he had obeyed the old law strictly. He had obeyed it as strictly as he understood it. To clear (justify) himself before Jesus he asked for a definition of it.

Jesus gave his definition by reciting the familiar story. Thus beginning with the germinal principle in the old law he developed his teaching of universal brotherhood; and at the same time he illustrated his claim that he had not come to destroy but to fulfil.

The lesson of the parable is made all the more vivid against the background furnished by Jesus in the story. First, he held up two types of character both of which contradicted the idea of true neighborliness. Both of these, by their association with the service of religion in the temple, should have been familiar with the spirit and intention of the law; but both had missed it. Contrasted with the failure of the priest and the Levite to realize and illustrate the ideal neighbor Jesus pictured the Samaritan. Of course he did not mean that every Samaritan would act as the man in this story. Nor did he intimate that every priest and Levite would fail as the characters he sketched seemed to do.

Between Jews and Samaritans

there was a bitter hatred inherited and transmitted from generation to generation from the days of Nehemiah onward. The Samaritan was not expected to entertain any feelings of tenderness toward the Jew and he did not expect any kindness from him. As the term neighbor was understood the Samaritan was as far from being a neighbor to the Jew who had fallen among thieves as it was possible to think. Yet, of the three characters in the parable he was the only one who acted the part of the neighbor. Thus Jesus impressed it upon his hearer that the relation of neighbor is not constituted either by kinship or by contiguity. It depends rather on the recognition of a common human nature with common human affections and needs.

And being independent of such conditions as blood relationship and nearness in residence, neighborliness is, according to Jesus, capable of cultivation. The exact words used by Jesus in bringing home the lesson to the lawyer were, "Which of these three thinkest thou became a neighbor unto him that fell among thieves?" In one sense all men are born neighbors to one another. But so far as they do not recognize this fact and are either gradually or suddenly awakened to its reality they become neighbors. This is further enforced by Jesus' direct exhortation: "Go, and do thou likewise."

Dec. 17—Jesus Among Friends and Foes

(Luke 10:38—11:54)

The connection between the story of the Samaritan and the incident at Bethany which immediately follows it in the narrative of Luke is not apparent. It has been suggested that the evangelist inserts the Bethany incident here as a further answer to the question, "What must one do to inherit eternal life?" Mere benevolence, such as that of the Samaritan, is not enough. It must be combined with and grow out of habitual communion with God. "The enthusiasm of humanity," if divorced from the love of God, is likely to degenerate into mere serving of tables. Whether this was or was not Luke's motive in putting the two stories together, their juxtaposition illustrates the fulness and breadth of Jesus' thought.

The most striking aspect of the visit of Jesus to the home at Bethany is the contrast of character and mind between the sisters, Martha and Mary. Jesus' answer to Martha's appeal that he bid Mary leave his side and help her with the housework has been variously interpreted as a rebuke to Martha for her exaggerated attention to the less important interests of life, or as an impartial adjudication of two types of service equally acceptable to the Master.[1] Whichever interpretation be accepted, Jesus appears in the affair as a friend among friends. It indicates the broad range of his circle of friendship and the possibilities of friendly ministry to him. It also shows how easily his friends may misunderstand and exclude one another from the circle to which they belong.

From this incident Luke's narrative, with some disregard for the time element, not unusual in him, turns to an earlier one, namely the giving of the so-called "Lord's Prayer," followed by an exposition of Jesus' view of prayer and its place in the kingdom of God. The thought moves in the realm of intimacy. Prayer both as offered and as heard and answered is the expression of mutual confidence and regard as between God and man.

But the section on prayer is followed by the recital of some facts bringing into view the adverse atti-

[1] For still another interpretation of the Martha-Mary episode see the REVIEW for September, 1922, p. 213.

tude of some men toward Jesus. The first of these was the casting out of a demon. Jesus' enemies attributed this miracle to a league with the chief of the demonic hosts. The bad logic of this judgment seems to have totally escaped the attention of the critics. Jesus asks them to note two flaws in their argument. The first is that applied to the general work of casting out demons prevalent among the Jews of the day the same principle would condemn all exorcists to the category of allies with Beelzebub. "If I by Beelzebub cast out demons, by whom do your sons cast them out?"

The second logical flaw in the thought of his critics pointed out by Jesus is in the argument itself. The judgment that he cast out demons by an alliance with the prince of the demons is self-contradictory. That Beelzebub should give such power to a man is unthinkable; for it would divide his own house and cause its collapse.

But illogical as it was, the thought of Jesus' critics represents a universal effort of mankind to explain some facts of life which demand explanation. God makes himself felt in power and in goodness. Jesus was bent on impressing upon men the goodness of God. When they failed to learn the lesson he was grieved. And when they perverted the meaning of the signs of God's goodness he became indignant and denounced those guilty of the perversion.

The last incident of the series shows Jesus' enemies as objectors to his disregard of the minute prescriptions of the ceremonial. Like the preceding occasion this too calls forth a scathing condemnation of loveless conduct. Against the ceremonial itself Jesus has nothing to say. In the words: "These ought ye to have done," he seems to give it his indorsement. It is the exaggerated and therefore exclusive devotion to the ceremonial as interpreted by tradition that he deprecates. His words are emphatic and strong. They insist upon a comprehensive ideal of religion, and condemning narrowness on one side, they inspire and encourage as a remedy the full expression of a well-balanced spiritual life.

Dec. 24—A Lesson in Trust and Preparedness
(Luke, chap. 12)

One of the main objects of Jesus' solicitude as a leader was the lack of a sense of proportion among men. Everywhere he noted an exaggerated interest in and devotion to unimportant matters and neglect of the essentials. And in the point of view of the Pharisees this perversion assumed such a dangerous form that Jesus felt constrained to warn his followers against the "leaven" of formalism with its inevitable sequel of "hypocrisy."

But the leaven of the Pharisees was not the only manifestation of the lack of a sense of proportion. The great majority of men show this lack when they fall under the fear of physical harm and sacrifice vital spiritual interests. They fear those that "kill the body" more than him who has power over the soul. Jesus points to the fact that they that "kill the body," whether they do this in the form of persecution and judicial murder or by the slower processes of industrial and commercial methods of compulsion to wrong and unfraternal action, can not pursue their victims beyond the portals of death. "After that they have no more that they can do." On the contrary, he who has the power of determining the destiny of the soul, and who has established laws of inexorable sequence of retribution for the evil-doer, can and does follow the soul into the after life.

Another manifestation of the distorted sense of proportion Jesus found in the prevalence of covetousness. Men set their affections upon the possession of earthly goods. A controversy between two brothers, regarding the distribution of the "inheritance" left them by their deceased father, furnished the occasion for Jesus to express his mind on this point. He put his teaching in the parable of the Rich Fool. To increase one's possessions is generally viewed as a very praiseworthy course. The abundance of the things which a man has is a sign of his security in life. It gives him the means of meeting vicissitude and possible adversities. Wealth is therefore a form of preparedness.

And yet, as Jesus endeavors to show in this parable, the exclusive pursuit of wealth may be the worst possible unpreparedness. The rich fool, a character undoubtedly among the truest to life and commonest in the world, was prepared to meet misfortune of a material type, but utterly unprepared to meet the developments following the death of his body. He had forgotten that he had a soul which might be required of him by its Creator at any time. True wealth is "riches toward God."

The same lesson is conveyed in a more direct and positive form in the words spoken by Jesus against being anxious. It may be scarcely necessary to observe that the term "anxious" is here used with a view to its exact meaning and not merely as a synonym of the term prudent. Prudence is not inconsistent with a calm trustfulness in God's goodness and care over his creatures. Anxiety is a harassing lack of confidence in God's willingness and power to provide all that is necessary for the welfare of his children. It is as unnecessary as it is useless. As against it Jesus recommends a realization of a better knowledge of God. He sends his hearers to the world of nature, where the evidences of God's goodness are so ample. He tells them to study the animals and plants which, without wasting energy in anxious forethought, find all the means of self-realization in God's provisions for them. For mankind there is something even better. "Seek ye first the kingdom of God."

Thus far Jesus had viewed life in its general and normal course as a movement toward a goal beyond itself. But life has also its crises. There are supreme moments of decision which must be met with a clear eye and a keen apprehension of their meaning. Such a critical moment requiring preparedness of a different sort was to be his own second coming. Jesus compares this moment to the return from a temporary absence of a master of men. It becomes the servants to greet the master upon his return. Therefore they must watch; for, in the nature of the case, the exact time of his return can not be foreseen. But Jesus does not intimate that this preparedness should take any other form than that of a faithful and orderly behavior in the household, such as is due at all times. It is not he who in his mind singles out the coming of the master, and forgets all else, that is the watchful servant, but he who works faithfully at his post. Such preparedness is simply the exercise of ordinary prudence similar to that which men use when they predict a shower or a season of warm weather.

Dec. 31—Review

The gospel story comprises data first concerning the preparation of the field of the Savior's work as well as of himself, secondly concerning the Savior at work, and thirdly concerning the Savior's plan to expand and perpetuate that work.

To the first class of data belong the birth and ministry of John the Baptist, and the birth, the boyhood, the baptism, and the temptation of Jesus himself. The narratives covering these matters are not only means of satisfying a natural human interest in the human personality of the Savior, but also necessary helps to the correct understanding and interpretation of his nature, his message, and his mission. They link him with the world of human life all about him. They show his identification with mankind to be a real and complete experience. They indicate that he became subject not only to the law in the technical sense attached to the term among the Jews, nor merely to the moral law as the expression of the will of his Father, but to the laws of nature as well. "It behooved him," as the author of Hebrews puts it, "in all things to be made like unto his brethren." A Savior injected into the order of history preternaturally, as the early Gnostic (Docetic) heretics taught, could not be a true Savior.

The historical and literary investigations of the last few generations have greatly enlarged the knowledge of men regarding the preparation of the world for Christ. They have brought into view a vast array of facts of exactly the same type and meaning as the gospel narratives of the birth and work of John the Baptist. John was the forerunner of Jesus. But other forerunners had preceded him. The language to be used by Jesus had been introduced among the Jews, the political conditions to confront him and constitute a part of his problem had been molded, the world of thought to serve as the vehicle and auxiliary of his ideas had grown up in the years immediately preceding his coming, the knowledge of these matters helps men to-day to affiliate Jesus with his environment and therefore to understand him all the better.

What is true of the preparation of the field of his labors is also true of the preparation of himself in boyhood and through his baptism and temptation. The gospel of Mark begins with a bare mention in a single sentence of this preparation. It illustrates what is absolutely indispensable to know of the Savior. But the gospels of Matthew and Luke not only fill the gap left vacant by Mark, but they also add vastly, yet not too much, to our understanding of Christ by prefixing accounts of his life before the beginning of his work.

Regarding the parts of the gospel story which portray the Savior at work, it is unnecessary to say anything more than that they show the universality of his interest and the comprehensiveness of his saving work. He ministered to the body by healing the diseases of men. He mingled with the poor and by sharing their poverty he instilled the conviction that poverty might be made a means of good. He ministered to the minds of men by training them to see God their heavenly Father in the world of nature about them as well as in the events of human history. His interest as a teacher did not lie in the facts he used as illustrations, but in the one great truth they illustrated, namely, the fatherly love and care of God. Then Jesus ministered to the souls of men. He preached the gospel of the kingdom. He persuaded men to accept God as their fatherly Ruler and live with other men in the relationship of brotherhood.

Finally, the gospel story shows the Savior as a far-seeing leader who had a vision of the world saved from sin and brought back to the knowledge and fellowship of God. Jesus realized that this plan would need the cooperation of a group of workers. He saw the harvest and it was great. Called for laborers and enjoined upon his disciples and helpers to pray the Lord of the harvest that he should thrust forth laborers into the harvest.

THE LATEST DEVELOPMENTS IN MOTION PICTURES

The Rev. ORRIN G. COCKS, Wellsboro, Pa.

Dec. 3—The Complex Problem

The motion-picture problem is slowly being solved by those who are closest to it, so far as it relates to the American people. It is too complicated for the layman to grasp sufficiently to permit him to offer many helpful suggestions regarding details and methods of improvement. He has served a useful purpose in speaking with increasing clarity of the kinds of pictures right-thinking theatergoers want or do not want. His words have had most weight when, in company with multitudes of his fellows, he has indicated his disapproval by refusing to look at a particular theater's offering of vulgar drama. This has happened with dramas dealing with super-sex themes, "vampire" themes, over-sensual society, and "bedroom" stuff, and also with the yellow and plotless crime picture. As a result of this simple registration of disapproval at the box-office most of these themes have gone the way of all evil things to a hell of their own, and some of the well-known actresses and actors have followed them.

The complexity of the problem is indicated when we remember that the picture is made on a national or international scale for adult, commercial amusement. People voluntarily pay their way into theaters from coast to coast to see the same picture simultaneously exhibited. They are designed for all classes of the public and necessarily seek those greatest common denominators of drama and humor to hold the largest numbers. The motion-picture is quite different from the spoken drama which plays in one city at a time until it has tested its popularity sufficiently to be duplicated in road shows. The film is finished before any audience sees it and starts simultaneously in from 75 to 150 places in approximately similar prints of the master copy. Moreover, in its method of construction it is far more complex than the stage play. Several entirely distinct hands have a share in the making of the picture, including writer, scenarist, director, actor, titler, critic, reviewer or censor, advertising agent, and exhibitor.

Each may have some modification in the strip of celluloid which superficially or fundamentally modifies the thought and plot of the original writer.

The values of pictures are far from uniform. It is customary to make an outlay of $40,000 to $50,000 for an ordinary photoplay of five reels. This cost may mount up to $250,000 for other stories of similar length or possibly seven reels. The drama, when put into circulation, may bring in little or no more than the more cheaply constructed film. These figures are the original costs "on the lot" or in the studio, for the negative from which many positives are made. They include salaries, scenery, rental of "locations," costumes, overhead, etc. By far the larger expense comes when the picture is put into circulation. Then are to be figured "exchange" and central office charges, advertising, publicity in trade and other papers, sales expenses, etc. Probably the most expensive department of the motion-picture business is that concerned with distribution of films to the cities and towns throughout the country. This fact explains several things little understood by the public.

Since every picture circulates in a territory of approximately 200 miles in radius, there is required, for the United States, for the pictures of a given motion-picture concern about thirty-five separate offices, each fully equipped with staff, fireproof vaults, film copies, and shipping facilities. Pictures are shot back and forth from distributor to exhibitor by fast express. The public, through the exhibitor, must pay these original and superimposed costs as well as bring a profit all along the line. The risks on individual pictures are enormous. About one in three proves to be sufficiently attractive to the playgoing public to bring in much over costs.

The producer, therefore, is intensely interested from a monetary standpoint in learning exactly what the playgoing public wants in the way of amusement. This desire to make the picture which will unquestionably earn much money explains the phenomenon of a succession of screen dramas dealing with the same general theme. One has been made which has been wonderfully successful financially and a dozen follow.

In the great expense of distribution is to be found the reason for the small number of agencies making and distributing pictures for the churches and other groups of nontheatrical users. They do not find enough renters or receive enough rental money in a given exchange territory to make it profitable for them to make new and fine films. Even in the most populous centers most of these non-theatrical renters are hard put to it to make a living. Many of them act as middlemen for pictures they do not own or which are old and discarded by the commercial agencies. The churches want pictures of the highest possible grade, but they are not willing to pay the price to make them, to purchase them, to rent them, or to handle them on a cooperative basis. Moreover, because of other reasons, chief of which are lack of vision and conservatism, the Church has allowed this powerful educational and inspirational medium to pass into the hands of professional showmen of a new type.

Steadily the photoplay has advanced in the hands of business men. Technically it is more connected in its dramatic construction, better photographed, more artistic in color and atmospheric effects, better staged, more cleverly and subtly acted, less obvious and less brazen in appeal. Its makers have found that the mentality of the ordinary person seeking entertainment in the United States is between twelve and thirteen years and, without blazoning abroad the fact, they have deliberately set themselves to exploit

it. They have searched the world for backgrounds and have given us sea, mountain, shore, plain, forests, northern snows, and out-of-the-way bits of artistic profusion and beautiful detail. Less can be said regarding the improvement in the story. This, after all, is the essential of the drama, whether spoken or silent. It is only fair to the picture-makers to say that they have tried many expensive experiments to enlist the public in support of the dramas requiring more mentality to appreciate. The losses on most of such stories have been sickening and have discouraged all but the more idealistic and wealthy individuals and corporations.

Among the studies which must be made concerning the motion-picture before any final judgment is given is one of the real wishes and wants of the American people, when they go out to be amused. Far too often those who debate this subject "poohpooh" any statements made along this line by sincere and shrewd students within the motion-picture business, who are staking fortunes on their investigations of the interests of the men and, especially, the women who attend the theaters. They are tired of the mushy twaddle they have to make and sell to the public, and would welcome, with grins and whoops, a new and finer type of picture.

Dec. 10—Young People and Motion Pictures

The screen draws all classes and ages. Among them, the group most attracted by the action, color, romance, and thrill of the picture is composed of the young people of both sexes between the ages of twelve and twenty. It is their adoption of the picture as a means of using leisure time and finding enjoyment that has caused thoughtful adults to demand that some modification of themes and treatment be made of the film dramas. This demand has usually taken the form of some kind of censorship. Every right-thinking person will support the movement for the protection of the youth if he is sure that harm is being done, and skilled leaders come forward with a method which will accomplish the results aimed at. The report of the Federal Council is the latest authoritative declaration which declares that politically appointed

State censors have not and can not protect the youth of the various States.

It would appear that far more serious thought should be given to the influences affecting this age-group than has yet been given. A surprising difference of opinion among experts has been found. So far as discovered, the romantic, emotional, society and love drama is of little interest to the average boy but abnormally appealing to the typical girl. The indifference to this form of story, dealing with sex, on the part of the boy and his enthusiasm for Western, frontier, detective, and sea stories deserves serious thought by workers with youth.

The motion-picture lure, as it affects boys and girls, is wrapped up in the whole question of the use of leisure time on the part of the young people. In most cases, the parents of the country have allowed their children to go to the picture theater because it was cheap. They have inquired little into the influence of the drama, designed for adults, on their young people. The boys and girls also have a glut of magazines, novels, autos, dress, dancing, jazz music, meals in public places, money to spend, and parties, with a minimum of oversight, work, responsibility, home pleasures, and association with parents in friendly ways. Few pictures would do them anything but good, if they were picked by father or mother and seen with them. Of the many things thrown in the way of boys and girls there are few which cause less harm than the motion-picture. All such absorbing pleasures contain more than a little moral dynamite!

Now, just what are the movies, which are holding our young people enthralled? They are conventional stories, presented on the theater screen, of the glamour of quick success, physical charm, heroism, adventure, beautiful women, easy money, much love; business, love, marriage and home stories. They introduce dress, rich background, public places, superabundant pleasure, sex appeal, and emotional touches. They usually contain the hero and heroine, the villain, the innocent party, the general public, and possibly the actor furnishing the humor. Almost without exception the moral is conventional and—sugary! They contain a maximum of action and a minimum of advice. The aim of most is to intersperse as

many thrilling situations as possible to make up for the lack of dialog.

All of these elements and many others not mentioned may be perfectly satisfactory, as a steady diet, for mature men and women, for whom they have been constructed; but they are not all right for the growing young person. Knowledge of "life" should come normally, slowly, wholesomely to young boys and girls. They are no more fitted to absorb the whole motion bill of fare than they are ready to be thrown against emotional avalanches. Wisdom cries aloud in the streets to-day, "If you intend to permit your young people to go regularly to the theater, be near enough to them to discuss the life questions presented and keep the lads and lasses seeing life whole and seeing it fine." The thoughtful parent will find in the motion-picture the natural introduction to many questions which must be discussed, if boys and girls are to go out into life properly equipped.

Social workers are recognizing generally over the country, that there are many wholesome influences operating as a result of the picture and the theater. They draw more youth of working age off the streets, throughout the year, in the evenings, than any three other forms of amusement. They are held inside, in company with other people, without feeling any restraints. The pictures give to almost every lively boy and girl the emotional thrill for which he and she are craving, after the monotonous work of the ordinary day; and they give it in a form which is not anti-social and which is followed by normal emotions before leaving the theater. This impersonal thrill is infinitely better than those coming to boys and girls alone together on the dark corners and in the parks. For the first time in the history of workers, they can find steady, wholesome amusement near at hand, for a cost which is not prohibitive. It may contain only an infinitesimal portion of education; but it contains sufficient to make working people turn more and more to the library, the newspaper, and the magazine. Such are the findings of social workers regarding the influence of pictures on the working-class young people.

For those of families where there is greater leisure, it may be well for parents to ask and answer the following questions: "Will you think hard and give your young people fine, simple and inspiring pleasures?" "Will you give them the facts of life they crave to know, in the fashion that only a parent knows?" "Will you pick and choose the pictures to be seen?" "Will you help to create a sentiment in favor of regular, selected motion-picture entertainments for all the young people of your town?" If you will pool your interest with other thoughtful parents of town, the motion-picture problem, as it affects boys and girls will have been solved; just as the library problem was solved by the introduction of the children's department.

Dec. 17—Regulation of Motion Pictures

The motion-picture captured the imagination and the attention of the common people of America some twenty years ago. They began to change their habits of using leisure time. The leaders of society discovered that a new form of family amusement had been evolved which contained elements more exciting than a horse-race, more gripping than the "ten, twenty, and thirty" melodrama, and as inexpensive as a trolley fare. It was as lurid, yellow, and blood-curdling as human ingenuity could make it. When the theaters began to dot the country like grocery stores, and to draw every member of the families of the working people, including the baby, then it was decided that the movies needed regulation of a radical kind. And it did! It was such a gold mine for its exploiters that all kinds of business men, junk-dealers, showmen, peanut venders, and gamblers set themselves to make and exhibit pictures. The wonder was that the decent people did not turn against it as they turn from the circus side-shows after being cheated a few times. They did demand that the gruesome, lurid, sickening, disgusting, sensual elements be taken out, but that the thrilling be retained.

One group of motion-picture critics demanded that the censoring be put, forthwith, into the hands of state boards, politically appointed, and instructed by law as to what should be eliminated or modified within the borders of the commonwealth. The other group was satisfied that the problem was so subtle and dipped so far into the realm of ethics that they could accomplish more by independent but intimate friendly

cooperation with the makers of pictures on the one hand and the consuming public on the other. They determined to gather the definite judgments of the adult public and apply them to pictures at the time when they were made by the manufacturers. This required agreements with the makers, a large corps of volunteer workers to examine pictures, and, most important of all, the probable misunderstanding of motives by those who wanted the impossible accomplished.

In some five States, namely, Ohio, Kansas, Pennsylvania, Maryland, and New York, the Boards were authorized by law and went to work. They have had plenty of time to demonstrate their ability to accomplish results; and in all cases have shown that the children could under no interpretation of the law be protected. They have construed the terms of the law, as public opinion has forced them to do, in terms of the demands of the more populous centers, the great cities, where interest in amusements has always been cosmopolitan and extremely tolerant. They, moreover, have adopted a policy of cutting or making a large number of eliminations to demonstrate their necessity as public agents. Many times, they have partially or completely destroyed the continuity of the drama, with no thought of dramatic requirements. They have found that the demands of the smaller city and the town were radically different from those of the metropolis. This has involved them in a criticism of themselves they were utterly unable to meet. Equally, they have discovered that there is a great variety of tastes on the subject of amusements, both inside their Boards and among the more responsible citizens of the State. Their attitude of regarding all pictures guilty until examined and found to be innocent, with the accompanying charges for censoring, has caused constant irritation among the owners of the pictures. This has caused, in turn, all kinds of efforts to punish them politically; and on their part a liberality in passing pictures which has sometimes been called favoritism. The other States,, which have investigated the workings of such long-established Boards, have been slow to undertake a work which appears to be a sword which easily may cut the hands which wield it.

The other group, represented by the National Board of Review, has proceeded since 1909 on the theory stated above, namely, of cooperative review and editing of all dramatic films. The bare expenses of maintaining a skilled staff, an office, and agencies for reaching the public have been met by a tax levied on each reel of film submitted for review by the owners. Decisions have been rendered by the volunteers who gather daily in the offices of the producing companies, and by agreement their action is final. This understanding has been adopted by the companies as a straight business policy. They prefer to have the work done cooperatively, at one time, in one place, by volunteers, for the country as a whole and with due recognition of story continuity as well as property values than by the method described above.

The owners and distributors of pictures are far from satisfied with any form of external dictation as to their product. They know, however, the nitroglycerin tucked away in some of their dramas; and now know the way wrath descends not upon the guilty head of the offender but upon the entire group. They must either give absolute guaranties that they can keep their entire house in order; accept meekly the rulings of State Boards; continue the relationships now existing with the National Board of Review; or make some radical change in their way of doing business such as the production and exhibition of pictures on a national scale for young people. This would be followed quickly and logically by the enactment and enforcement of laws prohibiting the attendance of boys and girls in the regular adult theater.

These horns of a dilemma on which they must sit have prompted the producers, first, to issue in 1921 a set of some thirteen statements referring to certain kinds of pictures they would insist should no longer be made, then to call upon Mr. Will Hays, late secretary of the Post-office Department, to act as director of an association of producers. They informed the public they would give to Mr. Hays almost absolute authority to make and keep the motion-picture screen clean. This group with Mr. Hays at its head can do many things in the studios of the cooperating companies to improve the quality of the product. It can perform many valuable kinds of service for the Church, for the school, for industry, and for the farmer in the shape of the larger production and more wide-spread distribution of the non-

dramatic film, containing education in correct and entertaining forms. It can not, however, restrain competing companies, nor can it convince the public that the interested parties can put as effective restraints on this kind of emotional product as other disinterested parties. Every churchman should give support to Mr. Hays in his undertaking.

The difficulties of a satisfactory regulation of photoplays may well be considered. The judgments of people on questions of taste and ethics are almost as numerous as the people. The small community has a community judgment on conduct and morals which is both different from that of the large city and that of the town of the same size in another part of the country. The person who has lived much has invariably a more tolerant opinion than the innocent and the ignorant. The points of view of the adult and the youth can never be the same, since one has lived through experiences and the other is simply dreaming about them. Motion-pictures are made for adult amusement. They circulate freely from the largest cities to the smallest villages in the course of twelve or fifteen months. They are seen by cultured and ignorant, by children and the mature.

The humble exhibitor in any town has learned this lesson far better than the most rabid reformer. He knows that he must modify his selections for his town and he does it constantly. The most persistent, effective, shrewd, and quiet censor or critic the motion-picture has is the man who wants to keep his neighborhood people coming to his house. He does his work in the following ways: He carefully considers the kinds of pictures made by several companies and makes a selection in the light of his clientele. He reads the trade papers and the opinions of other exhibitors. He sometimes goes to headquarters and examines the film for himself. He runs it through, when it arrives by express, at his theatre and takes out some incident he is afraid will prove offensive to his patrons. Then, finally, when the picture has been run, he forcefully informs his distributor whether or not he wants any more of a similar character.

The question of the establishment of a Federal Board of Censors of Motion-pictures has been canvassed by various national groups, including churchmen, women's clubs, educators, and social agencies. It has also been well pondered by political leaders in Washington. Thought is turning to another method of handling the public exhibition of pictures. This lifts the question out of the field of censorship and into that of selection.

In all this discussion of proper ways of handling pictures and their exhibitions it will be noted that every one recognizes that the ordinary photoplay is not designed for young boys and girls. They are equally certain that no form of regulation has appeared, either statutory or voluntary, either managed by the industry or by the public, which does much for the group needing the protection.

Evidently some other form of approach and treatment is needed. While the method of selection is only a partial solution, it is a long step in the right direction.

The extent to which it is carried is entirely a community question.

Dec. 24—Church Use of Motion Pictures

The picture is an ideal way to teach religious and ethical truths. It has infinite possibilities. It has already recorded many desirable facts about mission countries, Bible lands, science, art, etc. Some excellent film dramas have been made for the use of churches. A number of churches have picture projectors and are using films—when they can get them. All these things are true. They do not mean, however, that every church in this broad land can obtain satisfactory service and at a reasonable rate of rental.

Always the ministers must bear in mind that the film has been developed for commercial entertainment. As the years have passed large investments have been made in theater buildings by the exhibitors. They are the regular patrons of the distributors of motion pictures—those men who have figured to a nicety the profits of service and rental. They are all based on the theater demand for many pictures of a commonplace, dramatic type. The exhibitors do not want the "exchanges" to rent any large number of pictures to the churches for use, either in competing meetings where a charge is made or for strictly ethical purposes. The "exchange" men know they must please their regular clients. So they furnish nothing but fair words to the church-

man who tries to put in a modest order. This rule is broken over in just enough cases throughout the country to permit a fair number of ministers in the larger cities to declare that they are obtaining regular, long-sustained, and satisfactory service from the "commercial" distributors. There are also a few big national firms which are willing to fight the exhibitors in this respect.

Some producers have learned, as have the distributors, that there is no agreement among the churches as to what is a desirable film story. There is a well-supported theory among sincere makers of pictures that you antagonize more friends than you make by producing any kind of a religious film for Protestant America. They also tell you that the churches, except a negligible few, are unbusinesslike, slow pay, niggardly in haggling for special prices, and very widely scattered geographically. So they try to keep the friendship of churchmen without attempting to make religious or propaganda films, and with a minimum of rentals.

This throws the work of supplying the churches upon non-commercial agencies, film brokers, and—strangely enough—friendly local exhibitors. The two first have been successful in the regions of great populations, like Chicago, New York, St. Louis, and Boston. The reason is clear. The demand for service at decent rental rates is such that they can keep their pictures in circulation, and can make enough to buy or produce more. One or two such firms, like the Educational Film Corporation, have definitely turned from the non-commercial trade to make the same kind of film for the theaters. They find, now, a sufficient revenue to permit them to do more and finer things than under their original plan of supplying the churches.

The churches could be supplied generally from the film agencies if they abandoned the thought of competition with the theaters through admission charges. They can come to an understanding of the true costs of rental and obtain films in large numbers from the non-theatrical agencies. They can develop renting agencies of their own on a denominational or union basis which may be financed to make the kinds of photoplays and educational subjects desired. Or they can work with the commercial exhibitors in their various communities to have them obtain, occasionally, programs satisfactory to the church people. They can not hope to rent generally the best types of pictures for profit from the exchanges which draw their profit from the motion-picture theaters.

There is no doubt about the present supply of vast numbers of splendid dramatic subjects with high ethical content. They are being made in every studio of the country. The person living in any city or town does not realize this, because he sees only a few of those made by many companies. Moreover, the exhibitor may not be renting those which belong to this class. The National Committee for Better Films, in New York City, makes it its business to review and select pictures from the entire supply examined daily by the National Board of Review. Each year it has indicated some scores which are suitable for Sunday use. It segregates the titles of about 250 dramas as satisfactory for week-day entertainments in church houses. Moreover, it publishes a list of about 800 titles yearly of dramas, comedies, educationals, and magazine reels which are unusually good for selected family entertainments.

The constant effort of the producer of film dramas is to avoid any suggestion of preaching, propaganda, or advice. He claims that the action and the logical flow of the story must make individuals attracted or repellent. He has found that the method of indirection, through thrilling and dramatic incidents, is far more effective than any kind of preaching. So he is unwilling to allow the theaters to be drawn from their peculiar function of amusement.

While a few pictures have been made, like "From the Manger to the Cross," "The Stream of Life," "The Servant in the House," "Over the Hill," and "The Life of the Savior," which have made money, they are few and far between. There is now a series of Old Testament two-reel subjects being produced which are fairly good from the standpoints of history and interest. These may make enough for their producers to warrant their completion; but it will not be done without arranging for their release in the commercial theaters as contrasts to the dramatic entertainment (as what is known as "fillers").

It should also be noted that the production of dramas which are frankly ethical require different actors, technique, directors, and sales methods. The elements entering into the production of such pictures are infinitely more complex than those in the ordinary drama. The church people can not make them alone. They lack technique and sense of entertainment values. The showman can seldom make them; for he lacks vision, earnestness, and fundamental sincerity. In some way the two must be brought together to pool their talents, if fine pictures in large numbers are to be made for the churches.

The most expensive part of the motion-picture business is that of distribution. The best film in the world will fail to pay for the costs of production if it can not be rented constantly in from twenty-five to thirty-five centers of the country. Many pictures have been bought for small amounts because their owners had no way of renting them. They have then brought fortunes to their new owners who had exchange facilities. The churches need pictures. They must have them. But they will never have them for regular programs until there is sufficient demand for individual films to warrant the maintenance of a nation-wide system of exchanges. The most ambitious and progressive of the church film agencies, namely, The International Church Film Corporation, has learned that demand must be widespread if business is to prosper.

Dec. 31—What Our Town Can Do for Better Motion Pictures

You can have the finer kinds of motion-pictures in your town. Whatever the size or location, it is possible to obtain them.

But, you ask, what are "better pictures"? "Good" pictures are sincere and interesting studies of wholesome phases of life. They depict the joy of life and inspire us to seek a part of it. Some of them are set in an out-of-doors atmosphere and bring us the freedom and cleanliness of the hills, the woods, and the plains. They carry us into the midst of adventure, with its color, danger, and heroism. Others center around the simple routine of the home, bringing respect for womankind and the paramount value of family life. They present human and rollicking fun. Sometimes they are simply ridiculous. Besides these and more dramatic subjects with their color, thrill, and struggle, are pictures of travel, of nature, and of science, coupled with the news of the day. All these and more can be brought to your town if you want them and will support them on a town or community basis.

Last April the Southeastern Conference for Better Films was called by the Woman's Club of Atlanta, Ga., to formulate concrete ideas for the wholesome, playgoing public of six States. Together, they formulated certain conclusions. Among them were the following:

1. A real cooperation of the public, the exhibitor, and the exchange is possible in motion-picture exhibitions. Vision is required of each. We are resolved to work together.

2. With the exception of those attending the larger, downtown theaters, the audiences of town, village, and neighborhood houses want, principally, "family" pictures.

3. Thoroughly representative and tolerant better film committees are helpful in developing support for better pictures; but the exhibitor is the expert and is in control.

4. We recommend that monthly photoplay guides and other definite information about pictures be placed before the public in advance in newspapers, also in schools, libraries, clubs, etc. The facts should be given the public so that they can decide intelligently.

5. It is questionable to show pictures regularly to little children. The audience deserving the most attention is that composed of the adolescent group between 16 and 11 years. Where possible, this group should have special performances.

6. In all communities, down to the village, it is possible to have "family nights" in the theaters. In the smaller towns it may be necessary to hold these from week to week on different nights because of business contracts.

7. Adult performances should be shown to adults without any criticism expressed or implied.

9. There is a well-defined place for nontheatrical pictures which must be met. This applies also to films having educational, cultural, and inspirational values. The exhibitor should be given every chance to present these. If he will not or can not, other agencies should undertake it and receive the assistance of the exchanges in obtaining regular, satisfactory service.

10. It is agreed that the principle of "selection—not censorship" is the practical solution for most of the problems faced by the public in connection with motion-picture entertainment.

The Cleveland Cinema Club held a state convention in October where the same general plans were discussed. They have been in operation in that city for some years. An association has been formed for this kind of work on a state-wide basis in California. The Indiana Endorsers of Photoplays have performed a similar service for three or four years in the capital and in a number of towns and cities. In each case the aim is to select pictures and have them fully supported by enthusiastic audiences. Little is done to condemn or otherwise notice the poorly done, inartistic, and vulgar picture. This policy is reaching back to the producers of films and greater effort is being made to put out pictures which will bring entertainment "without regrets."

Here, Mr. Hays will perform a great service. He is passing on to the producers the unquestioned desires of the playgoing public for family pictures. It is well, however, to echo his warning to the public. Pictures have a life of from a year to two years and a half. Some made many months ago are now appearing in certain towns. Those made since the first of January, 1921, may fairly be said to reflect the newer point of view demonstrated when Mr. Hays was called from Washington to raise the standards of the entire motion-picture industry.

It is suggested, then, that the question be regarded as a community question. Second, that it be discussed fully by representative citizens, among whom will be included the theater owner. Third, that the motion-picture be regarded as a family entertainment. Fourth, that the entertainment needs of boys and girls be recognized as different from those of adults and met by special performances. Fifth, that better film committees be formed to arouse wide-spread public support of better pictures, and to cooperate with the theater owner in making finer pictures pay at the box-office. Sixth, that encouragement be given to the wider use of films for popular education; including travel, industry, science, history, and ethics.

THE MAKING AND USING OF MONEY[1]

*Take heed and keep yourselves from covet-
ousness: for a man's life consisteth not
in the abundance of the things which he
possesseth.—Luke 12:15.*

*Lay not up for yourselves treasures upon
earth, where moth and rust consume, and
where thieves break through and steal;
but lay up for yourselves treasures in
heaven, where neither moth nor rust doth
consume, and where thieves do not break
through nor steal; for where thy treasure
is, there will thy heart be, also.—Matt.
6:19-21.*

If there is kinship between sin and human
want, we should expect that the code of the
Mediator would contain some very definite
instruction concerning getting and using
money. The love of money being the root
of all evil, we should expect that any plan
for the eradication of evil would deal with
its root. Remembering the circumstances
under which Jesus taught—the intense reign
of covetousness in high life, the Hebrew
belief that riches are an evidence of God's
favor, and the unscrupulous methods that
were used to secure them—we shall be prepared for his denunciation of some of the
methods of finance, and his caution against
covetousness.

The Mediator's code does not prohibit one
from making a million dollars, or a hundred millions; but the manner in which it
is made and the uses to which it is applied
do come under very clear and unmistakable
principles. Man is a steward and not an
absolute owner, while money is a sacred
trust. The parable of the Wicked Husbandmen illustrates the outworking of these
principles. Throughout Jesus' teaching
there runs the great truth of accountability,
which is also applied to material wealth.
More than half his parables deal with matters of property.

"Godliness is profitable in all things," and
therefore must be profitable financially.
However, the gospels are not a recipe for
money-getting. The supreme purpose of

Jesus' teaching is to make character, not
to make money. Nevertheless, it is true
that economic conditions have much to do
with character-making. Power over one's
subsistence means power over his whole
moral being. The gospels deal with money
matters as of secondary importance, and
only as they minister to moral ends. "What
shall it profit a man to gain the whole world,
and lose his own soul?" The soul is that
which gives value to humanity, hence is of
supreme importance. To make a life is
infinitely more than to make a living. The
character and intelligence of its membership
measure the strength of a church; the
patriotism, intelligence, and character of
its citizens are the measure of a country's
power.

Ill fares the land, to hastening ills a prey
Where wealth accumulates and men decay.

Rome has shown us how, with the accumulation of wealth, men are likely to decay.
It is but an object lesson that has been repeated in every age and clime. Riches and
luxury bring about effeminacy and decay.
Poverty sinks into degradation and squalor,
and opens the way to sins and evils untold.
How wise is the prayer of the old Hebrew
philosopher, who said:

Give me neither poverty nor riches;
Feed me with the food that is needful for
    me;
Lest I be full and deny thee and say,
    Who is Jehovah?
Or, lest I be poor and steal,
And use profanely the name of my God.
    —Prov. 30:9.

It is not a question of more or less wealth,
but rather of its proper distribution, that
enters into the formation of proper conditions for character building and human welfare. Millions well distributed may fill a
proper mission, but millions at one extreme
and squalor at the other bring discontent
if not disaster. Many peoples have been
happy in poverty, when it was the common

[1]From *Jesus An Economic Mediator*, by JAMES E. DARBY. Fleming H. Revell Company,
New York, 1922.

lot. A right economic distribution makes happy lives, and saves from the dangers of great riches on the one hand and the temptations of extreme poverty on the other. That "the destruction of the poor is their poverty" is as true to-day as in the days of Solomon.

Jesus' first consideration of material wealth, in its bearing upon the formation of character, is as it affects the progress of the kingdom of God; and only secondarily upon the material things themselves. The treasure carries the heart and hence controls life's aspirations: "Where your treasure is, there will your heart be, also."

In his code, the acquisition of wealth is not set up as the chief object of life, nor a large bank account as the cure-all for human ills. We have seen that an inordinate desire for wealth is rebuked and its dangers are pointed out. Getting it at another's expense is severely denounced, and the folly of depending upon it for happiness is vividly exposed. However, the acquisition of treasure is assumed in the directions given for laying it up in heaven. To the Jew of Jesus' day no exhortation to accumulate was needed. The emphasis was needed upon just methods and right use of the accumulations.

One of the outstanding, axiomatic truths in his code is, "No man can serve two masters: ye can not serve God and mammon." Single-minded loyalty to God is demanded and no neutral ground is recognized. There is a deep psychological reason for this.

We can not have two chief centers of interest, or pursue two lines of effort at the same time. We are so constituted by nature that this is an impossibility. Those who have tried to do so in any line of endeavor have proved its truthfulness by their failure. In accordance with this law of our being, Jesus drew the lesson that one can not seek the things of the world with sufficient zeal to acquire great riches, and at the same time seek to establish the reign of God within himself and others. Two masters can not be served with success. One can not serve in two places at the same time, or give equal attention to two objects at the same moment.

Another difficulty is to rise from the narrow, selfish motives that blind one to all visions of larger truth. Ben Sira said, "An evil eye is grudging of bread." A penny before the eye hides the most beautiful landscape and shuts out the glory of a whole horizon. A mere selfish interest blinds one to opportunity, biases one's mind in matters of justice, and prejudices one against efforts for the larger good.

Dr. Charles Foster Kent has well said:

Complete acknowledgment of the rule of God in a man's economic, social, intellectual, moral, and religious life gives him a right conception of wealth and its use, a proper social consciousness, a normal relation to the universe, true ethical standards, and above all the knowledge that he has the approval of his divine King and Father.

We should expect, therefore, to find Jesus laying down the revolutionary doctrine that one can not serve God and mammon, and making the renunciation of mammon a first condition to membership in his kingdom. The first requirement is to seek the kingdom, and the great promise is that "all these things shall be added unto you." Thus those things necessary to life and godliness need not give one anxiety.

The danger of covetousness is greater with those who have had a taste of acquisition than with the rabble who care only for the next meal. Some of Jesus' followers were satisfied to be fed on loaves and fishes, but others had ambitions for the worldly emoluments of a kingdom. The Sermon on the Mount was necessary for the disciples. Many of them were from the comparatively well-to-do people of Galilee. James and John, with their father Zebedee, were prosperous fishermen, owning their own craft and employing servants. Peter possessed a boat, a home, and we know not what else. Matthew was called from a lucrative position at the receipt of customs, and Zacchæus, who must have been in quite prosperous circumstances, was accepted as a follower of the Master while in possession of at least half his fortune.

This shows that while Jesus possessed no fortune, cared little for money matters, and arose above the selfish consideration of worldly things, being content with the common treasury and the kindly ministration of women of means, who for sometime accompanied the group of disciples, he nevertheless associated with men of means and had about him those to whom the love of worldly possessions appealed. Peter was ready to say, "Lord, we have left all to follow thee; what shall we receive?" So natural was the question that Jesus did not give him a reproving answer, but lifted his mind to higher things, namely, the spiritual rewards.

In exercising the function of a Mediator in his interview with the rich young ruler, Jesus shows how wealth sometimes must be regarded as *impedimenta*. He did not require of others that they sell what they had. Perhaps there were two reasons for doing so in this case: The young ruler needed to rid himself of that which would divide his heart, and also to get into sympathy with the poor, if he were to follow Jesus. Barriers must be removed. He must learn to love the proletariat, if he is to help them. The Son of man needed to empty himself of his glory as he came to earth, to meet men and mingle with them—to put aside everything that would place a chasm between him and the helpless. The servant is not above his master, and ought to be willing to follow in his footsteps. That fine fortune, the circumstances of birth and early life, placed the rich young ruler in an entirely different realm from the common people.

The new birth upon which the Mediator insisted not only had its economic side, but on the spiritual side it demanded conditions favorable for spiritual growth. The new life must not be buried in the rubbish of covetousness and worldly cares, not crusht with the weight of material things, and not blighted and dwarfed by poverty, want, and unspiritual surroundings. "The deceitfulness of riches" must not choke it. "He that hath two coats, let him give to him that hath none." Let charitable action prepare the way for the reception of truth.

Then, to secure this growth, justice must prevail: "Take nothing unjustly from any man." When the disciples were astonished at the difficulties of the rich entering the kingdom of heaven, Jesus told them that what is impossible with men is quite possible with God: he could strike the fetters of gold from the shackled heart.

The true purpose of acquisition should be transportation, not hoarding, and not simply to spend it upon one's pleasures and vanities. The only way to transport treasure to heaven is to put it into the character and lives of people. They go into that realm and carry with them their spiritual development or deformity. That which is inwoven into

their development is thus transported and exchanged into the coin of the realm. Treasure may be invested in schools, in missions, in churches, in all worthy causes that make for the betterment of humanity and the glory of God. However, Jesus nowhere teaches that these offerings can atone for unjust dealings and economic oppression. If men have given large sums of money to charitable objects, hoping to merit salvation by generosity with ill-gotten gains, or to attempt to make the fruit of their business atone for the sins of their methods, such action finds no basis in the code of the Mediator. On the contrary, many large manufacturers with the purest of motives have conducted their business for the approval of the Mediator. A manufacturer recently said to the writer:

My ambition is to run these mills to the limit of their capacity, with a full complement of workmen; to pay each man a good living wage; and to have the family of each workman comfortably housed, in good, sanitary surroundings; to afford them good church and school facilities; to give them a quiet Sunday for rest and worship; and in proportion as I can do this, I am happy and regard my work as successful.

Was not that man making an investment in humanity? Many an act of economic justice brings more honor to the Father in heaven than lavish donations of money which has been wrung from opprest workmen.

In Luke's gospel there is a tone which might lead to the belief that all wealth is evil. He records the sayings of Jesus which indicate the dangers of greed and the tragic consequences of selfish materialism. He tells of the man who wanted Jesus to divide the inheritance. The request came from one who may have been laboring under a grievance or merely a grouch; but Jesus did not enter into the merits of the case. However, he did take occasion to sound a note of warning with the parable of the Rich Fool.

Commenting on this parable, Augustus Hare said:

There are more parables, I believe, in the New Testament against taking no thought for heavenly things, and taking too much thought about earthly things, than any other fault whatsoever."

It has been seen that the covetousness and exploitation practised by the Jewish rulers created a need for such teaching. A careful study will show, also, that in the parables there is a rich mine of economic truth.

The sixteenth chapter of Luke might be called the "money chapter." In the outset its shows that money may be used as to secure the favor of God and man. There the steward of a rich man was accused of mismanagement, and told to render an account. He practised his arts in the most unrighteous way, that he might make friends of those with whom he had been dealing and through them secure bread and shelter in the future. Jesus said he had acted wisely—not justly. If his ethics differed from ours, that does not weaken Jesus' commendation of his wisdom in preparing for the future.

I say unto you, make to yourselves friends by means of the mammon of unrighteousness; that when it shall fail, they may receive you into eternal tabernacles (Luke 16:9).

The use of money is a test of faithfulness, and "he that is faithful in a little is faithful also in much; and he that is unrighteous in a little is unrighteous also in much." What one would do with a million dollars can be told by what is done with the slenderest pay envelope: it would be an expenditure on a larger scale, but in the same direction.

The Pharisees, who were lovers of money, whose connection with the exploiting class made them supersensitive to the Mediator's denunciation of covetousness, heard him and began to scoff. He told them that they were trying to justify themselves in the sight of men, but that God knew their hearts and was displeased with them; that the things which they were exalting were an abomination to him. It was a cutting rebuke to their greed.

Luke follows this rebuke with the parable of Dives and Lazarus, showing the folly of ignoring the responsibility which wealth brings. There is no charge of fraud in securing the property, but there is a graphic picture of the idle rich—"clothed in purple and fine linen and faring sumptuously every day." The leisure which Dives enjoyed gave him opportunity to render fine service. In fact, when he did not seek the opportunity, circumstances brought it to his door in the person of Lazarus. His wealth gave him abundant ability to render service, but he lacked the disposition necessary. He failed to measure up to the responsibility which his accumulations placed upon him,

and "in hades he lifted up his eyes, being in torments, and seeth Abraham afar off and Lazarus in his bosom." The tables were turned, but his spirit was the same; he still demanded service, and put up a plea that Lazarus be sent to minister to him. Accustomed to being served, he had no thought of "not being ministered to, but ministering." Hell could not give him a heart to serve, since he had lived to be served.

When Archelaus went to Rome to seek a share of his father's kingdom, the Jews sent a deputation after him, to warn Cæsar that they would not have him to rule over them. Jesus used this well-known bit of history as a setting for his parable of the Pounds, in which he imprest the lesson of stewardship and responsibility. To each one was given a pound, and on the return of the master, settlement was demanded. Rewards and punishment were administered according as each one had used, or failed to use, "his lord's money." It was not his own, since he was but a steward to handle the treasure for another.[1]

The history of Christianity shows that the teaching of Jesus is not only in closest sympathy with struggling humanity, but that it is a leverage by which honest workers have been lifted into better conditions. From men of means, whose hearts are touched by the spirit of the Mediator, it brings kindlier cooperation and better opportunities for the struggling ones. It restrains the oppressive rich and encourages every worthy effort of the laborer. It cultivates the spirit and disposition, the industry and energy, which bring better living conditions and make humanity happier as well as holier. It encourages the workingman to

---

[1] To avoid lengthening this chapter unduly, the following references are given, with the suggestion that they be studied from the economic point of view:
Matthew 25:1-10: the folly of improvidence shown in oilless lamps.
Luke 14:28-30, 33: the importance of good business sense.
Luke 7:41-47: a warning against unjust dealing.
Luke 11:5-9: the duty of helping by a loan.
Matthew 20:1-16: gracious dealing with hired laborers.
Matthew 13:45-46: seeking the best value for one's money.
Luke 19:12-27: honest dealing; and losing what isn't used.
Luke: 12:16-52: the folly of overreaching.
Matthew 12:11-12: wisdom of saving property.
Many others will suggest themselves, as for example, the Unjust Steward, the Unprofitable Servant, the Wicked Husbandmen, etc., showing the economic value of Jesus' parables.

have a bank account and to own his home. A London paper once sneeringly remarked that "the poor do not go to church." Another replied, "Those who go to church do not remain poor." The church that faithfully presents the economic teaching of the Mediator has a spirit in its worship that naturally, and often unconsciously, cultivates thrift, inspires educational ideals, and leads to temporal betterment. These things are added as a natural result of the spiritual changes.

The profession of Christianity that makes no change in one's financial life is open to suspicion. The conversion of the "tight-wad" will be suspected until he loosens his purse strings; that of the industrial Shylock until he leaves off his pound of flesh; that of the gambler until he leaves his games and turns his revenue into the betterment of his home; that of the idler until he works, and that of the selfish man until he forsakes his selfishness and plans his finances for God and humanity!

CHRIST'S WELCOME TO THE PENITENT

The Rev. J. TEMPLETON, South River, Ont., Can.

Zacchæus, make haste and come down; for to-day I must abide at thy house.— Luke 19:5b.

Jericho is the scene of our discourse. We remember Bartimæus, the blind beggar, endowed with sight by the passing Jesus. Now we witness the transformation of a subverted man, whose moral blindness is suddenly enlightened by the vision of the holiness of being one with Christ. Zacchæus was probably the most detested man in Jericho. A collector of customs or "publican" was considered the lowest kind of fellow. As chief of the publicans, Zacchæus had sunk even further; and that he had become rich in the pursuit of his detested occupation was the crown of his degradation. Representing the Roman oppressor, he stood as one who was selling his own people.

But let us consider the man himself. He was a little man, full of animation, and possessed with a tremendous initiative. His shortness of stature prevented his seeing Jesus because of the thronging crowd. So he ran on ahead and climbed into a sycamore tree in order that he might have an uninterrupted view of the Savior. He refused to be cast down by obstacles. Rather, he endeavored to overcome them. More than that, too, he put himself in a position where he held the vantage ground. Thus when Jesus came opposite the tree where the little man was perched, he had an unobstructed view, tho little expecting the startling words that fell upon his bewildered ears—"Zacchæus, make haste and come down; for to-day I must abide at thy house."

Being a man of initiative, Zacchæus wasted no time in idle speculation, but immediately scrambled down the tree and "received him joyfully." Then, out of the fulness of his heart he stands manfully before the Lord and says: "Behold, Lord, the half of my goods I give to the poor; and if I have wrongfully exacted aught of any man, I restore fourfold."

Such is the simple gospel narrative. But let us look under the surface of this seemingly trivial incident in the life of our blessed Lord. First, it is something more than hysteria in an apparently abandoned reprobate. Notice that he desired to see Jesus. Desire usually conveys the idea of studied consideration and deliberate choice. But why should this hardened rogue, steeped in doubtful methods of getting rich, wish to see one with whom he held nothing in common? What was his object in desiring so eagerly to behold the face of the Great Healer, who but a few hours ago had performed that miracle of restoring sight to the blind beggar who had sat by the wayside this many a day, importuning the charity of the passers-by? The Greek gives us a clue to the reason. The word *esetoi* is used to denote "seeking eagerly with an earnest desire to find!" This translation lends a new and vastly different coloring to the bare word "see." It is not the idle curiosity of a loiterer in the street. It is the eager seeking of a man with an object vital and pressing.

The little outcast had been thinking, meditating. To the casual observer he was merely a cheap little blackguard, ready to make money scrupulously or otherwise, the ethics of a transaction not particularly affecting him. But the sacred narrative reveals a man torn with remorse and anguish of spirit. He is nauseated with the vileness of his coarse occupation. He sees his life in a new perspective. He had heard of the Christ—probably had witnessed the marvelous restoration of Bartimæus' sight that day, and a hidden, deep-lying chord in his cynical heart is struck. A haunting pain is in his heart. He feels the conviction of sin and desires something better, something worthier of his manhood. He desires Christ! and at once, without hesitation, takes special pains to see him.

The pressing crowd prevents him, for he is short in stature, but he finds a way to overcome this difficulty. His splendid initiative and determination show him the way even tho it may appear undignified, ridiculous. He runs on ahead and climbs a tree like some eager boy. That action of climbing the tree shows the clean boyishness lying underneath the veneer of callousness and unscrupulousness. And from the spreading branch he looks down eagerly, waiting for Jesus to come.

Strange it is that no word of condemnation is spoken by the Savior in his dealing with the little man. The murmur of disapproval comes presently from the crowd. But the Lord of life utters no word of harshness or contempt. He has caught the look of love reflected from the man's aching heart. He sees the sorrow that looks out as if from behind prison bars, and he knows of the unfulfilled longings in this despised little man's heart.

"Zacchæus, make haste and come down; for to-day I must abide at thy house." Oh, the power of Jesus! How instantly he recognizes the good in us, and how readily our hearts respond to that kindly recognition! So with Zacchæus. Joyfully he receives the Savior. We are not told what transpired between Christ and his latest desciple. That is not for curious ears. But we do know the result of that intimate conversation produced in the publican a deep desire to show his gratitude, and may we not say his love, in some practical way. Not only will he cheerfully make restitution of his ill-gotten gains, but he will gladly make provision for the poor. "Lord, the half of my goods I give to the poor, and if I have wrongfully

exacted aught from any man, I restore fourfold." The bars of callousness and greed are down! Gone the aching repression engendered, who can say, by fear of the gibes and sneers of his fellow publicans! Joyfully, gladly, he responds to the touch of the divine, and with the realization of his newly-found love he gladly and cheerfully tries to rectify his former errors.

So God deals with all of us. He awakens by his Holy Spirit, in this way or that, the aching desire for something worthier of our "high calling in God," something nobler than the sins "which so easily beset us." He stirs up our sin-laden hearts in earnest endeavor to attune our lives to the heavenly music. He recognizes the deep-hid love we bear him, tho for so long we have repress our holy desires. In the face of public opinion we had become callous to God's promptings, until in a very agony of desire we feel an insistent eagerness to seek him—to see him face to face. Instantly God responds. He knows our desire to seek him, and he understands how weak in faith we are—how the surging, pressing crowd of sins holds us back. Yet he awaits our attempt, however feeble, to come to him, and welcomes us again and again with "the best robe" and "the ring" and "the shoes," making merry with the song of feasting because the "prodigal" has returned. Let us but once stretch forth our hands, earnestly and sincerely, unto God and instantly he grasps them and hails us as brethren. No condemnation, no angry denunciation or scornful reproach! "Make haste and come down; for to-day I must abide at thy house." Abide! No mere formal visit, but taking up his abode (for that is what the word conveys) to-day, now!

Gladly will we respond, my brethren. Gladly will we make restitution for our former guilt. The sins which benefited us at the expense of others demand that we make amends as far as we are able. Do not we pray—"Forgive us our debts as we forgive our debtors"? How can we withhold our forgiveness and hope to be forgiven in the face of such wondrous love? Make restitution we must, even tho it may demand much that is dear to us.

Hard may be the struggle with self. It was hard for Zacchæus, but the love of God triumphed.

THE ONE THING

The Rev. F. W. Norwood, London, England

But one thing is needful.—Luke 10:42.

Jesus' explanation of life is not analytical —it is synthetical. He does not take it to pieces and explain its parts; he shows it to us whole—he makes us feel the wholeness of life as no one else does.

Nature is one great unity—there is a direct relationship between the farthest star and the smallest daisy. There is a direct connection between the bending of the stalk of a flower and the swing of a planet.

A friend of mine, who is both an artist and a naturalist, was explaining to me that every leaf upon a tree sends its tiny thread of woody matter down through the twig into the branches and the trunk itself, and even into the root. The growth of a tree is not upward only, the thickening comes down also from above; every leaf is not stuck on to the tree, but is part of the oneness of the tree, and the artist who would paint a tree truly must discern that. Many an artist has missed it; the genius of Turner never missed it.

For most people, life is a central stem of existence, with a heterogeneous mass of accidental things clinging to it. They would like to cut away a lot of things from their life, which seem to have no relation to its real purpose, and are not organic parts of one great whole.

For Jesus, life was a whole—it was "one thing." That is an expression we often hear upon his lips; it is a thought we often find in his parables. "Martha," he said, "but one thing is needful." These sisters had divided that one thing into two; the one showed the spirit of service, the other showed the spirit of worship, and these two were in conflict. To him they were one— life is both service and worship.

"One thing thou lackest," he said to the young man. It was not poverty he was recommending, but here was a man whose life was torn in two; his spiritual desires and his material possessions were in conflict; the man's life was not whole, and Jesus only put his finger upon the indicative thing to show where the divergence came in, and made an appeal for the unity of life.

I read to you just two of his parables; there is a whole cluster in this thirteenth chapter of Matthew:

The kingdom of heaven is like unto treasure hid in a field; the which, when a man hath found, he hideth, and for joy thereof goeth and selleth all that he hath, and buyeth that field.—That one thing.

Again, the kingdom of heaven is like unto a merchantman seeking goodly pearls; who, when he had found one pearl of great price, went and sold all that he had and bought it.—He bought the one thing.

Life is never right for anybody until it becomes one thing. What was the one thing in the mind of Jesus? I think we can not pause for a moment in doubt. If you had never seen the gospels, and I put them into your hand for the first time, especially the three synoptic gospels, and said to you, "Read that, and tell me what is characteristic of Jesus, what it was that dominated him," you would turn over the pages and say, "Why this man is always talking about the kingdom of God; it seems to be the one thought that possesses his mind."

Jesus spoke about the kingdom of God partly because everybody else was speaking about it; it was the question of the day; all men were dreaming about it. It was a thought that had come a long way down through history; it had been the theme of the prophets; it had been the theme of those later writers, whose writings for us have dropt out between the end of the canon of the Old Testament and the beginning of the canon of the New. Most of the prophetic writings had their origin about the time of the great exile of the Jewish people. In those days of exile, the prophets dreamed of a great day that was coming, when the kingdom of God would be set up on earth, and, as is natural in our wonderful human nature, when we are lowest down, hope shines brightest; when we are confronted with one trouble, we are always seeing through it and beholding the dawn of a new light. So the prophets spoke as if, when the exile should be over and the people should be restored again to the ancient land, the kingdom of God would come; the day would dawn at last when God would reign supreme, when Israel's ancient glory would come back to her, when there should be one faith throughout all the earth, when war should be no more, and swords and spears should be beaten into implements of peace. It would be a time when even nature herself would glow with additional beauty. The sun would be seven times brighter than before, the very wild beasts would lose their fierceness, and the lion would lie down with the lamb.

All these idyllic pictures charmed the minds of the people in the days of their bondage and punishment, but when at last they came back to the promised land, they did not find it all they had hoped. This people, who for seventy years or more had not known what it was to be free or to rule themselves, were now torn and rent with schisms, and it was not long before their weakness brought first the Greeks and then the Romans down upon them, and their holy city itself at last was dominated with foreign troops. A mood of pessimism settled down upon the people; they did not lose their faith in that day of God, but it took upon itself more somber colors, and the teachers who now arose spoke as if the world were utterly bad and could not be made right from within. God had forsaken them. But after a time, he would come again they said, he would break in from without, suddenly, with power, with flaming authority and rending cataclysm, and the kingdom would come at last.

When Jesus began his teaching, that is the way all men were talking, that was the way they were dreaming. They wanted to know more than anything else what he had to say about the kingdom of God. What he said was, "The kingdom of God is here; you have not to wait for it, it is here; the kingdom of God is among you; the kingdom of God is within you."

The kingdom is like—what? Like everything. Whatever his eyes rested upon, he said "The kingdom is like that." If he saw a sower sowing in the fields, he said "The kingdom of God is like that." If he saw men fishing in the lake, he said "The kingdom of God is like that." If he saw a woman at work in her kitchen, measuring her meal and mixing her leaven, he said "The kingdom is like that." The kingdom of God is like everything your eyes rest upon, if you can see it. It is there all the time; you have not to wait for something to break in from without. There is no

cataclysm, no divine rushing interference: the kingdom is here.

That was the message of Jesus, and when he talked like that, he was not blind to life's anomalies or to life's difficulties. He did not imagine that evil did not exist; he knew it was there; but he saw the oneness of the world beneath the diversities. He said, "The sower goes forth to sow; he sows one seed, but some of it falls on the wayside and is snatched away by the birds; some falls on shallow ground; some falls amidst thorns and is choked; some on good ground. But it is one truth."

The kingdom of God is like a man who sowed good seed, but an enemy sowed tares, and presently they said to him, "Behold the tares amidst the wheat; shall we pluck away the tares?" and he said, "Let both grow together till the harvest."

You can not get rid of evil like that; it will be there until the end; let them grow together. The kingdom of God is not absent because the tares are growing with the wheat. The harvest is one complete thing.

The kingdom of God is like a fisherman, who cast out his net, and lo, it encompassed a great multitude of fishes—some of them good and some bad. You must wait until the end before you separate the good from the bad. But the net is one.

The kingdom of God to him was not a thing that did not exist because evil remained; the kingdom was there in the midst of evil, if you had eyes to see.

"There is nothing new under the sun," said the pessimist long, long ago. There is nothing that man has found out in all the long centuries of his life upon the planet that was not there potentially in the beginning. All man's great discoveries have been simply discoveries of how to avail himself of things that were already there.

You remember the traditional tale of how Hans Lippershey, looking out through a shop window, accidentally placed in line two lenses which he held in either hand so that his sight, passing through the convex and concave glasses, saw the steeple of a neighboring church as it were drawn nearer to him. It was only the discovery of how to use old things that made new worlds swim into view.

When Fulton learned how to make the first steamship, you remember how he used to watch the ferry-man, a returned soldier who had lost his arms but yet wanted to earn a living. He had devised two paddles which he could work with his feet so that they turned in the water and propelled his boat. And Fulton said, "I want something that will drove a propeller like that and I shall have a ship." Steam was a most familiar thing—he had but learned how to use it.

Electricity is not a new thing; it was there in the days of Abraham; but at last men discovered how to avail themselves of it, and the world took on new characteristics. The kingdom had been there all the time, but men had not known how to live as its citizens.

When the minds of men opened to the wonders of wireless telegraphy, it was not because it was a new thing, it was only because they had found out the existence of an old thing.

There are wonders yet coming upon us which will make the triumphs of our day seem mere child's play. There are things men will do in the future, maybe in the near future, before which the imagination at this moment would reel in utter unbelief. But, whatever he does, he will never make a new thing—he will only discover and put himself into harmonious relationship with some old, old thing that the Creator placed, potentially at any rate, in the heart of his world when he launched it upon its course.

Jesus would have us believe it is the same with moral dynamics as it is with physical dynamics. You do not want God to break in with new and awful power, you only want to open your heart to him and put yourself in harmonious relationship with powers that already exist. The kingdom of God is among you, the kingdom of God is here!

Ah, but you say, "How can you talk like that in a world as we see it to-day? Are you blind; are you not conscious of the utter wretchedness, the starvation, the hatred, the turmoil, the unrest, that make the almost monotonous configuration of the world as we look out upon it?" Yes, I am conscious of all that. No man has a right to forget the background of the world's tragedy in these days, but still I repeat, the kingdom of God is here, it is among you, within you. The reason of that chaos is that men have not lived in this world as if the kingdom of God was really here. Some of them were teaching that the world was utterly bad, and as such was only doomed to judgment. Some were teaching that the economic laws were not consonant with religious faith. They have been dislocating the world; they have been treating it wrongfully, manipulating it, breaking its harmonies, destroying its music, and because it is the kingdom of God, it is all ajangle with discords. We have been acting in it as if it were a jungle of wild beasts, and the great discovery we have got to make and remake is how to live in it as citizens of God's kingdom—that is the only way. I am not blind to evil; I know its presence, I know its power, but the test of life and the essence of life, the last great purpose surely of the divine Being, is to bring into existence at last an ever-growing race of men and women who will live within the world that he has made like citizens of the kingdom of God.

We have to make a rediscovery of the power of moral forces; we have to learn that we must give ourselves to the discovery of moral dynamics with the same earnestness that we give ourselves to the mastery of physical power. We have to learn that God will flow in upon us in the realm of the soul as he flows in upon us when, with our lamps of knowledge, we enquire into the secret of the laws of nature. It is just the discovery that, in spite of all apparent contradictions, the kingdom of God is with us that is the supreme discovery to which our Lord referred so often in his parables.

I love this parable of the treasure hid in a field, but I love still more this parable of the pearl-seeker:

The kingdom of heaven is like unto a merchantman seeking goodly pearls, who, when he had found one pearl of great price, went and sold all that he had and bought it.

No pearl-seeker goes out to seek one pearl of great price; he goes out to seek pearls—any pearls. He is a lover of pearls, he will be interested in a pearl wherever he finds it, whether small or great; he will pay its appropriate price and gather it into his stock. It is a systematic search; it is a love for little pearls, for all manner of pearls, until one day his unceasing search at last brings him face to face with one great pearl. It is a parable of diligent search and of speculative faith, for it is one thing to buy a field and another thing to buy a pearl. You might not find a market for your great pearl; you must take the risk of that; but this man loves the beauty of pearls so much, is so fascinated by the grandeur and the loveliness of this one, that he takes the risk and sacrifices many a smaller thing that he may lay hold of this one great thing that makes the world beautiful for him.

The kingdom of God is not a lucky find—the kingdom of God is the reward of diligent search. The kingdom of God is a challenge to speculative faith, an appeal to heroism, an appeal to constructive ability; it is the laying out of life in a solemn conviction; it is a test everywhere; it is a battle all the time.

The kingdom of God is like my pulpit. I must occupy it if I can as if we were children of God, as if the supreme thing were to bring one another so far as possible into relation with God. If the day ever comes when that seems impossible, if the day ever comes when conscience leads one way and interest another, the kingdom of God may seem like a pearl of great price, and a man, if he be true, must sell all he has to keep his pearl.

The kingdom of God is like your business. Ah, but you say, "You do not know what business is like these days, with its keen competition, its unscrupulous buying and selling, its breaking of contracts, and its ruthless disregard of mere philanthropy —you do not know what business is like." Yes, I do, but that is where the test comes in. It may be you started in your business career with very high ideals, but when you faced facts and the pressure of things came down upon you, you surrendered your ideal and said, "I must do as other men do," and now the kingdom to you is a vague memory of bygone hopes. In short, you failed. You should have sold all that you had to be true to the kingdom; not recklessly, but even in the days when you were swept away by the power of the system, you should have battled to recover your feet. Even in the days when you went wrong and it seemed as if you could not help it, you should not have succumbed, you should have struggled back, for business itself is only possible in the long run by virtue of the principles of the kingdom of God. If you let go your moral restraint, you are only doing what, if everybody else did, would soon result in having no business to do at all.

The kingdom of God is no cheap, easy thing; Jesus never said so; what he said was, "It is here, and if men are brave enough, patient enough, persistent enough, loyal enough, they can enter into it."

H. G. Wells, in his *Outline of History*, says of Napoleon Bonaparte:

His fascination lies in his sheer unscrupulousness. He was a record—a record plunger. He was as few men are, or dare to be, a scoundrel, bright and complete. He had no religion; no moral conflict ever disturbed him; and this self-conceit and fundamental atheism made him at least magnificently direct. What we want to do secretly more or less he did in the daylight. Directness was his distinctive and immortalizing quality. In all history, there is no figure so completely antithetical to the figure of Jesus of Nazareth, whose pitiless and difficult doctrine of self-abandonment and self-forgetfulness we can neither disregard nor yet bring ourselves to obey. In that antithesis lies the essential historical importance of Napoleon.

I do not want to create in your minds a discussion concerning Napoleon, but we all know something of that spirit, the spirit that must have directness. There is the man who in his business would like to act according to the ethics of Christ, but there is one thing he wants still more, and that is wealth; he puts that first and misses the other. We would all like the principles of Christ brought into our national concerns. We have nearly wrecked the world with the other thing, and we are trying to feel our way back, but we like directness, and we say, "We must have our safeguards."

"Britannia must rule the waves."

"Germany must be over all."

"France must be secure against her ancient enemy, and have her natural frontiers."

"Russia must find her way to the sea."

"America must safeguard her Monroe Doctrine."

Yes, and we go the way of directness until we strike the rocks. Maybe, if we sought first the kingdom of God, all these things would be added to us. Maybe, if Germany had sought first the kingdom, her genius for organization might have given her a legitimate supremacy. She tried to gain it by the sword and lost. Maybe, if France would go the way of the kingdom of God, she would cease to have an ancient enemy and find instead a neighbor. Maybe, if Britain would go the way of the kingdom of God, she would be supreme upon the seas by reason of her native talent for seamanship, and would not need to keep it so much by the power of her blatant cannon. Maybe, if America would take her share more fully in human service, she would find her security not in the separating sea, but in the uniting force of brotherhood.

Maybe the way of the kingdom of God is the right way after all. Maybe we have not organized sufficiently our capacity for right; maybe we never explain our reasons, but we put second things first, until the world becomes a torn thing, and we say at last, "We can not reconcile the kingdom of God with the things we hold to be necessary." I know! That simply means we are not big enough, or intelligent enough yet, that is all.

Jesus did not despise the untoward elements that were in his life. He had a traitor at his very board, who betrayed him while he dipped his finger in the dish; but he did not hate the traitor, he took him as part of life. He had men all around him who were thirsting for his blood, but he did not hate them; he took them like the fisherman takes the bad fish with the good. He saw the cross looming up against the storm-swept sky, and he took it as part of the things that belong to the kingdom, and had faith enough to believe that even with the cross he could win through.

He was not so unpractical as men think. The facts are with him. He did build a kingdom which has lasted longer than any other kingdom the world has ever seen. He has proved for us that the world is a kingdom of God for those who will live in it like its citizens. It is not mere idealism I am preaching. I have had enough buffetings and seen enough of life to know that you can not talk the kingdom into existence, but it makes all the difference in the world when a man sees that, in spite of everything, this world is athrill with the divine presence, and all that is wrong with it is that we are not clean enough, not brave enough, not patient enough, not constructive enough in the things of the kingdom of God. It is a truth that once perceived, even amidst the storm, once grasped, even amidst the conflict, is like a pearl of great price. It is worth fighting for; it is worth holding on to; it is worth selling all that you have to make it clear at last to your own soul, if not to anybody else, that the world is not a jungle full of wolves, but is God's world, full of his spirit, and its basic thing after all is not hate, but love.

DOING THE IMPOSSIBLE

President Emeritus WILLIAM H. CRAWFORD, D.D., Allegheny College, Meadville, Pa.

I can do all things.—Phil. 4:13.

These words may sound to some like the utterance of a bold braggart. The ancients would think some god had spoken. The utterance is certainly striking. But if you could know the man—what he had in reserve, what his resources were and what were the circumstances—you would feel that the man could make good his claim, "I can do all things."

What a man does in this world depends largely on what he thinks he can do. If he thinks he can do nothing, that is what he does. If he has large confidence in himself, but not too large, he can achieve results worth while. There are certain things in life which we may do or not do, and it will make little difference. There are other things we must face as duties; we must do them or suffer loss. Sometimes we must suffer tremendous loss. On the other hand, if we do the things, we attain results in character and influence. This principle holds in all the affairs of our human life. Some men take a very serious view of life's activities. Others do not.

Have you noticed how men differ in the way they look at politics? Some say "Politics are bad. They are rotten. They can not be made good, and there is no use trying." Others seem to be born with the idea that they are to reform politics. Not all these reformers would go at their task in the same way. One man would begin by reforming his party. I saw in one of the papers the other day a statement that Senator Beveridge of Indiana would in all probability be the man who would clean house in the Republican party and so renovate the party that it would have a new lease of life and wield larger influence in the life of the nation than ever before. There are those in the Democratic party who say, and say openly, that the Republican party has lost its chance and that there is no hope for its future. Its sins are too many. "It is the Democratic party," they say, "with its true Jeffersonian simplicity, but under new management, which is the hope of the country if we are to right ourselves as we ought to in a way to meet our responsibilities to ourselves and to other nations." I do not pretend to say which is right. But I would rather take my stand with either one than with the man who says "We can do nothing." I would say the same thing about religion and morality and all social affairs. Just here may I ask, "What shall be your attitude and mine toward the fundamental institutions of our human society? What about the home? Shall we do something about it, or shall we do nothing? What about the school? Shall we do something about it, or do nothing? What about the Church? Shall we do something about it, or shall we do nothing? What shall we do about law and order? Shall we do something or nothing? I put these questions straight, for I want you to answer them. The answer which the American people gives to these questions will determine the future of the American nation. These are questions which can not be trifled with.

There is an infinite variety of possible human activities. They may be classified in various ways. For my purpose I propose this classification, that all human activities of whatever kind may be put into one of three groups. First, there are things which are easy to do. Second, there are the things which are hard to do, and third, there are the impossible things. There you have the three groups: the easy thing, the hard thing, the impossible thing! Some of you may be a bit startled that I include the impossible things in a program of life's activities. I do it with good reason, as I shall explain later. I want first to say something about the easy things and the hard things.

The greatest drag in human society to-day is that such a large number of people choose the easy thing. You have heard of the line of least resistance. Well, that is the line

they take. Life is a heavy burden for many people because of the number who shirk burdens. Life would be a very different thing if there could be an evening up in the bearing of responsibility. Because a multitude choose to do the easy thing there are others who must bear burdens too grievous to be borne. This is what causes a large part of the friction and disorder in a time of strikes such as the present. If every man was doing his part, his share, differences that arise could be settled much more easily. It is the shirkers who are largely responsible for throwing society out of joint. The trouble is that those "take-it-easy people" are in the majority. I do not pretend to say that none of this group is in what is called the working class. Many of them carry lunch baskets and dinner pails; they are in offices and mills and factories. But many of them are only marking time. They have no interest in their work. They get no promotions because they do not deserve promotion. They are the first to be laid off when the slack time comes.

What is true in what is called the labor world is true in the professions, in business, and in all the activities which go to make up the life of the community. They who choose to do the easy thing, or nothing, are in the church, in the school, in philanthropies, in social affairs, and in the home. Wherever they are, they are a burden. What they ought to do is laid on the shoulders of others. That is why so many people break down. They are carrying their own load and the load of other people.

I come now to the second group—those who choose to do the hard thing. These are the producers. They are the dependable ones. They are the people without whom human society could not get on. They are doing a large share of the world's work. Fortunately, we have a goodly number in this group. You see the spirit of the group in the boy. One of the proudest days of my life was in my early teens, when I was entrusted by my father to drive a span of horses alone and take a load of corn to market, fourteen miles away. It was a proud day because I had been given the chance to do a man's work, and I did it. I was down on one of the docks the other day where men were carrying sacks from the deck of a boat to the freight room. A son of one of the men was there and I saw him tug at a sack, which he finally got on his shoulder and carried it to the pile where the others were being carried. I wish you could have seen that boy's face as he dropped the sack to its place. One could see there the proud consciousness of having done something fine. He had done a man's task, perhaps for the first time. It was a proud moment for him. We are fortunate in having a very large number of boys of this type. They are the hope of the country. They will choose the hard thing if they see it is worth while. Show them the importance of the job and they'll tackle it.

Some years ago I sat one Sunday evening in the great St. James' Hall in West London. It was crowded to its capacity, gallery and all. At the time for the opening of the service the minister stepped to the front of the platform and said, "There are thousands of young men in West London to-night who are mourning the loss of a personal friend in the death of Mr. Quintin Hogg, founder of the Polytechnic. Before beginning our service I suggest that we all rise and remain standing while the band plays the Funeral March as a tribute of respect to the memory of our good friend who has gone from us." The band played and the audience rose and remained standing with visible and audible signs of deep emotion. Up to that night I had known almost nothing of Quintin Hogg. The next morning I went out Oxford Street as far as the Circus and then took Regent to the Polytechnic. There I found Charlie Studd, who told me the story of their founder. Quintin Hogg was the son of a wealthy merchant of West London. He was sent to Eton College to be educated. His record in college was good. He stood well in his studies and took active part in athletics. Eton was finished with credit to himself and his family. Coming back home he began to think of what he should do in life. He didn't have to do anything. He was the son of a rich man. But the spirit of work was in him. One day he saw a company of ragged boys at the side of the street playing marbles. He said to himself, "Something more ought to be done for the ragged boys of West London." He started to try to teach them in quarters down by the Thames Embankment. But he didn't get on. Finally he said, "The trouble is, I do not know the language of these boys." He spent a sleepless night walking about Trafalgar Square and the Strand. Next day he had on old clothes and a slouch hat and with a shoeblack's kit he was down in the street with the shoeshine boys. That day he shined shoes with the rest of the boys and at night he slept where they slept. He worked with them until he could say, "I know the language of these boys now and I know what they want." Then he went with the boys who hold horses, then with the street sweepers, and then with other groups until at last he could say, "I know now the language of all the ragged boys of West London, I know what they want and what they need." Then he founded a small school which grew to be the great Polytechnic. More than 6,000 boys had gone out into the various trades and occupations when I was there. Quintin Hogg knew every boy by name. He gave his entire fortune for the school and the boys. If you will go out Regent Street to-day you will find his form in heroic bronze and two of his boys with him. Quintin Hogg gladly gave his life to doing the hard thing, and his work has been a blessing to tens of thousands of boys. You know men and women, many of them, and so do I, who are doing just that kind of work. Jacob Riis did it here in New York City; Jane Addams is doing it in Chicago. One of the most conspicuous examples we have in the public life of this country was Theodore Roosevelt. They are the type who heed the Scripture, "Whatsoever thy hand findeth to do, do it with thy might."

I come now to the last group—they who do the impossible. Some years ago I was on a Mediterranean Line steamer. We stopped at Gibraltar. Since boyhood I had wanted to see that great rock fortress. As we were going up to the great chambers where the guns used to be, I saw far up on the side of the wall we were passing a beautiful flower. I said to the British soldier who was my guide: "My, but there is a beautiful flower. I stopped. I looked at it. Seeing my interest, the guide said, "Would you like to have it?" I said, "Would you be allowed to pluck it?" His answer was, "Oh, I think the law of the unclimbable wall would permit that." Almost before I knew it, he had the toe of his shoe in a crevice in the wall and then was up ten feet or more and then back with my flower. "The law of the unclimbable wall"? I had never heard the expression before. It meant for my guide that there was not another soldier in the fort who could do what he had done. For them it was the "unclimbable wall"—the impossible thing.

Not many years ago I was guest at a dinner of the American Society in London at the Hotel Cecil. Marconi was there. He had on a beautiful new decoration, given him only two days before by the King of Italy. Why were the King of Italy and all the world honoring Marconi at that time? It was because he had been sending quick messages without a wire. He had done what every one else regarded the impossible. We are just now mourning the loss of Graham Bell. Why is it that his name has gone so far? He transmitted the human voice by wire. He did the impossible. Why does such fame attach to the name of Andrew Carnegie? This is why. He introduced new method and organization into the manufacture of steel. I would suggest to every young man of ambition that he will do well to include the doing of the impossible into the program of his life's activities. It is seeing what others do not see and doing what others do not do which makes the truly great man.

But Paul meant more than this when he said, "I can do all things." In fact, he said more than I have quoted him as saying. He said, "I can do all things through Christ, who strengtheneth me." Paul believed in a strength divine which might be his in emergency. Paul had known some very trying experiences. He had been given up for dead more than once. Perhaps as he wrote he remembered the praise service in the jail at Philippi, how the people thought him a god when the cripple was healed at Lystra, the liberty given him on Mars Hill, or the power of the truth at Antioch. He certainly remembered that in all his long ministry not a day had gone by without some exhibition of a power more than human—a power that could take hold of a vile heart and change it, a profligate life and reform it, an ill-built character and reconstruct it. No wonder he could say, "I can do all things through Christ."

If there were time I might bring testimony from many. And I might select witnesses from each of the nineteen centuries since the gospel was preached in Jerusalem and in Rome.

I may be speaking to men who are standing here on the deck of this boat [1] who feel the need of more strength for their task. Some of you may feel that you are facing the impossible. May I earnestly commend to you my Christ, of whom the great apostle to the Gentiles said, "I can do all things through Christ, who strengtheneth me." I do not attempt to explain it, but there is a strength in Jesus Christ which is more than human. That strength is for you and me if we will have it.

---

[1] This sermon was preached on the steamer *De Witt Clinton* of the Hudson River Day Line.

THE CHRISTMAS LYRIC [1]

So interwrought are some compositions with certain impressive occasions or illustrious names that it is quite impossible to think of one and not the other. One seldom hears, for instance, the stately measures of the famous march in *Lohengrin* without thinking of a wedding, particularly a church wedding. The stirring hymn, "A Mighty Fortress Is Our God," suggests the name of Martin Luther. Thomas Knox's "Why Should the Spirit of Mortal Be Proud?" serves to recall the life of Abraham Lincoln, whose favorite poem it was. Comes Christmas—and the one passage of Scripture that the occasion invariably selects is Saint Luke's story of the birth of Jesus. Last night in many a home this story was read to children just before they said "Our Father Who Art in Heaven" or "Now I Lay Me Down to Sleep." In tens of thousands of churches this morning this Scripture will be read and made the basis of innumerable sermons.

Comment upon so flawless a production seems superfluous until one remembers that it is possible to praise this narrative extravagantly and at the same time not relate it in any practical way to present-day affairs or personal life. This is a peril always present, a tendency everywhere observable.

---

[1] From *When Jesus Wrote on the Ground*, by EDGAR DEWITT JONES. George H. Doran Company, 1922.

To-day, with tokens of the Christmas event on every hand and this place still vibrant with the melody of "Silent Night," we can do nothing better than to reflect on this Christmas lyric, for such it is—a hymn set to music by the Holy Spirit.

The poetry of this passage is exquisitely fine. Could anything of the kind be lovelier or more simply told than the birth of Jesus as chronicled by "the beloved physician." Here is an event—the most momentous of all history, yet in its telling there is no embellishment nor any tendency to lengthen out detail. The entire twenty verses tucked away in a corner of a modern newspaper would attract little attention and might easily be overlooked. In twelve sentences the world's greatest love-story is told; tho birth of humanity's most colossal figure described.

The scene here described is pastoral, and the locality already famed in Biblical lore. Over these same hills, hundreds of years before, David had tended his father's flock and fought successfully the lion and bear that attacked the sheep. Years later the shepherd king, familiar with both the sweets and the bitterness of renown, musing on his boyhood days, commemorated them in that psalm of psalms—the psalm of the shepherd's crook, of green pastures and still waters. On these identical hills, to the shepherds abiding in the fields and keeping watch over their flock, the good news came. Jesus' life was curiously linked with shepherds and the shepherding ministry. He called himself the Good Shepherd, spoke of his disciples as his flock, and said that he had "other sheep" not of the recognized fold.

Why were shepherds so signally honored as to be the first to hear the good tidings? Why was not this stupendous event communicated first to a group of learned rabbis or others of the wise, the renowned, and the great? Is God a respecter of persons? Was this high honor reserved for peasants just because they were poor? Was this distinction withheld from the learned, the great, the rich, just because they were learned, and great, and rich? I think not. There is, to be sure, a fitness in the fact that the first heralding of Jesus' coming should have been to the humble and the lowly. The great majority of the peoples of earth are poor and their lives a battle for bread and for shelter almost from the cradle to the grave. Even so, we may believe that this was not the chief reason that shepherds were the first to learn of the Savior's birth. Rather was it not because they were best fitted spiritually to receive the great word? Edersheim, learned author of one of the best-known lives of Christ, says that the flocks of sheep watched and tended in the vicinity of Jerusalem were for sacrifice in the temple and that their guardians were not ordinary shepherds. Whether he is correct or not, we can not be far wrong in assuming that the watchers of the flock that night of nights possessed a certain preparation of mind and affections to receive the revelation. The learned, the famous, the exalted of that day, as possibly of all other days, were troubled about many things. Their lives were already full and, after the manner of the inn at Bethlehem, they had no room for the great gift.

So it came about that the great light shone upon the shepherds as they kept watch by night over the sheep. An angel of the Lord stood by them and proclaimed the good tidings of great joy; then others of the celestial band appeared, and they praised God, saying—"Glory to God in the highest." Angels! How the word revives memories that bless and burn. Angels! Messengers of almighty God; visitants from a better order of society than this world of sin and death. Angels! Blessed belief that God has his messengers of mercy, his heralds of hope, his personal representatives who can go anywhere, at any time, under any conditions. Angels! The word vivifies my remembrance of a little girl, nearing the boundaries of the unseen and struggling for life; her speech no longer coherent but on her lips, clear and distinct one word was repeated over and over again—"Angels, angels, angels!" Oh, the exquisite poetry, the lovely language, the unending glory of this Christ lyric of Jesus' birth in Bethlehem.

It was not a mere contingency that the birth of Jesus should be inseparably linked with peace among men. Peace on earth is the note exultant in this lyric of Christmas. The New Testament is a book of peace, not of battles; a book that pronounces a blessing upon the peace-makers and promises that they shall be called the children of God. Between the peace spirit and ideals of the gospel and the history of nineteen centuries called Christian, there is something incongruous, discordant, and discouraging. Save for brief seasons and in restricted areas peace on earth has not yet prevailed. Christendom has much to her stock of credit—much that is glorious and monumental, but Christendom has yet to know the victory of peace on earth. No sadder spectacle has the world beheld than that of the followers of the Prince of peace hacking each other down with the sword, assailing each other with gases that scorch and shrivel the lungs, blasting each other to bits with bombs, drowning each other at sea by the wholesale, hymning hate against each other to the bitter end.

Peace on earth depends upon the good will between men. As long as hate reigns in the human heart, as long as covetousness crowds out the spirit of brotherliness, as long as jealousy and envy hold their sway over mankind, so long will wars endure. Mere limitation of armament is not enough —that of itself would be only a makeshift if the causes that produce war are not abolished. Destroy every battle-ship, scrap every submarine, wreck every bombing plane, muster out the soldiery now in ranks— do all this, but make no intelligent and consistent effort to create a new heart in man or open up a new outlet for his enthusiasms and ambitions, and some kind of war enginery, like the harvest of that famed crop of dragon teeth, will spring up over night. . . .

More people are thinking peace to-day than ever before. The voice of the people in solemn protest is being heard in the councils of the nations with a new insistence; but make no mistake, the millennium is not at hand. The voice of the profiteer, the militarist, the granite-hearted materialist who walks by sight and not by faith—their voices are still potent in behalf of armaments and a continuance of the old order. Not only so, but the motives for world peace must be deeper than for mere economic reasons if peace on earth endure.

If disarmament is desired chiefly because it would reduce taxes and produce a revival of business, we may believe that army and naval disarmament might come to pass, and we should have in its stead a commercial and industrial armament as deadly and as difficult to conquer as the old and familiar kind. Peace on earth—

well it simply can not come until there is good will among men. Good will among men is retarded by racial pride, handicapped by commercial jealousies, hindered by biased partizanship, crippled and hamstrung by a mean and narrow sectarianism. The core of Jesus' teaching is the supremacy of love and of sacrifice, the ministry of service and of mercy, the mightiness of right and justice. If we are to have peace among men, men must know the peace which is Christ's. His peace was an inward experience before it became an outward manifestation. His peace was a result of obedience to the laws of the spirit. He walked in full fellowship with the Father because from a child he learned obedience. It is possible for society to keep the laws in a formal way and still bend and break the laws of love and remain anarchists in the realm of the spiritual.

There will never be peace on earth until that gospel of good will which Jesus taught be mediated through the lives of those who accept his teaching, and narrow nationalism, racial hostilities, and sectarian bigotry give way to a Christian commonwealth—world-wide in its scope.

In the very center of this matchless story is the Child; the chief actor in this world drama is the Babe at Bethlehem. The shepherds, the angels, the manger, the star—these are all incidental. Christianity began with a child, and no teaching of Jesus is more fundamental than when he said: "Suffer the little children to come unto me; forbid them not, for of such is the kingdom of God." What gesture of Jesus was of more consequence than when, having been asked by his disciples who should be regarded as the greatest in the kingdom of heaven, he called to him a little child and set him in the midst of them, and said: "Verily, I say unto you, except ye turn and become as little children, ye shall in no wise enter into the kingdom of heaven." Childhood has been wronged terribly, and the rights of the child have been as flagrantly disregarded as the rights of womanhood. Babies have not always counted for much; there are places still where they count for little. There are corners of the earth where the gospel has not yet come where babies, especially girl babies, are slain ruthlessly and in great numbers; places where a puny or deformed baby is quickly put out of the way. There are plague spots of so-called

Christian countries where babies are not born, but damned into the world, with scarcely a chance to live, to love, and to be loved. It was the Christ himself who declared that it was not God's will that his little ones should perish. It is often man's will that the little ones suffer and die so young. Sometimes this is due to ignorance, sometimes to a perverse heart and a wrong conception of what Christianity is.

Yes, a baby is in the center and at the very heart of this lyric of Saint Luke's gospel. God's greatest gift to the world came as a child—a helpless babe, born amidst poverty and off to one side of the highways of the world. Theodore Parker once said that a baby is better for the heart than a whole academy of philosophers, and of course he was right. A young missionary madonna, after bending over her first-born, wrote to friends at home—"I had no idea being a mother was so wonderful." The advent of a child in a home is always occasion for wonderment, a never-ceasing miracle, and to the seeing eye every mother's man-child is haloed with a glory that only the mother-heart may know. Wordsworth was never more seer-like than when he wrote

Heaven lies about us in our infancy.

And there are other lines in the same noble ode that have peen praised much, but not too much—

Our birth is but a sleep and a forgetting:
The soul that rises with us our life's star—
    Hath had elsewhere its setting,
    And cometh from afar,
        Not in entire forgetfulness,
        And not in utter nakedness,
But trailing clouds of glory do we come
From God, who is our home.

There is something in the touch of the hand of a little child more enchanting than that of a fairy's wand. I can understand how the hard heart of the leading character in a famous story melted utterly when he felt a child's soft cheek against his, and the tiny fingers on his neck and behind his ears and in his hair. Then the trustfulness and the affection and the faith of a little child: what is there in all the world so irresistible?

Well do I remember arriving in the Union Station at St. Louis on a blustery winter night some years ago, and alighting from the car with me was a young mother and her baby, a beautiful child, possibly a year old. She was heavily burdened with baggage, and I offered to carry the child for her. She was a real mother, for she took a good look at me—a searching look—and then she handed the baby over to me. She expected to be met by some of her kinspeople in the station, so she informed me, no one appeared, and after we had waited and looked about for some little time she said, "Would you mind keeping baby while I call up my relatives here?" Time was when such a request would have set me quaking and filled me with a nameless sort of fear, but that time was a good ways in the past. Only five hours before I had said good-by to my own frisky five. So I kept baby, and his mother disappeared in the direction of a telephone booth. She was gone a good ten minutes, and during her absence I paced up and down the long waiting room holding the little fellow snug in my arms. He was a dear; he was content; he trusted me perfectly. He rested his velvety cheek against mine and gazed at me out of his big blue eyes as one who had absolute faith, never doubting but that even a stranger would protect him from the smallest harm. His little soft hand stole round my neck and rested there ever so lightly. I thought of these lines:

Softer it seemed than the softest down
On the breast of the gentlest dove,
And its timid press and its sweet caress
Were strong in the strength of love.

By and by and his mother returned. I helped her and her young son into a taxi and said good-night, and the little stranger vanished out of my life as quickly as he came into it, but he left a memory tender and precious.

God hath joined together the cradle and Christmas. Christianity has coronated childhood. God gives us children, but the molding of them for better or for worse—that ministry is our own. Christ put the child in our midst, but society has for a greater part set him to one side—neglected, slighted, and wronged him. If we want peace on earth there is a way to get it: train the child in the teachings of Jesus; train him to think peace, not war; rear him in the ideals of brotherhood; teach him the supremacy of service—but to do that successfully the child must have for environment a society that is Christian not only on Sunday but seven days in the week.

Christmas helps us to evaluate the children in our home at their truth worth. Surely the blessed birthday of our Lord is a family festival like unto no other. There is a story which inspired a much admired painting called "Content." A Chinese beggar is shown coming in before his king. With the beggar are two small sons. He claims to be penniless; he asks for money. The king promises to give him all his heart should desire, but there is one condition: the beggar must give in return one-half of his visible wealth. To this he readily agrees for he believes he has no wealth. Then the king mentions in detail his payment, and the first item he calls for is one of the lads. The beggar had not thought of his boys as wealth and he is staggered by the request. In the end, the mendicant goes away from the court with an arm about each boy, content with what he has. The story is good as far as it goes, but it does not go far enough. It is costly to rear children and give them a chance in the world. If society were really Christian, beggars would be rare, and rarer still the children of beggars, to be dwarfed, hindered, and cursed by poverty's blight.

Christmas in many a home this year can not but be different from Christmas a year ago. Oh, what a company of children whose shouts and merry laughter made music a year ago have since gone from us by way of the great pilgrimage of death. How small their feet and how brave to take that long journey with never a doubt or fear! Thrice blessed is the truth that the Christmas lyric includes not only poetry, charm, and color, but comfort as well. He whose birth we commemorate—he who said: "Suffer the little children to come unto me'—shall he not bless and comfort the heavy heart in the homes where Christmas to-day is not the same nor ever can be as it was ere the charmed circle was broken? It was the Christ who said of these little ones, "their angels do always behold the face of my Father who is in heaven."

O Christmas, merry Christmas!
    Is it really come again?
With its memories and greetings,
    With its joy and with its pain.
There's a minor in the carol,
    And a shadow in the light,
And a spray of cypress twining
    With the holly-wreath to-night.
And the hush is never broken
    By laughter, light and low,
As we listen in the starlight
    To the "bells across the snow."

O Christmas, merry Christmas!
    'Tis not so very long
Since other voices blended
    With the carol and the song!
If we could but hear them singing
    As they are singing now,
If we could but see the radiance
    Of the crown on each dear brow,
There would be no sighs to smother,
    No hidden tear to flow,
As we listen in the starlight
    To the "bells across the snow."

O Christmas, merry Christmas!
    This never more can be;
We can not bring again the days
    Of our unshadowed glee.
But Christmas, happy Christmas,
    Sweet herald of good will,
With holy songs of glory
    Brings holy gladness still.
For peace and hope may brighten,
    And patient love may glow,
As we listen in the starlight
    To the "bells across the snow."

THE CHILDREN'S SERVICE
THE CREATION STORY
The Rev. WAYLAND ZWAYER, Ridley Park, Pa.

God created the world a long, long time ago. How long ago we do not know, but it was so very long ago that no one has been able to find out when. Some people make guesses, but each man who writes a book about it makes a different guess. So all we know is that God made the world a long, long time ago.

And God spent a long, long time in making this world, and that is just exactly what you would expect him to do. He does not make boys and girls into men and women in a few minutes. He spends years and years helping them to grow up. That is God's way. If you plant an apple-seed in the spring you will not have apples by summertime. Nature is God's plan; it takes years to grow a tree big enough to bear apples.

When, in school, you study how trees and flowers grow, you are studying some of God's plans. When you study about the formation of coal in the earth, you are studying a long worked-out plan of God. He planned that through the years trees and other vegetation should be pressed down into black coal.

I have read to you a beautiful poem which is the first chapter in our Bible. It was written many years before the first Christmas. It was written long before people could look at the stars through great telescopes; long before people knew how coal was made; far, far back in the time when people thought that the earth was flat and that the sun moved around the earth. And that is just what makes it so wonderful a story. How wonderful, too, that the Hebrew people who knew nothing about what science has since taught us, that those Hebrew people thought God created the world and wrote about it in their literature!

And now I know you are going to ask me a question. You want to know how they knew that God created the world. God must have told them in their hearts. It is your heart that tells you the best things. How do you know that your mother is truly your mother? It is your heart that tells you it is not a lie. Oh, boys and girls, if man can close his eyes and create the thoughts of a beautiful poem; if he can create the undying melody of a song which before its birth was never heard; if Helen Keller, who never saw anything, who never heard anything, can of herself create thoughts and ideas; could not God make the sun and the moon and the stars?

> For the love of God is broader
> Than the measure of man's mind.

And that brings me to the very idea which that old Hebrew writer is trying to tell us. "The world is God's loving wish."[1] A loving God made the world. That is the first verse of the creation story, and the refrain is ever repeated, "God saw that it was good." And so the poem of the Hebrew writer is true in the sense in which he meant it.

Nature is God's book and the Bible is God's book. God put it into the heart of the writer of Genesis to tell us that God made the world, and God gives to other men intellect and imagination with which to study nature and find out how God made it.

[1] *What and Where Is God*, by Swain, p. 213.

And every day we are finding out new things about nature, new things which contradict the way in which old things were explained, but always a little nearer to the truth. Every new truth that we find out is fuller proof to our hearts that the world is God's loving wish.

In a history book which some of you use in school you are told that this creation story came to the Hebrews from the Babylonians. This, most likely, is true. For the Chaldeans and the Phenicians, the Egyptians and the Persians, the Greeks and the Romans, people north and people south, people east and people west, the Chinese, some of the American Indians, almost everybody, had traditions about the creation of the world. But when the writer of the Bible story took the tradition from the Babylonians, he changed it so that it should tell the truth which God had told him in his heart. Most people thought that the gods (for they believed in many gods) who made the world were not good gods. So, in this story of creation, the important thing was to tell the people that the God who made the world is a good God, a loving God, and that he made the world for our good. And just what this world is, and all about it, he left for us to find out.

Tryste Noël

The Ox he openeth wide the Doore,
And from the Snowe he calls her 'inne,
And he hath seen her Smile therefor,
Our Ladye without Sinne.
Now soone from Sleep
A Starre shall leap,
And soone arrive both King and Hinde;
        Amen, Amen:
But O, the Place co'd I but finde!

The Ox hath hush'd his voyce and bent
Trewe eyes of Pitty ore the Mow,
And on his lovelie Neck, forspent,
The Blessed layes her Browe.
Around her feet
Full Warme and Sweete
His bowerie Breath doth meeklie dwell:
        Amen, Amen:
But sore am I with Vaine Travel!

The Ox is host in Judah stall
And Host of more than onelie one,
For close she gathereth withal
Our Lorde her littel Sonne.
Glad Hinde and King
Their Gyfte may bring,
But wo'd to-night my Teares were there,
        Amen, Amen:
Between her Bosom and His hayre!
            —LOUISE IMOGEN GUINEY.

OUTLINES

The Utility of Faith

By faith, Moses, when he was grown up, refused to be called the son of Pharaoh's daughter, choosing rather to share ill-treatment with the people of God than to enjoy the pleasures of sin for a season.—Heb. 11:24-25.

This is the age of efficiency. What good is faith? Epistle written in answer to this very question. Faith fosters unmatched virtues.

I. Faith's resolute composure. "When he was come to years." The thing that makes a man a man. Half our sins arise from lack of it.

II. Faith's penetrating insight. Valuable and worthless: A race of serfs the people of God. Transient and permanent. A splendid court enduring a season. Right and wrong. The pleasures of sin in a "career."

III. Faith's indomitable courage. "Refused." The air of finality. Utter indifference to own comfort. Identification of self with the ideal.

Bad Reasons for Good Conduct

For he sacrificed unto the gods of Damascus, which smote him; and he said, Because the gods of the kings of Syria helped them, therefore will I sacrifice to them, that they may help me. But they were the ruin of him, and of all Israel.—2 Chron. 28:23.

Ahaz sent to Syria for help against Edomites. A man may have bad reason for doing good things.

I. This is a common sin. Many religious only for what they get. Pray only for selves. Go to church for business. Many a minister takes this motto. Frames vocation for livelihood. The religion of bargaining: Jacob—"If thou wilt . . . I will."

II. It is a mistaken course. Such never get what they expect. "It helped him not" —barren prayer. Some answers to prayer worse than none. This often God's only way. Less excusable than love of idols. Because selfish and false.

III. How escape this evil? Get right view of life. "That I may help them," not "That they may help me." Serve only that which you love.

The Disease of Sin

Which is easier, to say, Thy sins are forgiven thee; or to say, Arise and walk?—Luke 5:23.

In Bible sin is a disease. Life bears this out: like woman who touched his garment, we spend much money on physicians and are often worse than better in consequence.

I. Sin easily lends itself to this idea. 1. It is equally unnatural. Sin is not natural since the moral sense emerged and became a part of every normal man. 2. It is equally wasting. It begins in a small way and eats into a man's soul. It monopolizes the soul's nutrition. 3. It is similarly contracted. By infection: you don't seek it, you "get" it. Companions. Resorts. When you are at a low spiritual tone. You get the "flu" when run down.

II. Christ is the celestial surgeon. 1. He heals by spiritual suggestion. As a physician does by mental. 2. He infuses his own virtue and power.

Christ's Miracle in the Soul

I have been crucified with Christ; and it is no longer I that live, but Christ liveth in me.—Gal. 2:20.

Religion is fellowship—in all the phases of Christ's experience: Bethlehem, transfiguration, Golgotha.

I. The soul crucified: "I am crucified." 1. Christ's sufferings not only physical. 2. Christ's sufferings not only temporal. 3. Because spiritual and eternal they can be shared.

II. The soul risen: "Nevertheless I live." 1. All death ends in life. Caterpillar. 2. Always a higher life. Egg. Seed. 3. This verifiable in religious experience.

III. The soul immortal: "Yet not I, but Christ liveth in me." The joy of it. Perpetual, tho sullied. The power of it: can not sin because do not want to. The miracle of it: not new, but renewed.

The Christmas Contribution to World Peace

They shall beat their swords into plowshares. . . Let us walk in the light of the Lord.—Isa. 2:4, 5.

Ideas of world peace are not new. Here is one whose merit has preserved it through more than two thousand years of speculation and strife. Crystallized in the advent, it has grown in favor with the centuries.

I. Centers round a particular individual. Elaborated by highest ethical spirit. Vitalized by religious plan—from "mountain of the Lord's house." Late world conflict revealed futility of war. Every participating nation desired to evade responsibility for starting it. Given the law of righteousness as revealed in Christ, international peace could prevail easily.

II. Basis in world-wide brotherhood. "Wolf and lamb" (Isa. 11:6). William Penn's treaty with Indians. Canada's fortless boundary line. The economic benefit of "good will among men" seen in stock exchange and in mission fields.

III. Fellowship in glorious life-program; "walk in the light of the Lord." Opens channels for nobler service—"heroes of peace"—Grenfell, Sheldon Jackson, Paton, etc.

When the hand that sprinkles midnight
With its powdered drift of suns,
Has hushed this tiny tumult
Of sects and swords and guns;
Then hate's last note of discord
In all God's world shall cease;
In the conquest which is service,
In the victory which is peace.

Foregleams of Christmas

I see him, but not now. I behold him, but not nigh. A star shall arise out of Jacob, etc.—Num. 24:17.

In the springtime children sometimes say, "Forty weeks until Christmas; a long time." Yet here an example of the far-seeing longings of "seers" in the springtime of a spiritual religion. It is one of the far removed "foregleams" of the Christmas star.

I. Flashes from a smoldering fire of expectancy. "The hopes and fears of all the years" (P. Brooks). Contrast the gropings of heathendom.

II. World's longing for light. As eye created for sun's ray, so eye of the soul for rays from Bethlehem's star. Why wise men journeyed. Why thoughtful lives have responded through the succeeding centuries. "Light of the world."

III. World's need of authority. "Scepter as well as star." Sovereign of the soul. Stabilizing peaceful influence. "The Christ of the Andes" which reminds Chili and Argentina of neighborly relations.

A Wise Man's Christmas

We have seen his star . . . and are come to worship.—Matt. 2:2.

We need not confine our meditations to the oriental feelings of those first wise men. Let us broaden our horizon to see the later thousands of thoughtful ones who have paid reverential tribute to the Bethlehem manger. "Worship" implies ascription of "worthship."

I. Recognizing purity and simplicity of life. Pagan as well as Christian has admitted this—Pilate; the centurion, Rousseau. Rich and poor, wise and simple, find common grounds of respect.

II. Recognizing a unique helpfulness in righteousness, neighborliness, comfort, and hope—tests of true worship. Stimulates thought as to the possibilities of life, starting in the humblest.

III. Conceding an unusual form of authority, approaching truth from the experiential angle; introspective in conviction and enthusiastic in application. Wise men departed "another way" since they discerned an authority higher than Herod.

THEMES AND TEXTS

The Rev. WM. S. JEROME, White Pigeon, Mich

The Law of Necessity. "For where a testament is, there must of necessity be the death of him that made it."—Heb. 9:16.

The Fearful Followers. "They that followed were afraid."—Mark 10:32.

Present-day Scripture. "Ye are our epistle, written in our hearts, known and read of all men."—2 Cor. 3:2.

Personality and Providence. "Only, as the Lord hath distributed to each man . . . so let him walk."—1 Cor. 7:17.

Touching the Will. "Hath power as touching his own will."—1 Cor. 7:37.

A Divided Household. "Salute them of the household of Narcissus, that are in the Lord."—Rom. 16:11.

The Responsibility of Power. "I have power to release thee. . . . Pilate sought to release him."—John 19:10-12.

Proportion and Perspective. "Now in the things which we are saying the chief point is this."—Heb. 8:1.

· ILLUSTRATIONS AND ANECDOTES

Transforming the Ugly

A few days before Christmas I was walking down a communication-trench just as a heavy bombardment was ceasing. It was near four o'clock and the sun, a deep red, was almost touching the horizon. A German shell burst some little distance away, high in the air, and formed a black, ugly cloud. Slowly the rays of the sinking sun penetrated the cloud of smoke and turned it to a faint pink. As the pink deepened to rose the cloud expanded under the influence of the soft wind and within a few moments was transformed into a thing of beauty. It hung poised in mid-air, like a rose unfolding its fragrant petals, over the entrenched army. The black cloud was of man's making and revealed his hatred and spite; but its transformation into a thing of beauty and peace was of God's doing and revealed his love and good will as truly as did the rainbow to Noah. God's glorious sun, as it set in blood, turned man's cloud war into heaven's rose of peace.—THOMAS TIPLADY in *The Cross at the Front.*

Modifying Factors Affecting the Body

A Russian naturalist, Ogneff, shut up some goldfish in total darkness for three years, taking care to give them plenty of food and plenty of room. At the end of the three years they were quite blind; the rods and cones (the percipient elements) of the retina had disappeared. This was a negative modification, directly connected with the absence of light and the cessation of vision. A certain amount of functioning seems to be necessary if a normally active structure is to retain its position, its architectural stability.

A Japanese investigator subjected white rats to hard exercise for ninety to one hundred and eighty days, which is comparable to a period of seven to fourteen years in man, for the length of life in the white rat is about three years. What was the result? There was an increase in the weight of the heart, kidneys, and liver, on an average to about twenty per cent. This is an illustration of a modifying influence affecting several parts of the body in a similar way.

It has been shown (by Semper and de Varigny) that the young of the fresh-water snails (*Limonæus*) will develop into dwarfs in an aquarium where aeration is abundant, and food likewise, where indeed everything is satisfactory except that the surface does not give the animals sufficient room for exercise. This is surely a parable for our instruction.

The French have a wise proverb, "By force of striking one becomes a blacksmith" (*C'est à force de forger qu'on devient forgeron*); and this is equally true of the powerful wrist of the violinist. The results of physical exercises show the size and strength of a muscle may be greatly increased by persistent exercise. It seems that the muscle-fibers grow thicker and stronger; we believe we are right in saying that they do not become more numerous.—J. ARTHUR THOMSON, *The Control of Life.*

Light as an Element of Safety

When a lad in the primary department could not understand why my oldest brother wanted so much to go to India and leave "us." There was frequently a package arriving at our house from his strange mission field. It contained Indian trinkets, funny little shoes, and jewelry with a god or two. His letters and boxes from the banks of the Ganges constituted my first lessons in missions. Many years later, when he was back home and I was older and studying to be a preacher, I said to him, "Brother, tell me in ten words the supreme reason for taking the gospel to heathen people." His answer was: "As you multiply their light you increase their chances." Since then our government has recognized light as an element of safety. It sent an army of school-teachers to the Philippines to make the inhabitants safe. When we were boys the jewelry stores put great iron shutters over the windows of their establishments as night came on. With great iron bolts that were run through and fastened on the inside the shutters were made secure. That was their idea of making things safe. Now it is different. If you walk along by those same jewelry stores at night at the present time, you will see no iron shutters, but you will see the store brilliantly illuminated from one end to the other. That is the latest idea of safety.—EDGAR H. CHERINGTON in *The Line Is Busy.*

The Benefit of Hygiene

Since life is so precious and the human engine so valuable, all of our efforts to extend the average duration of each individual's usefulness and productivity are of infinite value. The average duration of human life is 51.5 years. Scientists figure that if we eliminate easily preventable diseases, this would be 60 years. If in addition we were to save the children that are now wasted needlessly in infancy, the country would have approximately twenty million more healthy grown-ups, each producing at least $3 a day. Therefore, it is plain that by simply raising our standard of hygiene, we may effect a saving of $60,-000,000 each and every 24 hours. Here is an economy worth practising, in view of the fact that the war, as wasteful as it was, cost us only $35,000,000 a day. Illiteracy costs us $50,000,000 a day, and industrial incompetence nearly as much.—FLOYD W. PARSONS in *The World's Work.*

The Boy Jesus

A boy of twelve in old Jerusalem one day realized that he had reached the age when he must think for himself and make decisions. Without false ideas of independence he went back to his home and workshop and did the things his parents thought best, but he began that day to live his own life and to make plans for helping the world. He was not ambitious to be rich or famous. He would not fight, and he hated meanness, cruelty, injustice, and hypocrisy. When he grew to manhood he healed sick people, comforted the sorrowful, pitied those who did wrong, divided his food with the hungry, strengthened the weak, and made friends with children. He loved the sea and boats, the hills and fields, flowers and birds. He was brave in danger, patient when persecuted, heroic in temptation, pure in heart, and so loving and unselfish that millions of people who never saw him love him and would lay down their lives for him. He did not preach long sermons—he never wrote a book. You could easily commit to memory all his recorded words. He died poor and almost friendless, and yet we celebrate his birthday throughout the world; we date our letters from the year of his birth; our law is founded on his book; we offer in our Congress and Parliaments prayers in his name. The history of his life is printed in more than five hundred languages, kings and emperors, presidents and judges, statesmen and scholars, peasants and slaves, declare this to be the greatest and best of all books. Thousands of magnificent buildings have been erected to him—abbeys, cathedrals, and churches. Our greatest colleges were dedicated to this poor boy who never went to college, never left his own little country, and died when he was only thirty-three years old. From his life and death painters, poets, orators, and musicians have gained inspiration.—*Everyland.*

Why He Succeeded

Some one tells of coming back to the place she had lived in as a child. Passing a fine big house she read a name on the brass plate upon the door.

"Who is Dr. Joseph Walker?" she asked.

"Why, don't you remember? He lived in a little house close to yours."

"What! Joe Walker who used to pick berries for us in the summer?"

"Do you remember anything about him?"

"No, except that my father said the berries Joe picked never had to be gone over a second time, and he never wasted a moment."

"Well, that's just what they say of him now. That's how he has got on."—*The Evangelical.*

The Divine Watcher

Behold he that keepeth Israel shall neither slumber nor sleep. Ps. 121:4.

Bishop Bashford, in one of his Episcopal tours in China, was one night compelled to sleep outdoors, under the trees, the hotel keeper warning him about marauders. Being watchful and wakeful awhile, he thought of these words of the Psalmist, and then said to the Lord, "There is no use both of us being awake," so he slept the sleep of the just. In the morning he saw a watcher standing guard under a tree; the heathen man was helping God guard his own.

When one asked Alexander the Great how he could sleep so soundly in the midst of danger, he replied, "Parmenio watched." So when we lie down to rest and awaken in the morning, we say, "I am still with him who giveth his beloved sleep." Jacob at Bethel resting on a stony pillow, far away from friends and companions, saw the ladder and the angel, and heard the divine voice saying, "Behold I am with thee and will keep thee in all places whither thou goest." How beautiful it is to know that when we go out to toil and come in to rest, or when we go out of this life into the next, we can say, "My soul, wait thou upon the Lord; he will sustain thee and keep thee. The sun shall not smite thee by day nor the moon by night, for the Lord is thy keeper."   E. W. C.

Types of Men

Three stonemasons working on a cathedral were asked in turn what they were doing. The first answered, "I am waiting until it is 5 o'clock"; the second said, "I am making seven dollars a day"; and the third answered, "I am building a cathedral." The first man was a drudge, the second was a money-maker, and the third was an idealist. The three men outwardly seemed to be doing the same thing, but inwardly they were far apart and were living in different worlds. These three men are ever with us and are at work on every job; and probably all three of them are in each one of us, one or another of them coming to the top on different days as we are in different moods.— *The Continent.*

Art and Personality

Great national ideals are set before the children in such pictures as those of Washington and Lincoln and are associated with song and story in the day school. A bronze statue of Abraham Lincoln stands on the plaza in front of the court-house in the city of Newark, N. J., and it is said that every day little children play about this statue. The figure of Lincoln is seated on a bench on which rests the tall hat that the president was accustomed to wear, and so natural is the pose of the figure that to the children it is like a companion and friend. Recently a passer-by saw three little girls there; one sat on one of Lincoln's knees, another leaned with crossed arms on the

other knee and looked up to the great benevolent face, and the third child, standing on the same knee, wound her arm lovingly against the bronze face. Facts are made clear by means of some pictures, while others are valued for their silent influence that is unconsciously absorbed. — *The Baptist.*

Acquired and Inherited Characteristics

PARABLE OF THE PEACH-TREES

The French biologist Brodage made careful observations on South European peach-trees which had been transplanted to Reunion in the West Indies. As has been noticed in similar cases, they became evergreen,—it took some of them twenty years. The individual constitution was altered; they stopped shedding their leaves in autumn. Now, when seeds of these false-evergreens, modification-evergreens, were sown in certain mountainous districts with a considerable amount of frost, they grew up into evergreen peach-trees. This looks at first sight like a demonstration of the transmission of an acquired character. But one has to remember that a seed is a complex thing with a considerable history behind it; it is not a germ-cell; it is a young plant. The body of the seed had probably been profoundly influenced by the body of the parent plant before separation took place. So it is in mammals and in man. It is necessary to distinguish between what is acquired or imprinted before birth and what is in the strict sense part of the inheritance.—J. ARTHUR THOMPSON, *The Control of Life.*

No Returning

Remember, three things come not back:
The arrow sent upon its track—
It will not swerve, it will not stay
Its speed, it flies to wound or slay;
The spoken word, so soon forgot
By thee, but it has perished not;
In other hearts 'tis living still,
And doing work for good or ill;
And the lost opportunity
That cometh back no more to thee;
In vain thou weepest, in vain dost yearn—
Those three will nevermore return.
—*From the Arabic.*

A HISTORY OF PSYCHOLOGY[1]

This is a very comprehensive work, the first of its kind in important respects, and useful in the highest degree to any one who seeks to show the origins and development of psychological thought. The only previous work that, in any sense, compares with it, is Siebeck's, but this was published thirty or more years ago, and many things have happened in psychology since then. Thus entire areas of psychological investigation, as in the fields of education, social life, mental pathology, the minds of animals and children, etc., have been opened up since Siebeck's work appeared. Such a comprehensive survey of the development of the science of mind, from the days of Thales and Anaximander, down to Wundt, James, Hall, and Dewey, is certain to fill a unique place in scientific literature and to command the interest of all serious students of the human mind.

The first volume is devoted to Ancient and Patristic psychology. In this section of the work, a man unfamiliar with current scientific psychology would inevitably have become lost in the speculations of those periods. But our author is not of that type. He has the genetic clue, and he is able to find in the crude beginnings of mental analysis the things significant for science. Thus throughout ten closely reasoned chapters of this first volume, from the analysis of primitive thought, up through the tortuous development of scientific viewpoints and methods among the Greeks, Hebrews, Alexandrians, and early Christian scholars, on down to Tertullian and Augustine, he shows the historical continuity of men's thoughts about their own minds, distinguishing as clearly as it is possible to distinguish between profitless metaphysical speculations and the well-accredited facts of human consciousness. The author's mental attitude and method are suggested in the opening sentences of the first chapter:

The evolution of thought has followed a course not unlike that which the ancient philosophers described when they traced the genesis of the world out of chaos. As the ordered world arose out of a previous chaotic condition of matter, so experience began with a chaos of facts, a distinctionless mass of data. . . . Psychology is itself a science that has been evolved out of a crude mass of thought by a slow process of specialization. . . . It is impossible to indicate exactly the time when the soul became a specific object of study. The origins of psychology are lost in that general confusion in which the origins of all things were mixed together and no one of them was distinct. To the body of knowledge existing at this stage of mental development we may assign the name Anthropology as indicating the time when there was a definite interest in man, but only an indirect interest in the soul as one of the parts of man. Psychology will then be understood as arising out of anthropology by that process of specialization which we have already mentioned, and the first stage of its history may be called the anthropological period as including popular views of the soul prior to the awakening of a scientific spirit.

The second volume deals with the Medieval and Early Modern Period of psychology. Here we have the same painstaking analysis applied to the influence of Christian theology, Arabian scholarship, early scientific thought in general, and all those beginnings of the modern mind to understand itself, as illustrated in Montaigne, Roger Bacon, Galileo, Francis Bacon, Newton, and all the rest. The more systematic thinkers along psychological lines receive careful attention, and the later divisions of the field of psychology are indicated in the works of Descartes, Hobbes, Spinoza, Comenius, Locke, etc. Part IV of this volume is taken up, first, with the classification of these great pioneers of modern psychological thought, according to nationality, and, second, with the influence and applications of their psychology. Thus the British psychologists, Locke, Berkeley, Hume, and Hartley are

[1] By George Sidney Brett. The Macmillan Company, New York, 1912-1921. Three volumes. 6 x 9 in. Vol. 1, 388 pp; Vol. II, 894 pp; Vol. III, 316 pp.

discussed; then, the French psychologists, Voltaire, Diderot, Candillac, and others; and, finally, the German psychologists, Leibniz, Wolff, Tetens, Tiedemann, and Kant are interpreted. As illustrating the applications of psychology during this period, the beginnings of the various specialized lines of psychological interest and study that are so prominent in our own day are indicated, as Comparative psychology, Physiological psychology, Social psychology, and Religious psychology.

The third volume treats of modern psychology. Here the long course of mental evolution is shown in its current fulfilment in all the manifold activities of the scientific mind in its attempts to interpret itself throughout civilization. There is not a mode of human self-expression, not an institution, that is not now being approached from the psychological point of view. The twentieth century, whatever else it may bring to light,

may well be characterized as an epoch in human thought when men, as individuals and as masses, are becoming self-conscious and are subjecting themselves, as never before, to psychological analysis. The steps in this great current psychological movement are traced by the author, through the new impulse given by the biological sciences of physiology, neurology, etc., under the influence of the evolutionary theory; and through the peculiar interests of the present in social psychology, child psychology, animal psychology, criminology, and psychoanalysis. Thus is rounded out in the third volume a survey of many centuries of mental evolution and an analysis of human forces that, at first revealing themselves in more or less childish questions as to the nature and meaning of man's soul, are now culminating in attempts to control the human mind and re-order civilization in harmony with its fundamental laws.   G. E. D.

THE HISTORY OF ARCHITECTURE[1]

The continuity or separateness of styles—whichever prevails in any national forms of historic structure—depends upon six conditions which are derived from geography, geology, climate, religion, social character, and history. Thus the situation of a special form like the Egyptian stretched along the Nile, or the limitations in space as in New York City, influences the character of the historic structures. Geology determines the materials of building—lasting stone in Egypt, mud bricks (sun-dried or baked in Mesopotamia, etc.). Climate determines the degree and kind of protection to the inhabitants. The close relationship of religion to architecture is witnessed by the attention given to temple, tomb, and church. Social conditions—slavery or serfdom in Egypt (once more) and freedom of thought and execution in Greece—have much to say as to the forms of structures private and public. The historic factor enters when proximity or conquest causes a style to pass, pure or modified, into a neighboring, a conquering, or a subjected country. In this way Egypt influenced Greek forms, and

these in turn passed into Italy, there to be repeated, modified, or combined with the Etruscan and to be used among peoples not then in existence. We are inclined to hold that still another condition exists—the innate genius of a people.

The volume by Sir Banister Fletcher is a new work, rewritten and modeled upon one put out by his father and himself jointly. The condensed results of two lifetimes of work are displayed in a full page illustration of the "tree of architecture." This is pictured as a mighty trunk from near the base of which upon separate branches (and so regarded as independent of each other) are placed as fruit of separate civilizations the architecture of the Peruvian, Mexican, Egyptian, Assyrian, Indian and Chinese-Japanese. In the trunk as it ascends are placed as genetically connected Greek, Roman, and Romanesque styles, while two branches issuing between Roman and Romanesque bear the Byzantine and Saracenic styles respectively. Above the Romanesque branch out on each side the Gothic structures which appear as Belgian-Dutch, Ger-

[1] A History of Architecture on the Comparative Method for Students, Craftsmen, and Amateurs. By Sir Banister Fletcher, 6th ed., rewritten and enlarged with about 3500 illustrations. New York, Scribner's, 1921. XXXIV—932 pp. $12.00.
   A Text-Book of the History of Architecture. By A. D. F. Hamlin. New (15th) ed; Longmans, Green & Co., New York, 1922. XXVIII—479 pp. $2.50.

man, French, Italian, English, and Spanish. Near the top of the tree two similar branches bear the name Renaissance with the same divisions as the Gothic, namely, Belgian-Dutch, German, etc. The crown of the tree is called "modern," and is varied in its branchlets by "revivals" of former styles, and here American architecture finds its place—with the Flatiron building, New York, as its representative!

This arrangement is the consequence of a painstaking investigation which embraces not only the general aspects but the structural details of the various styles and orders. The volume falls into two parts: The historical styles and the non-historical styles. The latter are so named because of their detachment from "Western art" and their paucity of influence upon it. They include Indian, Chinese, Japanese, Central American, and Saracenic. The author notes, however, the agency of Saracenic through the Moorish occupancy of Spain. On the contrary there is implied a historic stream of influence upon Western art by the Egyptian and West Asiatic forms of building.

The striking features of this massive volume are (1) its comprehensiveness; (2) its detailed examination of structural parts; (3) its wealth of illustrations (859 in all) making clear every discussion by line drawing, plan, or reproduced photograph. It is a splendid book for one who would have a reference book on the subject that was not too expensive.

An alluring feature not usual to this kind of book is its appreciation of American modes. The following quotation is typical of the author's attitude:

American architects, many of whom are first trained at the École des Beaux-Arts, Paris, have already advanced rapidly along new lines of adapted design, and have, in their various buildings, displayed that peculiar American freedom of character and outlook which enables them unconsciously to cut their way straight to the particular types of design most suitable for the wide variety of purposes, whether commercial, industrial, social, educational, municipal, religious, or domestic, of the up-to-date and untrammeled citizens of America. It is indeed only natural that the great country of the West, which was founded in religious freedom and was later established in political freedom, should to-day hand on the torch of freedom not only in religion and politics but also in literature and art.

Relatively unimportant for the subject of the volume, but to be taken account of in the historical relations, is the fact that the dates given by Sir Banister are now discarded by Egyptologists and Assyriologists. The dates now assumed for the early dynasties in Egypt and the kingdoms in Babylonia are lower by several centuries than those given in this book. Fortunately the relative chronology is not affected.

No better testimony to the high value of Professor Hamlin's text-book is needed than that this is the fifteenth printing. The reviewer over twenty years ago got his first systematic knowledge of historic architecture from an earlier edition. Since then the author within his self-prescribed limits has kept pace with progress and discovery. He has somewhat increased the number of pages and of illustrations, the latter now number 236. Certainly no better introduction to the history and forms of architecture can be found. For those who can not afford the larger work this will be a fairly acceptable substitute.

Both volumes are rich in bibliographical reference; Sir Banister Fletcher's is fairly complete in this respect. G. W. G.

———

What's Best Worth Saying. By RICHARD ROBERTS. George H. Doran Company, New York, 1922. 131 pp. $1.25.

The Untried Door. By RICHARD ROBERTS. George H. Doran Company, New York, 1921. xii—174 pp. $1.50.

At first glance the title of the first book is misleading and disquieting. Does the author assume that in this little book there is only what's best worth saying, and all of it? The memory harks back to the mild shock received when Dr. Joseph Parker issued a volume some years ago which he called *These Sayings of Mine*. In both cases the modesty of the authors is such that perhaps they themselves did not see the implication.

Dr. Roberts' plan is understood, and the newer shock is one of admiration at the felicity of the title when we read his quotation from Coventry Patmore:

In divinity and love
What's best worth saying can't be said.

His first sentence illuminates the title: "My quarrel with the creeds is not that they say too much, but that they say too little." The book is a collection of addresses delivered to college students. The author is the minister of the American Presbyterian Church of Montreal. The spirit of the addresses is reverent; the literary style is pleasing, and the book sparkles with quotable sentences and is rich with sermon material. How can one help reporting: "Faith is the will to live in the assumption that God is friendly to us"; "History is no more than the story of a lost child in search of its father. Revelation is the tale of a father in search of his lost child"; "The real test of a religion is whether it can be preached from a soap-box"; "Uplift, I am sick of hearing about it. Uplift indeed, and to what level? Our own of course"; "Athanasius said that Jesus came down from above. Arius said that he came up from below. They were both right." He declares that the proper place for a creed is behind us. He insists that it keep its place but also insists that it be there; that we are to gather up all that is past, and possess it.

There are ten short chapters, and young men and women, and some old ones as well, will be better furnished to live, and young preachers will be better equipped to preach after reading these chapters.

The Untried Door, according to its subtitle, is an attempt to discover the mind of Jesus for to-day. It has been adopted by the National Board of the Young Women's Christian Association, and is recommended as a text-book for study groups. While it is perhaps not as pungent and as arresting as the other volume it grows steadily upon the reader. The chapter heads and the Scripture verses to illustrate these chapters do not seem to have any logical sequence, but appear as isolated but brilliant fragments of exposition and paraphrase. This the author himself seems to realize as in the preface he suggests a redistribution of the chapters for the sake of unity. But orderly or informal the substance is choice, and the pastor who will give a series of prayer-meeting talks based upon the Scripture verses quoted, and inspired by the lucid comment, will lead his people into the high places, and feed and be fed upon spiritual vitamines.

The problem of life as Jesus gave the solution is not how to make the most of both worlds, which was the ideal of the last century, but how to live in both worlds at the same time. Whether a man thinks that the things worth living for are within him or without him is the distinction between spiritual and material values. In the world, we are told, there are two types of mind—one that builds walls, the other that pulls them down: tariff walls, creedal walls, caste walls—it is all the same, and the greatest breaker of walls ever known was Jesus Christ. The most of us are too busy with church organization, and card-indexes, and office details to mix with outsiders. The business of Jesus was to seek out this man and that man and tell him the "good news" and then let the "good news" work out its own consequences.

It is refreshing to find the great pastor of a great church recoiling at the modern Bolshevik theory of collectivity. According to the "Prolet-Kult" of sovietism even pictures and books must not be produced by individuals. The individual must be suppressed. Mass work even in the study and the *atelier.* This is the newest cult. The world must be saved sociologically, and in platoons and blocks of five. The soup-kitchen is to redeem the slums. Group meetings instead of prayer-meetings. Maybe the fad is passing. Maybe the individual is coming back to his kingdom. Maybe the world is to be saved by saving John Smith and Peter Robinson and sending them out to save the others. This was the program of Jesus. It has not been improved upon.

Smell, Taste, and Allied Senses in the Vertebrates. By G. H. PARKER, Professor of Zoölogy in Harvard University. J. P. Lippincott Co., Philadelphia, 1922. 192 pp. $2.50.

This book is one of a series of monographs on experimental biology. While written primarily for students of the biological sciences, it presents a line of experimentation, a technique, and a body of facts that should be interesting to most readers who are trying in these days to ground their thinking in fundamental realities. As the author says in his preface:

Sense organs have always excited general interest, for they are the means of approach to the human mind. Without them our intellectual life would be a blank. The deaf and blind show how serious is the loss of even a single set of these organs.

The significance of such a study for psychology, therefore, and for all the varied applications of psychology, is evident; for there is an urgent need of exact knowledge about the fundamentals of the human mind in a world so much given to superficial and vain speculations as to what the human mind is, and how it works.

The following chapter-headings will indicate the ground covered by the book: Nature of Sense Organs; Anatomy of the Olfactory Organ; Physiology of Olfaction; Vomero-nasal Organ, or Organ of Jacobson; The Common Chemical Sense; Anatomy of the Gustatory Organ; Physiology of Gustation; and Interrelation of the Chemical Senses.

It should not be inferred from the physiological terms used in such titles, that such a book has no psychological interest. Consider, for example, a few of the lines of inquiry bearing upon mental problems of fundamental importance:

(1) Absence or deficiency of a sense-organ.

A state of this kind implies a certain mental deficiency in the given individual. If a person has been blind from birth, no amount of description can supply to him the sensation of the wealth of color that the external world holds for the normal man.

(2) Unusual development of a sense-organ. While a lower animal may, in general, be inferior mentally to man, it may have powers of sense-perception far exceeding those of man. Thus a dog's sense of smell is incomparably superior to his master's, while a cat may hear tones of a pitch much too high for the human ear.

(3) Sense-organs entirely unknown to man, and therefore a mentality with factors quite outside human comprehension. Thus fish possess, in addition to the five classes of human sense-organs, certain so-called lateral-line organs, which give to the fish a wholly unique set of sensory relations. The bearing of all this upon both psychological facts and philosophical speculation as to different forms of consciousness is evident.

Studies in the Theory of Human Society. By PROFESSOR FRANKLIN H. GIDDINGS. The Macmillan Company, New York, 1922. 300 pp.

These studies deal with a phase of life that ought to be interesting to all intelligent people. To the man who comes in contact with audiences, with congregations, and who is willing to pay the price of careful reading and deep thinking, there is a real reward.

Sociology in the large sense as defined by the author is "the science of the production and distribution of adequacy, of man and in man." And adequacy comprises endurance, health, reproductive vigor, intelligence, self-control, ability to make adjustments with others and to get on helpfully with others in cooperation. Then comes a very important statement:

Society produces these factors of adequacy in the same sense in which the breeder produces desired qualities in animals, namely, by selecting them and providing the conditions under which they can survive. The practical manifestations of adequacy are: individual initiative, individual responsibility, and an individual participation that are efficient and helpful in collective endeavor.

We are reminded several times in these studies that while each person can come to know considerable about himself, all we know about the minds of our fellow men is what we learn from their conduct and that is why "there can be no other psychology of society than the behavioristic."

The volume is divided into three main parts: historical, analytical, and synthetic.

Les Penseurs de l'Islam. Vol. I. Les Souverains, l'Histoire et la Philosophie Politique. Vol. II. Les Geographes, les Sciences, Mathematiques, et Naturelles. By BARON CARRA DE VAUX. Librarie Paul Geuthner, Paris, 1921. 7 x 4½ in., 383, 400 pp. Both volumes, 12.50 fr. **l'Orient vu de l'Occident.** By E. DINET and SLIMAN BEN IBRAHIM. Librarie Paul Geuthner, Paris, 1921. 7 x 4½ in., 104 pp. 4 fr.

One has to be reminded occasionally that the Arabs of the late middle ("dark") ages were the transmitters and mediators of classical learning. The French follow the British in the number of Mohammedan subjects—in North Africa, Syria, and the Far East. It is natural, then, to find the French interested in Mohammedan literature. De Vaux's two handy volumes on *The Thinkers of Islam* deal in nineteen chapters with the royal patrons of literature, and with Arabic, Persian, Mongolian, and Turkish historians, philosophers, geographers, mathematicians, physicists, astronomers, etc. Here is a picture of the contributions—original and borrowed—made to human welfare by followers in faith of the Arabian prophet. Eminently readable—can a Frenchman write a dull book?—these volumes lack an index, about the only blemish on a book treating a subject little understood by Christians.

The little work by Dinet and Ben Ibrahim (a French and an Arab Mohammedan?) is designed to correct the Occidental views of the Orient and Islam in particular. These views, the authors say, are errant in part because they construe literally the picture language of the East and try to fit it within logical categories, in part because of undue stress on the argument for silence. The authors plead for fair play from critics of the Koran, Mohammed, and Islam, and protest urgently against applying the critical canons of the West to Eastern literature.

Jesus an Economic Mediator. By JAMES E. DARBY. Fleming H. Revell Company, New York, 1922. 256 pp. $1.50.

It is an encouraging sign of the times to find so much of present-day literature turning to the Master's teaching for the solution of all questions pertaining to the well-being of humanity. The book before us bears the sub-title of "God's Remedy for Industrial and International Ills" and twenty chapters are given over to a discussion of many aspects of this important question.

The author takes his stand on indisputable ground when he says only as Jesus becomes the mediator and helper of the individual can any improvement come to the great number of workingmen throughout the world.

The gospel of social redemption grows out of individual redemption as all human rights grow out of personal rights. Right relations with Jehovah bring right relations with one another, and weld together all interests.

The volume is a strong plea for the redemption of the whole person, spiritual, mental, moral, and physical.

Our readers will get an example of the method in the chapter on "The Making and Using of Money," see page 489.

When Jesus Wrote on the Ground. By EDGAR DEWITT JONES. George H. Doran Company, New York, 1922. 7¾x5½ in., 234 pp. $1.50.

The sub-title describes this collection as Studies, Expositions and Meditations in the Life of the Spirit, and as such they will prove helpful.

The presence of a fine, strong, brotherly spirit, intent in bringing the life of God into the lives of men, is a striking characteristic of the volume.

Dr. Charles C. Morrison of *The Christian Century* writes an appreciation of Dr. Jones. There are seventeen chapters altogether.

The final chapter we give in another department of this number.

PREACHERS EXCHANGING VIEWS

Facing the Facts on Christian Unity

Editor of THE HOMILETIC REVIEW:

In the June number of the REVIEW there is an article in the "Preachers Exchanging Views" under the caption "Facing the Facts on Christian Unity." This may be an earnest effort on the part of the writer to point out the way to a desired end, but as it does not suggest the real point of difficulty it could not indicate a plan of accomplishing the desired end, Christian unity. What the writer says about taking the Bible only and abolishing "human creeds," is in fact the same speech that Alexander Campbell started out with over a century ago, and has long since been worn threadbare, but has never yet effected a union anywhere, tho while launching a denomination out upon the mission to bring about union, it has itself become divided into three factions and each one still advocating unity on the same basis. The ultra immersionist insists that unless I am immersed as he was I can not be recognized as a church-member. Unless I will suffer the imposition of his creed on me I can not be a recognized member of a real church. I ask why is that? Then I am told that that is the only scriptural mode of baptism and I must ascribe to it. Of course that is only according to his view of the Scriptures. But I insist upon the privilege of studying the Bible myself; in fact, that is just what I have done. Now if it be demanded of me that I must be immersed or I can not be a member of a church, then I conscientiously could not be a member of any church making such demand, as I am not an immersionist, and having thoroughly examined every passage of Scripture bearing on the subject, I am fully persuaded in my own mind. Yet I do not insist that others must accept my view on the subject. Being satisfied myself I want every Christian to enjoy personal satisfaction, tho his view may not just correspond to mine, I give him the privilege I myself enjoy.

F. P. DEBOLT.

Dexter, Mo.

INDEX TO VOLUME LXXXIV

JULY TO DECEMBER, 1922

[Ed = Editorial Comment, Ill = Illustrations and Anecdotes, O = Outline, PEV = Preachers Exchanging Views, TT = Themes and Texts, Ser = Sermons, SC = Social Christianity, PM = Prayer Meeting, ISSL = International Sunday-school Lessons, CO = Comment and Outlook, SLTT = Side Lights on Themes and Texts.]

INDEX OF SUBJECTS

INDEX OF AUTHORS

INDEX OF TEXTS

LUME 84.   No. 2   JI 20 '22 S THE   U

'HOMILETIC

REVIEW

AUGUST, 1922

AN INTERNATIONAL MAGAZINE OF RELIGION, THEOLOGY, AND PHILOSOPHY.
EVERY PHASE OF THE MINISTER'S WORK DISCUSSED.

VOLUME 84. No. 3   SEPTEMBER, 1

THE
HOMILÉTIC
REVIEW

AN INTERNATIONAL MAGAZINE OF RELIGION, THEOLOGY, AND PHILOSOPHY.
EVERY PHASE OF THE MINISTER'S WORK DISCUSSED.

CANYON OF THE RIO DE LAS ANIMAS PERDIDAS ("RIVER OF LOST SOULS")

OLUME 84.　No. 4

S. 21 '22

THE

OCTOBER, 1

HOMILETIC
REVIEW

AN INTERNATIONAL MAGAZINE OF RELIGION, THEOLOGY, AND PHILOSOPHY.
EVERY PHASE OF THE MINISTER'S WORK DISCUSSED.

Our Service
Extends from Coast to Coast

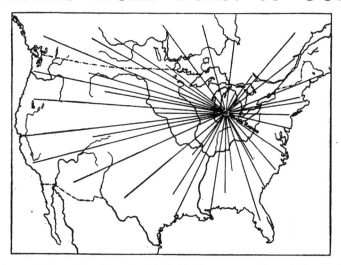

Volume 84
No. 6

CONTENTS

December
1922

TERMS OF SUBSCRIPTION

Terms for The Homiletic Review—Price per copy, 30 cents. Subscription, one year, $3.00. (Extra postage for foreign addresses, except Shanghai, 50 cents. No extra postage required to Shanghai, Cuba, Mexico, Canada, or to any territory of the United States.)

Receipts—The label pasted on the wrapper is a receipt for payment of subscription to and including the printed date.

Extension—The extension of a subscription is shown by the printed label the month after a remittance is received.

Discontinuance—We find that many of our subscribers prefer not to have their subscriptions interrupted and their files broken in case they fail to remit before expiration. Nevertheless, it is not assumed that continuous service is desired, but subscribers are expected to notify us with promptness if the magazine is no longer required.

Post-Office Address—Instructions concerning renewal, discontinuance, or change of address should be sent two weeks prior to the date on which they are to go into effect. The exact post-office address to which we are directing the magazine at the time of writing must always be given.

THE HOMILETIC REVIEW, Published Monthly by FUNK & WAGNALLS COMPANY
(Adam W. Wagnalls, Pres.; Wilfred J. Funk, Vice-Pres.; Robert J. Cuddihy, Treas.;
William Neisel, Sec.)
354-360 Fourth Ave., New York, N. Y. 133-134 Salisbury Square, Fleet Street, London, E. C.
Entered as second-class matter, March 5, 1899, at the Post-Office at New York, N. Y., under
the act of March 3, 1879. Copyright, 1922, by FUNK & WAGNALLS COMPANY

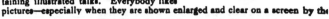

The Homiletic Revie

LOOKING TOWARD THE COMING

1923—PARTIAL PROSPECTUS—192

Health and long life are occasionally the lot of magazines as well as men. Aft forty years of service to the preachers of the world *The Homiletic Review* retains i vigor, initiative, and resourcefulness. It still enjoys a good measure of prosperity, an we trust also of influence and helpfulness. Experience has demonstrated that it is unwise at the beginning of the year to lay out a full program. We find it much more advantageous to our readers to hold ourselves in readiness to respond to any emergencies that may arise during the year to any conditions that call for consider: tion. These are usually matters not only of current interest but often of importanc to the preacher.

> An International magazine of religion, theology, and philoso-phy.
> Every phase of the min-ister's work discussed.

> The contributors t the Review are special-ists in Religion, Evan-gelism, Theology, Sociology, Psychology, Archeology, Comparative Religion, Mis sions, and Philosophy.

SOME MATERIAL OF PRIME IMPORTANCE FOR THI PREACHER'S PULPIT PREPARATION

Man's Place in Nature— Scientific and Religious Interpretations

The Health of the Whole Man—A Plea for an Old-Fashioned Sunday

The Preacher and the Old Testament

Beautiful Isle of Somewhere The Rose of the Plain

American Religious and Educational Interests in the Near East

An estimate and review of a recent work entitled "A History of the Church"

The Use of Art in Reli ious Education

Psycho-Analysis of Congr gations

Motion Pictures in th Church

Rosaries of the Great R ligions

Bible Study

These studies follow the lesson topics and passages of the International Sunday-School series. Preachers will find them practical, homiletical, and exegetical.

January to March—Jesus the World's Savior: Studies in Luke

April to June—Great Men and Women of the Bible. I. The Old Testament

July to September—Great Men and Women of the Bible. II. The New Testament

October to December—The Missionary Message of the Bible

Also other expository and exegetical contributions.

Social Christianity

The material in this department is discussed fro the Christian standpoint. A different subject is treate each month. This material keeps the preacher it formed on social movements of our time. Amo the topics to be discussed in the early part of t year are the following:

The Churches and Radio. The Ethical Aspects Work. A study of racial groups in Americ Mohammedanism and Christianity.

Hints on Church Design

1. The Importance of Good Design; 2. Wh Constitutes Good Design; 3. What Constitutes Ba Design; 4. The Difference Between Decoration an "Gingerbread"; 5. Architecture in its Relation Nature; 6. Construction in its Relation to Desig 7. Materials in Their Relation to Design; 8. Gener Principles of Design in their Relation to Churc Architecture.

1923

PRAYER-MEETING TOPICS FOR 1923

January—How to Get Your Heart's Desires
  What Is a Self?
  The Self and the Body
  The Thought Life of the Self

February—The Church's Effort for a Warless World
  Names One Can Respect—Lincoln, Washington
  Cyrus Hamlin of Turkey (*Missions*)

March—Lessons from the Book of Jeremiah
  Jeremiah's Inner Struggle
  Jeremiah's Loneliness
  Jeremiah's Message
  Tragedy and Triumph

April—The Practical Power of the Resurrection
  (*Easter*)
  Roots and Fruits
  What I Owe to a Good Book
  Rational Religion
  The Sacredness of Persons

May—The Kindly Treatment of Others' Imperfections
  Ideal Womanhood (*Mother's Day*)
  Robert Laws of Africa (*Missions*)
  Life Through Death (*Memorial Day*)

June—The Worth of Concentration (*Baccalaureate*)
  The Voice of the Child (*Children's Day*)
  Motives and Methods
  Order as an Element in Life

July—The Blessing of Liberty
  The Vacation that is Worth While
  Jesus in the Great Open Spaces
  A Mountain of Temptation
  Timothy Richard of China (*Missions*)

August—Some Gates of the Bible
  The Unrecognized
  The Wells of Human Life
  A Requirement of Man's Nature

September—Christ's Contribution to Economics
  (*Labor Day*)
  The Turning Point in a Life of Struggle
  Religion in the Market
  The Law of Habit
  The Control of Habit

October—A Study in Hope
  The Hope That Doubts
  The Hope That Sees From Afar
  The Hope That Arrives
  The Hope That Conquers Death

November—God's Civic Ministers (*Election Day*)
  The Christian View of Providence
  Seeing as God Sees
  The Sacrifices of Thanksgiving

December—Alexander Duff of India (*Missions*)
  Finding God in Our Sense of Duty
  Three Stages of Growth
  The Song of the Angels at Bethlehem (*Christmas*)
  Do It Now (*New Year's Day*)

Some of the Regular Features of the Review

Articles of high cultural value dealing with subjects that lie close to the preacher's pulpit preparation and successful pastoral work.

Reviews and Notices of the latest archeological investigations and discoveries.

Special Interviews with well-known Preachers, Thinkers, and Workers.

The Homiletic Review
Volume LXXXIV
Subscription Price
$3.00 per Year

Helpful Outlines and Illustrations for Sermons and Addresses.

Book Reviews that will keep you informed on the literature you need to know.

Selected Sermons from the Leading Preachers in America and Europe.

Every Number Contains a Brief Talk on Material for the Children's Service.
Brief Practical Articles on Church Methods.

OUR READERS' APPRECIATION OF THE HOMILETIC REVIEW

"I appreciate the Review and am delighted with its point of view."

"I have read the Review (with some interruptions) most of the time since about 1890 and can say conscientiously and without flattery that I find it more helpful now than even in the first years of my ministry. Your July (1922) number is, I think, the best you ever turned out."

"I am returning to The Homiletic Review after many years and am finding it abreast of this age."

"May I take this opportunity of expressing my appreciation of the Review, which I find increasingly helpful and inspiring."

"It is all good, just what we need. Thank you, sirs, a thousand times."

"I thank you for the truth and stimulus you get into the magazine. May you continue to be fruitful and happy in every good work."

"I am a reader of the Review for many years, and I always look forward with pleasure to every number, for as a rule it is a feast of good things."

"While I was in active work, I was a continual reader of your great magazine. Now I speak a good word for it to every young man that is beginning to preach."

FUNK & WAGNALLS COMPANY, Publishers, 354-360 Fourth Avenue, NEW YORK, N. Y.
LONDON OFFICE: 134 Salisbury Square

DEATH OF LYMAN ABBOTT

We regret to announce the death of Doctor Lyman
Abbott, who for forty-six years was editor-in-chief of
The Outlook. He died in New York City on October
22nd in the 87th year of his age.

The distinguished editor was born in Roxbury, Mass.,
December 18, 1835; graduated from New York University, 1853; admitted to the New York Bar in 1856;
ordained to the Congregational ministry in 1860; pastor
at Terre Haute, Ind., 1860-65; New England Church,
New York, 1865-9; Plymouth Church, Brooklyn, (succeeding Henry Ward Beecher), 1888-1899; author of
more than a score of religious books.

From *The Outlook* of November first we take the following:

He looked forward to this day without dread; he
even looked for it with curiosity; for he thought of it as
the beginning of a great adventure, as a time of falling
asleep and waking to find himself at home, as a passage
across the threshold to another room. He had fought a
good fight—he was willing to trust his comrades to continue the battle. He had finished his course—he was
willing to trust his message to those who would carry it
on. He had kept the faith—and he was willing to trust
that the faith would still be guarded. . . . .

Every problem of conduct, whether involving action
or national policy, he referred to those principles [su-
premely expressed in Jesus] for solution. He became
and remained, as he said, a student of one Book and
the follower of one Man.

Life he saw as a struggle, and the end of that struggle
was life. Conflict he neither sought nor avoided, but
when he found himself in the midst of battle he fought
for the peace of victory. This is the peace which he
sought in his own life, in the life of his own land, and
in the development of humankind.

Believing in the peace of victory, he found natural
comrades in those who, like himself, were doers as well
as preachers of the Word. So in his earlier years he
fought side by side with Beecher; so in his later years
he gave his trust and support to Roosevelt.

He was indifferent to partisan and factional labels. If
consistency meant stubborn adherence to what he found
to be false, he was willing to be inconsistent. He kept
his mind always open to new evidence and was unafraid
in the search for truth. He could change his opinions
without fear because he knew his convictions were un-
changeable. . . . . .

His power lay chiefly in his life. He not only preached
justice, mercy, and loyalty to the eternal; he was just,
merciful, and loyal in all that he did and all that he was.

That power is a living force today. Many times before
this he has gone, as now he has gone—into another room.
We are not reconciled to the loss of the sound of his
voice; we cannot so soon accustom ourselves to the
thought that we shall not see him again; but we shall not
be deprived of the power that he imparted, for that is
the power of his life.

THE LEXICOGRAPHER

☞ *The Lexicographer does not answer anonymous communications.*

"H. L. C.," New York, N. Y.—"Kindly advise the correct plural form of *apparatus*."

The dictionary gives the plural of *apparatus* as the same as its singular, or *apparatuses*, which it stigmatizes as rare, but which is much more frequently used to-day than the former.

"C. W. C.," New York, N. Y.—"Is it correct to use the expression 'most unique' and if not, is it even permissible to use it? In other words, are there any comparative or superlative degrees of uniqueness?"

Unique. An adjective meaning 'the only one of its kind,' frequently misused for 'odd,' 'rare,' 'unusual.'—*Mend Your Speech.*

"J. G. F.," Cleveland, O.—"Please give me the meaning of the word *synapse*."

Synapse is the junction between two nerve-cells. The word *synapse* is a variant form of *synapsis*. The word *synapsis* is defined as follows: "1. A stage in cell-division characterized by the massing of the chromatin at one side of the nucleus; fusion of the chromatin preparatory to gameto-genesis; mitapsis. 2. The intertwining of the dendron of a nerve-cell with the body or dendron of another cell."

"H. M. B.," Delta, Colo.—"Please explain the use of the words *toward* and *towards*. Is *towards* ever used in modern good English?"

The form *towards* is the earlier form of *toward*, antedating it by about a quarter of a century and dating from 860 or thereabouts. It occurs in Alfred the Great's paraphrase of Boethius's "Consolation" made about 884. In the United States the form *toward* is given preference over *towards*, but both are in use on the American continent, the Canadians preferring *towards*.

"J. E. R.," New York, N. Y.—"Kindly inform me whether it is ever correct to begin a sentence with the word *and*."

And has been used as an introductory, continuing the narration from a previous sentence, exprest or understood, since the year 855. You will find many examples of it in Shakespeare. See *King John*, Act iv, scene 1, line 40; Grote's "History of Greece," Volume I, chapter 1, page 29, Kingsley's "Hypatia," chapter 5, page 69; Lytton's "Pilgrimage on the Rhine," beginning, *"And the stars sat each upon his ruby throne, and looked with sleepless eyes upon the world."* See, also, definition 2 of *and* on page 105 of the NEW STANDARD DICTIONARY.

"B. N. G.," New York, N. Y.—"Your comments on the word *data* surprize me. *Data* is, of course, the plural of *datum* and should, therefore, take a plural verb. My experience convinces me that it is now accepted in business usage as a collective noun and used with a singular verb."

The point admits of no discussion. *Data* as a singular is bad English. The fact that such expression as, "Compile *this data*" and "When *this data* is available" are, as you say, "used constantly in letters received and sent from the best business houses in the city" is a sweeping assertion. No misapplications, based upon ignorance or corruption, should be cited in support of an erroneous use. Some careless persons use *memoranda* as a singular. The public in general is careless about these things, but carelessness is not privileged to establish incorrect forms as standard English.

By introducing a collective noun before it, *data* can be used in the manner suggested, as in such a sentence as "From all *this heap* of data it would not follow that it was necessary to remodel our plans."

Consult Goold Brown's "Grammar of English Grammars" (part 2, chapter 3, page 253): "Our writers have laid many languages under contribution, and those furnish an abundance of irregular words, necessary to be explained, but never to be acknowledged as English till they conform to our own rules. . . . Of nouns in *um*, some have no need of the plural; as, *decorum, odium,* etc. Some form it regularly; as, *asylums, mausoleums, vacuums.* Others take either the English or the Latin plural; as *memorandums, memoranda; stratums, strata.* A few have *the Latin plural only* as, *arcanum, arcana; datum, data.*"

The NEW STANDARD DICTIONARY says of *datum* that "the word is almost always used in the plural," and does not recognize, nor does any other dictionary recognize, the erroneous use introduced in careless commercial correspondence during the past ten years.

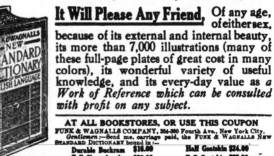

The CHRISTIAN CENTURY

A Journal of Religion

CHARLES CLAYTON MORRISON
and HERBERT L. WILLETT, Editors

Published Weekly   Four Dollars a Year

Dr. John Dewey's

criticism of China's Missionary Schools appeared in the New Republic some months ago.

"American missionary education [in China] has failed," thus Dr. Dewey quotes a Chinese student, "to develop independent energetic thought and character among even its most distinguished graduates. It has produced rather a subservient intellectual type, one which is characterized as slavish."

Dr. Guy W. Sarvis,

Professor of Economics and Sociology in the University of Nanking, replies to Dr. Dewey's criticism in one of the most trenchant and informing articles on Christian educational ideals in China that has yet appeared.

"Many of us who are in missionary educational work in China are former students of Dr. Dewey, or enthusiastic followers of his educational and philosophical doctrines. We believe he desires to aid China in every possible way. We do not understand why, on the basis of assumption and hearsay, he has used the weight of his influence to damage institutions which, with all their imperfections, are making possible the most important contribution of America to China."

Dr. Sarvis' reply will appear in a forthcoming issue of The Christian Century.

"Christianizing Public Opinion"
By SAMUEL McCREA CAVERT

The educational function of Christianity is not accomplished until the public opinion of the social order has itself been made Christian, so says Dr. Cavert in two articles about to appear in The Christian Century. These articles illuminate the concept of the social responsibility of the church.

"Studies in Sin" By H. D. C. MACLACHLAN

Using Tolstoi, Isben, Browning, Kipling, Bernard Shaw, Strindberg, Dostoiefsky, and A. S. M. Hutchinson as his background, Dr. Maclachlan is now beginning a series of articles on such subjects as "The Sin Against the Holy Ghost," "Sin and Atonement," "The Sin of Immaturity," "The Sin of the Secret Wish," "Sinning at Long Range," "Second Hand Sinning," "Sin and Punishment," and "Sin and Social Conventions." This will be a remarkable interpretation of literature and a unique discussion of the modern conception of sin.

"Christ and Modern Life"

Running currently with all other good things, the editors will continue to discuss and interpret the social aspects of the Christian gospel. Editorials and articles on such themes as these will be appearing each week:

"The Socialism That Is Christian"   "Jesus and Modern Industrialism"
"Christianity and Evolution"   "Christianity and Modern Science"
"When Will the Kingdom Come?"   "Is Modern Business Christian?"
"Christ Shows 'The Way Out' for the World"
"The Future of the Community Church." Etc, etc, etc.

The Christian Century is distinguished by its candid discussion of living issues in the light of the mind of Christ.

Fill out one of these coupons and mail today.
Extra postage outside U. S.

Just a Little Spice

Slightly Forgetful. — Kind Old Lady—"I beg your pardon, but you are walking with one foot in the gutter."

Absent Minded—"So I am; mercy, I thought I was lame!"—*Lampoon.*

Keeping the Sabbath. — MacTavish — "Ye'll have to change my caddy. I'll have no boy that desecrates the Sabbath by whistling!"—*Judge.*

Fellow Sufferers.—The "humorist" was laboring away in an after-dinner speech, in the midst of agonizing silence.

Finally one man near the further end of the table, who had been sitting with his hand cupped to his ear, called "Louder!"

And a man sitting immediately under the speaker's gesturing arm yawned and called out: "And funnier."—Adrian (Mich.) *Telegram.*

Plausible. — When Dr. Samuel Wilberforce, famous divine, was Bishop of Oxford, he happened to be present at a Sunday school where the passage was read which contains the story of Jacob's ladder. "Is there any little boy or girl," said the bishop, in his most persuasive tones, "who wishes to ask any question relative to the passage which has just been read?" As no response was given, the bishop repeated his question, in still more seductive tones, and after a short pause a small boy arose and said, "Please, sir, the angels must have had wings; why did they require a ladder?" "A most natural question," said the bishop, considerably puzzled as to a suitable reply. "Is there any other little boy or girl who can give an answer to that very reasonable question?" On which a little girl modestly suggested, "Perhaps, sir, they were molting!"—*The Methodist Recorder*, London.

Give It a Try.—"Grandpa, can you help me with this problem?"

"I could, dear, but I don't think it would be right."

"I don't suppose it would, but take a shot at it, anyway."—*Watchman-Examiner.*

Stole His Thunder.—The minister was preaching on the subject of Jonah. After about half an hour's discourse he came to the point of his story.

"Now, what kind o' a fush do you suppose it was that swallowed Jonah?" he said. "Maybe it was a herring? Aye, but it was no a herring. Maybe it was a salmon? Aye, but it was no a salmon. Then what sort of a fush was it? Was it a shairk?"

A member of the congregation, unable to remain silent any longer, quietly interjected, "Maybe it was a whale?"

The minister leaned over the pulpit.

"Och, yer blithering idiot," he shouted, "what do you mean by taking the word of God oot o' the mooth o' ain o' his ministers."—*The Humorist* (Canada).

In Remembrance. — Availing herself of her ecclesiastical privileges, the clergyman's wife asked questions which, coming from anybody else, would have been thought impertinent.

"I presume you carry a memento of some kind in that locket you wear?" she said.

"Yes, ma'am," said the parishioner. "It is a lock of my husband's hair."

"But your husband is still alive," the lady exclaimed.

"Yes, ma'am, but his hair is gone."—*The New York Times.*

Making It Peppy.—A woman reader of *The Continent* writes that a recent article by Dr. Barstow, "Make It Snappy," reminds her of an incident in her own household. "I with my three grandchildren, 7, 11 and 13 years, was at breakfast and together we said aloud the blessing 'Lord bless this food which now we take. And this we ask for Jesus' sake.' At its close, the youngest said, 'Grandmother, why do you say it so solemn? Why don't you put some pep in it and make it like a college yell?'"

Sunday Occupation.—A clergyman of a country village in New Jersey desired his clerk to give notice that there would be no service in the afternoon, as he was going to officiate with another clergyman. The clerk put it this way:

"I am desired to give notice that there will be no service this afternoon, as our minister is going off fishing with another clergyman."—*Christian Advocate.*

Temper Estimated.—An elderly Indian colonel used to boast that he had a tranquil disposition which nothing could ruffle. One day while playing a foursome he got into the worst bunker on the course and spent a terrible ten minutes trying to play out. He tried nearly every club in vain and at last, glaring like a demon, he smashed them one after another across a jagged rock.

"What are you doing?" cried one of the party above.

"It's all right," he snorted. "It's—it's better to break your clubs than to—to lose your temper." —*Continent.*

The Case Against War.—Visitor: "Who is that raving maniac waving the Turkish flag?"

Sanitarium Attendant: "That is a very sad case. The poor chap is a map publisher who had just finished revising the map of Europe when this new war broke out."—*New York Sun.*